TREATY SHOPPING IN INTERNATIONAL INVESTMENT LAW

INTERNATIONAL ECONOMIC LAW SERIES

International Economic Law series, established by the late Professor John H Jackson, addresses a range of issues in international economic law, which includes international trade law, international investment law, and the global financial order. The series aims to encourage interest in the broad contours of international economic law, heightening awareness of its significance across the globe as well as its continuous interactions with other areas. The series editors encourage quality submissions from a wide range of perspectives, including doctrinal, theoretical, empirical, and interdisciplinary viewpoints. Novel and cutting edge research is particularly welcome, as are contributions from both emerging and established scholars from around the world.

Series Editors

ANDREW D. MITCHELL
Professor at Melbourne Law School,
The University of Melbourne

TANIA VOON
Professor at Melbourne Law School,
The University of Melbourne

RECENT TITLES IN THE SERIES

Good Faith and International Economic Law
Edited by Andrew D. Mitchel, M Sornarajah, and Tania Voon

Development at the WTO
Sonia E. Rolland

The BRIC States and Outward Foreign Direct Investment
David Collins

Treaty Shopping in International Investment Law

JORUN BAUMGARTNER

OXFORD
UNIVERSITY PRESS

OXFORD
UNIVERSITY PRESS

Great Clarendon Street, Oxford, OX2 6DP,
United Kingdom

Oxford University Press is a department of the University of Oxford.
It furthers the University's objective of excellence in research, scholarship,
and education by publishing worldwide. Oxford is a registered trade mark of
Oxford University Press in the UK and in certain other countries

First Edition published in 2016
Impression: 1

Published in the United States of America by Oxford University Press
198 Madison Avenue, New York, NY 10016, United States of America

British Library Cataloguing in Publication Data
Data available

Library of Congress Control Number: 2016950214

ISBN 978–0–19–878711–2

Printed and bound by
CPI Group (UK) Ltd, Croydon, CR0 4YY

To my dad, who has always encouraged me to discover new horizons
May this book encourage Luca in a similar way later on

Series Editors' Preface

This is the first book to be published in the Oxford University Press Series on International Economic Law since the passing of its first editor, the great Professor John H Jackson. Professor Jackson was a warm and generous friend and mentor with a keen intellect and unending energy, who is recognized as the founder of the field of international economic law. We pay our respects to his family and friends and wish to acknowledge the enormous contribution he made to this field over his lifetime. As we continue our role as editors of the series, we cannot but feel his absence and only hope to be able to honour his legacy in small ways.

As relative newcomers to this role, our ambitions are modest. We hope to encourage interest in the broad contours of international economic law, heightening awareness of its significance across the globe as well as its continuous interactions with other areas, such as public policy concerning public health and the environment, international dispute settlement and other aspects of public international law, sustainable development, and other disciplines, including economics and political science. We encourage submissions to the series from senior scholars as well as newer voices, academics as well as practitioners, from doctrinal, theoretical and empirical perspectives, and from countries around the world.

While several of the debates today concerning international economic law perpetuate those of many decades, we believe that the current moment offers particularly exciting opportunities for thoughtful and rigorous scholarly contributions to have a meaningful impact on national and international law and policy. Developments in the World Trade Organization, new approaches to regional and plurilateral negotiations, and reform proposals in relation to investment treaty arbitration all offer room for a diversity of views that will benefit from engagement and collaboration. The current volume gets to the heart of a key legitimacy concern with international investment arbitration (and particularly investor–State dispute settlement): 'treaty shopping', which Baumgartner defines:

> to include all legal operations aimed at invoking or creating a qualifying nationality and/or a qualifying investment, eg by structuring or restructuring an investment or by otherwise conferring an entitlement or property right to an investment, with a view to benefitting from a particular international investment agreement granting an investor direct standing[.]

Treaty shopping in international investment law is surprisingly under-researched, with Baumgartner's work providing the first comprehensive English language study of the area. In particular, she delves into the complex problem of distinguishing between legitimate and illegitimate forms of treaty shopping, carefully analysing the principle of 'good faith' as a possible touchstone, as well as articulating various approaches to treaty drafting that may help minimize abusive practices.

Baumgartner's examination concerns a perennial problem in international investment law, while being all the more relevant today given increasing public scrutiny of investment treaties and investor–State dispute settlement (ISDS), the continuing accumulation of such treaties and disputes, and the uncertainty surrounding the current law. As an example of the current significance of treaty shopping in international investment law, awards of two tribunals only made public since the finalization of this manuscript accepted jurisdictional objections on the basis of 'abuse of process' in connection with corporate restructuring related to pre-existing disputes. In a jurisdictional award released to the public on 16 May 2016, the tribunal in *Philip Morris Asia Limited v Australia*, discussed in this book, found that the restructuring was undertaken when the claimant's dispute with Australia concerning standardized tobacco packaging was foreseeable, 'for the principal, if not sole, purpose of gaining Treaty protection'. Similarly, in an award dispatched to the parties on 2 June 2016, the tribunal in *Transglobal Green Energy LLC and Transglobal Green Panama SA v Panama* upheld Panama's jurisdictional objection 'on the ground of abuse by Claimants of the investment treaty system by attempting to create artificial international jurisdiction over a pre-existing domestic dispute'.

Such disputes are sure to continue. Baumgartner's piercing analysis offers valuable insights into the way in which they have been and are best handled, as well as suggestions for reducing uncertainty as to which side of the line particular conduct falls. The implications of the book also go further, given its consideration of broader public international law questions, and the growing potential for cross-treaty disputes, not only in the context of international investment law, but also extending to international trade law. These kinds of complications are likely to increase in both frequency and intensity as countries continue their fervour for negotiating more and bigger agreements, including the 'mega-regionals' such as the Trans-Pacific Partnership, Transatlantic Trade and Investment Partnership, and Regional Comprehensive Economic Partnership. This book provides an in-depth exploration of the issues surrounding treaty shopping to help better equip arbitrators, policy-makers, negotiators, and litigants in dealing with such issues at a crucial time.

Andrew D. Mitchell and Tania Voon

Acknowledgements

This book is a slightly revised and updated version of the doctoral thesis I defended at the University of Lausanne (Switzerland) in June 2015 under the same title. To see it published at Oxford University Press is an immense reward both to me as well as the persons who have contributed to making this a successful project.

I am indebted and sincerely grateful to many persons I have met along the way of this endeavour and who have contributed in one way or another, not least Professor Andreas Ziegler, my thesis supervisor, for the support and flexibilities granted during the period of writing, as well as Professor Marc Bungenberg, member of the PhD defence committee, for having always stood by with precious comments and advice. My gratitude extends to the other members of the PhD defence committee, Professor Christina Binder, Professor Andrea Bonomi and Professor Tarcisio Gazzini, for their valuable comments and for making my thesis defence a pleasurable and memorable experience.

I am also very thankful to my friends and colleagues who, over the years, have provided emotional support, reviewed drafts or given comments on the manuscript, in particular Tristan Gianora, Dr. Jörn Griebel, Caterina Arias Hernandez, Felix Imhof, Dr. Wolfgang Alschner, Ömer Keskin, Azadi Öztürk and Elisabeth Türk.

Many thanks are also due to the editorial team at Oxford University Press for their guidance, support and efficiency in bringing the book to press, to the Series Editors Professors Tania Voon and Andrew Mitchell for their kind support of the manuscript, as well as to the anonymous peer reviewers for their valuable comments.

This book has been revised to include investment arbitral jurisprudence until May 2016 (redacted *Philip Morris Asia v Australia* award). The opinions expressed in this book were written in my capacity as research fellow and are not necessarily those of my current, or any future, employer.

Finally, words are not enough to thank my family—my partner Pancho, our son Luca, my parents Viktor and Sylvia and my brother Peter—for the love, support and patience shown over these past years, without which this endeavour would not have been possible.

Geneva, October 2016

Table of Contents

Table of Cases xvii
Table of Treaties xxvii
Table of Abbreviations xxxv

Introduction 1

PART I. PLACING TREATY SHOPPING IN CONTEXT

1. Understanding the Practice of Treaty Shopping 7
1.1 Defining Treaty Shopping in International Investment Law 7
1.1.1 Perceptions and definitions of treaty shopping used in academic literature and arbitral jurisprudence 7
1.1.2 Possible scenarios of treaty shopping 12
1.1.2.1 Treaty shopping by natural persons 12
1.1.2.2 Treaty shopping by corporate structuring or restructuring 13
1.1.2.3 Treaty shopping by transfer of claims 14
1.1.3 The distinction between treaty and forum shopping 15
1.2 Reasons for the Occurrence of Treaty Shopping 19
1.2.1 Proliferation of investment treaties 20
1.2.2 Change from diplomatic protection to direct standing paradigm 27
1.2.3 Ease of incorporation of legal entities and high fungibility of shareholding 32
1.2.4 Absence of a doctrine of precedent? 32
1.3 Preliminary Conclusions 33

2. Is Anything Wrong with Treaty Shopping? 34
2.1 Introduction 34
2.2 Considerations in Favour of a 'Treaty Shopping-permissive' Approach 34
2.2.1 Sovereign consent 34
2.2.2 Access to justice? 37
2.3 Policy Concerns Against Treaty Shopping 39
2.3.1 Reciprocity 39
2.3.1.1 Reciprocity in public international law 40
2.3.1.2 Reciprocity in international investment law 42
2.3.2 Legitimacy concerns 49
2.3.2.1 The meaning of legitimacy in international law 49
2.3.2.2 Legitimacy concerns in international investment law 52
2.3.2.3 Legitimacy concerns and treaty shopping 58
2.3.3 Sustainable development 59
2.3.4 Regulatory chill 62
2.3.5 Lack of a 'level-playing' field 63
2.4 Preliminary Conclusions 65

PART II. SYSTEMATIC APPROACHES TO THE VALIDITY OF A CLAIM INVOLVING TREATY SHOPPING

3. The Customary International Law Relative to Changes of Nationality 69

3.1 Introduction 69
3.2 The Concept of Nationality 69
3.2.1 Natural persons 71
3.2.1.1 *Nottebohm* case 71
3.2.1.2 Discussion 72
3.2.2 Legal persons 74
3.2.2.1 Domestic law theories on the creation of legal persons 74
3.2.2.1.1 Incorporation theory 74
3.2.2.1.2 Seat theory 75
3.2.2.1.3 Control theory 77
3.2.2.2 Customary international law 77
3.2.2.2.1 *Barcelona Traction* case 77
3.2.2.2.2 Discussion 80
3.2.2.2.3 *Diallo* case 84
3.2.2.2.4 ILC 2006 Draft Articles on Diplomatic Protection 85
3.3 Continuous Nationality Requirement 86
3.4 Relevance of Customary International Law for the Practice of Treaty Shopping 88
3.5 Preliminary Conclusions 90

4. Jurisdiction *Ratione Personae* 92

4.1 Introduction 92
4.2 Natural Persons 92
4.2.1 'Genuine link' requirement in international investment law? 93
4.2.1.1 Single nationality 93
4.2.1.2 Dual nationality 95
4.2.2 Dual nationality of a natural person exercising 'foreign control' 97
4.2.3 Discussion 98
4.3 Legal Persons 99
4.3.1 Formal approach v 'piercing of the corporate veil' 101
4.3.1.1 So-called 'round-tripping' 102
4.3.1.2 So-called mailbox or shell companies 108
4.3.1.3 Discussion 111
4.3.2 Substantive link requirements 114
4.3.3 Denial of benefit clauses 116
4.3.3.1 Prospective or retrospective effect? 117
4.3.3.2 Discussion 119
4.3.4 Definition and scope of 'control' 120
4.3.4.1 Notion of 'foreign control' in the ICSID Convention 121
4.3.4.1.1 Which criteria can be used to define control? 122
4.3.4.1.2 Legal v effective control 123
4.3.4.1.3 Discussion 125

4.3.4.2 Level of control 127
4.3.4.2.1 First qualifying nationality found or ultimate controller? 127
4.3.4.2.2 Discussion 131
4.3.4.3 Notion of control in IIAs 134
4.3.4.3.1 Legal or effective control 134
4.3.4.3.2 Discussion 136
4.4 Preliminary Conclusions 138

5. **Jurisdiction *Ratione Materiae*** 140
5.1 Introduction 140
5.2 Notion of Investment in IIAs 140
5.2.1 Shareholding as investment 141
5.2.2 Indirect investments 142
5.2.2.1 Inclusion of indirect investments when the treaty text is silent? 143
5.2.2.2 Discussion 144
5.2.2.3 Exceptions 145
5.3 Notion of Investment in the ICSID Convention 147
5.4 Specific Problems Related to Treaty Shopping 150
5.4.1 Contribution requirement 150
5.4.1.1 Economic motivation 150
5.4.1.2 Transactions at nominal price or for free 151
5.4.2 Risk requirement 155
5.4.3 'Active contribution' requirement? 155
5.4.3.1 Cases 155
5.4.3.2 Discussion 158
5.4.4 Good faith as an element of the notion of investment? 160
5.4.4.1 Cases 160
5.4.4.2 Discussion 163
5.5 Preliminary Conclusions 164

6. **Jurisdiction *Ratione Temporis*** 166
6.1 Introduction 166
6.2 Timing of Nationality Requirement 167
6.2.1 ICSID Convention 167
6.2.2 Other investment treaties 168
6.3 Continuous Nationality Requirement 169
6.3.1 *Loewen Group Inc and Raymond Loewen v United States* 169
6.3.2 Discussion 171
6.4 Exclusion of Pre-existing Disputes 175
6.4.1 Why should a pre-existing dispute be excluded? 176
6.4.1.1 Treaty-based exclusion clauses 177
6.4.1.2 No treaty-based exclusion clauses 177
6.4.2 When has the dispute arisen? 182
6.4.2.1 Importance of the notion of dispute for a claim following a corporate restructuring 182

6.4.2.2 PCIJ and ICJ jurisprudence on the notion of 'dispute' 184
6.4.2.2.1 Cases 185
6.4.2.2.2 Discussion 187
6.4.2.3 Notion of 'dispute' in international investment law 188
6.4.2.3.1 Definition of dispute 188
6.4.2.3.2 'Objective' or 'subjective' approach to the notion of dispute? 190
6.4.2.3.3 *Philip Morris Asia v Australia* 194
6.4.2.3.4 Identity of disputes? 196
6.4.2.4 Discussion 199
6.5 Preliminary Conclusions 201

7. Objections on Grounds of an Abuse of Rights or Abuse of Process 202
7.1 Introduction 202
7.2 The Abuse of Rights or Abuse of Process Doctrine 202
7.3 The Timing of the Corporate Structuring or Restructuring and the Existence or Foreseeability of a Dispute 205
7.3.1 Cases 206
7.3.1.1 Société Générale v Dominican Republic 206
7.3.1.2 Cementownia v Turkey 207
7.3.1.3 Phoenix Action v Czech Republic 207
7.3.1.4 Aguas del Tunarí v Bolivia 208
7.3.1.5 Mobil v Venezuela 208
7.3.1.6 Pac Rim v El Salvador 210
7.3.1.7 Tidewater v Venezuela 211
7.3.1.8 ConocoPhillips v Venezuela 213
7.3.1.9 Lao Holdings v Laos 215
7.3.1.10 Cervin Investissements & Rhone Investissements v Costa Rica 215
7.3.1.11 Renée Rose Levy and Gremcitel SA v Peru 216
7.3.1.12 Philip Morris Asia v Australia 217
7.3.2 Discussion 219
7.3.2.1 Distinction between jurisdiction *ratione temporis* and abuse of process 219
7.3.2.2 The existence of an actual dispute and the foreseeability of a future dispute 222
7.3.2.3 The 'sole purpose' doctrine 227
7.3.2.4 Other factors that may influence whether a tribunal will be prepared to accept a corporate (re)structuring as 'legitimate corporate planning' or not 228
7.4 *Nemo Dat Quod Non Habet* 229
7.4.1 Cases 229
7.4.2 Discussion 231
7.5 Preliminary Conclusions 232
Conclusions of Part II 234

PART III. POSSIBLE SOLUTIONS TO THE INCONSISTENT APPROACHES TOWARDS TREATY SHOPPING

8. What States Can Do to Curb Treaty Shopping 239
8.1 'Political' Approaches to Treaty Shopping 239
8.1.1 Negotiation of a multilateral investment framework 239
8.1.2 Prescription of mailbox companies 240
8.1.3 Investment treaties without ISDS clauses 241
8.2 'Treaty Drafting' Approaches to Treaty Shopping 242
8.2.1 Joint interpretations 243
8.2.2 The role of the preamble 244
8.2.3 Notion of investor 246
8.2.3.1 Natural persons 246
8.2.3.1.1 Inclusion of the effective nationality principle 246
8.2.3.1.2 Exclusion of claims by host State nationals 248
8.2.3.1.3 Permanent residents as protected investors 248
8.2.3.2 Legal persons 249
8.2.3.2.1 'Anti-treaty shopping' nationality criteria found in IIAs 250
8.2.3.2.2 Denial of benefits clauses 251
8.2.3.2.3 Discussion 256
8.2.3.3 Notion of control 256
8.2.3.4 Foreign control as in Article 25(2)(b) ICSID Convention 260
8.2.4 Notion of investment 261
8.2.4.1 Protection of indirect investments 262
8.2.4.2 Specific criteria pertaining to the notion of investment 264
8.2.4.2.1 Specifications of the contribution requirement 264
8.2.4.2.2 Good faith requirement 264
8.2.4.2.3 'Active contribution' requirement 265
8.2.4.2.4 Origin of capital requirement 268
8.2.5 Temporal jurisdiction 269
8.2.5.1 Principle of non-retroactivity 269
8.2.5.2 Exclusion of disputes that have arisen prior to the entry into force of the IIA 270
8.2.5.3 Exclusion of acts or facts giving rise to a later dispute 271
8.2.5.4 Dispute settlement clause: notion of dispute 272
8.2.6 Inclusion of conditions under which a corporate restructuring is accepted 272
8.2.7 Inclusion of the abuse of process doctrine 274
8.2.8 Inclusion of the 'pre-existing/foreseeable dispute' jurisprudence 274
8.3 Preliminary Conclusions 276

9. The Role of the Principle of Good Faith in Treaty Shopping 278
9.1 Introduction 278
9.2 The Normative Status of the Principle of Good Faith and its Functions 279

9.3 The Interpretative Approach Towards Treaty Shopping 283
9.3.1 Ordinary meaning 284
9.3.2 Context 285
9.3.3 Object and purpose 285
9.3.4 Special case: *Phoenix Action v Czech Republic* 287
9.3.5 Discussion 290
9.4 Application of the Principle of Good Faith or One of its Concretizations 291
9.4.1 'Genuine link' theory 291
9.4.2 'Piercing of the corporate veil' doctrine 292
9.4.3 Fraud 298
9.4.4 The abuse of rights/abuse of process doctrine 301
9.5 A (More) Systematic Approach Towards the Use of the Principle of Good Faith and its Emanations in Cases of Treaty Shopping 303
9.6 Preliminary Conclusions 307
Conclusions 309

Annex 317
Bibliography 331
Index 351

Table of Cases

INVESTMENT ARBITRAL JURISPRUDENCE

(Unless otherwise indicated, all quoted decisions can be found on UNCTAD's Investment Dispute Settlement Navigator, <http://investmentpolicyhub.unctad.org/ISDS/FilterByCaseName>, or on www.italaw.com)

Abaclat and Others v Argentine Republic, ICSID Case No ARB/07/5, Decision on Jurisdiction and Admissibility (4 August 2011) (formerly known as Giovanna a Beccara and Others) 100, 280, 302–03

ABCI Investments NV v République Tunisienne, ICSID Case No ARB/04/12, Decision on Jurisdiction (French) (18 February 2011) 177–78, 191

Achmea BV v Slovak Republic, PCA Case No 13–2008, Award on Jurisdiction (26 October 2010) (formerly *Eureko BV v The Slovak Republic*) 25–26

ADC Affiliate Limited and ADC & ADMC Management Limited v Republic of Hungary, ICSID Case No ARB/03/16, Award (2 October 2006) . . . 14, 90, 106, 109, 284, 293, 297, 301

African Holding Company of America Inc et Société Africaine de Construction au Congo SARL v République Démocratique du Congo, ICSID Case No ARB/05/21, Sentence sur les déclinatoires de competence et la recevabilité (29 July 2008) 141, 197

Aguas del Tunarí SA v Plurinational State of Bolivia, ICSID Case No ARB/02/3, Decision on Respondent's Objections to Jurisdiction (21 October 2005) 8, 13–15, 47, 57, 126, 234, 208, 221, 245, 283–84, 286, 297

AIG Capital Partners Inc and CJSC Tema Real Estate Company Ltd v Republic of Kazakhstan, ICSID Case No ARB/01/6, Award (7 October 2003) 141–42

Alapli Elektrik BV v Republic of Turkey, ICSID Case No ARB/08/13, Award (16 July 2012) 157, 159, 161, 224, 278, 291, 306

Alapli Elektrik BV v Republic of Turkey, ICSID Case No ARB/08/13, Decision on Annulment (10 July 2014) 157, 159–61, 221, 224, 278, 291, 306

Alpha Projektholding GmbH v Ukraine, ICSID Case No ARB/07/16, Award (8 November 2010) 106, 149, 155

Alps Finance and Trade AG v Republic of Slovakia, UNCITRAL, Award (5 March 2011) 14, 115

Amco Asia Corporation, Pan American Development Limited, PT Amco Indonesia v Indonesia, ICSID Case No ARB/81/1, Award on Jurisdiction (25 September 1983) printed in (1993) 1 ICSID Rep 377 . . . . 101, 127, 133

Archer Daniels Midland Company and Tate & Lyle Ingredients Americas Inc v United States of Mexico, ICSID Case No ARB(AF)/04/5, Award (21 November 2007) 28

Ascom and Stati v Republic of Kazakhstan, SCC, Award (19 December 2013) 117, 286

Autopista Concesionada de Venezuela, CA (Aucoven) v Bolivarian Republic of Venezuela, ICSID Case No ARB/00/5, Decision on Jurisdiction (27 September 2001) printed in (2001) 16 ICSID Review-FILJ 469 . . . . 13, 101, 122–23, 130, 227, 273, 301

Azurix Corp v Argentine Republic, ICSID Case No ARB/01/12, Decision on Jurisdiction (8 December 2003) 142, 149, 183

Banro American Resources Inc and Société Aurifère du Kivu du Maniema SARL v Democratic Republic of Congo, ICSID Case No ARB/98/7, Award (1 September 2000) 173, 206, 214, 229–30, 232

Bayindir Insaat Turizm Ticaret Ve Sanayi AS v Islamic Republic of Pakistan, ICSID Case No ARB/03/29, Decision on Jurisdiction (14 November 2005) 148

Vladimir Berschader and Moise Berschader v Russian Federation, Arbitration V (080/2004) Award (21 April 2006) 146–47

Biwater Gauff Ltd v United Republic of Tanzania, ICSID Case No ARB/05/22, Award (24 July 2008) 149
Bosh International Inc and B&P Ltd Foreign Investment Enterprise v Ukraine, ICSID Case No ARB/08/11, Award (25 October 2012) 60
Bureau Veritas, Inspection, Valuation, Assessment and Control, BIVAC BV v Republic of Paraguay, ICSID Case No ARB/07/9, Further Decision on Objections to Jurisdiction (9 October 2012) 8
Burimi SRL and Eagle Games SH.A v Republic of Albania, ICSID Case No ARB/11/18, Award (29 May 2013) 13, 97, 99, 132, 285
Camuzzi International SA v Argentine Republic, ICSID Case No ARB/03/2, Decision on Objections to Jurisdiction (11 May 2005) 125
Caratube International Oil Company LLP v Republic of Kazakhstan, ICSID Case No ARB/08/12, Award (5 June 2012) 122–23, 126, 137, 150–52, 155, 162, 260, 285, 306
Cementownia "Nowa Huta" SA v Republic of Turkey, ICSID Case No ARB(AF)/06/2, Award (17 September 2009) 8, 18, 161, 169, 183, 204, 207, 227–28, 288, 298–300
CEMEX Caracas Investments BV and CEMEX Caracas II Investments BV v Bolivarian Republic of Venezuela, ICSID Case No ARB/08/14, Decision on Jurisdiction (30 December 2010) 145, 150, 158–59
Cervin Investissements SA and Rhone Investissements SA v Republic of Costa Rica, ICSID Case No ARB/13/2, Decision on Jurisdiction (Spanish) (15 December 2014) 183, 193, 215–16, 221, 227
Ceskoslovenska Obchodni Banka AS v Slovak Republic, ICSID Case No ARB/97/4, Decision on Objections to Jurisdiction (24 May 1999) 148, 155, 173
Champion Trading Company, Ameritrade International, Inc v Arab Republic of Egypt, ICSID Case No ARB/02/9, Decision on Jurisdiction (21 October 2003) (formerly *Champion Trading Company, Ameritrade International, Inc, James T Wahba, John Wahba, Timothy T Wahba v Arab Republic of Egypt*) 95–96, 98
CME Czech Republic BV v Czech Republic, UNCITRAL, Partial Award (13 September 2001) (*CME I*) 18, 53
CME Czech Republic BV v Czech Republic, UNCITRAL, Final Award (14 March 2003) (*CME II*) 18, 53
CME Czech Republic BV v Czech Republic, UNCITRAL, Svea Court of Appeal, Sweden (15 May 2003) 18, 53
CMS Gas Transmission Company v Argentine Republic, ICSID Case No ARB/01/8, Decision of the Tribunal on Jurisdiction (17 July 2003) 17–18, 31, 141–42, 196
Compagnie d'Exploration du Chemin de Fer Transgabonais v Republic of Gabon, ICSID Case No ARB/04/5, Decision on Jurisdiction (19 December 2005) printed in (2011) 26 ICSID Review-FILJ 153 .... 123, 125, 127–28, 132
Compañía de Aguas del Aconquija SA and Vivendi Universal SA v Argentine Republic, ICSID Case No ARB/97/3, Award (21 November 2000) (formerly *Compañía de Aguas del Aconquija, SA and Compagnie Générale des Eaux v Argentine Republic*) 17
Compañía de Aguas del Aconquija SA and Vivendi Universal SA v Argentine Republic, ICSID Case No ARB/97/3, Decision on Annulment (3 July 2002) (formerly *Compañía de Aguas del Aconquija, SA and Compagnie Générale des Eaux v Argentine Republic*) 17
ConocoPhillips Petrozuata BV, ConocoPhillips Hamaca BV, ConocoPhillips Gulf of Paria BV and ConocoPhillips Company v Boliviarian Republic of Venezuela, ICSID Case No ARB/07/30, Decision on Jurisdiction and the Merits (3 September 2013) 145, 190, 213–14, 219–21, 223–25, 227–28, 233, 280
Dawood Rawad v Republic of Mauritius, UNCITRAL, Notice of arbitration and statement of claim (9 November 2015) 99
El Paso Energy International Company v Argentine Republic, ICSID Case No ARB/3/15, Decision on Jurisdiction (27 April 2006) 173–74

Empresa Eléctrica del Ecuador, Inc v Republic of Ecuador, ICSID Case No ARB/05/9, Award (2 June 2009) 155
EnCana Corporation v Republic of Ecuador, LCIA Case No UN3481, UNCITRAL, Award (3 February 2006) (formerly *EnCana Corporation v Government of the Republic of Ecuador*) 174–75
Eureko BV v Republic of Poland, Partial Award (19 August 2005) 17, 25–26
Europe Cement Investment & Trade v Republic of Turkey, ICSID Case No ARB(AF)/07/2, Decision on Jurisdiction (13 August 2009) 18, 183, 228, 288, 298–300
Fedax NV v Bolivarian Republic of Venezuela, ICSID Case No ARB/96/3, Decision of the Tribunal on Objections to Jurisdiction (11 July 1997) printed in (1998) 37 ILM 1378 148
Marvin Roy Feldman Karpa v United States of Mexico, ICSID Case No ARB(AF)/99/1, Interim Decision on Preliminary Jurisdictional Issues (6 December 2000) 94, 98
Fraport AG Frankfurt Airport Services Worldwide v The Republic of the Philippines, ICSID Case No ARB/03/25, Award (16 August 2007) 149, 301
Vito G Gallo v Government of Canada, NAFTA/UNCITRAL, Award (15 September 2011) 169
Serafín García Armas y Karina García Gruber v Bolivarian Republic of Venezuela, UNCITRAL, PCA Case No 2013-3, Decision on Jurisdiction (Spanish) (15 December 2014) 96–97, 99, 247
Gas Natural SDG SA v Argentine Republic, ICSID Case No ARB/03/10, Decision on Jurisdiction (17 June 2005) 142
GEA Group Aktiengesellschaft v Ukraine, ICSID Case No ARB/08/16, Award (31 March 2011) 169, 183
Generation Ukraine Inc v Ukraine, ICSID Case No ARB/00/9, Award (16 September 2003) 178
Antoine Goetz & Consorts et SA Affinage des Métaux v République du Burundi, ICSID Case No ARB/95/3, Award (10 February 1999) 141
Gold Reserve Inc v Bolivarian Republic of Venezuela, ICSID Case No ARB(AF)/09/1, Award (22 September 2014) 111, 153
Guaracachi America Inc and Rurelec PLC v Plurinational State of Bolivia, UNCITRAL, PCA Case No 2011-17, Award (31 January 2014) 119–20, 145
Guardian Fiduciary Trust Ltd f/k/a Capital Conservator Savings & Loans Ltd v Former Yugoslav Republic of Macedonia, ICSID Case No ARB/12/31, Award (22 September 2015) 135
Gustav FW Hamester GmbH & Co KG v Ghana, ICSID Case No ARB/07/24, Award (18 June 2010) 265, 289
Helnan International Hotels A/S v Arab Republic of Egypt, ICSID Case No ARB/05/19, Decision of the Tribunal on Objection to Jurisdiction (17 October 2006) 148, 189
HICEE BV v Slovak Republic, PCA Case No 2009-11, UNCITRAL, Partial Award (23 May 2011) 146
Hulley Enterprises Limited (Cyprus) v Russian Federation, UNCITRAL, PCA Case No AA 226, Interim Award on Jurisdiction and Admissibility (30 November 2009) 18
ICS Inspection and Control Services Limited (United Kingdom) v The Republic of Argentina, UNCITRAL, PCA Case No 2010-9, Award on Jurisdiction (10 February 2012) 60
Impreglio SpA v Islamic Republic of Pakistan, ICSID Case No ARB/03/3, Decision on Jurisdiction (22 April 2005) 178, 188
Inceysa Vallisoletana SL v Republic of El Salvador, ICSID Case No ARB/03/26, Award (2 August 2006) 280, 299–300
Inmaris Perestroika Sailing Maritime Services GmbH and Others v Ukraine, ICSID Case No ARB08/8, Decision on Jurisdiction (8 March 2010) 149
International Thunderbird Gaming Corporation v United Mexican States, UNCITRAL, Award (26 January 2006) 123, 135–36
Invesmart BV v Czech Republic, UNCITRAL, Award (26 June 2009) 153
Ioannis Kardassopoulos v Republic of Georgia, ICSID Case No ARB/05/18, Decision on Jurisdiction (6 July 2007) 141, 145

Jan de Nul NV and Dredging International NV v Arab Republic of Egypt, ICSID Case No ARB/04/13, Decision on Jurisdiction (16 June 2006) 148, 197, 200
Joy Mining Machinery Limited v Arab Republic of Egypt, ICSID Case No ARB/03/11, Award on Jurisdiction (6 August 2004) 148
Kaiser Bauxite Company v Jamaica, ICSID Case No ARB/74/3, Decision on Jurisdiction (6 July 1975) 101
Khan Resources Inc, Khan Resources BV, CAUC Holding Company Ltd v Government of Mongolia, MonAtom LLC, PCA Case No 2011-09, Decision on Jurisdiction (25 July 2012) 117
KT Asia Investment Group BV v Republic of Kazakhstan, ICSID Case No ARB/09/8, Award (17 October 2013) 106, 111, 149, 151–52, 160, 278, 285, 293, 297, 306
Lanco International Inc v Argentine Republic, ICSID Case No ARB/97/6, Decision on Jurisdiction (8 December 1998) 142
Lao Holdings NV v Lao People's Democratic Republic, ICSID Case No ARB(AF)/12/6, Decision on Jurisdiction (21 February 2014) 13, 15, 177–78, 188, 190–91, 193, 215, 219–21, 224, 286
Ronald S Lauder v Czech Republic, UNCITRAL, Final Award (3 September 2001) 18–19, 53
LESI SpA and ASTALDI SpA v République Algérienne Démocratique et Populaire, ICSID Case No ARB/05/3, Decision (French) (12 July 2006) 149
Libananco Holdings Co Limited v Republic of Turkey, ICSID Case No ARB(AF)/06/8, Award (2 September 2011) 18, 298–99
Liberian Eastern Timber Corporation v Republic of Liberia, ICSID Case No ARB/83/2, Decision on Jurisdiction (24 October 1984) printed in (1994) 2 ICSID Rep 349 123
Liman Caspian Oil BV and NCL Dutch Investment BV v Republic of Kazakhstan, ICSID Case No ARB/07/14, Award (22 June 2010) 117, 286
Loewen Group Inc and Raymond Loewen v United States of Americas, ICSID Case No ARB(AF)/98/3, Award (26 June 2003) 14, 27, 90, 168–72, 174, 201
Empresas Lucchetti SA and Lucchetti Peru SA v Republic of Peru, ICSID Case No ARB/03/4, Award (7 February 2005) 188, 196–200, 223
Emilio Agustín Maffezini v Kingdom of Spain, ICSID Case No ARB/97/7, Decision on Objections to Jurisdiction (25 January 2000) 8, 19–20, 188–89, 271
Malaysian Historical Salvors, SDN, BHD v Government of Malaysia, ICSID Case No ARB/05/10, Award (28 May 2007) 148
Malaysian Historical Salvors, SDN, BHD v Government of Malaysia, ICSID Case No ARB/05/10, Decision on the Application for Annulment of the Award (16 April 2009) 149
MCI Power Group LC and New Turbine Inc v Republic of Ecuador, ICSID Case No ARB/03/6, Award (31 July 2007) 149, 178
Ioan Micula, Viorel Micula, SC European Food SA, SC Starmill SRL and SC Multipack SRL v Romania, ICSID Case No ARB/05/20, Decision on Jurisdiction and Admissibility (24 September 2008) 93–94, 98–99, 177
Mihaly International Corporation v Democratic Socialist Republic of Sri Lanka, ICSID Case No ARB/00/2, Award (15 March 2002) printed in (2002) 17 ICSID Review-FILJ 142 . . . . . 14, 206, 214, 229, 231, 232
Millicom International Operations BV and Sentel GSM SA v Republic of Senegal, ICSID Case No ARB/08/20, Decision on Jurisdiction of the Arbitral Tribunal (16 July 2010) 228, 297
Patrick Mitchell v Democratic Republic of Congo, ICSID Case No ARB/99/7, Decision on the Application for Annulment of the Award (1 November 2006) 148
Mobil Corporation, Venezuela Holdings BV, Mobil Cerro Negro Holding, Ltd, Mobil Venezolana de Petróleos Holdings, Inc, Mobil Cerro Negro, Ltd, and Mobil Venezolana de Petróleos, Inc v Bolivarian Republic of Venezuela, ICSID Case No ARB/07/27, Decision on Jurisdiction (10 June 2010) 14, 134, 142, 152–53, 204, 208–09, 212–13, 215, 219, 221, 231, 258, 280, 288, 300–01

Venezuela Holdings BV, Mobil Cerro Negro Holding, Ltd, Mobil Venezolana de Petróleos Holdings, Inc, Mobil Cerro Negro, Ltd, and Mobil Venezolana de Petróleos, Inc v Bolivarian Republic of Venezuela, ICSID Case No ARB/07/27, Award (9 October 2014) 190
Mondev International Ltd v United States of America, ICSID Case No ARB(AF)/99/2, Award (11 October 2002) 178
National Gas SAE v Arab Republic of Egypt, ICSID Case No ARB/11/7, Award (3 April 2014) 13, 15, 97–99, 127, 130–133, 285, 287, 305–06
National Grid plc v Argentine Republic, UNCITRAL, Decision on Jurisdiction (20 June 2006) 173–75
Niko Resources (Bangladesh) Ltd v People's Republic of Bangladesh, Bangladesh Petroleum Exploration & Production Company Limited ("Bapex") and Bangladesh Oil Gas and Mineral Corporation ("Petrobangla") ICSID Case No ARB/10/11 and 10/18, Decision on Jurisdiction (19 August 2013) 110, 301
Nova Scotia Power Incorporated v Bolivarian Republic of Venezuela, ICSID Case No ARB(AF)/11/1, Award (30 April 2014) 149
OI European Group BV v Bolivarian Republic of Venezuela, ICSID Case No ARB/11/25, Award (Spanish) (10 March 2015) 153
Eudoro Armando Olguín v Republic of Paraguay, ICSID Case No ARB/98/5, Award (26 July 2001) (unofficial English translation) 96, 98
Jan Oostergetel and Theodora Laurentius v Slovak Republic, UNCITRAL, Decision on Jurisdiction (30 April 2010) 94, 98–99, 149
Pac Rim Cayman LLC v Republic of El Salvador, ICSID Case No ARB/09/12, Decision on the Respondent's Jurisdictional Objections (1 June 2012) 115, 118–20, 178, 183–84, 190, 192–93, 210, 215–16, 218–20, 222–24, 226, 285, 288, 300–01
Pan American Energy LLP and BP Argentina Exploration Company v Argentine Republic, ICSID Case No ARB/03/13, Decision on Preliminary Objections (27 July 2006) 117, 286
Pantechniki SA Contractors & Engineers (Greece) v Republic of Albania, ICSID Case No ARB/07/21, Award (30 July 2009) 149
Perenco Ecuador Ltd v Republic of Ecuador and Empresa Estatal de Petróleos del Ecuador (Petroecuador) ICSID Case No ARB/08/6, Decision on Jurisdiction (30 June 2011) 153
Victor Pey Casado and President Allende Foundation v Republic of Chile, ICSID Case No ARB/98/2, Sentence Arbitrale (8 May 2008) 96, 98, 149, 189, 191
Philip Morris Asia Limited v Commonwealth of Australia, UNCITRAL, Australia's Response to the Notice of Arbitration (21 December 2011) 11, 302
Philip Morris Asia Limited v Commonwealth of Australia, UNCITRAL, PCA Case No 2012-12, Award on Jurisdiction and Admissibility (17 December 2015) (redacted version) 2, 13, 20, 58, 183, 194–96, 217, 219, 226–27, 255, 259, 276, 302, 305
Philip Morris Brands Sàrl, Philip Morris Products SA and Abal Hermanos SA v Oriental Republic of Uruguay, ICSID Case No ARB/10/7, Decision on Jurisdiction (2 July 2013) (formerly *FTR Holding SA, Philip Morris Products SA and Abal Hermanos SA v Oriental Republic of Uruguay*) 63, 149
Phoenix Action Limited v Czech Republic, ICSID Case No ARB/06/5, Award (15 April 2009) 11, 13, 141, 149–51, 160–61, 163–65, 178, 183, 204, 207, 210, 215, 220, 227, 231, 265, 279–80, 285–89, 296–300
Ping An Life Insurance Company of China, Limited and Ping An Insurance (Group) Company of China, Limited v Kingdom of Belgium, ICSID Case No ARB/12/29, Award (30 April 2015) 178
Plama Consortium Limited v Republic of Bulgaria, ICSID Case No ARB/03/24, Decision on Jurisdiction (8 February 2005) 117, 119–20, 135, 286
Plama Consortium Ltd v Republic of Bulgaria, ICSID Case No ARB/03/24, Award (27 August 2008) 265, 289
Polska Energetyka Holding SA v Republic of Turkey, UNCITRAL, Award (1 January 2009) (not public) 18

Quiborax SA, Non Metallic Minerals SA and Allan Fosk Kaplún v Plurinational State of Bolivia, ICSID Case No ARB/06/2, Decision on Jurisdiction (27 September 2012) 149, 153, 162, 285
Renée Rose Levy de Levi v Republic of Peru, ICSID Case No ARB/10/17, Award (26 February 2014). 154, 175, 228
Renée Rose Levy and Gremcitel SA v Republic of Peru, ICSID Case No ARB/11/17, Award (9 January 2015). 13, 169, 183, 193–94, 200, 216–217, 224, 226, 301, 306
Romak SA (Switzerland) v Republic of Uzbekistan, UNCITRAL, PCA Case No AA 280, Award (26 November 2009) 149
Rompetrol Group NV v Romania, ICSID Case No ARB/06/3, Decision on Respondent's Preliminary Objections on Jurisdiction and Admissibility (18 April 2008) 14, 105, 128, 173, 183, 284
RosInvestCo UK Ltd v Russian Federation, SCC Case No V079/2005, Final Award (12 September 2010) 155, 159
RSM Production Corporation v Grenada, ICSID Case No ARB/05/14, Award (13 March 2009). 149
Rumeli Telekom AS and Telsim Mobil Telekomunikasyon Hizmetleri AS v Republic of Kazakhstan, ICSID Case No ARB/05/16, Award (29 July 2008) 293, 297
Saba Fakes v Republic of Turkey, ICSID Case No ARB/07/20, Award (14 July 2010). 96, 162
Salini Costruttori SpA and Italstrade SpA v The Hashemite Kingdom of Jordan, ICSID Case No ARB/02/13, Decision on Jurisdiction (9 November 2004). 11, 177–78
Salini Costruttori SpA and Italstrade SpA v Kingdom of Morocco, ICSID Case No ARB/00/4, Decision on Jurisdiction (23 July 2001) 148–50, 155, 161, 264
Saluka Investments BV (The Netherlands) v Czech Republic, UNCITRAL, Partial Award (17 March 2006). 8, 14, 109, 150, 152, 155, 284
Sanum Investments Limited v Government of the Lao People's Democratic Republic, UNCITRAL, PCA Case No 2013-13, Award on Jurisdiction (13 December 2013). 19
Franz Sedelmayer v Russian Federation, Arbitration in Stockholm, Award (7 July 1998) 13, 143–45, 149, 286
Sempra Energy International v Argentine Republic, ICSID Case No ARB/02/16, Decision on Jurisdiction (11 May 2005) 141–42
Sergei Viktorovich Pugachev v Russian Federation, UNCITRAL, Notice of arbitration (21 September 2015) 99
Sergei Paushok, CJSC Golden East Company, CJSC Vostokneftegaz Company v The Government of Mongolia, Award on Jurisdiction and Liability (28 April 2011) 159
SGS Société de Surveillance SA v Islamic Republic of Pakistan, ICSID Case No ARB/01/13, Decision of the Tribunal on Objections to Jurisdiction (6 August 2003) 17
SGS Société de Surveillance SA v Republic of the Philippines, ICSID Case No ARB/02/6, Decision on the Tribunal on Objections to Jurisdiction (29 January 2004) 178
Waguih Elie George Siag and Clorinda Vecchi v Arab Republic of Egypt, ICSID Case No ARB/05/15, Decision on Jurisdiction (11 April 2007). 95, 98
Siemens AG v Argentine Republic, ICSID Case No ARB/02/8, Decision on Jurisdiction (3 August 2004) 142
Sociedad Anónima Eduardo Vieira v República de Chile, ICSID Case No ARB/04/7, Laudo Dictado (21 August 2007). 189–90, 197
Société Générale in respect of DR Energy Holdings Limited and Empresa Distribuidora de Electricidad del Este, SA v Dominican Republic, UNCITRAL, LCIA Case No UN 7927, Award on Preliminary Objections to Jurisdiction (19 September 2008). 13, 141, 149, 151, 169, 178, 183, 206, 215, 219, 221, 301
Société Civile Immobilière de Gaëta v République de Guinée, ICSID Case No ARB/12/36, Award (21 December 2015) (French). 115, 153
Société Industrielle des Boissons de Guinée (SIGB) v République de Guinée, Affaire CIRDI No ARB/12/8, Sentence (21 mai 2014) 126

Société Ouest Africaine des Bétons Industriels (SOABI) v République du Sénégal, ICSID Case No ARB/82/1, Decision on Jurisdiction (1 August 1984) printed in (1994) 2 ICSID Rep 164 . . . . 101, 127, 173
Hussein Nuaman Soufraki v United Arab Emirates, ICSID Case No ARB/02/7, Award (7 July 2004) 12, 100
ST-AD GmbH v Republic of Bulgaria, UNCITRAL, PCA Case No 2011-06, Award on Jurisdiction (18 July 2013). 38, 159, 177–78, 199, 230–31, 302–03
Standard Chartered Bank v United Republic of Tanzania, ICSID Case No ARB/10/12, Award (2 November 2012) 20, 40, 47, 155, 157–60, 245, 265–68, 286, 306
Teinver SA, Transportes de Cercanías SA and Autobuses Urbanos del Sur SA v Argentine Republic, ICSID Case No ARB/09/1, Decision on Jurisdiction (21 December 2012) 141–42, 145, 174
Telenor Mobile Communications AS v Republic of Hungary, ICSID Case No ARB/04/15, Award (13 September 2006) 11
Tidewater Inc, Tidewater Investment SRL, Tidewater Caribe, CA, Twenty Grand Offshore, LLC, Point Marine, LLC, Twenty Grand Marine Service, LLC, Jackson Marine, LLC and Zapata Gulf Marine Operators, LLC v Bolivarian Republic of Venezuela, ICSID Case No ARB/10/5, Decision on Jurisdiction (8 February 2013) 8, 13, 198, 211–12, 218–19, 223–28, 288, 301
Tokios Tokelés v Ukraine, ICSID Case No ARB/02/18, Decision on Jurisdiction (29 April 2004) 14, 64, 103–06, 109, 111–13, 128, 131, 188, 284, 286, 292–93, 297, 301
Toto Costruzioni Generali SpA v Republic of Lebanon, ICSID Case No 07/12, Decision on Jurisdiction (11 September 2009) 148
Tradex Hellas SA v Republic of Albania, ICSID Case No ARB/94/2, Award (29 April 1999) 106
TSA Spectrum de Argentina SA v Argentine Republic, ICSID Case No ARB/05/5, Award (19 December 2008) 105, 111, 128, 131–32, 135, 137, 259
Tza Yap Shum v Republic of Peru, ICSID Case No ARB/07/6, Decision on Jurisdiction (19 June 2009) 145
Ulysseas Inc v Republic of Ecuador, UNCITRAL, Interim Award (28 September 2010) 118–20, 134
United Parcel Service Inc v Government of Canada, UNCITRAL, Awards on the merits (24 May 2007) 178
Vacuum Salt Products Limited v Government of the Republic of Ghana, ICSID Case No ARB/92/1, Award (16 February 1994) printed in (1994) 9 ICSID Review-FILJ 72. . . . . 123–26, 129–32, 305
Vannessa Ventures Ltd v Bolivarian Republic of Venezuela, ICSID Case No ARB(AF)/04/6, Award (16 January 2013). 151, 162–63, 273, 278, 303, 305
Venoklim Holding BV v Bolivarian Republic of Venezuela, ICSID Case No ARB/12/22, Award (Spanish) (3 April 2015). 106–08, 113, 133, 284
Veteran Petroleum Limited (Cyprus) v Russian Federation, UNCITRAL, PCA Case No AA 228, Interim Award on Jurisdiction and Admissibility (30 November 2009) 155
Werner Schneider, acting in his capacity as insolvency administrator of Walter Bau AG (In Liquidation) v The Kingdom of Thailand, UNCITRAL, Award (1 July 2009) (formerly *Walter Bau AG (In liquidation) v The Kingdom of Thailand*) 178
Waste Management Inc v United Mexican States ("Number II"), ICSID Case No ARB(AF)/00/3, Award (30 April 2004) 142
Wena Hotels Limited v Arab Republic of Egypt, ICSID Case No ARB/98/4, Proceeding on the Jurisdiction (25 May 1999) printed in (2002) 41 ILM 881 . . . . 103, 133
Wintershall Aktiengesellschaft v Argentine Republic, ICSID Case No ARB/04/14, Award (8 December 2008) 28

Yaung Chi Oo Trading Pte Ltd v Government of the Union of Myanmar, ASEAN ID Case No ARB/01/1, Award (31 March 2003) 114, 289
Yukos Universal Limited (Isle of Man) v Russian Federation, PCA Case No AA 227, Interim Award on Jurisdiction and Admissibility (30 November 2009) 18, 106, 110–11, 117, 135, 137, 155, 174, 284, 286

PERMANENT COURT OF INTERNATIONAL JUSTICE

Acquisition of Polish Nationality (Advisory Opinion) [1923] PCIJ Series B No 7 111
Electricity Company of Sofia and Bulgaria (Belgium v Bulgaria) (Preliminary Objections) [1939] PCIJ Series A/B No 77 187
Factory at Chorzów (Germany v Poland) (Judgment) [1928] PCIJ Rep Series A No 17 28
Mavrommatis Palestine Concessions (Greece v United Kingdom) (Judgment) [1924] PCIJ Series A, No 2 . . . . 28, 178, 185, 191
Nationality Decrees Issued in Tunis and Morocco (Advisory Opinion) [1923] PCIJ Series B No 4 . . . . 70–71, 83
Panevezys-Saldutiskis Railway (Estonia v Lithuania) [1939] PCIJ Series A/B No 76 . . . . 28, 87, 175
Pecuniary Claims of Danzig Railways Officials who had Passed into the Polish Service (Advisory Opinion) [1928] PCIJ Rep Series B No 15 28
Phosphates in Morocco (Italy v France) (Preliminary Objections) [1938] PCIJ Series A/B No 74. . . . 186
Serbian Loans Issued in France (France v Serbia) (Judgment) [1929] PCIJ Series A No 20. 28
SS Lotus Case (France v Turkey) (Judgment) [1927] PCIJ Series A No 10 35
SS Wimbledon Case (United Kingdom and others v Germany) (Judgment) [1923] PCIJ Series A No 1 35

INTERNATIONAL COURT OF JUSTICE

Ahmadou Sadio Diallo (Republic of Guinea v Democratic Republic of the Congo) (Preliminary Objections) [2007] ICJ Rep 582. . . . . 31, 77, 84, 88–89, 296, 310
Ahmadou Sadio Diallo (Republic of Guinea v Democratic Republic of the Congo) (Judgment) [2010] ICJ Rep 639 . . . . 85, 88–89, 310
Anglo-Iranian Oil Co (United Kingdom v Iran) (Preliminary Objections) [1952] ICJ Rep 93 178
Applicability of the Obligation to Arbitrate Under Section 21 of the United Nations Headquarter Agreement of 26 June 1947 (Advisory Opinion) [1988] ICJ Rep 12 185
Barcelona Traction, Light and Power Company Ltd (New Application: 1962) (Belgium v Spain) (Preliminary Objections) [1964] ICJ Rep 6. 178
Barcelona Traction, Light and Power Co (Belgium v Spain) (Judgment) [1970] ICJ Rep 3. . . . . 3, 9, 19, 29–31, 44, 53, 68, 74, 77–90, 82–85, 88–89, 91, 101, 104, 109, 113, 116, 140–42, 234, 261–62, 292–93, 295–97, 310, 312
Certain Expenses of the United Nations (Advisory Opinion) [1962] ICJ Reports 151 290
Certain Property (Liechtenstein v Germany) (Preliminary Objections) [2005] ICJ Rep 6 185
East Timor (Portugal v Australia) (Judgment) [1995] ICJ Rep 90 185
Elettronica Sicula SpA (ELSI) (United States v Italy) (Judgment) [1989] ICJ Rep 15 . . . . 31, 144
Interhandel (Switzerland v United States of America) (Preliminary Objections) [1959] ICJ Rep 6. . . . . 28–29, 185–86
Interpretation of Peace Treaties with Bulgaria, Hungary and Romania (Advisory Opinion) [1950] ICJ Rep 65. . . . . 185, 188
Legality of the Threat or Use of Nuclear Weapons (Advisory Opinion) [1996] ICJ Rep 226 296
North Sea Continental Shelf (Germany v Denmark; Germany v Netherlands) (Judgment) [1969] ICJ Rep 3. . . . . 81, 178

Northern Cameroons (Cameroon v United Kingdom) (Preliminary Objections) [1963] ICJ Rep 15 185
Nottebohm (Liechtenstein v Guatemala) (Judgment) [1955] ICJ Rep 4 . . . . . 3, 9, 28, 68, 70–73, 79–83, 94–95, 282
Nuclear Tests (Australia v France) (Merits) [1974] ICJ Rep 253 . . . . . 279, 282
Oil Platforms (Iran v United States) (Judgment) [2003] ICJ Rep 161 296
Reparations for Injuries Suffered in the Service of the United Nations Case (Advisory Opinion) [1949] ICJ Rep 181 28
Right of Passage over Indian Territory (Portugal v India) (Preliminary Objections) [1957] ICJ Rep 125 185
Right of Passage over Indian Territory (Portugal v India) (Judgment) [1960] ICJ Rep 6. 187
South West Africa case (Ethiopia v South Africa; Liberia v South Africa), (Preliminary Objections) [1962] ICJ Rep 319 185

IRAN–UNITED STATES CLAIMS TRIBUNAL

Amoco International Finance Corporation v Iran, Case No 310-56-3 (14 July 1987) 15 Iran–US CTR 189 90
Case No A/18, Case No DEC 32-A18-FT (6 April 1984) 5 Iran–US CTR 251 72
Nasser Esphahanian v Bank Teheran, Case No 31-157-2 (29 March 1983) 2 Iran–US CTR 157 . . . . . 73, 296–97
Richard D Harza et al v Iran, Case No 232-97-2 (2 May 1986) 11 Iran–US CTR 76 296
Foremost Teheran Inc et al v Iran, Case No 220-37/231-1 (11 April 1986) 10 Iran–US CTR 228 296

OTHER INTERNATIONAL TRIBUNALS

Administrative Decision No V (United States v Germany) (1924) 7 RIAA 119 . . . . . 29, 86–87
Ambatielos Case (Greece v United Kingdom) (1956) 12 RIAA 119. 38–39
Beagle Channel (Argentina v Chile) (1977) 52 ILR 93 244
Canavero (Italy v Peru) (1912) 11 RIAA 397 72
Baron Frédéric de Born v Yugoslav State (1926) 4 Ann Dig 277 72
Flegenheimer (Italy v United States) (1958) 14 RIAA 327 . . . . . 72, 297
Eschauzier (Great Britain v Mexico) (1931) 5 RIAA 207 88
MOX Plant (Ireland v United Kingdom) ITLOS Provisional Measures Order (3 Dec 2001) 126 ILR 259 . . . . . 16, 27
MOX Plant (Ireland v United Kingdom) UNCLOS, Annex VII, Order No 3 (24 June 2003) 126 ILR 310 . . . . . 16, 27
Dispute Concerning Access to Information under Art 9 of the OSPAR Convention (Ireland v UK), Permanent Court of Arbitration, Final Award (2 July 2003) 126 ILR 334. 16

WTO PANEL AND APPELLATE BODY REPORTS

Appellate Body Report, *United States—Standards for Reformulated and Conventional Gasoline,* WTO Doc WT/DS2/AB/R (adopted 20 May 1996) 290
Appellate Body Report, *United States—Import Prohibition of Certain Shrimp and Shrimp Products,* WTO Doc WT/DS58/AB/R (adopted 6 November 1998) 280, 290
Appellate Body Report, *United States—Continued Dumping and Subsidy Offset Act of 2000,* WTO Doc WT/DS217/AB/R, WT/DS234/AB/R (adopted 27 January 2003) 282

EUROPEAN COURT OF JUSTICE

Cartesio (Case C-210/06) [2008] ECR I-9641 76
Centros (Case C-212/97) [1999] ECR I-1459 76
Commission v Austria (Case C-205/06) [2009] ECR I-1301 25
Commission v Finland (Case C-118/07) [2009] ECR I-10889 25
Commission v Ireland (Case C-459/02) [2006] ECR I-4635 27
Commission v Slovak Republic (Case C-264/09) Judgment of 15 September 2011 ECR I-08065 25
Commission v Sweden (Case C-249/06) [2009] ECR I-1335 25
Costa v ENEL (Case 6/64) [1964] ECR 585 27
Inspire Art (Case C-167/01) [2003] ECR I-10195 76
Kadi and Al Barakaat International Foundation v Council and Commission, (Joined Cases C-402/05 P and C-415/05 R) [2008] ECR I-6351 27
Paul Miles and Others v Ecoles européennes (Case C-196/09) [2011] ECR I-05105 27
Opinion 1/09 [2011] ECR I-01137 27
R v HM Treasury, ex parte Daily Mail and General Trust (Case 81/87) [1988] ECR 5483 74
Überseering BV v Nordic Construction (Case C-208-00) [2002] ECR I-9919 76
VALE (Case C-378/10) [2012] ECR 00000 76
Van Gend & Loos v Nederlandse Administratie der Belastingen (Case 26/62) [1963] ECR 1 27

EUROPEAN COURT OF HUMAN RIGHTS

Kemal Uzan and others v Republic of Turkey, Application No 18240/03, Decision (29 March 2011) 18
OAO Neftyanaya Kompaniya Yukos v Russian Federation, Application No 14902/04, Decision (29 January 2009) 18
OAO Neftyanaya Kompaniya Yukos v Russian Federation, Application No 14902/04, Judgment (20 September 2011) (rectified on 17 January 2012) 18

NATIONAL DECISIONS

The Atlantic Star v Bona Spes, House of Lords, 10 April 1973, AC (1974) 436 (1973, United Kingdom) 16

Table of Treaties

BILATERAL AND REGIONAL INTERNATIONAL INVESTMENT AGREEMENTS (INCLUDING PREFERENTIAL TRADE AGREEMENTS WITH INVESTMENT CHAPTERS)

1987 ASEAN Investment Agreement (Agreement among the Government of Brunei Darussalam, the Republic of Indonesia, Malaysia, the Republic of the Philippines, the Republic of Singapore, and the Kingdom of Thailand for the Promotion and Protection of Investments) 114

1998 Framework Agreement on the ASEAN Investment Area 106, 268

2009 ASEAN–Australia–New Zealand FTA (Agreement Establishing the ASEAN–Australia–New Zealand Free Trade Area) (Investment Chapter) 184, 247–48, 253, 270

2009 ASEAN–China Investment Agreement (Agreement on Investment of the Framework Agreement on Comprehensive Economic Cooperation between the People's Republic of China and the Association of Southeast Asian Nations) 184, 248, 251, 253, 262, 266, 269, 271

2009 ASEAN Comprehensive Investment Agreement 247, 253, 257, 262, 263, 266, 268, 271

2009 ASEAN–South Korea Investment Agreement (Agreement on Investment under the Framework Agreement on Comprehensive Economic Cooperation among the Governments of the Member Countries of the Association of Southeast Asian Nations and the Republic of Korea)

1997 Austria–Chile BIT (Agreement between the Republic of Chile and the Republic of Austria for the Promotion and Reciprocal Protection of Investment) 250–51, 270

1998 Austria–Mexico BIT (Agreement between the United Mexican States and the Republic of Austria on the Promotion and Protection of Investments) 245

2001 Austria–Armenia BIT (Agreement between the Government of the Republic of Austria and the Government of the Republic of Armenia for the Promotion and Protection of Investments) 252

2001 Austria–Jordan BIT (Agreement between the Hashemite Kingdom of Jordan and the Republic of Austria for the Promotion and Protection of Investments) 252

2001 Austria–Lebanon BIT (Agreement between the Lebanese Republic and the Republic of Austria on the Reciprocal Promotion and Protection of Investments) 252

2002 Austria–Libya BIT (Agreement between the Republic of Austria and the Great Socialist People's Libyan Arab Jamahiriya for the Promotion and Protection of Investments) 252

1988 Australia–China BIT (Agreement between the Government of Australia and the Government of the People's Republic of China on the Reciprocal Encouragement and Protection of Investments) 245, 248–49, 264

1992 Australia–Indonesia BIT (Agreement between the Government of Australia and the Government of the Republic of Indonesia concerning the Promotion and Protection of Investments) 248–49, 254, 259–60, 264, 266, 272

1993 Australia–Hong Kong BIT (Agreement between the Government of Hong Kong and the Government of Australia for the Promotion and Protection of Investments) 42, 259, 272

1995 Australia–Argentina BIT (Agreement between the Government of Australia and the Government of the Argentine Republic on the Promotion and Protection of Investments, and Protocol) 259, 261–62, 264, 266, 270–71, 289

1995 Australia–Peru BIT (Agreement between Australia and the Government of the Republic of Peru on the Promotion and Protection of Investments) 248–49, 254, 260

1996 Australia–Chile BIT (Agreement between the Government of Australia and the Government of the Republic of Chile on the Reciprocal Promotion and Protection of Investments) 248–49, 251, 254, 257, 259, 264, 271
1998 Australia–Lithuania BIT (Agreement between the Government of Australia and the Government of Lithuania on the Promotion and Protection of Investments) 248, 254, 259–60, 264, 266, 272
1999 Australia–India (Agreement between the Government of Australia and the Government of the Republic of India on the Promotion and Protection of Investments) 262, 264, 266, 272
2005 Australia–Mexico BIT (Agreement between the Government of Australia and the Government of the Republic of the United Mexican States on the Promotion and Protection of Investments) 245, 270
2011 Australia–New Zealand Investment Protocol (Protocol on Investment to the New Zealand–Australia Closer Economic Relations Trade Agreement) 251, 269
2012 Malaysia–Australia Free Trade Agreement (Investment Chapter) 44, 241, 247, 253
2014 Australia–South Korea Free Trade Agreement (Investment Chapter) 241
1994 Barbados–Venezuela BIT (Agreement between the Government of Barbados and the Government of the Republic of Venezuela for the Promotion and Protection of Investments) 211, 224
1989 Belgium–Luxemburg Economic Union-Russian Federation BIT (Accord entre les Gouvernements du Royaume de Bélgique et du Grand-Duché du Luxembourg, et le Gouvernement de l'Union des Républiques Socialistes Soviétiques, concernant l'Encouragement et la Protection Réciproques des Investissements) 147, 263
1990 Belgium–Luxemburg Economic Union-Bolivia BIT (Accord entre l'Union belgo-luxembourgoise et le Gouvernement de la République de Bolivie concernant l'encouragement et la protection réciproques des investissements) 143
1994 Bolivia–Chile BIT (Acuerdo entre la Républica de Bolivia y la Républica de Chile para la Promoción y Protección Recíproca de Inversiones) 245, 250–51, 262
2015 Brazil–Chile CFIA (Acuerdo de Cooperación y Facilitación de Inversiones entre la Républica Federativa del Brasil y la Réublica del Chile) 242
2015 Brazil–Colombia CFIA (Acordo de Cooperação de Investimentos entre a República Federativa do Brasil et a República da Colômbia) 242
2015 Brazil–Malawi CFIA (Investment Cooperation and Facilitation Agreement between the Federative Republic of Brazil and the Republic of Malawi) 242
1995 Cambodia–Thailand BIT (Agreement between the Government of the Kingdom of Cambodia and the Government of the Kingdom of Thailand for the Promotion and Protection of Investments) 245
1991 Canada–Argentina BIT (Agreement between the Government of Canada and the Government of the Republic of Argentina for the Promotion and Protection of Investments) 289
1996 Canada–Barbados BIT (Agreement between the Government of Canada and the Government of Barbados for the Reciprocal Promotion and Protection of Investments) 253
1996 Canada–Venezuela BIT (Agreement between the Government of Canada and the Government of the Republic of Venezuela for the Promotion and Protection of Investments) 260, 262
1998 Canada–Costa Rica BIT (Agreement between the Government of Canada and the Government of the Republic of Costa Rica for the Promotion and Protection of Investments) 253, 263
2006 Canada–Peru BIT (Agreement between Canada and the Republic of Peru for the Promotion and Protection of Investments) 247, 253, 269
2009 Canada–Jordan BIT (Agreement between Canada and the Hashemite Kingdom of Jordan for the Promotion and Protection of Investments) 253, 266

2010 Canada–Slovak Republic BIT (Agreement between Canada and the Slovak Republic for the Promotion and Protection of Investments) 253, 262, 266
2012 Canada–China BIT (Agreement between the Government of Canada and the Government of the People's Republic of China for the Promotion and Reciprocal Protection of Investments). 42, 141, 245, 253, 255–56
2013 Canada–Tanzania BIT (Agreement between the Government of Canada and the Government of the United Republic of Tanzania for the Promotion and Reciprocal Protection of Investments). 253
1998 Chile–South Africa BIT (Agreement between the Republic of Chile and the Republic of South Africa for the Promotion and Reciprocal Protection of Investments). 250–51
1991 Chile–Spain BIT (Acuerdo entre la Républica de Bolivia y el Reino de España para la Protección y Fomento Recíprocos de Inversiones). 197
2007 COMESA Investment Agreement (Investment Agreement For the COMESA Common Investment Area). 251, 263, 271
Comprehensive Economic and Trade Agreement (CETA). 24, 55, 240, 244, 247, 249, 251, 253, 264, 266, 272, 274
1989 Cyprus–Hungary BIT (Agreement between the Government of the Republic of Cyprus and the Government of the Hungarian People's Republic on Mutual Promotion and Protection of Investments). 109
2004 Dominican Republic–Central American Free Trade Agreement (CAFTA) 17, 55, 108, 118–120, 192, 211, 223, 247, 254, 269, 285
1997 Egypt–United Arab Emirates BIT 130
2000 EFTA-Mexico Free Trade Agreement (Free Trade Agreement between the EFTA States and the United Mexican States) (Investment Chapter). 142
1994 Energy Charter Treaty (ECT). 26, 117, 157, 168, 252
1972 France–Tunisia BIT (Décret no 72-974 du 25 octobre 1972 portant publication de la convention entre le Gouvernement de la République française et le Gouvernement de la République tunisienne sur la protection des investissements, signee à Paris le 30 juin 1972) 21
1993 France–Peru BIT (Décret no 96-898 du 9 octobre 1996 portant publication de l'accord entre le Gouvernement de la République française et le Gouvernement de la République du Pérou sur l'encouragement et la protection réciproques des investissements, signé à Paris le 6 octobre 1993) 154, 216
1999 France–Dominican Republic BIT (Accord entre le Gouvernement de la République française et le Gouvernement de la République Dominicaine sur l'encouragement et la protection réciproques des investissements). 206, 245
1959 Germany–Pakistan BIT (Treaty between the Federal Republic of Germany and Pakistan for the Promotion and Protection of Investments) 21
1976 Germany–Israel BIT (Treaty between the Federal Republic of Germany and the State of Israel concerning the Encouragement and Reciprocal Protection of Investments). 154, 216
1989 Germany–Soviet Union BIT (Federal Republic of Germany and Union of Soviet Socialist Republics, Agreement concerning the promotion and reciprocal protection of investments (with protocols)) 143, 145, 263
1997 Germany–United Arab Emirates BIT (Agreement between the Federal Republic of Germany and the United Arab Emirates for the Promotion and Protection of Investments) 263
1998 Germany–Antigua and Barbuda BIT (Treaty between the Federal Republic of Germany and Antigua and Barbuda concerning the Encouragement and Reciprocal Protection of Investments) 263
2002 Germany–Thailand BIT (Treaty between the Kingdom of Thailand and the Federal Republic of Germany concerning the Encouragement and Reciprocal Protection of Investments) 263

2007 Germany–Oman BIT (Agreement between the Federal Republic of Germany and the Hashemite Kingdom of Jordan concerning the Encouragement and Reciprocal Protection of Investments) 263, 271
1997 Israel–Czech Republic BIT (Agreement between the Government of the Czech Republic and the Government of the State of Israel for the Reciprocal Promotion and Protection of Investments) 183
1998 Japan–Russian Federation BIT (Agreement between the Government of Japan and the Government of the Russian Federation Concerning the Promotion and Protection of Investments) 261
2002 Japan–Korea BIT (Agreement between the Government of the Republic of Korea and the Government of Japan and for the Liberalisation, Promotion and Protection of Investment) 252, 262, 266, 271
2008 Japan–Uzbekistan BIT (Agreement between Japan and the Republic of Uzbekistan for the Liberalization, Promotion and Protection of Investment) 252, 257, 271
2011 Japan–Colombia BIT (Agreement between Japan and the Republic of Colombia for the Liberalization, Promotion and Protection of Investment) 247, 251, 257, 262, 264, 266, 271
2012 Japan–Iraq BIT (Agreement between Japan and the Republic of Iraq for the Promotion and Protection of Investment) 252, 254, 257, 271, 284
2012 Japan–Korea-China BIT (Agreement between the Government of Japan, the Government of the Republic Of Korea and the Government of the People's Republic of China for the Promotion, Facilitation and Protection of Investment) 266–67
1994 Lithuania–Ukraine BIT (Agreement between the Government of the Republic of Lithuania and the Government of Ukraine for the promotion and reciprocal protection of investments) 103–04
1986 Netherlands–Turkey BIT (Agreement on Reciprocal Encouragement and Protection of Investments between the Kingdom of the Netherlands and the Republic of Turkey) 157, 266–67
1991 Netherlands–Czech and Slovak Republic BIT (Agreement on Encouragement and Reciprocal Protection of investments between the Kingdom of the Netherlands and the Czech and Slovak Federal Republic) 245
1991 Netherlands–Venezuela BIT (Agreement on Encouragement and Reciprocal Protection of Investments between the Kingdom of the Netherlands and the Republic of Venezuela) 107–08, 113, 156, 158–59, 209, 213–14, 258, 263
1992 Netherlands–Argentina BIT (Agreement on Encouragement and Reciprocal Protection of Investments between the Kingdom of the Netherlands and the Argentine Republic) 100, 128, 131, 135
1992 Netherlands–Bolivia BIT (Agreement on Encouragement and Reciprocal Protection of Investments between the Kingdom of the Netherlands and the Republic of Bolivia) 134, 143
1994 Netherlands–Indonesia BIT (Agreement between the Government of the Kingdom of the Netherlands and the Government of the Republic of Indonesia on Promotion and Protection of Investment) 261, 266
1999 Netherlands–Costa Rica BIT (Agreement on Encouragement and Reciprocal Protection of Investments between the Republic of Costa Rica and the Kingdom of the Netherlands) 216, 222, 227
1999 Netherlands–Ecuador BIT (Agreement on Encouragement and Reciprocal Protection of Investments between the Republic of Ecuador and the Kingdom of the Netherlands) 270
1998 Netherlands–Macedonia BIT (Agreement on Encouragement and Reciprocal Protection of Investments between the Government of the Kingdom of the Netherlands and the Macedonian Government) 135

1998 Netherlands–Mexico BIT (Agreement on Promotion, Encouragement and Reciprocal Protection of Investments between the Kingdom of the Netherlands and the United Mexican States) 263
2001 Netherlands–China BIT (Agreement on Encouragement and Reciprocal Protection of Investments between the Government of the People's Republic of China and the Government of the Kingdom of the Netherlands) 266, 271
2002 Netherlands–Kazakhstan BIT (Agreement on Encouragement and Reciprocal Protection of Investments between the Republic of Kazakhstan and the Kingdom of the Netherlands) 111, 261, 267
2003 Netherlands–Lao People's Republic BIT (Agreement on Encouragement and Reciprocal Protection of Investments between the Lao People's Republic and the Kingdom of the Netherlands) 190, 261, 271
2006 Netherlands–Dominican Republic BIT (Agreement on Encouragement and Reciprocal Protection of Investments between the Kingdom of the Netherlands and the Dominican Republic) 263
2007 Netherlands–Burundi (Accord sur l'Encouragement et la Protection Réciproque des Investissements entre le Royaume des Pays-Bas et la République du Burundi) 263
2013 Netherlands–United Arab Emirates (Agreement on Encouragement and Reciprocal Protection of Investments between the Kingdom of the Netherlands and the United Arab Emirates) 260, 270
1992 North American Free Trade Agreement (NAFTA) 63, 94, 120, 135, 141, 168–72, 252, 254, 260, 262, 272, 304
1994 Peru–China BIT (Agreement between the Government of the Republic of Peru and the Government of the People's Republic of China Concerning the Encouragement and Reciprocal Protection of Investments) 262, 266–67
1994 Peru–Paraguay BIT (Convenio entre el Gobierno de la Républica del Peru y la República del Paraguay sobre Promoción y Protección Recíproca de Inversiones) 96
2000 Peru–Chile BIT (Convenio entre el Gobierno de la Républica del Peru y el Gobierno de la República de Chile para la Promoción y Protección Recíproca de la inversiones) 197
1995 Spain–Venezuela BIT (Acuerdo entre el Reino de España y la República de Venezuela para la Promoción y Protección Recíproca de Inversiones) 97
1961 Switzerland–Tunisia BIT (Traité entre la Confédération Suisse et la République Tunisienne relative à la protection et à l'encouragement des investissements de capitaux) 21
1974 Switzerland–Indonesia (Accord entre la Confédération Suisse et le Gouvernement de la République Indonésienne concernant l'encouragement et la protection réciproque des investissements) 263
1988 Switzerland–Uruguay BIT (Agreement between the Swiss Confederation and the Oriental Republic of Uruguay on the Promotion and Reciprocal Protection of Investments) 263
1990 Czech and Slovak Republic–Switzerland BIT (Agreement between the Czech and Slovak Federal Republic and the Swiss Confederation on the Promotion and Reciprocal Protection of Investments) 115
1991 Switzerland–Argentina BIT (Accord entre la Confédération Suisse et le République Argentine concernant la promotion et la protection réciproque des investissements) 250
1998 Switzerland–Ethiopia BIT (Agreement between the Swiss Confederation and the Federal Democratic Republic of Ethiopia on the Promotion and Reciprocal Protection of Investments) 263
2000 Switzerland–Costa Rica BIT (Agreement between the Swiss Confederation and the Republic of Costa Rica on the Promotion and Reciprocal Protection of Investments) 193, 216, 222, 250, 263
2006 Switzerland–Colombia BIT (Agreement Between the Republic of Colombia and the Swiss Federal Council on the Promotion and Reciprocal Protection of Investments) 247, 250, 271

2006 Switzerland–Saudi Arabia BIT (Accord entre la Confédération Suisse et le Royaume d'Arabie saoudite concernant l'encouragement et la protection réciproque des investissements). 250, 271
2008 Switzerland–Turkmenistan (Agreement between the Swiss Federal Council and the Government of Turkmenistan on the Promotion and Reciprocal Protection of Investments) 257, 263
2009 Switzerland–China BIT (Agreement between the Swiss Federal Council and the Government of the People's Republic of China on the Promotion and Reciprocal Protection of Investments). 250–51, 271
2011 Switzerland–Kosovo BIT (Agreement between the Swiss Confederation and the Republic of Kosovo on the Promotion and Reciprocal Protection of Investments) 264, 271
2012 Switzerland–Tunisia (Agreement between the Swiss Federal Council and the Government of the Republic of Tunisia on reciprocal promotion and protection of investments) 263, 271
1975 United Kingdom–Egypt BIT (Agreement between the Government of the United Kingdom of Great Britain and Northern Ireland and the Government of the Arab Republic of Egypt for the Promotion and Reciprocal Protection of Investments) 103
1994 United Kingdom–Tanzania BIT (Agreement between the Government of the United Kingdom of Great Britain and Northern Ireland and the Government of the United Republic of Tanzania for the Promotion and Reciprocal Protection of Investments) 156–58, 245, 260, 265, 286
2002 United Kingdom–Bosnia Herzegovina BIT (Agreement between the United Kingdom of Great Britain and Northern Ireland and Bosnia and Herzegovina for the Promotion and Reciprocal Protection of Investments) 269
2006 United Kingdom–Mexico BIT (Agreement between the Government of the United Kingdom of Great Britain and Northern Ireland and the Government of the United Mexican States for the Promotion and Reciprocal Protection of Investments) 249
1984 US–Zaire BIT (Treaty between the United States of America and the Republic of Zaire Concerning the Reciprocal Encouragement and Protection of Investment, with Protocol) (also US-Democratic Republic of Congo BIT) 197–98, 261
1986 US–Bangladesh BIT (Treaty between the United States of America and the People's Republic of Bangladesh Concerning the Reciprocal Encouragement and Protection of Investment) 43, 249
1986 US–Egypt BIT (Treaty between the United States of America and the Arab Republic of Egypt Concerning the Reciprocal Encouragement and Protection of Investment) 96, 257
1991 US–Argentina BIT (Treaty between the United States of America and the Argentine Republic Concerning the Reciprocal Encouragement and Protection of Investment) 117, 120, 249
1991 US–Czech Republic BIT (Treaty with the Czech and Slovak Federal Republic Concerning the Reciprocal Encouragement and Protection of Investment) 252
1993 US–Ecuador BIT (Treaty between the United States of America and the Republic of Ecuador Concerning the Reciprocal Encouragement and Protection of Investment) 118, 120, 134, 254
1994 US–Jamaica BIT (Treaty between the United States of America and Jamaica Concerning the Reciprocal Encouragement and Protection of Investment) 252
1994 US–Ukraine BIT (Treaty between the United States of America and Ukraine Concerning the Reciprocal Encouragement and Protection of Investment) 252, 254
1995 US–Albania BIT (Treaty between the Government of the United States of America and the Government of the Republic of Albania Concerning the Encouragement and Reciprocal Protection of Investment, with Annex and Protocol) 249, 257

1997 US–Azerbaijan BIT (Treaty between the Government of the United States of America and the Government of the Republic of Azerbaijan Concerning the Encouragement and Reciprocal Protection of Investment, with Annex) 249
1998 US–Bolivia BIT (Treaty between the Government of the United States of America and the Government of the Republic of Bolivia Concerning the Reciprocal Encouragement and Protection of Investment, with Annex and Protocol). . . . 119, 143, 188, 254
1999 US–Bahrain BIT (Treaty between the Government of the United States of America and the Government of the State of Bahrain Concerning the Encouragement and Reciprocal Protection of Investment, with Annex). . . . 249
2003 US–Chile FTA (Free Trade Agreement between the Government of the United States of America and the Government of the Republic of Chile) (Investment Chapter). . . . 55
2004 US–Australia FTA (Free Trade Agreement between the Government of the United States of America and the Government of the Australia) (Investment Chapter) 252
2005 US–Uruguay BIT (Treaty between the United States of America and the Oriental Republic of Uruguay Concerning the Encouragement and Reciprocal Protection of Investment) 249, 252, 266, 269
2006 US–Colombia FTA (Free Trade Agreement between the Government of the United States of America and the Government of the Republic of Colombia) (Investment Chapter) 252, 269
2008 US–Rwanda BIT (Treaty between the Government of the United States of America and the Government of the Republic of Rwanda Concerning the Encouragement and Reciprocal Protection of Investment) 247, 249, 252

DRAFT AND MODEL TREATIES

1948 Havana Charter for an International Trade Organisation 21
2005/2006 United Kingdom Model BIT. . . . 261, 266
2007 France Model BIT 267
2007 Norway Model BIT. . . . 17
2008 Germany Model BIT. . . . 76, 245
2012 United States Model BIT 17, 108
2015 India Model BIT 251, 253, 355, 262, 267, 271, 273
EU-Vietnam Free Trade Agreement. . . . 55, 240, 275
EU-Singapore Free Trade Agreement. . . . 274, 306
Trans-Pacific Partnership (TPP). . . . 242, 248, 253, 255, 266, 269
Transatlantic Trade and Investment Partnership (TTIP). . . . 24, 55, 57, 240, 242, 244, 251, 256, 275

WORLD TRADE ORGANIZATION AGREEMENTS

1994 General Agreement on Trade in Services (GATS). . . . 257–58
1994 Marrakesh Agreement Establishing the World Trade Organization 35, 280
1994 Understanding on Rules and Procedures Governing the Settlement of Disputes 280, 290

European Union legislation

Treaty of Lisbon (Treaty of Lisbon Amending the Treaty on European Union and the Treaty Establishing the European Community) (2009). . . . 24
Treaty on European Union (TEU) (Consolidated Version of the Treaty on European Union) 59
Treaty on the Functioning of the European Union (TFEU) (Consolidated Version of the Treaty on the Functioning of the European Union) 24–25, 27, 59
Regulation No 1219/2012 (Regulation (EU) No 1219/2012 of the European Parliament and of the Council of 12 December 2012 establishing transitional arrangements for bilateral investment agreements between Member States and third countries. . . . 25–26

OTHER INTERNATIONAL TREATIES AND RULES

Hague Convention on Certain Questions relating to the Conflict of Nationality Laws (1930) 70, 72
Charter of the United Nations (1945) 35, 280
Statute of the International Court of Justice (1945) 178, 185
Convention on the Recognition and Enforcement of Foreign Arbitral Awards (New York Convention) (1958) 45
Vienna Convention on Consular Relations (1963) 84–85
Convention on the Settlement of Investment Disputes between States and Nationals of Other States (1965) (ICSID Convention) 11, 23, 29, 45, 60, 92–93, 95–101, 104–07, 109, 111–14, 118, 120–21, 125–27, 129–30, 132–33, 137–38, 147, 149, 155, 157, 159, 161–64, 167–72, 174–75, 182–83, 189, 207, 210–11, 229–30, 235, 247–48, 256, 260–61, 264, 283–88, 290, 293, 302, 310–13
Vienna Convention on the Law of Treaties (1969) 35, 103, 117, 172, 243, 280
Declaration of the Government of the Democratic and Popular Republic of Algeria Concerning the Settlement of Claims by the Government of the United States of America and the Government of the Islamic Republic of Iran (1981) 268
Andean Commission of 1991, Decision 291, Regime for the common Treatment of Foreign Capital and Trademarks, Patents, Licensing Agreements and Royalties 268
European Convention on Nationality (1997) 70
Rome Statute of the International Criminal Court (1998) 280
United Nations Rules on Transparency in Treaty-based Investor-State Arbitration (2014) 56

Table of Abbreviations

a.m.	aforementioned
AF	Additional Facility
AJIL	American Journal of International Law
Am Soc Intl L Proc	Proceedings of the American Society of International Law
Am U Intl L Rev	American University International Law Review
Arb Intl	Arbitration International
ASEAN	Association of South East Asian Nations
Austr Year Book of Intl L	Australian Year Book of International Law
Baltic YIL	Baltic Yearbook of International Law
BEPS	Base Erosion and Profit Shifting
BIT	bilateral investment treaty
BRICS	Brazil, Russia, India, China, and South Africa
Bus L Intl	Business Law International
BYIL	British Yearbook of International Law
CAFTA	Dominican Republic–Central American Free Trade Agreement
CCP	Common Commercial Policy
CEO	Chief Executive Officer
CETA	Comprehensive Economic and Trade Agreement (between Canada and the European Union, final version February 2016)
CFIA	Cooperation and Facilitation Investment Agreement
Ch	Chapter
Chi J Intl L	Chicago Journal of International Law
Chin J Intl L	Chinese Journal of International Law
CMLR	Common Market Law Review
Colum J Transnatl L	Columbia Journal of Transnational Law
COMESA	Common Market for Eastern and Southern Africa
Cornell Int'l L J	Cornell International Law Journal
DOB	denial of benefits
DRC	State of Democratic Republic of the Congo
DSB	Dispute Settlement Body
DSU	Dispute Settlement Understanding
ECJ	European Court of Justice
ECT	Energy Charter Treaty
ECtHR	European Court of Human Rights
EFTA	European Free Trade Association
EIF	entry into force

EJIL	European Journal of International Law
EU	European Union
Europ Company L	European Company Law
FDI	foreign direct investment
FET	fair and equitable treatment
FIPA	Foreign Investment Promotion and Protection Agreement
Fordham L Rev	Fordham Law Review
FRG	Federal Republic of Germany
FTA	Free Trade Agreement
GATS	General Agreement on Trade in Services
GATT	General Agreement on Tariffs and Trade
Geo Wash Intl L Rev	George Washington International Law Review
Germ L J	German Law Journal
Germ YIL	German Yearbook of International Law
Harv Intl L J	Harvard International Law Journal
Harv L Rev	Harvard Law Review
ICC	International Chamber of Commerce
ICJ	International Court of Justice
ICJ Rep	ICJ Reports
ICLQ	International and Comparative Law Quarterly
ICSID	International Center for Settlement of Investment Disputes
ICSID Convention	Convention on the Settlement of Investment Disputes between States and Nationals of other States
ICSID Rep	Reports of ICSID Decisions and Awards
ICSID Review-FILJ	ICSID Review-Foreign Investment Law Journal
ICTR	International Criminal Tribunals for Rwanda
ICTY	International Criminal Tribunals for the former Yugoslavia
IIA	international investment agreement
ILC	International Law Commission
IMF	International Monetary Fund
Ind J Global Legal Stud	Indiana Journal of Global Legal Studies
Intl Org	International Organisations
Iran–US CTR	Reports of the Iran–United States Claims Tribunal
ISDS	investor–State dispute settlement
ITLOS	International Tribunal for the Law of the Sea
J Arb & Med	Journal of Arbitration and Mediation
J Intl Arb	Journal of International Arbitration
JDI	Journal du droit international
JICJ	Journal of International Criminal Justice
JIDS	Journal of International Dispute Settlement
JIEL	Journal of International Economic Law
JWELB	Journal of World Energy Law & Business
JWI	Journal of World Investment

JWIT	Journal of World Investment and Trade
JWT	Journal of World Trade
LCIA	London Chamber of International Arbitration
LIEL	Legal Issues of Economic Integration
LJIL	Leiden Journal of International Law
LPICT	Law and Practice of International Courts and Tribunals
LSE	London School of Economics
MAI	Multilateral Agreement on Investment
McGill L J	McGill Law Journal
Melb J Int L	Melbourne Journal of International Law
MFN	most-favoured nation
Mich J Intl L	Michigan Journal of International Law
MIT	Multilateral Investment Treaty
MNC	multinational company
MNE	multinational enterprise
NAFTA	North American Free Trade Agreement
NILR	Netherlands International Law Review
Nw J Intl L & Bus	Northwestern Journal of International Law and Business
NYU Environmental L J	New York University Environmental Law Journal
NYU J Intl L & Pol	New York University Journal of International Law and Policy
OECD	Organisation for Economic Cooperation and Development
OGEL	Oil, Gas & Energy Law Intelligence
OJ	Official Journal of the European Union
OUP	Oxford University Press
PCIJ	Permanent Court of International Justice
Penn St L Rev	Pennsylvania State Law Review
RIAA	UN Reports of International Arbitral Awards
Rich J Global L & Bus	Richmond Journal of Global Law and Business
S	Section
San Diego Intl L J	San Diego International Law Journal
SCC	Stockholm Chamber of Commerce
SME	small and medium-sized enterprises
Stan J L Bus & Fin	Stanford Journal of Law, Business and Finance
TDM	Transnational Dispute Management
TEU	Treaty on European Union
TFEU	Treaty on the Functioning of the European Union
TPP	Trans-Pacific Partnership
Transnatl Corporations	Transnational Corporations
TTIP	Transatlantic Trade and Investment Partnership

U Pa L Rev	University of Pennsylvania Law Review
UC Davis J Intl L & Pol	UC Davis Journal of International Law and Policy
UCL Journal of Law Jurisprudence and Jurisprudence	University College London Journal of Law and
UNCITRAL	United Nations Commission on International Trade Law
UNCLOS	United Nations Convention on the Law of the Sea
UNCTAD	United Nations Conference on Trade and Development
UNTS	United Nations Treaty Series
Va J Intl L	Virginia Journal of International Law
Vand J Transnatl L	Vanderbilt Journal of Transnational Law
VCLT	Vienna Convention on the Law of Treaties
Wash U L Re	Washington University Law Review
WIR	World Investment Report
World Dev	World Development
WTO	World Trade Organization
WTO DSB	World Trade Organization Dispute Settlement Body
Yale J Intl L	Yale Journal of International Law
ZaöRV	Zeitschrift für ausländisches öffentliches und Völkerrecht

Introduction

Is treaty shopping in international investment law 'legitimate nationality planning' or 'treaty abuse'? This is the question investment arbitral tribunals have been increasingly faced with over past years in investment treaty arbitration and which this book will attempt to answer.

As investment arbitrations have been soaring over the past decade, the practice of treaty shopping has gained continuous ground in foreign investment disputes. However, no universally accepted or authoritative definition of what constitutes treaty shopping exists in international (investment) law and for that matter treaty shopping can take on a variety of meanings. Investors may structure (or restructure) their investment in a favourable home State jurisdiction, thereby enabling them to invoke other investment treaties normally not available to them. Investors may transfer an investment claim to another (natural or legal) person holding a nationality enabling access to a (more) favourable investment treaty. Natural persons holding dual nationality may invoke one of the nationalities in an attempt to come under the protection of a specific (more favourable) investment treaty. As can be seen from the aforementioned examples, treaty shopping thus understood involves strategically changing or invoking a nationality, be it in the form of creating a (new) legal personality or invoking an existing (dual or multiple) nationality.

In its terminology, the notion of treaty shopping raises conspicuous associations with the practice of forum shopping, a practice hitherto mostly known from private international law litigation and employed by the claimant with a view to obtaining the most advantageous among various available fora. As for forum shopping, the notion of treaty shopping evokes rather negative connotations. It is certainly true that like forum shopping, the practice of treaty shopping poses certain important policy issues. Yet, fact is that nowhere in international law is there a universal prohibition of this practice nor for that matter of the vehicle commonly associated with it, the so-called mailbox or shell company. Any analysis of the legal issues at stake therefore needs to distinguish clearly between legal and policy arguments.

Any search for a more coherent approach towards treaty shopping should take into account the reasons for its occurrence. It is in particular the proliferation of investment treaties over past decades, culminating in currently over 3000 international investment agreements (IIAs), as well as the paradigm change from the protection of the foreign investor through diplomatic protection to its direct standing contained in virtually all modern investment treaties that renders treaty shopping not only possible, but also a highly attractive option for any investor wishing to enhance investment protection. Indeed, though investment treaties nowadays contain similarly worded key clauses (concerning in particular the question who qualifies as an investor and what qualifies as an investment), subtle differences often exist respectively are found to exist by arbitral tribunals, this latter fact also being a consequence of the lack of precedent in international investment arbitration. At the same time and in contradistinction to the customary law of diplomatic protection, investment treaties usually contain a very broad investor standing, protecting not only direct but also indirect shareholding, and often even minority shareholding. In particular, multi-jurisdictional corporate structures, such as multinational enterprises (MNEs), may in this way extend investment treaty protection considerably, with each and every entity within the corporate chain potentially having a separate standing of its own (provided the existence of a corresponding IIA concluded by the respective home and host States).

Arbitral tribunals' approaches towards the validity of a claim involving treaty shopping have for a long time mainly focused on the question of jurisdiction *ratione personae*, in other words, whether the corporate vehicle, the putative investor-claimant, qualified as protected investor under the invoked investment treaty. Respondent States have often tried to contest this on the basis of either the 'genuine link' or the 'piercing of the corporate veil' theories. They have also increasingly invoked denial of benefits clauses, where available under the IIA. Yet, as could be seen over more recent years, legal constructions and pleadings have become increasingly sophisticated, raising ever more questions pertaining to jurisdiction *ratione materiae* and *ratione temporis* as well as to the abuse of rights/abuse of process doctrine. Thus, is it enough for an investor, originally without a qualifying nationality, to acquire assets qualifying under the targeted investment treaty both as regards *ratione personae* and *ratione materiae*? Is it sufficient for the parent company to 'reshuffle' corporate assets so that one of its subsidiaries with a qualifying nationality becomes eligible under the intended treaty? In view of the protection of indirect investments under most investment treaties, may any entity along the corporate chain claim ownership or control of assets that any of its subsidiaries might hold? What, if the aforementioned operations occur in view of an investment dispute crystallizing at the horizon? And which are the legal limits to using corporate structures when the investor–claimant is a locally incorporated entity under 'foreign control'?

While arbitral tribunals have found more or less consistent approaches to some of the above questions, others remain unsettled and have produced a fair amount of inconsistency in jurisprudence. The importance of this practice transcends the outcome of concrete arbitral cases, though. In times of heightened public scepticism towards the current global economic governance system in general and the international investment system in particular, widely publicized 'treaty shopping' cases (such as the recent *Philip Morris v Australia* investment arbitration) may be perceived as contributing to a mounting 'legitimacy crisis' the international investment arbitration system has been facing for years (though that arbitral tribunal dismissed this case). This crisis, if further escalating, could indeed deeply impact on the system in its current form.

With the above-said in mind, this research undertakes a systematic analysis of customary international law, international investment law, and investment arbitral jurisprudence to identify and examine the legal questions and problems arising in the context of distinguishing 'objectionable' from 'unobjectionable' treaty shopping cases, and to make recommendations *de lege ferenda* on how to solve these problems. While starting out from the assumption that treaty shopping is a pervasive phenomenon with important systemic implications, no attempt at quantifying this practice will be made in this research, leaving this task to others.[1]

The research will proceed in the following way.

Being a notion in need of definition, Part I sets out to place the practice of treaty shopping in the wider context. To this end, Chapter 1 will approach the practice of treaty shopping by establishing a working definition and exploring in detail the causes for its occurrence, while Chapter 2 will analyse considerations in favour of a 'treaty shopping-permissive' approach, but also potential policy concerns arising from this practice.

Part II will then turn its attention to the legal approaches towards the validity of a claim involving treaty shopping, systematically analysing both customary international law and international investment law basis and jurisprudence. Thus, Chapter 3 will set out the customary international law basis for the question of changes of nationality, critically analysing among others the decisions rendered by the International Court of Justice (ICJ) in the *Nottebohm*, *Barcelona Traction*, and *Diallo* cases and their incidence for the question at issue under international investment law. Turning to investment arbitral jurisprudence, Chapters 4 to 7 will assess in a comprehensive way arbitral decisions according to whether key questions concern jurisdiction *ratione personae* (Chapter 4), *ratione materiae* (Chapter 5), *ratione temporis* (Chapter 6), or the abuse of rights/abuse of process doctrine (Chapter 7). These chapters will also determine which of these questions arbitral tribunals have treated in a consistent manner and for which questions this has not been the case.

Part III will finally examine which solutions may be at hand in particular for the remaining inconsistencies found through the systematic analysis of arbitral jurisprudence in Part II. States being the 'Masters of the Treaties', Chapter 8 will discuss the possibilities of States wishing to guard themselves against the practice of treaty shopping. While a coordinated, multilateral approach aimed at achieving consistency among the thousands of IIAs would be one of the most desirable solutions, its political feasibility remains at this point doubtful. Chapter 8 will thus focus on

[1] For quantitative analyses on the phenomenon see, eg, Eunjung Lee, 'Treaty Shopping in International Investment Arbitration: How often has it occurred and how has it been perceived by tribunals?' LSE Working Paper Series 2015, No 15–167, available at <http://www.lse.ac.uk/internationalDevelopment/pdf/Dissertations/WP167.pdf> (last accessed on 15 September 2016); see also UNCTAD, 'World Investment Report 2016, Investor Nationality: Policy Challenges' (United Nations 2016) 123ff, available at <http://unctad.org/en/PublicationsLibrary/wir2016_en.pdf> (last accessed on 15 September 2016).

'treaty-based' approaches, in other words how States may rein in treaty shopping by more rigorous treaty drafting, by comprehensively examining treaty practice and identifying possible formulations. Chapter 9 will finally assess the important role of the principle of good faith and some of its manifestations and concretizations in drawing the line between a 'legitimate nationality planning' and 'abusive treaty shopping'.

Preliminary conclusions will close each chapter, and each part will resume in a concise manner the main results of the analyses.

PART I

PLACING TREATY SHOPPING IN CONTEXT

'Treaty shopping' is a practice that has by now become part and parcel of any investment lawyer's toolbox, and accordingly arbitral tribunals have been increasingly confronted with the question of whether to dismiss claims brought on the basis of treaty shopping or not. However, as becomes evident from scholarship and jurisprudence, it is not always completely clear what is to be understood as treaty shopping and which policy issues this practice potentially raises.

Part I thus first aims at placing the practice of treaty shopping in context by elaborating a working definition of the notion under analysis, examining the reasons for its occurrence, and discussing potential policy issues arising in connection with this practice.

1

Understanding the Practice of Treaty Shopping

When approaching the subject of treaty shopping, what becomes readily apparent is the absence of any official, let alone universally valid, definition of what is considered treaty shopping. In fact, the term 'treaty shopping' is not even a legal term of art, but one that was arguably coined in relation to the well-known problem in international tax law where corporate structures are established in tax jurisdictions (so-called tax havens) for the sole purpose of benefitting from (more) favourable tax treaties.[1] With the rapid increase in investment treaties and investment arbitration around the turn of the century,[2] the practice of treaty shopping has also started to appear in investor–State dispute settlement (ISDS). With this, the first question that must be asked is: what is treaty shopping, what is characteristic of it, and why does this practice exist in investor–State dispute settlement?

1.1 Defining Treaty Shopping in International Investment Law

1.1.1 Perceptions and definitions of treaty shopping used in academic literature and arbitral jurisprudence

Looking at the notion of treaty shopping from the semantic side, the first thing that catches the reader's eye is the differing terms that commentators may use to denote one and the same phenomenon. While the term of 'treaty shopping' is most frequently used, some commentators prefer the word 'treaty planning',[3]

[1] See, eg, Stef Van Weeghel, *Improper Use of Tax Treaties* (Kluwer Law International 1998) 119–23; Luc de Broe, *International Tax Planning and Prevention of Abuse*, Volume 14 of Doctoral Series (Amsterdam IBFD 2008) 350, 353. On the international and multilateral (OECD, UN, etc.) efforts to restrict tax treaty shopping see OECD, 'Preventing the Granting of Treaty Benefits in Inappropriate Circumstances', Action 6 – 2015 Final Report (OECD 2015) available at <http://www.oecd-ilibrary.org/docserver/download/2315331e.pdf?expires=1461341716&id=id&accname=guest&checksum=3206A82136A7D3BE726F36C4B64C47CF> (last accessed on 15 September 2016). See also, eg, Christiana Panayi, *Advanced Issues in International and European Tax Law* (Hart Publishing 2015) 85–99; Brian Arnold, *International Tax Primer* (Kluwer Law International, 3rd edn 2016) 167–74.

[2] See section 1.2.1.

[3] Eduardo Zuleta, Andrea Saldarriaga, and Ana Vohryzek-Griest, 'Treaty Planning: Current Trends in International Investment Disputes that Impact Foreign Investment Decisions and Treaty Drafting', in Miguel Ángel Fernández-Ballesteros and David Arias (eds), *Liber Amicorum Bernardo Cremades* (Madrid La Ley 2010) 1207.

'nationality planning',[4] 'corporate manoeuvering',[5] or in turn, treat it right away as 'treaty abuse'.[6] As becomes apparent from the preceding quotations, depending on the term used, the user may show an inherent value judgment on what he or she may consider an acceptable ('treaty/nationality planning') or unacceptable ('treaty abuse') behaviour.[7] But even without such an explicit terminological choice, the notion of treaty shopping is beset more with negative connotations than positive ones.[8] This may be due to the association of the practice of treaty shopping with international tax law.[9] In investment arbitration, some arbitral tribunals have indeed attached a negative connotation to the notion of treaty shopping,[10] while others have taken a more neutral stance.[11] These characterizations should however not confuse the descriptive and the normative analysis,[12] the fact being that nowhere in international investment law is there a generally accepted definition, let alone a prohibition of treaty shopping.[13]

The same divergence in understanding may be seen with respect to the question of when, that is, at which point of time, treaty shopping usually takes place. Again, the use of the term 'corporate structuring', 'treaty planning', or 'nationality planning' seems to denote an operation undertaken (well) before any actual dispute may have arisen and thus has a relatively legitimate ring to it. After all, can you blame

[4] See, eg, Rudolf Dolzer and Christoph Schreuer, *Principles of International Investment Law* (Oxford University Press, 2nd edn 2012) 52; Sange Addison-Agyei, *Nationality Planning und Treaty Shopping im Internationalen Investitionsrecht* (Frankfurt aM, Peter Lang 2012).

[5] Tania Voon, Andrew Mitchell, and James Munro, 'Legal Responses to Corporate Manoeuvering in International Investment Arbitration' (2014) 5 JIDS 41.

[6] George Kahale III, 'The new Dutch sandwich: The issue of treaty abuse', *Columbia FDI Perspectives*, No 48 (10 October 2011) available at <http://ccsi.columbia.edu/files/2014/01/FDI_48.pdf> (last accessed on 15 September 2016).

[7] Similar Christoph Schreuer, 'Nationality Planning' in Arthur W Rovine (ed), *Contemporary Issues in International Arbitration and Mediation: The Fordham Papers 2012* (Martinus Nijhoff 2013) 17, 19.

[8] This is also what the differentiation between 'nationality planning' and 'treaty shopping' seems to suggest; see Addison-Agyei (n 4).

[9] Van Weeghel (n 1) 119: '[T]he term "treaty shopping" connotes a situation in which a person who is not entitled to the benefits of a tax treaty makes use—in the widest meaning of the word—of an individual or legal person in order to obtain those treaty benefits that are not available directly.'

[10] See, eg, *Emilio Agustín Maffezini v Kingdom of Spain*, ICSID Case No ARB/97/7, Decision on Objections to Jurisdiction (25 January 2000) para 63: 'a distinction has to be made between the legitimate extension of rights and benefits by means of the operation of the [MFN] clause, on the one hand, and *disruptive treaty-shopping* that would play havoc with the policy objectives of underlying specific treaty provisions, on the other hand' [emphasis added]. Similar *Saluka Investments BV v Czech Republic*, UNCITRAL, Partial Award (17 March 2006) para 240.

[11] See, eg, *Aguas del Tunarí SA v Plurinational State of Bolivia*, ICSID Case No ARB/02/3, Decision on Respondent's Objections to Jurisdiction (21 October 2005) paras 330, 332. Similar *Cementownia "Nowa Huta" SA v Republic of Turkey*, ICSID Case No ARB(AF)/06/2, Award (17 September 2009) para 117; *Tidewater Inc, Tidewater Investment SRL, Tidewater Caribe, CA, Twenty Grand Offshore, LLC, Point Marine, LLC, Twenty Grand Marine Service, LLC, Jackson Marine, LLC and Zapata Gulf Marine Operators, LLC v Bolivarian Republic of Venezuela*, ICSID Case No ARB/10/5, Decision on Jurisdiction (8 February 2013) para 184; *Bureau Veritas, Inspection, Valuation, Assessment and Control, BIVAC BV v Republic of Paraguay*, ICSID Case No ARB/07/9, Further Decision on Objections to Jurisdiction (9 October 2012) para 94.

[12] For this distinction with respect to the notion of forum shopping see Christopher Whytock, 'The Evolving Forum Shopping System' (2010–2011) 96 Cornell L Rev 481, 485 (FN 13).

[13] Dolzer and Schreuer (n 4) 52.

an investor (and his counsels) for being foresightful and plan ahead of time? The term 'treaty shopping', on the other hand, is less indicative of when the actual legal operation is taking place and might describe an action taken both before and after a dispute might have arisen. Already more indicative of a timing element is the term 'corporate restructuring'. As can be seen from this example, the use of certain terms, or more generally speaking the use of language,[14] though in the absence of binding definitions not authoritative, may have consequences for legal conclusions.[15]

Language, of course, is only the most visible manifestation of the core question at stake: why are some forms of treaty shopping considered to be (socially, or at least legally) acceptable while others are not? What is it exactly that makes a 'time-sensitive', 'belated' restructuring 'abusive'? And, as perceptively pointed out by Christoph Schreuer, why is nationality the 'eye of the needle' to access the benefits of an international investment agreement (IIA), while once this threshold has been crossed, any discrimination on the basis of nationality is forbidden?[16] Any attempt at explanation will certainly have to touch on the role of the concept of nationality, which will be explored more in detail in further chapters. As with everything else in today's world, the role of nationality is in flux. In more remote times, nationality was considered the 'bond of allegiance' linking a person and its State of nationality, and in return for this allegiance, the person could (potentially) enjoy protection against the wrongdoings of another State, namely through the instrument of diplomatic protection. 'Abuses' (or misues) were possible as the decision of the International Court of Justice (ICJ) in *Nottebohm*[17] shows, but not frequent. And even in 1970, the ICJ was not yet concerned by the phenomenon of mailbox companies and the effect of globalization, otherwise—who knows—it might have decided differently in the seminal *Barcelona Traction* case.[18] Nationality in modern times has changed, at least as regards international investment protection. It undoubtedly still remains important as Schreuer's observation shows. At the same time, we are faced with a peculiar paradox concerning nationality: on the one hand, it equips foreign investors with very powerful rights against State regulatory measures, providing them with (arguably originary) rights that elevate the individual to the status of a partial international law subject;[19] on the other hand, nationality (in particular corporate nationality) may be easily or even very easily acquired, one could even call it a 'commodity'. The protective function of nationality as relevant under the (customary) international law of diplomatic protection has thus given way to an—also protective, but above all—access-based function of nationality in international investment law. In an era of

[14] Timothy Endicott, 'Law and Language' in Jules Coleman and Scott Shapiro (eds), *The Oxford Handbook of Jurisprudence and Philosophy of Law* (Oxford University Press 2004) 935.

[15] See, eg, the difference Zachary Douglas, *The International Law of Investment Claims* (Cambridge University Press 2009) draws between treaty and forum shopping, paras 551, 866: '[T]reaty shopping can be condoned, whereas forum shopping must be repelled'. On this distinction see further in s 1.1.3.

[16] Schreuer, 'Nationality planning' (n 7) 17.

[17] *Nottebohm (Liechtenstein v Guatemala) (Judgment)* [1955] ICJ Rep 4.

[18] *Barcelona Traction, Light and Power Co (Belgium v Spain) (Judgment)* [1970] ICJ Rep 3.

[19] Douglas, *Investment Claims* (n 15) Rules 1 and 2, para 65. See also below s 1.2.2.

interlinked economies but also ever greater public scepticism towards the current economic governance system, this paradox does not leave the perception of the role of nationality untouched, forming the ground for changing value judgments on its uses in investment treaty arbitration.

So what is treaty shopping for purposes of this research? Most commentators seem to agree that treaty shopping presupposes a corporate structuring or restructuring decision of some sort with the aim of accessing a (more) favourable IIA with the host State.[20] One of the most comprehensive definitions was proposed by the Organisation for Economic Cooperation and Development (OECD), which considers treaty shopping to occur:

> when an investor structures an investment (through incorporation and possibly by restructuring certain business operations) in order to seek to qualify for protections conferred by particular investment treaties ... Since investors generally do not know the nature of (future) disputes when they are structuring their investments, they may seek to structure their investment in a way that provides potential coverage under several treaties with different characteristics – such as by using several intermediate holding companies in different jurisdictions ... Investors may seek to engage in treaty shopping for several reasons including: (i) to seek to ensure treaty protection where none would otherwise be available; (ii) to seek to benefit from specific substantive protections in particular treaties; or (iii) to seek to benefit from certain procedural or other aspects of the dispute settlement provisions of a particular treaty. Treaty shopping thus raises issue for ISDS as well as with regard to substantive investment law.[21]

Several preliminary conclusions can be drawn from the above sample of definitions.

First, no value judgment should be attached to the term 'treaty shopping' and it will thus be used interchangeably throughout this book with the terms 'nationality planning' or 'strategic use or change of nationality'.

Second, it becomes apparent that treaty shopping consists of a (legal) operation that is aimed at making certain (more beneficial) investment treaty provisions accessible to the investor. An investor would arguably not engage in treaty shopping if it did not result in providing him[22] with higher legal protection, either because his investment did not have any protection at all or because he seeks better

[20] See, eg, Roos Van Os and Roeline Knottnerus, *Dutch Bilateral Investment Treaties: A Gateway to 'Treaty Shopping' for Investment Protection by Multinational Companies* (SOMO 2011) 9, available at <http://papers.ssrn.com/sol3/papers.cfm?abstract_id=1974431> (last accessed on 15 September 2016); Matthew Skinner, Cameron Miles, and Sam Luttrell, 'Access and Advantage in Investor-State Arbitration: The Law and Practice of Treaty Shopping' (2010) 3 JWELB 260; Délphine Burriez, 'Le Treaty Shopping Procédural d'incorporation' (2010) 25 ICSID Review-FILJ 394–95; Peter Muchlinski, 'Corporations and the Uses of Law: International Investment Arbitration as a "Multilateral Legal Order"', Oñati Socio-Legal Series, Vol 1, No 4 (2011)—Socio-Legal Aspects of Adjudication of International Economic Disputes, 3, available at <http://papers.ssrn.com/sol3/papers.cfm?abstract_id=1832562> (last accessed on 15 September 2016).

[21] David Gaukrodger and Kathryn Gordon, *Investor-State Dispute Settlement: A Scoping Paper for the Investment Policy Community*, OECD Working Papers on International Investment, No 2012/3, 55, available at <http://www.oecd.org/daf/inv/investment-policy/WP-2012_3.pdf> (last accessed on 15 September 2016).

[22] For the sake of convenience, the masculine form or a gender-neutral form of 'investor' will mostly be used in this book.

investment protection in procedural and/or substantive terms.[23] This is the very *ratio* of treaty shopping. This being said, no legal consequences should be inferred from this fact alone. The objective of obtaining higher protection is the underlying motive in the practice of treaty shopping, but does not, beyond this and in abstract terms, carry any legal consequence.[24]

Third, one way to achieve this higher protection is by creating 'diversity of nationality',[25] which is needed to either accede ISDS at all (since ISDS is as a matter of principle not open to an investor national of the host State),[26] or to a more favourable investment treaty regime within the frame of an already existing access to ISDS. With the notion of 'nationality' being key, this can be achieved either by invoking a dual nationality, corporate structuring or restructuring or by a transfer of claims. Admittedly, there are no compelling (legal) reasons to limit the notion of treaty shopping to only these legal operations, given the absence of a legally binding definition of treaty shopping. Thus, if one laid the emphasis only on the objective of the benefitting from other, more favourable investment treaty provisions (whether in procedural or substantive terms), one might certainly consider the use of most-favoured nation (MFN) clauses in order to access other, more favourable treaty provisions as also having a treaty shopping effect.[27] The same would arguably apply to the accessing of other treaties through conflict of norms techniques.[28] In a similar vein, the attempt to access the protection under World Trade Organization (WTO) treaties through the use of the umbrella clause could arguably be considered as having a treaty shopping effect.[29] However, these techniques present problems that

[23] Similar Eunjung Lee, 'Treaty Shopping in International Investment Arbitration: How often has it occurred and how has it been perceived by tribunals?' LSE Working Paper Series 2015 (No. 15–167) 17, available at <http://www.lse.ac.uk/internationalDevelopment/pdf/Dissertations/WP167.pdf> (last accessed on 15 September 2016).

[24] Though the motive, or purpose, of the structuring or restructuring is not completely irrelevant either, as can be seen from the importance for an abuse of process finding, see Chapter 7.

[25] See, eg, *Phoenix Action Ltd v Czech Republic*, ICSID Case No ARB/06/5, Award (15 April 2009) para 34 [Respondent's position]: 'Phoenix is nothing more than an *ex post facto* creation of a sham Israeli entity created by a Czech fugitive from justice … to create diversity of nationality … this case represents one of the most egregious cases of "treaty-shopping" … this Tribunal should not elevate form over substance'.

[26] See Preamble of the Convention on the Settlement of Investment Disputes between States and Nationals of other States (ICSID Convention), entered into force on 14 October, 1966: 'Bearing in mind the possibility that from time to time disputes may arise in connection with such investment between Contracting States and nationals of *other* contracting States' [emphasis added]. But see for the exception in Art 25(2)(b) second clause ICSID in Chapter 4, at 4.3.4.

[27] See, eg, Alejandro Faya Rodriguez, 'The Most-Favored-Nation Clause in International Investment Agreements-A Tool for Treaty Shopping?' (2008) 25 J Intl Arb 89; Yannick Radi, 'The Application of the Most-Favoured-Nation Clause to the Dispute Settlement Provisions of Bilateral Investment Treaties: Domesticating the "Trojan Horse"' (2007) 18(4) EJIL 757. For arbitral tribunals' association of the use of the MFN clause with treaty shopping see, eg, *Maffezzini v Spain* (n 10) para 63; *Salini Costruttori SpA and Italstrade SpA v The Hashemite Kingdom of Jordan*, ICSID Case No ARB/02/13, Decision on Jurisdiction (9 November 2004) para 115; *Telenor Mobile Communications AS v Republic of Hungary*, ICSID Case No ARB/04/15, Award (13 September 2006) paras 91–101.

[28] See Wolfgang Alschner, 'Regionalism and Overlap in Investment Treaty Law: Towards Consolidation or Contradiction?' (2014) 17 JIEL 271, 292–97.

[29] See *Philip Morris Asia Limited v Commonwealth of Australia*, UNCITRAL, PCA Case No 2012-12, Australia's Response to the Notice of Arbitration (21 December 2011).

necessitate different solutions than treaty shopping through the strategic use or change of nationality, which would go beyond the scope of this book.

It is thus a deliberate decision of this author, for the purpose of this book, to limit the notion of treaty shopping to legal operations aimed at a strategic invocation, creation, or change of nationality with the aim of accessing more beneficial investment treaties (whether in procedural or substantive terms).

Treaty shopping should thus be understood to include all legal operations aimed at invoking or creating a qualifying nationality and/or a qualifying investment, for example by structuring or restructuring an investment or by otherwise conferring an entitlement or property right to an investment, with a view to benefitting from a particular international investment agreement[30] granting an investor direct standing (*ius standi*).

A final clarification seems necessary. Though this research sets out from the (broad) question of the 'validity' of treaty shopping in international investment law, it must in more precise terms be understood as the question of the validity of the *investment claim* involving treaty shopping. For the sake of convenience, the book may use these terms interchangeably.

With the above in mind, it is apposite to have a look at the different scenarios that may be understood as treaty shopping for the purposes of this research.

1.1.2 Possible scenarios of treaty shopping

1.1.2.1 Treaty shopping by natural persons

Treaty shopping is, in practical terms, almost exclusively relevant for legal persons only, though it is not excluded that natural persons strategically change nationalities or acquire dual (or multiple) nationalities needed for trying to come under the protection of different investment treaties.[31] International law is, as will be seen more in detail in Chapter 3, more restrictive in allowing natural persons to derive legal standing from multiple nationalities, thus making treaty shopping by natural persons normally more difficult.[32] However, this restriction is relativized by the fact that natural persons as investors can and often do structure their downstream investments through legal persons, thus presenting the same problems, in addition

[30] Whether bilateral, plurilateral, or multilateral investment treaties, including investment chapters contained in free trade agreements. For the sake of greater ease, this book will in the following use the term 'IIA(s)' to denote these investment agreements, unless an explicit specification is needed.

[31] In this sense also Robert Sloane, 'Breaking the Genuine Link: The Contemporary International Legal Regulation of Nationality' (2009) 50 Harv Intl L J 1, 41. Of note is also the fact that some countries 'sell' generous residency permits or even nationalities in return for investing into their country, see, eg, for the case of Malta <http://www.henleyglobal.com/citizenship-malta-citizenship/>, or for the case of Portugal <http://goldenvisa-portugal.com/FAQ.html> (both last accessed on 15 September 2016).

[32] This is also illustrated by the arbitral tribunal's doubtful *obiter dictum* in *Hussein Nuaman Soufraki v The United Arab Emirates*, ICSID Case No ARB/02/7, Award (7 July 2004) para 83, in which it stated, after finding that the claimant had not proven that he still possessed Italian nationality, that 'had Mr. Soufraki contracted with the United Arab Emirates through a corporate vehicle incorporated in Italy, rather than contracting in his personal capacity, no problem of jurisdiction would now arise'.

to the problems pertaining specifically to natural persons, as in the case of legal persons as investors.[33]

1.1.2.2 Treaty shopping by corporate structuring or restructuring

Corporate structuring or restructuring undoubtedly constitutes the main method to create diversity of nationality and to thus become eligible for protection under more favourable investment treaties.

As will be seen in more detail below, a corporate structuring or restructuring is governed by the laws of the national jurisdiction concerned.[34] For example, the investor who wants to come under the protection of a specific IIA can acquire shares of an already existing corporate structure that is a national under the targeted IIA. An investment claim may then be brought either by the existing corporate structure or by the investor having acquired its shares (as direct or indirect owner/controller of the investment), depending on the availability of corresponding IIAs and whichever contains more favourable conditions. Such was the case for example in *Banro American Resources v Democratic Republic of Congo*,[35] *Société Générale v Dominican Republic*,[36] *Aucoven v Venezuela*,[37] *Phoenix Action v Czech Republic*,[38] or *Philip Morris Asia v Australia*.[39] Though relatively rare, a corporate structure can also migrate from one jurisdiction to another one (having a more favourable investment treaty with the host State), as was the case in *Aguas del Tunarí v Bolivia*.[40] Furthermore, an investor can incorporate a new company in the target home State and interpose it (in particular in the form of a holding company) in its corporate structure. This happened for example in the cases of *Tidewater v Venezuela*[41] and *Lao Holdings NV v Lao Peoples Democratic Republic*.[42]

In these cases, questions concerning the validity of the claim involving a corporate structuring may arise when the company incorporated in one country having an IIA with the host State is effectively controlled by an investor national of that host State brought to arbitration. This practice, also called 'round-tripping',

[33] See, eg, *Franz Sedelmayer v Russian Federation*, SCC, Award (7 July 1998); *Burimi SRL and Eagle Games SH.A v Republic of Albania*, ICSID Case No ARB/11/18, Award (29 May 2013); *National Gas SAE v Arab Republic of Egypt*, ICSID Case No ARB/11/7, Award (3 April 2014); *Renée Rose Levy and Gremcitel SA v Republic of Peru*, ICSID Case No ARB/11/17, Award (9 January 2015).

[34] See Chapter 3, at 3.2.2.

[35] *Banro American Resources Inc and Société Aurifère du Kivu du Maniema SARL v Democratic Republic of Congo*, ICSID Case No ARB/98/7, Award (1 September 2000).

[36] *Société Générale in Respect of DR Energy Holdings Limited and Empresa Distribuidora de Electricidad del Este, SA ('EDE Este') v Dominican Republic*, LCIA Case No UN 7927, Award on Preliminary Objections to Jurisdiction (19 September 2008).

[37] *Autopista Concesionada de Venezuela CA (Aucoven) v Bolivarian Republic of Venezuela*, ICSID Case No ARB/00/5, Decision on Jurisdiction (27 September 2001).

[38] *Phoenix Action v Czech Republic* (n 25).

[39] *Philip Morris Asia Limited v Commonwealth of Australia*, UNCITRAL, PCA Case No 2012-12, Award on Jurisdiction and Admissibility (17 December 2015) (redacted version).

[40] *Aguas del Tunarí v Bolivia* (n 11).

[41] *Tidewater v Venezuela* (n 11).

[42] *Lao Holdings NV v The Lao People's Democratic Republic*, ICSID Case No ARB(AF)12/6, Decision on Jurisdiction (21 February 2014).

occurred in *Tokios Tokelés v Ukraine*[43] and in *Rompetrol v Romania*.[44] A company may also be incorporated in one country having an IIA with the host State and be effectively controlled by an investor national to a third-party state that does not have any IIA with the host State. Such was the case in *Saluka v Czech Republic*,[45] *ADC Affiliate Limited & ADMC Management Limited v Hungary*,[46] *Mobil v Venezuela*,[47] and the already mentioned *Aguas del Tunarí v Bolivia*.[48] Both variations are often discussed in relation with the question of treatment of 'shell' or 'mailbox companies', that is, companies that do not have any real economic activity in the State of incorporation.[49] The question may then arise whether tribunals should in those cases look at the substance of the relationship between the investor and the host State, rather than its form.[50] Manifold questions also arise in this context as to whether the investor has made a protected investment and whether the corporate structuring or restructuring occurred before or after the specific dispute has arisen.[51]

1.1.2.3 Treaty shopping by transfer of claims

The practice of what can be considered treaty shopping for the purposes of this book has also been discussed in relation to the transfer of treaty claims.[52] An investor may transfer or assign claims arising out of alleged violations of investment obligations by the host State to another investor covered by an IIA existing with the host State, thus creating the (appearance of) diversity of nationality characteristic of the notion of treaty shopping. Though there have been some early cases of transfer of claims such as in *Mihaly v Sri Lanka*[53] or *Loewen Group and Raymond Loewen v United States*,[54] treaty shopping by transfer of claims seems to have become rather rare compared to cases of corporate structuring or restructuring, probably in view of the potentially problematic timing element usually involved with this practice, as will be seen further below. However, as some claim that IIA claims potentially

[43] *Tokios Tokelés v Ukraine*, ICSID Case No ARB/02/18, Decision on Jurisdiction (29 April 2004).

[44] *Rompetrol Group NV v Republic of Romania*, ICSID Case No ARB/06/3, Decision on Respondent's Preliminary Objections on Jurisdiction and Admissibility (18 April 2008).

[45] *Saluka v Czech Republic* (n 10).

[46] *ADC Affiliate Limited & ADMC Management Limited v Republic of Hungary*, ICSID Case No ARB/03/16, Award (2 October 2006).

[47] *Mobil Corporation, Venezuela Holdings BV, Mobil Cerro Negro Holding, Ltd, Mobil Venezolana de Petróleos Holdings, Inc, Mobil Cerro Negro, Ltd, and Mobil Venezolana de Petróleos, Inc v Bolivarian Republic of Venezuela*, ICSID Case No ARB/07/27, Decision on Jurisdiction (10 June 2010).

[48] *Aguas del Tunarí v Bolivia* (n 11).

[49] See, eg, *Alps Finance and Trade AG v Slovak Republic*, UNCITRAL, Award (5 March 2011) paras 217ff.

[50] See more in detail in Chapter 4.

[51] See more in detail in Chapters 5, 6, and 7.

[52] William Kirtley, 'The Transfer of Treaty Claims and Treaty-Shopping in Investor-State Disputes' (2009) 10 JWIT 427.

[53] *Mihaly International Corporation v Democratic Socialist Republic of Sri Lanka*, ICSID Case No ARB/00/2, Award (25 March 2002).

[54] *Loewen Group Inc and Raymond Loewen v United States of America*, ICSID Case No ARB(AF)/98/3, Award (26 June 2003).

arising out of distressed investment projects are increasingly being traded,[55] it is not excluded to see some of these cases in the future.

1.1.3 The distinction between treaty and forum shopping

Both commentators and tribunals have in the past at times mixed up the terms 'treaty' and 'forum shopping'.[56] This may be due to the fact that, as the OECD has noted, '[f]orum shopping and treaty shopping are separate, but related practices undertaken by investors'.[57]

Forum shopping in international law is, in contrast to private international law, a rather recent phenomenon and in part due to the increasing availability of alternative judicial fora. In particular in the area of international criminal law, international human rights law, and international economic law, international tribunals have proliferated after the end of the Cold War, resulting in the creation of, among others, the ad hoc International Criminal Tribunals for the former Yugoslavia and Rwanda (ICTY and ICTR), the International Criminal Court, the Dispute Settlement Body of the WTO, the International Tribunal for the Law of Sea (ITLOS), and numerous regional tribunals (such as the African Court of Human Rights, the Inter-American Court for Human Rights, etc.).[58] The concerns of the academic community with respect to this development, in particular the danger of fragmentation of international law and inconsistency of judicial decisions, have been broadly and exhaustively addressed elsewhere.[59] Higher economic integration,

[55] Skinner, Miles, and Luttrell (n 20) 269: '[A]s a matter of commercial interest, it is worth noting that there is a growing market for BIT claims, and highly sophisticated investors dedicated to "trafficking in BIT claims" are now becoming active worldwide. The most commonly trafficked BIT claims are, it seems, distressed project investments in developing countries, but BIT claims relating to bonds are also traded'. This seems without prejudice to the trading of arbitration awards, see Gaukrodger and Gordon (n 21) 31–32: 'There is now a secondary market in arbitration awards, in particular in awards against States. This market has existed with regard to commercial arbitration awards for some time and now apparently extends to ISDS awards as well. Investors may be able to sell their award albeit at a discount. Firms such as hedge funds that acquire these awards typically engage in aggressive enforcement efforts in multiple jurisdictions.'

[56] See, eg, Mariel Dimpsey, *The resolution of international investment disputes* (Eleven International Publishing 2008) 71–73, who quotes two archetypical arbitral cases of treaty shopping (Tokios Tokelés and Aguas del Tunarí) as examples of forum shopping, yet rightly recognizes the problem and risk of multiple proceedings arising from the direct standing of each entity within a corporate group; similar Gus Van Harten, *Investment Treaty Arbitration and Public Law* (Oxford University Press 2007) 113–17. See also *Lao Holdings v Laos* (n 42) para 115.

[57] Gaukrodger and Gordon (n 21) 51; *National Gas v Egypt* (n 33) para 146.

[58] See, eg, Cesare Romano, 'The Proliferation of International Judicial Bodies: The Pieces of the Puzzle' (1998–1999) 31 NYU J Intl L & Pol 709.

[59] See, eg, Benedict Kingsbury, 'Foreword: Is the Proliferation of International Courts and Tribunals a Systemic Problem?' (1998–1999) 31 NYU J Intl L & Pol 679; Gilbert Guillaume, 'Advantages and Risks of Proliferation: A Blueprint for Action' (2004) 2 JICJ 300–303; same, 'The proliferation of international judicial bodies: The outlook for the international legal order', Speech by His Excellency Judge Gilbert Guillaume, President of the International Court of Justice, to the Sixth Committee of the General Assembly of the United Nations (27 October 2000) available at <http://www.icj-cij.org/court/index.php?pr=85&pt=3&p1=1&p2=3&p3=1> (last accessed on 15 September 2016); Rosalyn Higgins, 'A Babel of Judicial Voices? Ruminations from the Bench' (2006) 55 ICLQ 791.

both regionally and globally, have also led to an increase in transnational litigation, thus making concurrent jurisdictions more likely.[60]

So what is forum shopping? As for the notion of treaty shopping, there is no universal or authoritative definition of what constitutes forum shopping.

According to the OECD, forum shopping is 'the process throughout which one of the parties to a dispute attempts to bring a claim before the forum most advantageous to him or her'.[61] As in treaty shopping, a rational selection process thus takes place where a party, having the choice between several jurisdictions, will naturally select the one he/she considers most advantageous to his/her aims, only that it concerns not a particular treaty, but a particular forum.[62] However, despite its derogatory connotation, the notion of forum shopping should not from the outset be equated with inappropriate or even unlawful behaviour.[63] In this aspect, it seems misleading to state that 'treaty shopping is acceptable, forum shopping is not'.[64]

So is a distinction necessary, is it legally relevant, given the absence of authoritative definitions of either practice? This, it is submitted, will depend on whether forum shopping leads to a single or to multiple proceedings.

Indeed, in international investment law, the 'simple' forum shopping, that is, where forum shopping leads to the choice of one—the most advantageous—forum, is usually considered as unproblematic, as can be seen from investment treaty practice. States usually give investors of the Contracting Party a choice of several alternative fora where to bring their claim.[65] For example, Article X(3) of the 1991

[60] Andrew Bell, *Forum Shopping and Venue in Transnational Litigation* (Oxford University Press 2003) para 1.07. See, eg, the multiple MOX Plant litigations brought by Ireland against the United Kingdom: *MOX Plant (Ireland v UK)* ITLOS Provisional Measures Order (3 December 2001) 126 ILR 259; *MOX Plant (Ireland v UK)* UNCLOS, Annex VII, Order (24 June 2003) 126 ILR 310; *Dispute Concerning Access to Information under Art 9 of the OSPAR Convention (Ireland v UK)* Permanent Court of Arbitration, Final Award (2 July 2003) 126 ILR 334.

[61] Katia Yannaca-Small, 'Improving the System of Investor-State Dispute Settlement: An Overview' Working Papers on International Investment, No 2006/1 (OECD 2006) paras 79–80, available at <http://www.oecd.org/china/WP-2006_1.pdf> (last accessed on 15 September 2016).

[62] Gaukrodger and Gordon (n 21) 51; Whytock (n 12) 485.

[63] See Whytock (n 12) 485 (FN 13): 'However, it is important not to embed the definition of forum shopping with assumptions about whether it is an appropriate behaviour. To do so would conflate two distinct modes of analysis: (1) descriptive analysis of forum shopping and its consequences, and (2) normative analysis of forum shopping'. Similar 'Notes, Forum Shopping Reconsidered' (1989–1990) 103 Harv L Rev 1677–78: 'Any definition of forum shopping confronts a semantic difficulty. Forum selection is always a part of the legal process; at no clear point does it become forum "shopping". Thus, it is difficult for an observer to note definitely that forum shopping has occurred without analysing the litigant's motives. Indeed, a party makes a forum choice—through action or inaction—any time it can make a decision that would affect the forum for the dispute. Thus, the term "forum shopping", despite its clear derogatory connotations, has relatively limited descriptive content.' See also *The Atlantic Star v Bona Spes*, House of Lords, 10 April 1973, AC (1974) 436 (1973, United Kingdom) 471: 'Forum shopping is a dirty word; but it is only a pejorative way of saying that, if you offer a plaintiff a choice of jurisdictions, he will naturally choose the one in which he thinks his case can be most favourably presented: this should be a matter neither for surprise nor for indignation.'

[64] Douglas, *Investment Claims* (n 15) Rule 31, para 542.

[65] Gaukrodger and Gordon (n 21) 53. For a survey see ibid, 54 and 64: '56% of the sample treaties offer investors the possibility to forum shop between at least two arbitration fora, most frequently ICSID and UNCITRAL.'

bilateral investment treaty (BIT) between Canada and Argentina gives the investor a choice between arbitration under International Centre for Settlement of Investment Disputes (ICSID) Rules (including Additional Facility Rules) or arbitration according to United Nations Commission on International Trade Law (UNCITRAL) Rules or such rules as agreed by the parties. Similarly, the 2004 Dominican Republic–Central American Free Trade Agreement (DR-CAFTA) gives investors in its Article 10.16(3) a choice between arbitration under ICSID rules, ICSID Additional Facility Rules, or UNCITRAL Arbitration Rules. The same is the case for the 2008 German Model BIT[66] or the 2012 US Model BIT.[67] In these cases, it is clear that the investor has only an alternative ('or'), not a multiple choice. This form of forum shopping is included in virtually any IIA[68] and can therefore normally be assumed to be unproblematic for treaty-negotiating States. And while it may also raise some policy issues,[69] States concerns about this practice seem to remain overall rather limited.

This is arguably not what can be said of the kind of forum shopping that leads to multiple proceedings. The European Union (EU) is not the only one to be concerned by the risk of parallel claims.[70] Increasingly, States have been trying to counter multiple proceedings in a treaty-based manner for what arbitral tribunals have not found viable (and consistent) solutions.

For example, for the question of the effect of a contractual exclusive jurisdiction clause on treaty-based arbitral jurisdiction, arbitral jurisprudence has mostly found that the investor could pursue his claim for breach of treaty notwithstanding the existence of an exclusive jurisdiction clause in the investment contract, thus creating a problem of multiple proceedings.[71]

[66] See its Art 10(2), which gives a choice between ICSID arbitration (including under Additional Facility Rules), arbitration under UNCITRAL Rules or arbitration under Rules of the International Chamber of Commerce, the London Court of International Arbitration or the Arbitration Institute of the Stockholm Chamber of Commerce.

[67] See its Art 24(3), which gives a choice between ICSID arbitration (including under Additional Facility Rules), arbitration under UNCITRAL Rules and under any other rules as agreed by the parties.

[68] For an exception see Art 7 of the French Model BIT, which does not grant any choice, but only offers ICSID arbitration; similar Art 15(3) of the 2007 Norway Model BIT.

[69] Such as the concern about a 'level playing field' between domestic and foreign investors, see Gaukrodger and Gordon (n 21) 53–54. For further policy concerns see Yuval Shany, *The Competing Jurisdictions of International Courts and Tribunals* (Oxford University Press 2003) 131ff.

[70] European Commission, 'Factsheet, Investment Protection and Investor-to-State Dispute Settlement in EU agreements' (November 2013) 8: 'Preventing investors from bringing multiple or frivolous claims: Firstly, the EU will prohibit two types of claims being brought at the same time before different tribunals. Avoiding parallel claims will prevent investors potentially winning twice and also avoid a situation where two different tribunals come to different decisions based on the same facts', available at <http://trade.ec.europa.eu/doclib/docs/2013/november/tradoc_151916.pdf> (last accessed on 15 September 2016).

[71] See *Compañía de Aguas del Aconquija SA and Compagnie Générale des Eaux v Argentine Republic*, ICSID Case No ARB/97/3, Award (21 November 2000); *Compañía de Aguas del Aconquija SA and Vivendi Universal v Argentine Republic*, ICSID Case No ARB/97/3, Decision on Annulment (3 July 2002). This holding was broadly adopted by subsequent jurisprudence, see, eg, *CMS Gas Transmission Co v Argentine Republic*, ICSID Case No ARB/01/8, Decision of the Tribunals on Objections to Jurisdiction (17 July 2003); *SGS Société de Surveillance SA v Islamic Republic of Pakistan*, ICSID Case No ARB/01/13, Decision of the Tribunal on Objections to Jurisdiction (6 August 2003); *Eureko BV v Republic of Poland*, Partial Award (19 August 2005).

In a similar vein, arbitral tribunals have not really found a way to rein in multiple (be it parallel or consecutive) proceedings (usually in different fora/jurisdictions) arising from the same set of facts giving rise to the claim, but being brought by different investors from within the same corporate chain or group. Its root cause lying in an increasingly expansive reading of the notion of 'investor', granting direct standing under most IIAs to both direct and indirect investors and in the case of the latter often even non-controlling minority shareholders,[72] this leads to a situation where 'each and every member of the group of companies to which the claimant belongs might have standing to bring an investment treaty claim in respect of the same investment concurrently'.[73] Such has happened in for example the controversial *Lauder* arbitrations,[74] and in the diverse arbitrations and litigations of the Turkish Uzan family against the Turkish State[75] arising out of the same facts founding the investment dispute. The multiple arbitrations by certain shareholders against Russia in relation with the claims of expropriation of the Russian oil company Yukos Oil arguably also fall into this category.[76] Arbitral tribunals have in these situations tended to adhere to a strict reading of the 'triple identity' test, thus leaving classical litispendence tools such as *lis pendens* and *res judicata* without effect.[77] They have so far also dismissed the idea that the

[72] Douglas, *Investment Claims* (n 15) paras 574–77; Campbell McLachlan, Laurence Shore, and Matthew Weiniger, *International Investment Arbitration-Substantive Principles* (Oxford University Press 2007) para 4.118; Muchlinski, 'Corporations and the Uses of Law' (n 20) 3.

[73] Douglas, *Investment Claims* (n 15) para 575; see, eg, *CMS v Argentina* (n 71) para 86: '[I]t is not possible to foreclose rights that different investors might have under different arrangements'. Though the more remote along the corporate chain an entity is from the entity having suffered the direct damages, the more difficult it may get to calculate the indirect ('flow-through') damages.

[74] *Ronald S Lauder v Czech Republic*, UNCITRAL, Final Award (3 September 2001); *CME Czech Republic BV v Czech Republic*, UNCITRAL, Partial Award (13 September 2001) (CME I); *CME Czech Republic BV v Czech Republic*, UNCITRAL, Final Award, (14 March 2003) (CME II); *CME Czech Republic BV v Czech Republic*, UNCITRAL, Svea Court of Appeal, Sweden (15 May 2003).

[75] *Europe Cement Trade & Investment v Republic of Turkey*, ICSID Case No ARB(AF)/07/2, Decision on Jurisdiction (13 August 2009); *Cementownia v Turkey* (n 11); *Libananco Holdings Co Limited v Republic of Turkey*, ICSID Case No ARB(AF)/06/8, Award (2 September 2011); *Polska Energetyka Holding SA v Republic of Turkey*, UNCITRAL, Award (1 January 2009) (not public); *Kemal Uzan and others v Republic of Turkey*, ECtHR, Application No 18240/03, Decision (29 March 2011).

[76] *Yukos Universal Ltd (Isle of Man) v Russian Federation*, UNCITRAL, PCA Case No AA 227, Interim Award on Jurisdiction and Admissibility (30 November 2009); *Hulley Enterprises Ltd (Cyprus) v Russian Federation*, UNCITRAL, PCA Case No AA 226, Interim Award on Jurisdiction and Admissibility (30 November 2009); *Veteran Petroleum Ltd (Cyprus) v Russian Federation*, UNCITRAL, PCA Case No AA 228, Interim Award on Jurisdiction and Admissibility (30 November 2009); *OAO Neftyanaya Kompaniya Yukos v Russia*, ECtHR, Application No 14902/04, Decision of 29 January 2009 and Judgment of 20 September 2011.

[77] *Lauder v Czech Republic* (n 74) para 171. For a critical analysis see August Reinisch, 'The Issues Raised by Parallel Proceedings and Possible Solutions' in Michael Waibel, Asha Kaudal, Kyo-Hwa Chung, and Claire Balchin (eds), *The Backlash against Investment Arbitration* (Kluwer Law International 2010) 113; August Reinisch, 'The Use and Limits of Res Judicata and Lis Pendens as Procedural Tools to Avoid Conflicting Dispute Settlement Outcomes' (2004) 3 LPICT 37ff; Gilles Cuniberti, 'Parallel Litigation and Foreign Investment Dispute Settlement' (2006) 21 ICSID Review-FILJ 381; McLachlan, Shore, and Weiniger (n 72) paras 4.119–4.143; Douglas, *Investment Claims* (n 15) para 577.

bringing of multiple claims based on the same facts could amount to an abuse of rights.[78]

States have countered these problems by including in newly negotiated treaties clauses aimed at curbing multiple claims, such as consolidation clauses, fork-in-the-road clauses, and waiver clauses. In particular the latter may have the potential—provided they are properly worded—to capture precisely the problem of multiple proceedings arising from claims based on the same facts, but brought by different entities of the same corporate structure.[79]

So how can treaty and forum shopping be distinguished? First of all, treaty shopping may lead to forum shopping, both the simple and the multiple one. That is because when an investor engages in treaty shopping, he may access an investment treaty providing for a wider option of arbitral fora than normally available to him. He may then invoke one forum, that is, engage in one proceeding, and no real problem of forum shopping arises. Treaty and forum shopping in this case are clearly distinguishable, even though, as mentioned by the OECD, 'related practices'.[80]

It is different, however, when the investor structures or restructures an entity within his corporate group and has different of these entities bring multiple claims based on the same measure. It is here where the problem of multiple proceedings may arise and treaty and forum shopping may be difficult to distinguish.

In this case, it is submitted that solutions to the problem should be distinguished depending on whether it is the multiplicity of proceedings that is at stake or the legal standing of the investor–claimant(s). In the case of multiple proceedings, possible approaches have been discussed above. In the case of corporate structuring or restructuring, it is not the potential multiplicity of proceedings that is at stake, but rather the *Barcelona Traction* problematic, that is, the increasingly extensive reading of the notions of investor and investment and their potential for manipulation to fabricate legal standing for disputes that may have existed before the corporate structuring or restructuring. Possible approaches to this problem will be discussed in the Chapters 4 to 7.

1.2 Reasons for the Occurrence of Treaty Shopping

Before the turn of the last century, the notion of treaty shopping was, if not unknown, then largely inconsequential in investment arbitration. A first explicit mention of the practice of treaty shopping can be found in the *Maffezini* decision

[78] *Lauder v Czech Republic* (n 74) paras 176–80; see also *Sanum Investments Limited v Government of the Lao People's Democratic Republic,* UNCITRAL, PCA Case No 2013-13, Award on Jurisdiction (13 December 2013) paras 366–67. See also Andrew Mitchell, Tania Voon, and James Munro, 'Good Faith in Parallel Trade and Investment Disputes' in Andrew Mitchell, M Sornarajah, and Tania Voon (eds), *Good Faith and International Economic Law* (Oxford University Press 2015) 60.

[79] Similar Campbell McLachlan, *Lis Pendens in International Litigation* (Martinus Nijhoff 2009) 268; Charles Brower and Jeremy Sharpe, 'Multiple and Conflicting International Arbitral Awards' (2003) 4 JWI 211, 216–17.

[80] Gaukrodger and Gordon (n 21) 51.

handed down in 2000.[81] Ever since, claimants have discovered the advantages of and have increasingly been resorting to treaty shopping in investment arbitrations. Nowadays, tribunals are ever more called upon to decide upon the validity of this practice.[82]

Three (potentially four) factors are essentially responsible for the occurrence of and increase in treaty shopping.

Most importantly, the proliferation of investment treaties and the failure to negotiate one overarching multilateral investment agreement may arguably be seen as one of the main reasons for the increase in treaty shopping.[83] Intrinsically linked to the former is the paradigm change from the protection of the foreign investor by way of diplomatic protection to his direct standing contained in most if not all modern investment treaties, thus creating a direct right of access of the foreign investor to international arbitration against the host State in case of allegations of violations of his rights. Furthermore, it is the ease with which in particular legal entities may be brought into existence and thus acquire (corporate) nationality in many domestic jurisdictions, alongside the high fungibility of shareholding, that makes it possible to react relatively quickly to perceived changes in the investment climate of the host State. Finally, some have argued that the lack of a doctrine of precedent in international investment law, with its potential to further inconsistent decisions, can also be seen as a factor for the occurrence of treaty shopping.

1.2.1 Proliferation of investment treaties

In hardly any other area of international (economic) law exist nowadays a plethora and a network of treaties as dense as in international investment law. According to a recent United Nations Conference on Trade and Development (UNCTAD) study, a total of 3268 investment agreements were in force by the end of 2014, making this a threefold increase compared to the beginning of the 1990s.[84] It is submitted that treaty shopping would be largely impossible (or at least greatly reduced) if there was one overarching multilateral agreement on investment as is the case in world trade law.[85] In other words, treaty shopping thrives on the sheer number of similar,

[81] *Maffezini v Spain* (n 10) para 63: '[A] distinction has to be made between the legitimate extension of rights and benefits by means of the MFN clause ... and disruptive treaty-shopping'.

[82] See more recently, eg, *Philip Morris Asia v Australia*, Award (n 39); *Standard Chartered Bank v United Republic of Tanzania*, ICSID Case No ARB/10/12, Award (2 November 2012).

[83] Similar see Schreuer, 'Nationality Planning' (n 7) 27.

[84] UNCTAD, 'IIA Issues Note, Recent Trends in IIAs and ISDS', No 1 (February 2015) 2, available at <http://unctad.org/en/PublicationsLibrary/webdiaepcb2015d1_en.pdf>; UNCTAD, 'World Investment Report 2012—Towards a New Generation of Investment Policies' (United Nations 2012) 84, available at <http://unctad.org/en/PublicationsLibrary/wir2012_embargoed_en.pdf> (both last accessed on 15 September 2016).

[85] Similar Pieter Bekker, 'Is Arbitration Based on "Treaty Shopping" in Jeopardy' *Kluwer Arbitration Blog* (17 June 2009) available at <http://kluwerarbitrationblog.com/2009/06/17/is-arbitration-based-on-treaty-shopping-in-jeopardy> (last accessed on 15 September 2016); Kenneth Vandevelde, 'A Brief History of International Investment Agreements' (2005–2006) 12 UC Davis J Intl L & Pol 191; Rafael Leal-Arcas, 'Towards the Multilateralization of International Investment Law' (2009) 10 JWIT 865, 919.

yet in details differing investment treaties, thus giving investors the incentive to compare and try to access the most advantageous one(s).

As is well known, the proliferation of investment treaties we are witnessing today has to be seen in a historical perspective. Only the main traits of this historical development will be sketched here as fuller accounts of the historical development of the modern international investment law system can be found elsewhere.[86]

The first BITs (Germany–Pakistan BIT in 1959; Switzerland–Tunisia BIT in 1961; France–Tunisia BIT in 1972, etc.) came into being at a time when several multilateral attempts at creating a hard or soft law framework for the protection of foreign investment[87] had already failed or were doomed to fail due to already prevailing ideological differences.[88] These different ideologies (capitalism v anti-capitalism) clashed at their fullest in the 1960s and 1970s—often at the United Nations General Assembly—expressing a deep-rooted 'dichotomy between sovereignty and investment protection'[89] fed by 'existential conflicts about colonization, decolonization, industrialization, socialist revolution, ideological competition, nationalism, racism [and] foreign control over local resources'.[90]

However, the late 1980s and early 1990s brought about a fundamental paradigm change not only to the political world order, but as a consequence also to the international economic order. With the end of the Cold War, as evidenced by the fall of the Berlin Wall and the demise of the Soviet Union, investment policy lost its ideological division that had characterized the preceding decades and was replaced by more pragmatism and cooperation.[91] Economic liberalism got a fresh start—probably also not least with the negotiation of the 1994 Marrakech Agreement establishing the WTO and a modernized multilateral world trade order—and bilateral investment agreements went from being mere protection instruments to being equally aimed at liberalizing investment flows.[92]

[86] See, eg, Andrew Newcombe and Lluís Paradell, *Law and Practice of Investment Treaties, Standards of Treatment* (Kluwer Law International 2009) 3–41; Vandevelde (n 85); Andreas Lowenfeld, *International Economic Law* (Oxford University Press, 2nd edn 2008) 469–94.

[87] See, eg, the 1948 Havana Charter for an International Trade Organization, the 1949 ICC International Code of Fair Treatment for Foreign Investment, the Draft Statutes of the Arbitral Tribunal for Foreign Investment and the Foreign Investment Court by the International Law Association, the 1959 Draft Convention on Investments Abroad (Abs–Shawcross Draft Convention) or the 1961 Draft Convention on the International Responsibility of States for Injuries to Aliens (Harvard Draft), see Newcombe and Paradell (n 86) 19–22.

[88] Vandevelde (n 85) 167ff; Newcombe and Paradell (n 86) 41; M Sornarajah, 'Towards Normlessness, The Ravage and Retreat of Neo-Liberalism in International Investment Law' in Karl Sauvant (ed), *Yearbook on International Investment Law and Policy 2009–2010* (Oxford University Press 2010) 595, 598.

[89] Omar García-Bolívar, 'Sovereignty vs. Investment Protection: Back to Calvo' (2009) 24 ICSID Review-FILJ 464, 465; similar Stephan Schill, *The Multilateralization of International Investment Law* (Cambridge University Press 2009) 7: '[O]pposing views on State sovereignty and societal self-determination versus the protection of property, in particular foreign property'.

[90] Charles H Brower II, 'Reflections on the Road Ahead: Living with Decentralization in Investment Treaty Arbitration', in Catherine Rogers and Roger Alford (eds), *The Future of Investment Arbitration* (Oxford University Press 2009) 339, 356 (FN 13).

[91] Vandevelde (n 85) 182–83.

[92] Vandevelde, ibid (calling them 'instruments of globalization'); similar Rainer Geiger, 'The Multifaceted Nature of International Investment Law' in Karl Sauvant (ed), *Appeals Mechanism in*

Yet the reason why formerly opposed countries all of a sudden started to embrace economic liberalism may have been due more (or at least as much) to economic necessity than a true change of convictions: many developing countries were deeply affected by the drop in commodity prices and public debt crises of the 1980s, leading to a drop in sovereign lending and thus the drying up of hitherto traditional sources of foreign capital.[93] At the same time, the so-called Washington Consensus gained ground in the capitals of both developed and developing countries, imposing the adherence to neo-liberal economic policies, such as fiscal austerity, privatization, and market liberalization, often also as conditions for loans by the International Monetary Fund (IMF).[94] With the economic rise of the 'Asian tigers' and other emerging economies (such as the dubbed 'BRICS'—Brazil, Russia, India, China, and South Africa), ever more developing or transitioning countries increasingly became both capital importers and capital exporters.[95]

Nevertheless, the attempt at adopting a Multilateral Agreement on Investment (MAI) under the auspices of the OECD failed resoundingly at the end of the 1990s. As UNCTAD analysed the failure in hindsight:

> One reason for the failure of the MAI was a change in the political climate during the course of the negotiations and the emergence of a backlash against globalization ... negotiators underestimated the intensity of the public debate the MAI would provoke in some countries ... Thus, on the one hand, from the perspective of national decision makers there were no truly compelling problems of investment protection in the OECD area; they needed to consider the possibility that the MAI might lower the protection standards that had already been accepted in BITs (with the possible effects that this might have on the negotiation of future BITs); they were uncertain as to whether many developing countries would join an agreement (which, considering that the OECD was already largely liberalized, was seen by some as the real payoff of an agreement); and they realized that an agreement would not necessarily lead to improved market access in the OECD area (at least in the short term). On the other hand, national decision makers saw no strong support from the business community; faced broad opposition from NGOs, who saw the MAI as "a metaphor for all that was to be feared from globalization" (Sauvé, 1998, p. 5); and (in some countries) even expected difficulties within their own coalition Governments. On balance, therefore, a political cost/benefit calculation suggested to some Governments that the value-added of the MAI was limited.[96]

International Investment Disputes (Oxford University Press 2008) 17, 19; Newcombe and Paradell (n 86) 48.

[93] García-Bolívar, 'Sovereignty' (n 89) 467; Newcombe and Paradell (n 86) 48–49; M Sornarajah, 'A Coming Crisis: Expansionary Trends in Investment Treaty Arbitration' in Karl Sauvant (ed), *Appeals Mechanism in International Investment Disputes* (Oxford University Press 2008) 39, 46–47.

[94] Newcombe and Paradell (n 86) 48; Sornarajah, 'Coming Crisis' (n 93) 46–47; for more on IMF conditionality see, eg, Lowenfeld (n 86) 611–16 and 644–51.

[95] José Alvarez, *The Public International Law Regime Governing International Investment* (Martinus Nijhoff 2011) 144: 'Today's flows of investment are not merely unidirectional. In most years after WWII, the US has been the largest recipient of FDI [*foreign direct investment*] as well as the leading capital exporter. The US shares this duality with others, such as the so-called BRICs, Brazil, Russia, India and China—all leading recipients and exporters of capital'.

[96] UNCTAD, 'Lessons from the MAI', UNCTAD Series on Issues in International Investment agreements (United Nations 1999) 23ff, available at <http://unctad.org/en/docs/psiteiitm22.en.pdf> (last accessed on 15 September 2016). See also Reiner Geiger, 'Regulatory Expropriations

The consequence of this renewed failure was that States increasingly turned to bilateral and regional treaty-making. The trend to more regionalism is also a response to the deadlock of the Doha Development Round at the WTO, with States having started to address investment issues increasingly from the more comprehensive perspective of economic integration, making investment protection part and parcel of free trade or economic partnership agreements.[97]

With the rise in number of investment treaties, investment arbitration claims also soared, bringing the number of (known) investment arbitration cases every year to new record heights.[98] At the same time, discontent over the current investment law system started to grow among the users of the system, prompting several developing countries to withdraw from the ICSID Convention and/or denounce some of their BITs,[99] while others have become more wary to give their consent to investor–State dispute settlement.[100]

This 'legitimacy crisis' is nowadays not merely felt and discussed in academic circles,[101] but increasingly reverberates through the public domain, as can be seen from the vociferous opposition organized by parts of the civil society to free

in International Law: Lessons from the Multilateral Agreement on Investment' (2002) 11 NYU Environmental L J 94.

[97] UNCTAD, 'IIA Issues Note, The Rise of Regionalism in International Investment Policymaking: Consolidation or Complexity?' Issues Note No 3 (June 2013) 1ff, available at <http://unctad.org/en/PublicationsLibrary/webdiaepcb2013d8_en.pdf>; UNCTAD, 'WIR 2012' (n 84) 84; UNCTAD, 'International Investment Arrangements: Trends and Emerging Issues', UNCTAD Series on International Investment Policies for Development (United Nations 2006) 9, available at <http://unctad.org/en/docs/iteiit200511_en.pdf> (both last accessed on 20 September 2016).

[98] UNCTAD, 'World Investment Report 2014, Investing in the SDGs: An Action Plan' (United Nations 2014) 124, available at <http://unctad.org/en/publicationslibrary/wir2014_en.pdf> (last accessed on 20 September 2016).

[99] Eg, Bolivia denounced the ICSID Convention in 2007, Ecuador denounced the ICSID Convention in 2009, and Venezuela denounced the ICSID Convention in 2012. On the other hand, South Africa denounced many of its first-generation BITs, see Republic of South Africa, Department of Trade and Industry, 'Bilateral investment treaty policy framework review: government position paper' (Pretoria, June 2009); LE Peterson, 'South Africa Pushes Phase-Out of Early Bilateral Investment Treaties After At Least Two Separate Brushes with Investor-State Arbitration' *IA Reporter* (24 September 2012) available at <http://www.iareporter.com> (subscription required).

[100] See, eg, the Australian policy statement which aims at omitting in future investment treaties or chapters the ISDS clause, Australian Government, Department of Foreign Affairs & Trade, 'Gillard Government Trade Policy Statement: Trading our Way to More Jobs and Prosperity' (14 April 2011) available at <http://blogs.usyd.edu.au/japaneselaw/2011_Gillard%20Govt%20Trade%20Policy%20Statement.pdf> (last accessed on 15 September 2016); see also Jürgen Kurtz, 'The Australian Trade Statement on Investor-State Dispute Settlement', ASIL Insights Vol 15, Issue 22 (2 August 2011) available at <https://www.asil.org/insights/volume/15/issue/22/australian-trade-policy-statement-investor-state-dispute-settlement> (last accessed on 15 September 2016).

[101] See, eg, Susan Franck, 'The Legitimacy Crisis in Investment Treaty Arbitration: Privatizing Public International Law Through Inconsistent Decisions' (2004–2005) 73 Fordham L Rev 1521; Charles Brower, Charles Brower II and Jeremy Sharpe, 'The Coming Crisis in the Global Adjudication System' (2003) 19 Arb Intl 415; Charles Brower II, 'Structure, Legitimacy, and NAFTA's Investment Chapter' (2003) 36 Vand J Transnatl L 37; Catherine Rogers and Roger Alford (eds), *The Future of Investment Arbitration* (Oxford University Press 2009); José Alvarez and Karl Sauvant (eds), *The Evolving International Investment Regime: Expectations, Realities, Options* (Oxford University Press 2011); Michael Waibel, Asha Kaudal, Kyo-Hwa Chung, and Claire Balchin (eds), *The Backlash against Investment Arbitration* (Kluwer Law International 2010).

trade agreements with investment protection chapters such as the Comprehensive Economic and Trade Agreement (CETA) between the EU and Canada or the planned Transatlantic Trade and Investment Partnership (TTIP) between the EU and the United States.[102] In response to these concerns, many States—both capital-importing and capital-exporting ones—have been increasingly seeking to reassert 'their role in regulating and steering the economy'[103] and thus to re-conquer policy space.[104] In view of pressing key public policy issues such as public health, nuclear phase-out, or sovereign debt restructuring, this is a development that is likely to stay, even more so in times of tight public budgets.[105] The consequence is a move towards investment treaties that undertake to rebalance conflicting host State obligations and investor rights more evenly,[106] in particular through the use of more balanced preambles, more nuanced substantive protections, general exception clauses, etc.[107] Also, the policy objective of sustainable development has been taking on a more prominent role both in international law and in international investment law.[108]

Though attempts at creating a multilateral framework have thus failed, important developments have been ongoing on the EU level. As is well known, the Treaty of Lisbon conferred within the frame of its Common Commercial Policy (CCP) exclusive competence to the European Union in the subject matter of foreign direct investment.[109] It seems to transpire only gradually what this means in legal and practical terms for the multitude of intra-EU and extra-EU BITs EU members have concluded before their accession to the EU and/or before the entry into force of the Lisbon Treaty on 1 December 2009. In fact, despite the lingering economic crisis in the Eurozone, the European Union remains both the world's largest exporter

[102] BBC, 'TTIP trade deal: Germans rally in Hanover against EU-US trade deal' (23 April 2016) available at <http://www.bbc.com/news/world-europe-36120560> (last accessed on 15 September 2016).

[103] UNCTAD, 'WIR 2012' (n 84) 86.

[104] See in general Aikaterini Titi, *The Right to Regulate in International Investment Law* (Nomos 2014).

[105] UNCTAD, 'IIA Issues Note, Latest Developments in Investor-State Dispute Settlement', Issues Note No 1 (April 2012) 14, available at <http://unctad.org/en/PublicationsLibrary/webdiaeia2012d10_en.pdf> (last accessed on 15 September 2016).

[106] See, eg, Karl Sauvant, 'The times they are a-changin'—again—in the relationship between governments and multinational enterprises: From control, to liberalization to rebalancing' *Columbia FDI Perspectives*, No 69 (May 21, 2012) available at <http://ccsi.columbia.edu/files/2014/01/FDI_69.pdf> (last accessed on 20 September 2016); Wenhua Shan, 'Towards a Balanced Liberal Investment Regime: General Report on the Protection of Foreign Investment' (2010) 25 ICSID Review-FILJ 421–97.

[107] See, eg, Suzanne Spears, 'The question of more policy space in a new generation of international investment agreements' (2010) 13 JIEL 1037; Lars Markert, 'International Investment Law and Treaty Interpretation-Problems, Particularities and Possible Trends', in Rainer Hofmann and Christian Tams (eds), *International Investment Law and General International Law, From Clinical Isolation to Systemic Integration* (Nomos 2011) 53.

[108] UNCTAD, 'WIR 2012' (n 84) 9ff. UNCTAD, 'Investment Policy Framework for Sustainable Development 2015' (United Nations 2015) available at <http://unctad.org/en/PublicationsLibrary/diaepcb2015d5_en.pdf> (last accessed on 15 September 2016). On the United Nations' Sustainable Development Goals see Chapter 2, at 2.3.3.

[109] Arts 207(1), 3(1)(e) TFEU.

and leading recipient of international investments and EU member States' BITs account for over 1400 BITs in total.[110]

On 12 December 2012, the European Parliament and the Council issued 'Regulation No. 1219/2012 establishing transitional arrangements for bilateral investment agreements between Member States and third countries'.[111] This Regulation is legally binding upon the Member States of the European Union[112] and sketches the short to mid-term future of the extra-EU investment agreements, that is, those concluded between the Member States of the EU and third countries. While clarifying that these agreements 'remain binding on the Member States under public international law',[113] in this aspect corroborating earlier findings by the European Court of Justice (ECJ),[114] the long-term objective is clear: these extra-EU investment agreements are to be progressively replaced by investment agreements negotiated by the European Union.[115] In the meantime, however, the Regulation provides for notification and authorization mechanisms for the BITs signed before 1 December 2009, those signed between 1 December 2009 and 9 January 2013, as well as those signed after 9 January 2013.[116]

As for the future of intra-EU BITs not covered by this Regulation,[117] no official pronouncement exists as of yet. Arbitral tribunals seized by investors claiming violation of provisions of certain intra-EU BITs have so far persistently rejected the view that these intra-EU BITs were automatically terminated with the accession of the Member State in question to the EU.[118] Even the EU Commission conceded

[110] Julien Chaisse, 'Promises and Pitfalls of the European Union Policy on Foreign Investment—How will the New EU Competence on FDI affect the Emerging Global Regime?' (2012) 15 JIEL 52–53; Sergey Ripinsky and Diana Rosert, 'European Investment Treaty Making: Status Quo and The Way Forward (A Development Perspective)' (2013) 10 TDM 12, available at <http://www.transnational-dispute-management.com> (subscription required).

[111] 'Regulation (EU) No 1219/2012 of the European Parliament and of the Council of 12 December 2012 establishing transitional arrangements for bilateral investment agreements between Member States and third countries', OJ L 351/40 (20.12.2012) (in the following: 'Regulation').

[112] Art 288(2) Treaty on the Functioning of the European Union (TFEU).

[113] 'Regulation' (n 111) Recital 5.

[114] See, eg, *Commission v Slovak Republic*, Case C-264/09 [2011] ECR I-08065, paras 51–52: 'In the light of the foregoing, the Court finds that the preferential access granted to ATEL [*Aare-Tessin AG für Elektrizität*] may be regarded as an investment protected by the Investment Protection Agreement and that, under the first paragraph of Article 307 EC, it cannot be affected by the provisions of the EC Treaty ... it must be held that, even if it were to be assumed that the preferential access granted to ATEL were not compliant with Directive 2003/54, that preferential access is protected by the first paragraph of Article 307 EC [now Art 351 TFEU]'. Similar *Commission v Austria*, Case C-205/06 [2009] ECR I-1301, para 33; *Commission v Sweden*, Case C-249-06 [2009] ECR I-1335, paras 26–27; *Commission v Finland*, Case C-118/07 [2009] ECR I-10889, paras 33–34.

[115] 'Regulation' (n 111) Recital 5 and 6. Most of these agreements will most likely be so-called mixed agreements, touching also upon subject-matters that are not of exclusive competence of the EU, such as most prominently portfolio investment. On the latter see, eg, Marc Bungenberg, 'The Division of Competences Between the EU and its Member States in the Area of Investment Policies', in Marc Bungenberg, Jörn Griebel, and Steffen Hindelang (eds), *International Investment Law and EU Law, European Yearbook of International Economic Law*, Special Issue (Berlin, Springer 2011) 29–42; Angelos Dimopoulos, *EU Foreign Investment Law* (Oxford University Press 2011) 104–05 and 138ff.

[116] 'Regulation' (n 111) Arts 2ff.

[117] 'Regulation' (n 111) Recital 15.

[118] See, eg, *Eastern Sugar BV v Czech Republic*, UNCITRAL, SCC No 008/2004, Partial Award (27 March 2007) para 160; *Achmea BV v Slovak Republic* (formerly *Eureko BV v Slovak Republic*), PCA Case No 2008-13, Award on Jurisdiction (26 October 2010) paras 217ff; see also August Reinisch, 'Articles

this, all the while remarking that '[e]ventually, all intra-EU BITs will have to be terminated'.[119]

Of further interest may also be the future relationship between the Energy Charter Treaty (ECT)[120] and EU law, as similar questions with respect to the compatibility between the ECT, a multilateral investment treaty concluded in the early 1990s to which both the EU and its member States are parties, and both intra- and extra-EU BITs arise.[121] As Regulation 1219/2012 only concerns bilateral, not multilateral investment agreements, the 'roadmap' for ensuring the ECT's compatibility with future extra-EU BITs and with the continuing validity and applicability of intra-EU BITs is not clear yet.[122]

What are the implications for the sake of treaty shopping? As has been seen in this subsection, it is the multiplicity of agreements granting direct standing to investors that is a 'key ingredient' to the practice of treaty shopping. In other words, the more legal instruments for the protection of investments and the less coordinated or harmonized they are, the easier it is to try and come under the protection of one or several agreements thought most favourable for investors purposes. As long as both extra- and intra-EU BITs will continue to be in force, it is thus submitted that the potential and incentive for investors to treaty shop into European BITs will remain high.[123] This will only start to change with the gradual replacement of extra-EU and the termination of intra-EU BITs (though this will not eliminate the possibility of treaty shopping altogether).[124] It will also depend on which stance the EU Commission will take towards treaty shopping respectively round-tripping in

30 and 59 of the Vienna Convention on the Law of Treaties in Action: The Decisions on Jurisdiction in the Eastern Sugar and Eureko Investment Arbitrations' (2012) 39 LIEL 157; Michele Potestà, 'Bilateral Investment Treaties and the European Union. Recent Developments in Arbitration and Before the ECJ' (2009) 8 LPICT 225.

[119] *Achmea v Slovak Republic* (n 118) para 182; Reinisch, 'Eastern Sugar and Eureko Investment Arbitrations' (n 118) 161–62. See also the EU Commission's recent initiation of infringement proceedings against five EU members in an effort to hasten the termination of intra-EU BITs, LE Peterson, 'Infringement proceedings initiated by European Commission against five States over intra-EU BITs' *IA Reporter* (18 June 2015) available at <http://www.iareporter.com> (subscription required).

[120] Energy Charter Treaty (entered into force 17 December 1994) 35 ILM (1996) 509.

[121] Similar Jan Kleinheisterkamp, 'Investment Protection and EU Law: The Intra- and Extra-EU Dimension of the Energy Charter Treaty' (2012) 15 JIEL 103.

[122] Ibid, 104.

[123] See, eg, Ripinsky and Rosert (n 110) 9–10: 'European investors have been using the ISDS system actively. Out of the 451 publicly known arbitration cases around the world by the end of 2011, 219 (or 48%) were initiated by EU investors. Out of these 219 cases, ... 51 cases were launched by EU investors against other EU member states ... many of such claims have been based on intra-EU BITs. In sum, dispute settlement is much more common under BITs compared to EU IIAs'.

[124] Similar Chaisse (n 110) 61–62: '[T]he European Union has constituted a key example of a lack of uniformity in international investment regulation, and even a special case going beyond the fragmentation of international investment law and of public international law generally, as analysed by the International Law Commission. This legal situation, however, will change to a large extent in the future because of the new EU competence'. And ibid, 83: 'The new competence simultaneously contributes to reducing fragmentation of international investment regulation by first reducing the number of existing international instruments and, thus, ensuring a better homogeneity of the contents and these rules.' See also Ripinsky and Rosert (n 110) 12: 'Given that existing Member State BITs (1318 extra-EU and 177 intra-EU BITs) account for half of the world's BITs, the changes will indeed be dramatic, even if gradual. By reducing the overall number of treaties and creating more uniform rules, the EU's new agreements should lead to a considerable consolidation and harmonization of the international investment regime.'

future extra-EU investment agreements[125] and how the supremacy of EU law[126] and the quest of the ECJ to safeguard its exclusive jurisdiction to interpret EU law[127] will be upheld in future EU investment agreements with third States.

1.2.2 Change from diplomatic protection to direct standing paradigm

One of the single most important developments in modern investment law, essential for the purposes of the leading argument of this research, can undoubtedly be seen in the paradigm change that has removed investment protection (a priori) from the realm of diplomatic protection and has given the investor a right of its own, through the inclusion of investor–State dispute settlement clauses in IIAs, to bring a claim against the host State in case of violations of his rights.[128] It is submitted that without this paradigm change, treaty shopping would be, if not theoretically impossible, largely inconsequential as it is only the direct standing of investors that gives them, at its base, the possibility to enforce allegedly violated rights against the host State in the forum and treaty setting thought to be most advantageous. A brief review of the development from the diplomatic protection to the direct standing paradigm and its legal implications is therefore warranted.

The law on the protection of aliens was initially conceived of as part of the customary international law of State responsibility where only States had the right to take up a claim against another State in case the latter violated the foreign

[125] See LE Peterson, 'Brussels' thinking on future of extra-EU Investor-State Dispute Settlement comes into focus after much give and take with Member-States' *IA Reporter* (22 October 2012) available at <http://www.iareporter.com> (subscription required); Dimopoulos (n 115) 186: 'What is more problematic is how future EU IIAs will determine foreign nationality. Bearing in mind that primary EU law requires the consideration of foreign-controlled entities established in accordance with Art 54 TFEU as EU nationals, future EU IIAs should avoid including the control criterion in their definitions of foreign investment, so as not to raise issues of incompatibility similar to the ones raised by the FTA with Korea.'

[126] See *Van Gend & Loos*, Case 26/62 [1962] ECR 95; *Costa v ENEL*, Case 6/64 [1964] ECR 685.

[127] See Art 344 TFEU (ex-art 292 EC): '[M]ember States undertake not to submit a dispute concerning the interpretation or application of the Treaties to any method of settlement other than those provided for therein.' See also the *MOX Plant* arbitrations (n 60) and *Commission v Ireland* (Case C-459/02) [2006] ECR I-4635; Nikos Lavranos, 'Protecting its Exclusive Jurisdiction: The MOX Plant-Judgment of the ECJ' (2006) 5 LPICT 479–93; same, 'Is an international investor-to-state arbitration system under the auspices of the ECJ possible?' 6, available at <http://papers.ssrn.com/sol3/papers.cfm?abstract_id=1973491> (last accessed on 15 September 2016); *Kadi and Al Barakaat International Foundation v Council and Commission* (Joined Cases C-402/05 P and C-415/05 R) [2008] ECR I-6351; Stephan Schill, 'Luxembourg Limits: Conditions for Investor-State Dispute Settlement under Future EU Investment Agreements' (2013) 10 TDM 5–6, available at <http://www.transnational-dispute-management.com> (subscription required); Markus Burgstaller, 'Investor-State Arbitration in EU International Investment Agreements with Third States' (2012) 39 LIEL 207; *Opinion 1/09* [2011] ECR I-01137; *Paul Miles and Others v Ecoles européennes* (C-196/09) [2011] ECR I-05105.

[128] Douglas, *Investment Claims* (n 15) Rules 1 and 2, para 65: 'The fundamental assumption underlying the investment treaty regime is clearly that the investor is bringing a cause of action based upon the vindication of its own rights rather than those of its national state.' Similar Tillmann Rudolf Braun, *Ausprägungen der Globalisierung: Der Investor als partielles Subjekt im Internationalen Investitionsrecht, Qualität und Grenzen dieser Wirkungseinheit* (Nomos 2011) 85ff, 115. Different the arbitral tribunal in *Loewen Group Inc and Raymond Loewen v United States of America* (n 54) para 233: '[C]laimants are permitted for convenience to enforce what are in origin the rights of Party states.'

national's right.[129] In this aspect, international tribunals have wholeheartedly endorsed the seminal decision of the Permanent Court of International Justice (PCIJ) in the *Mavrommatis Palestine Concessions* case,[130] which regarded the right of diplomatic protection as the State's own right.[131] Already in the first half of the twentieth century, however, both international tribunals and scholars started to acknowledge the possibility that an international treaty could provide for direct rights of individuals, making diplomatic protection by a State of its own nationals thus only *one* possible form of invoking State responsibility.[132] Mixed Claims Commissions, in particular the (still working) Iran–US Claims Tribunal arguably also constituted important precursors for the development of the direct standing of investors in investor–State dispute settlement.[133] Article 33(2) of the 2001 International Law Commission (ILC) Draft Articles on the Law of State Responsibility (as codifying customary international law) also recognizes that secondary obligations arising from a breach of treaty could accrue directly in favour of a person or an entity other than a State if that treaty so provided.[134] This is the case under bilateral or regional investment protection agreements.[135]

[129] Chittharanjan Amerasinghe, *Diplomatic Protection* (Oxford University Press 2008), highlights the inherent link between the customary law of State responsibility and the customary law of diplomatic protection, 25–26: 'Under international law, a State is responsible for injury to an alien caused by its wrongful act or omission. Diplomatic protection is the procedure employed by the State of nationality of the injured person to secure protection of that person and to obtain reparation for the internationally wrongful act inflicted.'

[130] *Mavrommatis Palestine Concessions (Greece v United Kingdom) (Judgment)* [1924] PCIJ Series A, No 2.

[131] See, eg, *Panevezys-Saldutikis Railway* Case (Estonia v Lithuania) [1938] PCIJ Series A/B No 76; *Serbian Loans Issued in France (France v Serbia) (Judgment)* [1929] PCIJ Series A No 20; *Chorzów Factory* Case (Merits) [1928] PCIJ Series A No 17. Similar *Reparations for Injuries Suffered in the Service of the United Nations (Advisory Opinion)* [1949] ICJ Rep 181; *Nottebohm* (n 17); *Interhandel (Switzerland v United States of America) (Preliminary Objections)* [1959] ICJ Rep 6, 37.

[132] *Pecuniary Claims of Danzig Railways Officials who had Passed into the Polish Service (Advisory Opinion)* [1928] PCIJ Series B, No 15. See also Hersch Lauterpacht, 'Survey of International Law in Relation to the Work of Codification of the International Law Commission' (1949) UN Doc A/CN.4/1/Rev.1, 19–20: '[T]here is nothing in international law to prevent individuals from acquiring directly rights under a treaty provided that this is the intention of the contracting parties.' On the close relationship between international investment law and the law of State responsibility as codified in the 2001 ILC Draft Articles on the Law of State Responsibility see Jürgen Kurtz, 'The Paradoxical Treatment of the ILC Articles on State Responsibility in Investor-State Arbitration' (2010) 25 ICSID Review-FILJ 200, 207; James Crawford, 'Investment Arbitration and the ILC Articles on State Responsibility' (2010) 25 ICSID Review-FILJ 127.

[133] Ivar Alvik, *Contracting with Sovereignty, State Contracts and International Arbitration* (Oxford/Hart 2011) 23ff; similar Douglas, *Investment Claims* (n 15) paras 26–27. On the dual or hybrid character of the Iran-US Claims Tribunal see David Lloyd Jones, 'The Iran-United States Claims Tribunal: Private Rights and State Responsibility' (1984) 24 Va J Intl L 259.

[134] *Wintershall Aktiengesellschaft v Argentine Republic*, ICSID Case No ARB/04/14, Award (8 December 2008) paras 110–13; similar *Archer Daniels Midland Company and Tate & Lyle Ingredients Americas Inc v United States of Mexico* (NAFTA) ICSID Case No ARB(AF)/04/5, Award (21 November 2007) para 118: 'The customary international law that the ILC Articles codify do not apply to matters which are specifically governed by lex specialis ... Customary international law—pursuant to which only sovereign States may invoke the responsibility of another State—does not therefore affect the rights of non-State actors under particular treaties to invoke state responsibility. This rule is not only true in the context of investment protection, but also in the human rights and environmental protection arena.'

[135] James Crawford, *The International Law Commission's Articles on State Responsibility, Introduction, Text and Commentaries* (Cambridge University Press 2005) 210.

Bilateral investment treaties thus developed in response to the shortcomings of the law of diplomatic protection.[136] One major problem was the politicization of what often were minor (commercial) disputes between an individual and the host State before the home State of the investor espoused the claim.[137] It was precisely with this in mind that the ICSID Convention aims at depoliticizing investment disputes:

> Once an investor had been given the right to direct access to a foreign State, he should not have the right to seek the protection of his own State, and his State should not have the right to intervene on his behalf. The purpose ... was to remove disputes from the realm of diplomacy and bring them back to the realm of law.[138]

There were more reasons why the traditional law of diplomatic protection did not result in a satisfactory protection of foreign investors. First, diplomatic protection being a right of the State, not of its national, the State was free to exercise it or not, being by nature a discretionary proceeding.[139] An investor could thus never be certain whether his State of nationality *would* in fact espouse his claim. This clearly goes against the fundamental interest of a foreign investor for legal security. Furthermore, even if the State of nationality *did* espouse the investor's claim and managed to obtain some compensation, the former was under no *legal* obligation to refund the compensation to the investor.[140]

Second, it is generally accepted in customary international law that the investor in principle first has to exhaust local remedies before its State of nationality is allowed to potentially espouse the claim.[141]

Third and importantly, the law of diplomatic protection restricts a home State's capacity to bring a diplomatic protection claim on behalf of shareholders of an aggrieved corporation to few narrow exceptions. This was the finding of

[136] Jeswald Salacuse, 'The Emerging Global Regime for Investment' (2010) 51 Harv Intl L J 427, 436–39.

[137] Santiago Montt, *State Liability in Investment Treaty Arbitration* (Hart Publishing 2009) 3; Newcombe and Paradell (n 86) 3ff; Alvik (n 133) 15, 18.

[138] Convention on the Settlement of Investment Disputes between States and Nationals of Other States, Documents Concerning the Origin and the Formation of the Convention, Vol II (Washington DC 1968) 27.

[139] See *Barcelona Traction* (n 18) 44 (paras 78–79): '[W]ithin the limits prescribed by international law, a State may exercise diplomatic protection by whatever means and to whatever extent it thinks fit, for it is its own right that the State is asserting ... The State must be viewed as the sole judge to decide whether its protection will be granted, to what extent it is granted, and when it will cease. It retains in this respect a discretionary power the exercise of which may be determined by considerations of a political or other nature, unrelated to the particular case'. See also Alvik (n 133) 16; Peter Muchlinski, *Multinational Enterprises and the Law* (Oxford University Press 2007) 705.

[140] 'Administrative Decision No V, Mixed Claims Commission—United States and Germany: Opinion Dealing with Germany's Obligations and the Jurisdiction of the Commission' (1925) 19 AJIL 612, 626–27; Braun (n 128) 38.

[141] *Interhandel* (n 131) 27: 'Before resort may be made to an international court in such a situation, it has been considered necessary that the State where the violation occurred should have an opportunity to redress it by its own means, within the framework of its own domestic legal system'; Ian Brownlie, *Principles of Public International Law* (Oxford University Press, 5th edn 2008) 492ff; Chittharanjan Amerasinghe, *Local Remedies in International Law* (Cambridge University Press 2004) 69–72; Muchlinksi, *Multinational Enterprises* (n 139) 705; see also Arts 14 and 15 of the ILC's Draft Articles on Diplomatic Protection.

the ICJ in 1970 in the well-known *Barcelona Traction* case.[142] The Court drew a clear distinction between the company and its shareholders[143] and held that Belgium, as the State of nationality of the majority of shareholders, could not bring a diplomatic protection claim on their behalf against Spain, host State of the aggrieved company, for allegations of violations of the rights of the company.[144] It therefore authorized the State of incorporation of the company alone to bring such a claim (in that case Canada),[145] except where the company had ceased to exist in the place of its incorporation or where the State of incorporation was itself responsible for the injury on the company and the foreign shareholders' only means of redress on the international level was through their State of nationality.[146]

Under the traditional law of diplomatic protection, shareholders thus remain unprotected unless one of the stated exceptions is given. The ICJ itself acknowledged that this state of law may seem unsatisfactory, but pointed out that the protection of shareholders could be assured through specific treaty arrangements:

> Considering the important developments of the last half-century, the growth of foreign investments and the expansion of the international activities of corporations, in particular of holding companies, which are often multinational, and considering the way in which the economic interests of States have proliferated, it may at first sight appear surprising that the evolution of law has not gone further and that no generally accepted rules in the matter have crystallized on the international plane ... the law has been formed in a period characterized by an intense conflict of systems and interests. It is essentially bilateral relations which have been concerned, relations in which the rights of both the State exercising diplomatic protection and the State in respect of which protection is sought have had to be safeguarded. Here as elsewhere, a body of rules could only have developed with the consent of those concerned ... Thus, in the present state of the law, the protection of shareholders requires that recourse be had to treaty stipulations or special agreements directly concluded between the private investor and the State in which the investment is placed.[147]

The judgment of the ICJ triggered a flood of criticism at the time[148] and arguably continues to do so.[149] Some legal commentators see it as one of the main reasons

[142] *Barcelona Traction* (n 18); for a short description of the case see Chapter 3, at 3.2.2.2.1.

[143] *Barcelona Traction* (n 18) 34–35 (paras 41–42).

[144] *Barcelona Traction* (n 18) 36 (para 46), though acknowledging in para 47 that the situation was different if a direct right of the shareholders, such as their 'right to a declared dividend, the right to attend and vote at general meetings, the right to share in the residual assets of the company on liquidation' were violated.

[145] *Barcelona Traction* (n 18) 46–47 (para 88).

[146] *Barcelona Traction* (n 18) 40–48 (paras 64–92); International Law Commission (ILC), 'Fourth Report on Diplomatic Protection' Report of the Fifty-fifth Session (2003), UN Doc A/CN.4/530, para 7.

[147] *Barcelona Traction* (n 18) 46–47 (paras 89–90).

[148] See more in detail in Chapter 3, at 3.2.2.2.2.

[149] Arthur Watts, 'Nationality of claims: some relevant concepts', in Vaughan Lowe and Malgosia Fitzmaurice (eds), *Fifty Years of the International Court of Justice, Essays in honour of Sir Robert Jennings* (Cambridge University Press 1996) 424–38; Peter Muchlinski, 'The Diplomatic Protection of Foreign Investors: A Tale of Judicial Caution' in Christina Binder and others (eds), *Essays in Honour of Christoph Schreuer* (Oxford University Press 2009) 341, 359: '[The ICJ] is not persuaded that the extensive

why States developed and/or reinforced their BIT programmes.[150] Yet, despite all this criticism, the findings of the ICJ continue to be *lex lata* today.[151] The decision of the ICJ in the *ELSI* case[152] that might, on its face, seem like a reversal of its earlier decision in *Barcelona Traction*, was in reality a restatement of the opinion that effective protection of foreign shareholders can only be assured through recourse to specific treaty arrangements (as was the case in *ELSI* with the US–Italy Friendship, Navigation and Commerce Treaty).[153]

The traditional law of diplomatic protection has thus nowadays been largely replaced by a network of treaty-based investment protection,[154] to such extent that the ICJ in *Diallo* has argued that international investment law has in principle come to be considered *lex specialis* to the customary law of diplomatic protection.[155] However, this does not mean that the law of diplomatic protection has become completely obsolete in investment protection. As the *Diallo* case has shown, the customary law of diplomatic protection remains a residual mechanism that can be resorted to in the absence of applicable treaty protection recognizing a direct right of action by the individual investor.[156] This is also expressed by Article 17 of the Draft Articles on Diplomatic Protection which states that '[t]he present draft

treaty-based practice of States in the field of foreign investment law requires any change in the rules of diplomatic protection in this area … The ICJ has … chosen to ignore this extensive amount of State practice, and to treat the law as if it was frozen in time before State practice began to elaborate BITs and other IIAs.' See also Markus Perkams, 'Piercing the Corporate Veil in International Investment Agreements', in August Reinisch and Christina Knahr (eds), *International Investment Law in Context* (Eleven International Publishing 2008) 93, 101: '[I]t is remarkable that international law is deemed to have remained unchanged for 35 years despite the fundamental political and economic changes that took place since then … it seems to be problematic that the Commission relied on Barcelona Traction only and refused to at least discuss the recent developments in the international law of foreign investments.'

[150] Juliane Kokott, 'Interim Report on The Role of Diplomatic Protection in the Field of the Protection of Foreign Investment', in International Law Association, Report of the Seventieth Conference, New Delhi (2002) 26–27; ILC, 'Fourth Report on Diplomatic Protection' (n 146) paras 14–21, referring to the standard set by Barcelona Traction as 'unworkable'. See also Martins Paparinskis, 'Barcelona Traction: A Friend of Investment Protection Law' (2008) 8 Baltic YIL 105, 132.

[151] As evidenced by Arts 11 and 12 of the ILC Draft Articles on Diplomatic Protection; see also ILC, 'Fourth Report on Diplomatic Protection' (n 146) para 27: 'On the other hand, it must be acknowledged that, despite its shortcomings, Barcelona Traction is today, 30 years on, widely viewed not only as an accurate statement of the law on the diplomatic protection of corporations, but as a true reflection of customary international law. The practice of States in the diplomatic protection of corporations is today guided by Barcelona Traction … The writings of the most highly qualified publicists, to use the language of Art 38(1)(d) of the Statute of the ICJ, do not, in general, display an uncritical acceptance of Barcelona Traction. They do, however, treat it as the seminal decision on the diplomatic protection of corporations, the starting point of any discussion on the subject.'

[152] *Elettronica Sicula SpA (United States of America v Italy) (Judgment)* [1989] ICJ Rep 15. For a more general analysis see Sean Murphy, 'The ELSI Case: An Investment Dispute at the International Court of Justice' (1991) 16 Yale J Intl L 391.

[153] Amerasinghe, *Diplomatic Protection* (n 129) 128–29; Kokott (n 150) 26; Vaughan Lowe, 'Shareholders' Rights and to Control and Manage from Barcelona Traction to ELSI' in Nisuke Ando and others (eds), *Liber Amicorum Judge Shigeru Oda* (Kluwer Law International 2002) 269. In this sense see also the ICJ in *Ahmadou Sadio Diallo (Guinea v Democratic Republic of Congo) (Preliminary Objections)* [2007] ICJ Rep 582, 614 (para 87) (quoted: *Diallo* [2007]).

[154] Kokott (n 150) 27. [155] See also *Diallo* [2007] (n 153) 615 (para 90).

[156] *CMS v Argentina* (n 71) para 45; Muchlinski, 'Diplomatic Protection of Foreign Investors' (n 149) 341.

articles do not apply to the extent that they are inconsistent with special rules of international law, such as treaty provisions for the protection of investments.'

1.2.3 Ease of incorporation of legal entities and high fungibility of shareholding

The final 'ingredient' to the occurrence of treaty shopping in international investment law is the ease with which in particular legal entities may be brought into existence in many domestic jurisdictions, thus providing for the possibility to easily create diversity of nationality. Indeed, in many domestic jurisdictions, incorporation is sufficient for a legal entity to acquire legal personality and corporate nationality, often with little more requirements than proof of a postbox business address.[157] These entities may thus be easily set up and, if necessary, inserted into the corporate structure to maximize investment protection in the face of a changing political risks in the host State. Moreover, shareholdings are nowadays highly fungible, making it easy to transfer the shares in a (local) investment to an entity (whether recently set up or long-time existing) with the required nationality.

1.2.4 Absence of a doctrine of precedent?

Some scholars have considered the absence of the common law doctrine of precedent or *stare decisis* in international investment law[158] (as in international law in general)[159] as an additional factor for the occurrence of treaty shopping.[160] Indeed, as is well known, investment tribunals are not—at least not formally—obliged to follow previous decisions in similar matters under adjudication handed down by other investment tribunals, even if they often de facto do so.[161] The fact that investment tribunals may diverge (and have done so in the past)[162] in sometimes blatant

[157] On the so-called incorporation theory and its advantages and disadvantages see Chapter 3, at 3.2.2.1.1.

[158] On the doctrine of precedent in international investment law see, eg, Christoph Schreuer and Matthew Weiniger, 'A Doctrine of Precedent?' in Peter Muchlinski, Federico Ortino, and Christoph Schreuer, *Oxford Handbook of International Investment Law* (Oxford University Press 2008) 1189ff.

[159] On the doctrine of precedent in general international law see, eg, Gilbert Guillaume, 'The Use of Precedent by International Judges and Arbitrators' 2 JIDS (2011) 5.

[160] Skinner, Miles, and Luttrell (n 20) 261.

[161] Federico Ortino, 'Legal Reasoning of International Investment Tribunals: A Typology of Egregious Failures' (2012) 3 JIDS 31, 39; Jeffery Commission, 'Precedent in Investment Treaty Arbitration: A Citation Analysis of a Developing Jurisprudence' (2007) 24 J Intl Arb 129, 149; Judith Gill, 'Is There a Special Role for Precedent in Investment Arbitration?' (2010) 25 ICSID Review-FILJ 87; Lucy Reed, 'The De Facto Precedent Regime in Investment Arbitration: A Case for Proactive Case Management' (2010) 25 ICSID Review-FILJ 95; Tai-Heng Cheng, 'Precedent and Control in Investment Treaty Arbitration', in Andrea Bjorklund, Ian Laird, and Sergey Ripinsky (eds), *Investment Treaty Law: Current Issues III* (British Institute of International and Comparative Law 2008) 149; Andrés Rigo Sureda, *Investment Treaty Arbitration, Judging under Uncertainty* (Cambridge University Press 2012) 109. See also Andrea Bjorklund, 'The Emerging Civilization of Investment Arbitration' (2008–2009) 113 Penn St L Rev 1269, 1294ff, on why the development of a *jurisprudence constante* is better suited for investment arbitration than precedent.

[162] For examples see Ortino (n 161) 40–43.

ways on similar or even identical legal issues raises important concerns in terms of the uniformity and predictability, and thus more generally the legitimacy of the international investment law system.[163]

This, of course, is not specific to treaty shopping, but concerns the investment arbitration system as a whole. Though it might be argued that the lack of precedent creates an incentive to bring claims based on treaty shopping on grounds of sometimes widely diverging jurisprudence, it does in this author's opinion not, strictly speaking, enable or further treaty shopping. It therefore does not appear to be a reason for the occurrence of, or increase in, this practice.

1.3 Preliminary Conclusions

Treaty shopping has become a practice that is ever more widely recurred to due to its potential to cross the jurisdictional threshold of arbitral proceedings and/or 'import' more favourable procedural or substantive protections. What is precisely understood as treaty shopping is nowhere uniformly nor authoritatively defined. For the purpose of this analysis, treaty shopping should be understood as the practice undertaken by investors (natural or legal persons) that aims at invoking, creating, or changing a nationality, for example, through the structuring or restructuring of an investment, the transfer of an investment claim or the invocation of a dual nationality, with the aim of accessing more favourable procedural or substantive investment provisions. The question arbitral tribunals have been faced with in this respect is where to situate the distinguishing line between 'legitimate nationality planning' and 'abusive treaty shopping'. This question is difficult to answer in the abstract.

As seen, a distinction should also be made between treaty and forum shopping, being separate, but related practices that present potential problems necessitating differing answers. Treaty shopping may lead to forum shopping; but as long as no multiple (parallel or consecutive) proceedings arise, no particular (legal) problem is discernable.

Three factors are essentially responsible for the occurrence of and increase in treaty shopping in international investment law: the proliferation of investment treaties over past decades; the paradigm change from diplomatic protection to a direct investor standing; and the ease with which in particular corporate entities may be incorporated in many domestic jurisdictions, alongside the high fungibility of shareholdings.

[163] Ortino (n 161) 39. On the 'legitimacy crisis' of investment arbitration more generally see further Chapter 2, at 2.3.2.

2

Is Anything Wrong with Treaty Shopping?

2.1 Introduction

With a working definition established and a better understanding of the reasons for the occurrence of and increase in treaty shopping in investment arbitration, the question invariably arises: if treaty shopping is not prohibited, what is so bad about it? In other words, why should stakeholders of the international investment law system, in particular states and arbitral tribunals, take issue with it? As has already been pointed out in Chapter 1, judgments about its lawfulness and/or legitimacy may differ widely, depending on who makes the judgment. A responding State in an investment arbitration facing a claimant trying to gain access to the arbitration through a strategic use or change of nationality will naturally take a different stance on the 'validity' of a claim involving treaty shopping than the claimant himself who may use the technique in order to cross the jurisdictional threshold or invoke more favourable substantive protections.

It seems thus necessary to look in a first step at the considerations and arguments that may sustain treaty shopping as a perfectly legitimate and lawful practice, before examining potential (policy) concerns that may warrant a more restrictive stance towards treaty shopping.

2.2 Considerations in Favour of a 'Treaty Shopping-permissive' Approach

2.2.1 Sovereign consent

A traditional and State-centred argument that can be made in favour of a permissible stance towards the practice of treaty shopping is that States, when negotiating treaties among each other, are not only free in deciding whether they want to conclude the treaty, but in principle also its content. This principle, whose equivalent in private international law and international commercial arbitration would be the principle of party autonomy,[1] stems from the sovereign equality of States,

[1] See, eg, Alan Redfern and Martin Hunter, *Law and Practice of International Commercial Arbitration* (Oxford University Press 2004) paras 6.03ff; Yuval Shany, *The Competing Jurisdictions of International Courts and Tribunals* (Oxford University Press 2003) 144.

Treaty Shopping in International Investment Law. First Edition. Jorun Baumgartner. © Jorun Baumgartner 2016. Published 2016 by Oxford University Press.

a cornerstone of international relations and public international law.[2] Thus, the freedom to conclude treaties among each other is an attribute of the sovereignty of States, as already noted by the Permanent Court of International Justice (PCIJ) in the *SS Wimbledon* case:

The Court declines to see, in the conclusion of any treaty by which a State undertakes to perform or refrain from performing a particular act, an abandonment of its sovereignty … the right of entering into international engagements is an attribute of State sovereignty.[3]

And in the (often criticized) *SS Lotus* case, the PCIJ emphasized the importance of consent in the international legal order: 'International law governs relations between independent States. The rules of law binding upon States therefore emanate from their own free will.'[4]

From the principle of sovereign equality flow several observations pertinent for our purposes. First, States are free to conclude treaties with each other and may thus not be coerced into treaty relations. This is reflected in the Preamble of the Vienna Convention on the Law of Treaties (VCLT),[5] stipulating among others that 'the principles of free consent and of good faith and the *pacta sunt servanda* rule are universally recognized'.[6] It is also codified in the provisions of Articles 51 and 52 VCLT, providing for the invalidity of treaties concluded by coercion. Second, from the aforesaid follows that State obligations crucially depend on the States having consented to them.[7] In the absence of such consent—and leaving aside *ius cogens* obligations—States will not be bound by international obligations. Third, unless reasons exist that may invalidate State consent,[8] States will be held to the terms they have agreed upon.[9] This follows from the principle of good faith and is expressly provided for in Article 26 VCLT, anchoring the *pacta sunt servanda* rule firmly in the law of treaties.

This arguably puts the emphasis on the ability and skillfulness of treaty negotiators. As one commentator observed:

It is no good States complaining afterwards about the results that come out of the application of their treaties if they negotiated bad treaties in the first place. The responsibility for what goes into the text of a treaty is that of the negotiating parties and if, for example, a State decides to accept a particular clause proposed to it in a treaty without discussion, that

[2] See Art 2(1) UN-Charter: 'The Organization is based on the principle of the sovereign equality of all its Members.'

[3] *SS Wimbledon (United Kingdom and others v Germany) (Judgment)* [1923] PCIJ Series A No 1, 25.

[4] *SS Lotus (France v Turkey) (Judgment)* [1927] PCIJ Series A No 10, 18; Andrea Steingruber, *Consent in International Arbitration* (Oxford University Press 2011) para 5.04.

[5] Vienna Convention on the Law of Treaties (VCLT) (opened for signature 23 May 1969, entered into force 27 January 1980) 1155 UNTS 331.

[6] VCLT, Preambular Paragraph 3.

[7] Ian Brownlie, *Principles of Public International Law* (Oxford University Press, 5th edn 2008) 289–90; Marc Villiger, *Commentary on the 1969 Vienna Convention on the Law of Treaties* (Martinus Nijhoff 2009) 'Preamble' 48 (N 10).

[8] Such as error, fraud, etc.; see Arts 46–53 VCLT.

[9] Similar Rudolf Dolzer and Christoph Schreuer, *Principles of International Investment Law* (Oxford University Press, 2nd edn 2012) 23.

is something which has its consequences – namely, that the clause will be interpreted and applied in accordance with its terms. A central purpose of international law is to protect the sanctity of treaties and treaties must be taken to mean what they say.[10]

State sovereignty therefore also means that States may decide to limit their own sovereignty, in order words may 'trade away' aspects of their sovereignty.

The same is clearly valid for investment treaty negotiation.[11] When States decide to negotiate bilateral investment treaties with each other, they may thus agree to (implicitly) permit treaty shopping, for example by agreeing to extend international investment agreement (IIA) protection to the widest scope of investors possible, or by agreeing to extend the most-favoured nation (MFN) clause also to dispute settlement provisions, facilitating a treaty-shopping investor's access to investor–State dispute settlement (ISDS). Depending on particular policy considerations, they may on the other hand also agree to limit it, for example by restricting the consent to arbitration clause, by introducing the requirement of an economic link or substantial business activities, or by including a denial of benefits clause.[12] In any case, States are bound by the terms thus negotiated, and if the meaning of the wording of a given clause is unclear, its elucidation becomes a question of treaty interpretation,[13] but does not, a priori, call into doubt either the principle of sovereign equality of the State parties to the IIA or their free consent to it.

Not everybody would however agree on the above-mentioned view. Asha Kaudal for example criticizes IIA negotiations as a 'tool of state disempowerment' that allocates 'power to the international level and to private actors', thus circumscribing 'without any meaningful public debate or oversight … the sovereign sphere of governmental authority'.[14] Furthermore, she calls into question the reciprocal nature of IIA negotiations in the case of unequal negotiating powers, such as between the United States and any given less economically powerful country:

The US 'cookie-cutter' approach to BIT [bilateral investment treaty] negotiation results in a one-way conversation of imposed terms. A BIT negotiation is not a discussion between sovereign equals. It is more like an intensive training seminar conducted by the United States, on US terms, on what it would take to comply with the US draft.[15]

[10] Franklin Berman, 'Evolution or Revolution?' in Chester Brown and Kate Miles (eds), *Evolution in Investment Treaty Law and Arbitration* (Cambridge University Press 2011) 658, 670.

[11] Similar Susan Franck, 'The Legitimacy Crisis in Investment Treaty Arbitration: Privatizing Public International Law Through Inconsistent Decisions' (2004–2005) 73 Fordham L Rev 1521, 1591: 'Investment treaties do not trespass unnecessarily on sovereignty. Sovereigns choose to enter into investment treaties. In order to obtain the benefits arising from investment treaties, Sovereigns negotiate treaties and determine what rights they will cede and the responsibilities they will undertake. If Sovereigns wish to cede less sovereignty, Sovereigns should do so during negotiations.'

[12] See more in detail Chapter 8. On the legal nature of consent to arbitration see, eg, Christoph Schreuer, 'Consent to Arbitration' (2005) 2 TDM (updated February 2007) available at <http://www.transnational-dispute-management.com> (subscription required).

[13] On the significance of treaty interpretation see more in detail in Chapter 9, at 9.3.

[14] Asha Kaudal, 'Revisiting History: How the Past Matters' (2009) 50 Harv Intl L J 491, 512.

[15] Kaudal (n 14) 512, quoting José Alvarez, 'The Development and Expansion of Bilateral Investment Treaties: Remarks' (1992) 86 Am Soc Intl L Proc 532, 553. On the argument of reciprocity see further below at 2.3.1.

Samantha Besson levels a similar critique against the validity of the argument of sovereign consent. She not only calls into doubt 'the veracity of the sovereign consent that is given to most MITs and BITs' and criticizes the 'abusive lengths of the minimal period of duration in most of them',[16] but also evokes legitimacy concerns. In particular, she points out that:

> consent is no longer the only source of legitimacy in international law. Human rights, accountability and inclusion in the international law-making process also matter… Sovereignty is only protected to the extent that it is democratic and reflects popular will.[17]

This is an issue we will come back to more in detail further below. It is certainly true that unequal economic powers among negotiating States will in more cases than not lead to treaty clauses that, though on their surface reciprocal, have in fact been imposed by the economically stronger State. While it is thus necessary to discuss legitimacy concerns and the question of the reciprocal nature of IIA clauses as to their veracity and pertinence, this does however not, in this author's view, invalidate from the outset the fact that a State is not only free to conclude, but more importantly in principle also responsible for what goes into an IIA. The views advancing what are in essence legitimacy concerns of investor–State arbitration would seem to conflate the normative (Article 26 VCLT *pacta sunt servanda*) with a moral or policy analysis,[18] two levels that should in this author's view be analysed in separate steps.[19]

Without prejudice to the policy concerns examined further below, this means that the starting point of any analysis of the practice of treaty shopping should be the full acceptance of the principle of free and sovereign consent of the IIA-negotiating States, and in this sense a State should a priori be held to what it negotiated. Thus, if States take a treaty shopping-permissive approach in an IIA, in other words negotiate clauses that make their treaty respectively treaty network accessible to a de facto undetermined number of investors, this may be considered a reflection of the often-stated purpose and objective of investment treaties that is—often among others—the facilitation of investment flows and the best possible protection of foreign investors.

2.2.2 Access to justice?

Further, it may also be asked whether access to justice considerations would warrant a permissive stance towards treaty shopping.

[16] Samantha Besson, 'The Sovereign, the Investor and the Arbitrator' in Peter Gauch, Franz Werro, and Pascal Pichonnaz (eds), *Mélanges en l'honneur de Pierre Tercier* (Schulthess 2008) 745, 757.

[17] Ibid.

[18] Allen Buchanan, 'The Legitimacy of International Law' in Samantha Besson and John Tasioulas (eds), *The Philosophy of International Law* (Oxford University Press 2010) 79, 80: 'Assertions about legitimacy or illegitimacy of institutions (as opposed to reports about people's beliefs about their legitimacy) are moral evaluations, not statements of legal fact'.

[19] See below at 2.3.2.

As Shany has pointed out for the practice of forum shopping, in many civil law countries domestic forum shopping is regarded as a 'legitimate exercise of the right of access to the court system', and in deciding whether to permit or curb forum shopping, courts have to balance:

> between the interest of the plaintiff in controlling the conduct of the proceedings and pursuing his or her legitimate litigation advantages, on the one hand, and the need to ensure justice to the respondent, on the other hand.[20]

Jan Paulsson opined in his work on denial of justice that '[t]he right of access to courts is fundamental and uncontroversial; its refusal the most obvious form of denial of justice'.[21]

Could it thus be argued that taking a restrictive stance towards treaty shopping could under certain circumstances amount to a denial of justice? In other words, could it be argued that there is a right for the investor to choose the investment instrument most favourable to his or her purposes, which might result in access to a particular investment jurisdiction and if so, would such a right flow from the right of access to justice?

In international investment law, the access of the investor to investor–State arbitration is, as already seen further above, subject to States consenting to be sued before an arbitral tribunal for certain alleged breaches of investment obligations. As concisely expressed by the tribunal in *ST-AD GmbH v Bulgaria*:

> no participant in the international community, an international organization or a physical or legal person, has an inherent right of access to a jurisdictional recourse. For such a right to come into existence, specific consent has to be given ... the State can shape its consent as it sees fit by providing the conditions under which it is given – in other words, the conditions subject to which an 'offer to arbitrate' is made to the foreign investor.[22]

The above correctly shows that an investor has no inherent right to investment arbitration. This would therefore seem to dispose of the argument from the beginning that a treaty shopping-restrictive approach might under certain circumstances amount to a denial of justice.

It is also useful to consider the customary international law position in this aspect. Under customary international law, the right of access to justice is conceived of as a procedural minimum standard aimed at ensuring that the foreigner can effectively exercise his substantive rights.[23] An ad hoc tribunal held in this respect for example in the *Ambatielos* case:

> the foreigner shall enjoy full freedom to appear before the courts for the protection or defence of his rights, whether as plaintiff or defendant; to bring any action provided or authorized by law ... in short, to use the Courts fully and to avail himself of any procedural remedies

[20] Shany (n 1) 134–35.
[21] Jan Paulsson, *Denial of Justice in International Law* (Cambridge University Press 2005) 134ff.
[22] *ST-AD GmbH v Republic of Bulgaria*, UNCITRAL, PCA Case No 2011-06, Award on Jurisdiction (18 July 2013) para 337.
[23] Dolzer and Schreuer (n 9) 164.

or guarantees provided by the law of the land in order that justice may be administered on a footing of equality with nationals of the country.[24]

As becomes obvious from the above, the right of access to justice concerns a foreigner's access to *domestic* courts. The fact of an investor having no access to an IIA (respectively to a more favourable IIA) can therefore not justify a treaty shopping-permissive approach as long as the investor has a right of access to domestic courts (which he normally always has) and a procedural minimum standard is safeguarded. But even if a procedural minimum standard was not respected, the only remedy would, in the absence of investment protection, be diplomatic protection.

2.3 Policy Concerns Against Treaty Shopping

Having set out the principle of free and sovereign consent of treaty-negotiating States as point of departure that may warrant a permissive stance towards treaty shopping, several potential concerns have been discussed by scholarship and necessitate further critical analysis.

2.3.1 Reciprocity

An often-voiced concern is that treaty shopping violates the principles of reciprocity.[25]

Reciprocity certainly does play a role in the research of the limits to the practice of treaty shopping as understood for the purposes of this research. Indeed, when having to decide on the validity of a claim based on corporate structuring or restructuring or a transfer of claims, the essence of the question an arbitral tribunal has to ask itself is whether the investment treaty under interpretation was meant to cover the investor and the investment in its particular form and the (sometimes) particular timing of its acquisition.

But also the explicit reference to the notion of reciprocity in the titles and preambles of many IIAs reveals its importance for the question subject of this book,

[24] *Ambatielos Claim (Greece v United Kingdom)* (1956) 12 RIAA 83, 11.

[25] See, eg, Roos Van Os and Roeline Knottnerus, *Dutch Bilateral Investment Treaties, A Gateway to 'Treaty Shopping' for Investment Protection by Multinational Companies* (SOMO 2011) 11–12, available at <http://papers.ssrn.com/sol3/papers.cfm?abstract_id=1974431> (last accessed on 15 September 2016); Rachel Thorn and Jennifer Doucleff, 'Disregarding the Corporate Veil and Denial of Benefits Clauses: Testing Treaty Language and the Concept of "Investor"' in Michael Waibel, Asha Kaushal, Kyo-Hwa Chung, and Claire Balchin (eds), *The Backlash against Investment Arbitration* (Kluwer Law International 2010) 3, 20–21; David Gaukrodger and Kathryn Gordon, 'Investor-State Dispute Settlement: A Scoping Paper for the Investment Policy Community' OECD Working Papers on International Investment, No 2012/3, 57, available at <http://www.oecd.org/daf/inv/investment-policy/WP-2012_3.pdf> (last accessed on 15 September 2016); Paul Blyschak, 'Yukos Universal v Russia: Shell Companies and Treaty Shopping in International Energy Disputes' (2010–2011) 10 Rich J Global L & Bus 179, 195; John Lee 'Resolving Concerns of Treaty Shopping' (2015) 6 JIDS 1, 4–6.

as was correctly recognized by the arbitral tribunal in *Standard Chartered Bank v Tanzania*.[26] In this case, the tribunal had to decide whether an investor had to contribute 'actively' in order to make a protected investment. It found that this was the case, with the consequence that it would offend the BIT's reciprocal nature to:

> permit a UK national with subsidiaries all around the world to claim entitlement to the UK-Tanzania BIT protection for each and every one of the investments around the world held by these daughter or granddaughter entities. The BIT preamble says 'reciprocal protection' and 'reciprocal' must have some meaning.[27]

But which is the incidence of reciprocity in legal terms? How does it interact with the question of the validity or not of a claim based on treaty shopping, in particular which expressions does it find? May one really say that treaty shopping (or more precisely a claim involving treaty shopping) always violates the principle of reciprocity?

It seems apposite to first take a look at the notion of reciprocity in public international law in general, before analysing its role and its manifestations in international investment law more in particular.

2.3.1.1 Reciprocity in public international law

An analysis of the notion of reciprocity for the purposes of this research will have to start with the attempt to understand which aspect(s) of the notion is or are engaged in the negotiation of bilateral or multilateral treaties, reciprocity being a multifaceted and thus malleable notion without normative content.[28]

According to Simma's seminal research into the subject, reciprocity is 'a basic phenomenon of social interaction and consequently a guiding principle behind the formation and application of law' that increases in importance the lower the degree of institutionalization of a legal system is, and respectively decreases in importance in the presence of a highly institutionalized legal (enforcement) system.[29] He thus defines reciprocity in a broad way as 'the status of a relationship between two or more States under which a certain conduct by one party is in one way or another juridically dependent upon that of the other party'.[30] This is what he understands as the *objective* side of reciprocity, which he distinguishes from the *subjective* side of reciprocity, or in other words the 'subjective

[26] *Standard Chartered Bank v United Republic of Tanzania*, ICSID Case No ARB/10/12, Award (2 November 2012).

[27] Ibid, para 270.

[28] Bruno Simma, *Das Reziprozitätselement im Zustandekommen völkerrechtlicher Verträge* (Berlin, Duncker und Humblot 1972) 43 (FN 2) (Simma, *Reziprozitätselement*); Robert Keohane, 'Reciprocity in International Relations' (1986) 40 Intl Org 1, 3. But see Francesco Parisi and Nita Ghei, 'The Role of Reciprocity in International Law' (2003) 36 Cornell Int'l L J 93, 122, who consider reciprocity as a 'basic principle of customary law'.

[29] Bruno Simma, 'Reciprocity' in Rüdiger Wolfrum (ed), *Max Planck Encyclopedia of Public International Law* (Oxford University Press 2012) 651, N 1 (Simma, Reciprocity); Simma, *Reziprozitätselement* (n 28) 19ff.

[30] Simma, 'Reciprocity' (n 29) N 2.

interrelation of action and counteraction according to which the conduct of one party, whether consummated or expected, provides the motivation for that of the other'.[31] Closely linked hereto are the notions of *formal* versus *substantive* reciprocity, the former denoting the 'synallagmatic, *do ut des* ... nature of the respective rights and duties between two or more parties' that is present in every international treaty and is sanctioned by the general principle of *pacta sunt servanda*,[32] while the latter concerns the question of actual equivalence of the mutual advantages deriving from treaty performance. In this sense, 'parties may agree in a one-sided or unequal treaty because they expect to benefit from other aspects in the further legal or political relationship between the parties',[33] engaging both aspects of subjective and substantive reciprocity. A further distinction is sometimes made between legal and socio-political reciprocity, the former dealing 'with the more or less formal relationship between two obligations or duties and the respective rights, the obligation of one party being the right of the other', while the latter takes into account the power relationship between two more or less equal parties.[34]

The norm-stabilizing function of reciprocity in the formation and application of international law should not be underestimated. In the (continued) absence of a centralized (mandatory) enforcement mechanism in international law, reciprocity plays an important role in self-regulating treaty relations by striving to balance rights and obligations of the parties involved.[35] Reciprocity also constitutes a driving force behind the conclusion of international treaties and their continued respect by each party.[36] Thus, while subjective reciprocity is not a requirement in public international law for the validity of a treaty and the latter can only be invalidated on the grounds provided for by Articles 46ff VCLT, but not on grounds of (perceived or real) inequality of the respective rights and obligations,[37] the treaty in question has higher chances of being respected and fulfilled by the parties if these believe that they can realize the expected or hoped-for advantages, even though these may lie outside the legal framework properly speaking.[38] The motivations and expectations of the parties for concluding the treaty thus remain essential as a guarantor of the stability and effectiveness of the treaty.

[31] Ibid; Simma, *Reziprozitätselement* (n 28) 48, 73ff.

[32] Andreas Paulus, 'Reciprocity Revisited' in Ulrich Fastenrath and others (eds), *From Bilateralism to Community Interest-Essays in Honour of Judge Bruno Simma* (Oxford University Press 2011) 116–17; Simma, *Reziprozitätselement* (n 28) 50; Simma, 'Reciprocity' (n 29) N 4.

[33] Paulus (n 32) 117.

[34] Ibid, 118.

[35] Simma, 'Reciprocity' (n 29) 4; similar Paulus (n 32) 121: '[R]eciprocity is the hallmark of a decentralized legal system whose subjects cannot rely on a centralized reaction to breaches of the law'.

[36] Simma, *Reziprozitätselement* (n 28) 86; on reciprocity in customary international law see Bruno Simma, *Das Reziprozitätselement in der Entstehung des Völkergewohnheitsrechts* (Fink 1970); Parisi and Ghei (n 28) 120ff.

[37] On the theory of so-called unequal treaties see Simma, *Reziprozitätselement* (n 28) 69–70; see also Anne Peters, 'Unequal Treaties' *Max Planck Encyclopedia of Public International Law* (Oxford Public International Law) available at <http://opil.ouplaw.com>.

[38] Simma, 'Reciprocity' (n 29) N 4, 11; Simma, *Reziprozitätselement* (n 28) 73–74, 252–53.

2.3.1.2 Reciprocity in international investment law

Reciprocity may arguably come in differing forms depending on the subject area of international law in question. This is so because depending on the institutional development of the legal subject area and the scope of its addressees/beneficiaries entitled to demand performance respectively redress in case of breach, reciprocity plays a more or less important role in safeguarding respectively restoring the balance of rights and obligations agreed upon in the treaty.

For international investment law, a sub-system of public international law,[39] reciprocity functions in principle in the same way in the conclusion of investment treaties as described here above. Investment treaties establish mutual rights and obligations between and among the Contracting States. Most of the time, their titles and/or preambles are programmatic, stipulating reciprocity in promotion and protection of foreign investment in express terms.[40] In the case of a given IIA, both Contracting States are thus (normally) bound by the same set of obligations,[41] resulting both in a co-relativity of rights and obligations and formal and legal reciprocity.[42]

This of course does not necessarily mean, as mentioned above, that the mutual advantages arising from the IIA are actually equivalent, even though this raises the question as to which elements to take into account in order to define equivalence.[43] An investment treaty concluded between, say, the United States of America on

[39] See, eg, Campbell McLachlan, 'Investment Treaties and General International Law' in Andrea Bjorklund, Ian Laird, and Sergey Ripinsky (eds), *Investment Treaty Law: Current Issues III* (British Institute of International and Comparative Law 2008) 114. This statement is of course not to deny the 'hybrid nature' of investment arbitration as having evolved not only from the law of diplomatic protection, but also from international commercial arbitration, see, eg, Gus Van Harten and Martin Loughlin, 'Investment Treaty Arbitration as a Species of Global Administrative Law' (2006) 17 EJIL 121, 125ff.

[40] See, eg, the 1993 Agreement between the Government of Hong Kong and the Government of Australia for the Promotion and Protection of Investments, preambular paragraph 4: 'Recognizing that the encouragement and reciprocal protection under agreement of such investments will be conducive to the stimulation of individual business initiative and will increase prosperity in both areas' available at <http://investmentpolicyhub.unctad.org/Download/TreatyFile/152>. See also the 2008 German Model BIT, preambular paragraphs 2 and 3: '[I]ntending to create favorable conditions for investments by investors of either State in the territory of the other State, ... recognizing that the encouragement and contractual protection of such investments are apt to stimulate private business initiative and to increase the prosperity of both nations' available at <http://www.italaw.com/sites/default/files/archive/ita1025.pdf> (all last accessed on 15 September 2016).

[41] But see for 'asymmetrical' obligations, eg, the 2012 Canada–China BIT, which foresees different obligations in terms of transfers and exchange formalities and conditions precedent to the submission of a claim to arbitration, Annex B 12 and Annex C 21.

[42] But see Dolzer and Schreuer (n 9) 22–23, who question the reciprocity in BITs because of what they see as 'obligations placed solely on the host State without equal commitments on the parts of the home State and of the foreign investor'. See, however, on the possibility of counterclaims by host States for breach of obligations by investors, eg, Yaraslau Kryvoi, 'Counterclaims in Investor-State Arbitration', London School of Economics, Legal Studies Working Paper No 08/2011 (5 August 2011) available at <http://papers.ssrn.com/sol3/papers.cfm?abstract_id=1891935> (last accessed on 15 September 2016).

[43] See, eg, Keohane (n 28) 6–8.

the one hand, and Bangladesh on the other,[44] will clearly, as concerns the protection of foreign investment, be more beneficial to the US investors investing in Bangladesh than for Bangladeshi investors investing in the United States, due to the unequally higher probability of US investors having the capital to invest in Bangladesh than vice versa.[45] This does however not answer the question for potential advantages lying outside the treaty framework properly speaking that a capital-importing, in particular developing country may seek by concluding a IIA with a capital-exporting country.[46] Indeed, while the goal of investment protection has historically been the number one concern of capital-exporting countries,[47] the primary motivation for developing countries to conclude IIAs has become the promotion of foreign investment, in the hope that more capital and related technology would flow into and thus develop their economy.[48] Whether this 'bargain' has indeed turned out to be true is to date still controversial, with different empirical studies pointing to contradictory conclusions.[49] IIAs may also accompany democratization processes, helping in building stable and predictable regulatory environments. As long as capital-importing countries will thus be convinced of the overall advantages and benefits of signing investment treaties, they will more likely than not continue to conclude and respect investment treaties. By contrast, even though expectations linked to the conclusion of an IIA may have been frustrated, this will a priori not affect its validity.[50]

[44] Treaty between the United States of America and the People's Republic of Bangladesh concerning the reciprocal promotion and protection of investment (entered into force on 25 July 1989) available at <http://investmentpolicyhub.unctad.org/Download/TreatyFile/278> (last accessed on 15 September 2016).

[45] See also FA Mann's similar opinion already in 1981: 'It will be seen that these Agreements proceed from the principle of reciprocity: they apply to investments by the United Kingdom in the Philippines no less than to investments by the Philippines in the United Kingdom. In practice, of course, the latter type will be extremely rare and it is probably no exaggeration to suggest that reciprocity is to a large extent a matter of prestige rather than reality', in FA Mann, 'Notes: British Treaties for the Promotion and Protection of Investments' (1981) 52 BYIL 241.

[46] See also Simma, 'Reciprocity' (n 29) N 11.

[47] Including, sometimes, the goal of liberalization of developing countries' economies and the facilitation of entry and operation of the investments in the host country.

[48] Jeswald Salacuse and Nicholas Sullivan, 'Do BITs Really Work?' (2005) 46 Harv Intl L J 67, 77–78; Omar García-Bolívar, 'Economic development at the core of the international investment regime' in Chester Brown and Kate Miles (eds), *Evolution in Investment Treaty Arbitration and Law* (Cambridge University Press 2011) 586ff.

[49] For a positive correlation between the conclusion of BITs and the promotion of FDI, see Salacuse and Sullivan (n 48) 111ff; similar Eric Neumayer and Laura Spess, 'Do Bilateral Investment Treaties increase Foreign Direct Investment to Developing Countries?' (2005) 33 World Dev 1567, 1582; see also the positive assessment, though without further in-depth analysis, of inward and outward investment, European Commission, 'Communication, Towards a comprehensive European international investment policy', COM(2010)343 final (07.07.2010) 3, available at <http://trade.ec.europa.eu/doclib/docs/2010/july/tradoc_146307.pdf> (last accessed on 15 September 2016). Denying a positive correlation, Jason Webb Yackee, 'Do Bilateral Investment Treaties Promote Foreign Direct Investment?' (2010–2011) 51 Va J Intl L 397; Mary Hallward-Driemeier, 'Do Bilateral Investment Treaties Attract Foreign Investment?' in Karl Sauvant and Lisa Sachs (eds), *The Effect of Treaties on Foreign Direct Investment* (Oxford University Press 2009) 349–78.

[50] This is not to say that a case of frustrated expectations is not a case for potential concern, as this can lead to growing legitimacy concerns, see below at 2.3.2.

This does however not answer the question of what happens in case of breach of an international obligation. It is arguably in the case of (an alleged) breach of an international obligation where the role of reciprocity—in its objective or formal manifestation—becomes particularly palpable, as it denotes who is entitled to demand compliance (respectively compensation) in respect of the breached obligation.[51] Commentators have explained that if (only) the State(s) party (or parties) to the treaty can demand compliance, the obligation in question is strictly reciprocal. If, by contrast, any State (or for that matter any third party) can demand compliance from the breaching State, which is in particular the case when the obligation in question serves the more general interest of the international community, it can be considered 'beyond reciprocity', that is, 'beyond the bilateral relationship between the parties'.[52]

At the outset, it may be worth recalling a well-known passage by the International Court of Justice (ICJ) in the *Barcelona Traction* case. The Court held that:

> An essential distinction should be drawn between the obligations of a State towards the international community as a whole, and those arising vis-à-vis another State in the field of diplomatic protection. By their very nature, the former are the concern of all States. In view of the importance of the rights involved, all States can be held to have a legal interest in their protection; they are obligations *erga omnes*.[53]

The ICJ thus explicitly considered the right to exercise diplomatic protection, from which modern international investment law developed, as a strictly reciprocal right.[54]

However, modern international investment law has evolved precisely in view of the shortcomings of this (customary) law of diplomatic protection. As has been discussed in Chapter 1, modern international investment law has expanded the scope of beneficiaries beyond the realm of the classical subjects of public international law and has made the individual investor (both natural and legal persons)—not unlike under international human rights law—at least partially a subject under public international law, by granting the right, though usually linked to certain conditions, to sue the host State *directly*, that is, without any dependence from his home State's decision to this effect, in case of (alleged) breach of an investment obligation.[55] The vast majority of bilateral and plurilateral IIAs nowadays provide for such a direct standing of the foreign investor of the respective other Contracting party.[56]

[51] See in this sense also the ICJ in *Reparation for Injuries Suffered in the Service of the United Nations (Advisory Opinion)* [1949] ICJ Rep 181–82: 'Only the party to whom an international obligation is due can bring a claim in respect of its breach.'

[52] Paulus (n 32) 119; similar Antonio Cassese, *International Law* (Oxford University Press 2005) 14.

[53] *Barcelona Traction, Light and Power Co (Belgium v Spain) (Judgment)* [1970] ICJ Rep 3, 32 (para 33).

[54] On the historical development of international investment law see Chapter 1, at 1.2.1.

[55] See Chapter 1, at 1.2.2.

[56] For exceptions see, eg, the 2012 Australia–Malaysia Free Trade Agreement. See also the discussion in Chapter 8, at 8.1.3.

Does however the direct standing of the foreign investor mean that the investment relationship has become 'beyond reciprocity' in that it brings a third party into the equation? This alone will arguably not be enough to 'break' through reciprocity. In particular, it should be noted that the parties to an IIA grant the direct standing precisely in a reciprocal manner to the foreign investors of the respective other contracting party. This does of course a priori not mean that *any* foreign investor is entitled to demand redress from the host State, but only the one who qualifies as investor pursuant to the definition agreed upon by the parties to the IIA. It may thus probably be argued that the direct standing of the foreign investor, though atypical in the classical State–State treaty setting, ensures the balance of investment rights and obligations which is characteristic of reciprocal treaty relations, because without this direct right to sue, the protection of foreign investors would be largely ineffective in view of the shortcomings of customary international law as discussed above.[57]

Yet, there are also elements that warrant for a somewhat different, if less strict approach to reciprocity in international investment law. First, while international investment law remains, in the absence of a (permanent) multilateralized investment court,[58] a decentralized legal system, not presenting the same highly institutionalized level as for example WTO law, it undeniably offers foreign investors an enviably good enforcement system with arbitration under the International Centre for Settlement of Investment Disputes (ICSID) Convention.[59] As is well known, most investment arbitrations are conducted under the auspices of the ICSID Convention, which is currently ratified by 152 States (signed by 160 States).[60] But even arbitrations under other institutional rules, such as United Nations Commission on International Trade Law (UNCITRAL), International Chamber of Commerce, Stockholm Chamber of Commerce, London Chamber of International Arbitration arbitral rules, usually provide for enforcement of the arbitral awards under the 1958 New York Convention, admitting only a limited number of grounds on which the arbitral award may be set aside by a national court in whose jurisdiction the enforcement is sought.[61] One scholar, analysing the nature of reciprocity in WTO law, concluded with respect to the WTO dispute settlement procedure that:

> these two elements [dispute settlement procedure whose outcome can no longer be blocked by the defending party and the institutional type of implementation control] ... go beyond

[57] See Chapter 1, at 1.2.2.

[58] See for this proposal, eg, Gus Van Harten, *Investment Treaty Arbitration and Public Law* (Oxford University Press 2007) 180–84.

[59] Of particular note is the possibility of direct enforcement of the arbitral awards in countries that are members to the ICSID Convention, Art 54, and the limited grounds for review respectively annulment of the arbitral award, Arts 51, 52.

[60] See Status of Ratification (by 12 April 2016) available at <https://icsid.worldbank.org/apps/ICSIDWEB/icsiddocs/Documents/List%20of%20Contracting%20States%20and%20Other%20Signatories%20of%20the%20Convention%20-%20Latest.pdf> (last accessed on 15 September 2016). But for the recent denunciations by Venezuela, Ecuador, Bolivia, and Nicaragua see Chapter 1, at 1.2.1.

[61] Art V of the Convention on the Recognition and Enforcement of Foreign Arbitral Awards Done at New York, 10 June 1958 (entered into force on 7 June 1959) 330 UNTS 38 (1959 No 4739).

a strict reciprocity-type structure, where the parties to a deal can sort out any dispute by their own means.[62]

It could thus be argued that international investment law in a similar vein disposes in principle of sufficient own means in terms of enforcement, making reciprocity a more malleable, or even less necessary, concept than in other international law relationships.

Secondly, IIA-negotiating States can, and in virtually all IIAs do, include an MFN clause. An MFN clause extends certain concessions and advantages achieved by one negotiating party to a potentially indeterminate number of beneficiaries.[63] For the realm of WTO law, one scholar calls this the 'common interest dimension of international economic law'.[64] Another scholar also highlights the multilateralizing effect of the MFN clause and makes it one of the central arguments for his conclusion that modern international investment law is evolving towards a de facto multilateral system.[65] It can certainly be accepted that the MFN clause creates a quasi *erga omnes* effect that elevates the legal relationship of an IIA beyond strict reciprocity in the sense that *any* investor qualifying as national of the party to an IIA containing an MFN clause becomes eligible to request more favourable substantive protections or, depending on the wording of the MFN clause, more favourable procedural provisions that are contained in other, third-party IIAs negotiated by the State host to the foreign investor.

A similar effect can arguably also be observed in the formulation of the notion of investor in IIAs. As will be examined more in detail further below,[66] IIA-negotiating States may use differing criteria to establish the required nationality link of the foreign corporate investor wishing to attract the protection of the IIA. Most IIAs require that the legal person wishing to qualify as foreign investor under the IIA in question either be incorporated or organized in accordance with the law applicable in that Contracting Party, or have their main seat of business (*siège social*), sometimes alternatively expressed as the place of the central administration or effective seat in the territory of that Contracting Party, with some IIAs combining these criteria.[67] Since these criteria do not take into account the 'real' nature of the investment activity, they can be said to be formal (in the sense that they attach

[62] Peter-Tobias Stoll, 'The World Trade Organization as a Club' in Ulrich Fastenrath and others (eds), *From Bilateralism to Community Interest-Essays in Honour of Judge Bruno Simma* (Oxford University Press 2011) 183.

[63] See, eg, Art 3(1) of the 2008 German Model BIT: 'Neither Contracting State shall in its territory subject investments owned or controlled by investors of the other Contracting State to treatment less favourable than it accords to ... investments of investors of any third State.'

[64] Stoll (n 62) 177. On similarities and differences of national treatment in WTO law and international investment law see Nicholas DiMascio and Joost Pauwelyn, 'Nondiscrimination in Trade and Investment Treaties: Worlds Apart or Two Sides of the Same Coin' (2008) 102 AJIL 48.

[65] Stephan Schill, *The Multilateralization of International Investment Law* (Cambridge University Press 2009) 121ff, 362ff.

[66] See Chapter 8, at 8.2.2.

[67] For examples see Dolzer and Schreuer (n 9) 49ff; UNCTAD, 'Scope and Definition, A Sequel' UNCTAD Series on Issues in International Investment Agreements II (United Nations 2011) 80ff, available at <http://unctad.org/en/docs/diaeia20102_en.pdf> (last accessed on 15 September 2016).

to a formal criterion). If States negotiating an IIA want to avoid that companies without any real economic link to their home State benefit from the protection of the IIA, they may require in the IIA a 'bond of economic substance between the corporate investor and the state whose nationality it claims' [68] or include a so-called denial of benefits clause, which has the express purpose of excluding treaty shopping mailbox companies from the benefits of the advantageous treaty.[69] States may also include treaty language in the wording of protected investments to the effect that not any passive ownership of assets held through subsidiaries will be protected.[70]

By being able to define the scope and nature of foreign investors they wish to protect by the IIA, States may thus arguably modulate reciprocity as if on a sliding scale: the broader and more unqualified the notion of investor and/or investment, the more investors and investments will qualify for protection, independently of a potential economic bond with the host State, and thus the less reciprocity is contained in that IIA, while the more restricted and qualified the notion of investor and/or investment, the more the treaty relationship is brought back to strict reciprocity. The plethora of existing IIAs attests to this high variability in terms of 'scope of protection' criteria, not found in other areas of international law.

Does this mean that in the absence of restrictive treaty language, parties to an IIA must be presumed to have accepted investment obligations quasi *erga omnes*? This is what a former US negotiator seems to contend:

> Although each investment treaty is drafted as a bilateral set of obligations, to comply with those obligations the host state must treat them as obligations erga omnes: obligations owed to every state and every company. This conclusion stems from the fact that, under normal circumstances, host state officials will never know at the time they must take action whether a given company is covered by a given treaty. Where a host state has entered into BITs that cover indirectly layered controlled investments, there could be between one and 20 or more layers of intermediate holding companies that separate the company the host state officials see and the company which is a covered investor under the treaty … Under these circumstances, the only way to comply with the treaty is for the host state to assume that all investors—all companies—are covered by the highest standards of any BIT in force for the state. The reality that foreign capital is highly fungible and the breadth of the definitions of investor and investment thus combine effectively to transform the facially bilateral obligations of the BIT into an obligation that the host state must consider potentially applicable to all investors.[71]

[68] Dolzer and Schreuer (n 9) 51.

[69] See, eg, Loukas Mistelis and Crina Baltag, 'Denial of Benefits and Article 17 of the Energy Charter Treaty' (2008–2009) 113 Penn St L Rev 1301, 1302; Stephan Jagusch and Anthony Sinclair, 'Part II. Denial of advantages under Article 17(1)' in Graham Coop and Clarisse Ribeiro (eds), *Investment Protection and the Energy Charter Treaty* (Huntington JurisNet 2008) 18. On denial of benefits clauses see more in detail in Chapter 4, at 4.3.3.

[70] See, eg, *Standard Chartered Bank v Tanzania* (n 26) paras 267–70.

[71] Barton Legum, 'Defining Investment and Investor: Who is Entitled to Claim?' (2006) 22 Arb Intl 524ff. Similar the arbitral tribunal in *Aguas del Tunarí SA v Plurinational State of Bolivia*, ICSID Case No ARB/02/3, Decision on Respondent's Objections to Jurisdiction (21 October 2005) para 332.

It is true that the modern international investment law system offers a paradox unique in international law: while most IIA obligations are formally thought of as reciprocal, the broad investor standing and protection of indirect investments, coupled with the high fungibility of shares and the complexity of global corporate ownership structures make that de facto, host States cannot know in advance to whom investment treaty benefits will really accrue.

Yet, this does not mean that legally speaking, investment obligations should be thought of as *erga omnes* obligations. Indeed, if really States not having negotiated restrictive treaty language should be presumed to have accepted investment obligations quasi *erga omnes*, any objection to the tribunal's jurisdiction by the Respondent State would arguably come close to a *venire contra factum proprium*. Yet, it is clear that no Respondent could afford (and in reality would not be expected) to miss lodging objections on grounds of *ratione personae, ratione materiae, ratione temporis* or abuse of rights/abuse of process, depending on the circumstances of the case. Moreover, the fact that arbitral tribunals may, and under certain circumstances do, find a claim based on a strategic use or change of nationality to lack good faith (be it for example by interpreting the notion of investment to contain an 'active' contribution requirement or by inferring from the timing of the change of nationality an abuse of rights/abuse of process)[72] means that arbitral tribunals have a reserve power, even in the absence of explicit treaty language, to bring the legal relationship back to (strict) reciprocity.

What does the above mean for the purposes of this research? First, as the above has shown, reciprocity in international investment law must in principle be conceived of as being less strict (and probably less necessary) than in other areas of public international law. This is particularly due to the described specificities of international investment law (the 'built-in mechanisms' for the safeguard of the balance of rights and duties so to speak), but also to the fact that it is in principle within IIA-negotiating States' power to determine which scope they want to give to reciprocity in their legal relationship.

Second, in the absence of restrictive treaty language (such as a substantive business activities requirement, denial of benefits clause, etc.), the scope of reciprocity in a given IIA is difficult to determine in the abstract. It then becomes the arbitral tribunal's task to find out the intentions of the parties as concerns the scope of reciprocity by interpreting relevant notions (such as of investor or of investment) in accordance with the (customary) rules of treaty interpretation as codified in Articles 31 and 32 VCLT, taking into account the circumstances in bringing the claim based on a strategic use or change of nationality. Thus, when the arbitral tribunal decides to strike down a claim based on a corporate structuring or restructuring, be it on jurisdictional grounds or on grounds of abuse of rights/abuse of process, it arguably gives expression to what it understood to be the parties' intentions on the nature and scope of reciprocity in the IIA.

[72] See Chapter 9.

From the above seems to follow that reciprocity (in its objective or formal manifestation) functions in international investment law somewhat differently than in other fields of international law. One could term it 'reciprocity *à géométrie variable*', that is to say, parties to an IIA may agree on a stricter or a less strict conception of reciprocity by including corresponding treaty language. This also means that the cursory claim that treaty shopping always violates the principle of reciprocity is an inadequate reduction of the complexity of this notion and has to be examined in a more nuanced way and on a case-by-case basis.

Indeed, if the scope of reciprocity is largely in the hands of the parties, concerns with respect to possible 'violations' of the principle of reciprocity appear in principle secondary. If parties agree on broad notions of investor and investment and/or decide not to include a denial of benefit clause, they often (implicitly) decide to take a treaty shopping-permissive stance and reciprocity is therefore normally not an issue. Even where this is disputed between the parties to an investment arbitration (because the IIA under interpretation contains 'old-style' vague clauses), an arbitral tribunal has the reserve power to restore respectively enforce the reciprocity meant to govern the treaty relations (for example by applying the abuse of rights/abuse of process doctrine), making reciprocity concerns difficult to discern.

However, as has already been noted further above, reciprocity concerns may arise in terms of subjective reciprocity, possibly affecting the (perception of) legitimacy of the investment law system, as will be seen in turn.

2.3.2 Legitimacy concerns

In recent years, the investment arbitration system has also been under increasing criticism for what has been mostly and broadly termed so-called legitimacy concerns.[73] The following section will undertake to examine these legitimacy concerns with a view of determining whether they are pertinent for the practise of treaty shopping or not.

2.3.2.1 The meaning of legitimacy in international law

To examine the above-mentioned potential legitimacy concerns with respect to treaty shopping, it seems warranted to try and shed more light onto the notion of legitimacy itself.

[73] See, eg, Charles Brower, Charles Brower II, and Jeremy Sharpe, 'The Coming Crisis in the Global Adjudication System' (2003) 19 Arb Intl 415; Susan Franck, 'Legitimacy Crisis' (n 11) 1521; M Sornarajah, 'A Coming Crisis: Expansionary Trends in Investment Treaty Arbitration' in Karl Sauvant (ed), *Appeals Mechanism in International Investment Disputes* (Oxford University Press 2008) 39, 73; Charles N Brower II, 'Structure, Legitimacy, and NAFTA's Investment Chapter' (2003) 36 Vand J Transnatl L 37; Besson (n 16) 745; Barnali Choudhury, 'Recapturing Public Power: Is Investment Arbitration's Engagement of the Public Interest Contributing to the Democratic Deficit?' (2008) 41 Vand J Transnatl L 775; Olivia Chung, 'The Lopsided International Investment Law Regime' (2006–2007) 47 Va J Intl L 953. Though see also those contesting a 'legitimacy crisis', eg, Devashish Krishan, 'Thinking about BITs and BIT Arbitration: The Legitimacy Crisis that never was', in Todd Weiler and Freya Baetens (eds), *New Directions in International Economic Law, In Memoriam Thomas Wälde* (Brill/Martinus Nijhoff 2011) 107.

The attempt to approach the notion of legitimacy encounters its first difficulty due to its multifaceted content. As Carol Harlow has pointed out, 'legitimacy is … a vast and amorphous subject on which economists, sociologists, political scientists and lawyers have propounded differing views in different conceptual vocabularies', 'a portmanteau word', that 'lies in the eyes of the beholder'.[74] To Thomas Franck, one of the most prominent recent commentators on legitimacy in international law, legitimacy is a 'bracketing of many integral factors, which are related, but different'.[75] Accordingly, looking at it from a single perspective will not adequately capture its many possible facets.[76] For example, though it may be tempting for a lawyer to equate legitimacy with legality, a rule or decision that is legal will not necessarily also be considered legitimate, though the adherence to the rule of law, as mostly expressed in the respect of certain procedural safeguards, will more often than not contribute to a perception of legitimacy of the rule or decision in question.[77] Legitimacy and legality will therefore often coincide.[78]

The search for content encounters a further difficulty in that the meaning of legitimacy has changed over time with changing social and political conditions.[79] Thus, globalization, higher supra- and international institutionalization, their further reach into domestic affairs and the increasing involvement of the non-State actors (civil society, NGOs, etc.) in global governance issues have arguably also transformed and developed the notion and meaning of legitimacy in international law.[80] The traditional, state-centred concept of legitimacy that is based on the consent of the people, so-called democratic school, continues to be important, but does not seem to be in itself sufficient anymore to assess the legitimacy of international law and global governance institutions in modern times.[81]

Given the wealth of approaches towards the notion of legitimacy, anything more than a short overview of some of the most prominent theories and definitional attempts would be illusory, the aim for our purposes simply being to identify a set

[74] Carol Harlow, 'Concepts and Methods of Reasoning of the New Public Law: Legitimacy' LSE Working Papers 19/2010, 6, 11, 37, available at <http://papers.ssrn.com/sol3/papers.cfm?abstract_id=1713633> (last accessed on 15 September 2016).

[75] Thomas Franck, *The Power of Legitimacy Among Nations* (Oxford University Press 1990) 17.

[76] Similar Thomas Cottier, 'The Legitimacy of WTO Law' NCCR Trade Regulation Working Paper No 2008/19, 8, available at <http://phase1.nccr-trade.org/images/stories/publications/IP2/The_Legitimacy_of_WTO_Law_cottier_final%200808.pdf> (last accessed on 15 September 2016).

[77] Harlow, 'Legitimacy' (n 74) 6–8.

[78] Cottier (n 76) 7.

[79] On the historical development from a theocratic to a democratic understanding of the concept and notion of legitimacy see Jost Delbrück, 'Exercising Public Authority Beyond the State, Transnational Democracy and/or Alternative Legitimation Strategies?' (2003) 10 Ind J Global Legal Stud 29, 31–34.

[80] Delbrück (n 79) 34ff; Buchanan (n 18) 90; Kati Kulovesi, *WTO Dispute Settlement System, Challenges of the Environment, Legitimacy and Fragmentation* (Kluwer Law International 2011) 11ff, 29ff; Mattias Kumm, 'The Legitimacy of International Law' (2005) 15 EJIL 907, 913.

[81] Delbrück (n 79) 33, 40ff; see also Buchanan (n 18) 90–94; Allan Buchanan and Robert Keohane, 'The Legitimacy of Global Governance Institutions' in Lukas Meyer (ed), *Legitimacy, Justice and Public International Law* (Cambridge University Press 2009) 37; Harlow, 'Legitimacy' (n 74) 11ff; Benedict Kingsbury and Stephan Schill, 'Investor-State Arbitration as Governance: Fair and Equitable Treatment, Proportionality and the Emerging Global Administrative Law' IILJ Working Paper (2009/6) 42, available at <www.iilj.org/publications/documents/2009-6.KingsburySchill.pdf> (last accessed on 15 September 2016).

of factors that will help us in analysing the above-mentioned legitimacy concerns with respect to treaty shopping.

Most commentators writing on the issue seem to agree that legitimacy entails a sense or belief of the rightfulness and justified authority, which leads to a voluntary compliance with the rule or institution in question. Thus, according to Thomas Franck:

> Legitimacy is a property of a rule or rule-making institution which itself exerts a pull toward compliance on those addressed normatively because those addressed believe that the rule or institution has come into being and operates in accordance with generally accepted principles of right process.[82]

Samantha Besson defines legitimacy as 'the quality of what is justified and hence of what gives reason for action, i.e. has authority.'[83] Carol Harlow views legitimacy as 'involving arguments about the justification for and obedience to authority'.[84] Kati Kulovesi defines legitimacy largely as 'a belief in the rightfulness of the system or decision through which authority is exercised'.[85] Common to these definitions seems to be the sense of 'rightful authority' a system or decision perceived as legitimate will exude.

Commentators differ however as to the 'key ingredients' of what contributes to such a 'rightful authority'. Some distinguish between normative and sociological legitimacy. Thus, according to Allan Buchanan:

> An institution that attempts to rule (govern) is legitimate in the normative sense if and only if it has the right to rule … Calling an institution legitimate in the sociological sense is a misleading way of saying that it is widely believed to have the right to rule.[86]

A similar distinction can be found between formal legitimacy and social legitimacy other scholars adhere to. JHH Weiler for example defines formal legitimacy as implying that 'all requirements of law are observed in the creation of the institution or system'.[87] Social legitimacy, on the other hand, is understood by him as:

> a broad, empirically determined societal acceptance of the system. Social legitimacy may have an additional substantive component: legitimacy occurs when the government process displays a commitment to, and actively guarantees, values that are part of the general political culture, such as justice, freedom and general welfare.[88]

Still others distinguish between input and output legitimacy. Thomas Cottier defines input legitimacy as including 'the procedures by which rules and decisions are made and adopted', comprising '[t]ests of inclusiveness and participation, and fairness of discourse … applied in pluralist concepts of accountability'.[89] Output

[82] Thomas Franck (n 75) 16. [83] Besson (n 16) 751.

[84] Harlow, 'Legitimacy' (n 74) 8. [85] Kulovesi (n 80) 42.

[86] Buchanan (n 18) 79; similar Gráinne De Búrca, 'The Quest for Legitimacy in the European Union' (1996) 59 Modern Law Review 349: '[L]egitimacy has both a social aspect, in terms of being rooted in popular consent, and a normative aspect, in terms of the underlying values on which such consent is based.'

[87] Joseph HH Weiler, *The Constitution of Europe. Do the New Clothes Have an Emperor? And Other Essays on European Integration* (Cambridge University Press 1999) 80; Kulovesi (n 80) 43.

[88] Weiler (n 87) 80; Kulovesi (n 80) 44. [89] Cottier (n 76) 8.

legitimacy, on the other hand, 'assesses the effect of rules on society at large', the yardsticks including 'justice, fairness, welfare and the respect for human rights'.[90] More concisely, Samantha Besson defines input legitimacy as the 'background conditions' of a decision while output legitimacy relates to its 'results'.[91]

Finally, more 'constitutionalist' approaches propose a number of 'surrogates' for democratic legitimation, such as 'efficiency, transparency, accountability, ex post acceptance of public acts characterized by expertise, and rationality'.[92] Mattias Kumm for example identifies four elements that are in his view determinative of legitimacy, notably:

> the formal principle of international legality, the jurisdictional principles of subsidiarity, the procedural principle of adequate participation and accountability, as well as the substantive principle of achieving outcomes that are not violative of fundamental rights and are reasonable.[93]

As will be seen in the following literature review that specifically assesses legitimacy problems in investment arbitration, it seems that no single legitimacy theory mentioned above could alone explain what makes for a legitimate investment arbitration system; a combination of formal, procedural, and social and substantive elements seems thus warranted.[94]

2.3.2.2 Legitimacy concerns in international investment law

The current legitimacy critiques in international investment law are based on several crucial observations.

First, the so-called 'public–private divide' or 'public law challenge' makes the central claim that investment arbitration reaches (too) far into the domestic public order without for that matter being 'properly equipped' to respond to legitimacy concerns such as democratic legitimation, accountability, transparency, and other rule-of-law requirements.[95]

[90] Ibid; though see Harlow, 'Legitimacy' (n 74) 16–17, who points out the link between input and output legitimacy at the example of a 'better regulation', where in her view output legitimacy makes a case for efficiency and expertise, two elements that could be considered closer to input legitimacy.

[91] Besson (n 16) 752. [92] Delbrück (n 79) 40ff. [93] Kumm (n 80) 917ff.

[94] Similar Kulovesi for the realm of the WTO Dispute Settlement system (n 80) 52; see also Harlow, 'Legitimacy' (n 74) 8: 'Formal questions of legality, sovereignty, and primacy, largely procedural in character, lie at one end of a scale; at the other, lie questions of substance and values.'

[95] Van Harten, *Public Law* (n 58) 152ff; Besson (n 16) 758; Kate Miles, 'Reconceptualising International Investment Law' in Meredith Kolsky Lewis and Susy Frankel (eds), *International Economic Law and National Autonomy* (Cambridge University Press 2010) 295. Schill resumes the 'public law challenge' in the following terms: '[I]nvestment treaty arbitration restricts governmental action, and therefore concerns questions of public law, without relying on a dispute settlement mechanism that conforms to core public law values, including democracy, equal treatment, separation of powers, legal certainty and predictability, or in other words, the rule of law … it is not acceptable, in the view of critics, in the public law context, where the legality of a state's exercise of public power is reviewed under standards crafted by international arbitrators who are appointed by the disputing parties and have no genuine democratic legitimacy. International investment law, in this perspective, becomes a threat to state sovereignty, to the integrity of domestic public law and its values, and ultimately to national self-determination' in Stephan Schill, 'Enhancing International Investment Law's Legitimacy: Conceptual

Second, the lack of consistency and predictability of international investment law has been made out as a factor that can impact upon the perception of legitimacy of investor–State arbitration.[96] This relates in particular to the risk of conflicting interpretations of similar clauses and inconsistent arbitral decisions, which becomes most palpable in the case of multiple proceedings that are based on the same set of facts, but brought by different claimants within the same corporate structure, resulting in conflicting awards, as happened (in)famously in the *Lauder/CME* cases.[97]

This risk of conflicting interpretations relates on the one hand to the lack of binding precedent or *stare decisis* in international (investment) law.[98] On the other hand, it is also the vagueness and indeterminacy of the treaty texts that leave the arbitral tribunal much leeway for interpretation and that have, in the past, led to extensive and sometimes conflicting interpretations of core procedural or substantive clauses.[99] Susan Franck however very rightly points out that low textual clarity of the IIAs does not in itself result in a judgment of illegitimacy. Rather, it depends on who does the interpretation and how.[100] This has in turn raised the question of so-called arbitrator or institutional bias. In particular, some commentators have called into question the independence and impartiality of arbitrators and have argued that arbitrators have a natural or even personal interest to favour investor over host State interests.[101] Others have criticized the fact that arbitrators, traditionally coming from small elite

and Methodological Foundations of a New Public Law Approach' (2011–2012) 52 Va J Intl L 57, 67. Similar Naveen Gurudevan, 'An Evaluation of Current Legitimacy-based Objections to NAFTA's Chapter 11 Investment Dispute Resolution Process' (2004–2005) 6 San Diego Intl L J 399, 419ff.

[96] Gaukrodger and Gordon (n 25) 58.

[97] See, eg, Brower, Brower II, and Sharpe (n 73) 415, 424; similar Besson (n 16) 759. It has to be noted that it was precisely this risk of legal insecurity through the possibility of a multiplicity of claims by shareholders that led the ICJ in *Barcelona Traction* to reject in principle the direct standing of the shareholders under customary international law, see *Barcelona Traction* (n 53) 49 (para 96): 'The Court considers that the adoption of the theory of diplomatic protection of shareholders as such, by opening the door to competing diplomatic claims, could create an atmosphere of confusion and insecurity in economic relations. The danger would be all the greater in as much as the shares of companies whose activity is international are widely scattered and frequently change hands.' But see International Law Commission (ILC), 'Fourth Report on Diplomatic Protection' Report of the Fifty-fifth Session (2003) UN Doc A/CN.4/530, para 21: 'Why should the prospect of a multiplicity of claims by shareholders against a wrongdoing State create an atmosphere of confusion and insecurity in international economic relations?'

[98] Federico Ortino, 'Legal Reasoning of International Investment Tribunals: A Typology of Egregious Failures' (2012) 3 JIDS 31, 39. See also Chapter 1, at 1.2.4.

[99] Susan Franck, 'Legitimacy Crisis' (n 11) 1584–85; Brower II, 'Structure' (n 73) 59ff; Schill, 'Enhancing International Investment Law's Legitimacy' (n 95) 66; Charles Brower and Stephan Schill, 'Is Arbitration a Threat or a Boon to the Legitimacy of International Investment Law' (2009) 9 Chi J Intl L 471, 473ff.

[100] Susan Franck, 'Legitimacy Crisis' (n 11) 1585: 'By having an "authority recognized as legitimate" to provide clarification on the meaning and application of rules, interpretation can rectify textual indeterminacy. The success of such "interpretive determinacy", however, depends upon who does the interpretation, their authority to interpret, and the coherence of the decisions they reach. The issue facing investment arbitration is whether a neutral arbitral tribunal composed of private individuals, such as public international law experts who may be chosen by the parties, can and actually do apply investment rights in a correct and coherent manner'. Similar Brower II, 'Structure' (n 73) 71ff.

[101] Jan Wouters and Nicholas Hachez, 'The Institutionalization of Investment Arbitration and Sustainable Development' in Marie-Claire Cordonier Segger, Markus Gehring, and Andrew

circles, may receive multiple appointments and function as counsel in one arbitration and as arbitrator in the next, thus creating possible conflicts of interests.[102] Empirical studies have thus far not completely solved this controversy, but there seems to be ground to argue that the arbitrator bias reproach is exaggerated.[103]

Third, crucially building upon the first and second legitimacy critiques, the confidential nature of investor–state proceedings has raised important concerns.[104] Because of the fact that investor–state arbitration often touches on potentially sensitive matters of public interest, it has been considered as problematic that these restrictions of the exercise of public authority occur behind closed doors, without the possibility of participation of a larger public potentially affected by these decisions and often without even having knowledge of or access to these decisions.[105]

Newcombe (eds), *Sustainable Development in World Investment Law* (Kluwer Law International 2011) 628; M Sornarajah, 'Evolution or revolution in international investment arbitration? The descent into normlessness' in Chester Brown and Kate Miles (eds), *Evolution in Investment Treaty Law and Arbitration* (Cambridge University Press 2011) 631, 633; Peter Muchlinski, 'Corporations and the Uses of Law: International Investment Arbitration as a "Multilateral Legal Order"', Oñati Socio-Legal Series, Vol 1, No 4 (2011)—Socio-Legal Aspects of Adjudication of International Economic Disputes, 13–15, available at <http://papers.ssrn.com/sol3/papers.cfm?abstract_id=1832562> (last accessed on 15 September 2016); Choudhury (n 73) 787.

[102] Besson (n 16) 762; Brower II, 'Structure' (n 73) 65; Thomas Buergenthal, 'The Proliferation of Disputes, Dispute Settlement Procedures and Respect for the Rule of Law' (2006) 22 Arb Intl 495, 498: 'I have long believed that the practice of allowing arbitrators to serve as counsel, and counsel to serve as arbitrators, raises due process of law issues. In my view, arbitrators and counsel should be required to decide to be one or the other, and be held to the choice they have made, at least for a specific period of time. That is necessary, in my opinion, in order to ensure that an arbitrator will not be tempted, consciously or unconsciously, to seek to obtain a result in an arbitral decision that might advance the interests of a client in a case he or she is handling as counsel. ICSID is particularly vulnerable to this problem because the interpretation and application of the same or similar legal instruments (the bilateral investment treaties, for example) are regularly at issue in different cases before it. I also believe that repeated designations by counsel of the same arbitrator should be avoided. These revolving-door problems—counsel selecting an arbitrator who, the next time around when the arbitrator is counsel, selects the previous counsel as arbitrator—should be avoided. *Manus manum lavat*, in other words "you scratch my back and I'll scratch yours", does not advance the rule of law'.

[103] For studies challenging the bias reproach see Susan Franck, 'The ICSID Effect?' (2010–2011) 51 Va J Intl L 825, 852; same, 'Development and Outcomes of Investment Treaty Arbitration' (2009) 50 Harv Intl L J 435, 447; Daphna Kapeliuk, 'The Repeat Appointment Factor: Exploring Decision Patterns of Elite Investment Arbitrators' (2010) 96 Cornell L Rev 49. Similar Charles Brower and Stephan Schill, 'Regulating counsel conduct before international arbitral tribunals' in Pieter Bekker, Rudolf Dolzer, and Michael Waibel (eds), *Making Transnational Law Work in a Global Economy, Essays in Honour of Detlev Vagts* (Cambridge University Press 2010) 488, 492: 'Reputation is difficult to build up and is easily destroyed; these characteristics thus work against any incentive to taint one's decision making in favor of either party in order to secure future appointments'. For a study arguing empirical evidence of pro-investor bias see Gus Van Harten, 'Pro-Investor or Pro-State Bias in Investment-Treaty Arbitration? Forthcoming Study Gives Cause for Concern' Investment Treaty News (13 April 2012) available at <http://www.iisd.org/itn/2012/04/13/pro-investor-or-pro-state-bias-in-investment-treaty-arbitration-forthcoming-study-gives-cause-for-concern/>; and same, 'Arbitral Behaviors in Asymmetrical Adjudication: An Empirical Study of Investment Treaty Arbitration' Osgoode Hall Law School, Research Paper No 41/2012, available at <http://ssrn.com/abstract=2149207> (both last accessed on 15 September 2016).

[104] Witnessing its heritage from international commercial arbitration; see, eg, Ileana Smeureanu, *Confidentiality in International Commercial Arbitration* (Kluwer Law International 2011).

[105] UNCTAD, 'Transparency, A Sequel' UNCTAD Series on Issues in International Investment Agreements II (United Nations 2012) 8ff, available at <http://unctad.org/en/PublicationsLibrary/unctaddiaeia2011d6_en.pdf> (last accessed on 15 September 2016); Besson (n 16) 764; Choudury

Proposals on how to counter these challenges to the legitimacy of investor–state arbitration have been numerous and varying.

As for academic proposals on how to remediate the legitimacy concerns, some of them, in particular the earlier ones, stress the need for institutional and/or procedural reforms, thereby following more of a 'procedural legitimacy' approach. Thus, a solution to the lack of consistency and predictability of arbitral decisions has been seen for example in the establishment of an ad hoc or permanent investment court or tribunal,[106] permanent,[107] or ad hoc appellate structures or procedures.[108] The EU proposal[109] of the inclusion, in the Canada–EU CETA and the EU-Vietnam FTA, of an 'investment court system', with a roster of 'judges' appointed by the parties for a certain period of time similar to the WTO Dispute Settlement Body, is to counter the issue of 'repeat' appointments and practitioners acting both as counsels and as arbitrators, contributing the bias reproach.

Other scholars call for a 'renationalization' of investment disputes.[110] To enhance effectiveness of investor–state arbitration and public participation of concerned non-disputing stakeholders, arbitral institutions have been stressing the need to allow for greater transparency of the proceedings.[111] Both ICSID and UNCITRAL

(n 73) 789ff, 808ff; see also LE Peterson, 'Poland wins investment treaty arbitration with EU; Government sits on growing cache of unpublished rulings' *IA Reporter* (7 February 2012) who points out that in particular in the case of non-ICSID arbitrations, there is still a high percentage of non-published arbitrations, available at <http://www.iareporter.com> (subscription required).

[106] Van Harten, *Public Law* (n 58) 180ff.

[107] Miles (n 95) 298ff; David Gantz, 'An Appellate Mechanism for Review of Arbitral Decisions in Investor-State Disputes: Prospects and Challenges' (2006) 39 Vand J Transnatl L 39, 54ff; ICSID Secretariat, 'Possible Improvements of the Framework for ICSID Arbitration', Discussion Paper (22 October 2004) 14ff, available at <https://icsid.worldbank.org/apps/ICSIDWEB/resources/Documents/Possible%20Improvements%20of%20the%20Framework%20of%20ICSID%20Arbitration.pdf> (last accessed on 15 September 2016).

[108] See, eg, Annex 10-F of the CAFTA or Annex 10-F of the US-Chile FTA; also Joel Beauvais, 'Regulatory Expropriations under NAFTA: Emerging Principles and Lingering Doubts' (2002) 10 NYU Environmental L J 245, 263.

[109] EU Commission, 'Commission proposes new Investment Court System for TTIP and other EU trade and investment negotiations' Press Release (16 September 2015) available at <http://europa.eu/rapid/press-release_IP-15-5651_en.htm> (last accessed on 15 September 2016); see also LE Peterson, 'Analysis: European Commission's newly released investment treaty model departs in significant ways from recently concluded Canada Pact' *IA Reporter* (17 September 2015) available at <http://www.iareporter.com> (subscription required).

[110] Gus Van Harten and others, 'Public Statement on the International Investment Regime' (31 August 2010) available at <http://www.osgoode.yorku.ca/public-statement-international-investment-regime-31-august-2010/> (last accessed on 15 September 2016). For a multilevel reform approach see Besson (n 16) 768ff.

[111] OECD, 'Transparency and Third Party Participation in Investor-State Dispute Settlement Procedures' OECD Working Papers on International Investment (OECD 2005) 1, available at <http://www.oecd.org/daf/inv/investment-policy/WP-2005_1.pdf>. Similar NAFTA Free Trade Commission, 'Recommendation on Non-disputing Party Participation' (7 October 2004) available at <http://www.sice.oas.org/tpd/nafta/Commission/Nondispute_e.pdf>. See also ICSID, 'Suggested Changes to the ICSID Rules and Regulations' Working Paper of the ICSID Secretariat (12 May 2005) available at <https://icsid.worldbank.org/apps/ICSIDWEB/resources/Documents/Suggested%20Changes%20to%20the%20ICSID%20Rules%20and%20Regulations.pdf> (all last accessed on 15 September 2016).

Arbitration Rules have thus introduced or are contemplating to introduce the possibility of accepting *amicus curiae* briefs from non-disputing parties and to allow public access to arbitral hearings if the parties so agree.[112]

Some commentators have however voiced doubts as to whether institutional and/or procedural reform alone, in the absence of normative reform, that is, the creation of a multilateral framework, will be sufficient to remediate the concerns.[113] Moreover, the prospects for far-reaching institutional and normative reforms are generally being seen in a rather dim light given the recent reluctance of States to engage in multilateral solutions and their growing preference for regional or bilateral trade and/or investment agreements.[114] This has more recently led some scholars to propound more 'system-internal' solutions by advocating for a greater recourse to the legal framework of global administrative law[115] or a comparative public law approach to international investment law.[116] As can be seen, the above proposals tend to focus either on procedural or on more substantive–'constitutionalist' approaches towards legitimacy.

As for proposals that call for a greater democratic legitimation of investment arbitration, it has already been pointed out that the traditional democratic legitimation theories may not be sufficient in the case of global governance institutions,[117] investor–state arbitration arguably being considered a global governance institution as the adjudication of these disputes may reach far into the domestic public sphere and social life similar to a domestic court.[118] The consent of a State to an IIA alone probably cannot be argued to provide sufficient legitimizing authority to cover for possible malfunctions of the arbitral system. This is so because on the one hand the mere consent by a democratic government to an IIA does not solve the problem of

[112] UNCTAD, 'Transparency' (n 105) 10; ICSID Rules of Procedure for Arbitration Proceedings, as amended 10 April 2006 (ICSID Arbitration Rules) Rules 32(2) and 37(2); UNCITRAL Arbitration Rules, as amended 15 August 2010, Art 28(3). See also the recent UNCITRAL Rules on Transparency in Treaty-Based Investor-State Arbitration (entered into force on 1 April 2014).

[113] See, eg, Asif Qureshi, 'An Appellate System in International Investment Arbitration?' in Peter Muchlinski, Federico Ortino, and Christoph Schreuer (eds), *Oxford Handbook of International Investment Law* (Oxford University Press 2008) 1154; Donald McRae, 'The WTO Appellate Body: A Model for an ICSID Appeals Facility?' (2010) 1 JIDS 371.

[114] See, eg, Schill, 'Enhancing International Investment Law's Legitimacy' (n 95) 69.

[115] Nico Krisch and Benedict Kingsbury, 'Global Governance and Global Administrative Law in the International Legal Order' (2006) 17 EJIL 1. See also Kingsbury and Schill (n 81) 44: 'Key global administrative law principles for investor–State tribunals obviously include good process, legality and freedom from bias or arbitrariness in the decision-making process. More difficult to attain, because they introduce delay and higher costs, but probably inevitable in the future, are provisions for adequate review of the work of tribunals by a trusted independent mechanism … Of independent significance for legitimacy … is the requirement that arbitral tribunals address the issues and give reasons for their decisions and awards'; similar Van Harten and Loughlin (n 39) 121. For a criticism of the global administrative law approach see Carol Harlow, 'Global Administrative Law: The Quest for Principles and Values' (2006) 17 EJIL 187, 207ff.

[116] Schill, 'Enhancing International Investment Laws Legitimacy' (n 95) 85, 88; same (ed), *International Investment Law and Comparative Public Law* (Oxford University Press 2011).

[117] Buchanan (n 18) 80.

[118] Armin von Bogdandy and Ingo Venzke, 'Beyond Dispute: International Judicial Institutions as Lawmakers' (2011) 12 Germ L J 979, 990.

power imbalances among negotiating states.[119] On the other hand, investor–state arbitrations also suffer from the problem of 'bureaucratic distance',[120] meaning that even though a consenting democratic government may in principle confer some legitimacy onto the institutions, these engage in ongoing governance activities and are based on treaties that usually last for many years without regular processes of supervision respectively democratic participation.[121]

This being said, the current quest by States to recover policy space can also be seen as an attempt to regain some democratic legitimacy: by (re-)extending their regulatory powers (for example by recourse to general exception clauses) or defining the relevant clauses (that is, of investor, investment, MFN, etc.) more restrictively, States constrain the adjudicatory authority of arbitral tribunals. By having restricted authority that does not touch, or at least touches less, upon essential public issues potentially affecting large constituencies, arbitral tribunals (and the IIAs upon which their jurisdiction is based) may be perceived as more legitimate because their function may be seen as having been brought back to a more 'private', or less intruding, nature of international dispute settlement. And ironically enough, even regulatory measures taken by a given host government in reaction to pressure by its domestic constituency (such as the cancelling of licenses in response to public protests against tariff increases by private providers of essential public services such as water, etc.),[122] though possibly in violation of investors' rights, may in certain situations arguably be considered as restoring some democratic legitimacy to the investment law system—though the motivation may be populist. As could lately be seen from mushrooming protest movements acting in the context of the (loosely called) euro crisis and related austerity measures, constituencies heading to the streets do increasingly have the power, by their pressure, to influence important regulatory decisions, sometimes more so than through the regular electoral processes.[123] The same can be said of well-organized civil society and pressure groups with very efficient means and methods of communication that increasingly manage to mobilize opposition to the conclusion of new free trade/investment agreements, as can be currently seen in Germany with respect to the ongoing TTIP negotiations.[124]

[119] Buchanan (n 18) 91; Buchanan and Keohane (n 81) 37. Obviously, the consent by an autocratic state is even more dubious in terms of legitimizing authority.

[120] Buchanan (n 18) 91.

[121] Buchanan (n 18) 91; Buchanan and Keohane (n 81) 37; Kingsbury and Schill (n 81) 42.

[122] See, eg, the so-called 'Cochabamba Water Wars' that led to the investment arbitration *Aguas del Tunarí v Bolivia* (n 71).

[123] See, eg, the massive popular opposition in Cyprus to the first version of the rescue package in which all domestic depositors would have had to contribute without prejudice to the European savings' guarantee, Nicolai Kwasniewski, 'Anger in Cyprus: They Can't Just Penalize Us Because of the Banks' *Spiegel Online* (19 March 2013) available at <http://www.spiegel.de/international/europe/anger-in-cyprus-over-euro-crisis-bank-levy-plan-a-889724.html>. On social mass protests in Bulgaria over skyrocketing energy bills (though this has not led to a withdrawal of operating licences), see G.K., 'Protesting about power prices' *The Economist* (15 February 2013) available at <http://www.economist.com/blogs/easternapproaches/2013/02/bulgarias-electricity-prices> (both last accessed on 15 September 2016).

[124] See, eg, TJ/GSW, 'Thousands protest in Berlin against industralized farming' *Deutsche Welle* (17 January 2015) available at <http://www.dw.de/thousands-protest-in-berlin-against-industrialized-farming/a-18198089> (last accessed on 15 September 2016). See also Stephan Schill, 'Editorial: The German Debate on International Investment Law' (2015) 16 JWIT 1.

Critiques based on efficiency-centred legitimacy approaches (such as output legitimacy or constitutionalist legitimacy theories) have so far been rather sparse in the academic investment contributions. It could probably be argued that efficiency is rather high in investment arbitration, in particular in terms of expertise of the persons involved, though high costs and potentially long durations of the proceedings may somewhat invalidate this assessment.[125] This being said, it seems that criticism of factors of input legitimacy, namely the lack of transparency and the bias reproach, are prevalent.

2.3.2.3 Legitimacy concerns and treaty shopping

This leads us to the question: which legitimacy concerns may be triggered by the practice of treaty shopping?

Legitimacy concerns with respect to the public–private divide apply to the same extent to the practice of treaty shopping. They possibly even apply to a higher extent, as treaty shopping may make it easier for a claimant to challenge a State's regulatory authority in what may be essential public issues, as was the case in the recent investment treaty arbitration against Australia concerning the plain-packaging measures.[126]

Legitimacy concerns with respect to textual indeterminacy of IIA clauses also apply with respect to the practice of treaty shopping, the vagueness of treaty clauses being after all one of the main reasons for inconsistent interpretations. Inconsistent interpretations of treaty shopping-relevant notions may arguably further the practice of treaty shopping, as claimants may be tempted to 'push for limits' of treaty interpretation.

With respect to the confidential nature of investment arbitration, no legitimacy concerns seem to arise in the case of treaty shopping, the latter being a legal operation that is in any case performed before a potential proceeding has started. In a similar vein, though interpretations that recognize as sole object and purpose of an IIA the protection of the investor can result in decisions that condone certain forms of treaty shopping, arbitrator bias arguably does not seem to be a (systemic) legitimacy concern with respect to treaty shopping.[127]

In all of the afore-mentioned legitimacy concerns, States, it is submitted, play a primary role in remediating these concerns. As 'masters of the treaties', they have the power (and have started)[128] to restore 'interpretative sovereignty' by including in newly negotiated investment treaties more narrowly defined clauses and clarifications that leave less room for overly broad interpretations, thereby enhancing consistency and predictability of treaty interpretations[129] and taking the focus away

[125] On the cost argument see below at 2.3.3.

[126] See *Philip Morris Asia Limited v Commonwealth of Australia*, UNCITRAL, PCA Case No 2012-12, Award on Jurisdiction and Admissibility (17 December 2015) (redacted version).

[127] See also Chapter 9, at 9.3.4.

[128] See more in detail Chapter 8.

[129] Similar Brower and Schill, 'Is Arbitration a Threat or a Boon' (n 99) 474.

from the arbitrator bias reproach. By excluding certain regulatory matters from investment protection or otherwise recovering policy space, States may also counter the legitimacy critiques arising from the fact that an essentially private proceeding has the potential to intrude far into public regulatory matters.

2.3.3 Sustainable development

Another potential policy concern that has more recently started to get increased attention in international investment law is linked to the notion of sustainable development. The origins of the notion of sustainable development may be found in the 'Brundtland Report', which defined it as 'development that meets the needs of the present without compromising the ability of future generations to meet their own needs'.[130] Sustainable development has been the explicit objective in dozens of binding and non-binding international instruments ever since.[131] Its content is multi-faceted and has traditionally been understood as including three intersecting core areas: economic development, social development (including the respect for human rights), and environmental protection, with different instruments putting different emphases.[132] More recently, the United Nations adopted the 'Sustainable Development Goals', a set of seventeen overarching, cross-cutting objectives reaching from poverty reduction, more equitable access to food, health, education, and work to gender equality, 'green' energy, conservation of the environment, rule of law and the increasing role of public–private partnerships.[133]

As concerns international investment law, sustainable development is an objective that is increasingly taken into account and included in the negotiation of new investment agreements.[134] According to UNCTAD's recent research into the matter, the goal of sustainable development implies that:

> A treaty should (i) promote and protect those investments that are conducive to host-country development; (ii) provide treatment and protection guarantees to investors without hindering the government's power to regulate in the public interest (e.g. for environmental, public health

[130] Gro Brundtland, *Our Common Future: The Report of the World Commission on Environment and Development* (Oxford University Press 1987) ix.

[131] Markus Gehring and Andrew Newcombe, 'Introduction to Sustainable Development in World Investment Law' in Marie-Claire Cordonier Segger, Markus Gehring, and Andrew Newcombe (eds), *Sustainable Development in World Investment Law* (Kluwer Law International 2011) 4–5; see also UNCTAD, 'World Investment Report 2012—Towards a New Generation of Investment Policies' (United Nations 2012) 106–07, available at <http://unctad.org/en/PublicationsLibrary/wir2012_embargoed_en.pdf> (last accessed on 15 September 2016).

[132] Gehring and Newcombe (n 131) 6–8; see, eg, International Law Association, 'New Delhi Declaration on the Principles of International Law Related to Sustainable Development' (London, ILA 2002).

[133] See <https://sustainabledevelopment.un.org/sdgs> (last accessed on 15 September 2016).

[134] For the EU see, eg, European Commission, 'Communication, Towards a comprehensive European international investment policy' (n 49) 2, according to which investment policy is to contribute to the 'objectives of smart, sustainable and inclusive growth, as set out in the Europe 2020 strategy', and in 9: 'A common investment policy should also be guided by the principles and objectives of the Union's external action more generally, including the promotion of the rule of law, human rights and sustainable development (Art 205 TFEU and Art 21 TEU).' See also European Parliament, 'Resolution

or safety purposes); (iii) not overexpose a country to costly litigation and the risk of exorbitant financial liabilities; and (iv) stimulate responsible business practices by investors.[135]

In particular with respect to the a.m. policy requirement that an IIA should not overexpose a country to costly litigation and the risk of exorbitant financial liabilities, it seems arguable that concerns may arise. Investment arbitration usually generates very high defence costs.[136] Not only is a respondent State well advised to engage a highly specialized law firm if it wants to stand a chance to fend off claims (as claimants also are usually represented by highly specialized counsels). Specialized counsels' hourly fees go up to USD 1000, with full teams of lawyers usually working on the case that may take years before it comes to a conclusion (be it by settlement or by award respectively annulment proceedings).[137] Further costs to be borne by the parties (without prejudice to a cost decision imposing all costs on one particular party)[138] include the fees and expenses of the members of the arbitral tribunal and of experts, expenses incurred by the parties and in the case of ICSID proceedings, the charges for the use of the ICSID facilities.[139] Defence costs may quickly go into the millions of dollars,[140] and obviously multiply in the case of multiple proceedings. Thus, the survey conducted by the OECD Public Consultation shows that 'legal and arbitration costs for the parties in recent ISDS cases have averaged over USD 8 million with costs exceeding USD 30 million in some cases'.[141]

Money from the public treasury that has to be used for the defence of investment claims is money that may be missing for the implementation of policies in line with the objective of sustainable development, in particular in the case of claims for sovereign debt restructuring, where countries try to ward off bankruptcy. This affects not

of 6 April 2011 on the future European international investment policy' (2010/2203(INI)) para 27: 'Stresses that the EU's future policy must also promote investment which is sustainable, respects the environment (particularly in the area of extractive industries) and encourages good quality working conditions in the enterprises targeted by the investment; asks the Commission to include, in all future agreements, a reference to the updated OECD Guidelines for Multinational Enterprises', available at <http://www.europarl.europa.eu/sides/getDoc.do?pubRef=-//EP//TEXT+TA+P7-TA-2011-0141+0+DOC+XML+V0//EN>. Similar OECD, *Guidelines for Multinational Enterprises* (2011 Edition) 19: 'A. Enterprises should: 1. Contribute to economic, environmental and social progress with a view to achieving sustainable development', available at <http://www.oecd.org/daf/inv/mne/48004323.pdf> (all last accessed on 15 September 2016).

135 UNCTAD, 'WIR 2012' (n 131) 89.

136 Wouters and Hachez (n 101) 620.

137 Gaukrodger and Gordon (n 25) 20.

138 See more generally David Smith, 'Shifting Sands: Cost-and-Fee Allocation in International Investment Arbitration' (2010–2011) 51 Va J Intl L 749.

139 See, eg, Arts 59, 60(1), 61(2) ICSID Convention and Administrative and Financial Provisions, Chapter III, Regulations 14–19. For recent cost allocation decisions see, eg, *Deutsche Bank AG v Democratic Socialist Republic of Sri Lanka*, ICSID Case No ARB/09/2, Award (31 October 2012) paras 588–90; *Bosh International Inc and B&P Ltd Foreign Investment Enterprise v Ukraine*, ICSID Case No ARB/08/11, Award (25 October 2012) paras 291–92; *ICS Inspection and Control Services Limited (United Kingdom) v The Republic of Argentina*, UNCITRAL, PCA Case No 2010-9, Award on Jurisdiction (10 February 2012) para 340.

140 For the case of Argentina see, eg, Gaukrodger and Gordon (n 25) 19; LE Peterson, 'Argentina by the numbers: where things stand with investment treaty claims arising out of the Argentine financial crisis' *IA Reporter* (1 February 2011) available at <http://www.iareporter.com> (subscription required).

141 Gaukrodger and Gordon (n 25) 19. It is also noteworthy that fees and expenses incurred for legal counsel and experts are estimated to account for about 82 per cent of the total costs of a case, Gaukrodger and Gordon (n 25) 19; for a slightly lower estimation see UNCTAD, 'Investor-State Disputes: Prevention

exclusively, but in particular developing countries. Developing countries have so far also been the majority of Respondents in investor–State dispute settlement cases.[142] Though the problem of high defence costs is a general concern for developing countries, it seems arguable that treaty shopping may be an exacerbating factor in that it makes it easier for claimants to either bring a claim against the host State at all or to bring it on more favourable terms. In either case, however, the host State is more easily exposed to costly litigation, and even if the arbitral tribunal dismisses the claim based on treaty shopping on jurisdictional grounds, it usually does not—absent a finding of abuse of process or fraud—allocate Respondent's incurred costs onto the claimant.[143]

The same argument can arguably be made with respect to the damage awards, though as a caveat it should also be pointed out that the objective of sustainable development cannot be used to justify confirmed violations of investor rights. This being said, Respondent countries (and their taxpayers) may start to consider the total costs of investment arbitration (costs plus potential damage awards) as prohibitive and thus ever more illegitimate,[144] being based not only on what they may consider awards rendered by way of a dispute settlement procedure presenting legitimacy concerns,[145] but also in that taxpayers' money has to be used to satisfy damage awards where this money could be badly needed for social or environmental purposes, or where, especially in the case of sovereign debt restructuring, the population has to support harsh austerity measures and cuts into social budgets.[146] In such a situation, perceptions of illegitimacy may become ever more accentuated if the claimant obtains the award by way of treaty shopping.[147]

and Alternatives to Arbitration', UNCTAD Series on International Investment Policies for Development (United Nations 2010) 17, available at <http://unctad.org/en/Docs/diaeia200911_en.pdf> (last accessed on 15 September 2016), putting the average at about 60 per cent of the total costs.

142 Anne Joubin-Bret, Marie-Estelle Rey, and Jörg Weber, 'International Investment Law and Development' in Marie-Claire Cordonier Segger, Markus Gehring, and Andrew Newcombe (eds), *Sustainable Development in World Investment Law* (Kluwer Law International 2011) 18: 'ISDS cases have been launched against 74 countries from all regions, with Argentina topping the list (with 51 claims lodged against it). Other respondent countries include Mexico (with 19 claims), the Czech Republic (16), Ecuador (15), Canada, Ukraine, and the United States (14 each), Venezuela (11), Egypt and Poland (8 cases each), India (9), Kazakhstan, the Russian Federation and Turkey (8 each). As many as 90% of known disputes were initiated by firms headquartered in developed countries'. See also UNCTAD, 'World Investment Report 2015—Reforming International Investment Governance' (United Nations 2015) 115, available at <http://unctad.org/en/PublicationsLibrary/wir2015_en.pdf> (last accessed on 15 September 2016).

143 See also Chapter 9, at 9.5.

144 Similar Susan Franck, 'Rationalizing Costs in Investment Treaty Arbitration' (2010–2011) 88 Wash U L Rev 769, 774.

145 As concerns the 'public–private divide' and transparency concerns, see above at 2.3.2.2.

146 In this sense also Gaukrodger and Gordon (n 25) 23: '[T]he States that are Respondents in ISDS cases are accountable to their citizens regarding whether or not such expenditures are a good use of public funds.'

147 See, eg, the legitimacy argument made by Inna Uchkunova, 'Drawing a Line: Corporate Restructuring and Treaty Shopping in ICSID Arbitration' *Kluwer Arbitration Blog* (6 March 2013) available at <http://kluwerarbitrationblog.com/blog/2013/03/06/drawing-a-line-corporate-restructuring-and-treaty-shopping-in-icsid-arbitration/> (last accessed on 15 September 2016): 'I am looking into this question with the eyes of a tax-payer and—more importantly—of a citizen of Europe's poorest country [Bulgaria]. *I am therefore arguing that treaty-shopping in the above described situation amounts to abuse of process* and thus an ICSID tribunal will lack jurisdiction to consider the claim'; though that author's implicit conclusion that from the (perceived) illegitimacy of the potential damage by way of treaty shopping award follows the finding of abuse of process cannot be adhered to by this author.

2.3.4 Regulatory chill

It has also been argued that treaty shopping may lead to so-called regulatory chill in that the threat of investment arbitration—which may be heightened through the practice of treaty shopping—may prevent host governments from introducing domestic legislation because it may adversely affect the economic value of a foreign investment and thus raise the risk of investment claims.[148] The argument goes that in particular for those countries whose domestic regulatory framework in crucial areas (such as health, human rights, environmental protection, etc.) was weak at the time of concluding investment treaties, the threat of potentially looming investment arbitration may generate a chilling effect. This, according to these authors, would be compounded by the fact that international law hardly imposes any legally binding ('hard law') obligations on legal persons, creating a so-called governance gap.[149]

Whether the threat of investment arbitration causes regulatory chill remains a controversial question. Some authors deny any evidence of the causation of regulatory chill by the (perceived) threat of investment arbitration.[150] Others acknowledge that the current state of research has not yet come up with empirical results showing a correlation between investment arbitration and the occurrence of regulatory chill, without for that matter excluding this possibility.[151] A recent PhD study on the question of the impact of investment treaties on national regulatory autonomy comes to the conclusion that overall:

> The empirical evidence does not support the hypothesis on regulatory chill ... [though] there are some findings which raise the possibility of influence by IIA ISDS cases on the regulatory development process or trends in regulation ...[152]

[148] Van Os and Knottnerus (n 25) 12–13.

[149] Human Rights Council, 'Protect Respect and Remedy: a Framework for Business and Human Rights: Report of Special Representative of the Secretary-General on the issue of human rights and transnational corporations and other business enterprises, John Ruggie' (2011) UN Doc A/HRC/8/5, 3: 'The root cause of the business and human rights predicament today lies in the governance gaps created by globalization—between the scope and impact of economic forces and actors, and the capacity of societies to manage their adverse consequences. These governance gaps provide the permissive environment for wrongful acts by companies of all kinds without adequate sanctioning or reparation' quoted in Van Os and Knottnerus (n 25) 13. But see on counterclaims by host States Yaraslau Kryvoi, 'Counterclaims in Investor-State Arbitration' LSE Legal Studies Working Paper (5 August 2011) No 08/2011, available at <http://papers.ssrn.com/sol3/papers.cfm?abstract_id=1891935> (last accessed on 15 September 2016), arguing that contrary to conventional wisdom, counterclaims in investor–State arbitration are possible and are being done, even though it may be difficult to 'pierce the corporate veil' of the often undercapitalized local subsidiaries to reach the parent company.

[150] See, eg, Stephan Schill, 'Do investment treaties chill unilateral State regulation to mitigate climate change?' (2007) 24 J Intl Arb 469, 477; Julie Soloway and Chris Hollefson, 'NAFTA's Chapter 11: Investment protection, integration and the public interest' (2003) 9 Choices 1, 18, available at <http://www.envireform.utoronto.ca/conference/nov2002/tollefson-soloway.pdf> (last accessed on 15 September 2016).

[151] Sam Luttrell and Romesh Weeramantry, 'Submission in respect of the Trade and Foreign Investment (Protecting the Public Interest) Bill 2014' 6, available at <http://globalarbitrationreview.com/cdn/files/gar/articles/Submission_in_respect_of_the_Trade_and_Foreign_Investment_Protecting_the_Public.pdf> (last accessed on 15 September 2016).

[152] Christine Côté, *A Chilling Effect? The impact of international investment agreements on national regulatory autonomy in the areas of health, safety and the environment*, Doctoral thesis, London School of Economics (February 2014) 16, available at <http://etheses.lse.ac.uk/897/8/Cote_A_Chilling_%20Effect.pdf> (last accessed on 15 September 2016).

The difficulty lies of course in how to measure regulatory chill, as regulators may have many motives in retracting from a planned domestic regulatory measure, and even if they indeed do so in view of a perceived threat of investment arbitration, they are not likely to admit this publicly.[153] Yet, there may be cases in which the (perceived) threat of investment arbitration plays a preponderant role in chilling governmental regulatory action. Thus, planned tobacco restrictions in Canada both in 1994 and 2001 were allegedly thwarted because of threats by the tobacco industry to bring claims under NAFTA Chapter 11.[154] On the other hand, Australia did not retract from its plan to introduce them, to that date the toughest anti-tobacco legislation on earth, despite considerable pressure from the tobacco lobby beforehand and an (at the time already pending and in the meantime dismissed) investment arbitration against Uruguay based on similar grounds.[155] Instead, Australia announced its intention to abandon ISDS in future IIAs.[156] Though many States and public health stakeholders welcomed the dismissal of the claim against Australia on jurisdictional grounds, it remains to be seen in how far other States will be willing to enact similarly harsh anti-tobacco laws, which might expose them to similar investment claims.[157]

Based on these two examples, it would be difficult to claim that only developing countries may fall prey to the (perceived) threat of regulatory chill (if it exists), though it seems equally true that the less legal expertise and financial capacity a country has to fend off potential investment claims, the more likely its decision to withdraw a planned or existing domestic regulatory measure may be influenced by the (perceived) threat of arbitration.[158] Likewise, a government may back off in the face of looming investment arbitration, as it may not. This may depend on a host of motives and grounds. Yet, it does seem arguable that a country having negotiated in the past treaty shopping-permissive IIAs (and possibly being threatened with an investment claim) might consider a given regulatory measure twice before enacting it.

2.3.5 Lack of a 'level-playing' field

A further concern that has been voiced is that treaty shopping jeopardizes the 'level-playing field' between domestic and foreign investors in that foreign investors, through the possibility to access investment arbitration by recourse to treaty

[153] Kyle Tienhaara, 'Regulatory Chill and the Threat of Arbitration' in Chester Brown and Kate Miles (eds), *Evolution in Investment Treaty Law and Arbitration* (Cambridge University Press 2011) 606, 608.

[154] Ibid, 617 (FN 43).

[155] *Philip Morris Brands Sàrl, Philip Morris Products SA and Abal Hermanos SA v Oriental Republic of Uruguay*, ICSID Case No ARB/10/7, Award (8 July 2016) (formerly *FTR Holding SA, Philip Morris Products SA and Abal Hermanos SA v Oriental Republic of Uruguay*).

[156] Though it has been implementing this policy only in a selective way, see Chapter 8, at 8.1.3.

[157] In this sense also Côté (n 152) 194. Though the recent dismissal of the claim by Philip Morris against Uruguay's tobacco control measures on the merits (based on the customary law right to regulate) might encourage other States to enact similar measures.

[158] Tienhaara (n 153) 611–13. Similar Côté (n 152) 198–200.

shopping, are placed in a better position than domestic investors.[159] This is an argument that is reminiscent of the Calvo Doctrine, as Alvarez also points out:

> There is now considerable sympathy, including among members of the US Congress, for the Calvo-inspired notion that foreign investors should get no more favourable treatment than that accorded to national enterprises ... US policy-makers should be worried about: 1. Forum shopping [*sic*] by foreign investors. Stumberg points out that the US has a BIT with Panama and that Panama is seeking to become the legal domicile of companies because it is a tax haven. He suggests that companies may use their Panamanian operations to challenge domestic regulations in the US.[160]

This may seem ironic, after all, the US (and other Western capital-exporting States) had traditionally been fierce opponents to the Calvo Doctrine. It fits however well into the current trend, already described further above,[161] of host States recovering policy space and trying to curb resort to investor–State dispute settlement among others through the return of the local remedies requirement.[162]

Yet, the question may be asked whether it is really domestic investors that are now disadvantaged vis-à-vis foreign investors. After all, it is—in the absence of a restriction—precisely the practice of 'corporate nationality planning' that may make investor–State arbitration accessible also to domestic investors, if the corporate structuring is done in an anticipated, 'upstream' manner.[163] More than the dichotomy 'domestic–foreign investor', it seems it is the dichotomy 'small and medium enterprises (SME)-multinational companies (MNC)' that is at stake when discussing a 'level-playing field' in international investment law. This is so because first, the practice of treaty shopping by corporate structuring works best in case of a sufficiently large corporate structure potentially stretching over various countries. This tends to exclude, or at the very least seems to make it more difficult, for small or very small businesses to benefit from the practice of treaty shopping.[164] Secondly, both the corporate structuring advice and the bringing of an investment claim are cost-intensive as highly specialized advice is needed, making it more likely for MNCs than for SMEs to have the necessary financial resources.[165]

[159] See Gaukrodger and Gordon (n 25) 57.

[160] Testimony by Prof. Stumberg, Hearing on Investment Protection in US Trade and Investment Agreements, 34, available at <http://www.gpo.gov/fdsys/pkg/CHRG-111hhrg53473/pdf/CHRG-111hhrg53473.pdf> (last accessed on 15 September 2016).

[161] See Chapter 1, at 1.2.1.

[162] Christoph Schreuer, 'Calvo's Grandchildren: The Return of Local Remedies in Investment Arbitration' (2005) 4 LPICT 1; Wenhua Shan, 'From "North-South Divide" to "Private-Public Debate": Revival of the Calvo Doctrine and the Changing Landscape of International Investment Law' (2006–2007) 27 Nw J Intl L & Bus 631; Bernardo Cremades, 'Resurgence of the Calvo Doctrine in Latin America' (2006) 7 Bus L Intl 53.

[163] See, eg, *Tokios Tokelés v Ukraine*, ICSID Case No ARB/02/18, Decision on Jurisdiction (29 April 2004).

[164] Gaukrodger and Gordon (n 25) 17–18: 'Small investors can be ISDS claimants ... the survey shows that 22% of the claimants in both ICSID and UNCITRAL cases are either individuals or very small corporations with limited foreign operations (one or two projects) ... Medium or large multinational enterprises account for about half of the total sample'.

[165] Though not impossible, see Gaukrodger and Gordon (n 25) 23: 'High costs may preclude access to justice for small and medium investors (although the OECD survey of investor-claimants presented in section II.A suggests that this is not the case).'

2.4 Preliminary Conclusions

The above analysis suggests that while the principle of sovereign consent of States seems to warrant, at least at the outset, a permissive stance towards the practice of treaty shopping, several important policy concerns may arise.

It has been seen that reciprocity is a multifaceted notion and in the case of international investment law functions in a different, less strict manner than in other fields of public international law, due mainly to the specificities of international investment law (in particular the direct right of the investor to sue the host State) and the fact that it is largely left to the IIA-negotiating States to determine the scope of reciprocity in their treaty relations. However, the (unqualified) claim that treaty shopping violates the principle of reciprocity is an inadequate reduction of the complexity of this notion and cannot be upheld in this generality.

The most prevalent of the discussed policy concerns are arguably legitimacy concerns, in particular with respect to the so-called public–private divide. Indeed, treaty shopping may make it easier for a claimant to challenge a State's regulatory authority in what may be essential public issues, as could also be seen in the recent investment arbitration against Australia concerning tobacco control measures. Yet, important questions also arise with respect to the policy objective of sustainable development because of the high costs usually caused in order to defend against an investment claim. Finally, the threat of regulatory chill through the practice of treaty shopping seems arguable, though more difficult to prove, while a lack of 'level-playing field' arises in this author's opinion more likely between small/medium-sized and multinational companies than between domestic and foreign investors.

PART II

SYSTEMATIC APPROACHES TO THE VALIDITY OF A CLAIM INVOLVING TREATY SHOPPING

As treaty shopping (or the strategic use or change of nationality) aims primarily at passing the first hurdle in an investment arbitral proceeding, namely the tribunal's decision on its own jurisdiction, this is where the question of the validity of the treaty shopping will first and foremost be 'fought'.

Approaches to this question have in recent years seen an increasing legal refinement, due in part to the rapid increase in investor–State arbitrations and ever more highly specialized investment counsels seeking 'innovative strategies and counter-strategies' in litigating claims or defending against them.[1] There are thus a number of possible objections that Respondents may direct against an instance of treaty shopping.

Depending on the facts of the case and the framing of the questions, the question of validity of the strategic use or change of nationality may be broached from a jurisdictional angle, namely the eligibility of the investor as a covered national under the invoked investment agreement(s) (*ratione personae*), the scope of protection offered to the investment (*ratione materiae*), and/or the temporal scope of protection offered to the investor and its investment (*ratione temporis*). Increasingly, tribunals also treat the question of the validity of a strategic use or change of nationality from the angle of the prohibition of an abuse of rights/abuse of process.

Given these differing 'themes' of objections which, for the question of treaty shopping, each present different legal problems and are sometimes more, sometimes less settled, this author has chosen to adopt the same differentiation in examining the arbitral jurisprudence on the validity of treaty shopping, with the aim of rendering the analysis more systematic and in this way facilitate a better understanding of where the unsettled legal questions nowadays lie and how these could be responded to.

[1] Pierre-Emmanuel Dupont, 'The Notion of ICSID Investment: Ongoing Confusion or Emerging Synthesis' (2011) 12 JWIT 246, 248.

To this end, Chapter 3 will begin by analysing the (customary) international law of diplomatic protection as relevant for the question of changes of nationality. Investment arbitral tribunals, when having to decide on whether specific instances of a strategic use or change of nationality are valid or not, are often asked to determine whether certain leading cases referring to customary international law such as the ICJ *Nottebohm* or *Barcelona Traction* cases can be applied in the investment context. The question thus naturally arises whether the approaches taken by these courts and tribunals are, or should be, in any way influential for how investment arbitral tribunals are treating the issue of treaty shopping. Chapter 3 will thus first do a stocktaking of the customary international law position.

Chapters 4, 5, and 6 will then analyse investment arbitral jurisprudence on the legal issues and problems that usually arise with respect to the jurisdiction *ratione personae, ratione materiae*, or *ratione temporis* respectively, while Chapter 7 will assess the arbitral jurisprudence on the question of validity of treaty shopping by recourse to the abuse of rights/abuse of process doctrine.

The preliminary findings closing each chapter will form the basis of the review, in Part III, of how States may counter treaty shopping through more careful treaty drafting and which role the principle of good faith plays in the determination of whether a strategic use or change of nationality constitutes a 'legitimate nationality planning' or 'abusive treaty shopping'.

3

The Customary International Law Relative to Changes of Nationality

3.1 Introduction

As has been seen in Chapter 1, the practice of treaty shopping presupposes the deliberate decision of the investor to structure or restructure his investment vehicle in a particular way, or rather in a particular jurisdiction in order to come under the protection of another investment treaty thought to be more favourable in procedural and/or substantive terms.[1] Treaty shopping is thus aimed at a strategic use or change of nationality and the concept of nationality is a cardinal notion for these purposes.[2] Though this diversity of nationality is understandably more easily achieved in the case of legal persons, being creatures of law that can be (relatively easily) established and dissolved,[3] it is not completely excluded that natural persons strategically change nationality or invoke dual nationalities trying to obtain better legal protection.[4]

International tribunals have rendered several leading decisions dealing with the change of nationality and its effect under international law, as will be examined in turn.

3.2 The Concept of Nationality

International tribunals have been seized early on with respect to the question of how to regulate the 'international law of nationality', nationality being, as one commentator defines, 'the link between the individual and his or her state as

[1] See Chapter 1, at 1.1.1.

[2] Similar Campbell McLachlan, Laurence Shore, and Matthew Weiniger, *International Investment Arbitration-Substantive Principles* (Oxford University Press 2007) para 5.01.

[3] But see for the contrary opinion Maurice Mendelson, 'Runaway Train: The Continuous Nationality Rule from the *Panevezys-Saldutiskis Railway Case* to *Lowen*' in Todd Weiler (ed), *International Investment Law and Arbitration: Leading Cases* (Cameron May 2005) 97, 130.

[4] Robert Sloane, 'Breaking the Genuine Link: The Contemporary International Legal Regulation of Nationality' (2009) 50 Harv Intl L J 1, 40–42.

regards particular benefits and obligations. It is also the vital link between the individual and the benefits of international law'.[5] The reference to international law makes clear that questions of nationality arise often in the realm of diplomatic protection.[6]

At the same time, nationality is an inherently domestic legal concept. As the Permanent Court of International Justice (PCIJ) held in *Nationality Decrees Issued in Tunis and Morocco*:

> The question whether a certain matter is or is not solely within the jurisdiction of a State is an essentially relative question; it depends upon the development of international relations. Thus, in the present state of international law, questions of nationality are, in the opinion of the Court, in principle within this reserved domain.[7]

This principle has also been codified by the 1930 Hague Convention on Certain Questions Relating to the Conflict of Nationality Laws.[8] The European Convention on Nationality of the Council of Europe, dealing with nationality of natural persons, equally contains this principle.[9]

This does not mean, however, that international law may not set any limits as to the conferment of nationality by domestic law. This is particularly so in case of multiple nationalities. Indeed, any State is free to establish the connecting factors required for conferring its nationality on a given individual according to its domestic law. From the principle of sovereign equality of States thus follows that international law may not prohibit multiple nationalities in principle nor invalidate a nationality validly conferred under domestic law.[10] However, the conferment of nationality having potential (extraterritorial) legal effects with respect to other States, these States are not under all circumstances required to recognize the nationality in question (so-called principle of opposability),[11] as will be seen in turn.

International jurisprudence has established differing criteria in this respect for natural and legal persons.

[5] Malcolm Shaw, *International Law* (Cambridge University Press, 6th edn 2008) 808.

[6] See above Chapter 1, at 1.2.2; see also *Nottebohm (Liechtenstein v Guatemala) (Judgment)* [1955] ICJ Rep 4, 46 (Dissenting Opinion Judge Read): 'Nationality and diplomatic protection are closely inter-related. The general rule of international law is that nationality gives rise to a right of diplomatic protection.'

[7] *Nationality Decrees Issued in Tunis and Morocco (Advisory Opinion)* [1923] PCIJ Series B No 4, 7, 24; Ian Brownlie, *Principles of Public International Law* (Oxford University Press, 5th edn 2008) 383.

[8] See Convention on Certain Questions Relating to the Conflict of Nationality Laws (signed on 12 April 1930) 179 LNTS 89 [Hague Convention] (entered into force on 1 July 1937), Art 2.

[9] European Convention on Nationality (signed on 6 November 1997) 37 ILM 44 (entered into force on 1 March 2000), Art 3(1).

[10] Robert Jennings and Arthur Watts (eds), *Oppenheim's International Law*, Vol I Peace, Parts 2 to 4 (Longman, 9th edn 1996) para 378; similar Sange Addison-Agyei, *Nationality Planning und Treaty Shopping im Internationalen Investitionsrecht* (Frankfurt aM, Peter Lang 2012) 21.

[11] See Art 3(2) of the European Convention on Nationality: 'This law shall be accepted by other States in so far as it is consistent with applicable international conventions, customary international law and the principles of law generally recognized with regard to nationality.'

3.2.1 Natural persons

As regards natural persons, the paradigmatic case as to the question of whether a Respondent State must recognize a nationality of a natural person conferred by another State is the *Nottebohm* case decided by the International Court of Justice (ICJ).

3.2.1.1 Nottebohm *case*

In the *Nottebohm* case,[12] the ICJ had to decide whether Guatemala had to recognize the Liechtenstein nationality of Friedrich Nottebohm, a German national by birth, but having lived in Guatemala for decades. Nottebohm had in fact acquired Liechtenstein nationality under 'exceptional circumstances of speed and accommodation'[13] and renounced on his German nationality in October 1939 after the outbreak of the Second World War in order to evade the consequences of treatment as an enemy alien in Guatemala,[14] where he had been living since 1905 and building up his business. When Guatemala aligned itself with the Allies, Nottebohm, despite his Liechtenstein nationality, was eventually detained and expelled from Guatemala, was interned in the United States until the end of the war and his property in Guatemala seized and retained without compensation. Liechtenstein thus sought compensation for the damages caused to Nottebohm by the acts of the government of Guatemala.

The court, in having to decide upon the admissibility of the claim, reconfirmed the PCIJ's holding in *Nationality Decrees*, according to which:

> It is for Liechtenstein, as it is for every sovereign State, to settle by its own legislation the rules relating to the acquisition of its nationality, and to confer that nationality by naturalization granted by its own organs in accordance with that legislation. It is not necessary to determine whether international law imposes any limitations on its freedom of decision in this domain. Furthermore, nationality has its most immediate, its most far-reaching and, for most people, its only effect within the legal system of the State conferring it. Nationality serves above all to determine that the person upon whom it is conferred enjoys the rights and is bound by the obligations which the law of the State in question grants to or imposes on its nationals.[15]

However, this principle, according to the court, has to be distinguished from the question 'whether the act [the naturalization of Nottebohm] has the international effect here under consideration'.[16] After examining prior international jurisprudence and academic writings in the matter, the ICJ went on to state:

> Nationality is a legal bond having as its basis a social fact of attachment, a genuine connection of existence, interests and sentiments, together with the existence of reciprocal rights

[12] *Nottebohm* (n 6). [13] *Nottebohm* (n 6) 26.

[14] But critical on the Court's appraisal of Nottebohm's motive see *Nottebohm* (n 6) 48–49 (Dissenting Opinion Judge Read).

[15] *Nottebohm* (n 6) 20. [16] *Nottebohm* (n 6) 21.

and duties. It may be said to constitute the juridical expression of the fact that the individual upon whom it is conferred, either directly by the law or as the result of an act of the authorities, is in fact more closely connected with the population of the State conferring nationality than with that of any other State. Conferred by a State, it only entitles that State to exercise protection vis-à-vis another State, if it constitutes a translation into juridical terms of the individual's connection with the State which has made him its national.[17]

On this basis, the court found the 'genuine link', required for being able to oppose the Liechtenstein nationality to Guatemala, to be lacking, thereby dismissing Liechtenstein's claim.

3.2.1.2 Discussion

The *Nottebohm* judgment has not found unanimous agreement. Though there are scholars who embraced the findings of the ICJ,[18] numerous were those who underlined the lack of legal precedent of the application of a genuine or effective link requirement to the case of a single nationality as opposed to the case of dual nationality (for which indeed some judicial support could be found and which is now codified in Article 7 of the International Law Commission (ILC) Draft Articles on Diplomatic Protection).[19] It seems thus correct to make the difference as to whether single or dual nationalities are engaged.

Later jurisprudence appears to confirm the afore-said. Thus, the arbitral tribunal in *Flegenheimer* (decided only three years after *Nottebohm*) rejected the application of the 'genuine link' theory to the case of a single nationality.[20] On the other hand, the decision of the Iran–US Claims Tribunal in *Case No A/18* endorsed the *Nottebohm* holding and found that it only had jurisdiction over those claims brought by dual Iranian–US nationals 'when the dominant and effective nationality of the claimant during the relevant period from the date the claim arose until 19 January 1981 was that of the [non-Respondent] State'.[21] *Case No A/18* can thus

[17] *Nottebohm* (n 6) 23. [18] See, eg, Brownlie (n 7) 407–18.

[19] See, eg, Sloane (n 4) 15–16; *Nottebohm* (n 6) 42 (Dissenting Opinion Judge Read): 'It is noteworthy that, apart from the cases of double nationality, no instance has been cited to the Court in which a State has successfully refused to recognize that nationality, lawfully conferred and maintained, did not give rise to a right of diplomatic protection.' Similar *Nottebohm* (n 6) 59 (Dissenting Opinion Judge ad hoc Guggenheim); Chittharanjan Amerasinghe, *Diplomatic Protection* (Oxford University Press 2008) 95. For legal precedents of the 'genuine link' theory in the case of dual nationality see, eg, *Canavero (Italy v Peru)* (1912) 11 RIAA 397; *Baron Frédéric de Born v Yugoslav State* (1926) 4 Ann Dig 277. See also Art 5 of The Hague Convention: 'Without prejudice to the application of its law in matters of personal status and of any conventions in force, a third State shall, of the nationalities which any such person possesses, recognise exclusively in its territory either the nationality of the country in which he is habitually and principally resident, or the nationality of the country with which in the circumstances he appears to be in fact most closely connected.'

[20] *Flegenheimer (Italy-United States)* (1958) 14 RIAA 327, 377: 'when a person is vested with only one nationality, which is attributed to him or her either *jure sanguinis* or *jure soli*, or by a valid naturalization entailing the positive loss of the former nationality, the theory of effective nationality cannot be applied without the risk of causing confusion. It lacks a sufficiently positive basis to be applied to a nationality which finds support in a State law.' For further analysis see, eg, Florian Franke, *Der personelle Anwendungsbereich des internationalen Investitionsschutzrechts* (Nomos 2012) 101ff.

[21] *Case No A/18*, Case No DEC 32-A18-FT (6 April 1984) 5 Iran–US CTR 251, 265.

be read as being in line with customary international law, having dealt with dual nationality.[22]

In his dissenting opinion, Judge Read also pointed out the legal consequences of the application of the 'genuine link' theory that would de facto leave persons of single nationality living in another State than the one of their formal nationality without protection for the purposes of diplomatic protection.[23] Other scholars have shared this concern.[24] The potential lack of protection has also been of concern to the ILC, remarking in its First Report on Diplomatic Protection that:

> It would exclude literally millions of people from the benefit of diplomatic protection. In today's world of economic globalization and migration, there are millions of people who have drifted away from their State of nationality and made their lives in States whose nationality they never acquire. Moreover, there are countless others who have acquired nationality by birth, descent or operation of law of States with which they have a most tenuous connection.[25]

This led the ILC to state in the commentary to the 2006 Draft Articles on Diplomatic Protection that 'there were certain factors that served to limit *Nottebohm* to the facts of the case in question … This suggests that the Court did not intend to expound a general rule applicable to all States but only a relative rule'.[26] The ILC thus understood the *Nottebohm* holding as a case-specific test and rejected the application of a 'genuine link' test to cases of single nationality.

Interestingly, Guatemala also raised the objection of abuse of rights, which the majority of the court indeed did not rely on for its judgment. As two of the dissenting judges and later doctrinal opinion elaborated, the question of whether the conferment of a nationality of a State to which the person only has weak ties, while the same person continues to have strong ties to the State towards which it seeks to invoke the new nationality, should have rather been framed in terms of the principle of good faith respectively the abuse of rights doctrine than in terms of a 'genuine link' doctrine with questionable legal precedent.[27] This concerns in particular the question of whether the motive for the change of nationality, that is, the aim of benefitting from a more favourable legal framework, 'may vitiate the obligation of a respondent state to recognize an ascription in the context of the judicial espousal of a diplomatic protection claim'.[28] A similar question is, as will be seen in following

[22] Similar in *Nasser Esphahanian v Bank Tehran*, Case No 31-157-2 (29 March 1983) 2 Iran–US CTR 157, 166. See also George Aldrich, *The Jurisprudence of the Iran-United States Claims Tribunal* (Clarendon Press 1996) 54–57.

[23] *Nottebohm* (n 6) 44 (Dissenting Opinion Judge Read).

[24] See, eg, Mervyn Jones, 'The Nottebohm Case' (1956) 5 ICLQ 230, 239–40; Sloane (n 4) 17–18.

[25] International Law Commission, 'First Report on Diplomatic Protection', Report of the fifty-second session (2000) UN Doc A/CN.4/506, para 117.

[26] International Law Commission, 'Draft Articles on Diplomatic Protection with Commentaries', Report of the fifty-eighth session (2006) UN Doc A/CN 4/L 684, Art 4, para 5.

[27] *Nottebohm* (n 6) 37–38, 48–49 (Dissenting Opinion Judge Read, though rejecting an abuse of rights claim on the assumption that damage is required as a consequence of the abuse of rights); similar *Nottebohm* (n 6) 57–58 (Dissenting Opinion Judge Guggenheim); Sloane (n 4) 19ff; ILC, 'First Report on Diplomatic Protection' (n 25) paras 118–20.

[28] Sloane (n 4) 21.

chapters, of great interest for the discussion of possible limits to the practice of treaty shopping in international investment law.

3.2.2 Legal persons

As will be seen in the following section, customary international law is less strict in the case of legal persons than in the case of natural persons. A legal (or juridical) person may be defined as 'any object, association or institution which the law endows with the capacity of acquiring rights and incurring obligations and is not a natural being. Legal personality is not a natural phenomenon but a creation of law.'[29] As such, it depends on domestic law establishing the criteria according to which it can be endowed with legal personality.[30]

Like for natural persons, a distinction must thus be made between international and domestic law relative to nationality. This is also what the ICJ emphasized in the seminal decision of *Barcelona Traction*:

> In this field international law is called upon to recognize institutions of municipal law that have an important and extensive role in the international field. This does not necessarily imply drawing any analogy between its own institutions and those of municipal law, nor does it amount to making rules of international law dependent upon categories of municipal law. All it means is that international law has had to recognize the corporate entity as an institution created by States in a domain essentially within their domestic jurisdiction.[31]

It seems thus apposite to examine the various connecting factors States may use under their domestic laws in order to confer legal personality and thus nationality to legal persons.

3.2.2.1 Domestic law theories on the creation of legal persons

3.2.2.1.1 Incorporation theory

The incorporation theory is nowadays probably the most relevant theory for conferring legal personality upon legal persons. Originally mostly used in Anglo-Saxon countries, it can also increasingly be found in Continental European countries, and its importance has arguably further grown as a result of the European Court of Justice (ECJ) jurisprudence on freedom of establishment.[32] The incorporation theory is also considered as reflecting customary international law,[33] though not

[29] Amerasinghe, *Diplomatic Protection* (n 19) 138.

[30] See, eg, *R v HM Treasury, ex parte Daily Mail and General Trust* (Case 81/87) [1988] ECR 5483, para 19: 'It should be borne in mind that, unlike natural persons, companies are creatures of the law ... They exist only by virtue of the varying national legislation which determines their incorporation and functioning.'

[31] *Barcelona Traction, Light and Power Co (Belgium v Spain) (Judgment)* [1970] ICJ Rep 3, 33–34 (para 38).

[32] See further below at 3.2.2.1.2.

[33] *Barcelona Traction* (n 31) 42 (para 71); see also Art 9 Draft Articles on Diplomatic Protection: 'the State of nationality means the State under whose law the corporation was incorporated.'

everybody would wholeheartedly agree with this.[34] Be it as it may, the incorporation theory has its merits in that corporate nationality is easy to determine and transnational transfers of seat are possible without the necessity to re-incorporate, thus providing legal security and flexibility.[35] It also favours party autonomy in the choice of corporate law as shareholders may decide where to incorporate the company.[36] On the other hand, the incorporation theory favours the creation of mailbox companies and thus potentially the practice of treaty shopping.[37] Furthermore, the State of incorporation may not always be willing to provide diplomatic protection to a company in case of barely more than marginal connections.[38]

3.2.2.1.2 Seat theory

Some countries adhere to the seat theory in order to determine corporate nationality. In this sense, the seat of a company relates to the place where the effective management, that is, the centre of administration, takes place.[39] This is where 'the fundamental decisions of the company's management are actually executed into valid and externally focused management acts'.[40] A mere head office does thus not qualify as seat, nor does the statutory seat (though the former can of course coincide with the seat).[41]

The seat theory has the virtue that by requiring a more 'genuine link' with the State of operation, it may be able to prevent treaty shopping.[42] On the other hand, transfers of seat lead to changes in nationality, thus furthering legal insecurity.[43]

[34] Lawrence Jahoon Lee, 'Barcelona Traction in the 21st Century: Revisiting its Customary and Policy Underpinnings 35 Years Later' (2006) 42 Stan J Intl L 237, 247: 'But even this limited survey suggests that although the incorporation test from Barcelona Traction is widely used, it has not crystallized into a full-fledged rule of customary international law. Most states use the incorporation test, but a significant minority of states does not. Some states espouse claims on behalf of companies not incorporated in their territory. Second, at least one state asserts the right to refuse claims if no genuine link is present. Third, almost all states that use the incorporation test also require some sort of genuine link before espousing claims. All of this suggests that the incorporation rule is not the exclusive test for corporation nationality under customary law.'

[35] UNCTAD, 'Scope and Definition, A Sequel' UNCTAD Series on Issues in International Investment Agreements II (United Nations 2011) 82–83, available at <http://unctad.org/en/Docs/diaeia20102_en.pdf> (last accessed on 15 September 2016); Addison-Agyei (n 10) 26; similar Heinz Kussmaul, Lutz Richter, and Christoph Ruiner, 'Corporations on the Move, the ECJ off Track: Relocation of a Corporation's Effective Place of Management in the EU' (2009) 6 Europ Company L 246, 247; Lucius Caflisch, 'The Protection of Corporate Investments Abroad in the Light of the Barcelona Traction Case' (1971) 31 ZaöRV 162, 181.

[36] Justin Borg-Barthet, 'Free at Last? Choice of Corporate Law in the EU Following the Judgment in VALE' (2013) 62 ICLQ 503, 504.

[37] UNCTAD, 'Scope and Definition' (n 35) 82–83; Addison-Agyei (n 10) 26–27.

[38] UNCTAD, 'Scope and Definition' (n 35) 82–83; Zachary Douglas, *The International Law of Investment Claims* (Cambridge University Press 2009) 22 (para 45).

[39] UNCTAD, 'Scope and Definition' (n 35) 83; Brownlie (n 7) 420.

[40] Kussmaul, Richter, and Ruiner (n 35) 246.

[41] Addison-Agyei (n 10) 29.

[42] Addison-Agyei (n 10) 28; Kussmaul, Richter, and Ruiner (n 35) 246–47; M Sornarajah, 'Good Faith, Corporate Nationality, and Denial of Benefits' in Andrew Mitchell, M Sornarajah, and Tania Voon, *Good Faith and International Economic Law* (Oxford University Press 2015) 117, 139.

[43] Addison-Agyei (n 10) 29.

In addition, it may be difficult to determine the seat in the case of multinational companies.[44]

A further problem arises for EU Member States. In a series of important decisions starting with *Centros*, the ECJ increasingly removed barriers on the freedom of incorporation lawfully established in a EU Member State.[45] As one commentator pointed out:

> *Centros* and *Überseering* allowed promoters of new companies to choose the law under which the company would be established, regardless of the connecting factors required in the State in which the company would operate principally. In *Inspire Act*, it was held that Member States may not require pseudo-foreign companies to comply with their laws, thereby consolidating a nascent market for incorporations ... Following *VALE*, it is now clear that companies may convert to a new governing law in a single step through cross-border transformation. The result of these judgments is that party autonomy in corporate choice of law is now firmly established ... The only remaining power that Member States exercise over the autonomy of corporate decision-makers concerns the situation of the operational headquarters of companies established under their laws. Effectively, Member States may prescribe the connecting factors required of companies established under their laws and may require companies to retain those connections. This means that party autonomy is restricted in that the laws of States that employ the real seat theory are only available to companies that wish to establish their operational headquarters in said States.[46]

This development means that at least as concerns EU Member States, the seat theory has become legally almost unviable and European countries that used to adhere to the seat theory (such as Germany, Austria, Belgium, Denmark, etc.) had to adapt their domestic company laws in this respect as a consequence.[47] This has led to a notable increase of mailbox companies in the European Union.[48]

[44] Caflisch (n 35) 180.

[45] *Centros* (Case C-212/97) [1999] ECR I-1459; *Überseering* (Case C-208/00) [2002] ECR I-9919; *Inspire Art* (Case C-167/01) [2003] ECR I-10195; *Cartesio* (Case C-210/06) [2008] ECR I-9641; *VALE* (Case C-378/10) [2012] ECR 00000.

[46] Borg-Barthet (n 36) 508.

[47] Kilian Baelz and Teresa Baldwin, 'The End of the Real Seat Theory (Sitztheorie): the European Court of Justice Decision in Überseering of 5 November 2002 and its Impact on German and European Company Law' (2002) 3 Germ L J 1; Christoph Teichmann, 'Report from Germany' (2008) 5 Europ Company L 189–91; Erik Werlauff, 'A "Copenhagen Effect"? Denmark's Answer to Centros: A Far-Reaching Company Law Reform Aimed at Strengthening the "Free Movement of Companies"' (2009) 6 Europ Company L 160–68; Kussmaul, Richter, and Ruiner (n 35) 255–56.

[48] Erik Werlauff, 'Pro Forma Registration of Companies: Why a Brass Plate in the Host Country Is Enough in Some Respects, but Not in Others' (2010) 7 Europ Company L 25, 26; Christoph Teichmann, 'The Downside of being a Letterbox Company' (2012) 9 Europ Company L 180, 181. See also the adapted clause in Art 1(3)(a) of the 2008 German Model BIT: '(a) in respect of the Federal Republic of Germany [FRG]: ... any juridical person and any commercial or other company or association with or without legal personality which is founded pursuant to the law of the FRG or the law of a Member State of the European Union or the European Economic Area and is organized pursuant to the law of the FRG, registered in a public register in the FRG or enjoys the freedom of establishment as an agency or permanent establishment in Germany pursuant to Arts 43 and 48 of the EC Treaty.'

3.2.2.1.3 Control theory

The control theory means the nationality of a legal person will be determined by reference to the nationality of the person(s) controlling it.[49] This theory has the advantage of 'putting substance over form' by enquiring into the real economic links, which is what the doctrine of 'piercing the corporate veil' also does, thereby avoiding potential abuses of corporate structuring.[50] However, its principal weak spot is its indeterminacy and, in particular in the case of share companies, the risk of frequent changes of nationality as shares are generally freely transferable.[51] This is why the control theory can mostly be found in conjunction with other connecting factors, thereby rendering it more predictable.[52] More recently however, some commentators have been pointing out possible incompatibilities of primary EU law and the control theory.[53]

3.2.2.2 Customary international law

The customary international law on the protection of foreign investment has been crucially shaped by the seminal decision of the ICJ in *Barcelona Traction*.[54] This decision raises a host of highly important questions that are of relevance to the subject of this book and that, despite its shortcomings in the realm of development of (customary) international law, continues to constitute *lex lata*, as has been seen in the more recent decision of the ICJ in *Diallo* and the adoption of the 2006 ILC Draft Articles on Diplomatic Protection. These decisions and the new codification thus deserve a particularly close analysis of the points of interest in order to better understand modern international investment law's approach towards the treatment of investor.

3.2.2.2.1 *Barcelona Traction* case

To better understand the context of these questions, a brief summary of the facts in *Barcelona Traction* is warranted.[55]

Barcelona Traction, Light and Power Company Ltd (Barcelona Traction) was a holding company incorporated in 1911 in Canada, with its head office located in Toronto. Some of its subsidiary companies were located and registered in Spain, their business activities being the production and distribution of electric power in the Spanish province of Catalonia. Belgium claimed diplomatic protection on behalf of its Belgian shareholders in Barcelona Traction which at certain points in time allegedly made up eighty-eight per cent of the total shareholding, for actions

[49] UNCTAD, 'Scope and Definition' (n 35) 84; Addison-Agyei (n 10) 29.
[50] Addison-Agyei (n 10) 30; more on this doctrine see Chapter 9, at 9.4.2.
[51] UNCTAD, 'Scope and Definition' (n 35) 84; Caflisch (n 35) 180.
[52] UNCTAD, 'Scope and Definition' (n 35) 84.
[53] See, eg, Angelos Dimopoulos, 'The Compatibility of Future EU Investment Agreements with EU Law' (2012) 39 LIEL 447.
[54] *Barcelona Traction* (n 31).
[55] See *Barcelona Traction* (n 31) 7–11 (paras 8–24).

attributable to Spain that led to the declaration of bankruptcy of Barcelona Traction in 1948. After the bankruptcy declaration, both the Canadian and the Belgian governments (among others) intervened for several years diplomatically to the Spanish government, though to no avail, and only the Belgian government decided finally to refer the dispute to the ICJ.

The starting point for the analysis of the legal issues under review was the question of whether Belgium, as state of the majority shareholders, had, under customary international law, a right of diplomatic protection in favour of the shareholders of the bankrupt company, in other words, whether Belgium had *ius standi* and thus whether Belgium's claim was admissible.

The court first elaborated on the law applicable to the case. Stating that international law was silent on the treatment of companies while municipal law was not, it held that:

> Whenever legal issues arise concerning the rights of States with respect to the treatment of companies and shareholders, as to which rights international law has not established its own rules, it has to refer to the relevant rules of municipal law.[56]

Yet, the court denied that this meant drawing simple analogies from municipal law. It then went on to examine municipal law with respect to limited liability companies and underlined the principal characteristics of these companies being the clear distinction of legal personality between the company itself and its shareholders.[57] This, according to the court, meant that though a 'wrong done to the company frequently cause[d] prejudice to its shareholders', the 'mere fact that damage [was] sustained by both company and shareholder [did] not imply that both [were] entitled to claim compensation'.[58] Rather:

> Whenever a shareholder's interests are harmed by an act done to the company, it is to the latter that he [the shareholder] must look to institute appropriate action; for although two separate entities may have suffered from the same wrong, it is only one entity whose rights have been infringed.[59]

The court thus drew a distinction between shareholder interests and shareholder rights,[60] holding that only the latter gave an independent right of action.[61] It denied that such direct shareholder rights were at stake and thus turned to the question of whether there were instances under international law in which an attack on company rights, resulting in damage to shareholders, could be equated with the violation of their direct rights.

[56] *Barcelona Traction* (n 31) 33–34 (para 38).
[57] *Barcelona Traction* (n 31) 34–35 (paras 40ff).
[58] *Barcelona Traction* (n 31) 35 (para 44).
[59] Ibid.
[60] *Barcelona Traction* (n 31) 36 (para 46): 'Not a mere interest affected, but solely a right infringed involves responsibility, so that an act directed against and infringing only the company's rights does not involve responsibility towards the shareholders, even if their interests are affected.'
[61] *Barcelona Traction* (n 31) 36 (para 47). These rights include according to the court, eg, 'the right to any declared dividend, the right to attend and vote at general meetings, the right to share in the residual assets of the company on liquidation.'

This concerned the question of whether the court was allowed to 'lift the corporate veil' of the company in order to disregard the a.m. separation between the company and its shareholders. It thus referred to the:

Wealth of practice already accumulated on the subject in municipal law [indicating] that the veil is lifted, for instance, to prevent the misuse of the privileges of legal personality, as in certain cases of fraud or malfeasance, to protect third persons such as a creditor or purchaser, or to prevent the evasion of legal requirements or of obligations.[62]

It stated that this doctrine played a similar role in international law so that under exceptional circumstances, the lifting of the corporate veil in the interest of shareholders was justified.[63] Without relying on two specific scenarios in which the veil could be lifted—the treatment of enemy and allied property during the two World Wars, and the treatment of foreign property in the case of nationalizations—the court then recognized two scenarios as justifying the lifting of the veil under international law: 'the case of the company having ceased to exist and the case of the company's national State lacking capacity to take action on its behalf'.[64] It rejected the first case, stating that even though the company was in receivership, that is, in bankruptcy proceedings, it continued to exist.[65] As to the latter case, it had to decide which state was the company's national State. It thus had to decide on whether an analogy to the 'genuine/effective link' test of the *Nottebohm* case could be applied to corporations, thereby establishing, as Belgium had claimed, that the genuine connection of Barcelona Traction was with Belgium.

The court clarified that only a limited analogy was possible between the international law governing nationality of natural persons and the one governing nationality of legal persons and that the traditional theory was the incorporation theory. Acknowledging that the seat and the control theory could sometimes be applicable, it stated however that:

In the particular field of the diplomatic protection of corporate entities, no absolute test of the 'genuine connection' has found general acceptance. Such tests as have been applied are of a relative nature, and sometimes links with one State have had to be weighed against those with another. In this connection reference has been made to the *Nottebohm* case. In fact the Parties made frequent reference to it in the course of the proceedings. However, given both the legal and factual aspects of protection in the present case the Court is of the opinion that there can be no analogy with the issues raised or the decision given in that case.[66]

However, it then went on to examine the links Barcelona Traction had with the country of its incorporation, Canada, and concluded:

Thus a close and permanent connection has been established, fortified by the passage of over half a century. This connection is in no way weakened by the fact that the company engaged from the very outset in commercial activities outside Canada, for that was its declared object. Barcelona Traction's links with Canada are thus manifold.[67]

62 *Barcelona Traction* (n 31) 39 (para 56).
63 *Barcelona Traction* (n 31) para 58.
64 *Barcelona Traction* (n 31) 39–42 (paras 59ff, 64ff).
65 *Barcelona Traction* (n 31) 41 (para 67).
66 *Barcelona Traction* (n 31) 42 (para 70).
67 *Barcelona Traction* (n 31) 42 (para 71).

The court thus rejected an analogy with the genuine link requirement established by the *Nottebohm* case, thereby in the end also rejecting the possibility of 'lifting the veil'. Whether a third scenario existed under customary international law, justifying the lifting of the veil and giving the State of shareholders the right to intervene on their behalf when the respondent State was the national State of the company, was left open by the court.[68]

The ICJ thus held Belgium's claim on behalf of Barcelona Traction's shareholders to be inadmissible under customary international law, underlining the importance of 'treaty stipulations or special agreements directly concluded between the private investor and the State in which the investment is placed'.[69]

3.2.2.2.2 Discussion

The judgment in the *Barcelona Traction* case triggered a flood of criticism, not only from the academic quarter, but also from several of the judges involved in the case.[70] In fact, no fewer than eight judges, though supportive of the judgment as such, wrote separate opinions, while one judge, Judge ad hoc Riphagen, dissented. In particular, the majority's focus on the incorporation theory and the rejection of an analogy to the 'genuine link' theory of the *Nottebohm* case was criticized by some judges. Thus, for example, Judge Jessup stated that there were:

> two standard tests of the 'nationality' of a corporation. The place of incorporation is the test generally favoured in the legal systems of the common law, while the *siège social* is more generally accepted in the civil law systems ... It is not possible to speak of a single rule for all purposes.[71]

Likewise, Judge Fitzmaurice, though considering the incorporation theory as the 'better' theory, acknowledged that 'different tests have been applied for different purposes and ... an element of fluidity is still present in this field ... in such a case a different test of nationality should be applied'.[72]

With respect to the 'genuine link' theory, Judges Fitzmaurice, Gros, and Jessup all held the *Nottebohm* decision to be of relevance to the *Barcelona Traction* case, the latter judge even claiming that the link theory constituted a general principle of law.[73]

68 *Barcelona Traction* (n 31) 48 (para 92).

69 *Barcelona Traction* (n 31) 47 (para 90).

70 See the separate or dissenting opinions of Judges Bustamante y Rivero, Tanaka, Jessup, Gros, Riphagen, Morelli, Padilla Nervo, and Ammoun. For scholarly criticism see, eg, Georges Abi-Saab, 'The International Law of Multinational Corporations: A Critique of American Legal Doctrines' (1971) Annales d'études internationales—Genève 97; Herbert Briggs, 'Barcelona Traction: The Jus Standi of Belgium' (1971) 65 AJIL 327; AM Susman, 'Notes, The Barcelona Traction Case' (1971) 12 Harv Intl L J 91; FA Mann, 'The Protection of Shareholders' Interests in The Light of the Barcelona Traction Case' (1973) 67 AJIL 259; Rosalyn Higgins, 'Aspects of the Case Concerning the Barcelona Traction, Light and Power Company, Ltd.' (1971) 11 Va J Intl L 327; Richard Lillich, 'The Rigidity of Barcelona' (1971) 65 AJIL 522; Stanley Metzger, 'Nationality of Corporate Investment under Investment Guaranty Schemes: The Relevance of Barcelona Traction' (1971) 65 AJIL 532.

71 *Barcelona Traction* (n 31) 183–84 (paras 39–40) (Separate Opinion Judge Jessup).

72 *Barcelona Traction* (n 31) 83 (para 33) (Separate Opinion Judge Fitzmaurice).

73 *Barcelona Traction* (n 31) 80 (para 28) (Separate Opinion Judge Fitzmaurice); ibid, 280–81 (para 22) (Separate Opinion Judge Gros); ibid, 186 (para 44) (Separate Opinion Judge Jessup).

Some academic commentators also echoed the criticism with respect to the rejection of the *Nottebohm* analogy. Thus, Arthur Watts pointed out:

> It is surprising that the Court was so dismissive, in this context, of the relevance of the kind of 'genuine link' it had earlier asserted in relation to natural persons ... The Court's strict regard for the traditional rule and its reluctance to accept additional qualifications establishing an effective link sit uneasily beside its readiness in the *Nottebohm* case to prefer considerations of substance to those of form, and to invoke precedents from 'related' fields.[74]

In Ian Brownlie's view:

> There [was] a considerable body of opinion both on the Court and elsewhere in favour of the application of the *Nottebohm* principle to the diplomatic protection of limited companies. It would seem that the process whereby an individual embarks on a voluntary naturalization and the incorporation of a company in the country of choice are significantly similar.[75]

However, he also conceded that:

> Fears that the 'genuine' or 'effective' link principle will lead to instability and absence of diplomatic protection are by no means groundless. However, the *Nottebohm* principle is essentially the assertion that in referring to institutions of municipal law, international law has a reserve power to guard against giving effect to ephemeral, abusive and simulated creations. Moreover, there is probably a presumption of validity in favour of the nationality created by incorporation and, in the case of multi-national corporate bodies, no very exacting test of substantial connection should be applied.[76]

Lucius Caflisch also criticized the exclusive reliance on the incorporation criterion and opined that:

> Some minimum effectiveness is required ... If the basic idea expressed by the Court in the *Nottebohm* case and embodied in the resolution of the Institute of International Law is accepted, and if it is further conceded that this idea is also relevant for companies, it must be concluded that a State may not put forward a claim on behalf of a company having its nationality if the latter does not have at least some minimum effectiveness.[77]

Even recent authorities continue to level criticism. Peter Muchlinski, for example, criticized the lack of 'virtually uniform, extensive and representative'[78] state practice that is needed, alongside the *opinio iuris*, to form customary international law with respect to the incorporation theory.[79]

[74] Arthur Watts, 'Nationality of claims: some relevant concepts' in Vaughan Lowe and Malgosia Fitzmaurice (eds), *Fifty years of the International Court of Justice: Essays in Honour of Sir Robert Jennings* (Cambridge University Press 1996) 424, 432.

[75] Brownlie (n 7) 485–86. [76] Ibid. [77] Caflisch (n 35) 177–78.

[78] *North Sea Continental Shelf (Germany v Denmark; Germany v Netherlands) (Judgment)* [1969] ICJ 3, 43 (para 74).

[79] See, eg, Peter Muchlinski, 'The Diplomatic Protection of Foreign Investors: A Tale of Judicial Caution' in Christina Binder and others (eds), *Essays in Honour of Christoph Schreuer* (Oxford University Press 2009) 341, 351–52.

Zachary Douglas also critically remarked that:

In deciding whether or not to take up claims based on the corporate interests of their nationals, states are naturally preoccupied with the extent to which their own economy has been affected by the alleged violation of the state. Thus it is common for states to insist that the corporate interest comprises a dominant shareholding or beneficial ownership or a connection based on the *siege social* of the company.[80]

For Pia Acconci, the rejection of the relevance of the *Nottebohm* judgment for the *Barcelona Traction* case was not equivalent to the rejection of:

the relevance of effectivity as the criterion to be used for determining the relevant link at an international level. In this regard, the Court rejected only the existence of an 'absolute test' but not that of such a criterion.[81]

The court's *renvoi* to municipal law for international law purposes drew further criticism. Though the court denied drawing a simple analogy between municipal and international law as regards the treatment of corporations and shareholders, this is in essence what it precisely did. Judge Riphagen thus criticized that:

The considerations which determine the choice of a particular system of municipal private law with respect to what the Court has called 'the nature and interrelation' of 'the rights of the corporate entity and its shareholders' are completely foreign to the problems which are the concern of the rules of public international law relating to responsibility for the treatment of aliens.[82]

Judge Gros also rejected the idea that 'definitions taken from certain municipal systems of law' could be erected 'into a rule of international law'.[83] Judge Fitzmaurice leveled a similar criticism.[84] Rosalyn Higgins very aptly analysed that by referring to municipal law where international law was silent, the court denied 'any law-developing role' of its own and assumed that 'the functions of international law [were] the same as those of municipal law'.[85] More recently, Muchlinski called it the 'high point of judicial restraint in the development of a customary law of foreign investment'.[86]

[80] Zachary Douglas, 'The Hybrid Foundations of Investment Treaty Arbitration' (2003) 74 BYIL 151, 172. Similar Brownlie (n 7) 482–83: 'There is very little evidence in support of the view that a state may present a claim on behalf of a corporation on the sole basis of its incorporation under its law. In general the evidence supports a doctrine that some substantial and effective connection between the legal entity and the claimant state is required, but there is no certainty as to the criteria for determining such connection.'

[81] Pia Acconci, 'Determining the Internationally relevant Link between a State and a Corporate Investor' (2004) 5 JWIT 139, 147–48.

[82] *Barcelona Traction* (n 31) 336 (Separate Opinion Judge ad hoc Riphagen). For similar (more recent) criticism see also Markus Perkams, 'Piercing the Corporate Veil in International Investment Agreements' in August Reinisch and Christina Knahr (eds), *International Investment Law in Context* (Eleven International Publishing 2008) 93, 99–100.

[83] *Barcelona Traction* (n 31) 277 (Separate Opinion Judge Gros).

[84] *Barcelona Traction* (n 31) 66–68 (Separate Opinion Judge Fitzmaurice).

[85] Rosalyn Higgins, 'Aspects of the Case Concerning the Barcelona Traction, Light and Power Company, Ltd.' (1970–1971) 11 Va J Intl L 327, 331.

[86] Muchlinski, 'Diplomatic Protection of Foreign Investors' (n 79) 351–52.

The preceding criticism can only be endorsed. Article 38 of the ICJ Statute clearly and exhaustively enumerates the sources of public international law the ICJ is called upon to interpret in disputes brought before it, and municipal law is not one of them. Unless the practice of States in the realm of municipal law has transformed into custom or a general principle of law, it would seem that an unqualified *renvoi* to municipal law is difficult to justify, even if the starting point in the analysis can (or must) be the recognition by international law of legal persons created by domestic law. This is what the ICJ also did in *Nottebohm* (and the PCIJ in *Nationality Decrees*)—it started its analysis by recognizing the sovereign domain of the State to confer nationality upon natural persons according to its own criteria. However, from there, it drew legal consequences—whether rightly or wrongly—that pertained to international law. Would it have stayed, in its reasoning, de facto on the municipal law level, it would arguably have been difficult for it to deny the opposability of Nottebohm's Liechtenstein nationality to Guatemala.

With respect to the Court's treatment of the possibility under customary international law of 'lifting the (corporate) veil', a similar critique as concerns the a.m. *renvoi* to municipal law may in this author's opinion be made. The ICJ based its assumption of the existence of certain situations that give rise, under customary international law, to the possibility of 'piercing or lifting the veil' on a similarly mechanical transposition of municipal law instances in which such 'lifting of the veil' is allegedly permitted, without however providing for any further substantiation as to the exact conditions (beyond the approximate situations)[87] under which such lifting can be effected, nor any examples of corresponding municipal laws. Thus, not only may the municipal law *renvoi* be criticized,[88] but moreover, this *renvoi* is based on a figure that already under municipal law seems to be an inherently malleable, if not to say, unclear notion.[89] As will be examined more in detail further below, though the underlying common rationale is of course to ignore under certain circumstances the formally separate legal existence of parent and subsidiary companies, the figure of 'piercing or lifting the veil' can be used in municipal law for purposes as different as rendering the parent company liable for torts committed by its subsidiary[90] as for:

> Looking behind a company's State of incorporation to its shareholders and managers in identifying its nationality ... involving in the dispute an entity that is not a party to the relevant treaty or proceedings ... or investigating the ownership or control behind a company's incorporation in order to prevent the benefits of a treaty from accruing to investors of non-parties.[91]

[87] This can also be seen in the court's formulation: 'the veil is lifted, *for instance*' (emphasis added), *Barcelona Traction* (n 31) 38–39 (para 56).

[88] See also Perkams, 'Piercing the Corporate Veil' (n 82) 99–100.

[89] See also *Barcelona Traction* (n 31) 120–21 (Separate Opinion Judge Tanaka), where he criticized the 'figurative concept of "piercing the veil"' to be a 'slogan', 'a *petitio principia* and nothing more'. Similar Caflisch (n 35) 172–73; Tania Voon, Andrew Mitchell, and James Munro, 'Legal Responses to Corporate Manoeuvering in International Investment Arbitration' (2014) 5 JIDS 41, 44.

[90] See, eg, Howard Friedman, *Publicly Held Corporations, A Lawyer's Guide* (Oxford University Press 2011) 151ff.

[91] Voon, Mitchell, and Munro, 'Legal Responses' (n 89) 43–44.

It is equally not completely clear from where the ICJ took the two respectively three possible situations under which according to its opinion the veil could be lifted, in particular as it rejected any possible analogies to two instances of 'lifting the veil' recognized under customary international law.[92]

3.2.2.2.3 *Diallo* case

The recent *Diallo* case[93] confirms the big lines of the ICJ's holding in *Barcelona Traction.*

In this case, Guinea claimed diplomatic protection of its national Mr Diallo for acts attributable to the State of Zaire, the predecessor of the State of Democratic Republic of the Congo (DRC), that occurred between 1995 and 1996. In October 1995, Zaire issued an expulsion order to Mr Diallo, a long-time resident in Zaire and manager (*gérant*) and shareholder of two limited liability companies established under Zairean law (Africom–Zaire SPRL and Africontainers–Zaire SPRL), and kept him in detention for over two months before expelling him in January 1996 to Guinea. Guinea claimed that Mr Diallo suffered a number of damages both as an individual person (due to the illegal detention, alleged ill-treatment during detention, and the deprivation of his rights under the 1963 Vienna Convention on Consular Relations) and as a manager and shareholder of the two a.m. companies. As for the latter, Guinea based its claim both on the direct rights of Mr Diallo as a shareholder and manager, and on a right of protection 'by substitution'.[94]

The court endorsed in its decision on the preliminary objections the principal findings made almost forty years earlier in *Barcelona Traction*. As in that decision, it underlined the independent legal personality of companies from their shareholders and thus distinguished between the companies and the shareholders' direct rights, holding that as concerns Mr Diallo's direct rights as shareholder, the claim was admissible.[95] As regards Guinea's claim of protection of Mr Diallo 'by substitution' for the two companies, however, the court rejected an exception to the rule that only the national State of incorporation can exercise diplomatic protection when company rights were violated, thus holding that the claim was inadmissible.[96]

It clarified that:

> Since its dictum in the *Barcelona Traction* case, [it] has not had occasion to rule on whether, in international law, there is indeed an exception to the general rule 'that the right of diplomatic protection of a company belongs to its national State', which allows for protection of the shareholders by their own national State 'by substitution', and on the reach of any such exception.[97]

According to the court, the proliferation of international investment agreements—giving shareholders a direct standing of their own—was not so much expression of

[92] *Barcelona Traction* (n 31) 39–40 (paras 59–63).

[93] *Ahmadou Sadio Diallo (Guinea v Democratic Republic of Congo) (Preliminary Objections)* [2007] ICJ Rep 582, 614 (para 87) (quoted: *Diallo* [2007]; *Ahmadou Sadio Diallo (Republic of Guinea v Democratic Republic of the Congo) (Merits)* [2010] ICJ Rep 639 (quoted: *Diallo* [2010]).

[94] *Diallo* [2007] (n 93) 590–94 (paras 13–24).

[95] *Diallo* [2007] (n 93) 605–07 (paras 61–67).

[96] *Diallo* [2007] (n 93) 616 (para 95).

[97] *Diallo* [2007] (n 93) 614 (para 87).

the formation of customary international law, as rather proof of the fact that customary international law continued to be deficient in its granting of a direct standing to shareholders, and that their protection could, in the absence of the exceptions recognized by the court in *Barcelona Traction*, only be secured by recourse to international investment agreements.[98] It also found that the exception now contained in Article 11(b) of the 2006 ILC Draft Articles on Diplomatic Protection was not fulfilled in the case at issue.[99]

In its decision on the merits, the ICJ, examining whether direct rights of Mr Diallo's as shareholder and manager were violated, analysed DRC company law and, for each of the claimed shareholder and manager rights, found in the end no violation by the DRC.[100]

It thus adopted in *Diallo* its earlier approach in *Barcelona Traction* of a *renvoi* to municipal law instead of endeavoring to establish the contours of a customary minimum standard of treatment of aliens, thus consolidating the cautious approach of the ICJ towards customary international law of foreign investment.[101]

3.2.2.2.4 ILC 2006 Draft Articles on Diplomatic Protection

The Draft Articles on Diplomatic Protection that were adopted in 2006 by the ILC overall reaffirm the cautious approach of the ICJ established in *Barcelona Traction*, not however without a critical eye. Thus, even though Article 9 acknowledges the incorporation theory as default theory for the determination of the national state of a corporation, it goes further than the ICJ and also recognizes a right of diplomatic protection of the State of the shareholders under certain (cumulative) circumstances, namely:

> when the corporation is controlled by nationals of another State or States and has no substantial business activities in the State of incorporation, and the seat of management and the financial control of the corporation are both located in another State.[102]

This exception thus proposes a specific regulation for so-called mailbox or shell companies, combining various connecting factors mentioned above.[103] As one commentator points out, the control theory can be found twice—though in different forms—in this exception.[104] Article 11 of the Draft Articles also reaffirms two of the three exceptions potentially recognized by the ICJ in *Barcelona Traction* to give a right of diplomatic protection to the State of shareholders. [105] Article 12, finally, takes up the distinction drawn by the court between direct rights of the company and direct rights of the shareholder.

[98] *Diallo* [2007] (n 93) 615 (paras 89, 90).
[99] *Diallo* [2007] (n 93) 615–16 (paras 91–92). On the 2006 ILC Draft Articles on Diplomatic Protection see in the following subsection.
[100] *Diallo* [2010] (n 93) 673–91 (paras 99–159); this after finding violations of Mr Diallo's individual rights pertaining to the unlawful detention and deprivation of his rights under the Vienna Convention on Consular Rights, see *Diallo* [2010] (n 93) 691 (para 160).
[101] Similar Muchlinski, 'Diplomatic Protection of Foreign Investors' (n 79) 359.
[102] Art 9 Sentence 2 Draft Articles. [103] Addison-Agyei (n 10) 50. [104] Ibid.
[105] *Barcelona Traction* (n 31) 40–48 (paras 65–92).

3.3 Continuous Nationality Requirement

The question at which point in time the claimed nationality must exist in order to be opposable to the respondent State has arisen early on in international law. Indeed, if a change in nationality was possible without any limits at any time before or after legal proceedings have been brought, there would clearly be considerable potential for abuse, as Umpire Parker had already remarked in *Administrative Decision No V*:

Any other rule would open wide the door for abuses and might result in converting a strong nation into a claim agency on behalf of those who after suffering injuries should assign their claims to its nationals or avail themselves of its naturalization laws for the purpose of procuring its espousal for their claims.[106]

This concern seems valid for both natural and legal persons.[107] As will be seen further below, it is also—among others—relevant for the question of determining up to which point in time an investor may change his nationality or create diversity of nationality for purposes of treaty shopping without this change being considered an abuse. Two separate, but inter-connected questions must thus be asked: first, which is the (first) moment in time in which the claimed nationality must be present; and second, is there a continuity of nationality requirement, and if so, until which point does the claimed nationality have to be existent?

The foundations of a continuous nationality rule in customary international law can be traced back at least to the early twentieth century, if not already the nineteenth century.[108] Edwin Borchard, in his work on Diplomatic Protection, posited for example in the early twentieth century that a claim, in order to give rise to espousal, had to be national in origin, that is, at the time the claim arose, and did therefore not cover claims acquired by naturalization or assignment.[109]

In the 1925 *Administrative Decision No V*, the Umpire also confirmed that:

It is no doubt the general practice of nations not to espouse a private claim against another nation unless in point of origin it possesses the nationality of the claimant nation. The reason of the rule is that the nation is injured through injury to its national and it alone may demand reparation as no other nation is injured ... A third nation is not injured through the assignment of the claim to one of its nationals or through the claimant becoming its national

[106] *Administrative Decision No V (United States v Germany)* (1924) 7 RIAA 119, 141; ILC, 'Draft Articles on Diplomatic Protection with commentaries' (n 26) art 5 para 1. Similar Mendelson, 'Runaway Train' (n 3) 97, 105.

[107] Though for a critical view concerning natural persons see Guy IF Leigh, 'Nationality and Diplomatic Protection' (1971) 20 ICLQ 453, 546: 'One may question however, whether the fear that an individual will attempt to gain access to an international tribunal by means of naturalization is entirely realistic. There are surely few who would go to such lengths, and those only if their claims are extremely well founded and substantial. Moreover, it is not likely that a naturalizing State would lend itself to such a scheme.'

[108] See for a historical overview Eric Wyler, *La règle dite de la continuité de la nationalité dans le contentieux international* (Presses Universitaires de France 1990) 31–34.

[109] Edwin Borchard, *The Diplomatic Protection of Citizens Abroad or the Law of International Claims* (New York, The Banks Law Publishing 1927) 660–61.

by naturalization. While naturalization transfers allegiance, it does not carry with it existing State obligations.[110]

In 1929, the Survey on the State of International Law of the League of Nations that was drawn up in preparation of the 1930 Hague Conference for the Codification of International Law alleged that:

According to the opinion of the majority, and to international jurisprudence, the claim requires to have the national character at the moment when the damage was suffered, and to retain that character down to the moment at which it is decided.[111]

As Matthew Duchesne however convincingly shows, recognition of this rule was at that time far from unanimous.[112] Nevertheless, the PCIJ in 1939 explicitly endorsed in the *Panevezys-Saldutiskis Railway* case the date of injury as the (first) moment in time in which the claimed nationality must be present.[113]

It was however not so much this first moment in time, the date of the injury (so-called *dies a quo*), which was controversial.[114] Rather, much disagreement centred for a long time on the question up to which point in time the nationality had to be continuous (so-called *dies ad quem*).

Georg Schwarzenberger for example suggested that '[t]he times of presentation of a claim on the international level, submission to arbitral or judicial settlement, conclusion of the oral proceedings and the award or judgment are possibly relevant dates.'[115]

Ian Brownlie noted that '[t]he second part of the rule is variously stated in terms of nationality continuing until the "presentation of the award", or the filing of a claim before a tribunal, or the formal presentation of a diplomatic claim in the absence of submission to a tribunal.'[116]

[110] *Administrative Decision No V* (n 106) 140–41.

[111] League of Nations, '3 Bases of Discussion for the Conference Drawn up by the Preparatory Committee, Point XIII, National Character of the Claim' 140–45, reprinted in 2 League of Nations Conference for the Codification of International Law (1930) 567, quoted in Matthew Duchesne, 'The Continuous-Nationality-of Claims Principle, Its historical development and current relevance to investor-State investment disputes' (2004) 36 Geo Wash Intl L Rev 783, 793–94 (FN 57).

[112] Duchesne (n 111) 793–97.

[113] *Panevezys-Saldutiskis Railway Case (Estonia v Lithuania)* [1939] PCIJ Series A/B No 76, para 66: 'The Estonian Agent both in the written pleadings and in the oral arguments has endeavoured to discredit this rule of international law, if not to deny its existence. He cited a certain number of precedents, but when these precedents are examined it will be seen that they are cases where the governments concerned had agreed to waive the strict application of the rule, cases where the two governments had agreed to establish an international tribunal with jurisdiction to adjudicate on claims even if this condition as to nationality were not fulfilled. In the present case no grounds exist for holding that the Parties intended to exclude the application of the rule. The Lithuanian Agent is therefore right in maintaining that Estonia must prove that at the time when the injury occurred which is alleged to involve the international responsibility of … Lithuania the company suffering the injury possessed Estonian nationality.'

[114] See also Duchesne (n 111) 799: '[R]equiring a claimant to have the nationality of the espousing state at the time of his injury may well have become a rule of customary international law'.

[115] Georg Schwarzenberger, *International Law as Applied by International Courts and Tribunals*, Vol I (Stevens and Sons, 3rd edn 1957) 597.

[116] Brownlie (n 7) 479; Duchesne (n 111) 799.

Special Rapporteur John Dugard in his Seventh Report on Diplomatic Protection also pointed to the divergent opinions and practice in this respect.[117]

However, despite its doubtful customary status, the ILC in the end decided to retain the continuous nationality rule in the 2006 Draft Articles on Diplomatic Protection. Thus, according to these Articles, the nationality in question must exist 'from the date of injury to the date of the official presentation of the claim', with continuity being presumed 'if that nationality existed at both these dates'.[118] A change of nationality between these dates, for example through assignment of the claim, affects according to Brownlie the admissibility of the claim only if the principle of continuity is not respected.[119] This would supposedly mean that assignment of the claim to another person of the same nationality would not invalidate the claim. Whether a change of nationality between the *dies ad quem* and the making of the award is detrimental to the admissibility of the claim was left open by the Commentary, however seemingly showing sympathy to this possible conclusion.[120]

3.4 Relevance of Customary International Law for the Practice of Treaty Shopping

What does the above mean for the purposes of this research? The analysis of the evolution of the (customary) international law of diplomatic protection seems to suggest that it takes a restrictive approach towards the possibility of a strategic use or change of nationality. This might at first sight seem counter-intuitive—after all, the court in *Barcelona Traction* fully embraced the incorporation theory, which with its formalistic approach would seem to make nationality shopping at first sight easier.[121]

However, by restricting the possibility of diplomatic protection of shareholders to a few strict exceptions, it effectively took a restrictive stance towards nationality shopping. The rationale for this restriction seems to lie in the fear that:

> The adoption of the theory of diplomatic protection of shareholders as such, by opening the door to competing diplomatic claims, could create an atmosphere of confusion and insecurity in international economic relations. The danger would be all the greater inasmuch as the shares of companies whose activity is international are widely scattered and frequently change hands.[122]

The same conservative stance has been continued in the *Diallo* decision.[123]

[117] International Law Commission, 'Seventh Report on Diplomatic Protection' Report of the fifty-eighth session (2006) UN Doc A/CN.4/567, paras 39–40.

[118] See Arts 5(1) and 10(1) Draft Articles.

[119] Brownlie (n 7) 480.

[120] ILC, 'Draft Articles on Diplomatic Protection with commentaries' (n 26) Art 5, para 5 (with reference to Robert Jennings and Arthur Watts (eds), *Oppenheim's International Law*, Vol I, Peace, Introduction and Part I (London and New York, Longman, 9th edn 1996) 512–13 and the *Eschauzier claim (Great Britain v Mexico)* (1931) 5 RIAA 207.

[121] See above at 3.2.2.1.1.

[122] *Barcelona Traction* (n 31) 49 (para 96).

[123] See above at 3.2.2.2.3.

The ILC Draft Articles on Diplomatic Protection by and large adopt the line established in *Barcelona Traction* and confirmed in *Diallo*. More concretely, they reaffirm the incorporation test as main theory for establishing corporate nationality, the separate legal identities of the corporation and the shareholders, and the fact that shareholders cannot claim damages for violations of company rights except under certain circumstances. However, in an act of progressive development of the law, the Draft Articles also recognize under certain circumstances a right of diplomatic protection of shareholders in the case of mailbox companies, an exception not foreseen by the ICJ in its jurisprudence, thus de facto creating a fourth exception where the 'corporate veil may be pierced'. Hence, the Draft Articles overall retain a relatively restrictive approach towards nationality shopping, all the while providing for one further exception not included in ICJ jurisprudence.[124]

It is also noteworthy that neither the ICJ jurisprudence nor the 2006 Draft Articles define in an explicit way what customary international law considers as protected investment or property. Only with respect to shareholding has this question been implicitly treated by customary international law, more precisely by recourse to the distinction of the direct rights of the company and those of shareholders, and the fact that unless one of the exceptions recognized by the ICJ in *Barcelona Traction* is given, only the violation of a shareholder's direct rights gives (potentially) rise to diplomatic protection.

As for the continuous nationality requirement, it has already been pointed out further above[125] that a continuous nationality requirement serves the purpose of avoiding abuse through 'nationality shopping'. The respective ILC Draft Articles on Diplomatic Protection seem to have contributed to a certain clarification of the law in that the cut-off point of continuous nationality, the *dies ad quem*, is now firmly established by recourse to the date of the official presentation of the claim. Continuous nationality is therefore—in principle—required from the date of injury to the date of the official presentation of the claim. [126] Were this requirement, the *dies a quo*, not to exist at the time of the injury, the injured person (whether natural or legal) could easily change nationality before bringing a claim so as to take advantage of the best protections available.[127]

This first provisional result invariably raises the question of whether this (customary) international law is also relevant for the treatment of strategic uses or changes of nationality under international investment law. This boils down to the question of whether customary international law can help in the interpretation of the *lex specialis*, in other words, whether it can function as a 'gap-filler'.

The International Law Commission, treating this question among others in its 2006 Report on the Fragmentation of International Law, set out from the general principle that 'whenever two or more norms deal with the same subject matter,

[124] This may possibly be due to the higher topicality of mailbox companies today than in 1970.

[125] See above at 3.3.

[126] Without prejudice to the exceptions provided for in Arts 5(2)–(4) and 10(2) and (3) Draft Articles on Diplomatic Protection.

[127] Similar Mendelson, 'Runaway Train' (n 3) 105.

priority should be given to the norm that is more specific', with 'treaties often [acting] as *lex specialis* by reference to the relevant customary law and general principles'.[128] The fact that the *lex specialis* prevails over *lex generalis* does not however mean that the latter becomes extinguished or invalid. Rather, it remains valid and applicable in principle,[129] as has also been seen further above.

The gap-filling function of general law in the case of incompleteness of the special law is widely recognized in scholarship and international jurisprudence.[130] This gap-filling process is usually undertaken through the interpretive process of systemic integration by virtue of Article 31(3)(c) VCLT, which mandates that the interpreter of a treaty take into account 'any relevant rules of international law applicable in relations between the parties'.[131]

Importantly, however, the question whether the drafters of *lex specialis* treaty norms had left an intentional silence or an unintentional gap cannot be decided *in abstracto*. As the ILC 'Fragmentation Report' confirms:

> The relationship between the *lex specialis* maxim and other norms of interpretation or conflict solution cannot be determined in a general way. Which consideration should be predominant—i.e. whether it is the speciality or the time of emergence of the norm—should be decided contextually.[132]

From the aforesaid follows that the question whether customary international law may be of relevance to the treatment of strategic uses or changes of nationality in international investment arbitration cannot be answered in abstract and in advance. This is even more so given that the plethora of existing international investment agreements, though often very similar in the wording of their clauses, always have to be interpreted on a case-by-case basis. The following analysis, in Chapters 4 to 7, of how investment arbitral tribunals have treated the various facets of treaty shopping will thus also reveal whether and if so how arbitral tribunals have had recourse to customary international law to judge the validity of certain strategic uses or changes of nationality.

3.5 Preliminary Conclusions

As has been seen, customary international law takes an altogether rather restrictive approach towards strategic uses or changes of nationality.

[128] International Law Commission, 'Conclusions of the work of the Study Group on the Fragmentation of International Law: Difficulties arising from the Diversification and Expansion of International Law' Report of the Study Group of the International Law Commission, fifty-eighth Session (2006) A/CN/L.702 , para 5.

[129] Ibid, para 9.

[130] See ILC, 'Fragmentation of International Law' (n 128) para 15; Tarcisio Gazzini, 'The Role of Customary International Law in the Field of Foreign Investment' (2007) 8 JWIT 691, 710–11; *Amoco International Finance Corporation v Iran*, Case No 310-56-3 (14 July 1987) 15 Iran–US CTR 189, 222 (para 112); *Loewen Group Inc and Raymond Loewen v United States of America*, ICSID Case No ARB(AF)/98/3, Award (26 June 2003) para 226; *ADC Affiliate Limited & ADMC Management Limited v Republic of Hungary*, ICSID Case No ARB/03/16, Award (2 October 2006) para 483.

[131] ILC, 'Fragmentation of International Law' (n 128), paras 17–20.

[132] Ibid, para 6.

First, nationality—both for natural and for legal persons—is conferred according to municipal law, but international law has a reserve power for nationalities that can be considered 'of convenience' or acquired in an abusive fashion. In this aspect, it is noteworthy that the potential for abuse has traditionally—whether rightly or wrongly—been considered higher in the case of natural than legal persons.

Second, as concerns legal persons, no single theory for the conferral of nationality seems to constitute customary international law—contrary to the ICJ's holding in *Barcelona Traction* and the ILC's codification in its 2006 Draft Articles.

Third, customary international law recognizes a right of diplomatic protection in favour of shareholders only if direct shareholder rights have been violated or, if the former is not the case, if one of the limited exceptions for 'lifting the veil' (as also found in the 2006 Draft Articles) is fulfilled. This effectively limits considerably the possibility of States exercising diplomatic protection in favour of shareholders.

Fourth, a continuous nationality requirement exists under customary international law in order to guard against 'abusive nationality shopping'. While the exact extent of this requirement has for a long time been controversial, it seems by now settled that the invoked nationality has to be continuous from the date of the injury to the date of the official presentation of the claim, but not beyond that point.

Last but not least, the relevance of customary international law for the purpose of international investment law cannot be determined in the abstract, but will be analysed on a case-by-case basis in the following chapters.

4

Jurisdiction *Ratione Personae*

4.1 Introduction

When raising objections to jurisdiction *ratione personae*, respondents have often argued that the investor having brought the claim under a given investment treaty was not the 'real' investor who would ultimately benefit from a potentially positive outcome of the arbitral proceedings. For natural persons as investors, this has primarily translated into arguing that even absent a corresponding specific requirement in the applicable treaty, the tribunal should look for the 'effective' or 'genuine link' of the investor. For legal persons as investors, Respondents have clad this argument in terms of a so-called 'piercing of the corporate veil' principle or theory, asking the tribunal to identify the entity in control of the claiming investor as the 'real' investor. Respondents have also often argued that the tribunal should read implicit additional requirements into the definition of covered investors contained in the invoked investment agreement, thus disqualifying *ipso facto* so-called mailbox or shell companies. Arbitral tribunals have also sometimes had to decide whether a given 'denial of benefits' clause could be validly exercised against a mailbox company being the claimant. Finally, for locally incorporated claimants that the States party to the treaty have agreed to treat as foreign because of foreign control,[1] the objections have been centring on the exact meaning of the term 'control' and the question how far up the corporate tier the control has to be examined. Similar questions have arisen on the exact meaning of the notion of control contained in international investment agreement (IIAs).

4.2 Natural Persons

As mentioned above,[2] treaty shopping by natural persons is much less frequent than treaty shopping by legal persons. Indeed, the strategic *change* of nationality is normally much more difficult to perform in the case of natural persons than in the case of legal persons, natural persons usually having to fulfil higher requirements for the obtention of a specific nationality, contrary to the relatively rapid process of incorporation or constitution of legal persons. Treaty shopping by natural persons thus arguably plays out mainly through the invocation of an already existing dual nationality.

[1] Article 25(2)(b) second clause ICSID Convention.

[2] See Chapter 1, at 1.1.2.1.

In these cases, investment tribunals have—in particular in earlier cases—often been asked by Respondents to search for the 'effective' or 'genuine link' and dismiss the case on the grounds that the putative investor–claimant was not the 'real' investor. This has raised the question of whether an 'effective' or 'genuine link' doctrine could be applied in international investment law.

4.2.1 'Genuine link' requirement in international investment law?

As has already been pointed out further above,[3] international investment law, including the specific arbitral forum of International Centre for Settlement of Investment Disputes (ICSID), is considered to be the *lex specialis* to the (customary) international law of diplomatic protection, with the aim of providing for the protection of foreign investors where the law of diplomatic protection is deficient.

Article 25(2)(a) of the ICSID Convention[4] does not contain an 'effective link' requirement with respect to natural persons, but it excludes dual nationals from the protection of the Convention who also have the nationality of the respondent host State. And while some IIAs include an 'effective link' requirement in cases of dual nationals,[5] most are indeed silent on this question.

Despite the absence of such explicit requirements, parties to investment arbitrations have still often tried to argue in favour of a 'genuine link' requirement, either in order to disavow the claimant's nationality as an ineffective one or to claim that the claimant's host state's nationality was ineffective.

However, investment arbitral tribunals have thus far wholeheartedly rejected the application of an 'effective' or 'genuine link' theory both in the case of single as well as dual nationalities.

4.2.1.1 Single nationality

In *Micula v Romania*,[6] the claimants (two brothers among corporate claimants) were Romanians by birth, but renounced on their Romanian nationality when they acquired Swedish nationality, at different times, by marrying Swedish nationals and residing in Sweden for the duration required under Swedish law. Though acknowledging that only a single nationality was involved, the Respondent objected that Claimants presented, because of their frequent business trips to and stays in Romania, a more effective link with Romania, thus invoking the 'genuine link' doctrine. The tribunal noted in this respect that the role and status of this doctrine in public international law was 'disputable' at least as cases of single

[3] See Chapter 3, at 3.4.

[4] Convention on the Settlement of Investment Disputes (opened for signature 18 March 1965) 4 ILM (1965) 524 (entered into force 14 October 1966).

[5] See more in detail in Chapter 8, at 8.2.3.1.1.

[6] *Ioan Micula, Viorel Micula, SC European Food SA, SC Starmill SRL and SC Multipack SRL v Republic of Romania*, ICSID Case No ARB/05/20, Decision on Jurisdiction and Admissibility (24 September 2008).

nationality were concerned,[7] and it rejected the application of the 'genuine link' requirement in the context of ICSID proceedings in view of the clear wording of Article 25(2)(a) ICSID which 'does not require that a claimant only hold one nationality, so long as its second nationality is not that of the State party to the dispute'.[8] This, according to the tribunal, applied in the absence of an agreement by the parties to the bilateral investment treaty (BIT) on additional standards for the determination of nationality.[9] Nevertheless, this statement has to be somewhat relativized, as the tribunal—not unlike the International Court of Justice's (ICJ's) holding in the *Nottebohm* decision—left the door open to the application of the principle—even in the case of single nationality—'under exceptional circumstances'.[10]

The tribunal in *Jan Oostergetel and Theodora Laurentius v Slovak Republic* followed the decision in *Micula v Romania*.[11] In this case, the claimants were natural persons of Dutch nationality with permanent residence in Belgium. The Respondent claimed that because of the permanent residence in Belgium, the claimants were effectively Belgian. The tribunal noted in response that not only was there no 'effective link' requirement in Dutch law so that Dutch nationality was not lost for the mere reason of residing in another country,[12] but it also endorsed the already quoted holding of the *Micula* tribunal, attesting to the dubious status, under public international law, of the 'genuine link' theory in the case of single nationality except under exceptional circumstances.[13]

The decision in *Oostergetel* also seems to be conforming to the much earlier North American Free Trade Agreement (NAFTA) decision in *Feldman v Mexico*.[14] In that decision, Respondent objected to the jurisdiction of the tribunal on grounds of the claimant, of US nationality, permanently residing in Mexico, thus arguing the existence of an effective link with Mexico. The tribunal recalled that:

> Under general international law, citizenship rather than residence or any other geographic affiliation is the main connecting factor between a state and an individual. Residence, even permanent or otherwise authorized or officially certified residence, only fulfils a subsidiary function which, as a matter of principle, does not amount to, or compete with, citizenship.[15]

Thus, the tribunal continued:

> Dual nationality problems, including the search of the 'dominant or effective nationality', require[d] the existence of a double citizenship, connecting the same individual to two states with the legal bond of citizenship in the generally accepted meaning of the term.[16]

[7] Ibid, para 99. [8] Ibid, para 100. [9] Ibid, para 101.

[10] Ibid, para 104: '[W]hen dealing with a single nationality, the threshold for the Respondent State to show that the test is applicable is higher than in the cases of dual nationality and the use of the test should be limited to exceptional circumstances.'

[11] *Jan Oostergetel and Theodora Laurentius v Slovak Republic*, UNCITRAL, Decision on Jurisdiction (30 April 2010).

[12] Ibid, para 123. [13] Ibid, paras 131–32.

[14] *Marvin Roy Feldman Karpa v United States of Mexico*, ICSID Case No ARB(AF)/99/1, Interim Decision on Preliminary Jurisdictional Issues (6 December 2000).

[15] Ibid, para 30.

[16] Ibid, para 31.

This was however not the case here. Moreover, the tribunal continued, from the *Nottebohm* case followed that permanent residence in the Respondent State could only become a bar to invoking another nationality where that nationality had been acquired under exceptional or artificial circumstances, but not in the case of a nationality acquired under normal circumstances, for example by birth.[17] It thus implicitly also rejected the 'genuine link' theory.[18]

Finally, in *Siag and Vecchi v Egypt*,[19] the tribunal found that both claimants held Italian nationality, but had lost their Egyptian nationality for different reasons prior to the critical dates stipulated by Article 25(2)(a) ICSID Convention. Dealing with a single nationality, the tribunal discarded the 'genuine link' theory and underlined the *lex specialis* character of investment law, stating that:

> While it may be asserted that if this were a diplomatic protection case it could be argued differently, the parties have consented to have their dispute resolved under the ICSID Convention and it sets out a particular regime for the determination of jurisdiction ... Developments in international law concerning nationality of individuals in the field of diplomatic protection including, for example, greater flexibility in the requirement for the link of nationality, while of interest, must give way to the specific regime under the ICSID Convention and the terms of the BIT.[20]

It also noted that claimants had acquired the Italian nationality long before the bringing of the claim and for recognized reasons (i.e. marriage of an Italian citizen and reacquisition of the Italian nationality following the death of the Egyptian husband), not as sole purpose to access ICSID jurisdiction.[21]

4.2.1.2 Dual nationality

Arbitral tribunals were equally reluctant to accept the application of the 'genuine link' theory in cases of dual nationality.

In *Champion Trading v Egypt*,[22] the claimants (three brothers among corporate claimants) were US nationals by birth, but had also automatically acquired Egyptian nationality due to their father's Egyptian nationality. Bringing claims

[17] Ibid, para 32.

[18] Roberto Aguirre Luzi and Ben Love, 'Individual Nationality in Investment Treaty Arbitration: The Tension Between Customary International Law and Lex Specialis' in Andrea Bjorklund, Ian Laird, and Sergey Ripinsky (eds), *Investment Treaty Law: Current Issues III* (British Institute of International and Comparative Law 2008) 193.

[19] *Waguih Elie George Siag and Clorinda Vecchi v Arab Republic of Egypt*, ICSID Case No ARB/05/15, Decision on Jurisdiction (11 April 2007).

[20] Ibid, para 198; but see ibid, 62 (Prof. Orrego Vicuña's Dissenting Opinion): 'As the ICSID Convention does not define nationality, the principles of international law governing this matter come into play instantly. Cardinal among such principles is that of effectiveness. Ever since the *Nottebohm* case, this has been the accepted premise in international law and the recent work on the diplomatic protection of persons and property of both the International Law Commission and the International Law Association so confirms.'

[21] Ibid, para 200.

[22] *Champion Trading Company, Ameritrade International Inc v Arab Republic of Egypt*, ICSID Case No ARB/02/9, Decision on Jurisdiction (21 October 2003).

before an ICSID-constituted arbitral tribunal under the US–Egypt BIT, the claimants argued application of the effective link theory in order to disavow their prejudicial Egyptian nationality. The tribunal based itself on the *A-18* decision of the Iran–US Claims Tribunal,[23] which had held that the real and effective nationality was indeed relevant 'unless an exception [was] clearly stated'.[24] Such an exception, according to the tribunal, could be found in Article 25(2)(a) of the ICSID Convention, which contained 'a clear and specific rule regarding dual nationals'.[25] The tribunal did however not exclude that there could be 'situations where the exclusion of dual nationals could lead to a result which was manifestly absurd or unreasonable', such as 'where a country continues to apply the *ius sanguinis* over many generations',[26] thus excluding third- or fourth-generation dual nationals from the scope of the Convention.

In *Olguín v Paraguay*,[27] the claimant was a US–Peruvian dual national, bringing claims against Paraguay under the Peru–Paraguay BIT. Paraguay argued that the claimant's US nationality was his effective nationality, thus depriving the tribunal of jurisdiction *ratione personae*. The tribunal rejected the Respondent's contentions, stating that:

> What is important in this case in order to determine whether the Claimant has access to the arbitral jurisdiction based on the BIT, is only whether he has Peruvian nationality and if that nationality is effective. There is no doubt on this point.[28]

Similarly, in *Pey Casado v Chile*,[29] the tribunal also clarified that in the case of dual nationals, the question of whether one of the two nationalities was the effective or dominant one was not pertinent *de lege lata* in ICSID proceedings.[30] All the tribunal had to examine in view of Article 25(2)(a) was whether one of the two nationalities was that of the Respondent State at the critical times.[31] However, it also seemed prepared to accept an exception where 'la nationalité de l'Etat d'accueil paraîtrait totalement artificielle ou totalement dépourvue d'effectivité'.[32] This was however not the case.

Other tribunals have decided in a similar manner.[33]

In a recent case brought under the United Nations Commission on International Trade Law (UNCITRAL) arbitration rules, *Serafín García Armas y Karina García Gruber v Venezuela,* the arbitral tribunal also considered the international investment law system to constitute *lex specialis* vis-à-vis customary international law and

[23] *Case No A-18*, Case No DEC 32-A18-FT (6 April 1984) 5 Iran–US CTR 251, 265.

[24] *Champion Trading v Egypt* (n 22) 16. [25] Ibid. [26] Ibid, 16–17.

[27] *Euodoro Armando Olguín v Republic of Paraguay*, ICSID Case No ARB/98/5, Award (26 July 2001) (unofficial English translation).

[28] Ibid, para 61.

[29] *Victor Pey Casado and President Allende Foundation v Republic of Chile*, ICSID Case No ARB/98/2, Sentence Arbitrale (8 May 2008).

[30] Ibid, para 241. [31] Ibid.

[32] Ibid ('where the host State nationality would seem totally artificial or without any effect', translation by the author).

[33] See, eg, *Saba Fakes v Republic of Turkey*, ICSID Case No ARB/07/20, Award (14 July 2010) paras 71–76.

thus rejected the application of the 'genuine link' theory to the claim of Spanish–Venezuelan dual nationals brought against Venezuela in the absence of an explicit effective link requirement in the Spain–Venezuela BIT.[34] The tribunal also found its view confirmed by the fact that both Venezuela and Spain had negotiated other BITs containing an effective link requirement, while the Spain–Venezuela BIT did not contain any such requirement.[35] It therefore upheld jurisdiction, making a claim by dual nationals against their State of nationality possible under UNCITRAL arbitration rules.

4.2.2 Dual nationality of a natural person exercising 'foreign control'

As already mentioned in Chapter 1, treaty shopping by a natural person is not only thinkable through the strategic acquisition of a qualifying nationality (whether as single or dual nationality), but also through the structuring of downstream investments through intermediate companies, of which the natural person becomes the controller. If the (locally incorporated) investor brings an investment claim and the upstream (ultimate) controller holds dual nationality, one of which the host State nationality, the question may be asked whether this host State nationality invalidates possible 'foreign control' within the meaning of Article 25(2)(b) second clause.

Two arbitral tribunals have been very clear in giving an answer to this question. In *Burimi SRL and Eagle Games SH.A v Albania*,[36] one of the Claimants, Eagle Games, was an Albania-incorporated company whose majority shareholding was held by an Italian–Albanian dual national. The tribunal found that:

> While neither the ICSID Convention nor relevant precedents address the potential for a dual national invoking one of his two nationalities to establish jurisdiction over a claim brought in the name of a juridical person under the second clause of Article 25(2)(b), it strikes the Tribunal as anomalous that the principle against use of dual nationality in 25(2)(a) would not transfer to the potential use of dual nationality in 25(2)(b). Otherwise, any dual national who is a national of the Contracting State to a dispute could circumvent the bar on claims in Article 25(2)(a) by establishing a company in that state and asserting foreign control of that company by virtue of his second (foreign) nationality.[37]

This finding was endorsed by the tribunal in the *National Gas v Egypt* case, where the locally incorporated company was ultimately controlled by an Egyptian–Canadian dual national and the tribunal found the reasoning in *Burimi* to be 'based on established principles with a clear dividing-line, making for legal

[34] *Serafín García Armas y Karina García Gruber v República Bolivariana de Venezuela*, UNCITRAL, PCA Case No 2013-3, Decision on Jurisdiction (Spanish) (15 December 2014) paras 158, 167–75.

[35] Ibid, paras 176–206.

[36] *Burimi SRL and Eagle Games SH.A v Republic of Albania*, ICSID Case No ARB/11/18, Award (29 May 2013).

[37] Ibid, para 121.

predictability and certainty', without for that matter considering this legal construction as abusive.[38]

4.2.3 Discussion

The analysis of the cases decided by arbitral tribunals shows that the 'effective' or 'genuine link' theory has, as a matter of *lex lata*, so far unanimously been rejected in international investment arbitration, attesting—in the absence of express treaty-based requirements—to a formal approach to the notion of investor. This establishes the regulation in Article 25(2)(a) ICSID Convention firmly as *lex specialis*,[39] where the recourse to a gap-filling function by general international law does not seem permitted (notwithstanding the at any rate dubious status of a 'general link' doctrine in general international law as already discussed further above).[40]

This holds true both where the claimant only has a single nationality and the Respondent tries to either disavow the claimant's invoked nationality[41] or argue the existence of a 'more' genuine link to the host State,[42] as well as in the case of dual or multiple nationalities where, despite its 'anchorage' now in Article 7 of the Draft Articles on Diplomatic Protection, the 'genuine link' theory cannot be used in order for the Respondent to argue that one of two nationalities is more effective or predominant[43] or for Claimant to try and disavow a prejudicial host State nationality as non-effective.[44]

This appears to confirm the view that a nationality that does not exist according to domestic law cannot be construed, whether for purposes of the positive or the negative nationality requirement, by recourse to the 'genuine link' theory, be it by the Respondent or the Claimant.[45] The above analyses in *Feldman*, *Siag*, and *Olguín* also warrant the conclusion that a nationality acquired by birth or other 'legitimate' reasons such as marriage can normally—absent specific circumstances indicating the opposite and provided for proceedings under ICSID that it is not the host State nationality—be considered as 'effective' or 'genuine', barring recourse to the 'genuine link' theory.

Whether the 'effective' or 'genuine link' theory can, on the other hand, be used in order to disavow a Claimant's nationality because of weak links to the State of claimed nationality or because of exceptional circumstances as to the acquisition

[38] *National Gas SAE v Arab Republic of Egypt*, ICSID Case No ARB/11/7, Award (3 April 2014) paras 140, 146. On the incidence of the case for the interpretation of 'foreign control' within the meaning of Article 25(2)(b) second clause see below at 4.3.4.2.

[39] Lucy Reed and Jonathan Davis, 'Ratione Personae' in Marc Bungenberg, Jörn Griebel, Stephan Hobe, and August Reinisch, *International Investment Law, A Handbook* (CH Beck, Hart Publishing and Nomos 2015) 614, 627 (para 31).

[40] See Chapter 3, at 3.2.1.2.

[41] See, eg, *Siag v Egypt* (n 19); *Oostergetel v Slovak Republic* (n 11).

[42] See, eg, *Feldman v Mexico* (n 14); *Micula v Romania* (n 6).

[43] See, eg, *Olguín v Paraguay* (n 27); *Pey Casado v Chile* (n 29).

[44] See, eg, *Champion Trading v Egypt* (n 22).

[45] Cornel Marian, 'Who is Afraid of Nottebohm? Reconciling the ICSID Nationality Requirement for Natural Persons with Nottebohm's "Effective Nationality" Test' (2011) 28 J Intl Arb 326.

of nationality seems open to discussion. While some tribunals and scholars seem favourable to this conclusion,[46] others see the corrective to a potential manipulation of nationality for purposes of accessing ICSID jurisdiction rather in the application of the abuse of rights doctrine, of which the 'genuine link' theory would in reality only be an expression.[47]

What was said above with respect to the 'genuine link' theory would in principle also seem to apply to arbitrations under the UNCITRAL arbitration rules. Yet, as seen in the recent *Serafín García Armas* case, an important difference manifests itself due to the absence of 'host State bias' under UNCITRAL rules as the one contained in Article 25(2)(a) ICSID Convention. From this follows that the UNCITRAL rules are in this respect more treaty shopping-permissive for natural persons holding dual nationality and might in the future serve more often as arbitral framework for dual (host) State nationals wishing to bring a claim against their State.[48] This means that States wishing to exclude claims by dual nationals against their State of nationality may wish to consider including an explicit effective link requirement in the BIT and/or exclude claims by host State nationals.[49]

Finally, as seen in the *Burimi* and the *National Gas* decisions, the 'host State bias' contained in Article 25(2)(a) of the Convention will 'infect' the question of whether a dual national with host State nationality will be accepted as exercising 'foreign control' over a locally incorporated company for purposes of Article 25(2)(b) second clause,[50] a question that is not relevant for arbitration under other arbitral rules.

4.3 Legal Persons

As has been seen before, the possibility to take advantage of an often complex corporate structure and the less strict nationality requirements for legal persons

[46] *Micula v Romania* (n 6) para 104; *Oostergetel v Slovak Republic* (n 11) para 132; Marian (n 45) 324ff.

[47] Robert Sloane, 'Breaking the Genuine Link: The Contemporary International Legal Regulation of Nationality' (2009) 50 Harv Intl L J 136–37; Florian Franke, *Der personelle Anwendungsbereich des internationalen Investitionsschutzrechts* (Nomos 2012) 180; Robert Hunter, 'Is a Corporation's Entitlement to the Protection of an Investment Treaty a Question Solely of Form or is it also a Question of Substance?' in ILA German Branch, Working Group, *The Determination of the Nationality of Investors under Investment Protection Treaties*, Heft 106 (2011) 47–51, available at <http://telc.jura.uni-halle.de/sites/default/files/BeitraegeTWR/Heft%20106.pdf> (last accessed on 15 September 2016). For a more in-depth discussion of this question see Chapter 9, at 9.4.

[48] See in this respect also the recent arbitration proceedings *Sergei Viktorovich Pugachev v Russian Federation*, UNCITRAL, Notice of arbitration (21 September 2015) and *Dawood Rawad v Republic of Mauritius*, UNCITRAL, Notice of arbitration and statement of claim (9 November 2015). See also Joel Dahlquist and Luke Eric Peterson, 'Analysis: $12 billion arbitration vs. Russia by exiled oligarch may be next test case by arbitrators' willingness to let dual-nationals sue their own State' *IA Reporter* (23 September 2015) available at <http://www.iareporter.com>; Jarrod Hepburn, 'Mauritius to face first known BIT claim over revoked banking licence' *IA Reporter* (9 November 2015) available at <http://www.iareporter.com> (subscription required).

[49] See in Chapter 8, at 8.2.3.1.

[50] See below at 4.3.4.2.

makes treaty shopping (much) more likely for legal than for natural persons.[51] Indeed, ever since this phenomenon has come up, it has been discussed almost exclusively with respect to legal persons. Thus, the ease with which legal entities can be brought into being in some jurisdictions and the fact that many countries attribute standing to legal entities under investment treaties on the mere basis of incorporation make it easy for legal persons to qualify under certain investment treaties.[52]

Where a corporate group has subsidiaries in several national jurisdictions, several (or all of them) may potentially qualify as claimants provided the existence of applicable bilateral or multilateral investment agreements. A parent company seeking to bring an investment claim may thus have one of its subsidiaries, incorporated in a jurisdiction that has an advantageous investment treaty with the host State, bring the claim. If no subsidiary exists in this national jurisdiction, the parent company may decide to incorporate one in that jurisdiction and insert it into the corporate chain, if only for the sake of holding the (qualifying) investment and bringing the claim. This may raise questions of a varying nature, including whether this legal entity should have to be recognized on formal grounds or whether the tribunal should ignore it, looking instead to the 'real' investor.

A host State-incorporated company may exceptionally bring an investment claim of its own against the host State. This may happen based on a provision in the IIA recognizing an investor as a national protected under the IIA even where it is incorporated in a third or the host country, but is directly or indirectly controlled by a national of one Contracting Party.[53] A claim by a host State-incorporated company is also possible under the conditions of Article 25(2)(b) second clause of the ICSID Convention, provided the parties have agreed to treat the locally incorporated company as foreign 'because of foreign control'. Arbitral tribunals have in such cases often had to decide how exactly to define the notion of 'control' respectively 'foreign control'. Where the investment treaty under interpretation provides for the possibility of denying its benefits to the putative investor–claimant, the Respondent may exercise this right, raising however the question of whether this denial has retrospective or prospective effect only.

These issues will be examined in turn.

[51] In this sense also Maurice Mendelson, 'Issues Relating to the Identity of the Investor' in Arthur W Rovine (ed), *Fordham Papers 2010, Contemporary Issues in International Arbitration and Mediation* (Brill/Martinus Nijhoff 2011) 22, 27; Christoph Schreuer, 'Nationality Planning' in Arthur W Rovine (ed), *Contemporary Issues in International Arbitration and Mediation: The Fordham Papers 2012* (Martinus Nijhoff 2013) 17, 18; Jean-François Hébert, 'Abuse of Corporate Nationality' (2010) 1 J Arb & Med 123. This seems also confirmed by the arbitral tribunal's questionable dictum in *Hussein Nuaman Soufraki v The United Arab Emirates*, ICSID Case No ARB/02/7, Award (7 July 2004) para 83. As however Reed and Davis correctly point out, investment claims by individual claimants 'are likely to increase in number given the potential for tribunals to hear mass investor–State claims' as the one in *Abaclat and others v Argentina*, see Reed and Davis (n 39) 25.

[52] Similar Reed and Davis (n 39) 623 (para 20).

[53] See, eg, Art 1(b)(iii) of the Netherlands–Argentina BIT that defines the notion of covered 'investor' among others as 'legal persons, wherever located, controlled, directly or indirectly, by nationals of that Contracting Party'.

4.3.1 Formal approach v 'piercing of the corporate veil'

The question of whether tribunals should limit its interpretation of *ratione personae* clauses to a formal reading or instead endeavour to search for the 'real' investor by 'piercing the corporate veil' has featured prominently in arbitral jurisprudence, and in particular so with respect to the notion of nationality contained in Article 25(2)(b) first clause of the ICSID Convention, which has not been defined by the drafters of the Convention.[54]

One might recall that there was ample academic discussion during the drafting stages of the Convention as to which criteria should be determinative for defining nationality for purposes of Article 25(2)(b). While both the incorporation and seat theory were considered uncontroversial (and thus determinative), the main disagreement centred on the question as to whether the control test should be formally introduced into the provision of Article 25(2)(b). In the end, this proposal was not retained due to widespread criticism that:

> 'controlling interest' was too vague a term and would be unhelpful in the case where a company, incorporated in the host country, was controlled by foreign shareholders but with ownership widely scattered among numerous shareholders of different nationalities.[55]

Yet, the disagreement remained as to whether only the incorporation and seat theory or—implicitly—also the control theory could be used to determine nationality.

According to some scholars, the determination of nationality is restricted to the incorporation and seat theory.[56] Many—in particular early—arbitral decisions have in principle endorsed this view.[57]

Broches advocated for a more flexible approach. In his already quoted Hague Lectures, he set the decision of the ICJ in *Barcelona Traction* (which accepted the incorporation theory as the only relevant theory for determining nationality under customary international law) clearly apart from the determination of nationality of an investor for purposes of Article 25(2)(b) and underlined:

> The purpose of that provision [*art 25(2)(b)*], as well as of Article 25(1), is to indicate the outer limits within which disputes may be submitted to conciliation or arbitration under the auspices of the Centre with the consent of the parties thereto. Therefore the parties should be

[54] Aron Broches, 'The Convention on the Settlement of Investment Disputes between States and Nationals of other States' Académie de droit international (1972) 136 Recueil des Cours 331, 340.

[55] Broches (n 54) 359–60; see also Christoph Schreuer, Loretta Malintoppi, August Reinisch, and Anthony Sinclair, *The ICSID Convention: A Commentary* (Cambridge University Press 2009) 'Article 25' paras 695–96.

[56] See, eg, George Delaume, 'ICSID Arbitration and the Courts' (1983) 77 ASIL 784, 793–94; Stanislav Alexandrov, 'The "Baby Boom" of Treaty-Based Arbitrations and the Jurisdiction of ICSID Tribunals: Shareholders as "Investors" and Jurisdiction Ratione Temporis' (2005) 4 LPICT 19, 36–37; Schreuer and others, *ICSID Commentary* (n 55) 'Article 25' para 707.

[57] See, eg, *Kaiser Bauxite v Jamaica*, ICSID Case No ARB/74/3, Decision on Jurisdiction (6 July 1975) para 19; *Société Ouest Africaine des Bétons Industriels (SOABI) v République du Sénégal*, ICSID Case No ARB/82/1 (1 August 1984) para 29; *AMCO Asia Corporation and others v Indonesia*, ICSID Case No ARB/81/1, Award on Jurisdiction (25 September 1983) para 14 (iii) printed in (1993) 1 ICSID Rep 377; *Autopista Concesionada de Venezuela CA (Aucoven) v Bolivarian Republic of Venezuela*, ICSID Case No ARB/00/5, Decision on Jurisdiction (27 September 2001) para 108.

given the widest possible latitude to agree on the meaning of 'nationality' and any stipulation of nationality made in connection with a conciliation or arbitration clause which is based on a reasonable criterion should be accepted.[58]

Thus, in accordance with the principle that the consent of the parties constitutes the 'cornerstone of the jurisdiction of the Centre',[59] States may, and in virtually all cases nowadays do, define in a binding manner who, that is which investor, is to be considered protected by the investment agreement in question. If the IIA includes a clause giving the investor the right to investor–State arbitration (which almost every IIA does), the definition of investor contained in the IIA becomes part of the agreement on consent between the parties and is therefore directly relevant to the determination of the nationality requirements of Article 25(2)(b).[60] In accordance with the flexible approach quoted above, ICSID tribunals should hence accept 'any reasonable determination of the nationality of juridical persons'.[61]

States may thus define corporate nationality (for purposes of international investment agreements) either by recourse to the incorporation theory (which most States do), the seat theory, the control theory, substantial business activities, or a combination of the aforementioned,[62] which ICSID tribunals are bound to accept. The same applies to definitions of corporate nationality contained in national investment legislation.[63]

Recent decisions of importance for the purposes of treaty shopping have, for Article 25(2)(b) first clause cases, consistently endorsed this flexible, though formal and consent-centred, approach. In the absence of the inclusion of the requirement of control, substantial business activities, etc. in the notion of investor in the IIA, arbitral tribunals have, as will be seen, indeed mostly been reluctant to accept that an additional control element should be implicitly read into the definition of investor, thus favouring an approach that is permissive of treaty shopping by corporate structuring or restructuring.

4.3.1.1 So-called 'round-tripping'

The question of whether a tribunal should 'pierce the corporate veil', in other words search for the 'real' controller of the investment, has been raised in several important decisions concerning so-called 'round-tripping' cases. 'Round-tripping' exists when an investor national of the host State owns or controls a corporate entity incorporated in another country that has concluded an IIA with the host State. In such cases, it has thus been argued that a national of the host State is bringing an international investment claim against its own State of nationality through the vehicle of a formally distinct, foreign investor. Respondents have in such cases

[58] Broches (n 54) 360–61.
[59] ICSID, 'Report of the Executive Directors on the Convention on the Settlement of Investment Disputes between States and Nationals of Other States' ICSID Doc 2 (18 March 1965) para 23 at 8.
[60] Schreuer and others, *ICSID Commentary* (n 55) 'Article 25' para 723.
[61] Ibid.
[62] See more in detail Chapter 8, at 8.2.3.2.1.
[63] Schreuer and others, *ICSID Commentary* (n 55) 'Article 25' para 723.

therefore asked the tribunal to 'pierce the corporate veil' and dismiss the claim on grounds of lack of *ratione personae.*

An early case of 'round-tripping' can be seen in the decision in *Wena Hotels Limited v Egypt.*[64] In that case, the UK-incorporated claimant, owned and controlled by a natural person of Egyptian and UK nationality, brought a claim against Egypt. Egypt objected that the claimant should be treated as an Egyptian national given the Egyptian ownership, and based its argument on a provision in the Egypt–UK BIT in which the parties agreed to treat, for the purposes of the Convention, 'a company of one Contracting Party in which before such a dispute arises a majority of shares are owned by nationals or companies of the Contracting Party … as a company of the other Çontracting Party' in accordance with Article 25(2)(b) second clause of the Convention. Though acknowledging that Egypt's argumentation was 'plausible on [its] face', the tribunal rejected the argument, pointing out that Article 25(2)(b) second clause of the Convention was meant to expand, not limit ICSID jurisdiction in the case where an investment was made through a local, foreign-controlled company, which was not the case here and where no evidence was adduced that the parties to the BIT had wanted to exclude companies incorporated in one Contracting State but owned and controlled by nationals of the other Contracting State.[65]

One of the best-known 'round-tripping' cases, sparking a lot of controversy, is the arbitral decision in *Tokios Tokelés v Ukraine.*[66] In this case, the claimant, bringing a claim under the Ukraine–Lithuania BIT, was a Lithuania-incorporated company that was ninety-nine per cent owned by Ukrainian nationals. The Respondent argued that the claimant was not a 'genuine entity' of Lithuania as it was owned and controlled predominantly by Ukrainian nationals, and that allowing this claim would mean that nationals could pursue an international arbitration against their own State.[67] It therefore urged the tribunal to 'pierce the corporate veil', that is 'to disregard the Claimant's State of incorporation and determine its nationality according to the nationality of its predominant shareholders and managers'.[68]

In accordance with Article 31 Vienna Convention on the Law of Treaties (VCLT), the tribunal started by interpreting the ordinary meaning of the definition of 'investor' contained in the Ukraine–Lithuania BIT, setting apart this case from the case, also contained in the definition of 'investor', of entities incorporated in third states, but controlled by nationals of Ukraine or Lithuania and having their seat in one of these two countries. Basing itself on the preamble of the Ukraine–Lithuania BIT, it

[64] *Wena Hotels Limited v Arab Republic of Egypt,* ICSID Case No ARB/98/4, Proceeding on the Jurisdiction (25 May 1999).

[65] Ibid, 888–89. As a side note, had the claimant been a locally incorporated entity owned or controlled by a dual (host State) national and bringing a claim under Art 25(2)(b) second clause, the host State nationality would most likely have barred the claim (depending on the number of interposed corporate layers and tribunals' willingness to enquire into ultimate control, as will be seen more in detail below at 4.3.4.2), while since the claimant brought the claim under Art 25(2)(b) first clause, the dual (host State) nationality remained irrelevant.

[66] *Tokios Tokelés v Ukraine,* ICSID Case No ARB/02/18, Decision on Jurisdiction (29 April 2004).

[67] Ibid, para 22.

[68] Ibid, paras 22, 23.

held the object and purpose of the BIT to be the 'broad protection of investors and their investments'.[69] Then, reviewing other investment agreements that contained express inclusion of the requirement of substantial business activities and denial of benefits provisions, the tribunal noted:

> These investment agreements confirm that States parties are capable of excluding from the scope of the agreement entities of the other party that are controlled by nationals of third countries or by nationals of the host country. The Ukraine–Lithuania BIT, by contrast, includes no such 'denial of benefits' provision with respect to entities controlled by third-country nationals or by nationals of the denying party. We regard the absence of such a provision as a deliberate choice of the Contracting Parties. In our view, it is not for tribunals to impose limits on the scope of BITs not found in the text, much less limits nowhere evident from the negotiating history. An international tribunal of defined jurisdiction should not reach out to exercise a jurisdiction beyond the borders of the definition. But equally an international tribunal should exercise, and indeed is bound to exercise, the measure of jurisdiction with which it is endowed.[70]

For the tribunal, the crucial element was how the consent of the parties to arbitration was formulated, which the tribunal was not allowed to disregard unless the Convention was being used 'for purposes for which it clearly was not intended'.[71] Moreover, it found that the use of the control test without so being foreseen by the BIT would run counter to the declared purpose of the exception contained in the second alternative of Article 25(2)(b), which was to expand jurisdiction, not restrict it.[72]

As to the Respondent's request to 'pierce the claimant's corporate veil', the tribunal reviewed the ICJ's holding in this respect in *Barcelona Traction*[73] and found that none of the criteria mentioned by the ICJ were relevant in this case at hand.[74] It also discussed other arbitral decisions that had dealt with the 'piercing of the corporate veil' and, on the basis of different facts, set them clearly apart from the case at hand.[75] Finally, it rejected the existence of an origin of capital requirement under the ICSID Convention.[76]

The majority decision triggered a strong dissent by the Chairman of the arbitral tribunal Professor Prosper Weil who took issue with what he considered a wrong philosophy of the decision. Pointing out that the purpose of the ICSID Convention was to provide a forum for *international* investment disputes,[77] that is, for disputes between host States and *foreign* investors, he criticized that the decision expanded ICSID's jurisdiction 'beyond its outer limits' by not considering the origin of the capital, which was undisputedly Ukrainian. The object and purpose of Article 25(2)(b) second clause was to give effect to the genuinely international character of an

[69] Ibid, para 31. [70] Ibid, para 36. [71] Ibid, para 39.
[72] Ibid, paras 46–47.
[73] *Barcelona Traction, Light and Power Co (Belgium v Spain) (Judgment)* [1970] ICJ Rep 3, 38–39 (para 56).
[74] *Tokios Tokelés v Ukraine* (n 66) paras 53–56. [75] Ibid, paras 57–66.
[76] Ibid, paras 80–81.
[77] *Tokios Tokelés v Ukraine* (n 66) Dissenting Opinion Prof. Weil, para 5.

apparently national investment. According to him, the same rationale applied to an apparently foreign investment where, having the economic reality prevail over the legal structure, the investment would result in being national.[78] This is why methodologically, he contended, the tribunal should have examined first whether it had jurisdiction under Article 25 of the Convention and only in the affirmative should have examined whether the definition of investor under the BIT was fulfilled.

Most academic commentators rejected this critique,[79] though some sided with Professor Weil's reasoning.[80] Whatever however commentators supporting the minority opinion may argue, it is a fact that it has been rejected by the majority of subsequent arbitral jurisprudence except in *TSA Spectrum v Argentina* (which, as will be seen further below, can be distinguished on the facts of the case).[81]

Thus, the line taken by the majority decision in *Tokios Tokelés* was confirmed by the arbitral tribunal in *Rompetrol v Romania*,[82] a similar round-tripping case. In *Rompetrol v Romania*, a Netherlands-incorporated company owned and controlled by Romanian nationals brought claims against Romania under the Dutch–Romania BIT. The Respondent argued along Professor Weil's minority opinion.

The tribunal rejected Professor Weil's methodological critique, remarking that:

> Given the latitude granted to States under the ICSID Convention to settle the applicable nationality criteria, there is nothing illogical in looking first of all to whether the nationality criteria set forth in the BIT are satisfied before going on to examine whether there is anything in Article 25 of the Convention which stands in the way of giving effect to that.[83]

It added that ignoring the definition of investor contained in the BIT would amount to 'setting aside the clear language agreed upon by the treaty Parties in favour of a wide-ranging policy discussion'.[84] As for Respondent's request to disregard Claimant's Dutch nationality, the tribunal also rejected the view that there was in international law a 'general rule of "effective and genuine nationality" for determining the status of corporate entities'.[85]

The tribunal also gave a convincing argument on why it considered Professor Weil's critique in *Tokios Tokelés* as methodologically flawed as to the order of examination of the notion of investor contained in the BIT and the ICSID Convention. It pointed out that the ICSID forum was in most BITs only one of several possible

[78] Ibid, para 23.

[79] See, eg, Robert Wisner and Nick Gallus, 'Nationality Requirements in Investor-State Arbitration' (2004) 5 JWIT 927, 944; Alexandrov, 'Shareholders' (n 56) 37; Emmanuel Gaillard, 'Chronique des Sentences Arbitrales' (2009) JDI (Clunet) No 1, 355, 366–67.

[80] See, eg, Markus Burgstaller, 'Nationality of Corporate Investors and International Claims against the Investor's Own State' (2006) 7 JWIT 857; Délphine Burriez, 'Treaty Shopping par incorporation' (2010) 25 ICSID Review-FILJ 394, 399; Franke (n 47) 261; Engela Schlemmer, 'Investment, Investor, Nationality and Shareholders' in Peter Muchlinski, Federico Ortino, and Christoph Schreuer, *The Oxford Handbook of International Investment Law* (Oxford University Press 2008) 51, 80–81.

[81] See below at 4.3.4.2.

[82] *Rompetrol Group NV v Republic of Romania*, ICSID Case No ARB/06/3, Decision on Respondent's Preliminary Objections on Jurisdiction and Admissibility (18 April 2008).

[83] Ibid, para 82.

[84] Ibid, para 85.

[85] Ibid, para 92.

dispute fora in which to pursue an investment claim, one on an equal footing with other arbitral proceedings, whether under UNCITRAL or ad hoc arbitration rules. This meant that the ICSID Convention could not be argued to have an overriding effect for purposes of interpreting the BIT, as this would mean attaching to the BIT different interpretations, depending on whether the investor chose arbitral proceedings under the ICSID Convention or other institutional rules.[86]

A similar approach to 'round-tripping' was also taken by the tribunal in *Alpha Projektholding GmbH v Ukraine*.[87]

As pointed out by Professor Weil's minority opinion in *Tokios Tokelés*, the quintessential question in so-called 'round-tripping' cases is whether there is an (implicit) origin of capital requirement in international investment law in the sense that the origin of the capital invested defines the nationality of the investment. Though national security concerns have been on the rise as of late,[88] suggesting that it increasingly does matter to states where the capital is coming from, the by far prevailing opinion has, in the absence of an explicit origin of capital requirement in the invoked investment treaty,[89] thus far rejected an origin of capital requirement,[90] in the same manner as it has refused to 'pierce the corporate veil'.[91]

More recently, though, the arbitral tribunal in *Venoklim Holding BV v Venezuela* declined jurisdiction of a claim brought by a Netherlands-incorporated claimant

[86] Ibid, para 107.

[87] *Alpha Projektholding GmbH v Ukraine*, ICSID Case No ARB/07/16, Award (8 November 2010) paras 343–45. Similar in *KT Asia Investment Group BV v Republic of Kazakhstan*, ICSID Case No ARB/09/8, Award (17 October 2013) paras 111–39.

[88] Kalman Kalotay, 'Does it matter who invests in your country' *Columbia FDI Perspectives*, No 66 (April 30, 2012) available at <http://ccsi.columbia.edu/files/2014/01/FDI_66.pdf>; House of Commons Business, Innovation and Skills Committee, 2010. 'Mergers, Acquisitions and Takeovers: the Takeover of Cadbury by Kraft' Ninth Report of Session 2009–2010. HC 234, available at <http://www.publications.parliament.uk/pa/cm200910/cmselect/cmbis/234/234.pdf> (both last accessed on 15 September 2016).

[89] Such as, eg, Art 1 of the 1998 ASEAN Framework Agreement: 'For the purposes of this Agreement, "ASEAN investor" means—i. a national of a Member State; or ii. any juridical person of a Member State, making an investment in another Member State, the effective ASEAN equity of which taken cumulatively with all other ASEAN equities fulfills at least the minimum percentage required to meet the national equity requirement and other equity requirements of domestic laws and published national policies, if any, of the host country in respect of that investment.'

[90] See, eg, *Tradex Hellas SA v Republic of Albania*, Award, Case No ARB/94/2 (29 April 1999) para 105; *Tokios Tokelés v Ukraine* (n 66) paras 80ff; *Yukos Universal Ltd (Isle of Man) v Russian Federation*, UNCITRAL, PCA Case No AA 227, Interim Award on Jurisdiction and Admissibility (30 November 2009) para 432; *ADC Affiliate Limited & ADMC Management Limited v Republic of Hungary*, ICSID Case No ARB/03/16, Award (2 October 2006) para 360; see also Stephan Schill, *The Multilateralization of International Investment Law* (Cambridge University Press 2009) 228, 235. For a contrary opinion see, eg, Peter Muchlinski, 'Corporations and the Uses of Law: International Investment Arbitration as a "Multilateral Legal Order"', Oñati Socio-Legal Series, Vol 1, No 4 (2011)—Socio-Legal Aspects of Adjudication of International Economic Disputes, 19, available at <http://papers.ssrn.com/sol3/papers.cfm?abstract_id=1832562> (last accessed on 15 September 2016).

[91] Similar Rachel Thorn and Jennifer Doucleff, 'Disregarding the Corporate Veil and Denial of Benefits Clauses: Testing Treaty Language and the Concept of "Investor"' in Michael Waibel, Asha Kaushal, Kyo-Hwa Chung, and Claire Balchin (eds), *The Backlash against Investment Arbitration* (Kluwer Law International 2010) 3, 14.

against Venezuela on the grounds that this claimant was effectively controlled by Venezuelan nationals and companies.[92] A peculiarity of this case was that even though the claim could have in theory been based directly on the 1991 Netherlands–Venezuela BIT, the claimant invoked the Venezuelan Investment Law as legal basis for the tribunal's jurisdiction. According to Article 22 of this Investment Law, '[l]as controversias que surjan entre un inversionista internacional, cuyo país de origen tenga vigente con Venezuela un tratado o acuerdo sobre promoción y protección de inversiones ... serán sometidas al arbitraje internacional en los términos del respectivo tratado o acuerdo',[93] with 'international investor' being defined in its Article 3(4) as '[e]l propietario de una inversión internacional, o quien efectivamente la controle'[94] and 'international investment' in Article 3(2) as '[l]a inversión que es propiedad de, o que es efectivamente controlada por personas naturales o jurídicas extranjeras'.[95]

The tribunal found that in order to validly invoke the Venezuelan Investment Law, the claimant had to be an 'international investor' within the meaning of its Article 3(2) and (4). Even though it was undisputed that the claimant held majority shareholdings of five of the locally incorporated companies allegedly affected by the expropriation decree either directly or indirectly, the arbitral tribunal only analysed who held ultimate effective control over the claimant, finding that this ultimate effective control lay with several Venezuelan companies and nationals.[96] Though already having determined that the claimant did not qualify as international investor for purposes of the Venezuelan Investment Law, the tribunal also briefly touched upon Article 25 ICSID Convention and found that:

> Pretender que se considere como una inversión extranjera la efectuada por Venoklim por el solo hecho de ser esta una compañía incorporada en los Países Bajos, aunque la inversión objeto de la disputa sea en definitiva propiedad de personas jurídicas venezolanas, sería permitir que prevalezca el formalismo sobre la realidad y traicionar el objeto y el fin del Convenio CIADI.[97]

One arbitrator dissented from this majority decision, criticizing that the tribunal did not let suffice the criterion of 'ownership' (which would have been fulfilled in his view), that it did not take into account the definition of investor under the

[92] *Venoklim Holding BV v Bolivarian Republic of Venezuela*, ICSID Case No ARB/12/22, Award (Spanish) (3 April 2015).

[93] Ibid, para 44 ('The disputes that may arise between an international investor, whose home country has a treaty or agreement on the promotion and protection of investments in force ... will be submitted to international arbitration according to the terms of the respective treaty or agreement', translation by this author).

[94] 'The owner, or effective controller, of an international investment' (translation by this author).

[95] 'The investment that is owned, or effectively controlled, by foreign natural or legal persons' (translation by this author).

[96] *Venoklim Holding BV v Venezuela* (n 92) paras 144–48.

[97] Ibid, para 156 ('To pretend that one should consider the investment made by Venoklim as an foreign investment because of the simple fact that it is a company incorporated in the Netherlands, even though the investment object of the dispute is definitely owned by Venezuelan legal persons, would allow formalism to prime over reality and the object and purpose of the ICSID Convention to be betrayed', translation by this author).

Netherlands–Venezuela BIT, and that it effectively 'pierced the corporate veil' of the claimant without sufficiently arguing the existence of the circumstances potentially warranting such exceptional operation.[98]

4.3.1.2 So-called mailbox or shell companies

Tribunals also regularly have had to decide on whether the fact that the claimant is a so-called shell or mailbox company constitutes a bar to its jurisdiction, that is whether in such a case, it should look towards the 'real' investor owning or controlling the shell company. Often, the owning or controlling investor will be a third State or host State national, which is why the question of mailbox companies may overlap with the problems presented in 'round-tripping' cases, the vehicle used for 'round-tripping' often being a mailbox company.

As for the notion of treaty shopping, there is no universal definition of the notion of mailbox or shell company. The essence of what constitutes a mailbox or shell company may however be captured by recourse to typical denial of benefits clauses that deny the protection of the treaty to a company which does not have any substantial business activities in the home State territory and is owned or controlled by nationals either of the host State or of a non-Party.[99]

In a similar vein, Article 9 *in fine* of the 2006 International Law Commission (ILC) Draft Articles on Diplomatic Protection recognizes an exception to the incorporation theory in the case of mailbox or shell companies, which it defines in a more restrictive way as a:

> corporation ... controlled by nationals of another State or States and [which] has no substantial business activities in the State of incorporation, and the seat of management and the financial control of the corporation are both located in another State.

It can thus be extrapolated that typical characteristics of a mailbox or include at a minimum the absence of substantial business activities in the State of incorporation and the fact that it is owned or controlled by nationals of another State, in particular of the host State or a third State, though additional requirements in order not to qualify as a mailbox or shell company may be included by States in their agreements.

As it will be seen further below, States that wish to prevent mailbox companies from benefitting from treaty protection have thus the possibility to prescribe certain requirements the investor has to fulfil in order to be eligible as protected investor under the invoked treaty, or they may include a denial of benefits (DOB) clause in the treaty. In the absence of such requirements respectively clauses in the BIT, arbitral tribunals have thus far taken strictly formal approaches to mailbox or shell companies and have accordingly dismissed the contention that the mere

[98] *Venoklim Holding BV v Venezuela* (n 92) Concurring and Dissenting Opinion Arbitrator Enrique Gómez Pinzón, paras 22–23, 31, and 38.

[99] See, eg, Art 17(2) of the 2012 US Model BIT; similar Art 17(1) of the ECT; Art 10.12(2) of the 2004 CAFTA. On denial of benefits clauses see more in detail below at 4.3.3.

fact of the investor being a shell company constituted a bar to jurisdiction *ratione personae*.

In *ADC Affiliate v Hungary*,[100] the claimants, companies incorporated in Cyprus, but controlled by Canadian nationals, brought a claim under the Cyprus–Hungary BIT. Hungary objected that the claimants constituted mailbox companies aimed at providing access to ICSID jurisdiction for nationals of a State non-Party to the ICSID Convention (i.e. Canada) and therefore asked the tribunal to 'pierce the corporate veil' of the claimants. The tribunal rejected this contention, noting that:

> The BIT [was] governing, and in its Art. 1(3)(b), Cyprus and Hungary have agreed that a Cypriot 'investor' protected by that treaty includes a 'legal person constituted or incorporated in compliance with the law' of Cyprus, which each Claimant is conceded to be ... As the matter of nationality is settled unambiguously by the Convention and the BIT, there is no scope for consideration of customary law principles of nationality, as reflected in *Barcelona Traction*, which in any event are no different. In either case inquiry stops upon establishment of the State of incorporation, and considerations of whence comes the company's capital and whose nationals, if not Cypriot, control it are irrelevant.[101]

It also dismissed the contention that it should 'pierce the corporate veil', finding:

> no 'genuine link' requirement in the Cyprus-Hungary BIT either. While the Tribunal acknowledges that such requirement has been applied to some preceding international law cases, it concludes that such a requirement does not exist in the current case. When negotiating the BIT, the Government of Hungary could have inserted this requirement as it did in other BITs concluded both before and after the conclusion of the BIT in this case. However, it did not do so ... The Tribunal cannot read more into the BIT than one can discern from its plain text.[102]

It also concurred with the majority opinion in *Tokios Tokelés* which had held that the origin of capital was not a relevant factor in determining the Claimant's nationality, and stressed the fact that the Hungarian Government knew at all times in its dealings with the claimants that they were incorporated in Cyprus without having substantial business activities there.[103]

A similar consent-oriented and formal approach was taken by the tribunal in the decision *Saluka Investments BV v Czech Republic*.[104] In that case, the Respondent also objected to the tribunal's jurisdiction *ratione personae* on the grounds that the claimant was a shell company incorporated in the Netherlands without any substantial business activities there and owned or controlled by investors of a third State (Japan). Again, the tribunal strictly referred to the terms of the invoked investment treaty, holding that:

> To depart from that conclusion requires clear language in the Treaty, but there is none ... The parties having agreed that any legal person constituted under their laws is entitled to invoke the protection of the Treaty, and having agreed so without reference to any question

[100] *ADC Affiliate v Hungary* (n 90). [101] Ibid, para 357. [102] Ibid, para 359.
[103] Ibid, para 360; *Tokios Tokelés v Ukraine* (n 66) paras 80–81.
[104] *Saluka Investments BV v Czech Republic*, UNCITRAL, Partial Award (17 March 2006).

of their relationship to some other third State corporation, it is beyond the powers of the Tribunal to import into the definition of 'investor' some requirement relating to such a relationship having the effect of excluding from the Treaty's protection a company which the language agreed by the parties included within it.[105]

The tribunal also dismissed the contention that:

an investor—and particularly a portfolio investor—[showed] a lack of good faith in failing to disclose to the seller of shares, or to the host State's regulatory authorities, its ultimate objectives in entering into a share purchase transaction … In the Tribunal's view, it is both unreasonable and unrealistic to posit an obligation upon an investor to disclose its ultimate objectives in making a particular investment, whether through the purchase of shares or otherwise.[106]

The tribunal conceded that it had:

some sympathy for the argument that a company which has no real connection with a State party to a BIT, and which is in reality a mere shell company controlled by another company which is not constituted under the laws of that State, should not be entitled to invoke the provisions of that treaty. Such a possibility lends itself to abuses of the arbitral procedure, and to practices of 'treaty shopping' which can share many of the disadvantages of the widely criticized practice of 'forum shopping'.[107]

However, it found that:

The predominant factor which must guide the Tribunal's exercise of its functions is the terms in which the parties to the Treaty now in question have agreed to establish the Tribunal's jurisdiction. In the present context, that means the terms in which they have agreed upon who is an investor who may become a claimant entitled to invoke the Treaty's arbitration procedures. The parties had complete freedom of choice in this matter, and they chose to limit entitled 'investors' to those satisfying the definition set out in Art. 1 of the Treaty. The Tribunal cannot in effect impose upon the parties a definition of 'investor' other than that which they themselves agreed.[108]

Finally, it also attached importance to the fact that the Czech authorities knew at all times in their dealings with claimants that these were 'special-purpose vehicles set up for the specific and sole purpose of holding those shares'.[109]

Similar findings were made by the tribunals in *Yukos Universal Limited v Russian Federation*[110] and in the more recent case *Niko Resources (Bangladesh) Ltd v Bangladesh et al.*[111] The tribunal in the latter case also stressed the fact that Claimant's nature as 'vehicle of convenience' was at all times known to, and accepted by, the Respondent.[112]

105 Ibid, para 229. 106 Ibid, para 232. 107 Ibid, para 240.
108 Ibid, para 241. 109 Ibid, para 242. 110 *Yukos v Russia* (n 90) paras 399ff.
111 *Niko Resources (Bangladesh) Ltd v People's Republic of Bangladesh, Bangladesh Petroleum Exploration & Production Company Limited ("Bapex") and Bangladesh Oil Gas and Mineral Corporation ("Petrobangla")* ICSID Case No ARB/10/11 and 10/18, Decision on Jurisdiction (19 August 2013) para 203.
112 Ibid, para 182.

The reviewed cases confirm that in the absence of respective requirements, tribunals will not be prepared to depart from their formal approach to treaty interpretation. As the tribunal in *Yukos* remarked:

> The principles of international law, which have an unquestionable importance in treaty interpretation, do not allow an arbitral tribunal to write new, additional requirements—which the drafters did not include—into a treaty, no matter how auspicious or appropriate they may appear.[113]

Similarly, the tribunal in the recent *KT Asia v Kazakhstan* case (though properly speaking a 'round-tripping' case) noted that since the Netherlands–Kazakhstan BIT did not contain any additional requirements for the notion of investor, while other BITs concluded by Kazakhstan did, Claimant's nationality thus had to be determined by recourse to its place of incorporation only.[114] It also rejected Respondent's arguments that Claimant's corporate veil should be pierced, adhering to the majority opinion in *Tokios Tokelés*.[115]

4.3.1.3 Discussion

In cases where foreign-incorporated (mailbox) companies are claimants, the attempt to rely on Professor Weil's dissenting opinion in *Tokios Tokelés*, however desirable it may be from a policy point of view, does not convince in legal terms. In this sense, a clear distinction needs to be made between claims brought under Article 25(2)(b) first clause and those brought under Article 25(2)(b) second clause, for which a different solution may be warranted.[116] This distinction has not been sufficiently made in some of the *Tokios Tokelés* majority opinion critiques,[117] yet has crucial implications.

As already seen further above, the ICSID Convention means to leave the 'widest possible latitude to agree on the meaning of "nationality" and any stipulation of nationality made in connection with a conciliation or arbitration clause which is based on a reasonable criterion should be accepted'.[118] In this sense, parties may agree on a control criterion—usually to expand a tribunal's jurisdiction—and control

[113] *Yukos v Russia* (n 90) para 415, with reference to *Acquisition of Polish Nationality (Advisory Opinion)* [1923] PCIJ Series B No 7, 20: 'To impose an additional condition for the acquisition of Polish nationality, a condition not provided for in the Treaty ... would be equivalent not to interpreting the Treaty, but to reconstructing it'.

[114] *KT Asia v Kazakhstan* (n 87) para 123. Similar *Gold Reserve Inc v Bolivarian Republic of Venezuela*, ICSID Case No ARB(AF)/09/1, Award (22 September 2014) para 252.

[115] *KT Asia v Kazakhstan* (n 87) paras 126ff, 135ff.

[116] In this sense also *KT Asia v Kazakhstan* (n 87) para 132. For a discussion of the *TSA Spectrum v Argentina* case, see also below at 4.3.4.2.

[117] See, eg, Burgstaller, 'Nationality of Corporate Investors' (n 80) 866–71; Antoine Martin, 'International Investment Disputes, Nationality and Corporate Veil: Some Insights From Tokios Tokelès and TSA Spectrum de Argentina' (2011) 8 TDM 4, available at <http://www.transnational-dispute-management.com>; Omar García-Bolívar, 'The Issue of a Foreign Company Wholly Owned by National Shareholders in the Context of ICSID Arbitration' (2005) 2 TDM 6–7, available at <http://www.transnational-dispute-management.com> (subscription required).

[118] Broches (n 54) 360–61.

being considered a 'reasonable' criterion, tribunals are bound to accept it. However, when parties to the BIT decide to let a foreign-incorporated company qualify as potential claimant without any further restrictions and omit to include a denial of benefits clause, tribunals have in this author's opinion been correct—absent particular circumstances indicating fraud or abuse—in their objective to uphold the Contracting Parties' sovereign consent and not to let policy arguments prevail.

Already Professor Weil's methodological critique, according to which the arbitral tribunal should have first examined its jurisdiction under the ICSID Convention and only in a second step its jurisdiction under the BIT, does not persuade.[119] The tribunal can derive its jurisdiction at the outset only from the consent to arbitration clause contained in the BIT (the consent given by the Claimant by bringing the claim not being at stake here), and it is this same consent that makes proceedings under the ICSID Convention only possible (that is, if the conditions stipulated in the dispute settlement clause, with the specific meanings attached to them by the BIT, are fulfilled). The order taken by the majority opinion would therefore appear a logical necessity.

The dissenting opinion does not convince on grounds of treaty interpretation either. Commentators have rightly argued that, though interpretation in principle being a unitary process, the object and purpose of a provision is subordinate to the ordinary meaning and can thus not be used in order to 'arrive at a meaning that contradicts or displaces the clear meaning of a treaty text'.[120] This is however exactly what the dissenting opinion does, leading to a selective use of interpretative methods.[121] Though Professor Weil is right in underlining the objective of the Convention being the stimulation of private *international* investment, this sole objective would thus not be able to displace the clear agreement of the Contracting Parties of a reasonable criterion on nationality.

It should also be noted that Article 31(1) VCLT provides that '[a] treaty shall be interpreted in good faith in accordance with the ordinary meaning to be given to the terms of the treaty in their context and in the light of *its* object and purpose' (emphasis added). A provision contained in a BIT is thus in principle to be interpreted in the light of the object and purpose *of the BIT*, not in the light of the object and purpose of the ICSID Convention. In keeping with the double-barrelled test, this does not mean that the object and purpose of the ICSID Convention are insignificant. However, these are two separate methodological steps that should be kept apart. But even for the second leg of the examination, the question of whether the object and purpose of the ICSID Convention, that is the objective of providing a forum only for 'genuinely' international investments, would inherently bar claims brought by host or third State-controlled mailbox companies, Professor Weil's argumentation does not explain why—absent abusive circumstances—these

[119] *Tokios Tokelés v Ukraine* (n 66) Dissenting Opinion Prof. Weil, para 14.

[120] Romesh Weeramantry, *Treaty Interpretation in Investment Arbitration* (Oxford University Press 2012) paras 3.70–3.71. Similar Ian Sinclair, *The Vienna Convention on the Law of Treaties* (Manchester University Press 1984) 130; Richard Gardiner, *Treaty Interpretation* (Oxford University Press 2008) 190.

[121] Weeramantry (n 120) para 3.06.

companies would not qualify as foreign investors if these fulfil the nationality test required by the BIT in question, which on top is widely recognized by customary international law.[122] Indeed, as seen in the ICJ's holding in *Barcelona Traction*, incorporation *may* be considered as creating a 'close and permanent connection' with the State of incorporation.[123] At the time of the judgment, the world court was of course not yet very concerned by (or aware of) the potential problems created by mailbox companies, being a phenomenon that is intrinsically linked to the increased mobility of capital and thus to globalization. Yet, it would in this author's view seem wrong to attach a (negative) value judgment to an organizational form that is not only one of the most widely used in State practice, but remains in the absence of an international prescription also perfectly legal. In other words, it is not the form per se that renders a mailbox company potentially abusive, but the objective that is pursued with it. If States do not want to confer benefits to mailbox companies, they are free to exclude them from coverage.

Most of the above criticism would also seem to apply to the recent majority decision in *Venoklim Holding BV v Venezuela* where for the first time since the *Tokios Tokelés* dissenting opinion, the tribunal declined jurisdiction—in this author's opinion erroneously—for a claim by a foreign-incorporated investor because of ultimate host State control. Not only did the tribunal ignore the clear language of the domestic investment law in favour of an object and purpose-based interpretation, not letting qualify the Netherlands-incorporated company even though it held majority shareholding of the affected local companies, thus formally fulfilling the requirements.[124] As rightly remarked by the dissenting arbitrator, it also could not have enquired into the ultimate control without effectively 'piercing the corporate veil', yet any discussion of the necessary justification for 'piercing the veil' is blatantly absent from the tribunal's deliberations.[125]

Some have also suggested that the object and purpose of the ICSID Convention warranted the 'piercing of the veil' of a mailbox company in case of 'suspicion of host State control'.[126] Like Professor Weil's dissenting opinion, this argumentation uses the object and purpose-based interpretative method to justify the disqualification of the mailbox company, not however without conflating this interpretative method with an already vague figure of the 'piercing of the

[122] The same observation may be made with respect to a similar argumentation in M Sornarajah, 'Good Faith, Corporate Nationality, and Denial of Benefits' in Andrew Mitchell, M Sornarajah, and Tania Voon, *Good Faith and International Economic Law* (Oxford University Press 2015) 117, 122–25.

[123] *Barcelona Traction* (n 73) 42 (para 71).

[124] Even more so since Art 22 required ownership *or* effective control, not ownership *and* effective control, though admittedly the claimant had not raised the argument of ownership.

[125] As a side remark, the majority's interpretation of the definition of protected investor under Art 22 Venezuelan Investment Law, a unilateral instrument, had the effect of 'overriding' the scope of consent as to the definition of protected investor in the Netherlands–Venezuela BIT, a bilateral treaty. If this were correct, any State not happy with 'old-style' BITs could simply enact a domestic investment law with more restrictive investor definitions without having to pass through renegotiations and/or treaty terminations.

[126] Sange Addison-Agyei, *Nationality Planning und Treaty Shopping im Internationalen Investitionsrecht* (Frankfurt aM, Peter Lang 2012) 145–54.

veil'.[127] The proposal additionally raises the question—left unanswered by that commentator—of how the suspicion of host State control should be treated in procedural terms. In other words, should it translate into a reversal of the burden of proof onto the claimant as to the non-existence of host State control? This is not clear and seems difficult to argue in the absence of a treaty-based reversal of the burden of proof.

In the absence of a corresponding treaty-based requirement or a denial of benefits clause and absent circumstances that establish an abuse of the ICSID Convention, foreign-incorporated companies (whether mailbox or not) can in this author's opinion therefore not be barred from access to ICSID proceedings on the basis of the object and purpose of the ICSID Convention. This applies in this author's opinion regardless of whether the company is owned or controlled by host State or third State nationals.[128]

4.3.2 Substantive link requirements

As seen above, if States thus want to avoid extending protection to mailbox or shell companies, they have to prescribe explicitly the additional requirements an investor will have to fulfil in order to be eligible for protection under the treaty. Thus, some countries include the requirement that the investor has to have its 'real seat'/ 'effective management' or 'substantive business activities'/'real economic activities' in its home State to qualify as protected investor under the IIA.[129] Yet, in practice, it is not always clear how to interpret these terms.

One arbitral decision that discussed the additional requirement of 'effective management' contained in an investment treaty is the case *Yaung Chi Oo Trading Pte Ltd v Myanmar*.[130] In that case, the tribunal had to examine Article I(2) of the 1987 ASEAN Investment Agreement, according to which 'the term "company" of a Contracting Party shall mean a corporation, partnership or business association, incorporated or constituted under the laws in force in the territory of any Contracting Party wherein the place of effective management is situated'. Noting that the requirement of effective management of the investing company in the place of incorporation 'was primarily included in the 1987 ASEAN Agreement to avoid what has been referred to as "protection shopping", i.e. the adoption of a local corporate form without any real economic connection in order to bring a foreign entity or investment within the scope of treaty protection',[131] the tribunal found that 'the existence of a resident director and the required annual auditing of accounts [were] indicia of effective management', as well as a 'continuous procurement from … [and] an address in Singapore'.[132]

[127] See more in detail Chapter 9, at 9.4.2.

[128] But see the discussion at 4.3.4.2.2 below.

[129] For examples see Chapter 8, at 8.2.3.2.1.

[130] *Yaung Chi Oo Trading Pte Ltd v Government of the Union of Myanmar*, ASEAN ID Case No ARB/01/1, Award (31 March 2003).

[131] Ibid, para 52.

[132] Ibid.

More difficult to interpret is the notion of 'substantive business activities'. What qualifies as 'business activities' and when can they be said to be 'substantive'? Some authors find 'substantial business activities' to exist when the company is:

engaged in buying, selling, and contracting in that territory beyond the normal activities or functions required merely by the fact of its corporate existence (such as corporate registration and administration, including holding requisite board or shareholders' meetings and the payment of associated taxes and corporate registration fees). One would also expect such a company: (1) to have employees in the territory of the Contracting Party in which it is organized carrying out assignments in furtherance of the business; (2) to have resident managers involved in a hands-on manner in the actual decision-making of the business; (3) to be party to substantial transactions in the Area of the Contracting Party associated with the furtherance of the business; (4) to pay taxes to the treasury of that Contracting Party in relation to profits earned from these transactions; and (5) to engage in procurement locally of inputs for the business.[133]

The tribunal in *Pac Rim v El Salvador*[134] held that the requirement of 'substantial business activities', for a traditional holding company not to qualify as a prejudicial mailbox company, required 'usually a board of directors, board minutes, a continuous physical presence and a bank account' and an 'active holding of the shares in subsidiaries' as opposed to 'nominal, passive, limited and insubstantial activities'.[135]

The 'real economic activities' requirement under the 1990 Czech and Slovak Republic–Switzerland BIT was subject of Slovakia's objections against the claim of Switzerland-incorporated Alps Finance and Trade AG brought under ad hoc arbitral proceedings in the *Alps Finance and Trade v Slovak Republic* case.[136] The tribunal considered the proof adduced by the claimant as insufficient both as concerns the existence of claimant's seat as the existence of 'real economic activities' in Switzerland. The tribunal found that:

Proof of 'business seat', in the meaning of an effective center of administration of the business operations, [required] additional elements, such as the proof that: the place where the company board of directors regularly meets or the shareholders' meetings are held in [sic] Swiss territory; there is a management at the top of the company sitting in Switzerland; the company has a certain number of employees working at the seat; an address with phone and fax numbers are offered to third parties entering into contact with the company; certain general expenses or overhead costs are incurred for the maintenance of the physical location of the seat and related services, which would be a clear indication that a business entity is effectively organized at a given Swiss place.[137]

[133] Stephan Jagusch and Anthony Sinclair, 'Part II–Denial of advantages under Article 17(1)' in Graham Coop and Clarisse Ribeiro (eds), *Investment Protection and the Energy Charter Treaty* (Juris Publishing 2008) 20.

[134] *Pac Rim Cayman LLC v Republic of El Salvador*, ICSID Case No ARB/09/12, Decision on the Respondent's Jurisdictional Objections (1 June 2012).

[135] Ibid, paras 4.72 and 4.75.

[136] *Alps Finance and Trade AG v Slovak Republic*, UNCITRAL, Award (5 March 2011).

[137] Ibid, para 217. Similar see, eg, *Société Civile Immobilioère de Gaëta v République de Guinée*, ICSID Case No ARB/12/36, Award (French) (21 December 2015) para 144: 'Ce qui importe en

As for the requirement of 'real economic activities', the tribunal noted that:

> The 2007 tax return [indicated] a quite modest turnover and nothing [was] exhibited for the outstanding years. The Claimant was unable to establish number and type of its clients, type of its operations, kind of contracts it enters into, quantity and type of personnel, nature and composition of its managing bodies. It even admitted that it has no employees.[138]

It even found out that the telephone and fax numbers presented by the claimant 'belonged to a ... tax advisory service'.[139]

4.3.3 Denial of benefit clauses

If States want to avoid that mailbox or shell companies come under the protection of their investment treaties, they may include so-called denial of benefit—DOB—clauses into their IIAs. These clauses have in recent years increasingly crystallized as a possibility to keep at bay attempts by investors to take advantage of tribunals' mainly formal approaches to mailbox or shell companies and their overall refusal to 'pierce the corporate veil' and thus to come under the benefit of advantageous investment agreements by virtue of the corporate restructuring.[140]

Though clauses may slightly differ in their wording, they commonly deny the advantages of the invoked treaty (or parts of it) to companies that do not have substantial business activities either in their home State (or other States party to the invoked treaty), and that are owned or controlled by persons nationals of the host State or third States not party to the invoked treaty.[141] States have been increasingly including such denial of benefits clauses into investment treaties.[142]

DOB clauses clearly have the benefit of providing for *treaty-based* limitations to potentially abusive treaty shopping by way of mailbox/shell companies, giving expression to the Contracting Parties' intentions and thus guiding an arbitral tribunal's interpretive task to a considerable extent.[143] One author sees DOB clauses as a correlative to the increasingly expansive interpretation of the notions of investor and investment, leading to the direct standing of indirect investors, itself a consequence of the development of the law after *Barcelona Traction*.[144] However, in spite of this limitation of possible arbitral discretion, there remain to date important unsettled questions that arbitral tribunals have answered in disparate ways.

effet, c'est de rechercher où se trouve son principal établissement. Le fait pour une société d'avoir son principal établissement, ses organes de direction et ses services administratifs en France et de conclure ses contrats principaux en France est déterminant pour fixer le siège réel de la société en France' ('what is in fact important is to look for the principal place of business. For a company to have its principal place of business, its management organs and its administrative services in France and to conclude its principal contracts in France is determinative for confirming the real seat of the company in France', translation by the author).

138 Ibid, para 219.

139 Ibid, para 223.

140 Similar Panayotis Protopsaltis, 'The Challenge of the Barcelona Traction Hypothesis' (2010) 11 JWIT 561, 596.

141 Similar Thorn and Doucleff (n 91) 10.

142 See Chapter 8, at 8.2.3.2.2.

143 In this sense Mark Feldman, 'Setting Limits on Corporate Nationality Planning in Investment Treaty Arbitration' (2012) 27 ICSID Review-FILJ 281ff, 293ff.

144 Protopsaltis (n 140) 597.

4.3.3.1 *Prospective or retrospective effect?*

The question that interests most for the purposes of this research is whether the right to deny benefits or advantages arising out of the invoked investment agreement must be exercised by the respondent State and, if so, whether this exercise has only prospective or retrospective effect. It is clear that accepting retroactive effect of its invocation limits the possibility of treaty shopping.

One of the first cases in which this question was decided was *Plama v Bulgaria*.[145] In this case, the Respondent sought to deny the benefits under Part III of the ECT to the claimant, a Cyprus-incorporated company. The tribunal found that 'the interpretation of Article 17(1) of the Energy Charter Treaty (ECT) under Article 31(1) of the Vienna Convention [required] the right of denial to be exercised by the Contracting State'[146] and that 'a putative covered investor [having] legitimate expectations of such advantages until that right's exercise, … the object and purpose of the ECT [suggested] that the right's exercise should not have retrospective effect', but only prospective effect from the date's exercise onwards.[147]

Other arbitral tribunals have followed the *Plama* tribunal's holding. The tribunal in *Liman Caspian Oil v Kazakhstan* agreed that a notification requirement arose from the use of the word 'reserves the right to deny', implying that 'to reserve a right, it has to be exercised in an explicit way'.[148] It equally found that the object and purpose of the ECT being the promotion of the long-term cooperation in the energy field, a retroactive application of the DOB clause would be contrary to this declared objective and the principle of legal security more generally speaking.[149] The tribunal in the recent *Ascom and Stati v Kazakhstan* case also reconfirmed the *Plama* approach.[150] For the DOB clause under the 1991 US–Argentina BIT, the tribunal in *Pan American Energy v Argentina* also rejected retrospective application, referring to the *Plama* holding.[151] The arbitral tribunal in *Khan Resources and others v Mongolia*, another case under the ECT, has equally adhered to the *Plama* line of reasoning.[152]

Some commentators have criticized the *Plama* line of jurisprudence as rendering DOB clauses de facto meaningless, the host State often not even being aware:

> at the time of the existence of a new investment made in its territory let alone the nationality of that investor, the extent of its business activities in its home State, and the nationality of its underlying owners or controllers … The host State may only learn of the conditions that

[145] *Plama Consortium Limited v Republic of Bulgaria*, ICSID Case No ARB/03/24, Decision on Jurisdiction (8 February 2005).

[146] Ibid, para 158.

[147] Ibid, paras 161–62, 165.

[148] *Liman Caspian Oil BV and NCL Dutch Investment BV v Republic of Kazakhstan*, ICSID Case No ARB/07/14, Award (22 June 2010) para 224.

[149] Ibid, para 225; similar *Yukos v Russia* (n 90) paras 456–59.

[150] *Ascom and Stati v Republic of Kazakhstan*, SCC, Award (19 December 2013) para 745.

[151] *Pan American Energy LLP and BP Argentina Exploration Company v Argentine Republic*, ICSID Case No ARB/03/13, Decision on Preliminary Objections (27 July 2006) para 204.

[152] *Khan Resources Inc, Khan Resources BV and CAUC Holding Company Ltd v Government of Mongolia and MonAtom LLC*, PCA Case No 2011-09, Decision on Jurisdiction (25 July 2012) paras 410–31.

would justify invoking Art. 17 at such time as an investor notifies it that a dispute under the ECT has arisen and quite possibly not even then.[153]

Others have argued that the mere presence of a DOB clause in the invoked investment agreement should put the investor on notice and prevent the investor from building up legitimate expectations for the protection of his investment.[154]

Other tribunals have, on the other hand, implicitly or explicitly accepted a retrospective effect of the exercise of the DOB clause. Thus, in *EMELEC v Ecuador*, for a denial of benefits clause under the US–Ecuador BIT, the arbitral tribunal laconically found that the Respondent 'announced the denial of benefits to EMELEC at the proper stage of the proceedings, i.e. upon raising its objections on jurisdiction'.[155]

A year later, in *Ulysseas v Ecuador*,[156] the tribunal noted that the right to deny benefits under the US–Ecuador BIT could—in accordance with Article 21(2) UNCITRAL Rules—be exercised no later than in the statement of defence.[157] It thus found:

> no valid reasons to exclude retrospective effects. In reply to Claimant's argument that this would cause uncertainties as to the legal relations under the BIT, it may be noted that since the possibility for the host State to exercise the right in question is known to the investor from the time when it made its investment, it may be concluded that the protection afforded by the BIT is subject during the life of the investment to the possibility of a denial of the BIT's advantages by the host State.[158]

The treaty shopping-limiting potential of DOB clauses also becomes particularly obvious in the recent *Pac Rim v El Salvador* decision,[159] where the tribunal accepted the corporate restructuring as not constituting an abuse of process,[160] but dismissed the treaty-based[161] claims on the grounds of the DOB clause, in other words because the tribunal found that the claimant had no substantial business activities in any of the Dominican Republic–Central American Free Trade Agreement (CAFTA) Member States territories and was owned or controlled by investors of a non-CAFTA party. Though the tribunal did not explicitly pronounce on whether it considered the CAFTA DOB clause to have retrospective or prospective effect, it implicitly endorsed retrospective effect, and this with a very interesting argument. First of all, it found that, no explicit time limit for the exercise of the right to deny benefits existing in the DOB clause and the arbitration being brought under the ICSID Convention and Arbitration Rules, the right to deny benefits had to be

[153] Anthony Sinclair, 'Investment Protection for "Mailbox Companies" under the 1994 Energy Charter Treaty' (2005) 2 TDM 5, available at <http://www.transnational-dispute-management.com> (subscription required); similar Feldman (n 143) 300; Tania Voon, Andrew Mitchell, and James Munro, 'Legal Responses to Corporate Manoeuvering in International Investment Arbitration' (2014) 5 JIDS 41, 55; Protopsaltis (n 140) 597.

[154] See, eg, Thorn and Doucleff (n 91) 26; Jagusch and Sinclair (n 133) 17, 39.

[155] *Empresa Eléctrica del Ecuador, Inc v Republic of Ecuador*, ICSID Case No ARB/05/9, Award (2 June 2009) para 71.

[156] *Ulysseas Inc v Republic of Ecuador*, UNCITRAL, Interim Award (28 September 2010).

[157] Ibid, para 172. [158] Ibid, para 173. [159] *Pac Rim v El Salvador* (n 134).

[160] As will be analysed more in detail in Chapter 7, at 7.3.

[161] But it accepted jurisdiction for the claims based on the Salvadoran Investment Law, see Part 5 of the Decision.

exercised 'as early as possible' and 'no later than the expiration of the time limit fixed for the filing of the counter-memorial' in accordance with ICSID Arbitration Rule 41.[162] Secondly and more importantly, it accepted that 'Respondent's consent to ICSID Arbitration in CAFTA Article 10.16.3(a) [was] necessarily qualified from the outset by CAFTA Article 10.12.2 [the DOB clause]', so that—without prejudice to the afore-mentioned time limit—it could be exercised even after the commencement of an arbitration, for an investment that was made years before.[163]

The tribunal in the recent case *Guaracachi America Inc and Rurelec PLC v Bolivia* adopted a similar reasoning.[164] Finding that the claimant was 'a company that, for purposes of Article XII of the US–Bolivia BIT, "has no substantial business activities in the territory of the Party under whose laws it is constituted or organized"',[165] the tribunal went on to consider whether the exercise of the DOB clause was timely. As the tribunal in *Pac Rim*, this tribunal found that:

> Whenever a BIT includes a denial of benefits clause, the consent by the host State to arbitration itself is conditional and thus may be denied by it, provided that some objective requirements concerning the investor are fulfilled.[166]

By this very fact, it also rejected the idea that the investor had legitimate expectations to be protected under the BIT, taking into particular account the fact that the investor in this case—as opposed for example in the *Plama* case—made its investment before the US–Bolivia BIT even came into force.[167] As to the timing of its exercise, the tribunal found that the 'very purpose of the denial of benefits [was] to give the Respondent the possibility of withdrawing the benefits granted under the BIT to investors who invoke those benefits', adding that 'it [was] proper that the denial is "activated" when the benefits are being claimed'.[168] Endorsing the tribunal's reasoning in this respect in *Ulysseas v Ecuador*, it agreed that 'as a jurisdictional issue, [the denial of benefits objection] must be raised at the latest in the respondent's statement of defence'.[169]

4.3.3.2 Discussion

The above reviewed cases show two contradictory lines of jurisprudence: while for arbitrations under the ECT, tribunals have so far consistently accepted only prospective effect, thus limiting the utility of DOB clauses in constituting a counterweight to mailbox companies, other tribunals have accepted retrospective effect.

However, the difference in approaches of the quoted tribunals is difficult to explain.[170] It seems as though the wording of invoked DOB clauses in the above

[162] *Pac Rim v El Salvador* (n 134) para 4.85. [163] Ibid, para 4.90.

[164] *Guaracachi America Inc and Rurelec PLC v Plurinational State of Bolivia*, UNCITRAL, PCA Case No 2011-17, Award (31 January 2014).

[165] Ibid, para 370. [166] Ibid, para 372. [167] Ibid, paras 372ff, 380.

[168] Ibid, para 376. [169] Ibid, paras 381–82.

[170] But see for possible reasons Lindsay Gastrell and Paul-Jean Le Cannu, 'Procedural Requirements of "Denial-of-Benefits" Clauses in Investment Treaties: A Review of Arbitral Decisions' (2015) 30 ICSID Review-FILJ 78, 95–97.

cases would not necessarily warrant these divergent results as to whether the exercise of the DOB clauses should have prospective or retrospective effect. For example, while Article 10.12.2 CAFTA stipulates that 'a Party may deny the benefits', both Article 17(1) ECT and Article I (2) of the US–Ecuador BIT and the US–Argentina BIT enable each Contracting Party 'to reserve the right to deny' the benefits. The difference in wording 'may deny' and 'reserves the right to deny' does not appear to present any different meaning so as to support divergent conclusions, and in any case, even if this were the case, tribunals would have been incoherent in their analyses, as can be seen from juxtaposing the decisions under the ECT (*Plama*, etc.) and under the US–Ecuador BIT (*Ulysseas*)—which of course they can be, given the absence of a doctrine of precedent.

Neither does it seem possible to deduce crucial differences from the presence of explicit notification requirements in some[171] as opposed to the absence of such notification requirements in other DOB clauses.[172] However, if a tribunal considers, as did the tribunals in *Pac Rim* and in *Guaracachi and Rurelec*, that Respondent's consent to arbitration is 'qualified *from the outset*' (emphasis added) by the DOB clause, it becomes easy to see why it would not even bother to enquire about a potential prospective or retrospective effect, the consent being, according to this view, conditioned by the non-existence of the conditions permitting the exercise of the DOB clause. It remains to be seen whether this more recent line of jurisprudence that sets the cut-off point for invoking the DOB clause at the statement of defence respectively counter-memorial will gain ground in subsequent jurisprudence. For arbitrations under the ECT, the line taken so far by arbitral tribunals suggests that the objectives of the liberalization of the energy market and the protection of energy-related investments weigh heavier than any doubts as to whether the investor could really have any legitimate expectations protected.

In view of the uncertainty which approach an arbitral tribunal will take towards the question of retrospective or prospective effect of the exercise of the right to deny benefits, the utility of these clauses, in the absence of a treaty-based clarification seems greatly overrated.

4.3.4 Definition and scope of 'control'

As seen above, the question of how to define the notion of control may arise when a tribunal has to examine whether a locally incorporated company qualifies as a protected investor because of foreign control within the meaning of Article 25(2)(b) second clause ICSID Convention, this notion—like the notion of nationality—not having been defined by the drafters of the Convention.[173]

It may also arise when the IIA in question combines the incorporation and the control theories and recognizes as protected investor legal entities, wherever incorporated, but directly or indirectly controlled by a national of either Contracting Party, with

[171] Eg, Art 10.12.2 CAFTA; Art 1113(2) NAFTA.
[172] Eg, Art 17(1) ECT.
[173] Broches (n 54) 340.

IIAs (or protocols attached to it) sometimes clarifying further how to understand the notion of control. Finally, it would also seem to be relevant to determining, in the case of a denial of benefits clause, whether an investor without substantial business activities (i.e. a mailbox company) is controlled by a host State or third State national.

In these cases, respondents have often argued that the control exercised by the claimant had to be effective rather than purely legal or formal. This question tends to be particularly contentious in the case of minority shareholdings, where the tribunals have thus had to look at several elements that might justify a finding of control. Another contentious issue in this respect remains the question of up to which tier or level of control the tribunal has to look in order to find the requisite nationality. Does it have to stop in its enquiry once it has found the requisite nationality or does it have to continue and enquire about the nationality of the ultimate controller?

As it becomes apparent, these questions are highly relevant in the context of corporate structuring or restructuring. It is clear that the more of a formal approach a tribunal will take towards the notion of control and/or stop at the first level of control where it finds the requisite nationality, the more easily an investor will be able to come under the protection of the intended investment treaty through the interposition of a special purpose vehicle and thus cross the jurisdictional hurdle. By contrast, the more the tribunal looks for effective or actual control by the investor and the more it is willing to examine control up to the level of ultimate control, the more the tribunal may be disposed to dismiss the case, in particular if the ultimate controller turns out to be a host State national or national of a non-Contracting Party.[174]

4.3.4.1 Notion of 'foreign control' in the ICSID Convention

Article 25(2)(b) second clause of the ICSID Convention concerns the situation where a company incorporated in the host State may exceptionally be considered a 'foreign investor' and may thus bring a claim under the ICSID Convention if the parties have agreed to treat it as a protected investor because of its foreign control.[175] For the drafters of the ICSID Convention, the rationale of this exception was to find a balance between the interests of the host States and those of the investors: on the one hand, it means to ensure that investment disputes be international, thus a priori excluding claims by investors against their own State of nationality, while on the other hand it seeks to accommodate the fact that some host States require foreign investors to implement their investment through locally incorporated companies, which would thus, without this exception, exclude these investors from the ambit of the ICSID Convention.[176]

As has been seen further above, the drafters of the ICSID Convention refrained from defining the notion of nationality in Article 25(2)(b) so as to rely on the

[174] Similar Voon, Mitchell, and Munro, 'Legal Responses' (n 153) 57.
[175] See also ICSID, 'Report of the Executive Directors' (n 59) para 30.
[176] Schreuer and others, *ICSID Commentary* (n 55) 'Article 25' para 760.

consensual character of the Convention and grant the parties 'the widest possible latitude to agree on the meaning of "nationality"', with the consequence that any stipulation 'based on a reasonable criterion should be accepted'.[177] The parties may thus agree on any elements constitutive of control as long as these remain within the 'inner limits' of the Convention.[178]

4.3.4.1.1 Which criteria can be used to define control?

Various tribunals were thus called upon to decide whether the criteria the parties had agreed upon were reasonable or to the contrary, whether the parties purported to use the Convention for purposes for which it was not intended.

In *Aucoven v Venezuela*,[179] the claimant Autopista Concesionada de Venezuela (Aucoven) was a locally incorporated company (indirectly) owned and controlled by a Mexican conglomerate, ICA Holding. At the very beginning of the contract, Aucoven requested that the Venezuelan authorities agree to a transfer of seventy-five per cent of its shares to another wholly owned subsidiary of ICA Holding, the US-incorporated Icatech, to which the Venezuelan authorities eventually agreed. In the consent to arbitration clause of the concession agreement, Venezuela agreed to treat Aucoven as a foreign investor for the purpose of Article 25(2)(b) because of foreign control based on the criterion of direct shareholding. The reason for the transfer of shares was to internationalize ICA Holding's operations, which became necessary as a consequence of the 1995–6 Mexican peso crisis. In the ICSID proceedings, Venezuela objected to Aucoven's standing as foreign investor within the meaning of Article 25(2)(b) and asserted that foreign control within the meaning of this provision meant effective control.

The tribunal rejected this assertion, noting that:

> the drafters decided to give the parties wide discretion to determine under what circumstances a company could be treated as a national of another Contracting State because of foreign control. The concept of foreign control being flexible and broad, different criteria may be taken into consideration, such as shareholding, voting rights, etc.[180]

Though accepting that 'economic criteria often better reflect reality than legal ones', the tribunal felt itself obligated to enforce the parties' choice as long as the agreed-upon criteria were reasonable.[181] In the tribunal's view, direct shareholding was a reasonable, though not necessarily exclusive, test for control as '[d]irect shareholding confers voting rights, and, therefore, the possibility to participate in the decision-making of the company'.[182] The tribunal also rejected Venezuela's contention that the claimant's shareholder Icatech was a mere corporation of convenience, pointing out that it had been incorporated years before the conclusion of the

[177] Broches (n 54) 360–61.

[178] This does in principle not seem to be the case when the parties agree on the criterion of 'ownership' instead of 'control' in the BIT, see *Caratube International Oil Company LLP v Republic of Kazakhstan*, ICSID Case No ARB/08/12, Award (5 June 2012) paras 336–37, 380–81. See also in Chapter 8, at 8.2.3.4.

[179] *Aucoven v Venezuela* (n 57).

[180] Ibid, para 113.

[181] Ibid, paras 119–20.

[182] Ibid, para 121.

agreement and the authorization for the transfer of shares had been requested for reasons not linked with and well before the events giving rise to the dispute.

Other tribunals also recognized shareholding, voting rights, decision-making structures, nationality of the management or board of directors, technical know-how provided by a foreign national, etc., in principle as reasonable criteria for determining control.[183]

4.3.4.1.2 **Legal v effective control**

More difficult—and inconsistently decided by arbitral tribunals—is the question whether the notion of control means a legal/formal capacity to control (legal control) or the actual/effective exercise of control (effective control). In this aspect, tribunals have tended to make a distinction as to whether the investor asserting control held majority or minority shareholding.

In the abovementioned *Aucoven* case, the tribunal rejected Venezuela's contention that foreign control implied 'effective control' and accepted that direct (majority) shareholding, the criteria chosen by the parties to define foreign control, 'confers voting rights and, therefore, the possibility to participate in the decision-making of the company'.[184]

In *LETCO v Liberia*,[185] for the case of a one hundred per cent French ownership of the locally incorporated claimant, the tribunal examined also other elements such as the decision-making structure and management (though seemingly as evidence of the capacity to exercise control and not in application of an effective control test), finding not only one hundred per cent French shareholding, but also:

> effective control in the sense that, apart from the French shareholdings, French nationals dominated the company decision-making structure ... [and] a majority, if not all, of LETCO's directors, as well as the General Manager, were at all times French nationals.[186]

On the other hand, in *Caratube v Kazakhstan*,[187] the tribunal required proof of effective control despite the existence of majority shareholding. In this case, the tribunal had to decide whether the claimant, a locally incorporated entity, was an investment owned or controlled by a US citizen (in accordance with the invoked US–Kazakhstan BIT). Even though the tribunal held earlier that 'if majority ownership is shown, such a finding implies a presumption of control'[188] and the US citizen owned ninety-two per cent of claimant's shareholding and formally held a

[183] See, eg, *Vacuum Salt Production Limited v Government of the Republic of Ghana*, ICSID Case No ARB/92/1, Award (16 Feb 1994) printed in (1994) 9 ICSID Review-FILJ 72; *Liberian Eastern Timber Corporation v Republic of Liberia,* ICSID Case No ARB/83/2, Decision on Jurisdiction (24 October 1984) printed in (1985) 2 ICSID Reports 349, 351; *Compagnie d'Exploration du Chemin de Fer Transgabonais v Republic of Gabon*, ICSID Case No ARB/04/5, Decision on Jurisdiction (19 Dec 2005) para 40; *International Thunderbird Gaming Corporation v United Mexican States*, UNCITRAL, Award (26 January 2006) para 108. Similar Schreuer and others, *ICSID Commentary* (n 55) 'Article 25' para 864.

[184] *Aucoven v Venezuela* (n 57) paras 112 and 121.

[185] *Liberian Eastern Timber Corporation v Liberia* (n 183) 351.

[186] Ibid, quoted in Schreuer and others, *ICSID Commentary* (n 55) 'Article 25' para 855.

[187] *Caratube v Kazakhstan* (n 178).

[188] Ibid, para 382.

position as director of the claimant, giving him certain competences according to claimant's Charter and Incorporation Agreement, it found that a legal capacity to control a company, without evidence of actual control, was not sufficient for proving control within the meaning of Article 25(2)(b) second clause in this case.[189]

On the other hand, for minority shareholding, the tribunal had to decide in *Vacuum Salt v Ghana*[190] whether the locally incorporated claimant could be considered a foreign national because a Greek national owned a twenty per cent minority shareholding in the claimant while the remaining eighty per cent were owned by several Ghanaian natural and legal persons.

It first noted the flexible character of the notion of foreign control, finding that:

> 'Foreign control' within the meaning of the second clause of Art. 25(2)(b) does not require, or imply, any particular percentage of share ownership. Each case arising under that clause must be viewed in its own particular context, on the basis of all of the facts and circumstances ... It stands to reason, of course, that 100 percent foreign ownership almost certainly would result in foreign control, by whatever standard, and that a total absence of foreign shareholding would virtually preclude the existence of such control. How much is 'enough', however, cannot be determined abstractly. Thus, in the course of the drafting of the Convention, it was said variously that 'interests sufficiently important to be able to block major changes in the company' could amount to a 'controlling interest'; that 'control could in fact be acquired by persons holding only 25 percent of' a company's capital; and even that '51% of the shares might not be controlling' while for some purposes '15% was sufficient'.[191]

Yet, the tribunal conceded that:

> The smaller ... the percentage of voting shares held by the asserted source of foreign control, the more one must look to other elements bearing on that issue. As one authority has said, 'a tribunal ... may regard any criterion based on management, voting rights, shareholding or any other reasonable theory as being reasonable for the purpose'.[192]

Looking at other elements capable of inferring control, the tribunal found that:

> Nowhere does there appear to be any material evidence that [the Greek national] either acted or was materially influential in a truly managerial rather than technical or supervisory vein. At all times, he was subject to the direction of the Managing Director ... who himself apparently controlled the largest single block of shares, and who in turn responded to the board of directors, of which [the Greek national and his wife] were but two members. Nowhere in the proceedings is it suggested that [the Greek national], as holder of 20% of Vacuum Salt's shares, either through an alliance with other shareholders, through securing a significant power of decision or managerial influence, or otherwise, was in a position to steer, through either positive or negative action, the fortunes of Vacuum Salt. The fact that it was truly his 'brainchild' and, if such be the case, that his technical advice generally was heeded,

[189] Ibid, para 407.

[190] *Vacuum Salt v Ghana* (n 183).

[191] Ibid, para 43.

[192] Ibid, para 44, with reference to Chittharanjan Amerasinghe, 'Jurisdiction Ratione Personae Under the Convention on the Settlement of Investment Disputes Between States and Nationals of Other States' (1974–1975) 47 BYIL 227, 264–65.

and even proved to be indispensable, does not fuse with his 20% shareholding to render him capable of strongly influencing critical decisions on important corporate matters.[193]

It also remarked in passing that one could assume that a person having control in the sense of Article 25(2)(b) second clause should play a role in the decision to commence arbitration, while this, on the facts of the case, was not the case.[194] It thus found that this was a case in which the Convention would be used for purposes for which it was clearly not intended.[195]

In *Compagnie d'Exploration du Chemin de Fer Transgabonais v Gabon*,[196] the tribunal had to consider whether the combined minority shareholdings of investors in the local investment rose to the level of foreign control within the meaning of Article 25(2)(b) second clause. It found that the notion of control could be interpreted as:

pouvoir de décision, soit à travers la détention d'une part substantielle du capital, soit autrement, plusieurs éléments pouvant concourir au contrôle.[197]

It thus accepted that the decision-making power could be established either by recourse to majority shareholding or, in the case of minority shareholding, if several elements combined to rise to the level of a power to control. Importantly, the tribunal accepted that the foreign control could be calculated by 'teaming up' the shareholder interests of different foreign nationals of other Contracting States, and this even when there was no shareholder agreement between the different shareholders.[198] Though the formula used by the tribunal ('pouvoir de décision'/power to decide) is not completely unambiguous as to whether the tribunal considered the legal or the actual power to decide as the applicable test, the tribunal nonetheless seems to consider that in the absence of majority shareholding, other elements would need to be shown in order to confirm control, pointing to an actual or de facto control test.

4.3.4.1.3 Discussion

The above calls for a certain number of observations.

First of all, there seems hardly any doubt that elements like shareholding, voting rights, decision-making structure etc. constitute reasonable and adequate criteria for purposes of examining the notion of foreign control.[199]

Second, for the case of majority shareholding, conflicting jurisprudence exists with respect to the question of whether the tribunal should require purely legal

[193] Ibid, para 53. [194] Ibid, FN 31. [195] Ibid, para 54.

[196] *Compagnie d'Exploration du Chemin de Fer Transgabonais v Gabon* (n 183).

[197] Ibid, para 35 ('the power to decide, either through the holding of a substantial share of the capital or otherwise, as several elements may contribute to determining control', translation by this author).

[198] *Compagnie d'Exploration du Chemin de Fer Transgabonais v Gabon* (n 183) para 37; similar *Vacuum Salt v Ghana* (n 183) para 53; *Camuzzi International SA v Argentine Republic*, ICSID Case No ARB/03/2, Decision on Objections to Jurisdiction (11 May 2005) paras 38ff.

[199] Similar Chittharanjan Amerasinghe, 'Interpretation of Article 25(2)(b) of the ICSID Convention' in Robert Lillich and Charles N Brower (eds), *International Arbitration towards "Judicialization" and Uniformity?* (New York, Transnational Publishers 1994) 223, 240.

or (also) effective control. Though one may be tempted to assume that majority shareholding implies both legal and effective control (and tribunals have indeed established this presumption),[200] the decision in *Caratube* makes abundantly clear that tribunals may look for effective control if they have doubts about the true nature of the investor respectively his investment (as the tribunal did in the case at hand).[201]

This is equally (or even more) true for the case of minority shareholding where tribunals seem to rarely have let suffice a purely legal capacity to control,[202] but have rather mostly looked for proof of actual or de facto control by examining various elements that may be indicative of or combine to actual control. In particular the decision in *Vacuum Salt* is a case in point. In that case, the tribunal clearly expressed its view that to consider a (foreign) minority shareholder of twenty per cent of the shares without any more indicia as to actual control by him, while host State nationals held the majority shareholding, would be using the ICSID Convention for purposes for which it was not intended. This puts a particular focus, in the case of minority shareholding, on the necessity to examine additional criteria in order to confirm whether the claimant is actually 'capable of strongly influencing critical decisions on important corporate matters',[203] all the while not excluding that even a minority shareholder could exercise the necessary control.

Indeed, there is good reason to argue that the notion of 'foreign control' should be understood as meaning effective control as opposed to legal control.[204] First, already the drafters of the Convention 'considered the holding of a majority of shares not to be decisive … [and] agreed that even the holding of a minority of shares of even 15% could be sufficient to assume control if they conferred the right to block major changes'.[205]

Second, given the wide latitude to define control granted by the drafters of the Convention, any reasonable criterion is permissible, and to require criteria that establish de facto control does not only seem reasonable, but in some cases even necessary, in particular when there may be doubts whether the Convention is being used for purposes for which it was not intended. In such cases, it seems even

[200] *Caratube v Kazakhstan* (n 178) para 382; *Société Industrielle des Boissons de Guinée (SIGB) v République de Guinée*, Affaire CIRDI No ARB/12/8, Sentence (21 mai 2014) para 106.

[201] See more in detail Chapter 5.

[202] But see *Aguas del Tunarí SA v Plurinational State of Bolivia*, ICSID Case No ARB/02/3, Decision on Respondent's Objections to Jurisdiction (21 October 2005) para 264: 'In the case of a minority shareholder, the legal capacity to control an entity may exist by reason of the percentage of shares held, legal rights conveyed in instruments or agreements such as the articles of incorporation or shareholders' agreements, or a combination of these'.

[203] *Vacuum Salt v Ghana* (n 183) para 53.

[204] In this sense also Gaillard (n 79) 368; Albert Badia, *Piercing the Veil of State Enterprises in International Arbitration* (Kluwer Law International 2014) 159.

[205] Jan Asmus Bischoff and Richard Happ, 'Ratione Materiae' in Marc Bungenberg, Jörn Griebel, Stephan Hobe, and August Reinisch, *International Investment Law, A Handbook* (CH Beck, Hart Publishing and Nomos 2015) 495, 528 (para 90) with reference to Convention on the Settlement of Investment Disputes between States and Nationals of Other States, 'Documents Concerning the Origin and the Formation of the Convention' Vol II, Part 1, Documents 1–43 (Washington DC 1968) 359ff, 447ff, 538.

arguable that the search for actual or de facto control acts as a safeguard against abuse of the ICSID Convention. This also shows that the notion of foreign control has to be understood as a flexible notion and that 'no simple mathematical formula based on shareholding or votes alone' exists.[206]

Finally and importantly, the existence of foreign control is an objective requirement that has to be examined independently of the agreement of the parties to treat the locally incorporated company as foreign.[207] This makes it arguable that *foreign* control must effectively exist, thus favouring the de facto control test.

4.3.4.2 Level of control

Closely related to the question whether to apply a legal or actual control test is how far up the corporate tiers the tribunal should look in order to validate or invalidate the finding of foreign control. Should it stop once it has found the requisite nationality? Or should it continue up the corporate tiers until the ultimate level of control, even if this leads to the invalidation of foreign control, for example because the ultimate controller of the investment is a national of the host State?

4.3.4.2.1 First qualifying nationality found or ultimate controller?

Arbitral jurisprudence has so far been thoroughly inconsistent in treating this question. While some tribunals have stopped at the first tier of control,[208] others have accepted to look beyond the first tier.

This was, for example, the case in *SOABI v Sénégal*.[209] In this case, the claimant was a locally incorporated company, which was controlled by a Panamanian company, which in turn was controlled by Belgian citizens. Panama was not a Contracting State of ICSID when the arbitration consent was given, while Belgium was. The tribunal found that the objective of Article 25(2)(b) second clause was to facilitate foreign investments through locally incorporated vehicles and thus give them access to ICSID arbitration.[210] It thus considered as perfectly acceptable the decision of foreign investors to invest their funds through intermediary entities while retaining the same degree of control over the national company as they would have exercised as direct shareholders of the latter, therefore accepting second-tier control.[211]

The tribunal in *Compagnie d'Exploration du Chemin de Fer Transgabonais (CECFT) v Gabon* adopted a similar reasoning, finding that 'the verification of control should not be limited to the "first degree" of control, in particular where the investors, for various reasons, use an intermediary company organized under

[206] Schreuer and others, *ICSID Commentary* (n 55) 'Article 25' paras 864–65; similar Bischoff and Happ (n 205) 530 (para 101).

[207] See, eg, Schreuer and others, *ICSID Commentary* (n 55) 'Article 25' paras 813–25; *National Gas v Egypt* (n 38) paras 131–35.

[208] See, eg, *Amco Asia v Indonesia* (n 57) para 14 (iii).

[209] *Société Ouest Africaine des Bétons Industriels (SOABI) v Sénégal*, ICSID Case No ARB/82/1, Decision on Jurisdiction (19 July 1984).

[210] Ibid, para 35. [211] Ibid, para 37.

the laws of the host State'.[212] Interestingly, however, the tribunal did not stop there. It clarified that once foreign control by nationals of other Contracting States was found, the examination of who ultimately controlled the foreign entity should stop as it would be contrary to Article 25(2)(b), 'sauf peut-être dans le cas où ce contrôle retournerait vers l'Etat d'accueil'.[213]

This last *cas de figure* was precisely the issue in the controversial case *TSA Spectrum v Argentina*.[214]

In this case, the claimant was a locally incorporated company that was wholly owned by TSI Spectrum NV, a company incorporated in the Netherlands, which in turn was majority-controlled by an Argentinean national. The claimant brought a claim under the Netherlands–Argentina BIT for the termination of a concession contract in the administration, management, and control of the radio spectrum.

In the relevant jurisdictional objection, the tribunal had to decide whether the claimant qualified, because of foreign control, as foreign national within the meaning of Article 25(2)(b) of the Convention. The Netherlands–Argentina BIT defined in its Article 1(b)(iii) the notion of 'investor' as 'legal persons, wherever located, controlled, directly or indirectly, by nationals of that Contracting Party' and stipulated in Article 10(6) that '[a] legal person which is incorporated or constituted under the law in force in the territory of one Contracting Party and which, before a dispute arises, is controlled by nationals of the other Contracting Party shall, in accordance with Article 25(2)(b) of the Convention be treated for the purposes of the Convention as a national of the other Contracting Party'. Furthermore, a Protocol forming integral part of the aforementioned BIT clarified that for proving control within the meaning of Article 1(b)(iii):

> The following facts, inter alia, shall be accepted as evidence of the control: … ii. Having a direct or indirect participation in the capital of a company higher than 49% or the direct or indirect possession of the necessary votes to obtain a predominant position in assemblies or company organs.

The tribunal started by explaining the differences between the first and the second clause of Article 25(2)(b) of the Convention. With respect to the former, it held that as the first clause did not contain any reference to control or the possibility to pierce the corporate veil, its text 'may be interpreted in a strict constructionist manner'.[215] This, the tribunal found, was going 'against common sense in some circumstances', such as in cases as *Tokios Tokelés v Ukraine*[216] or *Rompetrol v Romania*,[217] where claimants were owned or controlled by host state nationals, siding with the minority dissenting opinion of Professor Weil and alleging that the majority opinion 'has not been generally accepted'.[218]

212 *Compagnie d'Exploration du Chemin de Fer Transgabonais v Gabon* (n 183) para 36.

213 Ibid ('except maybe where this control would revert to [a national] of the host State', translation by this author).

214 *TSA Spectrum de Argentina SA v Argentine Republic*, ICSID Case No ARB/05/5, Award (19 December 2008).

215 Ibid, para 145.

216 *Tokios Tokelés v Ukraine* (n 66).

217 *Rompetrol v Romania* (n 82).

218 *TSA Spectrum v Argentina* (n 214) para 146.

Turning its attention to the second clause and more concretely to the notion of 'foreign control', it wondered whether:

> it would be consistent with the text, if the tribunal, when establishing whether there is foreign control, would be directed to pierce the veil of the corporate entity national of the host State and to stop short at the second corporate layer it meets, rather than pursuing its objective identification of foreign control up to its real source, using the same criterion with which it started.[219]

It acknowledged that this question has so far not been treated in a unanimous manner by arbitral jurisprudence. Basing itself on the ICSID decision of *Vacuum Salt v Ghana* in which the tribunal denied there was 'foreign control' within the meaning of Article 25(2)(b), and citing an academic 'majority [that appears] to favour "piercing of the veil" and going for the real control and nationality of controllers',[220] the tribunal decided that 'in the application of Article 25(2)(b) it [was] necessary to pierce the corporate veil and establish whether or not the domestic company was objectively under foreign control'.[221] Finding that the ultimate controller of the claimant was the Argentinean national, it denied the existence of 'foreign control' within the meaning of Article 25(2)(b), 'whatever interpretation is given to the BIT between Argentina and the Netherlands, including the Protocol to the BIT'.[222]

One arbitrator criticized in his dissenting opinion that the majority opinion, while correctly starting from the premise that there were outer limits to the ICSID Convention that could not be done away with by party consent,[223] chose to obliterate the fact that the parties had expressly agreed on a definition of 'control' in Article 1(b)(iii) of the BIT by relying on the *Vacuum Salt* decision which he found fundamentally distinguishable from the case at issue.[224] By doing so, the dissenting arbitrator found, the majority ignored the basic principle of sovereign consent.[225]

Another arbitrator chose to clarify in a concurring opinion why he thought the claimant was not under Dutch foreign control. Interpreting the relevant part of the Protocol to the BIT, he first of all noted that there was a discrepancy between the English language version on the one hand and the Spanish and French ones on the other as to whether the following facts *must* (according to the English version) or *may* (according to the Spanish and French versions) be taken into account as evidence of the control.[226] Second, interpreting the notion of 'direct or indirect participation in the capital of a company higher than 49%' and thus finding that the notion of 'indirect participation' 'necessarily implie[d] the piercing of the second corporate layer', he wondered whether:

> If the text allows piercing the corporate veil to establish 'indirect' foreign control at a third or fourth remove, could it prohibit doing the same in order to infirm this foreign control, by establishing that real control is in the hands of nationals of the host State?[227]

[219] Ibid, para 147.
[220] Ibid, paras 150–52.
[221] Ibid, para 160.
[222] Ibid, para 162.
[223] Ibid, paras 134–36.
[224] Ibid, Dissenting Opinion Arbitrator Aldonas, paras 28ff.
[225] Ibid, para 34.
[226] Ibid, Concurring Opinion Arbitrator Abi-Saab, para 15.
[227] Ibid.

This, he acknowledged, was not clear and called for an interpretation, in which he did however not engage. Instead, he found that:

> The facts enumerated [in the Protocol] 'can' or even 'have to' be accepted, as a minimum, in the absence of any other evidence of foreign control; but not that they would prevail over other more ample and probative evidence or prohibit the Tribunal from admitting such evidence if it results from piercing the second corporate layer.[228]

In the recent *National Gas Company SAE v Egypt* award,[229] the arbitral tribunal also found the ultimate controller's nationality to be decisive. In this case, the claimant was a locally incorporated company controlled by two layers of shell companies incorporated in the United Arab Emirates and ultimately controlled by an Egyptian national. The arbitration being brought under the ICSID Convention, the Respondent argued that the claimant was not under foreign control within the meaning of Article 25(2)(b) second clause given the Egyptian nationality of the ultimate controller.

Reviewing relevant prior jurisprudence, in particular *Vacuum Salt v Ghana* and *Aucoven v Venezuela*, the tribunal confirmed that Article 25(2)(b) second clause established both a subjective and an objective test which had to be met cumulatively for jurisdiction to exist.[230] The subjective test concerning the agreement of the parties to treat a locally incorporated company as a national of the other Contracting Party, this requirement was fulfilled in the case at hand as Article 10(4) of the Egypt–UAE BIT contained this agreement.[231] However, the agreement on treating a local company as foreign alone not being sufficient, the question was whether there was foreign control objectively speaking. In this aspect, the tribunal recalled that while such an agreement could create a 'rebuttable presumption' as to the existence of foreign control, limits existed if the ICSID Convention was to be used 'for purposes for which it was clearly not intended', thus breaching its 'outer limits'.[232]

With this in mind, the tribunal found a 'significant difference' to exist in the case of 'control exercised by a national of the Contracting State against which the Claimant asserts its claim and … control by a national of another Contracting State'.[233] It thus found that '[t]he latter situation violates no principle of international law and is consistent with the text of the ICSID Convention', while:

> The former situation violates the general limitation in Article 25(1) and the first part of Article 25(2)(b) of the ICSID Convention in regard of both Contracting States and nationals (including dual nationals) [exclusion of host State nationals, the author]. In other words, the latter is consistent with the object and purpose of the ICSID Convention; but the former is inconsistent: it would permit the use of the ICSID Convention for a purpose for which it was clearly not intended and it would breach its outer limits.[234]

[228] Ibid, para 17.
[229] *National Gas v Egypt* (n 38).
[230] Ibid, paras 128–31.
[231] Ibid, para 132.
[232] Ibid, para 134.
[233] Ibid, para 136.
[234] Ibid.

Interestingly, though finding this to be a case in which the Convention would be used 'for a purpose for which it was clearly not intended', the tribunal passed no value judgment on the choice of corporate structure used:

> The Tribunal recognizes that his choice of corporate structure was made in good faith for legitimate fiscal reasons; it was not designed as an exercise in forum shopping [sic] under the Treaty; and whilst CTIP and REGI [the two UAE incorporated companies] are both shell companies, neither are sham entities.[235]

4.3.4.2.2 Discussion

Though still showing overall inconsistency (in particular with respect to earlier awards), the most recent case *National Gas v Egypt* seems to consolidate a line of jurisprudence that tends to decline jurisdiction on the grounds of Article 25(2)(b) second clause when the ultimate controller of a local investment is a host State national.[236] This also seems to be the solution advocated for by some scholars and practitioners.[237] If further reconfirmed, this line of jurisprudence would help curb the practice of treaty shopping by leaving the interposition of corporate vehicles that only formally qualify as foreign controllers de facto without effect for purposes of ICSID jurisdiction.

Some comments are nevertheless warranted.

For the *TSA Spectrum* case, there is first the statement that the majority opinion in *Tokios Tokelés* was supposedly not well accepted by commentators. Indeed, though there were commentators sympathetic to the minority opinion, the great majority supported the majority opinion.[238] And, except for the *TSA Spectrum* tribunal, no other tribunal has thus far endorsed the *Tokios Tokelés* minority reasoning, however much some of them may have sympathized with it from a policy point of view. The reference to the *Tokios Tokelés* case also seems to be misplaced under another aspect (though this was in the end correctly recognized by the *TSA Spectrum* tribunal): while the claim brought by Tokios Tokelés was one under Article 25(2)(b) first clause, the one brought by TSA Spectrum was one under Article 25(2)(b) second clause. Thus, while for the former case, the question of control (correctly) did not matter, for the latter case it did.[239]

Second, the heavy reliance on the decision in *Vacuum Salt* also seems doubtful because, though that tribunal did also dismiss the case, it was on different grounds.

[235] Ibid, para 146.

[236] Whether a natural or a legal person, see above at 4.2.2.

[237] See, eg, Schreuer and others, *ICSID Commentary* (n 55) 'Article 25' paras 849; Gaillard (n 79) 368.

[238] See above at 4.3.1.3.

[239] As a side note, one may of course wonder why the claim was not brought by the Netherlands-incorporated TSI. A possible explanation might be found in Art 1(b)(ii) Argentina–Netherlands BIT, giving standing to 'legal persons constituted under the law of that Contracting Party (meaning Netherlands) ... [that] actually [do] business under the laws in force in any part of the territory of that Contracting Party [meaning Netherlands] in which a place of effective management is situated'. Since TSI was a mailbox company, it did not meet these criteria and supposedly the only remaining possibility to bring a claim was therefore by TSA Spectrum under Art 1(b)(iii).

Indeed, in that case, there was only one layer of share ownership (among which the minority ownership of the Greek national and the majority ownership held by several host State nationals), as opposed to two upstream levels of ownership in the *TSA Spectrum* case. One could in this sense distinguish between vertical (in the case of two or more upstream corporate levels) as opposed to horizontal control (in the case of a single ownership level). The tribunal in *Vacuum Salt* thus did not (have to) enquire up to the ultimate controller of the locally incorporated claimant (beyond a formally qualifying entity), but rather had to examine whether the Greek national could be considered as holding (sufficient) control despite the fact that he only had a minority shareholding in the Claimant (twenty per cent) and no other elements were shown that could prove de facto control. If the *TSA Spectrum* tribunal had wanted to build on 'precedential' jurisprudence, it should have rather relied on the *Compagnie d'Exploration du Chemin de Fer Transgabonais (CECFT) v Gabon* where the tribunal was also faced with several layers of ownership and precisely envisaged the case, though hypothetical, of whether it should 'pierce the corporate veil' up to the ultimate controller if the control would turn out to revert to a host State national.[240]

The *TSA Spectrum* decision thus leaves the impression that the majority of the tribunal was guided more by policy than legal considerations, even more so as it failed to explain why the Dutch entity did not qualify as foreign controller for purposes of Article 25(2)(b) second clause even though it fulfilled the requirement constitutive of control for purposes of the BIT.

In this aspect, the argumentation brought forward by the tribunal in *National Gas* is more convincing. It seems undeniable that contrary to the case of a host State-controlled mailbox company bringing a claim under Article 25(2)(b) first clause,[241] in the case of a locally incorporated company under foreign control within the meaning of the second clause, the object and purpose of the ICSID Convention, namely the aim to encourage *international* investment (and thus to exclude claims by host State nationals), should have a role to play in interpreting the notion of 'foreign control'. The difference in this case is that Article 25(2)(b) second clause explicitly foresees the examination of the control criterion, thus making the relevance of the nationality of the controller evident. This applies even more so since, as seen further above,[242] the notion of foreign control should arguably be understood as actual or effective control, thus precluding corporate entities that only formally qualify as controlling the local investment. Furthermore, the argumentation of the *National Gas* tribunal was backed up by another important point of legal reasoning found in the *Burimi* decision. The latter tribunal correctly identified the possibilities of circumventing the requirements set out in Article 25(2)(a) by using downstream corporate structures controlled by natural persons (also)

[240] *Compagnie d'Exploration du Chemin de Fer Transgabonais v Gabon* (n 183) para 36.
[241] See above at 4.3.1.
[242] See above at 4.3.4.1.3.

holding host State nationality, and thus imported these underlying considerations into the analysis of 'foreign control'.[243]

Yet, though coming to the conclusion that the interposition of formally qualifying entities by an ultimately controlling host State national would be using the ICSID Convention 'for purposes for which it was not intended',[244] the tribunal in *National Gas* interestingly abstained from making a bad faith finding. Whether this was because the tribunal did not (have to) pass judgment on the timing of the interposition of the UAE-incorporated entities (which could have presented an issue in terms of jurisdiction *ratione temporis*),[245] is unclear. In any case, it raises the question how this tribunal would distinguish this case from the case of an abuse of the legal personality or the attempt to conceal the true ultimate controlling nationality, hypothesis that has already earlier been found by jurisprudence to warrant the enquiry into the nationality of the ultimate controller.[246]

Beyond the discussion of the concrete cases, the treatment of claims by locally incorporated entities ultimately controlled by host State nationals does show an important inconsistency compared to the treatment of claims by foreign-incorporated entities ultimately controlled by host State nationals. It has been seen that the interposition of corporate vehicles in the chain of ownership has the potential to enhance treaty protection, in other words to further treaty shopping. The inconsistency becomes most obvious in the case of dual nationals (with host State nationality) ultimately controlling foreign and/or locally incorporated entities.[247] Thus, while a claim by a foreign-incorporated entity controlled by a dual (host State) national does not encounter any problems, as seen in *Wena Hotels v Egypt*,[248] the claim by a locally incorporated entity ultimately controlled by a dual (host State) national will more likely than not lead to a dismissal of the case (at least in ICSID arbitrations), as seen further above. In such a chain of ownership, the chances of success for an investment claim to cross (at least) the first (jurisdictional) hurdle therefore largely depends on whether it is the foreign-incorporated or the locally incorporated entity bringing the claim. As seen above, this inconsistent treatment of foreign versus locally incorporated companies was intended by the drafters of the ICSID Convention, the *legal* conclusions, by arbitral tribunals, concerning the claims brought by foreign-incorporated entities can thus not be objected to. Yet, the potential for strategic decisions (or some might say manipulation) lying in this inconsistency cannot but be observed. As a consequence, the use and interposition of mailbox companies (in order to ensure there is a foreign-incorporated entity within the corporate structure) becomes even more attractive.

243 See also in Chapter 9, at 9.3.2.

244 *National Gas Company v Egypt* (n 38) para 136.

245 See in Chapter 6, at 6.4.

246 In this sense see already *Amco Asia v Indonesia* (n 57) 361–63.

247 Though it exists just as much in the case of legal persons.

248 See above sat 4.3.1.1. But see the discussion of the recent *Venoklim Holding v Venezuela* case (n 92) above at 4.3.1.3.

4.3.4.3 Notion of control in IIAs

4.3.4.3.1 Legal or effective control

For the notion of control contained in IIAs, arbitral tribunals have similarly discussed whether control should be understood as legal or effective control.[249] In this aspect, arbitral tribunals have also tended to make a distinction depending on whether the asserted control was based on majority or minority shareholding, based on the presumption that ownership normally implied control. Yet, like for the notion of 'foreign control', there have been arbitral tribunals willing to look for effective control even in case of majority shareholding when they had doubts about the true controller of the investment.

In *Aguas del Tunarí v Bolivia*,[250] the question was whether the locally incorporated claimant qualified as a Dutch national protected by the Netherlands–Bolivia BIT. Article 1(b)(iii) of the BIT defined a qualifying national as including 'legal persons controlled directly or indirectly, by nationals of that Contracting Party, but constituted in accordance with the law of the other Contracting Party'. Bolivia objected that the notion of (direct or indirect) control had to be interpreted as meaning the exercise of actual control, that is, the Dutch companies indirectly owning the claimant had to exercise actual control over the claimant for the latter to qualify as a Dutch national.

The tribunal rejected Bolivia's contention, finding that a test based on actual control was 'not practicable' and 'the resultant uncertainty would directly frustrate the object and purpose of the BIT'.[251] It concluded that:

> The phrase 'controlled directly or indirectly' means that one entity may be said to control another entity (either directly, that is without an intermediary entity, or indirectly) if that entity possesses the legal capacity to control the other entity. Subject to evidence of particular restrictions on the exercise of voting rights, such legal capacity is to be ascertained with reference to the percentage of shares held ... In the Tribunal's view, the BIT does not require actual day-to-day or ultimate control as part of the 'controlled directly or indirectly' requirement contained in Article 1(b)(iii) ... It is the Tribunal's conclusion, by majority, that, in the circumstances of this case, where an entity has both majority shareholdings and ownership of a majority of the voting rights, control as embodied in the operative phrase 'controlled directly or indirectly' exists.[252]

Similarly, in a case of majority shareholding, the tribunal in *Mobil v Venezuela* adopted a legal control test.[253]

For purposes of the notion of control in the DOB clause contained in Article I(2) of the US–Ecuador BIT, the tribunal in *Ulysseas v Ecuador* also adopted a legal control test.[254]

[249] While the notion of control is often relevant in the context of jurisdiction *ratione personae*, it is also sometimes discussed in the context of jurisdiction *ratione materiae*, more particularly for the question of 'ownership and control' in the case of indirect investments, in other words the link that has to exist between the investment and the investor, see Chapter 5.

[250] *Aguas del Tunarí v Bolivia* (n 202). [251] Ibid, para 246. [252] Ibid, para 264.

[253] *Mobil Corporation, Venezuela Holdings BV, Mobil Cerro Negro Holding, Ltd, Mobil Venezolana de Petróleos Holdings, Inc, Mobil Cerro Negro, Ltd, and Mobil Venezolana de Petróleos, Inc v Bolivarian Republic of Venezuela*, ICSID Case No ARB/07/27, Decision on Jurisdiction (10 June 2010) paras 159–60.

[254] *Ulysseas v Ecuador* (n 156) para 168.

In *Yukos v Russia*, the tribunal adopted a legal control test when interpreting the DOB clause under the ECT,[255] this even though the Understanding on Article 1(6) ECT clarifies that 'control of an Investment means control in fact', thus actual or effective control.[256]

On the other hand, the arbitral tribunal in *Guardian Fiduciary Trust v Macedonia*[257] required a showing of effective control despite the existence of majority shareholding. In this case, the New Zealand-incorporated claimant alleged being under the control of a Dutch entity for the purposes of Article I(b)(iii) of the Netherlands–Macedonia BIT. The tribunal noted that 'while ownership generally implie[d] the legal right or the capacity to exercise control',[258] the issue was complicated by the fact that control over the claimant was divided between an entity being the legal owner and another one, incorporated in the Marshall Islands, being the beneficial owner of the claimant. Judging the issue of control 'ultimately a matter of evidence',[259] the tribunal found that 'the Claimant, was in fact controlled by [the] Marshall Islands company, and its director and beneficial owner' and that it was also the latter 'who authorized the commencement of the arbitration on behalf of the Claimant and signed the powers of attorney of the Claimant's counsel',[260] thereby dismissing the claim.

Similarly, the tribunal in *TSA Spectrum v Argentina* (though deciding the case on the basis of Article 25(2)(b) second clause of the Convention) implicitly required an effective control test for the question whether the Argentinean company was controlled by a Dutch investor in conformity with Article 1(b)(iii) of the Netherlands–Argentina BIT, this in spite of the fact that the Protocol to this BIT accepted as evidence of control 'inter alia ... the direct or indirect participation in the capital of a company higher than 49% or the direct or indirect possession of the necessary votes to obtain a predominant position in assemblies or company organs', requirement which the Dutch entity fulfilled.[261]

For a case of minority shareholding, the tribunal in *International Thunderbird v Mexico*,[262] rejected Mexico's contention that Article 1117 NAFTA required a showing of legal control in the sense of majority shareholding. The term 'control' not being defined in the NAFTA, it found that control could be exercised in various manners, which is why effective or de facto control was in its view 'sufficient'.[263] In this case, however, it required a higher burden of proof, finding that 'in the absence of legal control ... *de facto* control must be established beyond any reasonable doubt'.[264]

[255] *Yukos v Russia* (n 90) paras 536–37; Voon, Mitchell, and Munro, 'Legal Responses' (n 153) 55.

[256] See in this sense *Plama v Bulgaria*, Decision on Jurisdiction (n 145) para 170: 'In the Tribunal's view, ownership includes indirect and beneficial ownership; and control includes control in fact, including an ability to exercise substantial influence over the legal entity's management, operation and the selection of members of its board of directors or any other managing body'.

[257] *Guardian Fiduciary Trust Ltd f/k/a Capital Conservator Savings & Loans Ltd v Former Yugoslav Republic of Macedonia*, ICSID Case No ARB/12/31, Award (22 September 2015).

[258] Ibid, para 131. [259] Ibid, para 134. [260] Ibid, para 137.

[261] *TSA Spectrum v Argentina* (n 214) paras 160–62.

[262] *International Thunderbird Gaming v Mexico* (n 183). [263] Ibid, para 106.

[264] Ibid (emphasis in the original).

It then gave important indicia as to which other circumstances could in its opinion contribute to a finding of effective control in the case of minority shareholding. It found that:

> It [was] quite common in the international corporate world to control a business activity without owning the majority voting rights in shareholders' meetings. Control can also be achieved by the power to effectively decide and implement the key decisions of the business activity of an enterprise and, under certain circumstances, control can be achieved by the existence of one or more factors such as technology, access to supplies, access to markets, access to capital, know how, and authoritative reputation. Ownership and legal control may assure that the owner or legally controlling party has the ultimate right to determine key decisions. However, if in practice a person exercises that position with an expectation to receive an economic return for its efforts and eventually be held responsible for improper decisions, one can conceive the existence of a genuine link yielding the control of the enterprise to that person.[265]

4.3.4.3.2 Discussion

As becomes apparent from the above, questions raised in the context of the notion of control in IIAs are similar to those raised in the context of Article 25(2)(b) second clause, in particular whether legal/formal control should suffice or actual/de facto control should be required. Thus, as in Article 25(2)(b) second clause cases, arbitral tribunals have often let suffice purely legal control in the case of majority shareholding, while usually requiring effective control in the case of minority shareholding. This points towards the same presumption as the one established already within the frame of Article 25(2)(b) second clause,[266] that is the presumption that majority shareholding—also understood as ownership—(usually) implies (effective) control, while this is more doubtful in the case of minority shareholding, which is why tribunals will tend to ask for proof of actual control.

Not all scholars see the necessity for an effective control test, though. Douglas for example criticized the use of the effective control test in the *Thunderbird* decision on the grounds that it risked becoming a 'subjective test that might, in future cases, simply be tailored to affirm jurisdiction'.[267] This critique should likely be read in light of his assessment that '[t]he strongest form of control that an individual or legal entity can acquire over tangible or intangible property is the right of ownership',[268] leading him to conclude that 'the question of control is a question of law' as opposed to a question of fact.[269] However, it seems reasonable to assume that the alternative possibility, contained in virtually every IIA, of establishing the required nexus between the investor and the investment by virtue of ownership *or* control is precisely meant to provide *also* for the possibility of effective control. Indeed, while it can be accepted that in many cases, the ownership of an investment will converge with both legal and effective control, there do remain cases in which ownership/

[265] Ibid, para 108. [266] See above at 4.3.4.1.

[267] Zachary Douglas, *The International Law of Investment Claims* (Cambridge University Press 2009) para 570.

[268] Ibid, para 557. [269] Ibid, para 558.

legal control and effective control may diverge.[270] This may be in particular the case where a corporate entity (in particular a shell company) is inserted into the corporate chain as a conduit or where the tribunal otherwise has doubts about the identity of the true controller.

Similarities notwithstanding, there are however grounds to distinguish the notion of foreign control as in Article 25(2)(b) second clause and the notion of control as contained in IIAs.

First of all, a distinction seems warranted because of the differing wording the notion of control appears in, depending on whether one examines the notion of control as in IIAs or as in Article 25(2)(b) second clause. In this aspect, it is notable that while the latter explicitly takes into consideration only control ('because of foreign *control*'), the former is mostly formulated in conjunction with ownership ('owned or controlled by').

Second, the interpretation of the notion of control as in IIAs will arguably depend on whether the IIA in question contains any further clarification on how to understand this notion. Indeed, many IIAs contain such clarifications, though some of the wordings used are in need of further interpretation as to whether they establish a legal or de facto control test.[271] What is not quite clear, however, is whether there might be differences in interpretation depending on the context in which the notion of control arises. In other words, is the notion of control as in the definition of protected investment the same as, for example, the notion of control in the DOB clause?[272] The interpretation by the tribunal in *Yukos v Russia* is a case in point: while Article 1(6) ECT clearly stipulates a de facto control test, the tribunal let suffice legal control for purposes of Article 17(1) ECT.[273] Was this justified by a differing interpretative context, or was it an interpretative lapse? This is not clear.

By contrast, foreign control as in Article 25(2)(b) second clause seems a (more) autonomous (though also more restrictive) test than the notion of control as in IIAs. This is arguably so because of the 'outer limits' of the ICSID Convention that cannot be exceeded even in the case of the parties agreeing on the notion of foreign control. This is not to say that the notion of control as contained in IIAs (and its clarifications, where existing) is completely irrelevant for the interpretation of the notion of foreign control.[274] Yet, even where an IIA may accept purely legal/formal control by an entity, this does not necessarily mean that ICSID jurisdiction will be established in the absence of effective foreign control. This means that the interposition, in the corporate structure, of a mailbox company with qualifying nationality

[270] Similar Bischoff and Happ (n 205) 530–31 (para 103).

[271] See more in detail in Chapter 8, at 8.2.3.3.

[272] Similar Loukas Mistelis and Crina Baltag, 'Denial of Benefits and Article 17 of the Energy Charter Treaty' (2008–2009) 113 Penn St L Rev 1301, 1314.

[273] *Yukos v Russia* (n 90) 536–37.

[274] See, eg, *Caratube v Kazakhstan* (n 178) para 333; *TSA Spectrum v Argentina* (n 214) Dissenting Opinion Judge Aldonas, para 10.

may be permissible under the BIT, but may not be so under the ICSID Convention (in the absence of effective control).[275]

This considerable uncertainty as to which interpretation a tribunal may take towards the notion of control seems to make the inclusion of a clarification in the IIA in question highly recommendable.[276]

4.4 Preliminary Conclusions

The preceding chapter has established that attempts by Respondent States to convince arbitral tribunals to dismiss claims on the grounds that the putative investor–claimant, whether a natural or legal person, was not the 'real' investor ultimately benefitting from the claim, have only very rarely been met with success.

With respect to natural persons, arbitral tribunals have so far uniformly rejected the application of the 'genuine link' test, whether for cases of single or multiple nationalities. The only bar to the invocation of a dual nationality may be found in the 'host State bias' contained in Article 25(2)(a) ICSID Convention. This means that claims under other arbitral rules (such as UNCITRAL) by a dual national holding host State nationality remain possible unless the invoked BIT contains an explicit exclusion to this effect. Arbitral tribunals have also started to recognize the potential for 'circumventions' of the 'host State bias' in Article 25(2)(a) ICSID Convention by the use of interposed corporate entities controlled by (host State) dual nationals, interpreting the notion of 'foreign control' in Article 25(2)(b) second clause in the light of Article 25(2)(a) ICSID Convention.

For legal persons as claimants within the meaning of Article 25(2)(b) first clause, arbitral tribunals have, in the absence of explicit additional requirements contained in the IIAs, virtually uniformly recognized the independence of legal entities in a corporate legal chain and have rejected arguments aimed at 'piercing the corporate veil', whether these entities are host State or third State-controlled. This attests to a formal, consent-oriented approach towards the notion of investor. Only under specific circumstances (such as fraud or instances of abuse of legal personality) do arbitral tribunals in principle appear to be ready to disregard the independent legal entity in favour of another corporate entity. States wishing to prevent treaty shopping should therefore prescribe additional substantive requirements for the investor to qualify as such, or include a DOB clause in the treaty. However, inconsistent jurisprudence as to whether the exercise of the latter clause has retrospective or prospective effect only may relativize the usefulness of this provision.

Inconsistent jurisprudence and thus uncertainty also exists with respect to whether the notion of (foreign) control as used in Article 25(2)(b) second clause and in IIAs should be defined as requiring purely legal or rather effective control.

[275] However, an arbitration under other arbitration rules, eg, UNCITRAL arbitral rules, would remain possible if so foreseen by the IIA.

[276] See in Chapter 8, at 8.2.3.3.

Tribunals have in this respect often established the presumption that majority shareholding (in other words ownership) implied (effective) control, while requiring a showing of effective control in the case of minority shareholding, but have under certain circumstances required a showing of actual control even in the case of majority shareholding when they had doubts about the true nature of the controller.

There is also inconsistency with respect to the question whether, once the requisite control qualifying as covered investor has been found, the tribunal may or even must continue to enquire into the nationality of the ultimate controller. Approaches taken by arbitral tribunals differ in this aspect, with formal versus substantive approaches militating against each other. There seems however a more recent trend in arbitral jurisprudence that dismisses jurisdiction when the ultimate controller of a local investment is found to be a host State national.

5

Jurisdiction *Ratione Materiae*

5.1 Introduction

In the context of corporate structuring, many questions have been increasingly arising with respect to the notion of investment or jurisdiction *ratione materiae*.

As is well known, the question of which investor qualifies for protection is inseparable from the question of which investment qualifies for protection under a given investment treaty, a putative investor–claimant not only having to prove that he holds the requisite nationality, but also that he has made an investment protected under the invoked investment treaty. This being so, the question arises as follows: is it enough for an investor, originally without a qualifying nationality, to acquire assets qualifying under the targeted investment treaty both as regards *ratione personae* and *ratione materiae*? What if the putative investor–claimant is part of a corporate group and the parent company simply reshuffles corporate assets so that the putative investor–claimant becomes eligible under the intended treaty?[1] And is it enough, in view of the protection of indirect investments under most modern investment treaties, for any entity along the corporate chain to claim ownership of assets that any of its subsidiaries might hold, or do putative investor–claimants have to make an 'active' contribution?

These and other questions have as of late come to the forefront of arbitral discussions on the validity of corporate structuring or restructuring, and will thus be examined in turn.

5.2 Notion of Investment in IIAs

As has already been seen,[2] States negotiating investment protection treaties have sought to overcome the restrictive effects of the *Barcelona Traction* jurisprudence with respect to investor standing by providing for generally broad definitions of the notion of investment and protecting not only direct, but also indirect, investments.[3]

[1] Tania Voon, Andrew Mitchell, and James Munro, 'Legal Responses to Corporate Manoeuvering in International Investment Arbitration' (2014) 5 JIDS 41, 53.

[2] See Chapter 1, at 1.2.2.

[3] Similar *Enron Corporation and Ponderosa Assets, LP v Argentine Republic*, ICSID Case No ARB/01/3, Decision on Jurisdiction (14 January 2004) para 46.

This combination has the effect—contrary to the decision in *Barcelona Traction*—of granting a direct right of action to any investor fulfilling the nationality requirement and whose investment qualifies under the investment treaty in question, even if the host State measure has only indirectly affected his investment.

The great majority of investment treaties have adopted the asset-based definition approach, usually followed by a non-exhaustive list of what is considered an investment by the treaty under examination.[4] Other countries have adopted a closed-list approach.[5] The North American Free Trade Agreement (NAFTA), by contrast, has adopted an enterprise-based definition of the notion of investment followed by an exhaustive list of covered investments.[6]

5.2.1 Shareholding as investment

What qualifies as protected investment has thus to be determined on a case-by-case basis, by recourse to the invoked investment treaties, and cannot be stated in a general manner. This being said, it seems safe to say that shareholding qualifies in virtually any investment treaty as protected investment, resolving, as it does, the a.m. *Barcelona Traction* problematic. Numerous tribunals have thus held that the mere ownership of shares qualifies in principle as a protected investment.[7]

The same usually applies to so-called portfolio investments, that is 'interests in assets of companies [which] do not involve the owner in participation in management or even entry into the state in which the assets are put to productive use'.[8] The term 'portfolio investment' thus typically captures non-controlling minority shareholdings. Many tribunals have indeed considered even non-controlling minority

[4] UNCTAD, 'Scope and Definition, A Sequel' UNCTAD Series on Issues in International Investment Agreements II (United Nations 2011) 21ff, available at <http://unctad.org/en/docs/diaeia20102_en.pdf> (last accessed on 15 September 2016).

[5] See, eg, the 2012 Canada–China BIT; Katia Yannaca-Small, 'Definition of "Investment": An Open-ended Search for a Balanced Approach' in Katia Yannaca-Small (ed), *Arbitration under International Investment Agreements* (Oxford University Press 2010) 243, 244.

[6] See North American Free Trade Agreement (opened for signature 17 December 1992) 32 ILM (1993) 296 and 695 (entered into force 1 January 1994) Arts 1139 and 201.

[7] *Antoine Goetz & Consorts et SA Affinage des Métaux v République du Burundi*, ICSID Case No ARB/95/3, Award (10 February 1999) para 89; *CMS Gas Transmission Co v Argentine Republic*, ICSID Case No ARB/01/8, Decision of the Tribunals on Objections to Jurisdiction (17 July 2003) para 56; *Sempra Energy International v Argentine Republic*, ICSID Case No ARB/02/16, Decision on Jurisdiction (11 May 2005) paras 123–24; *Ioannis Kardassopoulos v Republic of Georgia*, ICSID Case No ARB/05/18, Decision on Jurisdiction (6 July 2007) paras 123–24; *AIG Capital Partners and CJSC Tema Real Estate Company v Republic of Kazakhstan*, ICSID Case No ARB/01/6, Award (7 October 2003) para 9.4.8; *African Holding Company et Société Africaine de Construction au Congo SARL v République Démocratique du Congo*, ICSID Case No 05/21, Decision on Jurisdiction and Admissibility (29 July 2008) para 99; *Phoenix Action Ltd v Czech Republic*, ICSID Case No ARB/06/5, Award (15 April 2009) para 121; *Teinver SA, Transportes de Cercanías SA and Autobuses Urbanos del Sur SA v Argentine Republic*, ICSID Case No ARB/09/1, Decision on Jurisdiction (21 December 2012) para 230; *Société Générale in Respect of DR Energy Holdings Limited and Empresa Distribuidora de Electricidad del Este, SA ('EDE Este') v Dominican Republic*, LCIA Case No UN 7927, Award on Preliminary Objections to Jurisdiction (19 September 2008) paras 32–33.

[8] M Sornarajah, 'Portfolio Investments and the Definition of Investment' (2009) 24 ICSID Review 516.

shareholdings as protected investments.[9] However, some treaties explicitly exclude portfolio investments from protection.[10]

5.2.2 Indirect investments

Though the protection of shareholding is an important element in the possibility to access an advantageous bilateral investment treaty (BIT), treaty shopping would arguably not come to its full effect without the protection of *indirect* investments. In particular multinational companies with corporate structures covering several national jurisdictions may thus extend its potential treaty protection considerably, with each and every entity within the corporate chain potentially having a separate standing of its own (provided the existence of an international investment agreement (IIA) between its home and the host State) (see also Figure 5.1).[11]

As mentioned further above, virtually any BIT nowadays protects not only direct but also indirect investments, by virtue of including it either in the notion of investment or in the notion of investor.[12] Likewise, tribunals have usually rather unanimously found indirect investment to be covered by the investment treaties under interpretation.[13] Tribunals have also accepted that the investment may be structured through several corporate layers.[14] However, as Jan Asmus Bischoff and Richard Happ rightly point out, in those cases, the 'relationship of ownership and control has to be ascertained separately for each corporate layer'.[15]

[9] *CMS v Argentina* (n 7) para 51; *Lanco International Inc v Argentine Republic*, ICSID Case No ARB/97/6, Decision on Jurisdiction (8 December 1998) section 10ff; *Enron Corp and Ponderosa v Argentina* (n 3) para 49.

[10] See, eg, Article 45 of the 2000 EFTA–Mexico Free Trade Agreement (though not providing for ISDS): 'For the purpose of this treaty, investment made in accordance with the laws and regulations of the Parties means direct investment, which is defined as investment for the purpose of establishing lasting economic relations with an undertaking such as, in particular, investments which give the possibility of exercising an effective influence on the management thereof.'

[11] On the possible reasons for multilayered structuring by multinational companies see Patrick Fiedler, Robert Hunter, and Ulrich Klemm, 'Chapter H. Policy Issues: Is the Current Status of Law and Treaty Practice Satisfactory?' in ILA German Branch, Working Group, *The Determination of the Nationality of Investors under Investment Protection Treaties*, Heft 106 (2011) 79–86, available at <http://telc.jura.uni-halle.de/sites/default/files/BeitraegeTWR/Heft%20106.pdf> (last accessed on 15 September 2016).

[12] See Chapter 4 on the question of ownership and control. This leads to a certain blurring of the notions of indirect investor and indirect investment, as also noted by Martins Paparinskis, 'Barcelona Traction: A Friend of Investment Protection Law' (2008) 8 Baltic YIL 105, 121.

[13] *Azurix Corp v Argentine Republic*, ICSID Case No ARB/01/12, Decision on Jurisdiction (8 December 2003) paras 65, 73; *Sempra Energy International v Argentina* (n 7) paras 90ff; *Gas Natural SDG v Argentine Republic*, ICSID Case No ARB/03/10, Decision on Jurisdiction (17 June 2005) para 34; *Waste Management Inc v United Mexican States* ('Number II'), ICSID Case No ARB(AF)/00/3, Award (30 April 2004) paras 80, 85; *Teinver v Argentina* (n 7) paras 230–32.

[14] *Mobil Corporation, Venezuela Holdings BV, Mobil Cerro Negro Holding, Ltd, Mobil Venezolana de Petróleos Holdings, Inc, Mobil Cerro Negro, Ltd, and Mobil Venezolana de Petróleos, Inc v Bolivarian Republic of Venezuela*, ICSID Case No ARB/07/27, Decision on Jurisdiction (10 June 2010) para 165; *AIG Capital Partners v Kazakhstan* (n 7) para 9.4.8; *Siemens AG v Argentine Republic*, ICSID Case No ARB/02/8, Decision on Jurisdiction (3 August 2004) para 137.

[15] Jan Asmus Bischoff and Richard Happ,'Ratione Materiae' in Marc Bungenberg, Jörn Griebel, Stephan Hobe, and August Reinisch (eds), *International Investment Law, A Handbook* (CH Beck, Hart Publishing and Nomos 2015) (para 104).

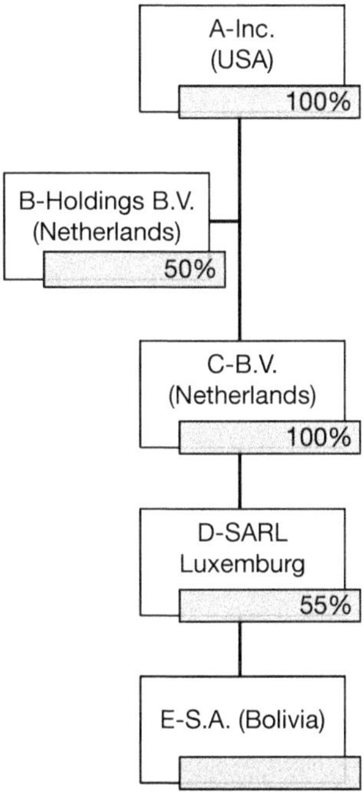

Figure 5.1 Example of an indirect ownership structure[a]

[a] In this hypothetical corporate structure, a claim could thus be theoretically brought under the 1998 US–Bolivia BIT by the US-incorporated parent entity, under the 1992 Netherlands–Bolivia BIT by the Dutch entities or under the 1990 BLEU–Bolivia BIT by the Luxemburg entity (though the latter requires the entity to have its 'real seat' in Luxemburg, Art 1(1)(b) BLEU–Bolivia BIT), if the respective treaties were in force at the time of the events giving rise to the alleged breach.

5.2.2.1 Inclusion of indirect investments when the treaty text is silent?

Even where IIAs are silent as to whether indirect investments should be covered, tribunals and scholars have mostly found that the use of the broad asset-based definition implied that indirect investments should be covered.[16]

One early case in which the arbitral tribunal found that a BIT that was silent on this issue protected an indirect investment was *Sedelmayer v Russian Federation*.[17] In this case, the Claimant, a natural person who invested in the Russian Federation through a corporate vehicle incorporated in the United States (SGC International) and wholly owned by him, brought arbitration proceedings against Russia based on the 1989 Germany–Soviet Union BIT. This BIT is defined in Article 1(1)(a) the notion of 'investment' as 'every kind of asset invested by an investor of one Contracting Party in the territory of the other Party in accordance with the latter's

[16] See, eg, Bischoff and Happ (n 15) 526 (para 84); for a contrary view see Zachary Douglas, *The International Law of Investment Claims* (Cambridge University Press 2009) 311.

[17] *Franz Sedelmayer v Russian Federation*, SCC, Award (7 July 1998).

legislation' and the notion of 'investor' in Article 1(1)(c) as meaning 'a natural person that has the permanent residence, or a legal entity that has its seat in the respective territories to which this Treaty applies, and that has the right to make investments'. Russia contested the Claimant's qualifying as an 'investor' within the meaning of the BIT terms, alleging that it was the US-incorporated entity that made the investment, if any.

The tribunal rejected this argument, holding that Mr Sedelmayer was not only:

> in full control of SGC International but also that SGC International was entirely dependent on financial contributions from him. These circumstances support Mr. Sedelmayer's allegation that SGC International was only a vehicle through which he transferred his own personal capital into Russia.[18]

It then wondered 'whether an individual who makes his investments through a company might be regarded as an investor—a *de facto* [sic] investor—under the Treaty. This question concerns the general issue to what extent the "theory of control" may be applied'.[19] This led the tribunal to remark that 'during recent years, there has been a growing support of the control theory ... to a large extent based on the judgment in the *ELSI* case'.[20] Accepting that it had to engage in the interpretation of the clause in question as to whether it could apply the control theory, it held:

> It is a fact that the Treaty does not contain any specific clause providing such application. On the other hand, there is nothing in the Treaty which excludes the applicability of the said theory. In the Tribunal's opinion, the mere fact that the Treaty is silent on the point now discussed should not be interpreted so that Mr. Sedelmayer can not be regarded as a *de facto* [sic] investor. In this context, not only the Treaty itself but also the Protocol attached to the Treaty is of interest. The Protocol contains a statement according to which an investor shall be entitled to compensation if the other Contracting Party interferes with the economic activities of an enterprise in which he is participating. This statement can be seen as an acknowledgment of the rights of a *de facto* [sic] investor. It should also be kept in mind that, as can be concluded from the text of the Treaty, the main aim of the Treaty is to promote, as far as possible, investments in the two countries concerned. Granting protection under the Treaty to the investments now discussed would be in line with the said purpose ...[21]

The Tribunal thus accepted that the claimant was an investor, even though formally it was the vehicle owned by him that made the investment.

5.2.2.2 Discussion

Correct as the result may be, the approach of the tribunal calls for several critical remarks.

First, it can be doubted that there was growing support for the control theory at the time of the judgment, and a mere reference to the—often-misunderstood—*ELSI* case clearly does not remedy any doubt in this aspect.

[18] Ibid, 57. [19] Ibid. [20] Ibid, 57–58. [21] Ibid, 58–59.

Second, the contention of what seems to be a new legal figure, i.e. the de facto investor, is as unfortunate—because lacking in clear contours—as the assumption of some commentators that the tribunal engaged in a form of piercing of the corporate veil.[22] The dissenting arbitrator correctly noted in this respect that 'the meaning attributed to the so-called "control theory" may be different in various instances and [that] this circumstance should be taken into account when a reference to this theory is made'.[23]

Indeed, the difficulties in this case did not arise from the definition of the notion of investor, which was easy to confirm. Rather, the difficulty lay in the fact that the Germany–Soviet Union BIT in question did not specify in its definition whether it covered indirect investments made by an investor through another country. Compare this with the 2008 German Model BIT, which stipulates now—maybe (also) as a consequence of the *Sedelmayer* award—clearly in its Article 1(1) that 'the term "investment" comprises every kind of asset which is *directly or indirectly invested* by investors of one Contracting Party'. The approach of the tribunal could also easily be misunderstood because commonly the control theory is invoked precisely to disavow the claimed nationality of the investor, not to ground it. Thus, the correct approach for the tribunal would have been to interpret the notion of 'investment' as found in Article 1(1)(a) of the BIT as to whether indirect investments were covered, which could have been confirmed by recourse to the same arguments as were otherwise correctly invoked by the tribunal.

It thus seems that there were good reasons for subsequent tribunals not to follow the *Sedelmayer* decision.[24] Instead, tribunals nowadays usually recognize indirect investment as protected based on the broad notion of investment contained in the treaties under interpretation.[25]

5.2.2.3 Exceptions

Tribunals have only found exceptions to this rule when this could be explicitly tied to treaty language.

[22] See, eg, Markus Perkams, 'The Determination of Nationality of Investors in International Investment Agreements (IIAs)—Taking Stock of the Criteria Used in Modern Investment Law' in ILA German Branch, Working group, *The Determination of the Nationality of Investors under Investment Protection Treaties* (March 2011) 13, 23, available at <http://telc.jura.uni-halle.de/sites/default/files/BeitraegeTWR/Heft%20106.pdf> (last accessed on 15 September 2016). For a critique of the theory of the 'piercing of the veil' see Chapter 9, at 9.4.2.

[23] *Sedelmayer v Russia* (n 17) Dissenting Opinion Prof. Zykin, 1.

[24] Similar Christoph Schreuer, 'Shareholder Protection in International Investment Law' (2005) 2 TDM 16, available at <http://www.transnational-dispute-management.com> (subscription required).

[25] See, eg, *Cemex Caracas Investments BV and Cemex Caracas II Investments BV v Bolivarian Republic of Venezuela*, ICSID Case No ARB/08/14, Decision on Jurisdiction (30 December 2010) paras 156–57; *ConocoPhillips Petrozuata BV, ConocoPhillips Hamaca BV and ConocoPhillips Gulf of Paria BV v Bolivarian Republic of Venezuela*, ICSID Case No ARB/07/30, Decision on Jurisdiction (3 September 2013) para 285; *Ioannis Kardassopoulos v Georgia* (n 7) para 124; *Tza Yap Shum v Republic of Peru*, ICSID Case No ARB/07/6, Decision on Jurisdiction (19 June 2009) paras 90–111; *Teinver v Argentina* (n 7) paras 209–35; *Guaracachi America Inc and Rurelec PLC v Plurinational State of Bolivia*, UNCITRAL, PCA Case No 2011-17, Award (31 January 2014) paras 352–53.

This has been the case for in for example *HICEE v Slovakia*.[26] The dispute arose out of State measures allegedly adversely affecting claimant's indirect investment, via a Slovakia-incorporated holding company, into two local companies in the health insurance business in Slovakia.

The tribunal first made some general remarks about the particular corporate structure used by the claimant, noting that:

HICEE's investment in the Slovak health insurance market is a structured one. This is not unusual, nor is there anything in the least reprehensible about it; structured investments are commonplace. The purpose is to secure advantages from incorporation or operation in a particular jurisdiction; the specific motives behind the incorporation of HICEE in the Netherlands are explained in the Claimant's Statement of Claim. The advantages anticipated often include the protection of particular bilateral (or other) treaties covering foreign investment.[27]

Interpreting the notion of investment contained in the BIT, which protects 'every kind of asset invested either directly or through an investor of *a third country*' [emphasis added],[28] the tribunal did not exclude claimant's possibility to claim for possible damages sustained by the Slovak holding company itself, this entity qualifying as a *direct* investment by the claimant. However, the claimant's *indirect* investment in the two local companies through a Slovak holding company was not protected because of the particular wording of the clause. The tribunal thus elaborated:

It is not enough for the Claimant to say that HICEE suffered a loss via the effect of national law on that business, unless the loss followed in some direct sense from a treaty breach. When the Claimant says that 'investment treaty jurisprudence' gives a shareholder standing to pursue claims for damage to the assets of a company in which it holds shares, that is not a proposition that can be upheld by the Tribunal in so sweeping a form, given the default position in international law that the corporate form is recognized as legally distinct from the shareholders, and confers on the corporate entity the capacity to assert claims for damage suffered to it or its property. The true position, as the Tribunal understands it, is that the admissibility of shareholder claims depends upon the provisions of the investment protection treaty in question, and that investment protection treaties very frequently make provision to allow for shareholder claims, either explicitly or by necessary implication. The position, in other words, is controlled by the treaty, and the Tribunal can see no justification for calling into play a supposed proposition of general law in order to change or override what the treaty itself provides.[29]

The above finding accords with the reasoning of the earlier *Berschader and Berschader v Russia* ad hoc arbitration.[30] As in the *HICEE* case, the BIT under interpretation, the 1989 Belgium–Luxembourg–Russia BIT, provided in relevant parts that the

[26] *HICEE BV v Slovak Republic*, UNCITRAL, PCA Case No 2009-11, Partial Award (23 May 2011).

[27] Ibid, para 103.

[28] Art 1(a) of the Netherlands–Slovak Republic BIT.

[29] *HICEE v Slovak Republic* (n 26) para 147.

[30] *Vladimir Berschader and Moise Berschader v Russian Federation*, Arbitration V (080/2004) Award (21 April 2006).

'term "investment" also means indirect investments made by investors of one of the Contracting Parties in the territory of the other Contracting Party *by the intermediary of an investor of a third state*' [emphasis added].[31] Since the claimants, two Belgian nationals, had made their investment in the Russian Federation through their wholly owned, Belgium-incorporated company Berschader International (BI), the tribunal rejected Claimants' contention that their indirect investment qualified under the Belgium–Luxemburg–Russia BIT. It also noted that it could not be assumed that indirect investments incorporated in Belgium or Russia be implicitly covered as the purpose of this provision, in the tribunal's view, was to provide protection to entities which would otherwise not enjoy any protection, whereas a Belgium entity investing in Russia would by itself qualify for protection under the BIT.[32] The fact that BI could no longer bring a claim of its own because of its bankruptcy was not considered sufficient by the tribunal to overcome the terms agreed between the Contracting Parties.[33]

5.3 Notion of Investment in the ICSID Convention

The practice of treaty shopping by corporate structuring also raises a number of important and highly contentious questions with respect to the notion of investment as contained in the International Centre for Settlement of Investment Disputes (ICSID) Convention.

As is well known, Article 25(1) of the Convention limits the Centre's jurisdiction *ratione materiae* to legal disputes 'arising out of an investment'. As with other notions contained in Article 25 of the Convention, their drafters also abstained from defining the notion of investment, because of a lack of agreement on the content of the notion as well as to allow for large flexibility by the Contracting Parties to define the notion and possible future progressive development of the law.[34]

While a comprehensive review of the divergent jurisprudence on the notion of investment in Article 25 would be beyond the scope of this book and can be gleaned from other academic contributions,[35] a short excursus seems necessary to lay the bases

[31] Art I(1) Belgium–Luxemburg Economic Union–Russian Federation BIT.

[32] Ibid, para 143. [33] Ibid, paras 148–49.

[34] UNCTAD, 'Scope and Definition' (n 4) 52; Aron Broches, 'The Convention on the Settlement of Investment Disputes between States and Nationals of other States', Académie de droit international (1972) 136 Recueil des Cours 331, 362; Yannaca-Small, 'Definition of "Investment"' (n 5) 248–49.

[35] See, eg, Pierre-Emmanuel Dupont, 'The Notion of ICSID Investment: Ongoing "Confusion" or "Emerging Synthesis"?' (2011) 12 JWIT 245; David Williams and Simon Foote, 'Recent developments in the approach to identifying an "investment" pursuant to Article 25(1) of the ICSID Convention' in Chester Brown and Kate Miles (eds), *Evolution in Investment Treaty Law and Arbitration* (Cambridge University Press 2011) 42; Yannaca-Small, 'Definition of "Investment"' (n 5) 248–51; Michael Reisman and Anna Vinnik, 'What Constitutes an Investment and Who Decides?' in Arthur W Rovine (ed), *Fordham Papers 2010, Contemporary Issues in International Arbitration and Mediation* (Brill/Martinus Nijhoff 2011) 50; Bischoff and Happ (n 15) 503–14.

for examining several elements that have been held to be critical in deciding whether a given situation of corporate structuring was to be considered lawful or prejudicial to the tribunal's jurisdiction.

There has been little controversy with respect to the fact that in order to confirm their jurisdiction *ratione materiae*, tribunals have to examine the existence of an investment both under the BIT in question and under Article 25 of the Convention (the so-called double keyhole test).[36]

Tribunals have however been consistently divided over the question whether the notion of investment contains objective elements not open to party consent (so-called 'objectivist' or 'objective approach'),[37] or whether the parties had full liberty in establishing what they would consider an investment for purposes of Article 25 of the Convention (so-called 'subjectivist' or 'subjective approach').[38]

The 'objective' approach has its origin in the *Fedax v Venezuela* decision[39] and has been further developed in the *Salini v Morocco* decision.[40] In the latter case, the tribunal identified four elements constitutive of an investment that came to be known by later tribunals as the '*Salini* criteria', namely:

> contributions, a certain duration of performance of the contract and a participation in the risks of the transaction ... In regarding the Conventions' preamble, one may add the contribution to the economic development of the host State of the investment as an additional criterion.[41]

Various tribunals adopted this 'objective approach', elevating these four criteria to the level of jurisdictional requirements.[42] Another tribunal, in the case *Phoenix Action v Czech Republic*, also adopted the 'objective approach', though adding to

[36] See, eg, *Ceskoslovenska Obchodni Banka AS (CSOB) v Slovak Republic*, ICSID Case No ARB/97/4, Decision on Objections to Jurisdiction (24 May 1999) para 68; *Fedax NV v Bolivian Republic of Venezuela*, ICSID Case No ARB/96/3, Award on Jurisdiction (11 July 1997) paras 28–29; *Joy Mining Machinery Limited v Arab Republic of Egypt*, ICSID Case No ARB/03/11, Award on Jurisdiction (30 July 2004) paras 43 and 48; *Toto Costruzioni Generali SpA v Republic of Lebanon*, ICSID Case No ARB/07/12, Decision on Jurisdiction (11 September 2009) para 66; *Malaysian Historical Salvors v Government of Malaysia*, ICSID Case No ARB/05/10, Award (28 May 2007) para 55; *Phoenix Action v Czech Republic* (n 7) para 74.

[37] Yannaca-Small, 'Definition of "Investment"' (n 5) 250; Veijo Heiskanen, 'Of Capital Import: The Definition of "Investment" in International Investment Law' in Anne Hoffmann (ed), *Protection of Foreign Investments through Modern Treaty Arbitration*, ASA Special Series No 34 (May 2010) 51, 509 available at <http://www.lalive.ch/data/publications/vhe_Of_capital_import;_The_definition_of_'investment'_in_international_investment_law.pdf> (last accessed on 15 September 2016).

[38] Yannaca-Small, 'Definition of "Investment"' (n 5) 251; Heiskanen 'Of Capital Import' (n 37) 59.

[39] *Fedax v Venezuela* (n 36).

[40] *Salini Costruttori SpA and Italstrade SpA v Kingdom of Morocco*, ICSID Case No ARB/00/4, Decision on Jurisdiction (23 July 2001).

[41] Ibid, para 52.

[42] See, eg, *Bayindir Insaat Turizm Ticaret Ve Sanayi AS v Islamic Republic of Pakistan*, ICSID Case No ARB/03/29, Decision on Jurisdiction (14 November 2005) para 130; *Jan de Nul NV and Dredging International NV v Arab Republic of Egypt*, ICSID Case No ARB/04/13, Decision on Jurisdiction (16 June 2006) para 91; *Helnan International Hotels A/S v Arab Republic of Egypt*, ICSID Case No ARB/05/19, Decision of the Tribunal on Objection to Jurisdiction (17 October 2006) para 66; *Patrick Mitchell v Democratic Republic of Congo*, ICSID Case No ARB/99/7, Decision on the Application for Annulment of the Award (1 November 2006) para 27; *Toto v Lebanon* (n 36) para 69; *Joy Mining v Egypt* (n 36) paras 50–53.

the aforementioned four criteria two additional ones, namely that the investment must have been made in accordance with host State legislation and that it must be made in good faith.[43]

Other tribunals have followed the 'subjective approach', leaving it to the parties' consent to define what should be considered as a protected investment.[44]

A more flexible approach, seeking to reconcile the former two approaches, can be found in an increasing number of recent decisions. This flexible approach rejects the character of jurisdictional requirements to the *Salini* criteria and considers them as mere 'typical characteristics' of an investment that may assist in identifying or excluding in extreme cases the existence of an investment.[45] Leaving wide latitude to parties' definitions of the notion of investment in BITs, it remains, however, circumscribed by an 'ordinary' or 'inherent' meaning of investment in Article 25, which must be fulfilled without prejudice to the notion of investment contained in the BIT.[46] Recent tribunals—some of them non-ICSID tribunals—have understood this 'inherent' meaning to require a contribution that extends over a certain period of time, and that involves some risk.[47] Many tribunals have by contrast been sceptical with respect to the criterion of contribution to the host State's development.[48]

It is noteworthy that although originally developed in the context of the notion of investment for the ICSID Convention, recent investment treaties have been

[43] *Phoenix Action v Czech Republic* (n 7) para 114; for an in-depth analysis of this case see in Chapter 7, at 7.3.1 and Chapter 9, at 9.3.4.

[44] See, eg, *Azurix v Argentina* (n 13) paras 62–65; *Enron v Argentina* (n 3) para 42; *Fraport AG Frankfurt Airport Services Worldwide v Republic of the Philippines*, ICSID Case No ARB/03/25, Award (16 August 2007) para 305; *Malaysian Historical Salvors, SDN, BHD v Government of Malaysia*, ICSID Case No ARB/05/10, Decision on the Application for Annulment of the Award (16 April 2009) para 58; *Inmaris Perestroika Sailing Maritime Services GmbH v Ukraine*, ICSID Case No ARB08/8, Decision on Jurisdiction (8 March 2010) para 130.

[45] See, eg, *MCI Power Group LC and New Turbine Inc v Republic of Ecuador*, ICSID Case No ARB/03/6, Award (31 July 2007) para 165; *Biwater Gauff Ltd v United Republic of Tanzania*, ICSID Case No ARB/05/22, Award (24 July 2008) paras 312–16; *Pantechniki SA Contractors & Engineers (Greece) v Republic of Albania*, ICSID Case No ARB/07/21, Award (30 July 2009) paras 36–47; *RSM Production Corporation v Grenada*, ICSID Case No ARB/05/14, Award (13 March 2009) para 241; *Alpha Projektholding GmbH v Ukraine*, ICSID Case No ARB/07/16, Award (8 November 2010) para 311; *Jan Oostergetel and Theodora Laurentius v Slovak Republic*, UNCITRAL, Decision on Jurisdiction (30 April 2010) para 162; *Philip Morris Brands Sàrl, Philip Morris Products SA and Abal Hermanos SA v Oriental Republic of Uruguay*, ICSID Case No ARB/10/7, Award (8 July 2016) para 206.

[46] See also *Nova Scotia Power Incorporated v Bolivarian Republic of Venezuela*, ICSID Case No ARB(AF)/11/1, Award (30 April 2014) paras 80–81.

[47] *Romak SA (Switzerland) v Republic of Uzbekistan*, UNCITRAL, PCA Case No AA 280, Award (26 November 2009) para 207; *Quiborax SA, Non Metallic Minerals SA and Allan Fosk Kaplún v Plurinational State of Bolivia*, ICSID Case No ARB/06/2, Decision on Jurisdiction (27 September 2012) paras 211–19; *KT Asia Investment Group BV v Republic of Kazakhstan*, ICSID Case No ARB/09/8, Award (17 October 2013) paras 165–70.

[48] See, eg, *Sedelmayer v Russia* (n 17) para 224; *LESI SpA and ASTALDI SpA v République Algérienne Démocratique et Populaire*, ICSID Case No ARB/05/3, Decision (12 July 2006) para 72; *Société Générale v Dominican Republic* (n 7) para 35; *Victor Pey Casado and President Allende Foundation v Republic of Chile*, ICSID Case No ARB/98/2, Sentence Arbitrale (8 May 2008) para 232; *Quiborax v Bolivia* (n 47) para 225; *KT Asia v Kazakhstan* (n 47) para 171.

including, mostly for greater clarity, in their definition of investment some or all of the above elements.[49]

Not seeking to take a definite stance on which of the above approaches should be considered the correct one by this author, the following section will discuss those elements of the notion of investment that have been controversial in the context of a strategic use or change of nationality.

5.4 Specific Problems Related to Treaty Shopping

5.4.1 Contribution requirement

Various arbitral tribunals (not all of them ICSID tribunals) have had to decide the question whether the payment of only a nominal price for the investment by the Claimant—often as part of a transfer of shares in the local investment within the corporate group—disqualified the investment from the ambit of jurisdiction *ratione materiae*. Respondents have in this respect in particular argued that the payment of only a nominal price was a strong indicator that the transfer or acquisition of the investment was only a 'sham transaction' aimed at accessing arbitral jurisdiction and—more in legal terms—that Claimant has thus not made a contribution within the meaning of the first *Salini* criterion.

This is a question that, as will be seen, partly intersects with the question of whether an investor needs to show an economic motivation when making the investment, whether he has to make an 'active' contribution, and whether he has assumed a certain risk with the investment.

5.4.1.1 Economic motivation

In cases where the investor–claimant acquired the investment for much less than it might objectively be worth, Respondents have sometimes tried to argue that the investment should not qualify because of a lack of an economic motivation by the investor–claimant.

The tribunal in *Saluka v Czech Republic* clarified that an investment did not disqualify only because the investor purchased shares 'as part of what might be termed bare profit-making or profit-taking transactions'.[50] However, while the tribunal in *Caratube v Kazakhstan* endorsed the *Saluka* holding in principle, it required the claimant to show 'the existence of an at least plausible economic motivation' in the alleged investment.[51]

[49] See in Chapter 8, at 8.2.4.2.

[50] *Saluka Investments BV v Czech Republic*, UNCITRAL, Partial Award (17 March 2006) para 209; similar *Phoenix Action v Czech Republic* (n 7) para 119.

[51] *Caratube International Oil Company LLP v Republic of Kazakhstan*, ICSID Case No ARB/08/12, Award (5 June 2012) para 466.

5.4.1.2 Transactions at nominal price or for free

As for the question of whether the payment of a nominal price qualifies as contribution, several cases are instructive.

In *Société Générale v Dominican Republic*,[52] Claimants acquired the shares in the local investment forming the object of the claim at nominal value. The tribunal did not find fault with this, finding that:

> If this were the only element involved in such a transaction, doubts could legitimately arise about its meaning, but in fact the transaction includes many other elements, such as the potential market value of the shares purchased, contract rights related to the concession and other claims and rights to benefits having an economic value.[53]

For the tribunal, the purchase of property at a nominal price was thus 'a normal feature of a global economy and the transfers are not as such disqualified from treaty protection'.[54]

The tribunal in *Caratube v Kazakhstan*,[55] though ultimately dismissing the claim on the particular facts of the case, took a similar position on whether the acquisition of shares at nominal value qualified as contribution. It held that:

> Payment of only a nominal price and lack of any other contribution by the purported investor must be seen as an indication that the investment was not an economic arrangement, is not covered by the term 'investment' as used in the BIT, and thus is an arrangement not protected by the BIT.[56]

One can deduce from this finding that the payment of a nominal price alone does not automatically disqualify the investment if there are other elements that convince the tribunal of the investor's intent to engage in a real investment. Thus, the tribunal in *Phoenix Action* also found that '[i]f there is indeed a real intent to develop economic activities on that basis, the existence of a nominal price is not a bar to a finding that there exists an investment.'[57]

More recently, the tribunal in *KT Asia v Kazakhstan*[58] was faced precisely with the question of whether a rearrangement of corporate assets at nominal price within entities ultimately controlled by the same person (though formally owned by different entities not forming a corporate group) was a normal and unobjectionable feature of the global economy, as the tribunal in *Société Générale* had held,[59] or whether the jurisdiction *ratione materiae* should be denied for lack of a contribution and thus lack of 'investment'. In this case, the claimant was a Netherlands-incorporated company that was ultimately controlled by a Kazakh national, Mr A.

[52] *Société Générale v Dominican Republic* (n 7). [53] Ibid, para 36.
[54] Ibid, para 44. [55] *Caratube v Kazakhstan* (n 51). [56] Ibid, para 435.
[57] *Phoenix Action v Czech Republic* (n 7) para 119; similar *Vannessa Ventures Ltd v Bolivarian Republic of Venezuela*, ICSID Case No ARB(AF)/04/6, Award (16 January 2013) para 122: 'The nominal purchase price does not of itself necessarily indicate that there was no real investment.'
[58] *KT Asia v Kazakhstan* (n 47).
[59] *Société Générale v Dominican Republic* (n 7) para 44.

What raised the tribunal's suspicions in this case was not only the fact that the purchase of shares was effected at nominal price, but that the sellers of the shares were two entities also owned by Mr A (though not forming a corporate group), that the claimant financed the purchase of the shares by a loan given by the selling entities, and that on top of this, this loan was never repaid, less even intended to be repaid.[60] This having been established by the tribunal, it continued to ask whether to establish an investment, the claimant must have made a contribution itself or whether it could benefit from a contribution made by someone else,[61] the claimant having argued that 'an internal group restructuring by definition does not result in a new injection of capital for the acquisition of an asset in the host State'.[62]

The tribunal left open the question of whether it could accept this argument in the case of a transfer of shares within the same corporate group, because it found that there was neither such corporate group structure nor even a single economic unity in the case at hand. Indeed, the tribunal found that 'the aggregation of assets in the form of a myriad of companies [was] in reality the antithesis of a group'[63] and qualified the purpose of the transfer of shares as an attempt by Mr A to 'use the companies as his "pockets" shifting assets from one to the other solely to suit his own purposes'.[64] Thus, while it agreed with the tribunal in *Caratube* that 'a payment of a nominal price for a shareholding [was] but one aspect out of a number of factors that may assist in ascertaining the existence of an investment',[65] the fact that 'Claimant agreed to pay a fraction of their value to buy the BTA shares and ultimately paid nothing at all for their acquisition'[66] led the tribunal to dismiss the contention that the claimant had made a contribution.

This decision is particularly interesting, giving important insights into a rather practical aspect of corporate restructuring that may be revealing of the claimant's (or its controller's) purpose of the restructuring. Though the tribunal explicitly abstained from passing judgment on the legality of the reshuffling of the assets, noting that '[t]here may be nothing unlawful in Mr. A treating the assets of companies formally owned by other persons as his personal property',[67] it still found fault with the particulars of the case, notably with the fact that the claimant acquired the shares potentially providing him with legal standing for free, and that he tried to appropriate the contribution that the ultimate controller may have made at the beginning. This point also becomes clear when the tribunal discusses and sets apart the decisions in *Mobil* or *Saluka* where the claimants had also been enabled to bring the claim following a transfer of shares, but either continued to invest after the transfer (*Mobil*) or where the obligation to repay its debt incurred for the financing of the purchase of shares remained real and effective (*Saluka*).[68]

Unfortunately, the decision does however not answer the question laid out by the tribunal, namely whether a mere 'reshuffling' of assets within a corporate group would be sufficient to meet the requirement of contribution, in other words whether the claimant can benefit from its parent company's original contribution

[60] *KT Asia v Kazakhstan* (n 47) paras 181–87.
[61] Ibid, para 192.
[62] Ibid, para 193.
[63] Ibid, para 197.
[64] Ibid, para 204.
[65] Ibid, para 203.
[66] Ibid, para 204.
[67] Ibid, para 205.
[68] Ibid, para 198.

or whether it has to make such contribution itself.[69] This is arguably a slightly distinct question from the above problem of whether a purchase at nominal price qualifies as contribution. The above-mentioned example of *Mobil*, though not explicit on whether the claimants have paid anything for the shares and if so how much, would seem to permit the conclusion—if only for the sake of the argument[70]—that even if the shares were transferred without payment at all, this would not automatically disqualify the investment *as long as* claimant made post-investment contributions.[71] This was visibly also the conclusion of the arbitral tribunal in *Gold Reserve Inc v Venezuela*, which refused to take issue with an intra-group share-to-share swap bringing the claimant into its ownership position, because it found that the claimant engaged in post-investment contributions.[72]

The question of whether an investment that was received for free qualifies as contribution was also discussed by the tribunal in the case *Quiborax v Bolivia*.[73] In this case, one of the claimants—holder of one single share—did not pay for his share but rather received it from the other claimants 'in order to comply with the minimum three shareholder requirement under Bolivian corporate law'.[74] The tribunal thus found that there was no evidence of either an original contribution or a subsequent contribution to exploit the mining concessions.[75] He therefore only benefited from the investment, without however making any contribution. This, the tribunal held to be insufficient to qualify as investment, noting that '[w]hile shares or other securities or title may be the legal materialization of an investment, mere ownership of a share is, in and of itself, insufficient to prove a contribution of money or assets.'[76]

The a.m. decisions would seem to establish that a gratuitous transfer of assets would, in the absence of any further contribution, not be sufficient to qualify as an investment and that some form of monetary contribution—whether for purposes of acquiring the investment or for maintaining it later on—is necessary.[77] This arguably raises the question of whether the fact of inheriting assets potentially qualifying as investment would fulfil the element of contribution or not.[78]

[69] For the related discussion of an 'active' contribution requirement see also below at 5.4.1.3.

[70] In practice, a donation of shares within a corporate group seems rather unlikely given both the tax advantages arising from the possibility to write off the debt of the loan and paid interests as well as an increasing sensitization of investors planning an internal corporate asset reshuffling to the potential necessity of a showing of contribution.

[71] In this sense see also *OI European Group BV v Bolivarian Republic of Venezuela*, ICSID Case No ARB/11/25, Award (Spanish) (10 March 2015) paras 204–11.

[72] *Gold Reserve Inc v Bolivarian Republic of Venezuela*, ICSID Case No ARB(AF)/09/1, Award (22 September 2014) paras 256–72.

[73] *Quiborax v Bolivia* (n 47). [74] Ibid, para 232. [75] Ibid.

[76] Ibid, para 233.

[77] Similar in *Société Civile Immobilière de Gaëta v République de Guinée*, ICSID Case No ARB/12/36, Award (French) (21 December 2015) paras 216–31. But see for a case where the arbitral tribunal refused to require a contribution by the investor–claimant *Invesmart BV v Czech Republic*, UNCITRAL, Award (26 June 2009) paras 183–89.

[78] The tribunal in *Perenco Ecuador Ltd v Republic of Ecuador and Empresa Estatal de Petróleos del Ecuador*, ICSID Case No ARB/08/6, Decision on Jurisdiction (30 June 2011) did not frame this question in these terms and accepted jurisdiction despite the fact that the putative investor–claimants had yet to prove that they inherited the shares constituting the investment. However, applying the above deliberations, this question arguably could have been asked.

Yet, this 'rule' is seemingly tempered in the case where no change of nationality is involved, as can be seen from the recent award in *Renée Rose Levy de Levi v Peru*.[79] In this case, the French national claimant acquired her shareholding in the Peruvian Bank BNM by assignment from her father, also a French national, without paying anything for the shares and five years after the contentious measures against the bank had occurred. In contradiction to the recent line of jurisprudence requiring a contribution of its own by the assignee as seen above, the tribunal did not find fault with the fact that the claimant had not paid anything for the shares, accepting that her father had fulfilled the criteria of the notion of investment when he made the investment.[80] The tribunal also rejected the abuse of process objection lodged by Peru, finding that the fact that the transfer was gratuitous was not enough to found an abuse of process objection, in particular in view of the fact that:

> This is a transfer between very close family members and, secondly, because the transfer occurred in July 2005 and it was not until five years later that the Claimant decided to resort to ICSID arbitration.[81]

It is quite obvious that what 'saved' the Claimant in this case from a (jurisdictional) dismissal was the fact that despite the gratuitous transfer of the shareholding, there was continuity of nationality contrary to the other reviewed cases.[82] The suspicion therefore springs to mind that the tribunal took more of a 'policy' than a legal approach to the question of the legality of the assignment, visibly finding that this was not an assignment of the 'wrong kind'.

While this is a bit unfortunate, not being helpful in clarifying the legal question at stake, the underlying rationale cannot be criticized and, what is more, would seem to serve as an important element to keep in mind in other cases as well: the question of whether a transfer of shares was 'of the wrong kind', that is, a potentially abusive manipulation of the investment arbitration system, does not pose itself when no strategic use or change of nationality and thus no other (more beneficial) treaty was involved. This means that the contribution requirement implicitly fulfils the function of safeguarding the reciprocity of the investment treaty only when there is a change of nationality. To the contrary, it is not necessary when there is no change of nationality.

Alternatively, in keeping with other possible approaches to the question of legality of treaty shopping,[83] one could equally argue that the 'sole purpose' of the transfer was not to obtain access to the investment arbitration system (given that this access already existed prior to the transfer), that there was no possible lack of jurisdiction *ratione temporis* (since the France–Peru BIT had been in force long before

[79] *Renée Rose Levy de Levi v Republic of Peru*, ICSID Case No ARB/10/17, Award (26 February 2014).
[80] Ibid, paras 146ff. [81] Ibid, para 154.
[82] In this sense see also Matthew Weiniger and Harry Ormsby, 'Treaty Column: Contrasting approaches to "contribution"' Global Arbitration Review, Vol 9, Issue 2, available at <http://www.globalarbitrationreview.com> (subscription required). On continuity of nationality see Chapter 6, at 6.3.
[83] As will be discussed more in detail in Chapter 7.

the transfer) and that the assignor assigned something he actually did possess, in contradistinction to the maxim of *nemo dat quod non habet*.

5.4.2 Risk requirement

As seen further above, arbitral tribunals have established, as part of the '*Salini* criteria', the requirement that the investment bear a certain transaction-related risk in order to qualify as investment within the meaning of Article 25 ICSID Convention.

For the purposes of this book, this argument has not figured prominently in arbitral jurisprudence in order to qualify the nature of the investment and, where it has been made, it has usually been linked to the discussion of whether a contribution has been made by the putative claimant-investor. Thus, the arbitral tribunal in *KT Asia v Kazakhstan* found *obiter* the element of risk inherent in the notion of investment to be lacking, as the claimant had made no contribution and thus had not incurred any risk of losing such contribution.[84]

5.4.3 'Active contribution' requirement?

A closely related question is whether in order to qualify as contribution, the claimant must show to have made an 'active contribution', or whether the passive or nominal (indirect) ownership or control of assets through one of claimant's subsidiaries is sufficient to qualify as investment.[85] This is a problem that arises in particular, though not exclusively, in relation with holding or shell companies whose only purpose is to hold a certain investment.

5.4.3.1 Cases

Many tribunals have in the past let suffice the purely passive or nominal (indirect) ownership of assets (in particular shares) to qualify as an investment.[86]

The tribunal in *Standard Chartered Bank v Tanzania* took a different stance on this question (though not in respect of the notion of investment as in Article 25(1) ICSID Convention, but of the consent to arbitration clause contained in the BIT).[87]

[84] *KT Asia v Kazakhstan* (n 47) paras 219–20. Similar the tribunal in *Caratube v Kazakhstan* (n 51) para 360.

[85] Voon, Mitchell, and Munro, 'Legal Responses' (n 1) 58.

[86] *Veteran Petroleum Ltd (Cyprus) v Russian Federation*, UNCITRAL, PCA Case No AA 228, Interim Award on Jurisdiction and Admissibility (30 November 2009) para 477; *RosInvestCo UK Ltd v Russian Federation*, SCC Case No V079/2005, Final Award (12 September 2010) paras 381, 388; *Alpha Projectholding v Ukraine* (n 45) paras 343–45; *CSOB v Czech Republic* (n 36) para 32; *Yukos Universal Ltd (Isle of Man) v Russian Federation*, UNCITRAL, PCA Case No AA 227, Interim Award on Jurisdiction and Admissibility (30 November 2009) para 430; *Saluka v Czech Republic* (n 50) paras 205, 211.

[87] *Standard Chartered Bank v United Republic of Tanzania*, ICSID Case No ARB/10/12, Award (2 November 2012).

In this case, the claimant brought its claim under the UK–Tanzania BIT claiming protection for a loan that one of its subsidiaries, a Hong Kong-based entity, had purchased from a Malaysian consortium that the latter had given to a Tanzanian entity for a local project that ran afoul. As confirmed by the tribunal, the claimant took no actions whatsoever concerning the Tanzanian Loans and claimed protection under the BIT merely based on its equity ownership of the Hong Kong entity.[88]

Article 8(1) of the UK–Tanzania BIT provided for consent to ICSID arbitration for any legal dispute arising between a Contracting Party and a national or company of the other Contracting Party 'concerning an investment *of* the latter in the territory of the former' [emphasis added]. The tribunal thus set out to enquire whether the claimant had made an investment in Tanzanian territory. Having examined the text and context, object, and purpose of the UK–Tanzania BIT, the tribunal found the BIT:

> to require an active relationship between the investor and the investment. To benefit from Article 8(1)'s arbitration provision, a claimant must demonstrate that *the investment was made at the claimant's direction, that the claimant founded the investment or that the claimant controlled the investment in an active and direct manner.* Passive ownership of shares in a company not controlled by the claimant where that company in turn owns the investment is not sufficient ... some activity of investing is needed, which implicates the claimant's control over the investment or an action of transferring something of value (money, know-how, contacts, or expertise) from one treaty-country to the other.[89]

Applying this standard to the facts of the case, the tribunal held that the activity of purchasing debt, which would qualify as investment under the BIT, was done by the Hong Kong subsidiary, not by the claimant, and that the claimant thus could not claim protection for this investment.[90]

Interestingly, the tribunal went to certain lengths to set this case apart from the issue of protection of indirect investments. Examining the example of *Cemex v Venezuela*, it pointed out that the Netherlands–Venezuela BIT provided for protection of indirect investments by virtue of the provision considering an entity, wherever incorporated, but directly or indirectly controlled by a national of either Contracting Party, as a national of such Contracting Party, while the UK–Tanzania BIT did not contain such a provision.[91]

Turning its attention to the question of whether the claimant exerted control over the subsidiary, it found that the claimant held both a majority shareholding in a subsidiary that in turn held a majority shareholding in the Hong Kong subsidiary, and a direct minority shareholding in the Hong Kong subsidiary. Yet, the tribunal admitted that:

> No bright line exists to determine how remote or near a corporate relationship should be in order to be relevant. The Tribunal attempts no such line-drawing, but merely indicates its hesitancy to find the type of indirect investment in *Cemex* was present in the instant case

[88] Ibid, paras 196–98.
[89] Ibid, paras 230, 232 (emphasis added).
[90] Ibid, paras 260, 277.
[91] Ibid, paras 247–50.

with respect to SC Sherwood [the subsidiary via which claimant held the majority ownership over the Hong Kong subsidiary].[92]

Noteworthy is finally also the tribunal's opinion that it would offend the BIT's reciprocal nature to:

permit a UK national with subsidiaries all around the world to claim entitlement to the UK–Tanzania BIT protection for each and every one of the investments around the world held by these daughter or granddaughter entities. The BIT preamble says 'reciprocal protection' and 'reciprocal' must have some meaning.[93]

The tribunal in the *Alapli Elektrik BV v Turkey* award (where one of the arbitrators was the same as in *Standard Chartered Bank*, Professor William Park) adopted a similar reasoning.[94] Though the award remains to date unpublished, some of its excerpts are contained in pertinent parts in the recent (published) Decision on Annulment and thus allow for some conclusions.[95] In this case, a Dutch entity (the putative investor–claimant) was inserted into the corporate chain of a Turkish–American joint venture for a proposed combined cycle power plant in Turkey at a time when problems with the Turkish authorities had already arisen. As the arbitral tribunal established:

A Turkish national, backed by an American multinational, seeing a dispute looming with his own government, established a Dutch entity which is claiming treaty protection for a proposed combined cycle power plant. The entirety of the financial contribution and technological know-how came from American backers, the [General Electric] Group, which advanced monies to realize an opportunity to provide equipment and services, taking all risk of loss if the Project never came to fruition. [Footnote omitted.] The Concession Contract, by which the host country agreed in principle to the Project's terms, was awarded to a Turkish company, Atam Elektrik.[96]

While the majority of the tribunal was in agreement to dismiss the case for lack of jurisdiction, the approaches taken to this end differed. While Arbitrator Professor Stern found fault with the timing of the restructuring that brought the Dutch entity into the ownership chain,[97] Arbitrator Professor Park focused on the question of 'contribution' which he understood as meaning that 'something of value' must have been transferred between the two countries.[98] Interpreting the wording of relevant clauses of the Energy Charter Treaty (ECT), the Netherlands–Turkey BIT and the ICSID Convention, he found that 'an investment "of" an investor

[92] Ibid, para 253.
[93] Ibid, para 270.
[94] *Alapli Elektrik BV v Republic of Turkey*, ICSID Case No ARB/08/13, Award (16 July 2012) reported by LE Peterson, 'In two recent arbitrations, Prof. William W. Park holds that wholly passive ownership is not enough for claimants to enjoy investment treaty protection' IA Reporter (18 January 2013) available at <http://www.iareporter.com> (subscription required).
[95] *Alapli Elektrik BV v Republic of Turkey*, ICSID Case No ARB/08/13, Decision on Annulment (10 July 2014).
[96] *Alapli Elektrik v Turkey*, Award (n 94) para 311.
[97] *Alapli Elektrik v Turkey*, Award (n 94) paras 393–99, 404–15.
[98] *Alapli Elektrik v Turkey*, Award (n 94) para 311.

must be characterized by an active contribution', which was not the case when simply owning some assets in Turkey, though 'engineered through a legitimate nationality structuring'.[99] This conclusion was seemingly also influenced by the finding that:

> The Claimant had not acquired any dominium over the funds which transited its accounts, and that the entire financial contribution came from the General Elektrik [*sic*] Group, which also ensured the technological expertise necessary for the project.[100]

5.4.3.2 Discussion

As has been seen in the presented cases above, the element of contribution as in the ICSID notion of investment fulfils an important, yet quite discreet, role in separating the investments of the 'wrong kind' from those of the 'right kind'. In this sense, it offers a fact-sensitive element that has the potential to detect a possible abuse of the arbitration system without explicitly naming it as such.[101] Moreover, it may (implicitly) invalidate a strategic use or change of nationality even where the timing aspect is not necessarily at stake (as was the case in *Standard Chartered Bank*).[102]

However, in particular the award in *Standard Chartered Bank* arguably raises more questions than it actually answers, the key question being, as also asked by that tribunal, where the line is to be drawn between a protected 'active' (indirect) investment and an unprotected 'passive' (indirect) investment. This distinction appears of essential importance in the case of multi-tiered, multi-jurisdictional corporate structures given the far-reaching consequences of potentially passing the jurisdictional hurdle or not. As can be seen from the award, the tribunal found the 'active contribution' requirement in a treaty-based formulation from which the tribunal deduced a qualification of the relationship between the investor and the investment in the sense that it must be 'active'. Two observations can be made in this aspect.

First, novel as this legal argument may be, the same cannot necessarily be said of the formulation in question, which can be found in many investment treaties.[103] The question is therefore whether and if so, how, *Standard Chartered* can really be distinguished from former cases where the arbitral tribunals protected indirect investments without requiring this active relationship between investor and investment. The tribunal set this case apart from the *CEMEX* case on the grounds that the Netherlands–Venezuela BIT granted *ius standi* to 'legal persons not constituted under the law of that Contracting Party but controlled, directly or indirectly, by ... legal persons [having the nationality of that Contracting Party]', while this was not the case in the UK–Tanzania BIT. However, it is undoubtable that the UK–Tanzania BIT protects indirect investments even in the absence of such specification in the

[99] Ibid.

[100] Ibid, paras 378–80.

[101] See also the discussion in Chapter 9, at 9.5.

[102] On the importance of the temporal aspects of a strategic change of nationality see Chapters 6 and 7.

[103] See more in detail in Chapter 8, at 8.2.4.2.3.

notion of investment,[104] even if it does not contain any expanded *ius standi* as in the Netherlands–Venezuela BIT. Indeed, the granting of *ius standi* to a legal entity controlled by a qualifying national extends the circle of eligible investor–claimants, but does a priori not change the scope of protection of indirect investments. It is therefore not clear whether the distinction made by the tribunal can really be justified with reference to the notion of investor.[105] Moreover, even the dispute settlement clause contained in the Netherlands–Venezuela BIT can be interpreted to impose an active relationship between the investor and the investment, yet the *CEMEX* tribunal let a passive one suffice.[106]

Second, the formulation used by the tribunal, 'that the investment was made at the claimant's direction, that the claimant founded the investment or that the claimant controlled the investment in an active and direct manner',[107] somewhat reminiscent of the principle of attribution under Article 8 of the International Law Commission (ILC) Draft Articles on State Responsibility,[108] should not divert attention from the fact that what is at stake in this constellation is the nature of the claimed investment and the extent of the claimed damage. Indeed, as also pointed out by the *ST-AD v Bulgaria* tribunal:

> An investor whose investment consists of shares cannot claim … that the assets of the company are its property and ask for compensation for interference with these assets. Such an investor can, however, claim for any loss of value of its shares resulting from an interference with the assets or contracts of the company in which it owns the shares.[109]

Following this reasoning, it becomes more easily understandable that if the claimant seeks compensation for alleged damages to an asset held by one of its subsidiaries, this is only possible if he has made a contribution himself (or has had an otherwise active role with respect) to *this asset*. Yet, whether this justifies the 'importation' of an unwritten ('active contribution') requirement into the treaty text, is another question.

As for the *Alapli Elektrik* Award and Decision on Annulment, conclusions are more difficult to draw, due also in part to the non-availability of the full award. However, it again shows the difficulty and related tension between accepting jurisdiction based on a formal reading of the IIA/ICSID Convention on the one hand,

[104] See above at 5.2.2.

[105] Even more so as in the *CEMEX* case, it was not even the (Cayman Islands-incorporated) entity controlled by Dutch companies that brought the claim, but the Netherlands-incorporated entities.

[106] See Art 9(1): '[D]isputes between one Contracting Party and a national of the other Contracting Party concerning an obligation of the former under this Agreement in relation to an investment *of* the latter' (emphasis added).

[107] *Standard Chartered Bank v Tanzania* (n 87) para 230.

[108] 'The conduct of a person or group of persons shall be considered an act of a State under international law if the person or group of persons is in fact acting on the instructions of, or under the direction or control of, that State in carrying out the conduct.'

[109] *ST-AD GmbH v Republic of Bulgaria*, UNCITRAL, PCA Case No 2011-06, Award on Jurisdiction (18 July 2013) para 282. Similar in *Sergei Paushok, CJSC Golden East Company, CJSC Vostokneftegaz Company v The Government of Mongolia*, Award on Jurisdiction and Liability (28 April 2011) para 202; *RosInvestCo v Russia* (n 86) para 608.

and arbitral attempts at preventing potential abuses that are rendered possible due to the wide protection of indirect investments under international investment law on the other. Indeed, the claimant/applicant criticized in its Application for annulment of the award that '[s]uch new legal requirement [the active contribution requirement] presents fundamental practical concerns in the context of modern international financial transactions, since funds often originate from a party other than the investor itself'.[110]

The possibilities created by multi-tiered corporate structuring to come under IIA protection are also apparent in the above *KT Asia* case. Interestingly, however, that case raises the inverse question to *Standard Chartered Bank*. While in this latter case, the question is whether the parent company may invoke for its own purposes the investment, that is, the contribution made by the subsidiary, in the former case the question is whether the subsidiary may invoke the investment/contribution made by the parent (or upstream) company. For both scenarios, these questions seemingly have started to get more attention only recently, but raise questions that are not sufficiently answered yet.

5.4.4 Good faith as an element of the notion of investment?

In all these cases of treaty shopping by corporate structuring or restructuring, the key question many tribunals have grappled with is how to determine whether the purpose of a specific corporate structure chosen was solely to obtain access to ICSID jurisdiction and/or more advantageous procedural or substantive protections. As will be also seen more in detail further below,[111] tribunals have in recent years increasingly resorted to the notion of good faith and more particularly the abuse of rights/abuse of process doctrine in order to draw the line between 'legitimate nationality planning' and 'abusive corporate structuring'. Tribunals have however differed in their approaches as to how to take into account a possible lack of good faith in the acquisition or transfer of an investment.

5.4.4.1 Cases

The *Phoenix Action v Czech Republic*[112] award has become known for its treating the absence of bad faith in the acquisition of the investment as an inherent element in the notion of investment. In this case, the Claimant was an Israel-incorporated entity that acquired the shares of two Czech Republic-incorporated companies (Benet Group and Benet Praha) and brought the claim for alleged treaty violations under the Czech Republic–Israel BIT. The peculiarity of this case was that both Czech companies and Claimant were owned by the same Czech owner or members of his family, that Claimant was incorporated shortly after this owner fled the Czech Republic on criminal charges of tax evasion, that Claimant notified Respondent of

[110] *Alapli Elektrik v Turkey*, Decision on Annulment (n 95) para 46.

[111] See Chapter 7.

[112] *Phoenix Action v Czech Republic* (n 7).

the existence of an investment dispute merely two months after the acquisition of the shares, and that the investment dispute concerned pre-existing disputes.

Setting out on a contextual analysis of the existence of a protected investment, the tribunal first noted that it also had to 'take into consideration the purpose of the international protection of the investment, whether it is the specific purpose of the ICSID system or the general purpose of the protection granted by international law'.[113] This purpose, it found, was the protection of foreign investments made in order to develop an economic activity, which was not the case when a national brought a claim against its own State or when an economic transaction was performed 'with the sole purpose of taking advantage of the rights contained in [the ICSID Convention/BITs], without any significant economic activity'.[114]

Thus finding that it had to prevent an abuse of the system of international investment protection under the ICSID Convention, it considered that the '*Salini* test' (which it endorsed in principle)[115] had to be supplemented by two additional criteria, namely the question of whether the investment has been made in accordance with host State laws, and in good faith.[116]

On the question of whether the investment was made in good faith, the tribunal, considering a number of factors, found not only that Claimant had bought an investment 'that was already burdened with the civil litigation as well as the problems with the tax and customs authorities',[117] but also that Claimant had admitted that 'its reason for attempting to bring this claim initially was to bring the pre-existing disputes involving [the two Czech companies] before [the ICSID tribunal]',[118] that Claimant notified the Czech Republic 'even before the registration of its ownership of the two Czech companies in the Czech Republic',[119] that 'all transfers were merely done inside the family of [the Czech owner]'[120] and finally that 'no business plan, no program of re-financing, no economic objectives were ever presented, no real valuation of the economic transactions were ever attempted.'[121]

All these elements led the tribunal to consider that:

> The whole operation was not an economic investment, based on the actual or future value of the companies, but ... simply a rearrangement of assets within a family, to gain access to ICSID jurisdiction to which the initial investor was not entitled.[122]

This, according to the tribunal, had to be considered an abuse of rights, leading to the dismissal of the claim.[123]

Most subsequent tribunals have not adopted the approach of the *Phoenix* tribunal to examine the notion of good faith as an element inherent to the notion of investment.[124] Indeed, many tribunals have ever since explicitly rejected the idea

[113] Ibid, para 79. [114] Ibid, paras 88, 93. [115] Ibid, paras 82ff.
[116] Ibid, paras 113–14. [117] Ibid, para 136. [118] Ibid, para 137.
[119] Ibid, para 138. [120] Ibid, para 139. [121] Ibid, para 140.
[122] Ibid. [123] Ibid, paras 143–45.
[124] But see *Cementownia "Nowa Huta" SA v Republic of Turkey*, ICSID Case No ARB(AF)/06/2, Award (17 September 2009) paras 154–57, and Arbitrator Stern's opinion in *Alapli Elektrik v Turkey*, Award (n 94) paras 390ff, quoted in *Alapli Elektrik v Turkey*, Decision on Annulment (n 95) paras 191 and 225–26.

that the principle of good faith should be part of the question of jurisdiction *ratione materiae*. Scholars have also mostly shared this scepticism.[125]

Thus, the tribunal in *Saba Fakes v Turkey* found that:

> [T]he principle of good faith and legality cannot be incorporated into the definition of Art. 25(1) of the ICSID Convention without doing violence to the language of the ICSID Convention: an investment might be 'legal' or 'illegal', made in 'good faith' or not, it nonetheless remains an investment.[126]

The tribunal in *Quiborax v Bolivia* argued in a similar manner:

> Likewise, the Tribunal is of the view that neither conformity to the laws of the host State nor respect of good faith are elements of the definition of investment ... recourse to treaty arbitration and substantive treaty protections may in certain circumstances breach the prohibition of abuse of rights which is an emanation of the principle of good faith. That does not mean that these elements are part of the definition of investment. An illegal or bad faith investment remains an investment. It may not be a protected investment, i.e. deserve protection in the sense that access to treaty arbitration and/or substantive treaty guarantees may not be granted, but that is a different matter.[127]

The same point was also argued by the Respondent in *Caratube v Kazakhstan*, but not decided by the tribunal on grounds of judicial economy.[128]

Most recently, the tribunal in *Vannessa Ventures v Venezuela* also dismissed the idea that the principle of good faith should be part of the definition of investment and found that even though an investment may have been made with the purpose of buying a legal claim against the host State, it still qualified as an investment for purposes of jurisdiction *ratione materiae* (though it dismissed the claim on the merits).

The decision is very interesting for purposes of this analysis because it spells out the possible ways, in procedural terms, of dealing with the objection of lack of good faith in the acquisition of the investment.

In this case, the Canada-incorporated claimant acquired the shares of a local investment in the Venezuelan mining business from another Canadian mining company, this in spite of a contractual requirement between the original partners that the shares could not be validly transferred without Venezuela's agreement. The tribunal thus wondered about the 'distinction between the making of an investment and the buying of a legal claim against the host State'.[129] Though it found a purchase of shares at nominal value not to be prejudicial to the finding of an investment, other factors raised the tribunal's doubts, namely the fact that the claimant and the Canadian vendor had agreed on a distribution of any proceeds recovered in the present arbitration, as well as the absence of any concrete technical or financial

[125] See, eg, Richard Kreindler, 'Are Tribunals Setting New Limits on Access to International Jurisdiction' (2010) 25 ICSID Review-FILJ 37, 41–43; Happ and Bischoff (n 15) 513–14 (para 41).

[126] *Saba Fakes v Republic of Turkey*, ICSID Case No ARB/07/20, Award (14 July 2010) para 112.

[127] *Quiborax v Bolivia* (n 47) para 226.

[128] *Caratube v Kazakhstan* (n 51) paras 458ff.

[129] *Vannessa Ventures v Venezuela* (n 57) para 121.

preparations that would have shown the intention to resume operations promptly after the purchase of the shares.[130] It thus laid out the question under which conceptual framework these facts should be taken into consideration:

> There is more than one way in which these factors might be addressed, and more than one way in which any lack of good faith might put a putative 'investment' outside of the scope of BIT protections. The 'reality' or 'genuineness' of the investment and the good faith of the investor are matters that might bear upon questions of jurisdiction, upon questions of admissibility, and upon questions of merits.[131]

Elaborating on this question, it first dismissed the idea that the '*intuitu personae* character' of the contracts between the vendor of the shares and its Venezuelan partner disqualified the investment from the ambit of the BIT.[132] With respect to the notion of good faith, the arbitrators were split as to whether the lack of good faith in the acquisition of the investment should be a question of jurisdiction *ratione materiae*, admissibility or the merits. It thus elaborated:

> One of us considers that, on the facts of this case, there was no good-faith investment and that the BIT does not cover investments not made in good faith, and accordingly the tribunal lacks jurisdiction. The majority accepts that good faith has an important role in the analysis but considers that, in the absence of a treaty provision ascribing some different effect to the principle of good faith, it is only in circumstances where the application of good faith as a principle of national law invalidates the acquisition of the investment that a lack of good faith means that there is no 'investment' for jurisdictional purposes. In other circumstances, the question of good faith does not go to jurisdiction but is a matter to be considered by the Tribunal when exercising its jurisdiction and to be applied in the context of admissibility and/or application of the substantive protections of the Treaty at the merits phase.[133]

Finding that 'good faith and public policy bear upon the question whether the acquisition by Claimant of its shareholding … was effective to transfer to Claimant an interest in [the local investment] that is protected by the BIT', it determined the issue of good faith to be a question of the merits.[134]

5.4.4.2 Discussion

Both the *Phoenix Action* and the *Vannessa Venture* decisions vividly emblematize the doctrinal difficulty surrounding the principle of good faith and its particularizations in being 'operationalized' in the context of corporate structuring or restructuring. While the latter decision takes note of the differing doctrinal 'currents' with respect to the question in which phase of the arbitral proceedings to take good faith (or rather a lack thereof) into account, the former decision is singular in its approach to read an implicit good faith requirement into the notion of investment under the ICSID Convention. However, it stands to reason to doubt the necessity

[130] Ibid, paras 122–23.
[131] Ibid, para 125.
[132] Ibid, para 154.
[133] Ibid, para 113.
[134] Ibid, paras 164, 169.

of an additional '*Salini*-esque' good faith criterion in determining whether a corporate structuring or restructuring was done in good or in bad faith.[135] Indeed, the same *Phoenix* tribunal did not hesitate further down in the decision to recur to the abuse of rights doctrine for finding that several elements and in particular the timing of the restructuring disqualified the claim.[136]

The examined cases thus show that there is no single way of dealing with a possible lack of good faith, materializing in different facts or criteria from which a potential lack of good faith will be inferred. Yet, as other scholars also rightly argue, this does not mean that a 'more principled' recourse to the principle of good faith and its particularizations could not be possible.[137]

5.5 Preliminary Conclusions

As for the notion of investment in IIAs, it has been seen that this notion is usually defined in a broad manner, thus normally covering both direct and indirect investment, and the latter even in the absence of a specific stipulation in the treaty. Tribunals have only accepted exceptions to the protection of indirect investments where this could be based on the clear language of the treaty. Respondents will thus find it hard to defend against what they may perceive as unacceptable corporate structuring by recourse to the notion of indirect investment as contained in IIAs. This broad protection of indirect investments is therefore inherently treaty shopping-permissive and also furthers the potential for multiple proceedings.[138]

As for the notion of investment in the ICSID Convention, beyond the continuing controversy as to whether an objective or a subjective approach should prevail, several important questions relevant to the issue of treaty shopping by corporate structuring remain unsettled. Though arbitral tribunals (including non-ICSID tribunals) have by now found a rather coherent line as to the fact that the payment of a nominal price for the investment alone—thus in the absence of further elements indicating a bad faith transaction—does in principle not disqualify the investment, it remains fairly unclear what qualifies as an 'active' as opposed to a 'passive'

[135] Similar Stephan Schill and Heather Bray, 'Good Faith Limitations on Protected Investments and Corporate Structuring' in Andrew Mitchell, M Sornarajah, and Tania Voon (eds), *Good Faith and International Economic Law* (Oxford University Press 2015) 88, 112. See also the discussion in this aspect in Chapter 9, at 9.3.4.

[136] *Phoenix Action v Czech Republic* (n 7) para 144. Though the decision could have already been decided on grounds of lack of jurisdiction *ratione temporis*, see the discussion in Chapter 7, at 7.3.2.1.

[137] Andrew Mitchell, James Munro, and Devon Whittle, 'Vannessa Ventures Ltd v The Bolivarian Republic of Venezuela' (2014) 15 JWIT 305, 312–13. See on this question also Chapter 9, at 9.5.

[138] See, eg, Dolores Bentolila, 'Shareholders' Action to Claim for Indirect Damages in ICSID Arbitration' (2010) 2 Trade, Law and Development 127ff; OECD, 'Roundtable on Freedom of Investment 18' (20 March 2013) 4ff, available at <http://www.oecd.org/investment/investment-policy/18thFOIRoundtableSummary.pdf> (last accessed on 15 September 2016); Walid Ben Hamida, 'The Notion of Investor: Comment of Sedelmayer v. Russia, Generation Ukraine, Inc. v. Ukraine, Tokios Tokelés v Ukraine, Plama Consortium Ltd. v. Bulgaria, and Petrobart Ltd. v. Kirghizstan' (2006) 4 OGEL 34.

contribution and how the latter relates to a (protected) indirect investment. Also, most tribunals have rejected the approach of the *Phoenix* tribunal to read an inherent good faith element into the notion of investment, raising the question of how to treat instead a possible investor *mala fide* with respect to corporate restructuring. As will be seen in the following chapters, arbitral jurisprudence has been increasingly focusing on the timing of the restructuring, raising questions of jurisdiction *ratione temporis* and of admissibility of the claim on grounds of abuse of rights/abuse of process.

6

Jurisdiction *Ratione Temporis*

6.1 Introduction

Questions in relation to the temporal scope of jurisdiction have become more prominent in recent years as arbitral tribunals have increasingly had to decide on the validity of instances of treaty shopping by corporate structuring or restructuring. In doing so, they have been focusing more and more on the timing of the corporate transactions, raising complex questions that have not always been clearly distinguished in arbitral jurisprudence and that to date remain under-researched in scholarship.

Thus, for one, there is the question of the timing of the nationality requirement. At which point in time does the investor have to possess the nationality under which he brings the claim? Moreover, is there a continuous nationality requirement in the sense that the investor must possess the claimed nationality in-between two distinct points in time, for example, the time of dispute or injury, and the time of bringing the claim or even the time of the award: what happens if the investor changes nationality in between these points in time?

Linked to these issues, the question may also arise whether the change of nationality has been implemented before or after a dispute has arisen or the events giving rise to the dispute have occurred, and if so what this mean in terms of jurisdiction *ratione temporis* (Figures 6.1 and 6.2). This is an important question in view of the customary principle of non-retroactivity, which provides that unless a different intention becomes apparent from the treaty, acts, or facts that have arisen before the treaty in question has become applicable to the investor are not covered by it. Scholarship and tribunals have been in disagreement as to whether the principle of non-retroactivity must be understood as also excluding disputes that have arisen before the entry into force of the international investment agreement (IIA). In any case, when a dispute exists or when events giving rise to a dispute have occurred is not always easy to determine, in particular in the case of continuous or composite acts, and has been subject to differing views by arbitral tribunals. If problems in the business relationship between the investor and the host State have been spanning over a longer period of time, straddling the time of the change of nationality, the question may also arise whether the dispute on the basis of which the investor is bringing the claim is the same as one that has already been existing before the change of nationality, or is a new one. Finally, the notion of dispute is also relevant (though in a subsidiary way) for deciding whether the corporate restructuring constitutes an abuse of rights or abuse of process, as will be seen more in detail in Chapter 7.

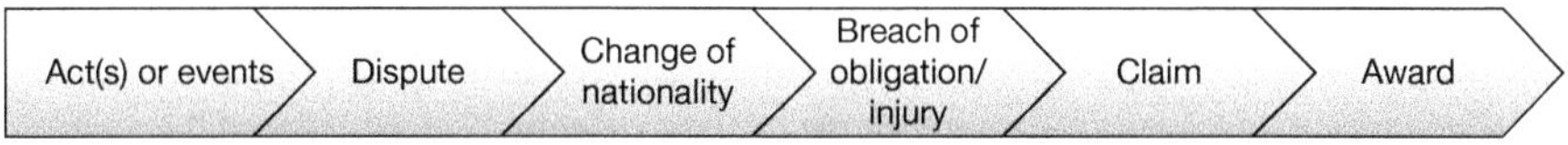

Figure 6.1 Dispute occurring before the change of nationality

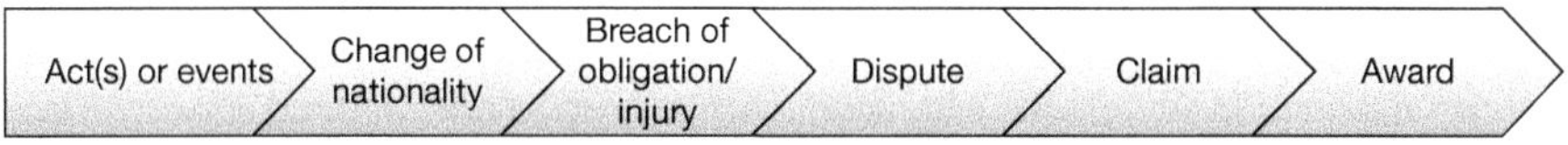

Figure 6.2 Dispute occurring after the change of nationality

As has already been seen, the question of the change of nationality can also be broached from the angle of the existence of an investment. This is so because in the case of a corporate structuring or restructuring, the change of nationality usually occurs with the acquisition, or the creation, of a corporate structure that holds the required nationality. For purposes of jurisdiction *ratione temporis*, the question can thus also be framed in terms of whether there was an existing investment at the time from which onwards the investor claims protection under the invoked IIA.

6.2 Timing of Nationality Requirement

At which point or points in time the investor has to possess the nationality of the State party to the investment treaty whose protection he seeks to invoke depends on the treaty in question. Different investment treaties may thus establish different requirements.

6.2.1 ICSID Convention

The ICSID Convention contains different timing requirements depending on whether the investor is a natural or a legal person. For natural persons, the investor has to have 'the nationality of a Contracting State other than the State party to the dispute *on the date on which the parties consented to submit such dispute to … arbitration as well as on the date on which the request was registered*' [emphasis added],[1] therefore providing for a double test of time.[2]

For legal persons, on the other hand, the investor only has to prove that he 'had the nationality of a Contracting State other than the State party to the dispute *on the date on which the parties consented to submit such dispute to … arbitration*' [emphasis added],[3] thus only requiring a simple test of time.[4] The same applies in

[1] Art 25(2)(a) ICSID Convention.

[2] On the discussions during the drafting of the Convention see Christoph Schreuer, Loretta Malintoppi, August Reinisch, and Anthony Sinclair, *The ICSID Convention: A Commentary* (Cambridge University Press 2009) 'Article 25' paras 680–81.

[3] Art 25(2)(b) first clause ICSID Convention.

[4] Schreuer and others, *ICSID Commentary* (n 2) 'Article 25' para 752.

principle to the locally incorporated investor whom the Parties have agreed to treat as a foreign investor because of foreign control.[5] In this respect, Schreuer points out that from a purely grammatical point of view, it could be considered unclear at which point in time the foreign control over the local investor must have existed.[6] He concludes however that since the agreement to treat a local investor as foreign relates to the fact of foreign control, the latter must have existed at the time of the agreement, which in turn is normally closely linked to the time of consent.[7] For both natural and legal persons, the date of consent respectively the date on which all the conditions for a valid consent have been met is therefore determinative, with the date of the registration of the request for arbitration pursuant to Article 28(3) of the Convention applying additionally to natural persons.

Many IIAs incorporate an additional timing requirement for determining foreign control, which may be recommendable not only in view of compulsory changes of control by the host State through expropriations, but also because it may set a limit to manipulative corporate structuring or transactions.[8]

6.2.2 Other investment treaties

Neither the North American Free Trade Agreement (NAFTA) Chapter 11 nor the Energy Charter Treaty (ECT) contain an explicit test of time at which the foreign investor has to hold his nationality. However, the fact that the substantive obligations of the NAFTA Chapter 11 or the ECT are owed to 'investors of a Party' implies that the investor must be a national of the qualifying State at the time of the injury, as otherwise there would be no breach of the treaty in question with respect to the investor.[9] In a similar vein, an implicit timing requirement can be found in dispute settlement clauses when they relate to the 'disputing investor' or 'claimant' being an 'investor of a Party' as the investor has to be a national of the qualifying State at the date of submitting the claim.[10] Thus, for a NAFTA claim, it may be argued that pursuant to NAFTA Articles 1116 or 1117, the investor must hold the invoked nationality at the date of the submission of the claim, and since NAFTA Article 1119 requires the submission by the 'disputing investor' of a notice of intent to submit a claim to arbitration at least ninety days before the actual submission, the investor has to hold the required nationality at the latest already at that point.

[5] Art 25(2)(b) second clause ICSID Convention.

[6] Schreuer and others, *ICSID Commentary* (n 2) 'Article 25' para 872.

[7] Ibid.

[8] Schreuer and others, *ICSID Commentary* (n 2) 'Article 25' paras 888, 891. For examples see Chapter 8, at 8.2.3.4.

[9] Maurice Mendelson, 'Runaway Train: The Continuous Nationality Rule, from the *Panevezys-Saldutiskis Railway Case* to *Lowen*' in Todd Weiler (ed), *International Investment Law and Arbitration: Leading Cases* (Cameron May 2005) 97, 132; Lucy Reed and Jonathan Davis, 'Ratione Personae' in Marc Bungenberg, Jörn Griebel, Stephan Hobe, and August Reinisch, *International Investment Law, A Handbook* (CH Beck, Hart Publishing and Nomos 2015) 633 (para 51); Meg Kinnear, Andrea Bjorklund and John Hannaford, *Investment Disputes under NAFTA: An Annotated Guide to NAFTA Chapter 11* (Kluwer Law International 2006) (last updated March 2008) 1116–22.

[10] Mendelson, 'Runaway Train' (n 9) 132–33; *Loewen Group Inc and Raymond Loewen v United States of America*, ICSID Case No ARB(AF)/98/3, Award (26 June 2003) para 226.

Similar arguments may arguably be made for IIAs that contain similar definitions, whether or not they follow the NAFTA model.

Arbitral jurisprudence has often confirmed that in order to claim substantive protection under an investment treaty, the putative investor–claimant must qualify as a national and have acquired a qualifying investment when the investment obligation was allegedly breached.[11]

6.3 Continuous Nationality Requirement

A related and equally important question with respect to treaty shopping by corporate structuring is whether there is a continuous nationality requirement in international investment law, either beyond the timing requirements contained in the ICSID Convention and some IIAs, or in the absence of such provisions as a matter of customary international law. As already pointed out, treaty shopping by corporate structuring aims at creating diversity of nationality in order to be eligible to more favourable investment protection (whether in procedural or substantive terms); a tactical change of nationality, by whichever means, is inherently necessary to obtain this objective. This thus raises the question whether there is a certain period during the timeline of events that is designed to be immune to such changes of nationality. In other words, is there a requirement of continuous nationality between the date of injury and the date the consent is perfected? And is there a requirement of continuous nationality between the date the consent is perfected and the award?

6.3.1 *Loewen Group Inc and Raymond Loewen v United States*

The question of whether the nationality has to be continuous between the date of the presentation of the claim and the date of the award was treated in a highly controversial decision by a NAFTA arbitral tribunal in *Loewen Group Inc and Raymond Loewen v United States*.[12] The arbitral proceedings arose out of a commercial dispute brought in the Mississippi State Court between the Canada-incorporated Loewen Group and its US subsidiary, Loewen Group International, on the one hand and a competitor in the funeral home and funeral insurance business, with a litigation value of approximately USD 5 million. In a court proceeding later judged flawed and discriminatory,[13] the Mississippi jury awarded to

[11] *Société Générale in Respect of DR Energy Holdings Limited and Empresa Distribuidora de Electricidad del Este, SA ('EDE Este') v Dominican Republic*, LCIA Case No UN 7927, Award on Preliminary Objections to Jurisdiction (19 September 2008) paras 106–07; *Cementownia "Nowa Huta" SA v Republic of Turkey*, ICSID Case No ARB(AF)/06/2, Award (17 September 2009) paras 112–14; *GEA Group Aktiengesellschaft v Ukraine*, ICSID Case No ARB/08/16, Award (31 March 2011) para 170; *Vito G Gallo v Government of Canada*, NAFTA/UNCITRAL, Award (15 September 2011) para 328; *Renée Rose Levy and Gremcitel SA v Republic of Peru*, ICSID Case No ARB/11/17, Award (9 January 2015) para 147.

[12] *Loewen v US* (n 10).

[13] Ibid, paras 119, 137.

Loewen's competitor USD 500 million in damages, including USD 75 million in damages for emotional distress and USD 400 million in punitive damages. Seeking to appeal the verdict, Loewen was required to post a USD 625 million bond within seven days to stay execution. This bond requirement effectively forced Loewen to settle the case at USD 175 million. In the arbitral proceedings brought in 1998, the Claimants, the Canadian Loewen Group and its founder, principal shareholder and CEO Raymond Loewen, thus sought damages against the United States on grounds of breaches of NAFTA Articles 1102 (national treatment), 1105 (minimum standard of treatment), and 1110 (expropriation) because of a discriminatory trial, grossly excessive verdict and the refusal to grant a reasonable bond. Well into the arbitral proceedings, in January 2002, Loewen Group filed a voluntary petition for relief under Chapter 11 of the US Bankruptcy Code and reorganized as a United States corporation.[14] Just before ceasing to exist, Loewen Group assigned however all of its rights, title, and interest to the NAFTA claim to a new Canada-incorporated corporation whose only business purpose was to pursue the NAFTA claim.

Though already having decided that the claim is unsuccessful because Claimants had not, according to the tribunal, exhausted all local remedies,[15] the tribunal continued and took issue with this change of nationality, finding *obiter dicta* that:

> In international law parlance, there must be continuous national identity from the date of events giving rise to the claim, which date is known as the *dies a quo*, through the date of the resolution of the claim, which date is known as the *dies ad quem*.[16]

It then noted that Articles 1116 and 1117 of NAFTA required nationality only to the date of submission of the claim, the *dies a quo*, whereas it was silent with respect to the *dies ad quem*. From this, it reasoned that '[i]t is that silence in the Treaty that requires the application of customary international law to resolve the question of the need for continuous national identity.'[17] Accepting that 'neither the language of the Treaty, nor any of the cases decided under it answers the question as to whether continuous nationality is required until the resolution of the claim',[18] it continued by stating that some treaties (such as the ICSID Convention) contained specific modifications of the continuous nationality requirement. However, this could not be to the benefit of the claimant:

> Whatever specificity ICSID has on the requirement of continuous nationality through the resolution of the dispute only points up the absence of such provisions in NAFTA. Claimants have not shown that international law has evolved to the position where continuous nationality to the time of resolution is no longer required.[19]

The tribunal also considered the legal effect of the assignment of the NAFTA claim to the newly incorporated Canadian entity. Finding that '[a]ll the benefits of any award would clearly inure to the American corporation', it declined to accept the new Canadian entity as a continuing national for the purposes of the proceedings,

[14] Ibid, para 220. [15] Ibid, para 217. [16] Ibid, para 225.
[17] Ibid, para 226. [18] Ibid, para 228. [19] Ibid, para 235.

refusing that it should 'pierce the corporate veil'.[20] It also refused to accept the reasons for the reorganization, though found legitimate, as justifying an exception to what the tribunal thought to be the *lex lata*.[21]

Without any in-depth discussion, it also disposed of Raymond Loewen's claim (who had submitted the claim both on his own behalf and on behalf of Loewen Group).[22]

6.3.2 Discussion

Academic commentators criticized the *Loewen* decision in a number of points, and in this author's view, rightly so.[23]

First of all, the tribunal erroneously assumed a continuous nationality requirement as a matter of customary international law until the date of the award. However, while it may be convincingly argued that there is sufficient support for the assumption that the claimant need to have the nationality invoked at the time of the injury (*dies a quo*)[24] and at the time of the presentation of the claim (*dies ad quem*), a continuous nationality requirement up to the time of the award has remained highly unsettled and should clearly not be considered as representing a rule of customary international law.[25] It can be considered as definitely outdated at least ever since the adoption of the 2006 ILC Draft Articles on Diplomatic Protection which took an equally critical point of view of the *Loewen* decision and adopted in its Articles 5 and 10 the official presentation of the claim as relevant *dies ad quem*. Furthermore, it has been doubted whether the nationality in question indeed has to be held continuously between the *dies a quo* and the *dies ad quem* or only at these precise key points.[26]

Secondly, the decision of the tribunal to fill a—perceived—gap in view of the silence of NAFTA text by recourse to customary international law also raises the question about the relationship between international investment law and the (customary) law of diplomatic protection and of treaty interpretation. While seemingly admitting the *lex specialis* character of specific timing requirements contained in BITs and the ICSID Convention,[27] it appears that the tribunal could not conceive of the possibility that the silence in the NAFTA text in this respect also be *lex specialis*, in other words that possibly the Contracting Parties had intended, at the time of the negotiation of the NAFTA, to specifically modify the continuous nationality requirement (in whichever terms and content the three Contracting Parties may have conceived it). That the United States, as Respondent in this case, argued in

[20] Ibid, para 237. [21] Ibid, para 238. [22] Ibid, para 239.

[23] But see William Kirtley, 'The Transfer of Treaty Claims and Treaty-Shopping in Investor-State Disputes' (2009) 10 JWIT 427, 438.

[24] Which the tribunal mistakenly stated to be the date of the submission of the claim, *quid non*.

[25] Mendelson, 'Runaway Train' (n 9) 110–23; Matthew Duchesne, 'The Continuous-Nationality-of Claims Principle, Its historical development and current relevance to investor-State investment disputes' (2004) 36 Geo Wash Intl L Rev 783, 787–801; Jan Paulsson, 'Continuous Nationality in Loewen' (2004) 20 Arb Intl 213, 214; Reed and Davis (n 9) 632 (para 44). See also in Chapter 3, at 3.3.

[26] Mendelson, 'Runaway Train' (n 9) 123. [27] *Loewen v US* (n 10) para 229.

favour of a continuous nationality rule extending to the date of the award, is of course an evident expression of self-interest and should not disguise the fact that the intention of the drafters of the NAFTA was not necessarily to include a continuous nationality requirement—and even less so one that is based on shaky customary law foundations. Indeed, as elaborated further above, there were good reasons for the body of modern international investment law to develop in departure from the law of diplomatic protection.[28] For one scholar it is thus 'difficult to conclude that modern investment agreements should be saddled with traditional notions of continuous nationality'.[29]

This alone does of course not exclude the possibility that despite the *lex specialis* character of international investment law, recourse may under certain circumstances be necessary to the gap-filling function of customary international law in interpreting a specific notion contained in an investment treaty.[30] This is however something that has to be determined in accordance with the (customary) rules of treaty interpretation as codified in Article 31 of the Vienna Convention on the Law of Treaties (VCLT) and cannot be simply assumed. One important element to take into account in this interpretation would certainly be the stated objective of the NAFTA (as also contained in similar terms in other investment treaties) to 'ensure a predictable commercial framework for business planning and investment'[31] and to 'increase substantially investment opportunities in the territories of the Parties',[32] thus the objective to foster the free and efficient flow and adequate protection of direct international investment. Scholars have agreed that this objective would militate against the assumption of a continuous nationality requirement building on a shaky legal foundation lacking in sufficient support and consensus.[33]

It thus appears that the *Loewen* decision, as concerns the question of existence of a continuous nationality requirement in the NAFTA agreement and in this respect the legal effect of a change of nationality after the institution of arbitral proceedings, is only difficult to maintain.[34] There has thus far not been another arbitral decision under the NAFTA agreement that has had to answer this same question so that it can at this point only be speculated whether a NAFTA arbitral tribunal would follow or reject the *Loewen* decision.

However, as concerns other investment treaties, commentators and arbitral tribunals seem to be unanimous in their rejection of a continuous nationality requirement as postulated by the *Loewen* decision. For the ICSID Convention, arbitral tribunals have been adamant that the (only) relevant date for determining

[28] See in Chapter 1, at 1.2.2. [29] Duchesne (n 25) 811.

[30] See in this respect, eg, International Law Commission, 'Conclusions of the work of the Study Group on the Fragmentation of International Law: Difficulties arising from the Diversification and Expansion of International Law' Report of the Study Group of the International Law Commission, Fifty-eighth Session (2006) A/CN/L.702, para 15; Tarcisio Gazzini, 'The Role of Customary International Law in the Field of Foreign Investment' (2007) 8 JWIT 691, 711–12.

[31] NAFTA Preamble 6th Indent. [32] NAFTA Art 102(1)(c).

[33] Paulsson (n 25) 215; Mendelson, 'Runaway Train' (n 9) 142; Duchesne (n 25) 811–15.

[34] Similar Schreuer and others, *ICSID Convention* (n 2) 'Article 25' para 756.

nationality was the one provided for in Article 25(2) of the Convention, thus (for legal persons) the date on which the consent was perfected.[35] Changes of nationality after this date have therefore been considered inconsequential for the jurisdiction of the arbitral tribunal.

Thus, the tribunal in *CSOB v Slovak Republic* found the assignment of the interest subject of the arbitral proceedings to be harmless to jurisdiction as this occurred after the institution of the proceedings:

> It is generally recognized that the determination whether a party has standing in an international judicial forum for purposes of jurisdiction to institute proceedings is made by reference to the date on which such proceedings are deemed to have been instituted. Since the Claimant instituted these proceedings prior to the time when the two assignments were concluded, it follows that the Tribunal has jurisdiction to hear this case regardless of the legal effect, if any, the assignments might have had on Claimant's standing had they preceded the filing of the case ... This conclusion is compelled by the consideration that absence of beneficial ownership by a claimant in a claim or the transfer of the economic risk in the outcome of a dispute should not and has not been deemed to affect the standing of a claimant in an ICSID proceedings.[36]

In a similar manner, the tribunal in *El Paso v Argentina* found the sale of the investment barely two weeks after the registration of the ICSID claim to be irrelevant, finding that:

> The reason for there not being such a rule [of continuous ownership of investment] in the ICSID/BIT context is that the issues addressed by those instruments are precisely those of confiscation, expropriation and nationalization of foreign investment. Once the taking has occurred, there is nothing left except the possibility of using the ICSID/BIT mechanism. That purpose would be defeated if continuous ownership were required.[37]

Yet, the tribunal conceded that some might find 'disturbing' the proximity of the dates of the bringing of the claim and the sale of the investment.[38]

In *National Grid v Argentina*, the tribunal also held the sale of the investment after the institution of the arbitral proceedings to be irrelevant to the investor's standing, attaching importance to the fact that the right to pursue the claim was part of the terms of the sale of the shares which had been approved by Argentina.[39]

[35] See, eg, *Société Ouest Africaine des Bétons Industriels (SOABI) v Sénégal*, ICSID Case No ARB/82/1, Decision on Jurisdiction (19 July 1984) para 29, and *Banro American Resources Inc and Société Aurifère du Kivu du Maniema SARL v Democratic Republic of Congo*, ICSID Case No ARB/98/7, Award (1 September 2000) para 1; *Rompetrol Group NV v Republic of Romania*, ICSID Case No ARB/06/3, Decision on Respondent's Preliminary Objections on Jurisdiction and Admissibility (18 April 2008) para 79.

[36] *Ceskoslovenska Obchodni Banka AS (CSOB) v Slovak Republic*, ICSID Case No ARB/97/4, Decision on Objections to Jurisdiction (24 May 1999) paras 31–32.

[37] *El Paso Energy International Company v Argentine Republic*, ICSID Case No ARB/03/15, Decision on Jurisdiction (27 April 2006) para 135.

[38] Ibid, para 136.

[39] *National Grid PLC v Argentine Republic*, UNCITRAL, Decision on Jurisdiction (20 June 2006) paras 114–21.

The tribunal in *EnCana v Ecuador* came to a similar conclusion, though with a different argument:

> The Claimant argues that a 'dispute' arises upon the taking of measures in breach of the Treaty which cause loss and damage to an investor, and that this is sufficient to found jurisdiction. The Tribunal agrees, both on the basis of the actual language of the BIT and its object and purpose. Provided loss or damage is caused to an investor by a breach of the Treaty, the cause of action is complete at that point; retention of the subsidiary (assuming it is within the investor's power to retain it) serves no purpose as a jurisdictional requirement, though it may be relevant to questions of quantum.[40]

For the ECT, the tribunal in *Yukos v Russia* explicitly rejected the holding in the *Loewen* decision and also found the date of the filing of the claim to be determinative.[41] The tribunal in *Teinver v Argentina* came to a similar conclusion.[42]

Many commentators have equally maintained that jurisdiction cannot be defeated by a change of nationality after the cut-off point of the institution of the proceedings.[43]

Yet, this opinion seems to be contrasted by the view held by others that the change, after the institution of the proceedings, to the host State nationality or the nationality of a non-Contracting State should defeat jurisdiction.[44] Indeed, for the case of determining foreign control of a locally incorporated investor, the Schreuer Commentary concedes that while 'the starting point should remain the date of consent', 'subsequent changes in control should be taken into account under certain circumstances'.[45] As the Convention was designed to exclude host State nationals of the Contracting Party as well as nationals of non-Contracting States, a voluntary change of control to either host State or non-Contracting State nationality, even after the institution of proceedings, should be considered relevant.[46]

The abovementioned tribunal's finding in *El Paso v Argentina* raises a similar question. The rationale invoked by the tribunal for rejecting a rule of continuous ownership[47] undoubtedly seems appropriate in the case which the tribunal

[40] *EnCana Corporation v Ecuador*, LCIA Case No UN3481, UNCITRAL, Award (3 February 2006) para 131.

[41] *Yukos Universal Ltd (Isle of Man) v Russian Federation*, UNCITRAL, PCA Case No AA 227, Interim Award on Jurisdiction and Admissibility (30 November 2009) paras 551–52.

[42] *Teinver SA, Transportes de Cercanías SA and Autobuses Urbanos del Sur SA v Argentine Republic*, ICSID Case No ARB/09/1, Decision on Jurisdiction (21 December 2012) para 255.

[43] Schreuer and others, *ICSID Convention* (n 2) 'Article 25' para 755; Chittharanjan Amerasinghe, 'International Centre for Settlement of Investment Disputes and Development Through the Multinational Corporations' (1976) 9 Va J Transnat L 793, 809–10; Rudolf Dolzer and Christoph Schreuer, *Principles of International Investment Law* (Oxford University Press, 2nd edn 2012) 41.

[44] George Delaume, 'Le Centre International pour le Règlement des Différends relatifs aux Investissements (CIRDI)' (1982) 109 JDI 797; Moshe Hirsch, *The Arbitration Mechanism of the International Centre for the Settlement of Investment Disputes* (Martinus Nijhoff 1993) 95–96.

[45] Schreuer and others, *ICSID Commentary* (n 2) 'Article 25' para 892.

[46] Ibid, paras 893–94.

[47] It is interesting that some tribunals phrased the problem of continuous nationality in terms of continuous ownership, such as in *El Paso v Argentina* (n 37) para 135 and in *National Grid v Argentina* (n 39) para 116. The tribunal in *EnCana v Ecuador* (n 40) correctly remarked in para 128 that these arguments 'are two ways of making the same point'; though the argument can also be made that while a change of nationality always also includes a change in ownership, the reverse is not necessarily true;

considers to be the typical cases of application of IIAs/ICSID Convention, namely involuntary deprivations of the investment that lead to the change in nationality, as the assumption of such a rule would otherwise deprive the investor of his (sometimes) last remedies. Though admittedly the tribunal in *National Grid v Argentina* was unimpressed by the question of whether the change of nationality was voluntary or involuntary,[48] the question seems nevertheless justified whether in the case of voluntary changes of nationality, the investor should in all cases continue to have a justified interest in legal protection in pursuing the arbitral proceedings, or whether, in accordance with the finding of the *EnCana* tribunal, this should only be a question of the merits/quantum.

Finally, while thus the *dies ad quem* in international investment law can be considered firmly and explicitly established to be the date of submission of the claim/perfection of the consent,[49] the *dies a quo* remains often implicit, namely the date of the injury respectively the (alleged) breach of the obligation. This seems to be in accordance with customary international law.[50] There seems to be unanimity that no continuity of nationality properly speaking is required between these points in time, but only that the invoked nationality has to be possessed at these precise key moments.[51] An assignment of an investment after the occurrence of a breach but before the bringing of a claim between persons holding the same nationality thus remains possible, as was correctly decided by the arbitral tribunal in the recent case *Renée Rose Levy de Levi v Peru*.[52]

6.4 Exclusion of Pre-existing Disputes

As we have seen, a putative investor–claimant has to possess the qualifying nationality and to have acquired a qualifying investment at the time of the alleged breach in order to enjoy treaty protection.

However, a question to be distinguished from when the investor has to possess the invoked nationality and the qualifying investment is the question whether and when an investment dispute has arisen. This is regularly important for determining whether the tribunal has jurisdiction *ratione temporis* in view of the change of nationality, in other words whether the temporal scope of the dispute settlement clause under interpretation is engaged. The question of whether the dispute already existed at the time of the change of nationality is part of an increasingly

there can be a change in ownership without necessarily having a change of nationality, see, eg, the case *Renée Rose Levy de Levi v Republic of Peru*, ICSID Case No ARB/10/17, Award (26 February 2014).

[48] *National Grid v Argentina* (n 39) para 119.

[49] This, it is submitted, is valid both for legal and natural persons. For the latter, the *dies ad quem* should be considered two-pronged in the case of Art 25(2)(a) ICSID Convention.

[50] See *Panevezys-Saldutiskis Railway Case (Estonia v Lithuania)* [1938] PCIJ Series A/B No 76 para 66; Duchesne (n 25) 799.

[51] Schreuer and others, *ICSID Commentary* (n 2) 'Article 25' paras 684–85; Mendelson, 'Runaway Train' (n 9) 128.

[52] *Renée Rose Levy de Levi v Peru* (n 47).

consolidated jurisprudence that dismisses jurisdiction *ratione temporis* if the dispute already existed at the time of the change of nationality or finds the claim inadmissible on grounds of abuse of rights/abuse of process if the dispute had not already existed, but was 'sufficiently' foreseeable for the investor.[53] A principled approach towards the notion of dispute is thus crucial, yet it is here where a lot of arbitral inconsistency reigns, making a clear distinction and definition of the questions at stake necessary.

In particular, in terms of issues *ratione temporis*, a preliminary question is why a pre-existing dispute should be excluded from jurisdiction *ratione temporis*. This question is straightforward when the IIA under interpretation contains a specific exclusion clause, but more controversial in the absence of an express limitation. Arbitral tribunals have also not always been clearly distinguishing between the acts or facts giving rise to the dispute, the dispute itself and the breach of the investment obligation and ensuing injury, all (or some) of which *may*, but need not necessarily occur at the same time. Moreover, even where tribunals make this distinction, they often enough apply the jurisprudence developed by the Permanent Court of International Justice (PCIJ), International Court of Justice (ICJ), and investment tribunals on the notion of 'dispute' in a haphazard way, or simply equate the timing of the (alleged) breach with the starting point of the dispute. Equating the (alleged) breach with the dispute renders the existing jurisprudence on the notion of dispute moot and begs the question why one should then distinguish between pre-existing and foreseeable disputes at all when deciding on the admissibility of corporate restructuring claims (instead of merely asking whether the dispute was foreseeable). These questions will be examined in turn.

6.4.1 Why should a pre-existing dispute be excluded?

As a preliminary issue, the question should be addressed on which legal doctrinal grounds jurisdiction *ratione temporis* may be dismissed because of a dispute having arisen before the change of nationality/restructuring. This is an issue that has to date not received sufficient scrutiny in scholarly contributions. In a similar vein, even where arbitral tribunals make the distinction between a pre-existing and foreseeable dispute, they most often do not sufficiently explain the legal dogmatic rationale for excluding a pre-existing dispute in the absence of an explicit exclusion clause or specific wording of the dispute settlement clause. This, however, seems important in order to achieve more consistency in the interpretation of the notion of dispute in restructuring cases, as will be seen more in detail below.

Two situations should be distinguished. On the one hand, the situation where the IIA under interpretation contains a treaty-based exclusion of disputes existing before its entry into force, and on the other hand, where the IIA under interpretation contains no such clauses.

[53] See on the second leg of the test more in detail in Chapter 7.

6.4.1.1 *Treaty-based exclusion clauses*

The answer to the above question seems rather straight-forward where the IIA under interpretation explicitly excludes from its temporal scope disputes that have arisen before its entry into force (so-called single exclusion clause), or excludes even the acts or facts giving rise to a later dispute that have occurred before its entry into force (so-called double exclusion clause).[54] Although one might argue that on a literal reading, the formulation used in these clauses ('before the entry into force of the treaty') only refers to the formal entry into force of the treaty within the meaning of Article 24 VCLT, it seems reasonable to let a teleological interpretation of such clauses prevail in the case of restructurings, to the effect that these clauses also apply to disputes existing before the entry into force of the IIA *with respect to the investor–claimant*, in other words the restructuring transaction that makes the investor–claimant an eligible national under the IIA in question. Indeed, a literal interpretation of (single or double) exclusion clauses would not seem to take into account the triangular relation, specific to international investment law, that gives a third party (not participating in the conclusion of the treaty, ie, the investor) a right based on a treaty concluded between two (or more) State parties.[55] Entry into force of the treaty should thus mean both its formal date of entry into force as well as its entry into force with respect to the investor. At least one arbitral tribunal has interpreted the single exclusion clause in this manner.[56]

In a similar vein, dispute settlement clauses providing for consent to settle 'disputes that may arise' or 'disputes that might arise' may also be interpreted as covering only future disputes, that is, those arising after the entry into force of the IIA.[57]

6.4.1.2 *No treaty-based exclusion clauses*

However, in the absence of an explicit limitation, the question as to whether disputes that have arisen before the entry into force of an IIA are excluded from a tribunal's jurisdiction remains controversial.

[54] For examples see Chapter 8, at 8.2.5.2 and 8.2.5.3.

[55] On the discussion whether this right is an originary or a derivative right see, eg, Zachary Douglas, *The International Law of Investment Claims* (Cambridge University Press 2009) Rules 1 and 2, paras 65ff.

[56] *ST-AD GmbH v Republic of Bulgaria*, UNCITRAL, PCA Case No 2011-06, Award on Jurisdiction (18 July 2013) para 300. In another case, the arbitral tribunal, though acknowledging the existence of a single exclusion clause, seems to have based its reasoning on the principle of non-retroactivity, see *Lao Holdings NV v Lao People's Democratic Republic*, ICSID Case No ARB(AF)12/6, Decision on Jurisdiction (21 February 2014) paras 76, 114.

[57] Schreuer and others, *ICSID Commentary* (n 2) 'Article 25' para 48; *Salini Costruttori SpA and Italstrade SpA v The Hashemite Kingdom of Jordan*, ICSID Case No ARB/02/13, Decision on Jurisdiction (9 November 2004) para 170; *Ioan Micula, Viorel Micula, SC European Food SA, SC Starmill SRL and SC Multipack SRL v Republic of Romania*, ICSID Case No ARB/05/20, Decision on Jurisdiction and Admissibility (24 September 2008) para 154; *ABCI Investments NV v République Tunisienne*, ICSID Case No ARB/04/12, Decision on Jurisdiction (French) (18 February 2011) para 154.

Under general international law, courts and many scholars have considered that in the absence of an express limitation, a court has jurisdiction over a dispute even if it has arisen prior to the entry into force of the treaty under interpretation.[58]

For investment arbitration, this question is more unsettled. Some tribunals have accepted that they could exercise jurisdiction over disputes that have arisen before the entry into force of the IIA.[59] However, many investment arbitral tribunals—many of them in treaty shopping/restructuring cases—have thus far decided that they did *not* have jurisdiction over pre-existing disputes, often despite the absence of an explicit exclusion clause.[60]

Two explanations are thinkable. One would be to argue that the exclusion of disputes that existed before the entry into force of an IIA has risen to the level of customary international law. This, however, seems difficult to maintain. As is well known, customary international law is a 'general practice accepted as law'[61] and requires virtually uniform, extensive, and representative State practice, as well as the legal conviction that a particular practice is carried out with a sense of legal obligation.[62] In view of thousands of differing IIAs, some of them containing explicit exclusion clauses, some of them not, the argument that there is sufficiently uniform and extensive State practice in this respect does not seem realistic. Indeed, the fact that some States do include (single or double) exclusion clauses would rather point to the (contrary) assumption that in the absence of such explicit

[58] *Mavrommatis Palestine Concessions (Greece v United Kingdom) (Judgment)* [1924] PCIJ Series A, No 2, 35; *Anglo-Iranian Oil Co (United Kingdom v Iran) (Preliminary Objections)* [1952] ICJ Rep 93, 106; Rosalyn Higgins, 'Time and the Law: International Perspectives on an Old Problem' (1997) 46 ICLQ 501, 502; Shabtai Rosenne, *The Law and Practice of the International Court 1920–2005*, Vol II, Jurisdiction (Martinus Nijhoff Publishers 2006) 752; Frédéric Dopagne, 'Article 28' in Olivier Corten and Pierre Klein, *The Vienna Conventions on the Law of Treaty, A Commentary*, Vol I (Oxford University Press 2012) para 11; ILC 'Commentary on Art 24 [now Art 28]' in International Law Commission, *Yearbook of the International Law Commission* (1966) Vol II, 212 (para 2). For a contrary view see Dissenting Opinion Judge Armand-Ugon, *Barcelona Traction, Light and Power Company Ltd (New Application: 1962) (Belgium v Spain) (Preliminary Objections)* [1964] ICJ Rep 6, 160–63.

[59] *Mondev International Ltd v United States of America*, ICSID Case No ARB(AF)/99/2, Award (11 October 2002) para 57; *United Parcel Service Inc v Government of Canada*, UNCITRAL, Award on the merits (24 May 2007) para 28; *SGS Société de Surveillance v Republic of the Philippines*, ICSID Case No ARB/02/6, Decision of the Tribunal on Objections to Jurisdiction (29 January 2004) paras 165–68.

[60] *Generation Ukraine Inc v Ukraine*, ICSID Case No ARB/00/9, Award (16 September 2003) paras 8.13, 17.1; *Salini v Jordan* (n 57) para 170; *Impreglio SpA v Islamic Republic of Pakistan*, ICSID Case No ARB/03/3, Decision on Jurisdiction (22 April 2005) para 300; *MCI Power Group LC and New Turbines v Republic of Ecuador*, ICSID Case No ARB/03/6, Award (31 July 2007) para 61; *Werner Schneider, acting in his capacity as insolvency administrator of Walter Bau AG (In Liquidation) v The Kingdom of Thailand*, UNCITRAL, Award (1 July 2009) para 9.67 (formerly *Walter Bau AG (In Liquidation) v The Kingdom of Thailand*); *Société Générale v Dominican Republic* (n 11) para 107; *Phoenix Action Ltd v Czech Republic*, ICSID Case No ARB/06/5, Award (15 April 2009) para 67; *ABCI Investments v République Tunisienne* (n 57) para 166; *Pac Rim Cayman LLC v Republic of El Salvador*, ICSID Case No ARB/09/12, Decision on the Respondent's Jurisdictional Objections (1 June 2012) para 2.99; *ST-AD GmbH v Bulgaria* (n 56) para 300; *Lao Holdings v Laos* (n 56) paras 76, 116–17; *Ping An Life Insurance Company of China, Limited and Ping An Insurance (Group) Company of China v Kingdom of Belgium*, ICSID Case No ARB/12/29, Award (30 April 2015) para 184.

[61] Art 38(1)(b) of the Statute of the International Court of Justice.

[62] *North Sea Continental Shelf cases (Federal Republic of Germany v Denmark; Federal Repblic of Germany v Netherlands) (Judgment)* [1969] ICJ Rep 3 (para 74).

exclusion clause, an arbitral tribunal's jurisdiction *ratione temporis* should cover pre-existing disputes.

The other possible explanation is the principle of non-retroactivity. Many of the abovementioned decisions base their argumentation directly on this principle.

The (customary) principle of non-retroactivity (also codified in Article 28 VCLT) provides that unless a different intention can be established, the treaty in question does not bind a party with respect to 'any act or fact which took place or any situation which ceased to exist before the date of entry into force of the treaty with respect to that party'. This principle is also reflected in Article 13 of the ILC's Draft Articles on State Responsibility, which states that 'an act of a State does not constitute a breach of an international obligation unless the State is bound by the obligation in question at the time the act occurs'.

The principle of non-retroactivity thus excludes from the temporal application those acts or facts or situations that occurred prior to the entry into force of the treaty, unless those acts or facts or situations continue thereafter, as may be the case for continuing or composite acts within the meaning of Articles 14(2) and 15 of the ILC's Draft Articles on State Responsibility.[63] It is thus directed at the substantive protection of the treaty or in other words at the merits. By contrast, jurisdiction *ratione temporis* concerns the question of whether the tribunal has (temporal) jurisdiction to hear the particular dispute, in other words whether the States party to the IIA have given their consent to the investor–State dispute settlement for pre-existing disputes.

The question is however whether an 'act or fact' having occurred before the entry in force of a treaty is the same as a 'dispute' having occurred before its entry into force. In this aspect, some authorities have pointed out that the question of whether certain acts or facts are excluded from the temporal scope of protection of the treaty on grounds of the principle of non-retroactivity may be different from the question of whether and in particular when a dispute has arisen.[64] As Rosalyn Higgins remarked, 'disputes, facts and situations may have occurred at different times'.[65]

There are in this author's opinion good arguments (if only for the sake of doctrinal underpinning) in favour of a clear distinction between the notion of dispute and 'acts and facts'. In investor–State arbitration (as in international dispute settlement more generally), an arbitral tribunal's jurisdiction is based on the parties' consent to submitting the dispute before the tribunal. For States, this consent is

[63] See more in detail Nick Gallus, *The Temporal Scope of Investment Protection Treaties* (British Institute of International and Comparative Law 2008) 31ff, 57ff; Stanislav Alexandrov, 'The "Baby Boom" of Treaty-Based Arbitrations and the Jurisdiction of ICSID Tribunals: Shareholders as "Investors" and Jurisdiction Ratione Temporis' (2005) 4 LPICT 19, 49.

[64] Higgins (n 58) 502. Similar Gallus (n 63) 133–41; Sadie Blanchard, 'State consent, temporal jurisdiction, and the importation of continuing circumstances analysis into international investment arbitration' (2011) 10 Wash U Global Stud L Rev 419, 429; Noah Rubins and Ben Love, 'Ratione Temporis' in Marc Bungenberg, Jörn Griebel, Stephan Hobe, and August Reinisch (eds), *International Investment Law, A Handbook* (CH Beck, Hart Publishing and Nomos 2015) 490 (para 38).

[65] Higgins (n 58) 502.

Table 6.1 Dispute settlement clause that only covers treaty claims (ie where jurisdiction *ratione temporis* and temporal scope of application are identical)

	JD *ratione temporis*	Temporal scope
Acts occurred before entry into force (EIF)	(-)	(-)
Acts occurred after EIF	(+)	(+)
Acts started before EIF but continued thereafter	(+)	(+)

usually contained in IIAs, often accompanied by a number of conditions the investor must fulfil before it may bring the investment claim. Though the investor must *claim* an (alleged) breach of a (treaty) obligation when bringing the claim, it is not until the merits phase that the claimed breach (and the question whether the State was bound by the obligation at the time of the alleged breach) will be actually examined, while it is a priori the existence of a *dispute* over the alleged breach (and the question when it arose) that must be determined for purposes of jurisdiction.[66] This is particularly true for the 'pre-existing dispute' jurisprudence. In other words, the 'pre-existing dispute' jurisprudence is a jurisdictional test not to be confounded with the question, relevant for the merits, whether the State will be held liable for an act that occurred before the entry into force (meaning the timing of the restructuring). Of course, the starting point of a dispute may coincide with the (alleged) breach, as it may not; a clear disentangling of the acts or facts leading to or constituting the breach (as relevant for the merits) and of the existence of a dispute (as relevant for jurisdiction) is, however, crucial.

Yet, this is not to say that the principle of non-retroactivity is completely disconnected from, or irrelevant for, jurisdiction *ratione temporis*. Whether the principle will have an incidence on the temporal jurisdiction of the arbitral tribunal may arguably depend on the wording of the dispute settlement clause contained in the IIA. Dispute settlement clauses may be (or look) very similar, yet in the end, an arbitral tribunal will have to interpret each clause in its own context and in light of its particular purpose, giving effect to the parties' intentions.

Indeed, several scholars have argued that if the dispute resolution clause only extends to claims that the measure has allegedly breached obligations of the IIA, the temporal jurisdiction is co-extensive with the temporal application of its substantive provisions.[67] In other words, in such a case, if the acts or facts have occurred prior to the entry into force of the IIA and have not continued thereafter, there is neither jurisdiction *ratione temporis* nor are the substantive provisions applicable for lack of temporal scope (see Table 6.1).

On the other hand, if the wording of the dispute resolution clause of the IIA is wider, covering also non-treaty claims, the temporal jurisdiction and the temporal

[66] See in this sense also Pierre-François Laval, *La compétence ratione temporis des juridictions internationales* (Thèse de droit, Université Montesquieu-Bordeaux IV 2011) 333–37.

[67] Dolzer and Schreuer (n 43) 36–37; Rubins and Love (n 64) 488 (para 30).

Table 6.2 Dispute settlement clause that not only covers treaty claims, but also non-treaty claims

	JD *ratione temporis*	Temporal scope
Acts occurred before entry into force (EIF)	(-) for treaty claims, (+) for non-treaty claims	(-) for treaty claims, (+) for non-treaty claims
Acts occurred after EIF	(+)	(+)
Acts started before EIF but continued thereafter	(+)	(+)

application of substantive provisions are not the same and non-treaty claims may remain possible despite the fact that the acts or facts in question may have occurred before the entry into force of the treaty (see Table 6.2).[68] The same should arguably apply *mutatis mutandi* in the case of broad dispute settlement clauses encompassing 'any legal dispute' between the host State and the investor concerning an investment in the territory of the former.

Applying the above assumptions in a consequent way, this would seem to mean that not *any* dispute existing before a corporate restructuring may automatically be excluded. This would then however call into question the pertinence of the first leg of the 'pre-existing/foreseeable dispute' jurisprudence. The complexities arising from the above distinctions (and in particular the reliance on the principle of non-retroactivity) may be the reason why arbitral tribunals tend to equate the timing of the (alleged) breach with the starting point of the dispute, irrespective of any analysis of the concrete wording of the dispute settlement clause under interpretation. It is certainly true that equating the timing of the (alleged) breach and the dispute is more predictable and in this sense furthers legal security. At the same time, the arbitral decisions adhering to this approach do not explain on which legal doctrinal grounds a pre-existing dispute should be excluded in the absence of an explicit exclusion clause, and they do not explain why, when equating alleged breach and dispute, this first leg of the 'pre-existing/foreseeable dispute' jurisprudence is then necessary at all. After all, a restructuring typically occurs *before* the actual (alleged) breach has taken place (when the investor experiences a deterioration of the business climate or a concrete disadvantageous measure is announced by the host government), so asking for a pre-existing dispute that (almost) invariably only starts after the breach makes this first leg of the test moot and, in passing, deprives the notion of dispute (and the existing jurisprudence on it) of its autonomous significance.

In view of these incongruities, a differentiated, factual approach towards the notion of dispute in restructuring cases seems dogmatically more convincing, despite the benefit of higher legal certainty when equating the timing of dispute and alleged breach. Yet, admittedly, even those tribunals that equate dispute and

[68] Rubins and Love (n 64) 489 (para 32).

alleged breach do not under all circumstances come to a wrong result as concerns the validity of a corporate restructuring claim, if and as long as they address the value judgment inherent in distinguishing 'legitimate nationality planning' and 'abusive treaty shopping' in the second leg of the test, that is, in the question of the foreseeability of the dispute, as will be seen more in detail in Chapter 7.

6.4.2 When has the dispute arisen?

6.4.2.1 Importance of the notion of dispute for a claim following a corporate restructuring

Without prejudice to the legal doctrinal grounds for excluding a pre-existing dispute in the case of a corporate restructuring, it becomes clear that it is crucial, for jurisdictional purposes, to determine whether the dispute in question has arisen before the investor acquired its nationality and investment.[69]

Indeed, the earlier a dispute is found to exist, less effective becomes a strategic change of nationality with respect to a specific existing dispute. Vice versa, the closer the relevant moment for the commencement of a dispute moves to the date of injury or even the date of the request for arbitration, though providing for a higher degree of legal certainty, the easier it becomes for the investor to perform a change of nationality that will be regarded as 'legitimate nationality planning' by the judging tribunal.[70]

As a practical consequence, the claimant will thus try to 'postpone' the date of existence of a dispute, while the respondent will try to do the opposite, that is, advance the date of existence of a dispute as much as possible.

Depending on the approach an arbitral tribunal takes towards the notion of dispute, this may also have an incidence on possible annulment proceedings. Wrongly rejecting or upholding jurisdiction *ratione temporis* could, for ICSID proceedings, constitute a manifest excess of power and thus give rise to annulment under Article 52(1)(b) of the ICSID Convention.[71] Both the failure to exercise jurisdiction (by wrongly assuming a pre-existing dispute at the time of the restructuring) as well as to (manifestly) exceed jurisdiction (by wrongly finding a dispute not to pre-exist) could potentially constitute the a.m. annulment ground.

Yet, arbitral jurisprudence has not been very coherent—even when interpreting the wording of the dispute resolution clauses in question—in determining the relevant point in time for the commencement of a dispute.

[69] Similar Tania Voon, Andrew Mitchell, and James Munro, 'Legal Responses to Corporate Manoeuvering in International Investment Arbitration' (2014) 5 JIDS 41, 46. The same question may be relevant for clauses in the BIT that agree to treat a locally incorporated investor as being under foreign control for purposes of Article 25(2)(b) ICSID Convention if, 'before a dispute arises, [it] is controlled by nationals of the other Contracting Party'.

[70] Similar Voon, Mitchell, and Munro, 'Legal Response' (n 69) 47.

[71] R Doak Bishop and Silvia Marchili, *Annulment under the ICSID Convention* (Oxford University Press 2012) paras 6.46ff.

In some cases, investment tribunals have found the date of the notification of the claim or, in accordance with Article 25 of the ICSID Convention, the request for arbitration to be the relevant date for the commencement of a dispute.[72] Others have focused on the date of the harm or injury or on the date of the (alleged) breach of the investment treaty obligations, both of which will often coincide.[73]

The often incoherent or imprecise use of relevant, potentially differing points in time—if only as concerns its terminology—is well illustrated by the holding of the *Phoenix Action* tribunal. In explaining why the strategic change of nationality cannot apply to pre-existing disputes, the tribunal argued that '[t]he Tribunal is limited *ratione temporis* to judging only those *acts and omissions occurring* [emphasis added] after the date of the investor's purported investment'.[74] Shortly after, it concluded that it 'has no jurisdiction *ratione temporis* over any alleged *claims* [emphasis added] that predate the decision of Phoenix to invest in the Czech companies on December 26, 2002'.[75] The tribunal thus used the term 'claims' as a synonym for 'dispute' and visibly equated the principle of non-retroactivity with the exclusion of pre-existing disputes (this in spite of the absence of a corresponding exclusion clause in the Israel–Czech Republic BIT). Though the conclusion of the tribunal cannot be objected to, the imprecise use of the above-shown different points in time may be a matter of concern, potentially leading to incoherent jurisprudence, as will be seen further below.

This is not to say that the notion of dispute should be understood as a static concept. Different points in time may indeed be of relevance when determining the starting point of a dispute in the case of a corporate restructuring.

In a typical one-time act, such as the passing of an expropriation decree or law constituting the (alleged) breach of the investment obligation, the act or event giving rise to the dispute will normally occur at the same time as the breach of the obligation (which is also often synonymous with the occurrence of the injury or harm).[76] In this case, a dispute will often only come into being once the measure constituting the (alleged) breach of the investment obligation has occurred.[77]

[72] Voon, Mitchell, and Munro, 'Legal Responses' (n 69) 47; *Azurix Corp v Argentine Republic*, ICSID Case No ARB/01/12, Decision on Jurisdiction (8 December 2003) para 55; *Rompetrol v Romania* (n 35) para 79.

[73] Douglas, *Investment Claims* (n 55) Rules 31–32; Kirtley (n 23) 437; Voon, Mitchell, and Munro, 'Legal Responses' (n 69) 48; *Pac Rim v El Salvador* (n 60) para 2.109; *Cementownia v Turkey* (n 11) paras 122–23; *Europe Cement Trade & Investment v Republic of Turkey*, ICSID Case No ARB(AF)/07/2, Decision on Jurisdiction (13 August 2009) para 140; *GEA Group v Ukraine* (n 11) para 170; *Phoenix Action v Czech Republic* (n 60) para 92; *Société Générale v Dominican Republic* (n 11) para 109; *Cervin Investissements SA & Rhone Investissements SA v La República de Costa Rica*, ICSID Case No ARB/13/2, Decisión sobre Jurisdicción (15 December 2014) para 278; *Renée Rose Levy and Gremcitel v Peru* (n 11) para 149.

[74] *Phoenix Action v Czech Republic* (n 60) para 68.

[75] Ibid, para 71.

[76] See 2001 ILC Draft Articles on Responsibility of States for Internationally Wrongful Acts (2001 ILC Draft Articles on State Responsibility) Art 14(1). See also Gallus (n 63) 48–50.

[77] In this sense also *Philip Morris Asia Limited v Commonwealth of Australia*, UNCITRAL, PCA Case No 2012-12, Award on Jurisdiction and Admissibility (17 December 2015) (redacted version) para 532.

However, this reasoning is not mandatory under all circumstances. Indeed, some scholars have pointed out that the existence of the possibility of provisional measures under the major bodies of arbitration rules respectively many investment treaties confirms that a dispute may arise even before the injury or harm has actually occurred.[78] This argument would seem to be correct in any case for those clauses that allow for provisional measures even before the institution of the investment claim as such.[79]

It is thus thinkable that even in the case of a one-time act, a dispute may already arise before the measure is taken, for example when the measure has been announced and without the breach of the obligation already having taken place, the investor has started to engage with the host State on a conflict level with respect to the announced measure that would qualify as 'dispute' under the investment treaty and arbitral jurisprudence.

In other cases, such as in the case of a continuous act[80] which may span over months or even years, the determination of the existence/starting point of a dispute may become more difficult.[81] An example of a continuous act is the non-issuance of a permit or licence over a certain period of time.[82] In particular, when a business relationship gradually deteriorates between a foreign investor and the host State, a dispute may and indeed often does come into being before the actual breach of the investment obligation and/or injury or harm occurs.

The timing of a dispute thus may, but need not necessarily, be identical with the timing of the (alleged) breach of the obligation. Yet, in particular in restructuring cases, arbitral tribunals have shown a tendency to equate the starting point of the dispute with the occurrence of the (alleged) breach. A thorough analysis of the arbitral jurisprudence on the notion of dispute, including in restructuring cases, seems therefore warranted. As the investment jurisprudence on the notion of 'dispute' essentially builds on corresponding PCIJ and ICJ jurisprudence, this latter will be reviewed first before turning to the interpretation of the notion of 'dispute' in international investment law.

6.4.2.2 PCIJ and ICJ jurisprudence on the notion of 'dispute'

The jurisprudence on the notion of 'dispute' is certainly one of the most recurrent and developed ones in the dealings of the PCIJ and ICJ, being courts whose jurisdiction must be recognized by the States who refer disputes to it. The recognition of the jurisdiction of the PCIJ/ICJ can be general (for all disputes) or ad

[78] Voon, Mitchell, and Munro, 'Legal Responses' (n 69) 48.

[79] See, eg, Art 14(7) of the 2009 ASEAN–China Investment Agreement: 'No Party shall prevent the disputing investor from seeking interim measures of protection, not involving the payment of damages or resolution of the substance of the matter in dispute before the courts or administrative tribunals of the disputing Parties, prior to the institution of proceedings before any of the dispute settlement fora referred to in Paragraph 4 [ICSID, UNCITRAL etc], for the preservation of its rights and interests.' Similar Art 18(12) of the 2009 ASEAN–Korea BIT and Art 22(2) of the ASEAN–Australia–New Zealand FTA.

[80] See 2001 ILC Draft Articles on State Responsibility, Art 14(2).

[81] Similar Hervé Ascencio, 'Abuse of Process in International Investment Arbitration' (2014) 13 Chin J Intl L 763, 773–74.

[82] See, eg, *Pac Rim v El Salvador* (n 60) para 2.92.

hoc (for one precise dispute) and may be conditional or unconditional.[83] When States accede(d) to the PCIJ and the ICJ, they often accepte(d) jurisdiction only for disputes arising after a certain date, mostly the entry into force of the consent to jurisdiction instrument. Some States additionally exclude(d) situations or facts giving rise to a dispute if these occur before the consent instrument has become valid.

6.4.2.2.1 Cases

One of the earliest and most quoted definitions of the notion of 'dispute' can be found in the *Mavrommatis* case where the PCIJ defined the notion of 'dispute' as 'a disagreement on a point of law or fact, a conflict of legal views or of interests between two persons'.[84]

Similarly influential has been the ICJ's definition in the *Interpretation of Peace Treaties with Bulgaria, Hungary and Romania* case, finding a dispute to exist where 'the two sides hold clearly opposite views concerning the question of the performance or non-performance of certain treaty obligations'.[85]

Other decisions of the ICJ found that a requirement of negotiations was inherent in the notion of dispute,[86] that the contested decision must not necessarily be in force for a dispute to exist,[87] and that where one party formulated complaints of fact and law and the other party denied those complaints, there was a dispute by virtue of this denial, no matter whether the 'real dispute' was with this or another Party.[88] In other instances, the ICJ also found a dispute to exist where the Respondent did not negate the existence of a dispute, either by not advancing any arguments to justify its conduct claimed by the claimant party to constitute a breach or by otherwise not responding to the demands of the other party.[89]

The question of when a dispute exists was also dealt with in the *Interhandel* case.[90] In that case, Switzerland sought, on behalf of the Swiss company Interhandel, the restitution of company assets that had been confiscated by the United States during

[83] See Art 36 of the Statute of the International Court of Justice and Art 36 of the Statute of the Permanent Court of International Justice.

[84] *Mavrommatis Palestine Concessions* (n 58) 11.

[85] *Interpretation of Peace Treaties with Bulgaria, Hungary and Romania (Advisory Opinion)* [1950] ICJ Rep 65, 74; similar *South West Africa (Ethiopia v South Africa; Liberia v South Africa) (Preliminary Objections)* [1962] ICJ Rep 319, 328; *Northern Cameroons (Cameroon v United Kingdom) (Preliminary Objections)* [1963] ICJ Rep 15, 27.

[86] *Right of Passage over Indian Territory (Portugal v India) (Preliminary Objections)* [1957] ICJ Rep 125, 149.

[87] *Applicability of the Obligation to Arbitrate Under Section 21 of the United Nations Headquarter Agreement of 26 June 1947 (Advisory Opinion)* [1988] ICJ Rep 12, 29–30 (para 42).

[88] *East Timor (Portugal v Australia) (Judgment)* [1995] ICJ Rep 90, 99–100 (para 22); *Certain Property (Liechtenstein v Germany) (Preliminary Objections)* [2005] ICJ Rep 6, 18–19 (para 25); Gallus (n 63) 117–20.

[89] *Applicability of the Obligation to Arbitrate* (n 87) 28; Christoph Schreuer, 'What is a Legal Dispute?' in Isabelle Buffard, James Crawford, Alain Pellet, and Stephan Wittich (eds), *International Law between Universalism and Fragmentation: Festschrift in Honour of Gerhard Hafner* (Martinus Nijhoff 2008) 959, 963–65.

[90] *Interhandel (Switzerland v United States of America) (Preliminary Objections)* [1959] ICJ Rep 6.

the Second World War. The United States objected to the ICJ's jurisdiction on the grounds that it had recognized the ICJ's compulsory jurisdiction only for disputes arising after 26 August 1946 and that the present dispute had arisen before that date. However, the court attached importance to the fact that while in the years between 1945 and 1948 there had been exchanges of view between Switzerland and the United States relating to the Swiss or German character of Interhandel within the framework of the collaboration agreed upon in the Washington Accord, it was for the first time in a note dated 4 May 1948 that Switzerland formulated its claim for the restitution of Interhandel's assets and the United States rejected that claim by note dated 26 July 1948. As the court noted, 'the divergent views of the two Governments were concerned with a clearly-defined legal question, namely the restitution of Interhandel's assets in the United States', thus placing the date of the dispute at 26 July 1948 and dismissing the United States' objection.[91] Several judges dissented, however, on the grounds that they found the real dispute to lie in the question of whether *Interhandel* was of enemy or neutral character.[92] And as Judge Sir Spender remarked:

> A dispute may, as not infrequently happens, enter upon a new phase. An entirely separate dispute may of course arise between the parties with which the existing dispute is only casually connected. But if the substance of the dispute remains the same, the fact that it has entered upon a new phase or that other issues directly connected with and relevant to the dispute in which the parties are also in agreement are subsequently added or appear, or that new claims of relief are presented, cannot alter the problem as such as is here presented to the Court. Were it otherwise, legal ingenuity would usually be able to transmute a dispute which clearly enough was beyond the jurisdiction of the Court, into one within its competence. The Court should concern itself with substance, not form.[93]

Other decisions also dealt with the question whether the situations or facts giving rise to a dispute occurred before the (accordingly formulated) consent instrument of the concerned Party (or Parties) became valid, thus depriving the tribunal of its jurisdiction.

Thus, in the *Phosphates in Morocco* case, the PCIJ had to decide whether the situations or facts giving rise to the dispute between Italy and France—in this case the monopolization of phosphates deposits in Morocco, the decision to reject an Italian's claim for rights in such deposits and France's subsequent obstruction of attempts to challenge the decision—occurred before or after the ratification of the consent instrument. For this purpose, the tribunal asked for the 'source' respectively the 'real causes' of the dispute.[94] Confronted with two alternative submissions by Italy, it took for both submissions a broad view of the dispute at issue, finding that for both the monopolization of phosphates (which was based on legislation from 1920) and the decision in 1925 of the Mines Department not to grant exploitation rights to the Italian national,

[91] Ibid, 21. [92] Gallus (n 63) 122.

[93] *Interhandel* (n 90) 60 (Dissenting Opinion, Judge Sir Percy Spender); Gallus (n 63) 122.

[94] *Phosphates in Morocco (Italy v France) (Preliminary Objections)* [1938] PCIJ Series A/B No 74, paras 29 and 32.

these constituted situations or facts that arose before the consent to the PCIJ's jurisdiction became valid in 1931.

The 'source' or 'real cause' test was subsequently confirmed by the PCIJ in the *Electricity Company of Sofia and Bulgaria* case[95] and by the ICJ in the *Case concerning Right of Passage over Indian Territory*.[96] These latter cases have in common that the respective consent to jurisdiction instruments foresaw similarly phrased clauses, providing jurisdiction only for disputes arising after a certain date and with regard to situations or facts arising subsequent to that date. Consent instruments that use similarly phrased clauses have arguably the effect of making it more difficult for the claimant to prevail in the jurisdictional phase because the consent to jurisdiction is more restrictively conditioned.

The 'source' or 'real cause' test may also be helpful in determining which of several situations or facts underlying the relationship between Claimant and Respondent is relevant. As emphasized by the PCIJ in the *Electricity Company of Sofia and Bulgaria* case:

> It is true that a dispute may presuppose the existence of some prior situation or fact, but it does not follow that the dispute arises in regard to that situation or fact. A situation or fact in regard to which a dispute is said to have arisen must be the real cause of the dispute.[97]

This led the Permanent Court to regard an earlier arbitral award which was the source of the rights claimed by one of the Parties, but which had given rise to no difficulty prior to the facts constituting the subject of the dispute as not constituting the situation which was the 'source' or 'real cause' of the dispute.[98]

The ICJ, in the *Rights of Passage* case, used the same test in order to determine which ones of the several situations and facts pitting Portugal and India against each other were at the source of the dispute and determined that while there may have been minor incidents up to 1954 with respect to Portugal's right of passage over Indian territory to its enclaves, the dispute arose only in 1954 when the controversy started as to both 'the existence of a right of passage to go into the enclaved territories and to India's failure to comply with obligations which, according to Portugal, were binding upon it in this connection'.[99]

6.4.2.2.2 Discussion

As can be seen from the relevant jurisprudence, to establish when a specific dispute has arisen may be a fact-sensitive endeavour, often rendered more complicated by exclusion clauses in need of interpretation.[100] The PCIJ and ICJ have tried to counter this difficulty by developing the 'clear claim' and 'real cause' tests, aimed at rendering the process of establishing the existence of a dispute more objective.

[95] *Electricity Company of Sofia and Bulgaria* case (*Belgium–Bulgaria) (Preliminary Objections)* [1939] PCIJ Series A/B No 77, para 87.

[96] *Right of Passage over Indian Territory (Portugal v India) (Judgment)* [1960] ICJ Rep 6, 34–35.

[97] *Electricity Company of Sofia and Bulgaria* (n 95) para 87.

[98] Ibid.

[99] *Right of Passage* [1960] (n 96) 35.

[100] Stanimir Alexandrov, *Reservations in Unilateral Declarations Accepting the Compulsory Jurisdiction of the International Court of Justice* (Martinus Nijhoff 1995) 40–53.

However, both the 'clear claim' and the 'real cause' tests, unambiguous as they may seem, are not free from uncertainty. While the 'clear claim' test may have the merit of greater legal security, making the occurrence of a dispute more easily traceable to a concrete behaviour or action, it is more susceptible to 'procrastinatory' manipulation or tactical behaviour, as the Claimant has a greater leeway in influencing when a dispute will be considered to have arisen, for example by delaying to state the claim in sufficiently clear terms.

The 'real cause' test, on the other hand, while laudable in its attempt to be concerned by substance, not merely form, uncovers the inherent subjectivity that very often lies in trying to find the real causes of the dispute, despite the ICJ's holding in the *Interpretation of Peace Treaties* case that 'whether there exists an international dispute is a matter for objective determination'.[101]

6.4.2.3 Notion of 'dispute' in international investment law

Having reviewed in all brevity the relevant PCIJ/ICJ jurisprudence on the notion of dispute, an analysis of how arbitral tribunals have interpreted the notion of dispute in international investment law is warranted. Indeed, just as the PCIJ and ICJ, investment arbitral tribunals are often faced with the crucial question of when a specific investment dispute has actually started.

Though, as mentioned above, some IIAs contain provisions excluding disputes (or acts or facts giving rise to a dispute) having arisen prior to their entry into force, not a single IIA defines in its dispute settlement clause what is to be understood as 'dispute' for the purposes of an investment claim. As seen further above, dispute settlement clauses simply define the extent of the consent to jurisdiction by the Contracting Parties, for example over a dispute over 'an alleged breach of an obligation of the [host State] under Part III',[102] or over a 'dispute between a Party and a national or company of the other Party arising out of or relating to an investment authorization, an investment agreement or an alleged breach of any right conferred, created or recognized by this Treaty with respect to a covered investment',[103] seemingly taking for granted that the arbitral tribunal will know how to interpret the notion of dispute.

6.4.2.3.1 Definition of dispute

Investment arbitral tribunals have often relied on the jurisprudence of the PCIJ and ICJ on the notion of 'dispute' as being 'a disagreement on a point of law or fact, a conflict of legal views or of interests between two persons' or 'a situation in which two sides hold clearly opposing views concerning the question of the performance or non-performance [of a legal obligation]'.[104]

[101] *Interpretation of Peace Treaties* (n 85) 74.

[102] Art 26(1) ECT.

[103] Art IX (1) of the 1998 US–Bolivia BIT.

[104] See, eg, *Emilio Agustín Maffezini v Kingdom of Spain*, ICSID Case No ARB/97/7, Decision on Objections to Jurisdiction (25 January 2000) para 94; *Empresas Lucchetti SA and Lucchetti Peru SA v Republic of Peru*, ICSID Case No ARB/03/4, Award (7 February 2005) para 48; *Tokios Tokelés v Ukraine*, ICSID Case No ARB/02/18, Decision on Jurisdiction (29 April 2004) para 106; *Impreglio v Pakistan* (n 60) paras 301–03; *Lao Holdings v Laos* (n 56) para 120.

Noteworthy is also the definition of 'legal dispute' contained in the 'Report of the Executive Directors on the ICSID Convention', according to which:

Conflicts of rights are within the jurisdiction of the Centre, mere conflicts of interests are not. The dispute must concern the existence or scope of a legal right or obligation, or the nature or extent of the reparation to be made for breach of a legal obligation.[105]

It has been recognized by arbitral tribunals early on that not any divergence of opinion or disagreement necessarily qualifies already as a 'dispute'.[106] Thus, the investment tribunal in *Maffezini v Spain* acknowledged that:

There tends to be a natural sequence of events that leads to a dispute. It begins with the expression of a disagreement and the statement of a difference of views. In time these events acquire a precise legal meaning through the formulation of legal claims, their discussion and eventual rejection or lack of response by the other party. The conflict of legal views and interests will only be present in the latter stage, even though the underlying facts predate them. It has also been rightly commented that the existence of the dispute presupposes a minimum of communications between the parties, one party taking up the matter with the other, with the latter opposing the Claimant's position directly or indirectly.[107]

In *Helnan v Egypt*, the arbitral tribunal also found a difference to exist between the notion of divergence and the notion of dispute:

In the case of a divergence, the parties hold different views but without necessarily pursuing the difference in an active manner. On the other hand, in case of a dispute, the difference of views forms the subject of an active exchange between the parties under circumstances which indicate that the parties wish to resolve the difference, be it before a third party or otherwise. Consequently, different views of parties in respect of certain facts and situations become a 'divergence' when they are mutually aware of their disagreement. It crystallizes as a 'dispute' as soon as one of the parties decides to have it solved, whether or not by a third party.[108]

Beyond the difference between divergence and dispute, the *Maffezini* and *Helnan* quotes also confirm the world courts' approaches that for a dispute to exist, it is usually necessary that the claim is capable of being stated in concrete terms and that the parties' positions positively oppose each other.[109] Similarly, the arbitral tribunal in *Sociedad Anónima Eduardo Vieira v Chile* found that a dispute was characterized among others by a minimum of communication between the parties, the fact that one of the parties has formulated the problem respectively the claim to the other party in concrete terms, that the parties were positively opposed over a point of fact

[105] ICSID, 'Report of the Executive Directors on the Convention on the Settlement of Investment Disputes between States and Nationals of Other States' ICSID Doc 2 (18 March 1965) para 26.

[106] This does of course not exclude the possibility that the IIA in question also excludes explicitly 'divergences' that arise before its entry into force, see, eg, Art 12 of the 1999 Denmark–Egypt BIT.

[107] *Maffezini v Spain* (n 104) para 96.

[108] *Helnan International Hotels A/S v Arab Republic of Egypt*, ICSID Case No ARB/05/19, Decision of the Tribunal on Objection to Jurisdiction (17 October 2006) para 52.

[109] *Victor Pey Casado and President Allende Foundation v Republic of Chile*, ICSID Case No ARB/98/2, Sentence Arbitrale (8 May 2008) para 446; *Lao Holdings v Laos* (n 56) para 121.

or of law creating a conflict of interest etc.[110] This positive opposition can lie in a protest, by the investor, against announced measures that will later form the basis of the claim, as the arbitral tribunal found in the recent *Mobil v Venezuela* award.[111]

However, in particular this latter requirement (positive opposition) appears to present a considerable margin of manoeuvre for the Claimant to control the beginning of a dispute. Indeed, if a dispute is not found to exist by arbitral tribunals as long as the parties' positions are not positively opposed, it is thinkable for a (well-advised) Claimant to tactically postpone his voicing of opposing views or withdraw a protest until a later moment thought more suitable for him, for example after a corporate restructuring has been finished.[112]

6.4.2.3.2 'Objective' or 'subjective' approach to the notion of dispute?

Whether an arbitral tribunal will find a dispute will also depend on whether it endeavours to establish the existence of a dispute in an objective, autonomous manner or whether it accepts parties' submissions as to whether in their view a dispute existed or not. In some important recent restructuring cases, arbitral tribunals have shown a tendency to place (possibly too) much emphasis on the investor's horizon on whether a dispute existed, with the consequence of equating the existence of a dispute with the timing of the alleged breach.

The decision in *Lao Holdings v Laos* is a case in point. In this case, the claimant, a company incorporated under the laws of the Netherlands Antilles, acquired on 17 January 2012 one hundred per cent of the ownership in Macao-incorporated Sanum, which had an investment in the gambling business in the Lao People's Democratic Republic. The tribunal was tasked to decide whether the incorporation of Claimant and the acquisition of the shareholding in Sanum happened at a time when a dispute with the Lao Government over the measure alleged to constitute a violation of the BIT (the non-extension of a flat tax agreement) already existed. The Netherlands–Laos BIT contains a single exclusion clause.

The arbitral tribunal started out by noting that:

> The test for determining the critical date is objective and that the relevant question is not whether the [Respondent] subjectively believed the legal dispute to have arisen, or whether the Claimant subjectively believed it had not, the question is whether the facts, objectively analysed, establish the existence of a dispute and if so at what time did it arise, and was it resolved … before the Treaty came into force as between the [Respondent] and the Claimant?[113]

[110] *Sociedad Anónima Eduardo Vieira v Chile*, ICSID Case No ARB/04/7, Laudo Dictado (21 August 2007) para 249.

[111] *Venezuela Holdings BV, Mobil Cerro Negro Holding, Ltd, Mobil Venezolana Petróleos Holding Inc, Mobil Cerro Negro Ltd and Mobil Venezolana Petróleos Inc v Bolivarian Republic of Venezuela*, ICSID Case No ARB/07/27, Award (9 October 2014) paras 206–10.

[112] See, eg, Respondent's submission in *Pac Rim v El Savaldor* (n 60) para 2.100, highlighting this precise problem; see also *ConocoPhillips Petrozuata BV, ConocoPhillips Hamaca BV and ConocoPhillips Gulf of Paria BV v Bolivarian Republic of Venezuela*, ICSID Case No ARB/07/30, Decision on Jurisdiction (3 September 2013) para 278, where the Claimants withdrew their early protest against a measure and the tribunal thus found that there was no dispute at that early stage.

[113] *Lao Holdings v Laos* (n 56) para 124.

However, as the competent government ministry apparently left the investor in the dark in the months leading up to the final decision as to whether the flat tax agreement would be extended or not, the arbitral tribunal found that the Claimant had 'a reasonable expectation that the decision of the Minister of Finance was just a stepping stone in a longer process' and that it was only when the final decision not to grant the flat tax extension to the Claimant was adopted at the highest level that the dispute arose.[114]

So contrary to its professed allegiance to an objective test on when a dispute comes into being, the investor horizon visibly did matter for this arbitral tribunal, making this test not so objective after all. This, however, begs the question: if a dispute is 'a disagreement on a point of law or fact, a conflict of legal views or of interests between two persons',[115] if a dispute crystallizes when the points of views are expressed, confronted and positively oppose each other,[116] why should only the highest and ultimate decision-making instance, the Prime Minister's office, matter, in particular when the Ministry of Finance—a State organ capable of attribution of State responsibility—has already issued a negative decision on the issue? Does the fact that there were negotiations over many months inherently mean that there were opposing points of view?[117] Indeed, what would prolonged negotiations be good for except to try and find a solution for opposing points of view or interests? It seems arguable that *this* was the objective element for the finding of a dispute, not the (subjective) investor horizon on whether the (negative) decision of the Minister of Finance should be considered as one foreshadowing the final one by the Prime Minister.

Another point is worth noting. The fact of placing too much emphasis on the investor horizon as to the existence of a dispute visibly had the effect that the tribunal equated the final (negative) decision by the Prime Minister to extend the flat tax to the Claimant with the existence of a dispute.[118] However, by doing so, it confounded the existence of a dispute with the (alleged) breach of the investment obligation in the case of a continuous act. As has already been stated further above,[119] depending on the facts of the case, a dispute may of course arise only at the time or after the measure at issue constituting the (alleged) breach of the investment obligation has been taken, but it need not be so in all cases.

Indeed, it is submitted that in cases where there are prolonged negotiations between the investor and the host State before the latter takes the final decision constituting the measure at issue, chances are that there have been (sufficiently) opposed points of view and thus a dispute exists within the meaning of the jurisprudence both of the PCIJ/ICJ and investment arbitral tribunals before the measure is taken. This is thus what the tribunal should examine when determining the existence of a dispute.

[114] *Lao Holdings v Laos* (n 56) paras 139, 146.
[115] *Mavrommatis Palestine Concessions* (n 58) 11.
[116] *Pey Casado v Chile* (n 109) para 441.
[117] See in this sense also *ABCI Investments NV v République Tunisienne* (n 57) para 176.
[118] *Lao Holdings v Laos* (n 56) 146.
[119] See above at 6.4.2.1.

A similar analysis can be made of the tribunal's reasoning in *Pac Rim v El Salvador*. In this case, the claimant was a US-incorporated company wholly owned by the Canada-incorporated Pacific Rim Mining Corporation which claimed that its investments in El Salvador aimed at obtaining permits for mining gold and silver had been frustrated by the Salvadoran authorities. At issue was the practice of continued withholding and non-issuing of mining permits and the vague and uncertain stance of the authorities in this respect over a period stretching from as early as 2005 to March 2008 (period in which the claimant and Respondent's authorities maintained regular and increasingly conflictive communication and negotiations), when the President of El Salvador for the first time openly took a public stance against mining.

On 13 December 2007, the ownership interest in the local investments was transferred from a Cayman Islands-incorporated entity to the US-incorporated Claimant, thus making the latter in principle eligible for investment protection under the CAFTA (Dominican Republic–Central America–United States Free Trade Agreement), this in contrast to its Canadian parent company. In relevant parts, the Respondent objected to the claim both on grounds of lacking *ratione temporis* as well as on grounds of abuse of process.[120] The claimant explicitly claimed damages only for the period of March 2008 onwards, thus raising the question for the tribunal to decide whether at the time of the corporate restructuring, in December 2007, a dispute already existed (this despite the fact that CAFTA does not contain a single or double exclusion clause).

The tribunal found in relevant parts:

> The Claimant was here alleging a known opposition to its interests by the Salvadoran Government by 2005; and it had already objected to the conduct of the Salvadoran authorities as to the non-granting of new mining permits by 2007, before its change of nationality one year later.[121]

And:

> (i) before 13 December 2007, the Claimant was aware of difficulties in obtaining the permit and concession; (ii) discussions with Salavadoran authorities to resolve those difficulties extended at least until mid-2008, after President Saca's speech ... and (iv) the fact that ... no formal decision was taken by the Respondent terminating such [administrative] proceedings likewise suggests that these proceedings were still live at the beginning of 2008.[122]

It therefore found no pre-existing dispute at the time of the restructuring.[123]

One further observation is noteworthy. Though it may be accepted that the determination of a dispute cannot be completely disconnected from the (subjective) perceptions of the disputing parties, governing their actions and reactions that ultimately give rise to the dispute, laying too much emphasis on (either) party's perception of the existence of dispute makes the finding vulnerable to manoeuvrings

120 On the discussion of the abuse of process objection see Chapter 7.

121 *Pac Rim v El Salvador* (n 60) para 2.82.

122 Ibid, para 2.85.

123 Ibid, para 3.36.

and selective pleadings. Indeed, the established jurisprudence on the notion of dispute would become meaningless if it was only the (subjective) parties' perception of whether a dispute exists or not that counted in this respect. Thus, though acknowledging that there is no static formula to the notion of dispute and there remains a margin for arbitral discretion, its finding should correctly be based on as objective criteria as possible, as laid out by the jurisprudence shown above. Claimant's beliefs or expectations as to whether permits might still be granted (and government authorities' behaviour in this respect) should rather be taken into account as a question of the merits, in particular as part of the legitimate expectations under the fair and equitable treatment (FET) standard.

A similar case is *Cervin Investissements & Rhone Investissements v Costa Rica* brought under the 2000 Switzerland–Costa Rica BIT (no single or double dispute exclusion clause).[124] In this case, the owner of the claimants, a Mexican group, started to intervene with the Ministry of Economy as early as 2007 with respect to several measures affecting the distribution and retailing market of liquefied petroleum gas in Costa Rica, some of them only announced, others already taken by the time of the restructuring in March 2010. Though the Respondent pleaded the necessary elements to enable the tribunal to examine the existence of a dispute prior to the change of nationality and prior to the alleged breaches, the tribunal also equated the existence of a dispute with the alleged breaches[125] and rejected the Respondent's insistence on the conflictive chronology prior to the change of nationality, finding that:

> No hay duda de que las Demandantes sí han identificado hechos posteriores a la inversión como alegada fuente de la responsabilidad de la Demandada y que las Demandantes no han invocado conductas cometidas anteriormente ...[126]

As in *Lao Holdings v Laos* and *Pac Rim v El Salvador*, the arbitral tribunal thus also focused only on the subjective investor horizon and contented itself with the respective investor pleadings, without enquiring in a more objective manner as to whether the prior litigious context warranted the finding of a pre-existing dispute. The fact that it considered the dispute to be synonymous with the alleged breaches may indeed have clouded its view on the importance of an objective determination of when the dispute came into being.

The above shows that even though international jurisprudence has come up with tests to determine the existence of a dispute, arbitral tribunals, though sometimes invoking this jurisprudence, do not always seem to follow through in their analysis and instead often tend to mix the question of the existence of a dispute with the occurrence of the (alleged) breach of the investment obligation.[127] It has also been

[124] *Cervin Investissements SA & Rhone Investissements SA v Costa Rica* (n 73).

[125] Ibid, para 278.

[126] Ibid, paras 284–85 ('[T]here is no doubt that the Claimants have identified facts having occurred after the investment was made as alleged source of the Respondent's responsibility and that the Claimants have not invoked conduct that happened before'; translation by this author).

[127] See in this sense also *Renée Rose Levy and Gremcitel v Peru* (n 11) para 149.

seen that the more an arbitral tribunal is willing to accept the investor's horizon on the starting point of a dispute, the more likely it will equate the timing of the dispute with the timing of the (alleged) breach.

6.4.2.3.3 *Philip Morris Asia v Australia*

The most recent decision on 'time-sensitive' restructuring, *Philip Morris Asia Ltd v Australia*,[128] warrants a separate consideration of the tribunal's reasoning in view of the important public policy interests that were at stake and the main objection by Australia that the corporate restructuring undertaken by the claimant occurred at a time when a dispute already existed or was at least foreseeable.

In this case, the claimant, Philip Morris Asia Ltd, a Hong Kong-incorporated company, challenged the so-called plain packaging legislation that Australia enacted in November 2011 on the allegation that this legislation violated the intellectual property rights of the Australian Philip Morris subsidiaries (Philip Morris Australia and its wholly owned subsidiary Philip Morris Limited) under the 1993 Hong Kong–Australia BIT (no dispute exclusion clause) and therefore constituted an indirect expropriation as well as unfair treatment of its investment (ie the shareholding) into these two subsidiaries. Importantly, the claimant acquired this shareholding on 23 February 2011. The conflictive history started earlier, though. In particular, plans and public discussions on the introduction of tobacco plain packaging measures started as early as 2008/2009, the Australian Government announced its intention to introduce this legislation on 29 April 2010 and published a timetable on 7 July 2010, and the legislation was finally enacted on 21 November 2011. During this whole period, the Australian Philip Morris companies, as well as the ultimate parent Philip Morris International, opposed this planned legislation 'by stating their opposition during government consultations in 2009 and in various other communications to Australia's Health Minister and Minister for Trade, and public speeches from 2009 to 2011'.[129]

For the relevant objection by Australia that the tribunal lacked jurisdiction *ratione temporis* because of a pre-existing dispute at the time of the restructuring, the tribunal set out by confirming that the distinction 'between the *ratione temporis* objection and the abuse of rights objection' was now reasonably settled.[130]

Responding to Claimant's submission that a distinction must be made between jurisdiction *ratione temporis* and the temporal application of the substantive standards, the tribunal found that 'while correct in principle, the Tribunal is of the view that the distinction is unnecessary when the cause of action is founded upon a treaty breach.'[131] Referring to the earlier award of *Renée Rose Levy and Gremcitel v Peru*, it confirmed that tribunal's view that 'whenever the cause of action is based on a treaty breach, the test for a *ratione temporis* objection is whether a claimant made a protected investment before the moment when the alleged breach occurred.'[132]

[128] *Philip Morris Asia v Australia*, Award (n 77).

[129] *Philip Morris Asia v Australia*, UNCITRAL, PCA Case No 2012-12, Procedural Order No 8 (14 April 2014) para 40 (footnotes omitted).

[130] *Philip Morris Asia v Australia*, Award (n 77) para 527.

[131] Ibid, para 528.

[132] Ibid, para 529.

Thus turning to the question when the dispute at issue arose, the Tribunal conceded:

The date of the *dispute* is not necessarily identical to that of the alleged breach. Rather, at least as far as one-time acts are concerned, the dispute normally follows the alleged breach (it arises when an aggrieved investor 'positively opposes' the measures adopted or any claim of the other party that derives from them).[133]

It concluded that '[f]or purposes of the *ratione temporis* objection the critical date is the date when the State adopts the disputed measure, which in this case is the date of *enactment* of the TPP [Tobacco Plain Packaging] Act, as before that moment the Claimant's right could not be affected',[134] therefore confirming its jurisdiction *ratione temporis*.[135]

Long-awaited by the investment arbitration community and interested stakeholders, this award provides for a number of welcome clarifications and confirms some of the findings of the doctoral dissertation on which this book is based.[136] However, as concerns the question of jurisdiction *ratione temporis*, respectively the question whether a dispute existed before the restructuring, some of the incongruities observed further above remain. First, like former tribunals, the tribunal also based the analysis of jurisdiction *ratione temporis* on the principle of non-retroactivity. This led it, as seen above, to posit that in the case of treaty claims (ie claiming an alleged breach of an IIA), jurisdiction *ratione temporis* should be determined by reference to the moment when the alleged breach occurred, without however examining the dispute settlement clause at issue, which in the case of the Hong Kong–Australia BIT is a broad one, covering 'a dispute between an investor of one Contracting Party and the other Contracting Party concerning an investment of the former in the area of the latter'. This is presumably also why it, like several tribunals before it, equated the starting point of the dispute with the timing of the alleged breach, even though it conceded that dispute and alleged breach are not necessarily identical, but then did not really enquire into whether the dispute may have started before the alleged breach. While it is correct that in the case of a one-time act, a dispute will often follow the measure constituting the alleged breach, a dispute may also already arise before that point, and, applying jurisprudence on the notion of dispute, the question is not whether the claimant 'positively opposed' the measure at issue, but whether (and when) conflicting legal views/positions were 'positively opposed'. This, it seems arguable, was already the case by virtue of the unequivocal position of the Australian Government to introduce plain packaging legislation and the Philip Morris International Group's resistance and lobbying efforts over a period of more than a year before the restructuring.

Of course, one might argue that the dispute (if it was found to exist before the restructuring) pitted a different actor than the actual claimant against the

[133] Ibid, para 532 (emphasis in original). [134] Ibid, para 533 (emphasis in original).

[135] On the analysis by the tribunal of the foreseeability of the dispute see Chapter 7, at 7.3.1 and 7.3.2.

[136] In particular with respect to the abuse of rights objection, see Chapter 7, at 7.3.2.

Respondent, given that before the restructuring, the claimant was not a protected investor and thus not part of the conflict. While formally correct, this would seem to be an artificial argument (given that the dispute concerns in any case the same corporate group) and would reduce the first leg of the 'pre-existing/foreseeable dispute' test completely *ad absurdum*, since in that case, a pre-existing dispute would never exist for a 'restructured' claimant.

Yet, as already mentioned further above, even if an arbitral tribunal takes an undifferentiated approach towards the notion of dispute, it may still exercise the value judgment inherent in the distinction between 'legitimate nationality planning' and 'abusive treaty shopping' in the second leg of the test, namely the question of the foreseeability of the dispute, as the *Philip Morris* tribunal also did.[137]

6.4.2.3.4 Identity of disputes?

An equally important question, in particular in situations where the business relationship turns sour gradually and over a series of host State acts and measures affecting the investor, may be whether the tribunal is faced with one single (broadly framed) or two (or more) separate (thus more narrowly framed) disputes. This is as essential for determining whether a dispute existed at the time of the corporate (restructuring) as for finding whether it is the same dispute as one that existed before the change of nationality. As has been pointed out, depending on whether the tribunal frames the dispute in a broad or a narrow way, it may confirm or reject its jurisdiction, thus creating considerable legal uncertainty.[138]

Arbitral tribunals have had to determine in a number of cases (though most of them not restructuring cases) whether they were confronted with one single or two separate disputes.

In *CMS v Argentina*, the tribunal was faced with the question whether (specific) measures taken by Argentina in the wake and during the peak of the economic crisis between 2000 and 2002 and aimed at suspending the tariff adjustment formula for gas transportation, constituted one single continuing or (two) separate disputes. Setting these measures apart from the questions of general economic policy, the tribunal held:

> The argument that the background to the so-called two disputes is different is also not a deciding factor as to whether there are one or two disputes. What the Tribunal has to look at is the nature of the dispute or disputes; their background may be different but again, what counts is whether the rights of the investor have been affected or not and whether the claims arise directly out of the same subject-matter.[139]

Finding that the measures related to the same subject-matter, it confirmed its jurisdiction.

In *Lucchetti v Peru*,[140] the tribunal had to decide whether the dispute brought before it in 2003 was the same as the one that had opposed the Claimants and

[137] See Chapter 7. [138] Voon, Mitchell, and Munro, 'Legal Responses' (n 69) 49.

[139] *CMS Gas Transmission Co v Argentine Republic*, ICSID Case No ARB/01/8, Decision of the Tribunals on Objections to Jurisdiction (17 July 2003) para 111.

[140] *Lucchetti v Peru* (n 104).

the involved Peruvian municipalities already in 1997 and 1998 over Claimants' application to build a pasta factory in an environmentally sensitive area. This was important because the Peru–Chile BIT on which Claimants based their claims entered into force on 3 August 2001 and contained a clause excluding 'differences or disputes that arose prior to its entry into force'.[141] The tribunal thus found that:

> Whether the focus is on the 'real causes' of the dispute or on its 'subject-matter', it will in each instance have to determine whether or not the facts or considerations that gave rise to the earlier dispute continued to be central to the later dispute.[142]

Noting that one of the Decrees in question referred explicitly to the measures taken by the municipal authorities to force Claimants to comply with the environmental and zoning requirements,[143] it concluded that the two disputes had the 'same origin or source: the municipality's desire to ensure that its environmental policies are complied with and Claimants' efforts to block their application to the construction and production of the pasta factory',[144] thus dismissing the case.

The test established by the *Lucchetti* tribunal was also used in the *Jan de Nul v Egypt* arbitration.[145] Here, however, the tribunal set the case apart from the *Lucchetti* decision on the facts of the case, finding that though 'the previous dispute [was] one of the sources of the present dispute, if not the main one', the intervention of a new actor, the Ismailia Court, was a decisive factor for deciding that the dispute was a new dispute different from the previous one.[146]

Similarly, the tribunal in *Sociedad Anónima Eduardo Vieira v Chile* used the *Lucchetti* test in order to determine whether the dispute had arisen before the entry into force of the Chile–Spain BIT. Finding that the dispute concerned the right of the Claimant to fish in a specific zone and that this dispute arose before the entry into force of the BIT in 1994, it continued to enquire whether the present dispute before the ICSID tribunal was the same dispute as the aforementioned. It concluded that the facts that gave rise to the earlier dispute continued to be central in the present dispute, thus dismissing the case.[147]

In *African Holding Company et Société Africaine de Construction au Congo v République Démocratique du Congo*,[148] the tribunal had to decide whether the facts giving rise to the dispute occurred before the first Claimant (African Holding Company) had acquired the interest in second Claimant (Société Africaine de Construction au Congo) in 2000. This was important because of Article VII(6) of the 1984 US–Zaire BIT, which grants standing to a locally incorporated company if it is owned or controlled by nationals of the other BIT Contracting Party prior

[141] Art 2 of the 2000 Peru–Chile BIT. [142] *Lucchetti v Peru* (n 104) para 50.

[143] Ibid, para 52. [144] Ibid, para 53.

[145] *Jan de Nul NV and Dredging International NV v Arab Republic of Egypt*, ICSID Case No ARB/04/13, Decision on Jurisdiction (16 June 2006).

[146] Ibid, paras 127–28.

[147] *Sociedad Anónima Eduardo Vieira v Chile* (n 110) paras 266–303.

[148] *African Holding Company et Société Africaine de Construction au Congo v République Démocratique du Congo*, ICSID Case No ARB/05/21, Sentence sur les déclinatoires de competence et la recevabilité (29 July 2008).

to the events giving rise to the dispute. It thus had to decide whether the events occurred before 2000 or, if they occurred after that, whether there was a 'continuum' between the events or not.[149] The question raised was therefore whether the dispute concerned the payment of bills unpaid ever since the beginning or whether the dispute arose after the critical date when the State of Democratic Republic of the Congo (DRC) refused to pay.[150] The tribunal concluded that:

La nature du différend concerne le fait que des travaux ont été exécutés sous contrat et que leur coût n'a pas été réglé pendant une longue période de plus de quinze ans. Que la RDC ait officiellement refusé de payer ou ait gardé le silence, est sans importance pour la nature du différend. Le fait est que la RDC a manqué à ses obligations aux termes du contrat, ce qui se rattache donc à une situation d'inexécution envisagée à l'article 7.1.1 des Principes d'UNIDROIT. Aux termes de ce même article, l'inexécution comprend l'exécution défectueuse ou tardive. En outre, le fait que la RDC offrait de renégocier les créances et de ne payer qu'une fraction de leur valeur ne peut pas être assimilé à un refus official. Même si la RDC avait accepté de payer, et n'a en fait pas payé, la nature du différend serait toujours restée la même: avant comme après la date critique: le montant des travaux exécutés n'a pas été réglé.[151]

The majority of the tribunal thus visibly considered the (continued) non-payment of the contractual debts as the events giving rise to the dispute pursuant to Article VII(6) of the 1984 US–Zaire BIT, which happened before the American investor acquired the interest in the Congolese subsidiary.

In *Tidewater v Venezuela*,[152] the claimants complained against the seizure of their operations and assets by Venezuela in May 2009, which was preceded by a dispute over payment arrears by, and contractual negotiations with, Venezuela in 2008 and 2009 for marine support services to the oil industry in Venezuela. Having to determine whether a dispute existed at the time of the restructuring in February/March 2009, thus prior to the seizure, the tribunal adopted the test proposed by the *Lucchetti* tribunal that had found:

The critical element in determining the existence of one or two separate disputes is whether or not they concern the same subject matter … whether the focus is on the 'real causes' of the dispute or on its 'subject matter', it will in each instance have to determine whether or

[149] Ibid, para 116. [150] Ibid, para 120.

[151] Ibid, para 121 ('The nature of the dispute concerns the fact that works have been executed under contract and that their costs have not been settled for a long period of over 15 years. Whether the DRC officially refused to pay or remained silent is without importance to the nature of the dispute. Fact is that the DRC failed its contractual obligations, which can therefore be considered a situation of non-performance foreseen by Article 7.1.1 of the UNIDROIT principles. Within the meaning of this same Article, non-performance includes defective or late performance. Moreover, the fact that the DRC offered to re-negotiate the debts and to pay only a fraction of their value cannot be assimilated to an official refusal. Even if the DRC had accepted to pay, and did in fact not pay, the nature of the dispute would have stayed the same: before as after the critical date: the non-payment of executed work'; translation by this author).

[152] *Tidewater Inc, Tidewater Investment SRL, Tidewater Caribe, CA, Twenty Grand Offshore, LLC, Point Marine, LLC, Twenty Grand Marine Service, LLC, Jackson Marine, LLC and Zapata Gulf Marine Operators, LLC v Bolivarian Republic of Venezuela*, ICSID Case No ARB/10/5, Decision on Jurisdiction (8 February 2013).

not the facts or considerations that gave rise to the earlier disputes continued to be central to the later dispute.[153]

This in mind, the tribunal rejected Venezuela's contention that the contractual payment dispute was part of the expropriation dispute, attaching importance to the fact that claimants' local investment was under no contractual obligation to continue to supply services beyond the end of any contractually agreed period, that the assets of some thirty-nine service providers, thus not only claimants' investments, were seized, as well as to the fact that the Minster of Energy and Petroleum had denied that the reason for the enactment of the expropriatory legislation was the disputes with suppliers over payments.[154]

In the recent *ST-AD GmbH v Bulgaria* case,[155] the arbitral tribunal did not even (have to) use the *Lucchetti* test in order to find that the dispute a Bulgarian investor had fought through the national judicial instances without success before the German investor acquired some shares of the investment was the same as the dispute the latter investor brought again before the Bulgarian tribunals shortly after the acquisition. It held in the clearest terms that:

> A tactic based on the resubmission of an application that has been denied before a claimant becomes an investor after it has acquired such status is unacceptable. It created an illusion of an event that happened when a protected investor was on the scene ... nothing new of any relevance was presented by LIDI-R in its second application to set aside Decision 1153, when it had a German shareholder. Rather, this application can be considered ... as a 'repackaging' of the first application to set aside that same Decision 1153, rendered six years before the Claimant became an investor in Bulgaria. The Tribunal reiterates that it is not acceptable for a claimant to artificially create a new act of the State allegedly interfering with its rights by simply 'mirroring' events that occurred before it became a protected investor ... if a claimant, before coming under the protection of a given BIT, had asked for and been refused a license, it could not simply purport to create an event posterior to it becoming a protected investor by presenting the very same request for a license that would, no doubt, be similarly refused.[156]

6.4.2.4 Discussion

As can be seen from the consecutive analysis of PCIJ/ICJ and investment arbitral jurisprudence on the notion of dispute, investment arbitral tribunals seem to have indeed found inspiration in PCIJ/ICJ jurisprudence on the notion of dispute, without for that matter always explicitly quoting it. Thus, like the world courts, investment arbitral tribunals have in principle adopted an autonomous test for the notion of dispute, which aims at laying down objectifiable criteria for the question as to whether a dispute exists.

As also seen, however, in corporate restructuring claims arbitral tribunals often do not follow through with this analysis, showing a considerable degree of arbitral

[153] Ibid, para 149.
[154] Ibid, paras 190–91.
[155] *ST-AD GmbH v Bulgaria* (n 56).
[156] Ibid, paras 317, 331–32.

discretion. To which extent specificities of the IIA under interpretation (eg the exact wording of the dispute settlement clause, the explicit inclusion of the principle of non-retroactivity or of an exclusion clause) play a role in these conclusions is also not always clear. The complexity of these elements shows that the finding of a dispute necessarily remains fact-sensitive, yet creates a certain tension with respect to the claim of an 'objective' test. It seems however arguable that the more an arbitral tribunal accepts the (subjective) pleadings on claimants' perceptions as to whether a dispute exists or not (instead of enquiring in an objective way), the easier it will equate the timing of the (alleged) breach with the starting point of the dispute. Again, this need not be wrong under all circumstances, but should be kept in mind by arbitral tribunals in view of potentially important consequences in the case of restructurings, that is, the crossing of the jurisdictional hurdle.

Another point is worth noting. It is of course correct that 'a claimant bringing a claim based on a Treaty obligation must have owned or controlled the investment when that obligation was allegedly breached'.[157] Yet, this is arguably the latest possible moment in time for the acquisition of the invoked nationality without incurring a problem in terms of non-retroactivity, but does not per se mean that a dispute could not have started before this moment.

Rather, by 'pegging' the notion of dispute to the notion of the (alleged) breach, the former is divested of its autonomous significance and the ample jurisprudence on the notion of dispute becomes de facto meaningless. Though the timing of the (alleged) breach admittedly provides for a more legally secure test, equating the existence of a dispute with the (alleged) breach of an investment obligation also defeats the purpose of explicit, that is treaty-based, exclusion clauses as any strategic restructuring before the actual measure is taken would normally remain possible in terms of jurisdiction *ratione temporis*. But even in the absence of an explicit exclusion clause, equating the two notions risks blurring the jurisprudential and the treaty-based notions of dispute and leaves a sensitive time frame open to strategic restructurings.

On the question of whether to frame a dispute in a broad or a narrow way, the analysis of the jurisprudence shows that many tribunals seem intent on looking for the 'source' or the 'real cause' of the dispute in order to determine whether there is one single or several separate disputes, confirming a willingness to look more for substance than form even in cases where the treaty under interpretation does not explicitly exclude the acts or facts giving rise to a later dispute. This should however not mask the fact that the application of these tests also remains highly fact-sensitive and leaves a large margin of discretion to arbitrators, thus leading to potentially contradictory findings.[158]

[157] See *Renée Rose Levy and Gremcitel v Peru* (n 11) para 147.

[158] Similar John Gaffney, 'Jurisdiction ratione temporis of ICSID Tribunals: Lucchetti and Jan de Nul considered' (2006) 3 TDM 12: 'The ambiguity that lies at the centre of the test applied in Lucchetti is also a crucial factor in explaining why the respective Tribunals [*Jan de Nul and Lucchetti tribunals*] reached very different decisions regarding their jurisdiction ratione temporis', available at <www.transnational-dispute-management.com> (subscription required).

6.5 Preliminary Conclusions

The analysis above has shown that the temporal scope of protection is an important factor to reckon with when examining the validity of corporate restructuring claims. This is not so much because of the timing of the nationality requirement, which varies depending on the treaties concerned, but does not function as an effective bar against treaty shopping. Nor is it because of the (customary) continuous nationality requirement. Indeed, despite the *Loewen* tribunal's *dicta* to the contrary, the invoked nationality only has to be shown at the moment of the injury (*dies a quo*) and the presentation of the claim/perfection of the consent to arbitration (*dies ad quem*), but not beyond that point, and it need not be continuous properly speaking.

Rather, it is because of the central importance of the notion of dispute, in particular the question from which moment on a dispute can be said to exist and whether in a series of contentious issues, the tribunal is faced with one single (broadly framed) or two or more (narrowly framed) disputes. These questions are crucial as the existence of a (specific) dispute, according to an increasingly settled line of jurisprudence, most often sets the time limit for a strategic change of nationality.

Yet, uncertainties remain. For one, basing the exclusion of pre-existing disputes (in the absence of explicit temporal limitations) on the principle of non-retroactivity raises questions in the context of the application of the first leg of the 'pre-existing/foreseeable dispute' jurisprudence that have not been sufficiently addressed by arbitral tribunals. Second, arbitral tribunals have shown a certain lack of consistency in determining the relevant point in time for the commencement of a dispute. Indeed, despite the existence of a well-established jurisprudence of the world courts on the notion of dispute, investment arbitral tribunals have not always applied it consistently and have instead often equated the existence of a dispute with the (alleged) breach of the investment obligation, which may be correct in certain cases, but not necessarily in all cases, as restructurings typically occur in a deteriorating business climate, but before the (alleged) breach of the obligation.

To conclude, the interpretation of the notion of dispute creates considerable legal uncertainty because of the potential for manipulation and subjectivity inherent in this notion. But the notion of dispute is (indirectly) also relevant for determining whether a strategic change of nationality must be considered an abuse of rights or abuse of process, as will be seen in Chapter 7.

7

Objections on Grounds of an Abuse of Rights or Abuse of Process

7.1 Introduction

Respondents in investment treaty arbitration have in recent years increasingly invoked the abuse of rights or abuse of process doctrine in order to contest the validity of a corporate transaction that made specific investment treaties accessible to the putative investor–claimant. Arbitral tribunals were thus called upon to distil criteria or principles that would clarify the link between a claim based on a corporate structuring or restructuring and a possible *mala fide*.

This chapter will review and analyse how arbitral tribunals have tried to draw the line between 'legitimate nationality planning' and 'treaty abuse' by recourse to the abuse of rights or abuse of process doctrine.

7.2 The Abuse of Rights or Abuse of Process Doctrine

The doctrine of the prohibition of abuse of rights (or *abus de droit*) is an important particularization of the principle of good faith and is overwhelmingly accepted, by scholarship and international jurisprudence, as a general principle of law or as part of customary international law.[1] However, as such, its content remains vague and is thus in need of further concretization before it can become operational.[2]

The doctrine of prohibition of abuse of rights fulfils an important social ordering function. First, no right is a priori absolute and ever more closely interconnected legal relationships, rights, and obligations of States and persons endowed

[1] Marion Panizzon, *Good Faith in the Jurisprudence of the WTO* (Hart Publishing 2006) 30; Robert Kolb, *La Bonne Foi en Droit International Publique* (Presses Universitaires de France 2000) 463; Bin Cheng, *General Principles of Law as Applied by International Courts and Tribunals* (Stevens and Sons 1953) 121ff; Hersch Lauterpacht, *The Function of Law in the International Community* (Clarendon Press 1933) 298; Michael Byers, 'Abuse of rights: An Old Principle, A New Age' (2002) 47 McGill L J 391, 397. But see Georg Schwarzenberger and Edward D Brown, *A Manual of International Law* (Professional Books, 6th edn, 1976) 84; Steven Reinhold, 'Good Faith in International Law' (2013) 2 UCL Journal of Law and Jurisprudence 40, 52–53.

[2] Kolb, *Bonne Foi* (n 1) 463; Panizzon (n 1) 30.

with international legal personality have an increasing potential of restricting each other.[3]

Second, when a right crystallizes, law, as a means of resolving social conflicts, incorporates an inherent bias in favour of the individual interest contained in the right as opposed to the general interest of the community. In the case of an anti-social use of the right, the abuse of rights doctrine helps in readjusting the balance of countervailing interests 'as soon as policy decides that it is socially more advantageous to restrict a right in favour of an interest which henceforth becomes a legal right'.[4] This function is ever more important in a system where absent an authoritative world legislator, international law is in need of a flexible tool to adapt the law to changed conditions.[5] Its importance thus increases to the same extent as a given body of international law has not yet incorporated this balance of interest or resolution of normative conflicts.[6]

Some scholars have in the past questioned the necessity for an abuse of rights doctrine.[7] Byers however convincingly argues that it is 'supplemental to the principle of good faith' in that 'it provides the threshold at which a lack of good faith gives rise to a violation of international law, with all the attendant consequences' and that contrary to the principle of good faith, 'one need not imply malice in order to establish that an abuse has occurred'.[8] Yet, even proponents of the doctrine like Lauterpacht caution against its over-use for risk of endowing tribunals with too much power.[9] Panizzon also underlines the subsidiary character of the abuse of rights doctrine, which should only be called upon once treaty interpretation has been unsuccessful in finding the required balance of countervailing interests.[10] This establishes the abuse of rights doctrine as a legal tool of 'last resort'.

To give the doctrine of the prohibition of abuse of rights content, scholarship, and international jurisprudence have developed various categories of situations of abuses of rights.

First, a right being the legal protection of a legitimate interest, its malicious, arbitrary, or fictitious exercise, that is, for the sole purpose of causing injury to another or for the purpose of evading a rule of law or a contractual obligation, even without

[3] Kolb, *Bonne Foi* (n 1) 436–37; Cheng (n 1) 131.

[4] Lauterpacht, *Function of Law* (n 1) 296; similar Kolb, *Bonne Foi* (n 1) 438–39.

[5] Lauterpacht, *Function of Law* (n 1) 299–300; Panizzon (n 1) 32; Byers (n 1) 429.

[6] Byers (n 1) 417–18; John O'Connor, *Good Faith in International Law* (Dartsmouth 1991) 121.

[7] See, eg, Anthony D'Amato, 'Good faith' in Rudolf Bernhardt (ed), *Encyclopedia of Public International Law* (North Holland Publishing Company 1992) Vol 2, 600; Jean-David Roulet, *Le Caractère Artificiel de la Théorie de l'Abus de droit en Droit International Public* (Neuchâtel, Editions de la Baconnière 1958).

[8] Byers (n 1) 411–12.

[9] Hersch Lauterpacht, *The Development of International Law by the International Court* (Stevens and Sons 1958) 164. Similar in Robert Jennings and Arthur Watts (eds), *Oppenheim's International Law*, Vol I Peace, Parts 2 to 4 (Longman, 9th edn 1996) para 124: 'the delimitation of its function is a matter of delicacy … It may be said that it is a useful agent in the progressive development of the law, but that, as a general principle, it does not exist in positive law. Indeed, it is doubtful if it could safely be recognised as an ambulatory doctrine, since it would encourage doctrines as to the relativity of rights and result, outside the judicial forum, in instability.'

[10] Panizzon (n 1) 34; similar Byers (n 1) 421–22.

clearly violating another State's or person's right, cannot be considered as worthy of protection and is thus prohibited as an abuse of rights.[11]

Second, rights and obligations being interdependent, where the exercise of a right would impinge on an obligation assumed, that right must be exercised reasonably and in good faith. Thus, the doctrine of abuse of rights, 'while protecting the legitimate interests of the owner of the right, imposes such limitations upon the right as will render its exercise compatible with that party's treaty obligations, or, in other words, with the legitimate interests of the other contracting party'.[12]

Third, the abuse of rights doctrine also sanctions an abuse of discretion. Also known by the term 'détournement de pouvoir', it commands that 'where the right confers upon its owner a discretionary power, this must be exercised honestly, sincerely, reasonably, in conformity with the spirit of the law and with due regard to the interests of others.'[13] In particular, it protects the finality of a norm against actions that would run counter to this finality.[14]

Finally, a further concretization of the abuse of rights doctrine is sometimes undertaken for procedural aspects. According to Robert Kolb, abuse of process:

> consists of the use of procedural instruments or rights by one or more parties for purposes that are alien to those for which the procedural rights were established, especially for a fraudulent, procrastinatory or frivolous purpose, for the purpose of causing harm or obtaining an illegitimate advantage, for the purpose of reducing or removing the effectiveness of some other available process or for purposes of pure propaganda. To these situations, action with a malevolent intent or with bad faith can be added.[15]

As becomes obvious from the above categorizations, it is thus the purpose (found to go against certain social or legal 'conventions') pursued with the exercise of a specific right that may be sanctioned by the abuse of rights/abuse of process doctrine. To determine the validity of a claim based on corporate structuring or restructuring, tribunals have therefore often asked whether the (sole) purpose of the transaction was to manufacture international jurisdiction for a claim where none would otherwise exist, in which case it was a *mala fide* transaction not deserving the protection under the International Centre for Settlement of Investment Disputes (ICSID) and/or the international investment agreement (IIA).[16] This boils down to trying

[11] Cheng (n 1) 122–23; Andrew Mitchell, 'Good Faith in the WTO Dispute Settlement' (2006) 7 Melb J Intl L 339, 350; Panizzon (n 1) 31; similar Kolb, *Bonne Foi* (n 1) 468–69.

[12] Cheng (n 1) 124ff, 129; similar Alexandre Kiss, 'Abuse of Rights' *Max Planck Encyclopedia of Public International Law* (Oxford Public International Law) para 4, available at <http://opil.ouplaw.com>. But seemingly different O'Connors (n 6) 122: 'the potential value of the principle [of good faith] in reconciling the co-existence of two legal rights (*as distinct from the abuse of a legal right*)' (emphasis added).

[13] Cheng (n 1) 130; Panizzon (n 1) 31.

[14] Kolb, *Bonne Foi* (n 1) 464–65; Kiss (n 12) para 5.

[15] Robert Kolb, 'General Principles of Procedural Law' in Andreas Zimmermann, Christian Tomuschat, and Karin Oellers-Frahm (eds), *The Statute of the International Court of Justice: A Commentary* (Oxford University Press, 2nd edn 2012) 904 (para 49); similar John Gaffney, 'Abuse of Process in Investment Treaty Arbitration' (2010) 11 JWIT 515, 518.

[16] See, eg, *Phoenix Action Ltd v Czech Republic*, ICSID Case No ARB/06/5, Award (15 April 2009) para 92; *Cementownia "Nowa Huta" SA v Republic of Turkey*, ICSID Case No ARB(AF)/06/2, Award (17 September 2009) para 117; *Mobil Corporation, Venezuela Holdings BV, Mobil Cerro Negro*

to make sense of an investor's motives for the transaction in order to determine whether the latter was done in good or in bad faith. The problem is of course that motives inherently pertain to the subjective sphere, making them—in particular in the absence of a clear admission of the (real) reasons for the transaction—difficult to establish in an objective, respectively objectifiable manner.[17] Investment arbitrators encounter in this aspect arguably a similar problem as criminal judges, having to establish intent respectively intention by way of circumstantial evidence.[18]

Wary of the gravity of accusing a party of bad faith, arbitral tribunals have thus often tried to infer the motives of the corporate transaction from certain facts, in particular the timing of the transaction and the question whether it was done with respect to an existing or foreseeable dispute, as will be seen in the next section 7.3. In a few decisions, arbitral tribunals have looked at whether the former owner of an investment transferred claims or rights pertaining to the investment in order to establish jurisdiction where otherwise none would have existed (maxim of *nemo dat quod non habet*). Sometimes, several of the aforementioned arguments overlap, blurring the lines between different legal approaches. These approaches will be presented and discussed in turn.

7.3 The Timing of the Corporate Structuring or Restructuring and the Existence or Foreseeability of a Dispute

As will be seen in turn, arbitral jurisprudence has over past years focused on two salient aspects when deciding whether a corporate structuring or restructuring was an abuse of process or not: the timing of the (re)structuring, and the question whether a specific dispute existed or was foreseeable at that moment in time. While a certain refinement of treating these questions can be observed over the years, several inconsistencies remain.

As will be seen, three submissions will be particularly important: first, a distinction should necessarily be made between objections directed at the jurisdiction *ratione temporis* and those directed at abuse of process; second, the 'foreseeability doctrine' remains hardly foreseeable despite some developments in recent arbitral decisions; and third, the question whether the sole purpose of the corporate transaction was to obtain protection under an international investment scheme is in its essence nothing more than the above question of whether a specific dispute existed or was foreseeable at the time of the (re)structuring, emphasizing the particular importance of the notion of 'dispute' and its potential for subjectivity.[19]

Holding, Ltd, Mobil Venezolana de Petróleos Holdings, Inc, Mobil Cerro Negro, Ltd, and Mobil Venezolana de Petróleos, Inc v Bolivarian Republic ofVenezuela, ICSID Case No ARB/07/27, Decision on Jurisdiction (10 June 2010) paras 204–05.

[17] Similar Daniel de Andrade Levy, *L'abus de l'ordre juridique arbitral: Contributions de la doctrine de l'abus de droit à l'arbitrage international*, Thèse de doctorat (Université Panthéon Assas 2013) 476–77.

[18] See, eg, *Cassese's International Criminal Law* (revised by Antonio Cassese, Paola Gaeta, Laurel Baig, Mary Fan, Christopher Gosnell, and Alex Whiting) (Oxford University Press, 3rd edn 2013) 57.

[19] See also Chapter 6.

To this end, since the examined cases are complex and often touch upon several crucial issues, they will be presented in a first step (see section 7.3.1), while the conclusions to be drawn from the cases will be discussed in a second step (see section 7.3.2).

7.3.1 Cases

7.3.1.1 Société Générale v Dominican Republic

In this case,[20] the France-incorporated Claimant, through a complex ownership structure extending over six corporate tiers, brought claims under the 1999 France–Dominican Republic bilateral investment treaty (BIT) for damages allegedly caused to its indirect investment in the Dominican Republic by a series of acts qualifying as (direct or indirect) expropriation. The Dominican Republic objected among others that 'the acts and events complained of … preceded the date on which the investment was acquired by the Claimant as a French national'.[21]

The tribunal found that the relevant clauses of the BIT showed clearly that 'the treaty violations falling under the Tribunal's jurisdiction must have occurred after the entry into force of the Treaty and [after] the investor became its beneficiary as an eligible national of the relevant Contracting Party'.[22] It thus confirmed jurisdiction only over acts and events that took place after the Claimant acquired the investment, 'at which time the investment became protected under the Treaty to the benefit of French nationality and companies only'.[23] It found its rationale confirmed by the principle, rooted in the law of diplomatic protection subsidiarily applicable, 'that a claimant must have the nationality of the relevant Contracting Party at the time of the breach' which, according to the tribunal, remained valid unless a different rule was expressed.[24] Then, turning to the corporate structuring itself, it held:

> This finding does not mean that transfers of rights eventually giving rise to claims under a Treaty cannot take place, but questions of nationality … set a limit to the application of investment treaties to these transactions. One such limit is that the transaction in question must be a *bona fide* transaction and not devised to allow a national of a State not qualifying for protection under a treaty to obtain an inappropriate jurisdictional advantage otherwise unavailable by transferring its rights after-the-fact to a qualifying national, as occurred in *Mihaly* and *Banro*. While AES at the time did not have the benefits of any treaty protection and the Claimant in this case has such benefits as a French national under the Treaty, nothing suggests that the transaction that took place here was designed to obtain an inappropriate jurisdictional advantage.[25]

It thus confirmed its jurisdiction, though conditioned by the percentage of its indirect ownership of the investment.[26]

[20] *Société Générale in Respect of DR Energy Holdings Limited and Empresa Distribuidora de Electricidad del Este, SA ('EDE Este') v Dominican Republic*, LCIA Case No UN 7927, Award on Preliminary Objections to Jurisdiction (19 September 2008).
[21] Ibid, para 68. [22] Ibid, para 105. [23] Ibid, para 107. [24] Ibid, para 109.
[25] Ibid, para 110. [26] Ibid, para 121.

7.3.1.2 *Cementownia v Turkey*

The tribunal in the *Cementownia v Turkey*[27] case also had to look at the timing of the alleged corporate transaction and the question of whether the latter constituted an abusive attempt of treaty shopping. It found:

> The date of 12 June 2003 assumes importance in the tribunal's consideration of the claimed transaction, because that is the date on which the measures complained of culminated with the termination of the concession ... The timing of the claimed transaction is important because for any share transfers taking place after 12 June 2003, the purchaser would be deemed to be aware of the reduction in value of the shareholdings resulting from the acts of termination.[28]

Acknowledging that Claimant's avowed motive of the share transfer was to protect its interests, it held:

> This, if true, is unabashedly treaty shopping ... treaty shopping *per se* is not in principle to be disapproved of, but in some instances it has been found to be a mere artifice employed to manufacture an international dispute out of a purely domestic dispute. Given the dispute's history and the temporal aspects of the case (a mere twelve days elapsed between the claimed acquisition of shares in companies already on notice of potential termination of the concessions and the actual termination measures themselves), had the Tribunal found that the share transfer actually did occur on May 30, 2003, it would have held that this case fell within the category of an artifice. Even if they did occur, the share transfers would not have been *bona fide* transactions, but rather attempts (in the face of government measures dating back some years about to culminate in the concessions' termination) to fabricate international jurisdiction where none should exist.[29]

7.3.1.3 *Phoenix Action v Czech Republic*

Similarly, in the already discussed *Phoenix Action*[30] case, the tribunal also took issue with the timing of the corporate structuring and held that:

> According to ICSID case law, a corporation cannot modify the structure of its investment for the sole purpose of gaining access to ICSID jurisdiction, after damages have occurred. To change the structure of a company complaining of measures adopted by a State for the sole purpose of acquiring an ICSID claim that did not exist before such change cannot give birth to a protected investment.[31]

Interpreting the ordinary meaning, the context and the object and purpose of the ICSID Convention and the BIT, it inferred the applicability of '*the international principle of good faith as applied to the international arbitration mechanisms of ICSID*',[32] thus finding that it had to 'prevent an abuse of the system of international investment protection under the ICSID Convention, in ensuring that only investments that are made in compliance with the international principle of good faith and do not attempt to misuse the system are protected'.[33] It thus found that the

[27] *Cementownia v Turkey* (n 16). [28] Ibid, paras 122–23. [29] Ibid, para 117.
[30] *Phoenix Action v Czech Republic* (n 16). [31] Ibid, para 92.
[32] Ibid, para 113 (emphasis in original). [33] Ibid.

elements examined, such as the timing of the investment and the claim, the substance of the transaction, the true nature of the operation, all pointed to the 'same conclusion of an abuse of rights'.[34]

7.3.1.4 Aguas del Tunarí v Bolivia

In *Aguas del Tunarí v Bolivia*,[35] the tribunal, confronted with the objection by Bolivia that the timing of the corporate restructuring in November and December 1999 suggested that it was done in anticipation of the events that followed in spring 2000, remarked almost in passing that:

> a. the planning of a joint venture of the scale of the venture between Bechtel Enterprises Holding Inc. and Edison SpA in November-December of 1999, of which the transfer was a part, likely predated the transfer by at least several months, …
>
> c. the present record does not establish that the severity of the particular events that would erupt in the Spring of 2000 were foreseeable in November or December of 1999.[36]

Though acknowledging that treaty shopping could not be accepted in cases of abuse or fraudulent multi-jurisdictional structuring,[37] it also rejected Bolivia's contention that the December 1999 restructuring was an abusive device to assert jurisdiction under the BIT, finding that:

> c. a decision as to where to locate a joint venture is often driven by taxation considerations, although other factors such as the availability of BITs can be important to such a decision;
>
> d. it is not uncommon in practice, and – absent a particular limitation – not illegal to locate one's operations in a jurisdiction perceived to provide a beneficial regulatory and legal environment in terms, for examples, of taxation or the substantive law of the jurisdiction, including the availability of a BIT.[38]

7.3.1.5 Mobil v Venezuela

The case of *Mobil v Venezuela*[39] was the first in a row of decisions coming up with a refined approach as to the question of the timing of the corporate restructuring. The claim has to be seen against the background of the increasing resource nationalism in Venezuela that, after a period of liberalization in the 1990s, led in the years between 2001 and 2007 to the enactment of various laws (in particular the 2001 Hydrocarbons Law) and measures aimed at regulating the petroleum industry more tightly. Some of these measures included the increase of the royalty rates in October 2004, the enactment of an extraction tax of thirty-three-and-a-third per cent in May 2006, the increase of the income tax to fifty per cent in August 2006 and finally in January 2007 the announcement of the nationalization

[34] Ibid, para 143–44.
[35] *Aguas del Tunarí SA v Plurinational State of Bolivia*, ICSID Case No ARB/02/3, Decision on Respondent's Objections to Jurisdiction (21 October 2005).
[36] Ibid, para 329. [37] Ibid, paras 237, 245. [38] Ibid, para 330.
[39] *Mobil v Venezuela*, Decision on Jurisdiction (n 16).

of all projects and companies that had been operating outside the framework of the 2001 Hydrocarbons Law.[40] The two projects of the Claimants, Cerro Negro and La Ceiba, were thus nationalized and no amicable settlement was achieved.

Central to the Respondent's objection was the creation, in October 2005, of a new entity under the laws of the Netherlands, Venezuela Holdings, and its insertion into the corporate chain for the Cerro Negro and La Ceiba projects in February 2006 and November 2006 respectively. This thus inserted corporate entity became the indirect owner of the locally incorporated investments.[41]

In analysing the lawfulness of Claimants' corporate manoeuver, that is, the insertion of the Netherlands-incorporated entity into the chain of ownership of the two projects, the tribunal first examined whether Claimants qualified as protected nationals and had a protected investment under the Netherlands–Venezuela BIT, which it quickly confirmed.[42]

Turning to the objection of abuse of rights, the tribunal first took pains with couching the principle within an international law framework and giving shape to it by referring to manifold international jurisprudence, including in public international law, World Trade Organization law, European law as well as investment law.[43] Then, applying the findings to the case, it found that:

> The main, if not the sole purpose of the restructuring was to protect Mobil investments from adverse Venezuelan measures in getting access to ICSID arbitration through the Dutch-Venezuela BIT. Such restructuring could be 'legitimate corporate planning' as contended by the Claimants or an 'abuse of rights' as submitted by the Respondents. It depends upon the circumstances in which it happened.[44]

On the facts of the case, the tribunal noted that while not being contractually obliged to receive approval from the Venezuelan authorities for the planned restructuring, Mobil did not hide it and notified the Venezuelan authorities of the changed ownership structures in the Cerro Negro and La Ceiba projects on 16 October 2006 and 7 March 2007 respectively.[45] It also considered that while the lion share of the investment in the Cerro Negro Project was made between 1999–2002 and for the La Ceiba project in 2007, the fact that in the years 2005 and 2006 the investment was financed virtually without external funding was not prejudicial to a good faith finding.[46] Finally, turning to the question of the existence of a pending dispute at the time of the corporate restructuring, it found that there were pending disputes with respect to the increase of royalties and income taxes,[47] but clearly set these disputes apart from the nationalization measures taken from January 2007 onwards, holding that no such dispute existed at the time of the corporate restructuring between the parties.[48] From this finding, the tribunal concluded that:

> The aim of the restructuring of their investments in Venezuela through a Dutch holding was to protect those investments against breaches of their rights by the Venezuelan authorities by gaining access to ICSID arbitration through the BIT. The Tribunal considers that this was a perfectly legitimate goal as far as it concerned future disputes. With respect to pre-existing

[40] Ibid, para 19. [41] Ibid, paras 23–24. [42] Ibid, paras 153–65.
[43] Ibid, paras 169–85. [44] Ibid, paras 190–91. [45] Ibid, para 192.
[46] Ibid, paras 193–98. [47] Ibid, para 202. [48] Ibid, para 203.

disputes, the situation is different and the Tribunal considers that to restructure investments only in order to gain jurisdiction under a BIT for such disputes would constitute, to take the words of the *Phoenix* Tribunal, 'an abusive manipulation of the system of international investment protection under the ICSID Convention and the BITs'. The Claimants seem indeed to be conscious of this, when they state that they 'invoke ICSID jurisdiction on the basis of the consent expressed in the Treaty only for disputes arising under the Treaty for action that the Respondent took or continued to take after the restructuring was completed'.[49]

The Tribunal thus confirmed jurisdiction for 'any dispute born after 21 February 2006 for the Cerro Negro project and after 23 November 2006 for the La Ceiba project, and in particular with respect to the pending dispute relating to the nationalization of the investments'.[50]

7.3.1.6 Pac Rim v El Salvador

The basic facts to this case[51] have already been laid out in Chapter 6.[52] For the purposes of this chapter, the arbitral tribunal had to examine whether the corporate restructuring, by the claimant on 13 December 2007, constituted an abuse of process in view of the conflictive history between the parties.

On the question of abuse of process, the tribunal thus set out to examine:

whether the relevant measure(s) or practice, which (as the Claimant alleges) caused damage to its investments from March 2008 onwards, took place before or after the change in nationality on 13 December 2007. This approach in turn requires the Tribunal to ascertain the legal nature of the relevant measure(s) or practice alleged by the Claimant.[53]

Finding it had to distinguish between the President's speech in March 2008 'as the alleged culminating point of a pre-existing practice and the effective beginning of a practice causing injury to the Claimant and its Enterprises',[54] the tribunal turned to customary international law as codified in the International Law Commission (ILC) Articles on State Responsibility in order to classify the de facto mining ban of the Salvadoran authorities and infer its legal consequences.

Thus, the tribunal found that the de facto ban, necessarily comprising several acts and omissions, could not be classified as a one-time act.[55] It also rejected the classification as a composite act because it was, in its view, impossible 'to characterize the ban as a different legal animal from the several acts that comprise it'.[56] Concluding that 'an omission that extends over a period of time and which, to the reasonable understanding of the relevant party, did not seem definitive should be considered as a continuous act under international law',[57] it found the act:

started at a certain moment of time after the Claimant's request for environmental permits and an exploitation concession but before the Claimant's change of nationality in December 2007 and … continued after December 2007, being publicly acknowledged by President's

[49] Ibid, paras 204–05. [50] Ibid, para 206.

[51] *Pac Rim Cayman LLC v Republic of El Salvador*, ICSID Case No ARB/09/12, Decision on the Respondent's Jurisdictional Objections (1 June 2012).

[52] See Chapter 6, at 6.4.2.3.2. [53] *Pac Rim Cayman* (n 51), para 2.52.

[54] Ibid, para 2.61. [55] Ibid, para 2.86. [56] Ibid, para 2.88.

[57] Ibid, para 2.92.

Saca [sic] speech in March 2008; or in other words, that the alleged practice continued after the Claimant's change of nationality on 13 December 2007.[58]

With this determination, the tribunal next had to decide on the relevant point in time when a change of nationality could become an abuse of process. The parties had proposed several possible dividing lines:

(i) where facts at the root of a later dispute have already taken place and that future dispute is foreseen or reasonably foreseeable; (ii) where facts have taken place giving rise to the actual dispute; and (iii) where facts have taken place giving rise to an actual dispute referable under the parties' relevant arbitration agreement.[59]

Rejecting the third proposal as too late,[60] the tribunal went on to state that:

The dividing-line occurs when the relevant party can see an actual dispute or can foresee a specific future dispute as a very high probability and not merely as a possible controversy … before that dividing-line is reached, there will be ordinarily no abuse of process; but after that dividing-line is passed, there ordinarily will be.[61]

Importantly, the tribunal found a material difference between the relevant test for determining an abuse of process and the one for determining *ratione temporis*. As for the latter, the tribunal decided that it would have jurisdiction over that part of the continuous act that lasted after the change of nationality, regardless of events or knowledge by the Claimant of an existing or future foreseeable dispute before that date.[62] However, as for the abuse of process objection, the tribunal held that the relevant date must be necessarily earlier in time, precluding:

the exercise of such jurisdiction … if the Claimant had changed its nationality during that continuous practice knowing of an actual or specific future dispute, thus manipulating the process under CAFTA [Dominican Republic–Central American Free Trade Agreement] and the ICSID Convention in bad faith to gain unwarranted access to international arbitration.[63]

Based on this finding, the tribunal decided in a somewhat cursory manner that as the de facto mining ban had only become known to the Claimant from the public report of the President's speech in March 2008, an actual or specific future dispute with the Respondent was not known to or foreseeable by the Claimant at the time of the change of nationality, thus dismissing Respondent's objection of abuse of process.[64]

7.3.1.7 Tidewater v Venezuela

This case[65] concerned a claim brought under the 1994 Barbados–Venezuela BIT[66] with respect to a dispute concerning Claimants' investment in marine support

[58] Ibid, para 2.94. [59] Ibid, para 2.96.
[60] Ibid, para 2.99. [61] Ibid, para 2.99. [62] Ibid, para 2.104.
[63] Ibid, para 2.107. [64] Ibid, paras 2.109–10.
[65] *Tidewater Inc, Tidewater Investment SRL, Tidewater Caribe, CA, Twenty Grand Offshore, LLC, Point Marine, LLC, Twenty Grand Marine Service, LLC, Jackson Marine, LLC and Zapata Gulf Marine Operators, LLC v Bolivarian Republic of Venezuela*, ICSID Case No ARB/10/5, Decision on Jurisdiction (8 February 2013).
[66] As well as under Art 22 of Venezuela's Investment Law, whose wording did not, according to the tribunal, allow the conclusion that Venezuela had given its advance consent to submit all investment

services to the oil industry in Venezuela, arising from the enactment, on 7 May 2009, of the 'Organic Law that Reserves to the State the Assets and Services Related to Primary Activities of Hydrocarbons', which led to the seizure of Claimants' operations and assets in Venezuela.[67] Prior to the seizure of Claimants' assets, the parties were already engaged in contractual negotiations in 2008–2009 due to the Venezuelan counterpart struggling to meet its payment obligations. As relevant for the purposes of this analysis, in February 2009, a new entity was incorporated under the laws of Barbados—Tidewater Investment SRL or Tidewater Barbados—and inserted into the chain of ownership of the Tidewater corporate structure on 9 March 2009, becoming the indirect owner—through Tidewater Caribe—of the locally incorporated investment SEMARCA. Venezuela objected that the corporate restructuring in March 2009 constituted an abuse of the BIT.

Based on Article 8(1) of the BIT, which requires that there be a dispute 'between one Contracting Party and a national or company of the other Contracting Party', the tribunal started out on the premise that as Claimant could not expect to obtain protection for pre-existing disputes, the question hinged on whether at the time of the corporate restructuring, that is, in March 2009, there was a pre-existing dispute, or alternatively, whether the dispute was reasonably foreseeable.[68]

On the facts of the case, the tribunal first considered the stated reasons by Claimants of the restructuring and accepted the tax rationale as sufficient motivation alongside the wish to protect the investment from future risk of expropriation.[69] Reconfirming *Mobil* jurisprudence, it found that:

> It [was] a perfectly legitimate goal, and no abuse of an investment protection treaty regime, for an investor to seek to protect itself from the general risk of future disputes with a host state [by way of corporate restructuring].[70]

It then turned its attention to the question of whether the contractual dispute was part of the same dispute as the expropriation dispute, or alternatively, whether that latter dispute was reasonably foreseeable.

Having found that the contractual dispute was not the same as the expropriation dispute,[71] the tribunal, though acknowledging that one of the reasons for the restructuring was the wish to protect itself against the risk of nationalizations, rejected the idea that the spectre of nationalization was 'imminent' (and thus foreseeable) at the moment of the restructuring.[72] In particular, it underlined the fact that the claimants had been in this business in Venezuela for fifty years, that they continued to invest in its Venezuelan business and bid for new business with other oil companies operating in Venezuela, and that the Reserve Law had been introduced without any warning and passed into law over just three days (from 4–7 May 2009), with the seizure taking effect on the following day.[73] Neither

disputes with nationals of other ICSID Contracting States to the jurisdiction of the Center, see *Tidewater v Venezuela* (n 65) paras 73–141.

[67] Ibid, para 6. [68] Ibid, paras 143–48. [69] Ibid, para 183.
[70] Ibid, para 184. [71] Ibid, paras 190–91. See also Chapter 6, at 6.4.2.3.3.
[72] Ibid, para 194. [73] Ibid, paras 194, 196.

did the tribunal consider the seizure of the assets of an unrelated oil company in January 2009 as foreshadowing an imminent nationalization, finding that that other nationalizations 'post-dated the Claimants' decision to restructure their holding'.[74] The tribunal thus dismissed Respondent's objections and confirmed its jurisdiction over the treaty claims.

7.3.1.8 ConocoPhillips v Venezuela

This case[75] interestingly presents facts largely similar as in the *Mobil v Venezuela*[76] case. In this case, the claimants brought claims under the 1991 Netherlands–Venezuela BIT[77] against a series of measures enacted by Venezuela, in particular a royalty rate increase announced by Venezuela on 10 October 2004, a thirty-three-and-a-third per cent extraction tax enacted on 16 May 2006, an income tax increase from thirty-four to fifty per cent announced in June 2005, amended on 29 August 2006 and entered into effect on 1 January 2007, and finally the announcement of nationalizations on 8 January 2007.

Against this background, three Netherlands-incorporated entities were inserted into the ConocoPhillips corporate structure for each of the concerned oil projects. The first, ConocoPhillips Petrozuata B.V. (CPZ), concerning the Petrozuata project, was incorporated on 26 July 2005 and the relevant ownership interest transferred to it on 27 July 2005. The second, ConocoPhillips Gulf of Paria B.V. (CPG), concerning the Corocoro project, was incorporated on 26 July 2005 and the relevant ownership interest transferred to it on 11 August 2005. And the third, ConocoPhillips Hamaca B.V. (CPH), concerning the Hamaca project, was incorporated on 17 July 2006 and the relevant ownership interest transferred to it on 22 September 2006. Venezuela objected to the tribunal's jurisdiction on the basis that Claimants were 'corporations of convenience' created in anticipation of litigation for the sole purpose of gaining access to ICSID and that the thus created entities could not claim protection for measures that occurred before they qualified as protected investors under the BIT.

Discussing possible limits to 'corporations of convenience', aka mailbox companies, the tribunal reviewed prior case law and acknowledged that 'the principal reason that tribunals have given for not treating compliance with formal or technical requirements as being sufficient is to avoid the misuse of power conferred by law.'[78] The fact that corporate entities were being placed on an equal footing with States in investor–State dispute settlement was for the tribunal 'a further factor

[74] Ibid, para 195.

[75] *ConocoPhillips Petrozuata BV, ConocoPhillips Hamaca BV and ConocoPhillips Gulf of Paria BV v Bolivarian Republic of Venezuela*, ICSID Case No ARB/07/30, Decision on Jurisdiction (3 September 2013).

[76] *Mobil v Venezuela* (n 16).

[77] As well as under Art 22 of the Venezuelan Investment Law, which the tribunal again stroke down as not providing the necessary consent to arbitration, *ConocoPhillips v Venezuela* (n 75) para 262.

[78] *ConocoPhillips v Venezuela* (n 75) para 273.

supporting the growing body of decisions placing some limits on the investor's choice of corporate form, even if it complies with the relevant technical definition in the treaty text', though recognizing that the standard for finding bad faith was a high one.[79]

On the facts of the case, the tribunal first noted that 'the transfers of ownership in 2005 and 2006 did not attempt to transfer any right or claim arising under ICSID or a BIT from one owner to another',[80] thus presumably setting this case apart from decisions such as *Mihaly* and *Banro*. Indeed, ConocoPhillips had withdrawn its only claim of breach at the time of the restructuring and the first action in relation to the later dispute was undertaken by ConocoPhillips in May 2006.

The tribunal then noted that 'the only business purpose of the restructuring, as acknowledged by the Claimants' principal witness on this matter, was to be able to have access to ICSID proceedings'.[81] This, however, was not considered by the tribunal as prejudicial to the claim as 'no claim had been made at the time of the restructuring and, subject to the qualification made in respect of the claims by [ConocoPhillips Hamaca] about the two measures taken in 2006, none was in prospect at the times of the restructurings.'[82] For its finding against treaty abuse, it also attached particular importance to the fact that the Claimants continued to heavily invest into its local investments both after the enactment of the restrictive measures as after the corporate restructuring.[83]

Turning its attention to the objection *ratione temporis*, the tribunal only discussed the case of the corporate restructuring of ConocoPhillips Hamaca (finalized on 22 September 2006), examining the question of whether it had temporal jurisdiction with respect to the extraction tax and the income tax increase. Noting that it was unchallenged that Claimants could not make any claim with respect to measures taken before they acquired the relevant ownership interest, it held that ConocoPhillips Hamaca could not make any claim with respect to the extraction tax that came into force on 24 May 2006.[84] However, with respect to the income tax increase, the tribunal had to decide whether the relevant date was the one of the enactment (which was August 2006, thus before the corporate restructuring), or the entry into effect of the amendment (which was the 1 January 2007 and thus after the corporate restructuring). Arguing that a breach of an obligation could not occur until the law at issue was actually applied in breach of that obligation, the tribunal found the later date to be controlling and thus confirmed its jurisdiction *ratione temporis* with respect to the claims made by ConocoPhillips Hamaca in relation to the income tax increase.[85] The same applied also to the nationalizations announced in January 2007.

[79] Ibid, paras 274–75. [80] Ibid, para 278. [81] Ibid, para 279.
[82] Ibid. [83] Ibid, para 280. [84] Ibid, paras 287–88.
[85] This despite the fact that Art 10 of the Netherlands–Venezuela BIT contains a 'single' exclusion clause, that is, excludes disputes that have arisen before the entry into force of the BIT.

7.3.1.9 Lao Holdings v Laos

The basic facts to this case[86] are also laid out in Chapter 6. Of particular relevance to this chapter was the fact that the Respondent explicitly limited its objection to the tribunal's jurisdiction *ratione temporis* and argued that Claimant's abuse of process should be found by the tribunal 'solely for the purpose of allocating fees and costs at the end of the arbitration', not in order to dismiss the entire arbitration.[87]

As in former arbitral decisions,[88] the tribunal distinguished between an objection to jurisdiction *ratione temporis* and an objection on grounds of abuse of process in deciding whether the timing of the corporate structuring constituted a bar to its jurisdiction.

Heavily relying on the relevant parts of the *Phoenix*, *Mobil*, and *Pac Rim* decisions, it acknowledged that:

> The time frame corresponding to a finding of abuse of process is not the same as the time frame corresponding to an objection *ratione temporis*. More precisely, if a company changes its nationality in order to gain ICSID jurisdiction at a moment when things have started to deteriorate so that a dispute is highly probable, it can be considered an abuse of process, but for an objection based on *ratione temporis* to be upheld, the dispute has to have actually arisen before the critical date to conform to the general principle of non-retroactivity in the interpretation and application of international treaties.[89]

It went on to find:

> In the present case, as in *Phoenix*, it is difficult to discern any fresh economic investment arising out of the restructuring that would advance the purposes of the Treaty which, according to its preamble, exists 'to extend and intensify the economic relations between [the Parties], particularly with respect to investments by the nationals of one Contracting Party in the territory of the other Contracting Party.[90]

However, since the Respondent had not raised the abuse of process objection in relation to the entire arbitration, but only the objection to jurisdiction *ratione temporis*, the tribunal considered itself limited to examining only whether a dispute existed at the time of the structuring, instead of also examining whether a dispute was at that time also foreseeable.[91] Since the Respondent failed to adduce sufficient proof that the dispute arose before the change of nationality, the tribunal upheld its jurisdiction.

7.3.1.10 Cervin Investissements & Rhone Investissements v Costa Rica

Again, the basic facts to this case[92] are laid out in Chapter 6.[93]

86 *Lao Holdings NV v The Lao People's Democratic Republic*, ICSID Case No ARB(AF)12/6, Decision on Jurisdiction (21 February 2014).

87 Ibid, para 81.

88 Eg, *Société Générale v Dominican Republic* (n 20); *Pac Rim v El Salvador* (n 51).

89 *Lao Holdings v Laos* (n 86) para 76.

90 Ibid, para 79.

91 Ibid, para 83.

92 *Cervin Investissements SA & Rhone Investissements SA v La República de Costa Rica*, ICSID Case No ARB/13/2, Decisión sobre Jurisdicción (15 December 2014).

93 See Chapter 6, at 6.4.2.3.2.

The Respondent pleaded that the dispute concerning the alleged breaches had arisen, or at least was reasonably foreseeable, before the corporate restructuring involving the Swiss entities occurred at the end of March 2010. However, the tribunal rejected the objection *ratione temporis* as seen further above.[94] The tribunal also rejected the abuse of process objection, finding that the burden of proof lay effectively with the Respondent to prove that the restructuring was done with the sole purpose of obtaining an inappropriate procedural advantage.[95] Though admitting that the Claimants had not pleaded more precise reasons than tax and financing reasons for the restructuring, the arbitral tribunal found that they did not need to explain themselves in this aspect given the burden of proof for an abuse of process lying on the Respondent and given the fact that before obtaining protection under the Switzerland–Costa Rica BIT, the investment had already been protected under the Netherlands–Costa Rica BIT.[96] Finally, the arbitral tribunal also found that the transaction through which the restructuring took place was not done via 'fictitious or nominal payment', but that it was proven that the Claimants paid over 20 million USD for the investment.[97]

7.3.1.11 Renée Rose Levy and Gremcitel SA v Peru

In this case,[98] the claimants initiated investment arbitration under the France–Peru BIT, alleging that a '2007 resolution setting the boundaries of an archaeological site defeated the claimants' legitimate expectations to develop a tourism and real estate project ... on Peru's Pacific coast'.[99] Peru objected that the French national, Renée Rose Levy, acquired the shares at a time when a dispute already existed or alternatively a future dispute was foreseeable with a view of internationalizing it, thus constituting an abuse of process.

Having found that it had jurisdiction *ratione temporis* (by equating the moment of the alleged breach with the starting point of the dispute),[100] the arbitral tribunal set out to examine the abuse of process objection. Leaving open the question whether the abuse of process objection was a jurisdictional or an admissibility issue,[101] the tribunal reviewed the leading cases on corporate restructuring and endorsed the foreseeability test proposed by the *Pac Rim* tribunal, finding that '"a specific future dispute" must be "foresee[able] ... as a very high probability and not merely as a possible controversy"'.[102] Acknowledging that the threshold for a

[94] See Chapter 6, at 6.4.2.3.2.

[95] *Cervin Investissements & Rhone Investissements v Costa Rica* (n 92) para 292 ('La Demandada tiene la carga de probar que efectivamente, la inversión se reestructuró con el único propósito de lograr indebidamente una ventaja procesal').

[96] Ibid, paras 294–96. [97] Ibid, para 299.

[98] *Renée Rose Levy and Gremcitel SA v Republic of Peru*, ICSID Case No ARB/11/17, Award (9 January 2015).

[99] Clovis Trevino, 'Arbitrators toss out ICSID claim against Peru due to abusive restructuring of investment' *IA Reporter* (18 January 2015) available at <http://www.iareporter.com> (subscription required).

[100] *Renée Rose Levy and Gremcitel v Peru* (n 98) para 161.

[101] Ibid, para 181. [102] Ibid, para 185.

finding of abuse of process was high, it reasoned that 'the closer the acquisition of the investment is to the act giving rise to the dispute, the higher the degree of foreseeability will normally be'.[103]

With this in mind, it found that 'it [was] clear that the Claimants could foresee that the 2007 Resolution was forthcoming'.[104] Though a report issued in 2005 by a Historical Commission, on which the land delimitation through the 2007 Resolution was largely based, was never officially communicated to the Claimants, relevant witnesses for the Claimants admitted to knowing that 'the Historical Commission had been created "at the end of 2004"' and that one of them—acting on behalf of Gremcitel—'had seen the Historical Commission's Report shortly after it was issued'.[105] Moreover, the tribunal was convinced that this person acting on behalf of Gremcitel learned sometime in 2007 that the office in charge 'was about to formalize the land delimitation and, in the ordinary course of events must have informed the Levys accordingly'.[106] Noting that the 'claimants were unable to furnish any reasonable explanation' as to the transfer of shares, it concluded that 'the only purpose of the transfer was to obtain access to ICSID/BIT arbitration, which was otherwise precluded' and that thus 'the Levys could foresee the 2007 Resolution as a very high probability when Ms. Levy was inserted into Gremcitel's ownership'.[107] It therefore dismissed the claim on grounds of an abuse of process.

7.3.1.12 Philip Morris Asia v Australia

The basic facts of this case[108] are laid out in Chapter 6.[109] As a reminder, Australia objected that the corporate restructuring on 23 February 2011 occurred at a time when the dispute already existed or, alternatively, was foreseeable for the claimant, thus constituting an abuse of rights.

The tribunal having found that a dispute did not exist at the time of the restructuring,[110] it turned to the question whether the Claimant's invocation of the treaty constituted an abuse of rights.

As preliminary underpinning, the tribunal confirmed that:

> The threshold for finding an abusive initiation of an investment claim is high. It is equally accepted that the notion of abuse does not imply a showing of bad faith. Under the case law, the abuse is subject to an objective test and is seen in the fact that an investor who is not protected by an investment treaty restructures its investment in such as fashion as to fall within the scope of protection of a treaty in view of a specific foreseeable dispute. Although it is sometimes said that an abuse of right might also exist in the case of restructuring in respect of an existing dispute, if the dispute already exists, then a tribunal would normally lack jurisdiction *ratione temporis*.[111]

[103] Ibid, para 187. [104] Ibid, para 189. [105] Ibid. [106] Ibid, para 190.
[107] Ibid, para 191.
[108] *Philip Morris Asia Limited v Commonwealth of Australia*, UNCITRAL, PCA Case No 2012-12, Award on Jurisdiction and Admissibility (17 December 2015) (redacted version).
[109] See Chapter 6, at 6.4.2.3.3. [110] *Philip Morris Asia v Australia* (n 108) para 534.
[111] Ibid, para 539.

Reviewing prior jurisprudence and comparing their reasonings, it found:

Case law has articulated legal tests on abuse of right that are broadly analogous, revolving around the concept of foreseeability. In the tribunal's view, foreseeability rests between the two extremes posited by the tribunal in *Pac Rim v El Salvador*—'a very high probability and not merely a possible controversy' … the initiation of a treaty-based investor-State arbitration constitutes an abuse of rights (or abuse of process, the rights abused being procedural in nature) when an investor has changed its corporate structure to gain the protection of an investment treaty at a point in time when a specific dispute was foreseeable … a dispute is foreseeable when there is a reasonable prospect, as stated by the *Tidewater* tribunal, that a measure which may give rise to a treaty claim will materialize …[112]

Applying this test to the facts of the case, the tribunal reviewed the conflictive history and found that:

As early as 2009, it had informed the Australian Government that plain packaging would interfere with its property rights, and its internal memoranda made it clear that it was considering the matter in legal terms. On 29 April 2010, Australia's Prime Minister Rudd and Health Minister Roxon unequivocally announced the Government's intention to introduce Plain Packaging Measures. In the Tribunal's view, there was no uncertainty about the Government's intention to introduce plain packaging as of that point. Accordingly, there was at least a reasonable prospect that legislation equivalent to the Plain Packaging Measures would eventually be enacted, which would trigger a dispute. The Tribunal is not convinced that political developments after 29 April 2010 were such that the Claimant could reasonably conclude that the enactment of Plain Packaging Measures and the ensuing dispute were no longer foreseeable.[113]

As a matter of general comment, the tribunal also observed that 'the length of time it takes to legislate is not a decisive factor in determining whether the legislation is foreseeable',[114] and that 'in April 2010, long before the restructuring, the Australian Government announced it would introduce Plain Packaging Measures and never withdrew from that position even though political leaders changed and the Government became a minority government'.[115] It thus concluded that at the time of the restructuring, the dispute that materialized subsequently was 'reasonably foreseeable'.[116]

Interestingly, however, the tribunal did not stop there. Rather, it went on to enquire at length into Claimant's alleged other reasons for the restructuring, showing its inclination to acknowledge in principle that a legitimate and credible reason for the restructuring could invalidate an otherwise abuse of rights finding. Thus, the tribunal found that:

It would not normally be an abuse of right to bring a BIT claim in the wake of a corporate restructuring, if the restructuring was justified independently of the possibility of bringing such a claim. The Tribunal acknowledges the reality that corporate groups—and particularly multinationals—are routinely restructured for a variety of reasons.[117]

[112] Ibid, para 554.
[113] Ibid, para 566.
[114] Ibid, para 567.
[115] Ibid, para 568.
[116] Ibid, para 569.
[117] Ibid, para 570.

However, after thorough examination, it concluded that it was 'not persuaded that tax or other business reasons were determinative factors for the Claimant's restructuring'.[118] It based this conclusion on the fact that 'no witness who was familiar with the rationale of the restructuring was presented by the Claimant in the proceedings' and that the Tribunal was not presented 'with contemporaneous corporate memoranda or other internal correspondence sufficiently explaining the business case for the restructuring in detail',[119] thereby essentially dismissing these arguments on grounds of lack of proof. It concluded that 'the main and determinative, if not sole, reason for the restructuring was the intention to bring a claim under the Treaty, using an entity from Hong Kong'.[120]

7.3.2 Discussion

7.3.2.1 Distinction between jurisdiction ratione temporis *and abuse of process*

As can be seen from the reviewed cases, in corporate structuring or restructuring cases, the necessity to distinguish between objections directed at the tribunal's jurisdiction *ratione temporis* and objections on grounds of abuse of rights or abuse of process can by now be considered as reasonably settled,[121] and rightfully so. However, not all decisions were as explicit and methodological in making this distinction (and elaborating on its consequences) as were the ones in *Société Générale, Pac Rim* and in *Lao Holdings*. For example the decision in *Mobil v Venezuela*, though influential for subsequent decisions in its distinction as to whether the restructuring occurred with respect to pre-existing or future disputes, failed to elaborate on this distinction, even though it must have implicitly made it. The same can be said of the decisions in *Tidewater* and *ConocoPhillips*.

Beyond this fairly straightforward distinction, an important submission can be made based on the *Pac Rim* and *Lao Holdings* tribunals' findings with respect to where the dividing line between an objection to jurisdiction *ratione temporis* and an abuse of process objection lies. While the *Pac Rim* tribunal considered that it 'would have jurisdiction *ratione temporis* over that portion of the continuous act that lasted after that date', that is, the change of nationality, regardless of events or knowledge by the investor of an existing or future foreseeable dispute, it considered that the change of nationality 'knowing of an actual or specific future dispute' would constitute an abuse of process.[122] The *Lao Holdings* tribunal, on the other hand, distinguished jurisdiction *ratione temporis* and abuse of rights/abuse of process depending on whether there was an existing dispute at the time of the change of nationality, in which case jurisdiction *ratione temporis* would not be engaged, while if there was a future foreseeable dispute, the change of nationality would constitute an abuse of process.

Two conclusions can be drawn from the aforesaid.

[118] Ibid, para 582. [119] Ibid. [120] Ibid, para 584.
[121] See in this sense now also *Philip Morris Asia v Australia* (n 108) para 527.
[122] *Pac Rim v El Salvador* (n 51) paras 2.104, 2.107.

First, it would seem that the question of jurisdiction *ratione temporis* is a purely factual one, independent of any subjective factors pertaining to the investor horizon such as knowledge of an actual or presaging of a future dispute. The question is thus solely whether at the time of the change of nationality, a dispute existed, and in the case of a gradually souring business relation whether it is the same as a former one (though as seen in Chapter 6, even so there remains enough potential for subjectivity in the notion of dispute).

Second, for a change of nationality to be considered an abuse of process, in contrast to jurisdiction *ratione temporis*, the investor horizon is primordial and translates, as seen above, into the question whether the investor was aware of an actual or could foresee a future dispute at the time of the strategic change of nationality.[123] This is so because in order to determine an abuse of rights/abuse of process, the purpose pursued with the exercise of the right is crucial, as has been seen in this chapter. The purpose being 'hidden' in motives, this subjective element needs 'objectification' in order to become workable for arbitral tribunals. This is how the investor horizon, that is, the awareness of an existing or foreseeable dispute, comes into the equation. And how to objectify an investor's awareness of an existing or a foreseeable dispute? By recourse to (objective) timing elements and other similarly objectifiable facts.

However, where the *Lao Holdings* reasoning wins in its logic over the *Pac Rim* reasoning is with respect to the existence of an actual dispute and the abuse of process objection. Indeed, if at the time of the change of nationality an actual dispute existed, jurisdiction *ratione temporis* is not established, independently of whether the investor knew or did not know of an actual dispute. In this case, thus, the arbitral tribunal does not need to enquire further into whether an abuse of rights or abuse of process could be established, also given the subsidiary nature of the abuse of rights/abuse of process doctrine.[124] This distinction has also not been made in the *Phoenix Action v Czech Republic* award.[125]

From this follows that the abuse of rights/abuse of process objection is really only relevant for the question whether a future dispute was foreseeable or not, but not for the question whether a dispute existed at the time of change of nationality. This is also why the *Pac Rim* tribunal should have examined first whether there was an existing dispute at the time of the corporate restructuring, and only in case it did not find an existing dispute, further enquire into whether a future dispute was foreseeable, but not vice versa.[126] This is so because of the distinction between objections directed at the jurisdiction of the tribunal and those directed at the admissibility of the claim, with jurisdiction preceding the admissibility of the claim.[127] Tribunals' approaches

[123] Similar Tania Voon, Andrew Mitchell, and James Munro, 'Legal Responses to Corporate Manoeuvering in International Investment Arbitration' (2014) 5 JIDS 41, 47.

[124] Panizzon (n 1) 34; Byers (n 1) 421–22; Lauterpacht, *Development of International Law* (n 9) 164.

[125] *Phoenix Action v Czech Republic* (n 16) paras 67–68, 113.

[126] The same applies to the *ConocoPhillips* decision (n 75), which did however not enquire into the foreseeability of a future dispute.

[127] Eric De Brabandere, '"Good Faith", "Abuse of Process" and the Initiation of Investment Treaty Claims' (2012) 3 JIDS 609, 613.

have in this respect not always been coherent as to whether an objection on grounds of abuse of rights or abuse of process should be treated as a question of jurisdiction of the tribunal or of the admissibility of the claim.[128]

Based on this conclusion, it becomes apparent that though influential for the development of the distinction between an existing and a future foreseeable dispute, the decision in *Mobil v Venezuela* may be criticized, not only because it considered that the change of nationality in case of an existing dispute constituted an abuse of rights, but also for its lack of enquiring into whether a future dispute was foreseeable.[129]

Similarly, the tribunal in *Société Générale*, though visibly aware of the potential of manipulation of restructuring, after finding no actual dispute at the time of the change of nationality, contented itself with stating, absent any closer analysis, that nothing *suggested* that 'the transaction that took place ... was designed to obtain an inappropriate jurisdictional advantage'.[130] Interestingly, the very early decision of *Aguas del Tunarí* did briefly consider the foreseeability of the dispute with respect to an abuse of process objection, but quickly disposed of it without any in-depth discussion.[131]

The above findings lead to a further observation. As can be seen from the *Lao Holdings* decision, the distinction between jurisdiction *ratione temporis* and abuse of rights/abuse of process objections may have important consequences depending on how these objections are phrased and presented. Thus, the Respondent having failed to extend the abuse of process objection to the dismissal of the entire arbitration (instead of only concerning the costs finding), the arbitral tribunal considered itself barred from examining the more far-reaching question of whether a future dispute was foreseeable at the time of the restructuring.[132] Respondents will thus be well advised to raise the abuse of process objection with respect to the entire arbitration, even though this is no guarantee that the tribunal will effectively treat this objection, as can be seen from the *ConocoPhillips* decision where the Respondent had raised the abuse of process objection with respect to the entire arbitration,[133] yet the tribunal completely failed to examine the foreseeability of disputes with respect to the different measures at issue.

The same can be said of the *Cervin Investissements & Rhone Investissements* decision where the Respondent also raised the abuse of process objection, yet the tribunal only focused its attention on the 'sole purpose' doctrine and failed to examine the foreseeability of the dispute. This was visibly the case because the tribunal gave the

[128] De Brabandere (n 127) 617; Gaffney, 'Abuse of Process' (n 15) 531–32. See also *Alapli Elektrik BV v Republic of Turkey*, ICSID Case No ARB/08/13, Decision on Annulment (10 July 2014) paras 224–27. See also the discussion in Chapter 9, at 9.4.4.

[129] *Mobil v Venezuela* (n 16) paras 190–91, 204–05.

[130] *Société Générale v Dominican Republic* (n 20) para 110.

[131] *Aguas del Tunarí v Bolivia* (n 35) paras 329–30.

[132] *Lao Holdings v Laos* (n 86) para 83.

[133] *ConocoPhillips v Venezuela* (n 75) para 216: 'Claimants CPZ, CPH and CGP are merely corporations or convenience created for the purpose of obtaining ICSID jurisdiction in this case in an abuse of the corporate form and therefore jurisdiction under the Dutch Treaty should be rejected'.

Claimants credit for the fact that even before the restructuring, the Costa Rican investment was protected through Dutch entities under the Netherlands–Costa Rica BIT and that the Respondent had not alleged that this latter BIT was more favourable. However, in this author's opinion, this argument misses the point. Indeed, even if it is true that the Dutch investors *could* have brought an investment claim under the Netherlands–Costa Rica BIT, this does not free the arbitral tribunal from its task of examining its jurisdiction *under the BIT under which the claim was brought*, in this case merely and solely the Switzerland–Costa Rica BIT. By adhering to the 'sole purpose' doctrine, the tribunal thus substituted legal for policy arguments.

7.3.2.2 The existence of an actual dispute and the foreseeability of a future dispute

The aforesaid confirms that the question of whether an actual dispute exists or whether a future dispute was foreseeable at the time of the change of nationality takes on a primordial importance.[134]

It has already been seen in Chapter 6 that the determination of the existence of a dispute is saddled with a relatively big amount of subjectivity.[135] This uncertainty is compounded in international investment arbitration by differing tests developed by arbitral tribunals as to when a future dispute is foreseeable.

Thus, the decision in *Pac Rim* leaves one wondering why a dispute was only found to exist with the public acknowledgment of the de facto mining ban by the Salvadoran President even though the difficulties in obtaining mining permits and exchanges in this respect with the authorities had been ongoing for three years. This seems to be due to the fact that the tribunal qualified the measure at issue, the de facto mining ban, as a continuous act in accordance with Article 14(2) of the ILC, which provides that 'the breach of an international obligation by an act of a State having a continuous character extends over the entire period during which the act continues and remains not in conformity with the international obligation', and found that the dispute only started to exist with the public acknowledgment, that is, the (alleged) breach of the obligation.

This, however, confounds the closely related, yet still separate questions of when a continuous act has been completed (respectively when the breach of the obligation started and when it ended) and when the dispute has arisen.[136] Indeed, as has already been pointed out in Chapter 6, a dispute may, but need not necessarily arise with the (alleged) breach of an obligation only. Often it arises already prior to that point, in particular when a government has announced certain prejudicial measures and the investor has started to undertake action, short of investment arbitration, to

[134] Similar Utku Topcan, 'Abuse of the Right to Access ICSID Arbitration' (2014) 29 ICSID Review-FILJ 1, 20.

[135] Similar Christoph Schreuer, 'Nationality Planning' in Arthur W Rovine (ed), *Contemporary Issues in International Arbitration and Mediation: The Fordham Papers 2012* (Martinus Nijhoff 2013) 17, 26.

[136] Similar Florian Franke, *Der personelle Anwendungsbereich des internationalen Investitionsschutzrechts* (Nomos 2012) 289, though it cannot be adhered to that author's view that the question of when a dispute exists depends solely on the investor's (subjective) sphere, ibid.

preserve his interests. Whether the arbitral tribunal in *Pac Rim* equated the existence of a dispute with the (alleged) breach of the obligation consciously in view of the wording used in Article 10.16(1)(a)(i) CAFTA is unclear. Arbitral tribunals have in any case shown themselves, if not unaware of, then at the very least often imprudent in handling these different time tests, seemingly using them synonymously where they are not synonymous.[137]

Applying the various tests distilled from PCIJ, ICJ, and investment arbitral jurisprudence on the notion of 'dispute', which find a dispute to exist in particular when a disagreement over a point of law or of fact has formed and parties have expressed clearly and positively opposite views, the fact that Claimant was aware of 'a known opposition to its interests by the Salvadoran Government by 2005 … [and that] it had already objected to the conduct of the Salvadoran authorities as to the non-granting of new mining permits by 2007',[138] should at least have induced the tribunal to a critical analysis of this question. If it can be accepted that the President's speech in March 2008 was the culminating point of the disputed practice, this does by no means signify that the dispute only started at this point (in particular in view of aforementioned established jurisprudence on the notion of 'dispute').

Yet, even if one took this view, a necessary follow-up question should have been whether the acts and omissions that occurred before December 2007 were part of the same or a different dispute, for which jurisprudence has mostly looked at the 'source' or 'real cause' of the dispute. Again, it seems that to reject the 'source' or 'real cause' to lie in the acts prior to December 2007 would at least have necessitated a discussion.

The decision in *Tidewater* confirms the risk of subjectivity inherent in determining the existence of a dispute. It will be remembered that that tribunal held that the payment dispute was not the same as the expropriation dispute. Applying the *Lucchetti* test as the tribunal did, thus searching for whether the 'facts or considerations that gave rise to the earlier dispute continued to be central in the later dispute',[139] one could however have argued that the 'real' cause of the payment dispute was not only about continuity of service, but *also* about the payment arrears and the related demands by Venezuela to negotiate the debts. This seems even more so as Claimant continuously reaffirmed its will to continue performing its services, but under the condition of payment of the arrears. Now, as transpires quite clearly from various parts of the decision, Venezuela's concern was to force the foreign oil companies to agree to considerably lower rates. Thus, the Minister of Energy and Petroleum stated on 6 March 2009 that 'the Executive will not permit the oil industry to be paralyzed', that PDVSA [the competent Venezuelan petroleum authority] 'was in the process of revising all [of its] cost and expense structures', and that the 'amount of debt that PDVSA would pay those contractors [depended] on negotiations'.[140] Later in May 2009, President Hugo Chávez was reported as saying that the expropriations would save USD 700 million per year.[141] The Minister of

[137] See also in the decision *ConocoPhillips* (n 75).
[138] *Pac Rim v El Salvador* (n 51) para 2.82.
[139] Ibid, para 149.
[140] Ibid, para 167.
[141] Ibid, para 174.

Energy and Petroleum also admitted on 9 May 2009 that the 'expropriations were driven by the concern that the service companies might remove their vessels from Venezuela',[142] as had already happened earlier in response to the non-payment of arrears.[143] So by asking for the real cause of the dispute and framing the question in a slightly different way, it seems arguable that the real cause of the expropriation dispute lay (also) in the payment disputes (which did not only concern Claimant) and that thus the facts relative to the payment dispute continued to be central to the expropriation dispute.[144]

Finally, the decision in *ConocoPhillips* also uncovers the immense potential for uncertainty and subjectivity that exists when it is not clear which relevant point of time is to be used for judging the validity of the change of nationality and when moreover different tests are used quasi-synonymously. While the tribunal considered for two of the three claimants as relevant that at the time of the change of nationality, 'no claim had been made' (in particular because the only claim had been withdrawn in time by the visibly well-advised claimant),[145] it found for the third claimant that the (alleged) breach of the obligation was the relevant time test, leading it to conclude that the corporate restructuring claim had to be judged not by the date of the enactment of the income tax increase law, one month before the change of nationality, but only by its entry into force, subsequent to the change of nationality.[146]

As for the foreseeability of future disputes, four different arbitral tribunals have produced four slightly differing foreseeability tests, which is particularly surprising given that one of the arbitrators sat in all of these arbitrations. Thus, while the *Pac Rim* tribunal asked whether a future dispute was 'foreseeable as a very high probability and not merely as a possible controversy',[147] the tribunal in *Tidewater* enquired whether a future dispute was 'reasonably foreseeable'.[148] The *Lao Holdings* tribunal, though ultimately not engaging in the foreseeability test, asked whether 'a dispute [was] highly probable'.[149] In the *Alapli* award, on the other hand, the test was whether, at the time of the restructuring, 'the relevant party can see an actual dispute or can foresee a specific future dispute as a high probability and not merely as a general future controversy.'[150]

Though the tests produced by the *Pac Rim, Lao Holdings*, and *Alapli* tribunals are admittedly very similar (yet may still leave room for diverging interpretations), the test developed by the *Tidewater* tribunal stands out as the more objective one.

[142] Ibid. [143] Ibid, para 158.

[144] Similar Voon, Mitchell, and Munro, 'Legal Responses' (n 123) 50–51. This submission is even without prejudice to the double exclusion clause contained in Art I of the Barbados–Venezuela BIT which excludes 'disputes arising from acts or occurrences which have taken place before [the] entry into force [of the BIT]', which the tribunal seemingly has not examined (or if it has, it has not mentioned it in the decision).

[145] *ConocoPhillips v Venezuela* (n 75) para 279. [146] Ibid, para 289.

[147] *Pac Rim v El Salvador* (n 51) para 2.99. This test was also endorsed by the tribunal in *Renée Rose Levy and Gremcitel v Peru* (n 98) para 185.

[148] *Tidewater v Venezuela* (n 65) para 193. [149] *Lao Holdings v Laos* (n 86) para 76.

[150] *Alapli Elektrik BV v Turkey*, Decision on Annulment (n 128) para 225; *Alapli Elektrik BV v Republic of Turkey*, ICSID Case No ARB/08/13, Award (16 July 2012) para 403.

Indeed, to ask whether the investor could foresee a future dispute as a (very) high probability arguably places too much emphasis on the investor horizon and lacks an objective element that may be needed as a corrective to avoid abuse. It clearly seems too easy for an investor to contend that in spite of continuing problems in the business relationship, he never thought of a future specific dispute as very likely ... An objectifying element thus lies in the 'reasonably foreseeable' test, which does not make the foreseeability judgment entirely dependent on the investor horizon, but introduces the assessment of whether a *reasonable* investor would have been able to foresee a future dispute.

However, even the application of the 'reasonably foreseeable dispute' test does not eliminate all unpredictability as to which conclusion the arbitral tribunal will come to in this respect.

Already with respect to the *Tidewater* decision, some doubts seem arguably justified. In a general macroeconomic and socio-political setting like Venezuela's prevailing in the years from 2004 onwards, can it be argued that a reasonable investor could (or should) not have foreseen the increasing clamp-down on foreign oil multinationals and impending nationalizations? Shouldn't any foreign investor operating in the oil business in Venezuela have been increasingly alarmed by the series of royalty rate and income tax increases and the nationalizations implemented from 2004 on? Indeed, they certainly were, as attests the wish for 'risk mitigation' which Claimants openly admitted among a tax rationale. This, of course, does not necessarily nor automatically mean that a *specific* future dispute was always already foreseeable. However, depending on the circumstances of the case, it seems to this author that the fact of other nationalizations in the oil industry (though touching other investors) already having occurred should not be completely devoid of importance for a finding of whether a future dispute was *reasonably*, thus not only from the purely subjective investor horizon, foreseeable. Indeed, the general awareness of the increasing government clampdown on foreign investments was such that the *Forbes* magazine published on 30 January 2009 (thus three months before the nationalizations) an article, warning of a 'natural progression of asset nationalization' in Venezuela.[151]

This doubt seems even greater in the case of the *ConocoPhillips* decision where several of the contentious measures were announced before the change of nationality, yet any discussion as to whether these future disputes were foreseeable is blatantly absent. Indeed, the income tax increase was announced in June 2005, thus one respectively two months *before* the corporate restructuring of ConocoPhillips Petrozuata and ConocoPhillips Gulf of Paria, and more than a year before the corporate restructuring of ConocoPhillips Hamaca. Under such circumstances, one cannot help but wonder why the tribunal did not at least raise the question whether this timing sequence did not make a specific future dispute sufficiently foreseeable (under whichever foreseeability test). For the tribunal, the situation with respect to ConocoPhillips Petrozuata and ConocoPhillips Gulf of Paria—surprisingly—seems

[151] *Tidewater v Venezuela* (n 65) para 158.

to have been so clear as to not even necessitate a separate mention in the analysis. However, if a concrete measure that is going to give rise to a later specific claim is announced by the government before the corporate restructuring takes place, shouldn't this, at least according to the foreseeability standards established in *Pac Rim* and *Tidewater*, automatically raise the question whether the dispute was foreseeable or not? A fortiori, does not the fact that the income tax increase was already enacted, though not yet in force at the time of the restructuring, make a future dispute *ex post facto* even more foreseeable if this is exactly what the investor will challenge after the restructuring? The tribunal is admittedly right in saying that a breach of an obligation can only happen once the law breaching it is in force. However, as already pointed out, these are two separate questions, and even more so when the question is aimed at the foreseeability of a specific future dispute.

Interestingly, the tribunal in *Renée Rose Levy and Gremcitel v Peru* was the first one in actually confirming the foreseeability of a future dispute and thus tossing out a claim on grounds of an abuse of process. This is particularly surprising as it adhered, following the *Pac Rim* tribunal, to the very restrictive foreseeability test, though, as it turns out, ended up setting a higher bar to the investor horizon as to a possible unforeseeability of a future dispute, not letting suffice meager explanations by the claimants and memory gaps of key witnesses ('I don't recall. It is *likely*, it is *probable*, but I don't recall').[152] This seems to indicate that the arbitral tribunal was aware that it had to be particularly attentive in incorporating the value judgment with respect to the change of nationality in the foreseeability test (even more so since, as seen in Chapter 6, it had equated the starting point of the dispute with the (alleged) breach). A similar conclusion can be drawn in the *Philip Morris Asia v Australia* case. Though that arbitral tribunal also (rather summarily) equated the timing of the (alleged) breach with the starting point of the dispute, it adopted the here favoured 'reasonably foreseeable' test, thereby injecting an objectifying element into the analysis that led to the dismissal of the case. If the foreseeability test is to become a functional tool in making the abuse of process doctrine operational in the question of the admissibility of corporate restructuring claims, this can only be welcomed.

A further observation seems noteworthy. As has by now become sufficiently clear, the question of whether a dispute existed or was foreseeable at the time of the restructuring is a concretization of the value judgment inherent in the distinction between 'legitimate nationality planning' and 'abusive treaty shopping', in other words, of the good faith in bringing the particular claim. As will also be examined more in detail in Chapter 9, this value judgment may be exercised in different ways when making this distinction. In particular for the notion of dispute and its foreseeability, *Philip Morris Asia v Australia* shows well that, giving due consideration to the conflictive history and existing jurisprudence on the notion of dispute, the tribunal could have already found the existence of a dispute before the restructuring,

[152] *Renée Rose Levy and Gremcitel v Peru* (n 98) para 189 (emphasis in original).

but that, in the absence of such finding, it still came to the (in this author's opinion) correct conclusion by virtue of adopting the 'reasonably foreseeable' test.

7.3.2.3 The 'sole purpose' doctrine

As has been seen in this chapter, in particular earlier tribunals, in trying to decide whether a change of nationality was abusive or not, have shown a tendency to ask whether the 'sole purpose' of the transaction was to gain access to ICSID jurisdiction where none would otherwise exist.[153] It almost seemed as though it would be enough for the investor–claimant to invoke additional reasons, such as tax or other corporate reasons, to dispel any doubts as to the validity of the restructuring.[154] The difficulty with focusing too much on whether the 'sole purpose' of the transaction was to gain access to investment arbitration is obvious and has already been mentioned further above: the motives of a corporate restructuring pertain inherently to the investor's horizon and are thus difficult to establish in the absence of objective criteria permitting the affirmation of bad faith.

It seems therefore commendable, as the *ConocoPhillips* tribunal has implicitly done, to lay the 'sole purpose' test to rest. By way of reminder, in that decision, the tribunal found that even though the fact of gaining access to ICSID jurisdiction was the avowed and single purpose of the restructuring, the tribunal's only concern was to examine whether at the time of the restructuring, claims were made or in prospect.[155]

Unfortunately, however, it was 'resurrected' by the tribunal in *Cervin Investissements & Rhone Investissements*. That tribunal accepted tax and financing reasons as sufficient explanation for the restructuring visibly in view of the fact that even before the restructuring, there was investment protection under the Netherlands–Costa Rica BIT. Yet, as pointed out further above, in doing so the tribunal let prevail a policy argument over what should have been a factual determination as to whether the dispute was (sufficiently) foreseeable.

A shift from asking for the purpose of the change of nationality to whether a dispute existed (or was foreseeable at the time of the restructuring) has the advantage of circumventing the highly subjective question of motivations, without of course eliminating altogether the risk of subjective decisions pertaining to the notion of dispute and its foreseeability, as seen further above. The tribunal's approach in *Philip Morris Asia v Australia* towards the admissibility of the corporate restructuring claim, on the other hand, does correctly acknowledge that any abuse of rights finding remains based on a case-by-case examination.[156] This must not be reason for concern as long as the adjudging tribunal maintains a high threshold for

[153] See, eg, *Phoenix Action v Czech Republic* (n 16) para 92; *Cementownia v Turkey* (n 16) para 117.

[154] See, eg, *Autopista Concesionada de Venezuela CA (Aucoven) v Bolivarian Republic of Venezuela*, ICSID Case No ARB/00/5, Decision on Jurisdiction (27 September 2001) paras 123–26; *Tidewater v Venezuela* (n 65) para 183.

[155] *ConocoPhillips v Venezuela* (n 75) para 279.

[156] *Philip Morris Asia v Australia* (n 108) para 582.

accepting proof as to other possible reasons for the restructuring. However, it is not excluded that future claimants will quickly adapt to these heightened standards of proving alternative reasons, leading again to a blurring of the jurisprudence. The benefit of relying on the 'sole' or 'main purpose' doctrine remains therefore in this author's opinion questionable.

7.3.2.4 Other factors that may influence whether a tribunal will be prepared to accept a corporate (re)structuring as 'legitimate corporate planning' or not

Finally, it has been seen from the above decisions that some facts were considered by arbitral tribunals to strengthen investors' case when examining whether a corporate restructuring should be accepted as 'legitimate corporate planning', while others had the contrary effect.

As to the latter, it is no surprise whatsoever that the determination of fraud constitutes a factor to strike down a feigned corporate restructuring, as can be seen in the *Cementownia* and *Europe Cement* cases.[157] But the tribunal in *Millicom v Senegal* also identified—but did not find on the facts of the case—any hidden structuring operations or those 'under artificial conditions' as constituting an 'abusive solution'.[158]

On the other hand, it has also been seen that some tribunals have considered the fact of continuing to invest despite problems in the business relationship as a sign of good faith, visibly influencing arbitral tribunals' judgment in deciding whether a future dispute was foreseeable for the investor–claimant. Thus, in *Tidewater*, the tribunal clearly gave Claimants much credit for the fact of continuing to invest even at a time when the contractual payment dispute was already afoot.[159] Does this however mean that an investor who continues to invest despite lingering business problems can be assumed not to foresee a future dispute? This argument would seem to imply *a contrario* that any investor bringing an ICSID claim against the host State is willing to burn bridges and stop its investment in the host State after the arbitration proceedings. Whether such an assumption has already been empirically verified is unknown to this author. It seems however that while it may undeniably be a sign of good faith to continue to invest, it is usually motivated by sound business reasons, without excluding for that matter that a specific future dispute may already be reasonably foreseeable for the investor.

Finally, it has been confirmed in several arbitral decisions that a corporate restructuring remains innocuous even after the occurrence of a dispute if it does not lead to a change of nationality.[160]

[157] *Cementownia v Turkey* (n 16) paras 156–59; *Europe Cement Trade & Investment v Republic of Turkey*, ICSID Case No ARB(AF)/07/2, Decision on Jurisdiction (13 August 2009) paras 163–75.

[158] *Millicom International Operations BV and Sentel GSM SA v Senegal*, ICSID Case No ARB/08/20, Decision on Jurisdiction of the Arbitral Tribunal (16 July 2010) para 84.

[159] Similar the tribunal in *ConocoPhillips v Venezuela* (n 75) para 280.

[160] See, eg, *Millicom v Senegal* (n 158) para 84; *Renée Rose Levy de Levi v Peru* (n 98) para 154.

7.4 *Nemo Dat Quod Non Habet*

In a few cases thus far, arbitral tribunals have examined the lawfulness of a claim based on a change of nationality by recourse to the rather figurative maxim of *nemo dat quod non habet* or *nemo potiorem potest transfere quam ipse habet.*

7.4.1 Cases

Its first (explicit) appearance was in the early case *Mihaly International Corporation v Sri Lanka.*[161] In this case, Canada-incorporated Mihaly company assigned a 'claim' it alleged to have against Sri Lanka on grounds of sunken pre-investment expenditures on a power plant proposal to its US-incorporated subsidiary, given that Canada at that time was not a party to the ICSID Convention while the United States were. In the decision that was only published in excerpts, the tribunal found:

> It follows that as neither Canada nor Mihaly (Canada) could bring any claims under the ICSID Convention, whatever rights Mihaly (Canada) had or did not have against Sri Lanka could not have been improved by the process of assignment with or without, and especially without, the express consent of Sri Lanka, on the ground that *nemo dat quod non habet* or *nemo potiorem potest transfere quam ipse habet.* That is, no one could transfer a better title than what he really has. Thus, if Mihaly (Canada) had a claim which was procedurally defective against Sri Lanka before ICSID because of Mihaly (Canada)'s inability to invoke the ICSID Convention, Canada not being a party thereto, this defect could not be perfected vis-à-vis ICSID by its assignment to Mihaly (USA). To allow such an assignment to operate in favour of Mihaly (Canada) would defeat the object and purpose of the ICSID Convention and the sanctity of the privity of international agreements not intended to create rights and obligations for non-Parties ... A claim under the ICSID Convention with its carefully structured system is not a readily assignable chose in action as shares in the stock-exchange market or other types of negotiable instruments, such as promissory notes or letters of credit ...[162]

It accepted however that Mihaly (USA) might be able to establish rights and interests of its own in the failed investment that would enable it to bring a claim in its own name,[163] yet dismissed the case in the end on grounds of lack of jurisdiction *ratione materiae.*

Already two years earlier, the tribunal in *Banro American Resources Inc and Société Aurifère du Kivu et du Maniema SARL (SAKIMA) v Democratic Republic of Congo*[164] can arguably be said to have used this maxim,[165] even though it did not explicitly name

[161] *Mihaly International Corporation v Democratic Socialist Republic of Sri Lanka*, ICSID Case No ARB/00/2, Award (15 March 2002).

[162] Ibid, para 24.

[163] Ibid, para 26.

[164] *Banro American Resources Inc and Société Aurifère du Kivu du Maniema SARL v Democratic Republic of Congo*, ICSID Case No ARB/98/7, Award (1 September 2000).

[165] In this sense also Schreuer, 'Nationality Planning' (n 135) 22.

it as such. In this case, the parent company of the locally incorporated SAKIMA, the Canada-incorporated Banro Resource, transferred its shares in SAKIMA to its US-incorporated subsidiary Banro American. Though it is not known when this transfer of shares took place,[166] it can be assumed that it was at a time when a dispute already existed, but before the claim was brought before the ICSID tribunal. This is so because Canada not being a Contracting Party to ICSID at the relevant time,[167] the Canadian parent company could not have brought a claim under ICSID, while the US subsidiary could, the United States being a Contracting Party to ICSID.

The tribunal rejected jurisdiction (among others) on the basis that in the investment contract that contained the consent to ICSID jurisdiction, the Congolese State had consented to submit to ICSID arbitration disputes involving Banro Resource and SAKIMA, but not disputes involving Banro American Resources, Inc.[168] It clarified:

> In order to consider the right of access to ICSID arbitration, available under Article 35 [of the Mining Convention], as 'extended' or 'transferred' to Banro American by applying other provisions of the Mining Convention, it would still be necessary that such right existed first for the benefit of the entity Banro Resource. Such is not the case, given that Banro Resource, a Canadian company, never had, at any time, *jus standi* before ICSID. Having never existed for the benefit of Banro Resource, the right of access to ICSID cannot be viewed as having been 'extended' or 'transferred' to its affiliate, Banro American.[169]

It also did not accept the proposition that 'beyond procedural appearances', the Canadian parent company could be considered as a valid claimant by 'piercing the corporate veil' of the group's structure and 'allowing financial reality to prevail over legal structures', finding that in that case, 'the requirement that a Claimant, a juridical person, have the nationality of a Contracting State', is not met, Canada not being a party to the ICSID Convention.[170]

In the recent case *ST-AD GmbH v Republic of Bulgaria*,[171] the arbitral tribunal also used the 'general principle of *nemo dat quod non habet*'.[172] In this case, the Germany-incorporated claimant acquired shares in a Bulgarian investment from the Bulgarian owner at a time when the Bulgarian Supreme Court had dismissed the claim of the Bulgarian owner against the measures allegedly affecting the investment.

Even though the tribunal had already found that it lacked jurisdiction *ratione temporis* because the dispute had arisen before the acquisition of shares,[173] it continued to treat all objections raised by the Respondent, including the abuse of

[166] Which may be due to the fact that the decision is published only in excerpts.

[167] Canada ratified the ICSID Convention only in 2013, see <https://icsid.worldbank.org/apps/ICSIDWEB/Pages/News.aspx?CID=18&ListID=74f1e8b5-96d0-4f0a-8f0c-2f3a92d84773&variation=en_us> (last accessed on 15 September 2016).

[168] *Banro American Resources and SAKIMA v DRC* (n 164) para 4.

[169] Ibid, para 5.

[170] Ibid, paras 7–8.

[171] *ST-AD GmbH v Republic of Bulgaria*, UNCITRAL, PCA Case No 2011-06, Award on Jurisdiction (18 July 2013).

[172] Ibid, para 411.

[173] Ibid, para 333.

process objection, which it conceptually divided into the issue of 'systemic abuse' or 'bad faith in the initiation of the arbitration'[174] on the one hand, and 'procedural abuse' or 'bad faith in the conduct of the arbitration' on the other hand.[175] Thus, in accordance with the '*nemo dat quod non habet* principle', it considered that, a Bulgarian investor not having a right to international arbitration against his own State of nationality, that investor could not transfer a right to international arbitration to a German investor, resulting in an attempt at manipulation of the investment arbitration system.[176] Examining whether the claimant could bring a claim of its own, the tribunal, heavily relying on the decisions in *Mobil v Venezuela* and *Phoenix Action v Czech Republic*, reaffirmed that 'all of the damaging facts occurred years before the Claimant acquired its investment'[177] and found that 'the Claimant sought to manufacture jurisdiction by introducing a German investor in LIDI-R once all of its domestic legal options had failed'.[178] This, it concluded, would be:

> an abuse of the system of international investment arbitration … to accept jurisdiction in this case would go against the basic objectives underlying bilateral investment treaties. The Tribunal has to ensure that the BIT mechanism does not protect investments that it was not designed to protect, that is, domestic investments disguised as international investments or domestic disputes repackaged as international disputes for the sole purpose of gaining access to international arbitration.[179]

7.4.2 Discussion

The above decisions arguably leave more questions open than they answer. First and foremost, the necessity and *raison d'être* of a *nemo dat quod non habet* 'principle' is more than doubtful. What does this 'principle' add that cannot be achieved by recourse to objections to jurisdiction *ratione temporis* or the abuse of rights or abuse of process doctrine? Its superfluousness is particularly patent in the *ST-AD* case where the tribunal had already confirmed the lack of jurisdiction *ratione temporis* because the dispute (respectively the facts giving rise to the dispute) had arisen prior to the acquisition of shares. Did the tribunal decide to treat all the objections, contrary to the possibility to exercise judicial economy, in order to try and contribute to a clarification of the law? Did it treat the abuse of process objection in order to be able to order the Claimant to bear all the costs, including those of the Respondent? If this was the tribunal's objective, it is doubtful that it had to go to such (doctrinal) length, mixing several different conceptual approaches to the question of the validity of treaty shopping. Moreover, while the idea expressed by this maxim can arguably be accepted in a case like the one in *Mihaly*, that is, where a non-qualifying investor assigns an ICSID claim to a potentially qualifying investor, it seems incorrect in the case of *ST-AD* where the Bulgarian investor did not transfer a claim, but rather shares in the investment. Petty as may seem this

[174] Ibid, paras 404–05.
[175] Ibid, paras 404, 406.
[176] Ibid, paras 407–11.
[177] Ibid, para 419.
[178] Ibid, para 422.
[179] Ibid, para 423.

differentiation, he thus transferred something he actually *did* possess, only that this did not give rise to a right to international arbitration with respect to this particular, pre-existing dispute. In a similar vein, in the *Mihaly* case, a simple argument based on jurisdiction *ratione temporis* most likely would have provided for a clear-cut and conceptually correct answer. Similar arguments can arguably be made with respect to the *Banro* decision.

In conclusion, it seems like the maxim of *nemo dat quod non habet* is nothing more than a figurative expression of the abuse of rights or abuse of process doctrine. Its utility is particularly doubtful given that the legal problem pertaining to it can be perfectly captured by recourse to arguments *ratione temporis*. Moreover, as has been proposed further above, in cases where a change of nationality fails on grounds of lack of jurisdiction *ratione temporis* because of an existing dispute, the use of the abuse of rights or abuse of process doctrine should be reserved only for the question of whether a specific future dispute was sufficiently foreseeable.[180]

7.5 Preliminary Conclusions

As has been seen in this chapter, the abuse of rights or abuse of process doctrine does have an important role to play in determining whether a strategic change of nationality is a 'legitimate corporate planning' or a 'treaty abuse'. Arbitral tribunals have over the past years refined their approaches and criteria in order to draw this dividing line, though decisions remain often incoherent in specific details, raising new questions. Of particular importance is in factual terms the increased focus on the timing of the transaction, being an objectifiable element in the question of whether the purpose pursued with the claim based on a strategic change of nationality constitutes an abuse of rights/abuse of process. Based on this question, arbitral tribunals have developed the line of jurisprudence that asks whether at the time of the change of nationality, a dispute existed or was (sufficiently) foreseeable. In legal terms, this has translated into the distinction between objections directed at jurisdiction *ratione temporis* and objections on grounds of abuse of rights or abuse of process.

However, as has been shown above, the question of whether a dispute existed at the time of the change of nationality is an issue that is already captured by the question of jurisdiction *ratione temporis*,[181] so that the abuse of rights or abuse of process doctrine should be reserved only for the question, absent an existing dispute,

[180] There is arguably also no reason why the pre-existing/foreseeable dispute jurisprudence should not also be applicable in principle where the tribunal's jurisdiction is based on domestic investment legislation or investor–State contracts (as opposed to IIAs) if one accepts the proposition found in an increasing number of arbitral decisions that pre-existing disputes are excluded from the temporal jurisdiction of a tribunal even in the absence of a corresponding exclusion clause, see Chapter 6, at 6.4.1.2.

[181] Similar Stephan Schill and Heather Bray, 'Good Faith Limitations on Protected Investments and Corporate Structuring' in Andrew Mitchell, M Sornarajah, and Tania Voon (eds), *Good Faith and International Economic Law* (Oxford University Press 2015) 88, 112.

of whether a future specific dispute was foreseeable for the investor at the time of the change of nationality. Arbitral jurisprudence on whether a dispute was foreseeable remains to date rather incoherent, with two lines being apparent, one setting a rather high and subjective standard ('foreseeability as a very high probability'), while the other one is more objective ('*reasonably* foreseeable') and thus preferable.

As has also been seen, the necessity and utility of what this author considers a particularization of the abuse of rights or abuse of process doctrine, the maxim of *nemo dat quod non habet*, should also be questioned in the context of determining whether a change of nationality constitutes a 'legitimate corporate planning' or a 'treaty abuse'. In a similar vein, the 'sole purpose' doctrine should be laid to rest, being a test that is doctrinally unclear, prone to manipulation and, with its focus on the motives for the restructuring, more correctly captured by the 'pre-existing/foreseeable dispute' jurisprudence.

In more general terms, this chapter has once more highlighted the preeminent importance of the notion of dispute, as has also been seen in Chapter 6. From the notion of dispute (respectively the finding of an existing dispute) thus depends whether the tribunal should look into an abuse of rights or abuse of process objection (ie whether a future dispute was foreseeable) or not. This however further highlights the uncertainty that still belies the question of when a dispute starts, and in particular the lack of precision with which different possible tests of time (such as acts giving rise to a dispute, breach of an obligation, injury, bringing of the claim)—sometimes with, sometimes without respective backing in the wordings of investment treaties—are at times used in quasi-synonymous ways. This uncertainty may prompt some investors to proceed in a tactical fashion in order to try and postpone or post-date a dispute, such as by withdrawing claims (as happened in *ConocoPhillips*) or by not protesting against the measure at issue before the corporate restructuring has been implemented.

Conclusions of Part II

As seen in Chapter 3, customary international law, wary of preventing possible abuses, takes an altogether restrictive approach towards the issue of treaty or nationality shopping. The answers it has found are germane to general international law. It has, as seen in *Barcelona Traction*, adopted a restrictive stance towards the question of shareholder standing, strictly distinguishing the separate legal personalities of companies and their shareholders. Though accepting in principle the possibility to look for the 'real' beneficiary of the claim ('genuine link' theory; 'piercing of the veil'), it has also altogether applied these theories in a restrictive—albeit not always uncontroversial—manner. By applying a continuous nationality requirement from the date of injury to the date of the presentation of the claim, customary international law also considerably reduces the possibility of strategic changes of nationality after an injury has occurred (though it does not necessarily prevent the strategic change of nationality if the injury has not yet occurred, but a dispute has already arisen).

International investment law, on the other hand, though not being a self-contained system, has developed markedly different rules and approaches to the question of a strategic change of nationality. Yet, it is not hermetically sealed off to general rules and principles of customary international law.

First of all, though the exact detail may vary depending on the IIAs, it has embraced a quasi-omnipresent shareholder standing, clearly departing from the customary international law's *Barcelona Traction* position.

Second, arbitral tribunals have, in the absence of explicit treaty-based restrictions and notwithstanding few exceptions, declined to look for the 'true' investor when the investor–claimant is foreign-incorporated, thus rejecting to import into international investment law the customary international law-based 'genuine link' or 'piercing of the veil' doctrines or legal figures. In these first two aspects, international investment law as *lex specialis* is in principle more permissive of the possibility of treaty shopping than customary international law. Uncertainty exists however with respect to whether the notion of (foreign) control as used in Article 25(2)(b) second clause or in IIAs should be defined by recourse to a legal or a de facto control test and whether, once the requisite control qualifying as covered investor has been found, the tribunal may or even must continue to enquire into the nationality of the ultimate control. More recent arbitral jurisprudence would seem to suggest that the latter is the case if evidence is available showing ultimate control by a host State national.

Third, international investment agreements have been increasingly incorporating the treaty-based denial of benefits clauses in order to deny the advantages of the treaty to investors that do not have any substantive business activities in the country of their incorporation, while being controlled by host State or third State investors. Jurisprudence with respect to the interpretation of denial of benefits clauses remains ambiguous, with no clear trend crystallizing as to whether the exercise of these clauses will be accorded retrospective or prospective effect only.

Fourth, arbitral tribunals, trying to draw the line between acceptable and unacceptable treaty shopping, have in recent years increasingly shifted their attention to questions of *ratione materiae*, an issue customary international law is silent on. While it seems mostly clear by now that tribunals will accept to take a holistic view at the investment and will not invalidate it on grounds of a mere nominal payment for its acquisition, a nominal payment will normally prompt a tribunal to have a closer look at the circumstances of the acquisition. However, what remains to date the most unsettled question is how to distinguish an 'active' as opposed to a 'passive' (and thus not protected) contribution in the case of indirect investments. In particular in the context of multi-layered investments, this seems an outrightly primordial question.

Fifth, for ICSID arbitrations, special provisions apply in Article 25 ICSID Convention with respect to the question of when the claimed nationality must be shown to exist, thus superseding the (customary) continuous nationality requirement. However, the main difficulty when dealing with temporal issues lies in the clean differentiation of different concepts *ratione temporis*, such as the temporal application of an IIA's substantive provisions, its temporal jurisdiction, the existence of a dispute and other timing requirements or restrictions explicitly or implicitly provided for by investment treaties. It is also not quite clear whether the customary rule of non-retroactivity, which excludes in principle acts or facts having occurred before the entry into force of the treaty, also excludes disputes having arisen before the entry into force of the treaty. In any case, the notion of 'dispute' takes on a key importance, and in particular the question from which moment on a dispute can be said to exist and whether in a series of contentious issues, the tribunal is faced with one single (broadly framed) or two or more (narrowly framed) disputes. These questions are crucial as the existence of a (specific) dispute most often sets the time limit for a strategic change of nationality, yet create considerable legal uncertainty because of the potential for manipulation and subjectivity that is inherent in the notion of 'dispute'. Problematic seems in this author's opinion in particular the tendency of arbitral tribunals to equate the existence of a dispute with the timing of the (alleged) breach of the obligation, which may be correct, but need not in all cases.

Finally, the abuse of rights or abuse of process doctrine has an important role to play in determining whether a strategic change of nationality is a 'legitimate corporate planning' or 'treaty abuse'. To this end, arbitral tribunals have increasingly put their focus on the timing of the change of nationality, thus trying to infer whether the latter was done in good or in bad faith. In legal terms, this has translated into the distinction of whether an actual dispute existed at the time of the change of nationality (in which case jurisdiction *ratione temporis* would be denied) or whether a future dispute was foreseeable (in which case the bringing of the claim based on the change of nationality would be considered an abuse of rights or abuse of process). The importance of the notion of dispute, though also its potential for subjective decisions, must once more be underlined. In a similar vein, arbitral jurisprudence on the foreseeability of future disputes remains, to date, rather incoherent.

PART III

POSSIBLE SOLUTIONS TO THE INCONSISTENT APPROACHES TOWARDS TREATY SHOPPING

As we have seen in Part II, the treatment, by arbitral tribunals, of cases of strategic uses or changes of nationality has produced some rather coherent approaches in some aspects, while leaving quite a few questions open in many other aspects.

The question that Part III will turn its attention to is therefore which solutions exist to remedy the inconsistencies observed in the preceding chapters.

To this end, Chapter 8 will begin by examining what States can do in order to curb treaty shopping. The chapter will first examine possible 'political' approaches towards the question of treaty shopping, before analysing more in detail treaty-based solutions that consist essentially in the negotiation of more restrictively formulated IIA clauses. This analysis seeks to take into account the arbitral inconsistencies analysed in preceding chapters and propose formulations, where possible, that might remedy these inconsistencies, including examples found in existing treaty practice.

Chapter 9 will then treat the question which role the principle of good faith plays in judging whether a strategic use or change of nationality constitutes a 'legitimate nationality planning' or 'treaty abuse' before presenting the conclusions of this research.

8

What States Can Do to Curb Treaty Shopping

It has already been seen in Chapter 2 that while States may have certain policy concerns with respect to the practice of treaty shopping, they remain the 'Masters of the Treaties'. This means that any solution to the problems created by the practice of treaty shopping lies to a great extent in the hands of the same States.

Two possible approaches can be identified and will be discussed: on the one hand, 'political' approaches as in multilateral initiatives or in national decisions to leave out investor–State dispute settlement (ISDS) in future investment treaties (8.1); and 'treaty drafting' approaches in investment treaties or chapters that make States less vulnerable to treaty shopping practices (8.2). A remark seems necessary at the outset as regards the choice of the terms 'political' versus 'treaty drafting approaches'. It is clear that any decision by States to include in future investment treaties more restrictive language is a policy, and thus political, decision. The term 'political approaches' was chosen with the aim of setting the proposals mentioned in the corresponding subsection apart from the detailed discussion of possible ways of drafting relevant investment treaty clauses more restrictively.

8.1 'Political' Approaches to Treaty Shopping

8.1.1 Negotiation of a multilateral investment framework

As discussed in Chapter 1, the plethora of investment treaties can be seen as the key ingredient to the practice of treaty shopping. The negotiation of one single multilateral investment framework, replacing (at least) the great majority of the currently existing and often overlapping international investment agreements (IIAs), would thus greatly reduce the possibility of treaty shopping. If, in addition, a permanent investment court were to be established within this multilateral investment framework, this could arguably greatly further the consistency of the jurisprudence, working against current 'legitimacy' critiques.[1]

[1] Gus Van Harten, *Investment Treaty Arbitration and Public Law* (Oxford University Press 2007) 180–84; UNCTAD, 'Investor-State Dispute Settlement, A Sequel' UNCTAD Series on Issues in International Investment Agreements II (United Nations 2014) 194–95, available at <http://unctad.org/en/PublicationsLibrary/diaeia2013d2_en.pdf> (last accessed on 15 September 2016).

However, the proposal of negotiating a multilateral investment framework is probably not entirely realistic under current political circumstances, at least for the foreseeable future.[2] Indeed, the failure of the Multilateral Agreement on Investment (MAI) under the auspices of the Organisation for Economic Cooperation and Development (OECD) has already shown that too great cleavages and conflicts of interests still exist between States in order to agree on a common set of multilateral investment rules. Though united in their wish to reform their IIAs, current proposals by States show a variety of approaches,[3] making it difficult to imagine a consensus on one single set of multilateral investment protection rules.

Moreover, with the virtual deadlock of the multilateral trading system, the sign of the time is called 'regionalism' and 'plurilateralism': States have been ever more focusing on regional and plurilateral treaty-making, increasingly integrating investment chapters into highly complex, so-called 'WTO [World Trade Organization] plus'/'WTOextra' FTAs[4] [free trade agreements] and thus contributing to a 'spaghetti bowl' of overlapping treaties.[5] The process of the European Union of consolidating and harmonizing the extra-EU bilateral investment treaty (BIT) network, due to the conferral of the new foreign direct investment (FDI) competence under the Lisbon Treaty, must in this context arguably be seen as a regional initiative, not as a forebearer of a more general development of multilateral investment treaty-making.[6]

8.1.2 Prescription of mailbox companies

As has been seen in preceding chapters, it is mainly (though not exclusively) through the use of so-called mailbox or shell companies that (in particular multinational) companies implement the strategic change of nationality needed to come under the protection of a specific investment treaty. The question thus arises as to whether the use of mailbox companies should be prescribed on a universal level.

[2] Similar UNCTAD, 'Investor-State Dispute Settlement' (n 1) 195 (though see the proposal ibid that 'a standing investment court may well start as a plurilateral initiative, with an opt-in mechanism for those States that will wish to join').

[3] See, eg, UNCTAD, 'Taking stock of IIA Reform' IIA Issues Note No 1 (March 2016) available at <http://unctad.org/en/PublicationsLibrary/webdiaepcb2016d1_en.pdf> (last accessed on 15 September 2016).

[4] WTO, 'World Trade Report 2011, The WTO and preferential trade agreements: From co-existence to coherence' (WTO 2011) available at <http://www.wto.org/English/res_e/booksp_e/anrep_e/world_trade_report11_e.pdf> (last accessed on 15 September 2016).

[5] Wolfgang Alschner, 'Regionalism and Overlap in Investment Treaty Law: Towards Consolidation or Contradiction?' (2014) 17 JIEL 271, 274.

[6] Yet the new EU approach towards investor–State dispute settlement, that is, the introduction of a so-called 'Investment Court System', has the ambition of potentially being the basis for a multilateralized investment court, see, eg, Art 8.29 CETA (version February 2016) available at <http://trade.ec.europa.eu/doclib/docs/2014/september/tradoc_152806.pdf> (last accessed on 15 September 2016); Art 15 (Chapter 8, Section 3, Sub-section 4) of the EU–Vietnam Free Trade Agreement, available at <http://trade.ec.europa.eu/doclib/docs/2016/february/tradoc_154210.pdf> (last accessed on 15 September 2016); or Art 12 (Chapter II, Section 2, Section 3, Sub-section 4) of the draft TTIP Investment Chapter, available at <http://trade.ec.europa.eu/doclib/docs/2015/september/tradoc_153807.pdf> (last accessed on 15 September 2016).

In this latter aspect, the current discussions and developments at the OECD with respect to the Base Erosion and Profit Shifting (BEPS) methods employed in particular by multinational companies are noteworthy.[7] However, novel as may seem the sudden unanimity among States as to the harmfulness and undesirability of these tax saving schemes in which the interposition of mailbox companies in the corporate structure usually plays a vital part, the universal prescription of mailbox companies appears clearly not around the corner, if ever. This is also so because the decision of each State whether to confer corporate nationality on the sole basis of incorporation (or on other, more substantive factors) remains a sovereign one.

This proposal is thus not only unrealistic, but also unnecessary given the possibility to restrict the circle of protected investors by combining the incorporation theory with additional requirements, such as the seat and/or substantive business activities in order to prevent the use of mailbox companies, as will be seen further below.

8.1.3 Investment treaties without ISDS clauses

The conclusion of future investment treaties (or chapters) without an ISDS clause would arguably constitute one of the most efficient ways to curb the practice of treaty shopping. Indeed, as seen in Chapter 1, alongside the proliferation of investment treaties, it was the paradigm change from the practice of diplomatic protection of foreign investors to their direct right to sue against the host State that furthered the practice of treaty shopping. The direct right to sue is normally contained in the dispute settlement clause of the investment treaty giving the Contracting Parties mutual consent to this method of dispute settlement. If States now decided not to include ISDS clauses in future investment treaties anymore, this would greatly reduce the practice of treaty shopping, though only under the condition that the great majority of States (and not only some States) would take this decision.

Only few States have so far decided to opt out of ISDS. In 2011, Australia announced its intent to omit the ISDS clause in future investment treaties or chapters and concluded the 2012 Australia–Malaysia FTA without it;[8] yet, the investment chapter contained in the Australia–South Korea FTA, concluded in late 2013, does again contain an ISDS clause.[9] Brazil, never a big friend of IIAs,[10] has in the

[7] See, eg, OECD, *Action Plan on Base Erosion and Profit Shifting* (OECD 2013) available at <http://www.oecd.org/ctp/BEPSActionPlan.pdf> (last accessed on 15 September 2016).

[8] It is noteworthy that already the Investment Chapter of the 2005 Australia–USA FTA contained no ISDS mechanism.

[9] Leon Trakman, 'Investor-State Arbitration: Evaluating Australia's Evolving Position' (2014) 15 JWIT 152, 166; Liang-Ying Tan and Amal Bouchenaki, 'Limiting Investor Access to Investment Arbitration-A Solution without a Problem?' (2014) 11 TDM 8, available at <http://www.transnational-dispute-management.com> (subscription required). For an analysis of the 2004 Australia–United States Free Trade Agreement that does not contain an ISDS clause either see, eg, William Dodge, 'Investor-State Dispute Settlement Between Developed Countries: Reflections on the Australian-United States Free Trade Agreement' (2006) 39 Vand J Transnatl L 1.

[10] Brazil signed at least 7 BITs between 1995 and 1999 containing classical ISDS clauses, however never ratified them, see UNCTAD's International Investment Agreements search at <http://investmentpolicyhub.unctad.org/IIA/AdvancedSearchBITResults>.

recent past concluded a series of so-called Cooperation and Facilitation Investment Agreements (CFIAs), which replaces the investor's right to sue with institutional cooperation and dispute prevention mechanisms.[11] Other restrictions to ISDS are more piecemeal (but revealing of a more recent trend to 'treaty drafting *à géometrie variable*'). For example, in the recently concluded Trans-Pacific Partnership (TPP), Australia and New Zealand excluded in a side letter reciprocally their nationals' right to ISDS that is in principle contained in the Investment Chapter.[12]

The question is of course whether the conclusion of future investment treaties or investment chapters without ISDS clauses would really be desirable. Some scholars indeed argue that the renouncement on ISDS clauses would be a regression.[13] It is certain that while the current investment arbitration system is undeniably not perfect and abuses (or attempts at abuses) do exist, it has developed for good reasons and, though some may disagree, the great majority of States do not seem to fundamentally call it into question. This should of course not prejudice reform efforts depending on their political feasibility, among which the possibility to (re)negotiate more strictly formulated treaty language in order to curb treaty shopping.

In summary, political approaches towards the curbing of treaty shopping do not seem promising under current political circumstances, shifting the focus instead to possibilities of treaty-based approaches.

8.2 'Treaty Drafting' Approaches to Treaty Shopping

As has been seen in the preceding chapters, arbitral tribunals have over past years increasingly refined their approaches towards novel legal constructions or 'creative' pleadings by investors and their counsels in order to access (procedural or substantive) protections under given investment treaties. Some of these approaches have been shown to be reasonably settled to date, leaving few questions open (such as the approaches with respect to 'round-tripping' and mailbox companies), while other approaches may still lack in consistency and/or raise more questions than they actually answer.[14]

The question is therefore in how far States have adapted (or more generally speaking might adapt) their treaty frameworks to counter the possibility of treaty

[11] See, eg, the 2015 Brazil–Chile CFIA, Brazil–Colombia CFIA, Brazil–Malawi CFIA, etc.

[12] See <https://www.tpp.mfat.govt.nz/assets/docs/side-letters/New%20Zealand-Australia%20Side%20Letter%20Relationship%20between%20TPP%20and%20Other%20Agreements.pdf> (last accessed on 15 September 2016).

[13] See, eg, Rafael Leal-Arcas, 'Towards the Multilateralization of International Investment Law' (2009) 10 JWIT 865, 918–19. Similar Stephen Schwebel, 'In defense of bilateral investment treaties' *Columbia FDI Perspectives*, No 135 (2014) available at <http://ccsi.columbia.edu/files/2013/10/No-135-Schwebel-FINAL.pdf> (last accessed on 15 September 2016). But see for a different view concerning the necessity of ISDS in the TTIP agreement, eg, Jan Kleinheisterkamp, 'Is there a need for Investor-State Arbitration in the Transatlantic Trade and Investment Partnership?' (14 February 2014) available at <http://papers.ssrn.com/sol3/papers.cfm?abstract_id=2410188> (last accessed on 15 September 2016).

[14] See Chapters 4, 5, 6, and 7.

shopping by investors, presuming a corresponding policy decision has been taken by the government(s) in question. That States are increasingly wary of too vaguely formulated treaty clauses that may easily permit treaty shopping has also been seen when the European Union proclaimed in its recent Investment Policy that the newly negotiated BITs or FTAs with investment chapters would aim at preventing 'abusive claims', meaning among others treaty shopping.[15] In view of these concerns, the United Nations Conference for Trade and Development (UNCTAD) has also advocated in its World Investment Reports 2014 and 2015 for introducing selective adjustments in new investment treaties, among others by limiting investor access to ISDS.[16] As many IIAs already have or will soon come up for termination, States may also consider the renegotiation of too vaguely formulated treaty clauses.

Based on the critical appraisal of investment tribunals' jurisprudence on approaches towards the practice of treaty shopping, this Chapter will examine a non-exhaustive, exemplary selection of IIAs in order to assess whether, and if so how, States have chosen to protect themselves against treaty shopping.[17] The analysis will largely follow the order found in Chapters 4 to 7.

8.2.1 Joint interpretations

A tool that is finding increasing attention in the current quest of States to regain 'interpretative control' over IIAs is the possibility of joint interpretations.[18] Joint interpretations may be binding or non-binding, and they may be based either on general principles of treaty interpretation or on explicit clauses contained in IIAs. Indeed, even without an explicit treaty clause, joint interpretations are possible as a way of 'subsequent agreement between the parties regarding the interpretation of the treaty or the application of its provisions' within the meaning of Article 31(3)(a) Vienna Convention on the Law of Treaties (VCLT), which has to be taken into account, alongside with the other elements of treaty interpretation, by treaty interpreters.[19] Some of the newer IIAs (concluded or under negotiations) moreover

[15] European Commission, 'Fact Sheet, Investment Protection and Investor-to-State Dispute Settlement in EU Agreements' (November 2013) 8, available at <http://trade.ec.europa.eu/doclib/docs/2013/november/tradoc_151916.pdf> (last accessed on 15 September 2016).

[16] UNCTAD, 'World Investment Report 2014, Investing in the SDGs: An Action Plan' (United Nations 2014) 129, available at <http://unctad.org/en/publicationslibrary/wir2014_en.pdf>; UNCTAD, 'World Investment Report 2015—Reforming International Investment Governance' (United Nations 2015) 148, available at <http://unctad.org/en/PublicationsLibrary/wir2015_en.pdf> (both last accessed on 15 September 2016).

[17] Unless specified, all investment treaties examined in this chapter can be found in the UNCTAD treaty database of the UNCTAD Investment Policy Hub at <http://investmentpolicyhub.unctad.org/IIA/AdvancedSearchBIT>.

[18] UNCTAD, 'WIR 2015' (n 16) 148.

[19] See on the key implications David Gaukrodger, 'The legal framework applicable to joint interpretive agreements of investment treaties' OECD Working Papers on International Investment 2016/1 (OECD 2016) 7ff, available at <http://www.oecd-ilibrary.org/docserver/download/5jm3xgt6f29w.pdf?expires=1462177183&id=id&accname=guest&checksum=A771D43EF45E3E523C7FAB28E46E7C17> (last accessed on 15 September 2016). See also the work undertaken by the International Law Commission, 'Treaties over time/Subsequent agreements and subsequent practice in relation to interpretation of treaties' and International Law Commission, 'First Report on subsequent agreements

explicitly include the possibility to issue binding interpretations, usually done by Joint Committees established by the treaty Parties.[20]

Joint interpretations offer the advantage of promoting 'evolutionary and sustainable treaty interpretations without requiring legal amendments (recontracting strategies) or political attacks (delegitimizing strategies)'.[21] They could therefore be particularly useful for 'recalibrating' broad and vague treaty clauses contained in existing 'old-style' IIAs, such as the key clauses of importance in the practice of treaty shopping (investor, investment, etc.), awaiting formal renegotiation of the IIA.[22]

8.2.2 The role of the preamble

Though preambles have no binding force in international law,[23] their interpretative value for purposes of investment arbitration should not be completely overlooked. As preambles often contain the policy rationale(s) for the conclusion of the treaty,[24] 'they may be relevant and important as guides to the manner in which the Treaty should be interpreted, and in order, as it were, to "situate" it in respect of its object and purpose' as the *Beagle Channel* arbitration already confirmed.[25] The interpretive purpose of the preamble is also captured in Article 31 VCLT, which states in relevant parts:

> 1. A treaty shall be interpreted in good faith in accordance with the ordinary meaning to be given to the terms of the treaty in their context and in the light of its object and purpose.
> 2. The context for the purpose of the interpretation of a treaty shall comprise, in addition to the text, including its preamble and annexes:
>
> ...

and subsequent practice in relation to treaty interpretation' Report of the sixty-fifth session (2013) UN Doc A/CN.4/660.

[20] See, eg, Article 8.31(3) CETA (version February 2016): 'Where serious concerns arise as regards matters of interpretation that may affect investment, the Committee on Services and Investment may, pursuant to Article 8.44.3(a), recommend to the CETA Joint Committee the adoption of interpretations of this Agreement. An interpretation adopted by the CETA Joint Committee shall be binding on a Tribunal established under this Section. The CETA Joint Committee may decide that an interpretation shall have binding effect from a specific date.' Similar in Article 13(5) of the draft TTIP Investment Chapter (Chapter II, Section 2, Section 3, Sub-section 4).

[21] Anthea Roberts, 'Power and Persuasion in Investment Treaty Arbitration: The Dual Role of States' (2010) 104 AJIL 179.

[22] On the question of the effect of such joint interpretations on third parties, in particular investors, see Gaukrodger (n 19) 11ff.

[23] See, eg, Makane Moise Mbengue, 'Preamble' *Max Planck Encyclopedia of Public International Law* (Oxford Public International Law) para 11, available at <http://opil.ouplaw.com>; Romesh Weeramantry, *Treaty Interpretation in Investment Arbitration* (Oxford University Press 2012) para 3.91.

[24] Sir Gerald Fitzmaurice, 'The Law and Procedure of the International Court of Justice 1951–54: Treaty Interpretation and Other Treaty Points' (1957) 33 BYIL 203, 228; Mbengue, 'Preamble' (n 23) para 11.

[25] *Beagle Channel (Argentina v Chile)* (1977) 52 ILR 93, 132 (para 19).

A specific policy rationale can thus enter the interpretative process through the context-based method, as explicitly mentioned in Article 31(2) VCLT. It may however also help in clarifying the object and purpose of a treaty, one of the interpretive methods mentioned in Article 31(1) VCLT.[26]

Investment arbitral tribunals have often recognized the significance of the preamble for identifying the object and purpose of a treaty under interpretation.[27] Thus, the arbitral tribunal in *Aguas del Tunarí v Bolivia* stated that 'it [was] widely accepted that the preamble language of a treaty can be particularly helpful in ascertaining the motive, object and circumstances of a treaty'.[28]

The tribunal in the already quoted *Standard Chartered Bank v Tanzania*, on the other hand, used the preamble to confirm a conclusion it arrived at by engaging in interpretation under Article 31 VCLT. Having concluded that the BIT under interpretation required an active relationship between the investor and the investment as opposed to a purely passive ownership of shares, the tribunal highlighted the explicit mention, in the preamble of the UK–Tanzania BIT, of the reciprocal nature of the treaty, leading it to confirm that:

> In the absence of text in the BIT expressing a contrary intent and on a record indicating no involvement or control of the UK national over the investment, it would be unreasonable to read the BIT to permit a UK national with subsidiaries all around the world to claim entitlement to the UK-Tanzania BIT protection for each and every one of the investments around the world held by these daughter or granddaughter entities. The BIT preamble says 'reciprocal protection' and 'reciprocal' must have some meaning.[29]

A specific emphasis by the interpreting tribunal on the reciprocal nature of the treaty thus can, as seen, contribute to thwart treaty shopping attempts by putative investor-claimants. Many treaties indeed carry the expectation of reciprocal protection already in the title of the treaty[30] or in the preamble.[31] Surprisingly, however,

[26] Richard Gardiner, *Treaty Interpretation* (Oxford University Press 2008) 186–87.

[27] See also Chapter 9, at 9.3.3.

[28] *Aguas del Tunarí SA v Plurinational State of Bolivia*, ICSID Case No ARB/02/3, Decision on Respondent's Objections to Jurisdiction (21 October 2005) para 241.

[29] *Standard Chartered Bank v United Republic of Tanzania*, ICSID Case No ARB/10/12, Award (2 November 2012) para 270.

[30] See, eg, the 1988 Agreement between the Government of Australia and the Government of the People's Republic of China on the *Reciprocal* Encouragement and Protection of Investments; the 2005 Agreement between the Government of Australia and the Government of the United Mexican States on the Promotion on *Reciprocal* Protection of Investments; the 1994 Acuerdo Entre la República de Bolivia y la República de Chile Para la Promoción y Protección *Recíproca* de Inversiones; the 2012 Agreement between the Government of Canada and the Government of the People's Republic of China for the Promotion and *Reciprocal* Protection of Investments; the 2003 Accord Entre le Gouvernement de la Répubique Française et le Gouvernement de la République Dominicaine sur l'Encouragement et la Protecton *Réciproques* des Investissements; the 2008 Model Treaty of the Federal Republic of Germany; the 1991 Agreement on Encouragement and *Reciprocal* Protection of Investments between the Kingdom of the Netherlands and the Czech and Slovak Federal Republic (all emphases added).

[31] See, eg, the 1998 Austria–Mexico BIT, 3rd indent: 'CONSIDERING that a bilateral agreement is aimed at granting and assuring equal treatment of investors of both Contracting Parties in accordance with the principles of international reciprocity'; the 1995 Cambodia–Thailand, 3rd indent: 'Recognizing that the encouragement of investments and the reciprocal protection of

it took until 2012 for a tribunal to explain the dismissal of a case for the first time (among other) with the expectation of reciprocity that would be frustrated if the tribunal accepted the claimant's argument. Why former tribunals examining cases of treaty shopping by corporate structuring have never invoked this argument is unknown to this author. While it is thus probably not in any case one of the sharpest-cutting knives for States wishing to curb treaty shopping, the inclusion of the expectation of the reciprocal protection in the title and/or preamble still seems apt to set the larger picture for an arbitral tribunal to take the expectation of reciprocity of protection into account when engaging in treaty interpretation.

8.2.3 Notion of investor

8.2.3.1 Natural persons

With respect to natural persons as investors, the analysis in Chapter 4 allows two main observations pertinent for the purposes of this research. As IIAs define who qualifies as eligible investor, States may, depending on their policy choices, decide to keep the circle of protected natural persons restricted, or they may instead decide to widen it. In the former case, knowing that treaty shopping by natural persons presupposes dual nationality from which to choose,[32] the fact of restricting the circle of eligible investors makes treaty shopping more difficult, while in the latter case, widening the circle makes treaty shopping more easy.

If States thus want to restrict the circle of eligible natural persons, they should include the requirement of effective nationality in case of dual nationalities and/or explicitly exclude claims by host State nationals.[33] The problem arising from including permanent residents in the scope of protected investors will also be addressed.

8.2.3.1.1 Inclusion of the effective nationality principle

As has been seen in Chapter 3, the status of the 'genuine link' theory under customary international law has been controversial and can nowadays only be considered confirmed with respect to multiple nationalities.[34] Even if one thus assumes the correctness of the 'genuine link' theory under customary international law, this

investments under international agreement [sic] will be conducive to the stimulation of individual business initiative and will increase prosperity in both States.'

[32] The strategic change of nationality from one nationality to another one, not leading to dual nationality, is, contrary to the strategic change of nationality by legal persons, much more seldom in the case of natural persons as it is more difficult to plan and would probably, in the context of treaty shopping, mostly be broached from the angle of whether the strategic change of nationality occurred in view of an existing or future but foreseeable dispute, thus from the *ratione temporis* or abuse of rights angle. This author is not aware of any case where a natural person has sought to access treaty protections through a strategic change of nationality not involving the invocation of a (pre-existing) dual nationality.

[33] In the case of single nationality, some treaties restrict the coverage of natural persons by including the requirement of permanent residency in the territory, see, eg, Art 1(3)(b) of the 1976 Germany–Israel BIT.

[34] See Chapter 3, at 3.2.1.2.

does however not mean, in view of the intricate relationship between international investment law as *lex specialis* and customary international law as *lex generalis*, that an arbitral tribunal would automatically find it applicable to a natural person holding multiple nationalities and seeking to qualify as protected investor under the invoked BIT.

Neither investment law (in the form of BITs) nor the ICSID Convention has an inherent bias against dual nationality. Indeed, for the latter, only the (dual) nationality of the host State is prejudicial.[35] As seen in Chapter 4, other arbitral rules (such as United Nations Commission on International Trade Law (UNCITRAL) arbitration rules) do not contain this 'host State bias', therefore rendering claims by dual nationals against their own State possible.[36]

However, it is within the negotiating States' power to agree on a different position towards dual nationality. If States want to ensure that a natural person holding dual nationality only qualifies for protection under the treaty concluded by the State with whom he has an effective link, they are thus well advised to include the requirement of effective nationality, and this in particular in treaties where investors also have the possibility of choosing UNCITRAL arbitral proceedings.

Only few IIAs specifically and explicitly include an effective nationality principle with respect to dual nationality, while the great majority of IIAs does not.

Thus, Canada has incorporated in some of its IIAs the effective nationality principle. For example, the 2006 Canada–Peru BIT provides in Article 1 that 'a natural person who is a dual citizen shall be deemed to be exclusively a citizen of the State of his or her dominant and effective citizenship'. In a similar vein, the investment chapter of the final Comprehensive Economic and Trade Agreement (CETA) text provides in Article 8.1 that:

> A natural person who is a citizen of Canada and has the nationality of one of the Member States of the EU shall be deemed to be exclusively a natural person of the Party of his or her dominant and effective nationality ...[37]

In a similar vein, the investment chapter of the 2004 Dominican Republic–Central America Free Trade Agreement (CAFTA), the 2008 US–Rwanda BIT, the investment chapters of the 2013 Australia–Malaysia FTA and the 2014

[35] Note, however, that some IIAs explicitly exclude claims brought by persons holding also the host State nationality, see, eg, Art 29(2) of the 2009 ASEAN Comprehensive Agreement: 'A natural person possessing the nationality or citizenship of a Member State shall not pursue a claim against that Member State under this Section.' Similar see Art 18(3) of the ASEAN–Australia–New Zealand FTA. Other IIAs allow claims of persons also holding the host State nationality only under certain circumstances, see, eg, Art 1(b) Note 2 of the 2011 Japan–Colombia BIT: 'This Agreement shall not apply to investments of natural persons who are nationals of both Contracting Parties unless such natural persons have at the time of the investment and ever since been domiciled outside the Area of the Contracting Party in which they made such investments'. Similar in the 2006 Switzerland–Colombia BIT.

[36] As could be seen in the recent case *Serafín García Armas y Karina García Gruber v República Bolivariana de Venezuela*, UNCITRAL, PCA Case No 2013-3, Decision on Jurisdiction (Spanish) (15 December 2014).

[37] CETA (version February 2016).

Australia–Korea FTA also contain the effective nationality principle for dual nationals.

8.2.3.1.2 Exclusion of claims by host State nationals

As seen in Chapter 4, there is no bar in arbitral rules other than the ICSID Convention to dual nationals also holding host State nationality bringing an investment claim against the host State.[38] It may thus be advisable for States wishing to exclude the possibility of claims by dual (host State) nationals to include a corresponding explicit exclusion to avoid that such claims be brought under other arbitral rules than ICSID. Such exclusion clauses can for example be found in some of the Australian BITs or in some of the Association of Southeast Asian Nations (ASEAN) Investment Agreements.[39] The Investment Chapter of the Trans-Pacific Partnership (TPP) excludes claims by a natural person 'who is a permanent resident of a Party and a national of another Party … against that latter Party', in other words his host State.[40]

8.2.3.1.3 Permanent residents as protected investors

A few countries, mostly those with liberal immigration policies, not only protect their nationals as eligible investors under investment treaties, but also include permanently residing non-nationals, thus widening the circle of eligible investors. This is, for example, the case in Australia.[41] The 2009 ASEAN–China Investment Agreement also includes permanent residents within the scope of protected investor, albeit providing for specifications and exceptions for certain Parties.[42]

As the circle of protected investors widens, the potential for treaty (and potentially forum) shopping also increases. The inclusion of permanent residents within the scope of protected investor makes both the agreement of the State of permanent residence as well as the agreement of the State of nationality—if existing—potentially available. The investor could thus choose which one to invoke. He could even first invoke the agreement of his State of permanent residence before invoking the agreement of his State of nationality if the first proceeding was not to his liking.

Australia has recognized this problem early on and has thus included in most of its older BITs a safeguard aimed at preventing multiple proceedings with respect to the same matter. Thus, the 1995 Australia–Argentina BIT provides in its Article 2(3)(a):

[38] See Chapter 4, at 4.2.2.

[39] See, eg, Art III(6)(b) of the 1993 Australia–Indonesia BIT; Art 2(5)(b) of the 1998 Australia–Lithuania BIT; Art 2(5)(b) of the 1995 Australia–Peru BIT; Art 18(2) of the 2009 ASEAN–Korea Investment Agreement; Art 18(3) of the Investment Chapter of the 2009 ASEAN–Australia–New Zealand FTA; Art 14(2)(b) of the 2009 ASEAN–China Investment Agreement.

[40] Art 9.1 Investment Chapter of TPP (text released on 5 November 2015 and undergoing legal review and translation before signature) available at <http://www.mfat.govt.nz/assets/_securedfiles/Trans-Pacific-Partnership/Text/9.-Investment-Chapter.pdf> (last accessed on 15 September 2016).

[41] See, eg, the 1995 Australia–Argentina BIT; 1996 Australia–Chile BIT; 1988 Australia–China BIT; 1992 Australia–Indonesia BIT; 1995 Australia–Peru BIT.

[42] Art 1(1)(i) of the 2009 ASEAN–China Investment Agreement.

In respect of Australia, this Agreement shall not apply to a natural person who is a permanent resident but not a citizen of Australia where:

(a) the provisions of an investment protection agreement between the Argentine Republic and the country of which the person is a citizen have already been invoked in respect of the same matter; ...[43]

It does therefore not prevent the investor from choosing which investment treaty to invoke, but it does prevent him from invoking the Australian investment treaty if the treaty of the State of nationality has already been invoked in the same matter.[44] This would seem to suggest that in the absence of a similar provision in the treaty of the State of nationality, an investor could arguably first invoke the Australian treaty and, if he is not satisfied with the result, invoke the treaty of his State of nationality after that, but not vice versa.

Under the final CETA text, permanent residents are also, under certain conditions, covered natural persons. This is the case for Canada and on the European Union side for Latvia. However, in order to avoid that (covered) permanent residents holding also host State (ie EU or Canadian) nationality could claim against their State of nationality, Article 8.1 foresees that:

A natural person who has the nationality of one of the Member States of the European Union or is a citizen of Canada, and is also a permanent resident of the other Party, shall be deemed to be exclusively a natural person of the Party of his or her nationality or citizenship, as applicable.

8.2.3.2 Legal persons

As has already been seen in Chapters 3 and 4, it is up to States to decide the criteria—to be found in domestic company laws—based on which legal persons will be accorded legal personality and therefore home State nationality. In the BITs, on the other hand, the negotiating States agree on the criteria based on which a legal person will be accorded protection as an investor.

States may thus decide to accord protection on a purely formal basis, letting suffice incorporation or constitution under the domestic law of a Contracting State. This is, for example, the case of UK BITs[45] or of US BITs.[46] Other investment treaties adhering to the incorporation theory only include for example the 2009 ASEAN–Korea Investment Agreement. These BITs can a priori be considered inherently treaty shopping-friendly (in particular in the absence of denial of benefits clauses)[47]

[43] Similar provisions can, eg, be found in the 1996 Australia–Chile BIT; 1988 Australia–China BIT; 1992 Australia–Indonesia BIT; or 1995 Australia–Peru BIT.

[44] A similar provision exists with respect to legal persons, see below at 8.2.4.1.

[45] Virtually all UK BITs adhere to the incorporation theory except the 2006 UK–Mexico BIT, which requires aside from incorporation also 'business activities in the territory of the Contracting Party', Art 1.

[46] See, eg, the 1989 US–Bangladesh BIT; 1991 US–Argentina BIT; 1995 US–Albania BIT; 1997 US–Azerbaijan BIT; 1999 US–Bahrain BIT; 2005 US–Uruguay BIT; or 2008 US–Rwanda BIT.

[47] Such as in the case of UK BITs, see below at 8.2.3.2.2.

and arbitral tribunals have—with few exceptions—taken purely formal approaches towards the notion of investor contained in these BITs, not accepting any arguments aimed at 'piercing the corporate veil'.[48]

States may also decide to prescribe additional criteria *ratione personae* that require a more substantive link of the investor with its home State. The more substantive criteria they prescribe, the more difficult it will become for an investor to create and use a corporate vehicle for the sole purpose of bringing a claim as an eligible investor under a given investment treaty. The inclusion of denial of benefits (DOB) clauses has in theory a similar effect, though this effect is in practice tempered by the uncertainty, already observed further above,[49] about whether tribunals will accord the exercise of the DOB clause a retrospective or prospective effect only.

8.2.3.2.1 'Anti-treaty shopping' nationality criteria found in IIAs

Seat requirement

Countries that want to ensure a more substantive link between the investor and its home State may require that in addition to being incorporated or constituted according to the law of one of the Contracting Parties, the investor also have its seat in the territory of the Contracting Party in question. This requirement can be alternatively expressed in terms of having its 'principal place of business', 'registered office', or 'central administration' in the territory of the home State.

Many older European (eg German and Austrian) BITs used to contain this additional requirement, but it had to be abandoned after several European Court of Justice decisions have found it to be incompatible with EU (company) law.[50]

Nowadays, the seat requirement can still be found in a select few (non-EU member States) IIAs, such as for example the 2006 Switzerland–Saudi Arabia BIT or the 1994 Chile–China BIT, but is becoming less frequent.

Substantial business activities

States have also been increasingly incorporating the (additional) requirement of substantial business activities in order to prevent so-called mailbox or shell companies established on their territory from benefitting from treaty protection.

One country that has been including rather consistently the requirement of real economic activities is Switzerland. Indeed, many IIAs concluded by Switzerland will require real economic activities on the territory of the State of claimed nationality for the legal person to be granted status as protected investor.[51]

Chile has also rather consistently included the requirement of substantial economic activities.[52] Other investment treaties requiring substantial business activities

[48] See Chapter 4, at 4.3. [49] See Chapter 4, at 4.3.3.

[50] See Chapter 3, a 3.2.2.1.2.

[51] See, eg, the 1991 Switzerland–Argentina BIT Ad Art. 1(1); 2006 Switzerland–Colombia BIT; 2009 Switzerland–China BIT. But see for BITs that do not contain this requirement, eg, the 2000 Switzerland–Costa Rica BIT (only seat requirement).

[52] See, eg, the 1994 Bolivia–Chile BIT; 1997 Austria–Chile BIT; 1998 Chile–South Africa BIT.

include the 2011 Japan–Colombia BIT, the 2009 ASEAN–China Investment Agreement, the 2007 Common Market for Eastern and Southern Africa (COMESA) Investment Agreement for the COMESA Common Investment Area, and the CETA. The draft Transatlantic Trade and Investment Partnership (TTIP) equally foresees a substantial business activities requirement.[53]

Some countries combine the requirements of incorporation, seat, and substantial economic activities, thus setting an even higher standard for legal persons to qualify as protected investors under the invoked IIA. This is, for example, the case of the 1994 Bolivia–Chile BIT, the 1997 Austria–Chile BIT, the 1998 Chile–South Africa BIT, and the 2009 Switzerland–China BIT.

While most treaties use the term 'substantial business activities',[54] some vary slightly in terminology, requiring 'real economic activities',[55] 'effective economic activities',[56] or simply 'commercial or business activities'.[57] Though the latter can probably be regarded as less stringent requirement, it is doubtful whether any substantive difference can be found between the terms 'substantial business activities', 'real economic activities', and 'effective economic activities'. Yet, it is by far not always clear what is precisely meant by these terms, hardly ever being defined in the investment treaties.

One exception in this aspect is the 2007 COMESA Investment Agreement that gives the following criteria for finding 'substantial business activity':

> The concept of 'substantial business activity' requires an overall examination, on a case-by-case basis, of all the circumstances, including, inter alia,
> (a) the amount of investment brought into the country;
> (b) the number of jobs created;
> (c) its effect on the local community; and
> (d) the length of time the business has been in operation.[58]

8.2.3.2.2 Denial of benefits clauses

Another possibility to restrict the access of foreign investors to investment arbitration is to include a DOB clause. Many IIAs have nowadays recourse to this possibility.

[53] See Art 1-1(3)(c) draft TTIP, Chapter 'Trade in Services, investment and e-commerce' available at <http://trade.ec.europa.eu/doclib/docs/2015/july/tradoc_153669.pdf> (last accessed on 15 September 2016).

[54] See, eg, the CETA (version February 2016) or the 2007 COMESA Investment Agreement. Similar Art 1.5 of the 2015 India Model BIT (adopted in December 2015) available at <http://finmin.nic.in/the_ministry/dept_eco_affairs/investment_division/ModelBIT_Annex.pdf> (last accessed on 15 September 2016). The 2015 draft India Model BIT included the requirement of 'real and substantive business operations', Art 1.2(ii), but was subsequently changed to 'substantial business activities' in the adopted Model BIT.

[55] See the Swiss BITs quoted above.

[56] See, eg, 1997 Austria–Chile BIT and 1998 Chile–South Africa BIT.

[57] See 1996 Australia–Chile BIT; 2014 Australia–Korea FTA; 2013 Australia–New Zealand Investment Protocol.

[58] Art 1(4)(ii) of the 2007 COMESA Investment Agreement.

While formulations may slightly vary, the DOB clauses examined can overall be distinguished according to two aspects of interest to this research. First, they can be distinguished according to whether the benefits are denied only to mailbox companies owned or controlled by investors of a non-Party or whether it also includes those owned or controlled by investors of the host State. Secondly, they can be distinguished according to whether they provide in any explicit way for the way and time limit according to which the DOB must be exercised.

Addressees of the DOB clause

Variously described as investors of a 'non-Party', a 'non-Contracting Party', or a 'third State', many IIAs give the possibility to deny the benefits of the investment treaty, or specific aspects thereof, to investors of a Party when these are owned or controlled by investors of a non-Party.

For example, Article 1113(2) of the North American Free Trade Agreement (NAFTA) provides that:

> Subject to prior notification and consultation ... a Party may deny the benefits of this Chapter to an investor of another Party that is an enterprise of such Party and to investments of such investors if investors of a non-Party own or control the enterprise and the enterprise has no substantial business activities in the territory of the Party under whose law it is constituted or organized.

In a similar vein, Article 17 of the Energy Charter Treaty (ECT) provides that:

> Each Contracting Party reserves the right to deny the advantages of this Part to:
>
> a legal entity if citizens or nationals of a third state own or control such entity and if that entity has no substantial business activities in the Area of the Contracting Party in which it is organized ...

Similar DOB clauses can be found in many Japanese investment treaties or chapters, such as the 2002 Japan–Korea BIT, the 2008 Japan–Uzbekistan BIT, the 2012 Japan–Iraq BIT, or the 2012 Japan–Mexico FTA. Those Austrian BITs that contain a DOB clause also only extend to investors of non-Parties.[59]

Other IIAs provide for the possibility to deny benefits not only to mailbox companies owned or controlled by investors of a non-Party, but also to those owned or controlled by host State nationals.

While older US BITs have seemingly extended the DOB clauses to investors of third States only,[60] the newer IIAs extend them more often also to investors of host State nationality.[61] Many of the recently negotiated ASEAN investment

[59] See, eg, the 2001 Austria–Libya BIT; 2002 Austria–Lebanon BIT; 2001 Austria–Jordan BIT; 2001 Austria–Armenia BIT.

[60] See, eg, the 1991 US–Czech Republic BIT; 1994 US–Ukraine BIT; 1994 US–Jamaica BIT.

[61] See, eg, the 2005 US–Uruguay BIT; 2006 US–Colombia FTA; 2004 US–Australia FTA; 2008 US–Rwanda BIT.

agreements also extend the DOB clauses to both investors of non-Parties and host State investors.[62] The same applies to the 2013 Australia–Malaysia FTA.

The TPP also extends the DOB clause to mailbox companies owned or controlled by either investors of non-Parties or host State nationals.[63]

Canadian treaty practice seems to follow a rather case-by-case approach with respect to the DOB clause: while some BITs do not contain any DOB clause at all,[64] some contain a DOB clause extending to third State investors only,[65] while others extend to both third State and host State investors.[66] The CETA, on the other hand, does not contain the possibility to deny the benefits to a mailbox company owned or controlled by third State or host State investors,[67] which is consequent in so far as the notion of investor (respectively 'enterprise of a Party'), according to its Article 8.1, only covers legal persons 'constituted or organized under the laws of [one] Party and [having] substantial business activities in the territory of that Party'.

States thus far not having negotiated any DOB clauses in their treaties include the UK, Switzerland, and the Netherlands. At least for Switzerland, this absence can presumably be explained by the consequent inclusion of a 'real economic activities' requirement within the notion of investor.[68]

The 2015 India Model BIT proposes a novel ground for giving the right of the host State to exercise the DOB clause:

A Party may at any time, including after the institution of arbitration proceedings in accordance with Chapter IV of this Treaty, deny the benefits of this Treaty to:-

(i) an investment or investor owned or controlled, directly or indirectly, by persons of a non-Party or of the Host State; or
(ii) an investment or investor that has been established or restructured with the primary purpose of gaining access to the dispute resolution mechanisms provided in this Treaty.

Thus, India envisages reserving the right to deny the benefits of the treaty in the case of treaty shopping. However, as with arbitral jurisprudence that has been asking whether the structuring or restructuring has been implemented with the 'sole purpose' of accessing international arbitration, the problem with asking for the

[62] See, eg, the 2009 ASEAN Comprehensive Agreement; 2009 ASEAN–China Investment Agreement; 2009 ASEAN–Korea Investment Agreement; ASEAN–Australia–New Zealand FTA Investment Chapter.

[63] See Art 9.14(1) of the TPP: 'A Party may deny the benefits of this Chapter to an investor of another Party that is an enterprise of such other Party and to investments of that investor if the enterprise:

(a) is owned or controlled by a person of a non-Party or of the denying Party; and
(b) has no substantial business activities in the territory of any Party other than the denying Party'[.]

[64] See, eg, 1996 Canada–Barbados BIT; 1998 Canada–Costa Rica BIT.

[65] See, eg, the 2006 Canada–Peru BIT; 2009 Canada–Jordan BIT; 2010 Canada–Slovak Republic; 2013 Canada–Tanzania BIT.

[66] See, eg, the 2012 Canada–China BIT.

[67] But the possibility to deny benefits exists if an investor of a non-Party owns or controls the enterprise and if the denying party adopts or maintains measures with respect to the non-Party that are typically related to (economic) sanctions, Art 8.16 CETA (version February 2016).

[68] See above at 8.2.3.2.1.

'primary purpose' is the difficulty in establishing in an objective manner whether the access to international arbitration was the 'primary' or only an 'accessory' purpose of the (re)structuring, thereby reducing the utility of the formulation.[69]

Conditions for the exercise of the right to deny benefits

As has been seen above,[70] arbitral jurisprudence has thus far been very incoherent as to when a DOB clause must be exercised and whether to accord retrospective or prospective effect only to this exercise. Hardly any investment treaty contains an explicit stipulation as to when and how a DOB clause must be exercised so that an investor-claimant may be validly denied the benefits in a looming or ongoing investment arbitration.

Thus, many DOB clauses simply provide that '[e]ach Party reserves the right to deny to a company of the other Party the benefits'[71] without clarifying in any way how and in particular when this right must be exercised in order to become effective.

Other DOB clauses contain notification and consultation requirements before the DOB clause may be invoked. Article 1113(2) of NAFTA for example provides that benefits may be denied 'subject to prior notification and consultation in accordance with Articles 1803 (Notification and Provision of Information) and 2006 (Consultations)'.[72] In a similar vein, the 2009 ASEAN–Korea Investment Agreement provides that:

> The denying Party shall, to the extent practicable, notify the other Parties concerned before denying the benefits. If the denying Party provides such notice, it shall consult with the other Parties concerned at the request of such other Parties.[73]

The formulation of these notification and consultation provisions makes clear that these are not strict and absolute conditions for the exercise of the DOB clauses, but only obligations of means.[74]

Other IIAs do not provide for a right to deny benefits, but only for the possibility to consult with the other Contracting Party with respect to the decision of a denial of benefits. Thus, some Australian BITs provide that:

> Where an investor of a Party is owned or controlled by a citizen or a company of any third country, the Parties may consult with a view to deciding not to extend the rights and benefits of this Agreement to such investment.[75]

[69] See more in detail Chapter 7, at 7.3.2.3.

[70] See Chapter 4, at 4.3.3.

[71] Art XII of the 1998 US–Bolivia BIT; similar Art I(2) of the 1994 US–Ukraine BIT; Art I(2) of the 1993 US–Ecuador BIT; Art 17 ECT.

[72] Similar, eg, Art 10.12(2) of the 2004 CAFTA; Art 23(2) of the 2012 Japan–Iraq BIT.

[73] Art 17(2) of the 2009 ASEAN–Korea Investment Agreement.

[74] See, eg, Art 1803(1) NAFTA: 'To the maximum extent possible, each Party shall notify any other Party with an interest in the matter of any proposed or actual measure that the Party considers might materially affect the operation of this Agreement or otherwise substantially affect that other Party's interests under this Agreement'; Art 2006(5) NAFTA: 'The consulting Parties shall make every attempt to arrive at a mutually satisfactory resolution of any matter through consultations under this Article or other consultative provisions of this Agreement.' Similar Art 18.3 of the 2004 CAFTA.

[75] Art III(3) of the 1992 Australia–Indonesia BIT. Similar in the 1998 Australia–Lithuania BIT; 1995 Australia–Peru BIT; 1996 Australia–Chile BIT.

In none of the quoted DOB clauses, any explicit time limit for the exercise of the denial of benefits has been included, leading arbitral tribunals to the divergent approaches discussed further above.[76]

It is thus here where a clarification in newly negotiated investment treaties could be of great help to remedy this uncertainty. A progressive example that is becoming more frequent can be found in the 2012 Canada–China BIT, which provides:

> A Contracting Party may, at any time including after the institution of arbitration proceedings in accordance with Part C, deny the benefits of this Agreement to an investor of the other Contracting Party ...[77]

In a similar vein, the already mentioned DOB clause contained in the 2015 India Model BIT also clarifies that the clause may be exercised 'at any time, including after the institution of arbitration proceedings'.

Admittedly, the aforementioned formulations does not explicitly stipulate that the exercise of the DOB clause will have retrospective effect. However, an interpretation in good faith, respecting the *effet utile* of the clause,[78] would seem to warrant that if benefits can be denied even after the institution of proceedings, this concerns the investor-claimant with respect to the present dispute and not only prospectively with respect to future disputes. States wishing to ensure that the denial of benefits to a mailbox company be effective even after the institution of arbitral proceedings by the latter would therefore be well-advised to include this clarification in a newly negotiated IIA.[79]

Alternatively, as proposed by UNCTAD, States might 'formulate a denial-of-benefits clause as automatic ("benefits shall be denied")' or 'issue a declaration (or attach it to the treaty at the time of conclusion) expressly denying the benefits of the IIA (or IIAs) to all those investors that fall within the ambit of the clause'.[80]

An interesting comparative analysis may be made of the two different DOB clauses contained in the TPP. While Article 9.14 (Investment Chapter) provides for a 'classical' DOB clause without a clarification on when it may or must be exercised, Article 29.5 of the 'Exceptions Chapter' contains a specific DOB clause covering challenges to tobacco control measures with the clarification that 'a Party may elect to deny benefit during the [investor–State arbitration] proceedings'. The rationale for such a differentiation is—beyond the obvious topicality because of the *Philip Morris Asia v Australia* case—doubtful, even more so as it will be difficult to argue, in view of the consciously different wording, that Article 9.14 was meant to imply a right to exercise the DOB clause even after the commencement of the proceedings.

[76] See Chapter 4, at 4.3.3. [77] Art 16(2) of the 2012 Canada–China BIT.

[78] See International Law Commission, *Yearbook of the International Law Commission* (1966) Vol II, 219: 'When a treaty is open to two interpretations, one of which does and the other does not enable the treaty to have appropriate effects, *good faith and objects and purposes* of the treaty demand that the former interpretation should be adopted.'

[79] Similar see Art 20.1 of the draft India Model BIT.

[80] UNCTAD, 'Scope and Definition, A Sequel' UNCTAD Series on Issues in International Investment Agreements II (United Nations 2011) 98–99, available at <http://unctad.org/en/docs/diaeia20102_en.pdf> (last accessed on 15 September 2016).

8.2.3.2.3 Discussion

To include the requirement of substantial business activities (and seat) is a good way to ensure that treaty protection is only extended to entities that are 'real' nationals, that is those that contribute to the economy of their home State.[81] In this way, the Contracting Parties ensure strict reciprocity as between their investors and reduce the risk of treaty shopping considerably. This presupposes however that the IIA includes a clarification on how the notion of substantial business activities should be interpreted by arbitral tribunals.

Indeed, the inclusion of the requirement of substantial business activities in the notion of investor has one important advantage over the inclusion of DOB clauses. If an investor only qualifies as such under a given investment treaty if he exercises substantial business activities in the territory of his incorporation or constitution, the consent to arbitration is *ex ante* conditioned on the investor qualifying as such. If he does not qualify as such because of a lack of substantial business activities, there is thus no consent to arbitration and no discretion for arbitral tribunals to decide otherwise.[82] In the case of DOB clauses, on the other hand, arbitral tribunals have, as has been seen, considerable discretion in deciding whether the exercise of a DOB clause should have retrospective or prospective effect only. The uncertainty created by this discretion can arguably be remedied by clarifying, as for example the 2012 Canada–China BIT does, that the DOB clause can be invoked at any time and even after the institution of arbitral proceedings.

This does not mean that the risk of treaty shopping is completely thwarted, as in particular multi-layered corporate investors may manipulate corporate nationality through the notion of investment, more precisely by shifting qualifying corporate assets to entities holding the required nationality or claiming control of assets held by downstream corporate entities, as has been seen in Chapter 5. However, it is the first in a series of legal loopholes to close if States want to clamp down on treaty shopping.

8.2.3.3 Notion of control

As discussed in Chapter 4, arbitral jurisprudence remains incoherent with respect to the question of whether the notion of control found in many IIAs (including in DOB clauses) or in Article 25(2)(b) of the ICSID Convention should be interpreted as meaning purely legal (or formal) or rather effective (or de facto) control. Requiring effective control as opposed to legal control is a more probing test for the claimant and enables tribunals to look more easily for the 'true' controller of the investment, thus 'unmasking' corporate structures that may have been set up with the aim of treaty shopping.

To guide arbitral tribunals in interpreting the notion of control, some investment treaties have therefore included clarifying provisions.

[81] Similar 'Public Consultation on Investor-State Arbitration in TTIP- Comment' 6, available at <http://www.kent.ac.uk/law/downloads/ttip_isds_public_consultation_final.pdf> (last accessed on 15 September 2016).

[82] However, contrary to the DOB clause, the requirement of substantial business activities does not prevent ultimate ownership/control possibly reverting to host State or third State nationals.

Some of them have explicitly and unambiguously opted for the inclusion of effective or de facto control. Thus, the Understanding with respect to Article 1(6) ECT defines the notion of control as meaning de facto or effective control, emphasizing the case-specific nature of a finding of control and naming several factors to be taken into account in this exercise:

For greater clarity as to whether an Investment made in the Area of one Contracting Party is controlled, directly or indirectly, by an Investor of any other Contracting Party, control of an Investment means control in fact, determined after an examination of the actual circumstances in each situation. In any such examination, all relevant factors should be considered, including the Investor's

(a) financial interest, including equity interest, in the Investment;
(b) ability to exercise substantial influence over the management and operation of the Investment; and
(c) ability to exercise substantial influence over the selection of members of the board of directors or any other managing body.

Where there is doubt as to whether an Investor controls, directly or indirectly, an Investment, an Investor claiming such control has the burden of proof that such control exists.

In a similar vein, the 1996 Australia–Chile BIT provides for a de facto control test:

Una persona jurídica que sea propietaria o *controle efectivamente* una inversión en el territorio de la otra Parte Contratante donde esa persona jurídica … está constituida en conformidad con la legislación de un tercer país pero es propiedad de o es controlada efectivamente por un inversionista como el que se define en los incisos (a) y (b) de este párrafo [emphasis added].[83]

Some of the US BITs also clarify that mere legal control is not sufficient for the purposes of the notion of control contained in the BIT. Thus, para 2 of Protocol to the US–Egypt BIT clarifies that '[c]ontrol means to have a substantial share of ownership rights *and* the ability to exercise decisive influence' [emphasis added]. The US–Albania BIT, in its letter of submissal, also explains that 'ownership of over fifty percent of the voting stock of a company would normally convey control, but in many cases the requirement could be satisfied by less that that proportion, or by other arrangements'.[84]

Other BITs are more ambiguous as to which control test they adopt. A clause that can be found in many investment treaties (and which is seemingly inspired by the nearly identical clauses contained in Article XXVIII lit. n General Agreement on Trade in Service (GATS)) provides that a legal person is:

(i) 'owned' by an investor if more than fifty (50) percent of the equity interest in it is owned by the investor; and
(ii) 'controlled' by an investor if the investor has the power to name a majority of its directors or otherwise to legally direct its actions.[85]

[83] Art 1(2)(c) of the 1996 Australia–Chile BIT.
[84] Treaty Doc 104–19 (6 September 1995) VII.
[85] See, eg, in the 2008 Switzerland–Turkmenistan BIT; 2008 Japan–Uzbekistan BIT; 2011 Japan–Colombia BIT; 2012 Japan–Iraq BIT; similar in the 2009 ASEAN Comprehensive Agreement.

Should the power to name a majority of the directors be understood as the legal power to name a majority of the directors, or should it be understood as the effective power to do so? This is not clear, as both interpretations seem possible.[86] But the alternative formulation is not free from ambiguity either: the power to 'otherwise legally direct its actions' could again be understood as the *legal* power to direct the actions of the investment, interpretation that could be corroborated by the addition of the word '*legally* direct' [emphasis added], or it could be understood as meaning the effective power to do so, depending on which interpretation one has opted for in the first alternative and corroborated by the use of the word 'otherwise'. It would also seem that since the ownership test is based on majority shareholding and thus on a formal position akin to the legal control test, it would go against the *effet utile* of the alternative control clause to equally restrict it to the legal control test. Indeed, as already seen further above, while ownership/majority shareholding usually coincides with effective control, this is not always the case, and in these cases, it seems only logical that the alternative control clause should capture a different scenario than the ownership clause, even more so as most BITs use the formulation 'owned *or* controlled', not 'owned *and* controlled'.

The formulation used in the Protocol to the Netherlands–Venezuela BIT is not free from ambiguity either. It provides in its Ad Article 1(b)(iii) that:

A Contracting Party may require legal persons referred to in Art. 1(b) (iii) to submit proof of such control in order to obtain the benefits provided for in the provisions of this Agreement. For example, the following may be considered acceptable proof:

(a) that the legal person is an affiliate of a legal person constituted in the territory of the other Contracting Party;
(b) that the legal person is economically subordinated to a legal person constituted on the territory of the other Contracting Party;
(c) that the percentage of its capital owned by natural or legal persons of the other Contracting Party makes it possible for them to exercise control.[87]

While letters (a) and (b) can arguably more easily be interpreted to mean legal control, letting suffice a purely formal legal relationship between the covered investor and the controlled entity, letter (c) seems more equivocal. Should the requirement that the percentage of owned capital makes it possible for the putative investor-claimant to exercise control be understood as the abstract, for example formal, possibility to exercise control? This is what the arbitral tribunal decided in *Mobil v Venezuela*, refusing to consider 'whether or not such control was exercised in fact'.[88] However, the possibility to exercise control could in this author's view also

[86] Tania Voon, Andrew Mitchell, and James Munro, 'Legal Responses to Corporate Manoeuvering in International Investment Arbitration' (2014) 5 JIDS 41, 57. Similar for Art XXVIII lit. n GATS see Rüdiger Wolfrum, Peter-Tobias Stoll, and Clemens Feinäugle (eds), *WTO-Trade in Services* (Martinus Nijhoff 2008) 'Art XXVIII' N 50.

[87] Ad Art 1 (b)(iii) of the Protocol to the 1991 Netherlands–Venezuela BIT.

[88] *Mobil Corporation, Venezuela Holdings BV, Mobil Cerro Negro Holding, Ltd, Mobil Venezolana de Petróleos Holdings, Inc, Mobil Cerro Negro, Ltd, and Mobil Venezolana de Petróleos, Inc v Bolivarian Republic of Venezuela*, ICSID Case No ARB/07/27, Decision on Jurisdiction (10 June 2010) para 160.

be interpreted as meaning the opposite, that is, the possibility to actually exercise control.[89] This was what the tribunal in *TSA Spectrum v Argentina* (implicitly) found for a somewhat similar clause.[90]

Some other countries have defined the notion of control by reference to whether the investor had a 'substantial interest' in the investment. Thus, several Australian BITs provide that:

> A natural person, company or legal person shall be regarded as controlling a company, legal person or an investment if the natural person, company or legal person has a substantial interest in the company, legal person or the investment ...[91]

However, since the term 'substantial interest' is a rather malleable term, some of these Australian BITs—though not all of them[92]—include clarifying provisions for the interpretation of the notion of control. The Protocol to the 1995 Australia–Argentina BIT provides for example:

> 1. The Contracting Parties acknowledge that the question of control with respect to an investor will depend on the factual circumstances of the particular case.
> 2. The Contracting Party in whose territory the investments are undertaken may require proof of the control invoked by the investors of the other Contracting Party.
> 3. The following facts, inter alia, shall be accepted as evidence of control:
>   (a) a level of direct or indirect participation in the capital of a legal person or of a company which allows for control, such as a direct or indirect participation higher than 50% of the capital or a majority shareholding; or
>   (b) a direct or indirect control of the voting rights allowing for:
>   (i) the exercise of a decisive power over management and operations; or
>   (ii) the exercise of a decisive power over the composition of the Board of Directors or any other managing body.
> 4. Where there is doubt as to whether an investor exercises effective control, the investor shall be responsible for demonstrating that such control exists.

Similar clarifying provisions can be found in the Protocol to the 1996 Australia–Chile BIT, which, as may be remarked on the sideline, unambiguously opts for the effective control test:

> The Contracting Parties acknowledge that the question of effective control with respect to an investor will depend on the factual circumstances of the particular case. The following facts, inter alia, shall be accepted as evidence of such control:
>
> (a) a substantial direct or indirect participation in the capital of the legal entity which allows for effective control, such as, in particular, a direct or indirect participation of more than 50% of the capital or a majority shareholding; or

[89] Indeed, as seen in Chapter 4, even minority shareholding may under certain circumstances confer decisive control.

[90] See Chapter 4, at 4.3.4.2.1.

[91] Art 1(4) of the 1995 Australia–Argentina BIT. Similar, eg, in the 1992 Australia–Indonesia BIT; 1998 Australia–Lithuania BIT.

[92] For an exception see, eg, the 1993 Australia–Hong Kong BIT. For an interpretation of the term 'substantial interest' see *Philip Morris Asia Limited v Commonwealth of Australia*, UNCITRAL, PCA Case No 2012-12, Award on Jurisdiction and Admissibility (17 December 2015) (redacted version) para 502.

(b) direct or indirect control of voting rights allowing for:
 (i) the exercise of a decisive power over management and operations; or
 (ii) the exercise of a decisive power over the composition of the board of directors or of any other managing body.

Where there is doubt as to whether an investor exercises effective control, the investor shall be responsible for demonstrating that such control exists.

The inclusion of a clause reversing the burden of proof in case of doubt as to the effective control also seems an appropriate way to exclude the interposition of conduits in particular in the case of indirect investors and thus seems recommendable for States who wish to restrict treaty shopping.[93]

8.2.3.4 Foreign control as in Article 25(2)(b) ICSID Convention

Since international investment arbitration is in principle not open to domestic investors, locally incorporated legal persons may normally not bring investment claims, but are limited to domestic proceedings. For ICSID arbitration, this principle is inherent in Article 25(2)(a) and (b) of the Convention, which excludes host State nationals from bringing investment claims. Some investment treaties or chapters also stipulate explicitly that (local) investments may not bring claims.[94]

However, some host countries require that a foreign investment be channelled into their territories via local investments. This is why many IIAs make an exception to the rule that locally incorporated legal persons cannot bring an investment claim and include a provision recognizing, for purposes of Article 25(2)(b) second clause of the ICSID Convention, locally incorporated investments or legal persons as protected under the invoked IIA if the latter are controlled by investors of the other Contracting Party.[95] However, some IIAs provide that locally incorporated legal persons will be treated as nationals of the other Contracting Party for purposes of ICSID proceedings if 'the majority of shares are *owned* by investors of the other Contracting Party' [emphasis added].[96] Whether this criterion is still within the 'outer limits' of the ICSID Convention is doubtful.[97] As has been seen in the *Caratube* decision, majority ownership does not in all and any cases translate into (actual) control.[98]

Article 25(2)(b) second clause of the Convention is not explicit on the question at which time the foreign control of the locally incorporated investment must exist.

[93] A similar reversal of the burden of proof for showing control can be found in the Annex to Art I(f) of the 1996 Canada–Venezuela BIT, requiring that the 'investor *demonstrably* controls, directly or indirectly, the enterprise which owns the asset'.

[94] See, eg, Art 2(5) of the 1995 Australia–Argentine BIT; Art III(4) of the 1992 Australia–Indonesia BIT; Art 2(3) of the 1995 Australia–Peru BIT; Art 2(3) of the 1998 Australia–Lithuania BIT. Similar Art 1117(4) NAFTA.

[95] On the criteria for establishing foreign control see Chapter 4, at 4.3.4.1.1.

[96] See, eg, Art 9(5) of the 2013 Netherlands–United Arab Emirates BIT; Art 9 of the 1994 Netherlands–Peru BIT; or Art 8(2) of the 1994 United Kingdom–Tanzania BIT.

[97] See Chapter 4, at 4.3.4.1.3.

[98] *Caratube International Oil Company LLP v Republic of Kazakhstan*, ICSID Case No ARB/08/12, Award (5 June 2012) paras 336–37, 380–81.

As has been seen above, the conclusion seems allowed that under normal circumstances, the foreign control has to be established at the same time as the nationality of the locally incorporated investment, for example 'on the date on which the Parties consented to submit the dispute to … arbitration'.[99] Some investment treaties have incorporated this date as relevant date for the showing of foreign control.[100]

However, in view of the fact that changes in foreign control of a local investment may be intransparent and happen quickly, thus favouring strategic changes of nationality, many IIAs have included the requirement that the invoked foreign nationality must exist 'before the dispute arises'.[101] This is undisputedly an appropriate way to curb strategic corporate restructuring in view of an existing dispute. However, it does not prevent strategic changes of nationality in view of a future, but foreseeable dispute, and it does of course not eliminate the difficult question of when an actual dispute started.[102]

For the contentious question as to whether an arbitral tribunal, in search of foreign control within the meaning of Article 25(2)(b) of the ICSID Convention, can or even must enquire into the nationality of the ultimate controller,[103] none of the examined investment treaties contains any treaty-based provision or clarification. In view of the uncertainty created by inconsistent arbitral decisions in this respect (and despite a more recent, seemingly developing line of jurisprudence), States should consider including a clarification in newly negotiated investment treaties as to whether they will let suffice any first-found qualifying nationality or rather want the arbitral tribunal to enquire into ultimate ownership.

Alternatively, the clarification that 'foreign control' should (also) be understood as meaning actual/effective control has a similar (though not identical) effect as asking the tribunal to enquire into the nationality of ultimate control. However, while in most cases effective control will coincide with ultimate control (and the quest for effective control therefore fulfils the policy goal of ensuring that only 'real' nationals of the other treaty Party benefit from the rights contained in the treaty), the possibility remains that even an entity with the qualifying nationality and exercising effective control be ultimately controlled (eg by a natural person) with host State nationality.

8.2.4 Notion of investment

As has been seen both in Chapters 1 and 5 above, the limited standing, under customary international law, of shareholders as seen in the *Barcelona Traction* judgment

[99] Christoph Schreuer, Loretta Malintoppi, August Reinisch, and Anthony Sinclair, *The ICSID Convention: A Commentary* (Cambridge University Press 2009) 'Article 25' para 872.

[100] See, eg, Art 9(5) of the Netherlands–Indonesia BIT; similar Art 11(5) of the 1998 Japan–Russian Federation BIT.

[101] See, eg, Art 9 of the 2002 Netherlands–Kazakhstan BIT; Art 9 of the 2003 Netherlands–Laos BIT; Art 9 of the Netherlands–Jordan BIT; Art 8(2) of the 2005/2006 UK Model BIT; Art 13(5) of the 1995 Australia–Argentina BIT; Art 26(7) ECT; Art VII(6) of the 1984 US–Democratic Republic of Congo BIT.

[102] See Chapters 6 and 7.

[103] See Chapter 4, at 4.3.4.2.

of the International Court of Justice (ICJ) was one of the main reasons for States to include the protection of indirect investments in BITs, most notably in the form of shareholding. This broad and often unqualified protection of indirect investments makes treaty shopping much easier, in particular for multinational companies with corporate structures covering several national jurisdictions.

If only for theoretical purposes, a (rather far-reaching) proposal included in the former 2015 draft India Model BIT[104] seems worth mentioning. Clearly concerned by the practice of treaty shopping, the draft India Model BIT proposed to exclude from treaty protection not only portfolio investments,[105] but also holding or investment companies as protected investment.[106] As also seen in the specification that 'real and substantial business operations do not include: ... (ii) the passive holding of stock',[107] the objective of the Indian Government was visibly to close the door to corporate vehicles that are easily set up and interposed in the corporate structures and thus normally grant easy access to investment protection. Though a legitimate policy decision, one may in this author's opinion wonder whether this would not have been almost a return to the times of *Barcelona Traction*. The adopted Model BIT has only retained the exclusion of portfolio investment, but not the exclusion of holding companies.[108]

8.2.4.1 Protection of indirect investments

In essence, two approaches can be found in the formulation of the protection of indirect investments in international investment law.

The first approach usually defines covered investment as 'investment owned or controlled directly or indirectly by an investor of [another] Party'.[109] In this approach, the protection of direct or indirect investments can thus be found in the same definition of 'investment'. Sometimes the notion of investment is specified to mean 'every kind of *asset* owned or controlled, directly or indirectly, by an investor' [emphasis added].[110]

The definition is often qualified, such as by the requirement that the investment be made in the territory of the other Contracting Party[111] and/or the requirement that the investment be made in accordance with the laws and/or investment policies of the other Contracting Party.[112] Some investment treaties additionally

[104] 2015 draft India Model BIT, available at <https://mygov.in/sites/default/files/master_image/Model Text for the Indian Bilateral Investment Treaty.pdf> (last accessed on 15 September 2016).

[105] Art 1.7 of the draft India Model BIT.

[106] Art 1.8 of the draft India Model BIT: 'For the purposes of this Treaty, a holding company or an investment company shall not be considered an Investment nor shall such companies be considered as protected assets of an Investment.'

[107] Art 1.2.2 of the draft India Model BIT.

[108] Art 1.4 of the 2015 India Model BIT.

[109] Art 1139 NAFTA.

[110] See, eg, in the 2002 Japan–Korea BIT; 2011 Japan–Colombia BIT.

[111] See, eg, 1994 US–Kazakhstan BIT; 1995 Australia–Argentina BIT; 2009 ASEAN Comprehensive Investment Agreement; 2010 Canada–Slovak Republic BIT.

[112] See, eg, the 1994 Peru–China BIT, the 1994 Bolivia–Chile BIT, the 1999 Australia–India BIT, the 1996 Canada–Venezuela BIT, the 2009 ASEAN–China Investment Agreement.

require that the investment be approved in writing in order to qualify as covered investment.[113]

The second approach, on the other hand, can mainly be found in (partly older) European BITs such as in Swiss BITs or many German and Dutch BITs. This approach often omits the inclusion of direct or indirect investment in the definition of investment, simply defining the notion of protected investment broadly as 'every kind of asset', usually followed by a non-exhaustive list of protected assets. In the definition of protected investor, however, some will include, aside from natural persons qualifying as nationals and legal persons incorporated or constituted according to the law of one Contracting Party (often with additional substantive requirements), those legal entities that are established under the law of a non-Contracting Party but controlled by natural or legal persons of one Contracting Party, thus leading to a broader *ius standi*. This is the case of virtually all Swiss BITs.[114] Most Dutch BITs also follow this approach.[115]

Under both approaches, some IIAs restrict the protection of indirect investments to those owned 'through an investor of a third State'.[116] Others only protect those indirect investments constituted on the territory of one of the Contracting Parties.[117]

On the other hand, some IIAs do not explicitly include the protection of indirect investments. This is the case for example of all UK BITs, as well as some German BITs.[118] However, as has been seen in Chapter 5 above, arbitral tribunals have rather unanimously found that even in the absence of an explicit mention of indirect investments, the latter were protected.

As has been seen in Chapters 1 and 5 above, the broad protection of indirect investments leads to the possibility—in particular for multi-jurisdictional corporate structures—to bring separate investment claims (either in parallel or consecutively) in their own right for what is the same measure. Most States seem to try to counter the risk of multiple proceedings by recourse to procedural (consolidation, waiver, or fork-in-the-road) requirements.[119] By contrast, only few States explicitly limit the possibility of treaty shopping inherent in the protection of indirect investments. One country that has been wary of this risk is Australia, whose BITs often provide that:

> This Agreement shall not apply to a company or legal person organized under the law of a third country within the meaning of paragraph 1(d)(ii) of Article 1 where the provisions of

[113] See, eg, in the 2009 ASEAN–Korea Investment Agreement; 2009 ASEAN Comprehensive Investment Agreement; 2007 COMESA Investment Agreement.

[114] See, eg, the 1974 Switzerland-Indonesia BIT; 1988 Switzerland–Uruguay BIT; 1998 Switzerland–Ethiopia BIT; 2000 Switzerland–Costa Rica BIT; 2008 Switzerland–Turkmenistan BIT; 2012 Switzerland–Tunisia BIT.

[115] See, eg, the 1991 Netherlands–Venezuela BIT; 2006 Netherlands–Dominican Republic BIT; 2007 Netherlands–Burundi BIT.

[116] See, eg, 1991 Netherlands–Slovak Republic BIT; 1989 Belgium–Luxemburg–Russian Federation; 1998 Canada–Costa Rica BIT.

[117] See, eg, 1994 US–Kazakhstan BIT; 1998 Netherlands–Mexico BIT.

[118] See, eg, the 1989 Germany–Soviet Union BIT; 1998 Germany–Antigua and Barbuda BIT; 1997 Germany–United Arab Emirates BIT; 2002 Germany–Thailand BIT; 2007 Germany–Oman BIT.

[119] See Chapter 1, at 1.1.3.

an investment protection agreement with that country have already been invoked in respect of the same matter.[120]

8.2.4.2 Specific criteria pertaining to the notion of investment

As has been seen in Chapter 5, more recent arbitral jurisprudence has started to read specific requirements into the notion of investment in order to decide whether a claim based on a corporate structuring or restructuring should be dismissed or not. In particular the questions of how the notion of contribution should be understood, whether the notion of investment contains a good faith requirement and whether it should be interpreted as containing an 'active' contribution requirement remain contentious.

As for the notion of investment under Article 25(1) of the ICSID Convention, it has been seen above that as of yet no consensus exists among arbitral tribunals as to whether the notion of investment should be understood to contain some inherent criteria or characteristics or not. Seemingly in view of this uncertainty, many newer IIAs now include some of the so-called *Salini* criteria, namely the commitment of capital or other resources, the expectation of gain or profit, and the assumption of risk, while mostly omitting the contentious criteria of the contribution to the economic development of the host State. This is, for example, the case in the 2011 Japan–Colombia BIT, the 2011 Switzerland–Kosovo BIT, the 2012 Japan–Iraq BIT, and the CETA.

8.2.4.2.1 Specifications of the contribution requirement

Arbitral jurisprudence has also further specified how the notion of investment under Article 25(1) of the ICSID Convention should be understood, in particular whether an economic motivation is necessary or a nominal payment is sufficient in order to qualify as a contribution.[121] However, none of the examined investment treaties has thus far included any of these findings, likely in view of their highly case-specific nature.

8.2.4.2.2 Good faith requirement

As for the contentious question whether good faith properly speaking should be part of the notion of investment (be it for purposes of the ICSID Convention or for purposes of the BIT),[122] hardly any investment treaty provides for a treaty-based clarification. A notable exception in this aspect seems to constitute Ad Article 1(b)(iii) of the 2013 Netherlands–UAE BIT, which provides that '[a]n investor of one Contracting Party having a subsidiary with a *bonafide* business *lawfully* established in the other Contracting Party shall with regard to its investments benefit from the protection of this Agreement' [emphasis added].

[120] See, eg, Art 2(2) of the 1995 Australia–Argentina BIT. Similar the 1988 Australia–China BIT; 1996 Australia–Chile BIT; 1999 Australia–India BIT; 1992 Australia–Indonesia BIT; 1998 Australia–Lithuania BIT; 1995 Australia–Peru BIT.

[121] See Chapter 5, at 5.4.1.

[122] See Chapter 5, at 5.4.4.

However, as the exact meaning of this concretization '*bonafide* business' is not clear, arbitral tribunals will be hard-pressed to fill this notion with more concrete content. Indeed, the discussions by the arbitral tribunal in *Phoenix Action v Czech Republic* spring to mind (even though in that case, the arbitral tribunal could not rely on a treaty-based good faith requirement). As will be discussed more in detail further below,[123] in the case of a strategic change of nationality, an explicit good faith requirement attached to the notion of investment does not seem to have much added value as it is normally not the investment as such that must be disapproved of, but the purpose pursued with it. There may however be cases in which the investment itself can be considered tarnished, such as in the case of the violation of transnational public policy.[124] Though some arbitral tribunals have in such cases applied the principle of good faith (sometimes in its concretization of transnational public policy) even in the absence of a treaty-based notion (the latter usually being in the form of an 'in accordance with host State law' clause),[125] the inclusion of such notion may guide an arbitral tribunal in its reasoning.

8.2.4.2.3 'Active contribution' requirement

Unclear is also the question whether the investor must have made an 'active contribution' in order to qualify for protection. This question arises in particular in multi-level corporate structures where, because of the protection of indirect investments, normally either the parent company or any of its subsidiaries could claim protection under select investment treaties based on qualifying assets any of the subsidiaries might hold. As has been seen above, the tribunal in *Standard Chartered Bank v Tanzania* was the first one to read an 'active contribution' requirement into the dispute settlement clause of the UK–Tanzania BIT, interpreting the formulation 'concerning an investment *of* the latter in the territory of the former' [emphasis added] to require that the Claimant had some active role either in the process of making or administering the investment.[126]

Though that tribunal's findings remain in need of further clarification in particular with respect to the question how precisely an 'active' investment can be distinguished from a 'passive' one, it nevertheless stands to reason that some treaty-based formulations can more easily be interpreted to contain an inherent 'active contribution' requirement than others. Valuable clues on the nature of the relationship required between the investor and the investment can indeed often be found either in the clause defining the notion of investment or in the dispute settlement clause. Arguably, it is sometimes a question of fine nuances in wording that may tilt an arbitral tribunal's 'interpretative balance' towards one or the other conclusion.

[123] See Chapter 9, at 9.3.4.

[124] Such as in the case of acquisition of the investment through corruption or bribery.

[125] See, eg, *Gustav FW Hamester GmbH & Co KG v Ghana*, ICSID Case No ARB/07/24, Award (18 June 2010) paras 123–24; *Plama Consortium Ltd v Bulgaria*, ICSID Case No ARB/03/24, Award (27 August 2008) para 133. See also Carolyn Lamm, Brody Greenwald, and Kristen Young, 'From World Duty Free to Metal-Tech: A Review of International Investment Treaty Arbitration Cases Involving Allegations of Corruption' (2014) 29 ICSID Review-FILJ 328, 342ff.

[126] *Standard Chartered Bank v Tanzania* (n 29) para 230.

Thus, in the classical passive-voice formulation 'every kind of asset, owned or controlled, directly or indirectly, by an investor', found in many investment treaties,[127] it seems more difficult to read an active relationship requirement into the plain words of the clause. The use of the passive voice 'controlled by' seems to indicate that the drafters of the treaty would accept a purely passive ownership or control by an investor-claimant, even over several layers of corporate structures, in particular in the absence, in the IIA, of any 'effective control' requirement.

The active-voice formulation 'every kind of asset that an investor *owns or controls*, directly or indirectly [emphasis added]' that some of the most recent IIAs use,[128] would seem to make it (a little bit) easier to argue that the investor must have a more active role than claiming protection simply on the basis of a (passive) indirect ownership or control over a qualifying asset. Yet, even this latter formulation may leave one wondering where the distinguishing line between an unprotected passive indirect ownership or control and a protected active one exactly lies.[129]

This distinction seems clearer in the formulation 'every kind of asset *invested* by investors of one Contracting Party [emphasis added]' found in some IIAs,[130] which would seem to impose a more active relationship between the investor and the investment than the mere ownership or control, namely by requiring that the investor have actually invested in the asset on whose basis protection is being claimed, in other words have contributed some of his capital all the while assuming the risks inherent in an investment.

That there may be a difference between the act of owning or controlling the asset and the act of investing in it also becomes apparent through the formulations found in some BITs that combine the two requirements. Thus, some Australian BITs define covered investment as 'every kind of asset owned or controlled, *and invested* by an investor of one Contracting Party in the territory of the other Contracting Party [emphasis added]'.[131] Requiring alternatively a passive or an active investment, the 2010 Canada–Slovak Republic BIT defines investment as 'any kind of asset *held or invested* either directly or indirectly by an investor of one Contracting Party [emphasis added]', thus making a clear distinction between the (passive) holding of an investment and the (active) act of investing.

Some definitions of the notion of covered investment do not permit a conclusion as to whether a more active relationship between the investor and the investment is required. This is in particular the case for the 'Continental' style clauses, which, as

[127] See, eg, Art 2(2) of the 1986 Netherlands–Turkey BIT; Art 1(1)(a) of the 1998 Australia–Lithuania BIT; Art 1(2) of the 2002 Japan–Korea BIT; Art 1(a) of the 2005/2006 UK Model BIT; Art 4(c) of the 2009 ASEAN Comprehensive Agreement; Art 1(s) of the 2009 Canada–Jordan BIT; Art 1(a) of the 2011 Japan–Colombia BIT.

[128] See, eg, Art 1 of the 2005 US–Uruguay BIT; Art 1(1) of the 2012 Japan–Korea–China BIT; Art 8.1 of the CETA (version February 2016); Art 9.1 of the TPP Investment Chapter.

[129] See *Standard Chartered Bank v Tanzania* (n 29) para 253.

[130] See, eg, Art 1(1) of the 1994 Peru–China BIT; Art 1(1) of the 1994 Netherlands–Indonesia BIT; Art 1(c) of the 1999 Australia–India BIT; Art 1(1) of the 2001 Netherlands–China BIT; Art 1(1)(d) of the 2009 ASEAN–China Investment Agreement.

[131] See, eg, Art 1(1)(a) of the 1992 Australia–Indonesia BIT; Art 1(1)(a) of the 1995 Australia–Argentina BIT.

seen further above, usually define the notion of investment broadly as 'every kind of asset', followed by a (usually non-exhaustive) list of protected assets. In this case, dispute settlement clauses may sometimes need to be looked into in order to find an 'active contribution' requirement.

Formulations in dispute settlement clauses that can arguably be interpreted to contain such a requirement include:

Any legal dispute arising between that Contracting Party and a national of the other Contracting Party concerning an investment *of* that national in the territory of the former Contracting Party,[132]

Disputes between a Contracting Party and an Investor of another Contracting Party relating to an Investment *of* the latter in the Area of the former, which concerns an alleged breach of an obligation of the former under Part III,[133]

A dispute between an investor of one Contracting Party and the other Contracting Party concerning an investment *of* the former in the area of the latter which has not been settled,[134] or

A dispute between a Contracting Party and an investor of another Contracting Party that has incurred loss or damage by reason of, or arising out of, an alleged breach of any obligation of the former Contracting Party under this Agreement with respect to the investor or *its* investments in the territory of the former Contracting Party.[135] [All emphases added.]

In all these examples, the active relationship required between the investor and the investment becomes apparent in the emphasized formulations. Worth mentioning is also the formulation in the 2015 draft India Model BIT, which for the notion of protected investor not only explicitly excluded the passive holding of stock and holding respectively investment companies from the scope of protection,[136] but also required that the investor 'has made *and* owns or controls an Investment in the Host State [emphasis added]'.[137] This formulation has again not made it into the Model BIT.

By contrast, the following formulations lack this very information, thus making it difficult to attach the requirement to the wording of the treaty:

Any dispute between an investor of one Contracting Party and the other Contracting Party *in connection with an investment* in the territory of the other Contracting Party,[138]

... any dispute *concerning the investments* occurring between one Contracting Party and a national or company of the other Contracting Party,[139] or

... an alleged breach of any right conferred or created by this Treaty *with respect to an investment*[140] [all emphases added].

States wishing to prevent the possibility of investors claiming protection on the basis of qualifying assets held by a subsidiary as in *Standard Chartered Bank v*

[132] Art 9 of the 2002 Netherlands–Kazakhstan BIT.

[133] Art 26(1) ECT.

[134] Art 10 of the 1993 Hong Kong–Australia BIT.

[135] Art 15(1) of the 2012 Japan–Korea–China BIT.

[136] See Arts 1.2.2 and 1.8 of the draft India Model BIT.

[137] Art 1.9 of the draft India Model BIT.

[138] Art 8 of the 1994 Peru–China BIT.

[139] Art 7 of the 2007 France Model BIT.

[140] Art VI(1) and (4) of the 1992 US–Kazakhstan BIT; similar Art 8(1)(b) of the 1986 Netherlands–Turkey BIT.

Tanzania should therefore consider to include wording that expresses the requirement of a more active relationship between the investor and the investment, as shown above. Given the novelty of the legal argument and the remaining uncertainties concerning the distinguishing line between a 'passive' and an 'active' investment, the inclusion of such requirement does of course not guarantee that arbitral tribunals will in every case follow the jurisprudence as in *Standard Chartered* and require an active relationship between the investor and the investment. Yet, it will increase chances that a deciding arbitral tribunal will do so, also in view of the now probably heightened awareness of arbitral tribunals with respect to this kind of legal arguments.

8.2.4.2.4 Origin of capital requirement

As seen in Chapter 4, it is only where a treaty provides for an explicit origin of capital requirement that an arbitral tribunal can impose this requirement on the investor.

Only very few treaties contain an origin of capital requirement, mandating that the capital or equity originate in the State of claimed nationality. An origin of capital requirement can for example be found in Article VII(1)(b) of the Iran–US Claims Settlement Declaration of 1981, which gives standing to:

> A corporation or other legal entity which is organized under the laws of Iran or the United States or any of its states or territories, the District of Columbia or the Commonwealth of Puerto Rico, if, collectively, natural persons who are citizens of such country hold, directly or indirectly, an interest in such corporation or entity equivalent to fifty per cent or more of its capital stock.[141]

In a similar manner, Decision 291 of the Andean Commission of 1991 on the 'Regime for the Common Treatment of Foreign Capital and Trademarks, Patents, Licensing Agreements and Royalties' defines the term 'national enterprise' as:

> An enterprise established in the recipient country, more than eighty percent of whose equity capital belongs to national investors, provided that, in the judgment of the competent national agency, that share is reflected in the technical, financial, administrative and commercial management of the company.[142]

However, while the 1998 Framework Agreement on the ASEAN Investment Area contained a requirement for 'effective ASEAN equity',[143] the 2009 ASEAN Comprehensive Investment Agreement has done away with it.

[141] Declaration of the Government of the Democratic and Popular Republic of Algeria Concerning the Settlement of Claims by the Government of the United States of America and the Government of the Islamic Republic of Iran (Claims Settlement Declaration) 19 January 1981, available at <http://www.iusct.net/General%20Documents/2-Claims%20Settlement%20Declaration.pdf> (last accessed on 15 September 2016).

[142] Andean Commission of 1991, Decision 291, 'Regime for the Common Treatment of Foreign Capital and Trademarks, Patents, Licensing Agreements and Royalties' Art 1, available at <http://www.wipo.int/wipolex/en/text.jsp?file_id=223259> (last accessed on 15 September 2016).

[143] See its Art 1(ii).

Although the inclusion of an origin of capital requirement is undoubtedly a possibility to maintain or restore strict reciprocity as between the Contracting Parties, it does not seem to reflect, nor attend to, the nature and necessities of modern international financial transactions. It is probably for this reason that an origin of capital requirement is not found in any more recent investment treaties.

8.2.5 Temporal jurisdiction

As has been seen in Chapters 6 and 7, several important questions arise when examining whether a claim based on a strategic change of nationality may be dismissed for lack of jurisdiction *ratione temporis* or is inadmissible on grounds of the abuse of rights or abuse of process doctrine.

Thus, the question of whether disputes existing at the time of the change of nationality are excluded from the temporal scope of application of the invoked IIA even without the explicit inclusion of a provision to this effect, that is, as a matter of customary international law, remains controversial. While some States restrict themselves to re-stating the customary international law principle of non-retroactivity as found in Article 28 of the VCLT, others explicitly exclude disputes having arisen prior to the entry into force of the BIT in question. This however raises in turn the highly subjective question at which time the specific dispute has arisen and, in case of a gradually souring business relationship, whether it is the same as an earlier dispute. As will be seen, none of the revised IIAs provides for treaty-based guidelines or clarifying provisions in this respect.

8.2.5.1 Principle of non-retroactivity

Some IIAs restate the principle that the provisions of the IIA in question do not bind either Party in relation to any act or fact that took place or any situation that ceased to exist before the BIT entered into force. This is, for example, the case of many US BITs,[144] the 2002 UK–Bosnia-Herzegovina BIT, the 2004 CAFTA, the 2006 Canada–Peru BIT, the 2009 ASEAN–China Investment Agreement, the 2013 Australia–New Zealand Investment Protocol, or the TPP Investment Chapter.

Whether the explicit inclusion of the principle of non-retroactivity is necessary in view of its customary nature is doubtful, yet has the merit of clearly stating the intention of the treaty parties to exclude pre-existing acts, facts or situations from the scope of protection. However, as discussed in detail in Chapter 6, it does in any

[144] See, eg, Art 2(3) of the 2005 US–Uruguay BIT; similar Art 10.1(3) of the Investment Chapter of the 2006 US–Colombia FTA. See also the US position in this respect: 'The dispute settlement procedures in a BIT generally do not apply retroactively. In other words the dispute settlement mechanisms—as well as the other obligations—in a BIT do not apply to any act or fact which took place before the BIT entered into force. However, if the act or fact began in the past but continues after the BIT entered into force, the BIT may apply' available at <http://tcc.export.gov/Trade_Agreements/All_Trade_Agreements/exp_002699.asp> (last accessed on 15 September 2016).

case not resolve the controversy as to whether the principle of non-retroactivity (whether as treaty or customary law) also excludes disputes that have arisen before the entry into force of the BIT, in particular in the absence of an explicit exclusion clause.

As already mentioned in Chapter 6, this arguably depends on how the dispute settlement clause defines the notion of dispute.[145] As a reminder, the principle of non-retroactivity excludes acts, facts or situations that occurred or ceased to exist before the entry into force of the treaty. These acts, facts or situations constitute the basis of the (alleged) breach of the investment obligation and are therefore a question of the substantive scope of investment protection or in other words of the merits.

Now, if the notion of dispute in the dispute settlement clause is defined (only) with reference to the (alleged) breach of an investment obligation, the principle of non-retroactivity may arguably be interpreted as excluding pre-existing disputes even in the absence of an explicit corresponding exclusion clause. By contrast, if the notion of dispute in the dispute settlement clause is not only defined with reference to the notion of breach of an investment obligation, the principle of non-retroactivity may arguably not be interpreted as also excluding pre-existing disputes even in the absence of an explicit corresponding exclusion clause.

The above shows a considerable uncertainty in relation with the explicit inclusion of the principle of non-retroactivity, depending on how the dispute settlement clause is worded. This is not to say that States should not explicitly include the principle of non-retroactivity. Indeed, as already mentioned, despite its customary nature, the explicit inclusion leaves no doubt about the fact that the parties had wanted to exclude acts, facts or situations that have occurred or have ceased to exist before the entry into force of the IIA. The problem rather arises from not additionally including a (single or double) exclusion clause, as seen in the following.

8.2.5.2 Exclusion of disputes that have arisen prior to the entry into force of the IIA

In view of this uncertainty, it may be advisable for States to include a clause that explicitly excludes disputes that have arisen before the entry into force of the IIA with respect to the party (so-called single exclusion clause).

This is what many States have done. Exact wordings may vary, such that some IIAs exclude 'disputes' that have arisen before the entry into force of the IIA.[146] Some also exclude 'differences'[147] that have arisen before the IIA has entered into force. Others additionally exclude 'claims' that have arisen before the entry into force of the IIA, with a few excluding claims that have been settled or that were

[145] See Chapter 6, at 6.4.1.2.

[146] See, eg, 2001 Australia–Uruguay BIT; 2005 Australia–Mexico BIT; 1999 Netherlands–Ecuador BIT; 2013 Netherlands–United Arab Emirates BIT; 2009 ASEAN–Australia–New Zealand FTA; 1998 Germany–Mexico BIT; 1997 Austria–Chile BIT.

[147] See, eg, 1996 UK–Chile BIT; 1995 Australia–Argentina BIT.

already under judicial or arbitral process before the entry into force of the IIA.[148] As has been argued in Chapter 6, 'entry into force' of the treaty should be understood as covering also the 'entry into force with respect to the investor-claimant'.[149]

The explicit exclusion of pre-existing disputes is a good and first step for States wishing to prevent strategic changes of nationality solely in view of a concrete and existing dispute. It does however not solve the subjectivity involved with finding the existence (or not) of a dispute, as shown in Chapter 6. The exclusion of 'differences or disputes' that have arisen before the entry into force of the IIA may be an appropriate means to bring the relevant cut-off point for the change of nationality forward, as a 'difference' usually represents a lesser conflict level[150] and thus can arguably be more easily found to exist than a dispute. A strategic change of nationality thus becomes more difficult to be upheld by an arbitral tribunal.

8.2.5.3 Exclusion of acts or facts giving rise to a later dispute

Another possibility to reduce the subjectivity inherent in finding a dispute is the exclusion of acts or facts giving rise to a later dispute that have occurred before the entry into force of the IIA (so-called double exclusion clause). In a similar way as the exclusion of 'differences', the exclusion of acts or facts giving rise to a dispute that have occurred before the entry into force of the IIA has the advantage of bringing forward the relevant cut-off point for a strategic change of nationality. However, even more than the exclusion of 'differences', it literally goes to the root of the dispute, that is, the relevant acts or facts that constitute the backbone of the dispute and the later claim. When these acts or facts have occurred is a question that is open to a more objective determination than the existence of a dispute and is therefore clearly advisable if States want to restrict the possibility of a strategic change of nationality.

Switzerland has a consistent policy of excluding 'claims or disputes arising out of events' which have occurred before the entry into force of the BIT.[151] Japan has also concluded various BITs that exclude 'claims arising out of events' which occurred before the entry into force of the BIT.[152]

Other IIAs excluding acts or facts giving rise to a dispute that have occurred before its entry into force include for example the 2009 ASEAN Comprehensive Agreement, the 2009 ASEAN–China Investment Agreement, the 2009 ASEAN–Korea Investment Agreement, the 1996 Australia–Chile BIT, and the 1998 Netherlands–Chile BIT. A similar clause can also be found in the 2015 India Model BIT.

[148] See, eg, 1990 UK–Argentina BIT; 1995 Australia–Argentina BIT; 2003 Netherlands–Laos BIT; 2007 Germany–Oman BIT; 2001 Netherlands–China BIT; 2007 COMESA Agreement.

[149] See Chapter 6, at 6.4.1.1.

[150] See in this sense, eg, *Emilio Agustín Maffezini v Kingdom of Spain*, ICSID Case No ARB/97/7, Decision on Objections to Jurisdiction (25 January 2000) para 96.

[151] See, eg, 2006 Switzerland–Saudi Arabia BIT; 2006 Switzerland–Colombia BIT; 2007 Switzerland–Syria BIT; 2009 Switzerland–China BIT; 2010 Switzerland–Egypt BIT; 2011 Switzerland–Kosovo BIT; 2012 Switzerland–Tunisia BIT.

[152] See, eg, 2002 Japan–Korea BIT; 2012 Japan–Iraq BIT; 2008 Japan–Uzbekistan BIT; 2011 Japan–Colombia BIT. It should be noted, however, that even the inclusion of a double exclusion clause does not address the question of the foreseeability of the dispute; it thus only goes half-way.

No exclusion clauses of whichever kind exist for example in the 1992 Australia–Indonesia BIT, the NAFTA Chapter 11, the 1999 Australia–India BIT, the 1993 Australia–Hong Kong BIT, the 1998 Australia–Lithuania BIT, and the CETA.

8.2.5.4 Dispute settlement clause: notion of dispute

As seen in Chapter 6, the notion of dispute is prone to arbitral subjectivity, thus creating a considerable amount of legal uncertainty. It may therefore come as somewhat of a surprise that although the notion of dispute is omnipresent in ISDS (and more generally speaking in international adjudication), at the same time it appears to be one of the least defined notions. Indeed, none of the revised investment treaties contains a definition properly speaking of what is to be understood as 'dispute', all the while determining which kinds of investment disputes are covered by States' consent to investor–State arbitration.

This obviously raises the question: should States include a clarification of the notion of dispute, for instance one along the lines of the jurisprudence of the Permanent Court of International Justice or ICJ?

The inclusion of clarifications may be an adequate means in certain specific matters for ensuring that arbitral tribunals will be guided, in their interpretations, by what the parties had intended to understand by the notion in question. For example, for the question of how to understand indirect expropriation, with several different interpretations existing,[153] a clarification guides arbitral tribunals in their interpretation and limits possible arbitral discretion. However, in the case of the notion of dispute, it is not necessarily existing differing arbitral interpretations of the notion itself that is problematic, but rather the application of the jurisprudence on the notion to the facts of the case. In other words, the finding of a dispute will to a certain extent always remain fact-specific. This being said, States wishing to reduce arbitral discretion in this aspect might include a clarification to the effect that prolonged negotiations or protests about a measure (or part of a measure) that will later form the basis of investment claim may be considered as constituting a dispute for the purposes of the jurisprudence on corporate structuring or restructuring.

8.2.6 Inclusion of conditions under which a corporate restructuring is accepted

Finally, there is the possibility to include in domestic investment legislation or investor–State agreements the requirement that the competent host State authorities must approve a planned transfer of shares. This was, for example, the case in

[153] See, eg, August Reinisch, 'Expropriation' in Peter Muchlinski, Federico Ortino, and Christoph Schreuer (eds), *Oxford Handbook on International Investment Law* (Oxford University Press 2008) 407–58; Brigitte Stern, 'In Search of the Frontiers of Indirect Expropriation' in Arthur W Rovine (ed), *Contemporary Issues in International Arbitration and Mediation, The Fordham Papers 2007* (Martinus Nijhoff 2008) 29–51; W Michael Reisman and Robert Sloane, 'Indirect Expropriation and its Valuation in the BIT Generation' (2003) 74 BYIL 115.

Aucoven v Venezuela, where the Concession Agreement concluded between the Parties contained such requirement.[154] A similar requirement was contained in the Shareholders' Agreement between the original investor and the competent Venezuelan authority in *Vannessa Venture v Venezuela*.[155]

In a similar vein, Schill and Bray propose that 'host States [should] clearly set the conditions in which corporate restructuring is acceptable in their domestic laws or in investor-State contracts, as a question relating to the admission of foreign investments'.[156] To this proposal might arguably be added the inclusion of the obligation to disclose ownership structures—in particular before a potential investment claim might be raised—so as to enable the host State (and the arbitral tribunal in the case of a dispute) to determine the nationality of the ultimate controller.

The inclusion of a requirement to have any corporate restructuring approved by the competent authorities or of the obligation to disclose ownership structures for the investment to remain covered seems in principle an appropriate way for host State authorities to keep track of possible changes in the corporate structure of foreign investors that might be implemented with the aim of bringing an investment claim. However, in particular the first proposal presupposes the capacity, in terms of infrastructure and resources, of host State authorities to follow up on these approval requests and would seem to be pertinent above all for investor–State contracts (such as concession agreements), where there is already a particularized relationship between the foreign investor and the host State. For IIAs, where such a relationship does a priori not exist, it would seem that the inclusion of an approval requirement could theoretically be linked to a (separate) admission or registration requirement, yet again subject to the caveat of practical feasibility. An obligation to disclose claimant's ultimate ownership and control structures to the host State (possibly subject to certain confidentiality requirements) as a pre-condition to the right to bring an investment claim, as proposed by the 2015 draft India Model BIT,[157] would on the other hand not depend on infrastructure or resources and could therefore be an adequate and easy-to-implement tool to ensure that arbitral tribunals dispose of knowledge on ultimate ownership and control structures, if necessary for the decision.

The clarifying inclusion, in IIAs, of the conditions under which a corporate restructuring is acceptable also seems a possibility to reduce the uncertainty created in this respect by arbitral jurisprudence. Though a clarification would not seem to have much added value with respect to the question of whether a pre-existing

[154] *Autopista Concesionada de Venezuela CA (Aucoven) v Bolivarian Republic of Venezuela*, ICSID Case No ARB/00/5, Decision on Jurisdiction (27 September 2001) para 92.

[155] *Vannessa Ventures Ltd v Bolivarian Republic of Venezuela*, ICSID Case No ARB(AF)/04/6, Award (16 January 2013).

[156] Stephan Schill and Heather Bray, 'Good Faith Limitations on Protected Investments and Corporate Structuring' in Andrew Mitchell, M Sornarajah, and Tania Voon (eds), *Good Faith and International Economic Law* (Oxford University Press 2015) 88, 114.

[157] Arts 8 and 10 of the 2015 draft India Model BIT foresaw obligations to disclose ownership structures, their changes and sources of funds as a condition to benefit from ISDS, but these obligations were also softened in the final Model BIT text and disconnected from ISDS.

dispute is excluded, this question being adequately covered by a corresponding exclusion clause,[158] it could be very useful for the question which foreseeability test to use in order to determine whether a future dispute was (sufficiently) foreseeable for the investor and the corporate restructuring thus constituted an abuse of rights/abuse of process. However, any inclusion of such clarification should not mask the fact that these questions remain highly case-specific, as will be seen in turn.

8.2.7 Inclusion of the abuse of process doctrine

A novel approach in investment treaty drafting is the inclusion of an express mention to the prohibition of an abuse of process. An example therefore is the CETA. Its Article 8.18(3) clarifies that:

> For greater certainty, an investor may not submit a claim to arbitration under this Section where the investment has been made through fraudulent misrepresentation, concealment, corruption, or conduct amounting to an abuse of process.

As can be seen from the above formulation, the clause seems to have mainly declaratory value ('for greater certainty'), aimed at ensuring that the arbitral tribunal will be guided towards the abuse of process objection in cases of abusive corporate restructuring. However, it is clear that even without this inclusion, a tribunal should examine an abuse of rights/abuse of process objection given its nature as general principle of law and the applicable law clause that usually includes applicable rules of international law. Though not adding much in substantive terms, its inclusion is still useful as a guidance to the arbitral tribunal, and it has the advantage of explicitly covering other possible procedural 'misbehaviours'.

8.2.8 Inclusion of the 'pre-existing/foreseeable dispute' jurisprudence

Another innovative approach seeking to address potentially abusive changes of nationality can be found in the Investment Chapter of the EU–Singapore FTA. Its Article 9.17(6) provides:

> For greater certainty, a tribunal shall decline jurisdiction where the dispute had arisen, or was very likely to arise, at the time when the claimant acquired ownership or control of the investment subject to the dispute, and the tribunal determines based on the facts that the claimant has acquired ownership or control of the investment for the main purpose of submitting the claim to arbitration under this Section. This is without prejudice to other jurisdictional objections which could be entertained by the tribunal.[159]

[158] See Chapter 7, at 7.3.2.1.

[159] EU–Singapore Free Trade Agreement (initialled agreement, authentic text as of May 2015) Chapter 9, available at <http://trade.ec.europa.eu/doclib/docs/2014/october/tradoc_152844.pdf> (last accessed on 15 September 2016).

The draft text of the TTIP Investment Chapter under negotiation and the Investment Chapter of the EU–Vietnam FTA contains identically or similarly-worded clauses, entitled 'Anti-circumvention'.[160]

As becomes obvious, the drafters of the aforementioned FTAs have incorporated the essence of the line of jurisprudence described in Chapters 6 and 7 above that distinguishes as to whether at the time of change of nationality, there was a pre-existing dispute or whether a future dispute was foreseeable. This seems to reflect the wish of the Contracting Parties to guide an arbitral tribunal's interpretation in this respect.

The attempt to 'codify' this line of jurisprudence in the FTA is not without problems, though. For one, though the drafters seem to understand it as a clarification ('for greater certainty'), likely with declaratory value only, the wording '*shall* decline' would seem to imply that a tribunal must decline its jurisdiction if the conditions found in the clause are fulfilled. Does it also mean that an arbitral tribunal would be prevented from applying its own interpretation of the 'pre-existing/foreseeable dispute' jurisprudence, in other words, that it would be obliged to apply the conditions set by Article 9.17? This is not clear.

Second and related to the first remark, the wording chosen implies that both objections (pre-existing respectively foreseeable future dispute) are jurisdictional objections, even though as elaborated in Chapter 7 and will be in Chapter 9, the foreseeability objection should be understood as the test for the finding of an abuse of process, which itself should be correctly seen as an admissibility objection.

Third, the wording 'was very likely to arise', though clearly aimed at capturing the idea of foreseeability of the dispute, introduces yet another variation of the test and risks placing too much emphasis on the subjective investor horizon.[161]

Fourth and importantly, by explicitly including the 'sole purpose' doctrine and seemingly establishing it as an additional requirement for the finding of an abusive restructuring ('*and* the tribunal determines … for the main purpose of submitting the claim to arbitration [emphasis added]'), the clause may arguably be interpreted as excluding a finding of abusive restructuring even where the tribunal has established that the restructuring occurred at a time when a dispute already existed or a future dispute 'was very likely to arise', if the investor can credibly invoke other important reasons, such as tax reasons, for the restructuring. As has already been explained in Chapter 7, the 'sole purpose' doctrine is problematic because of the difficulty in establishing in a more objective manner why the investor has undertaken the change of nationality. It is arguably because of this difficulty that arbitral tribunals have developed the line of jurisprudence that looks in particular at the timing of the change of nationality and the question whether at that time, a dispute existed or was foreseeable, this in order to infer the purpose from objective facts. Even though this approach acknowledges (as did the arbitral tribunal in *Philip*

[160] Art 15 (Chapter II, Section 2, Section, 3, Sub-section 4) Investment Chapter of the draft TTIP; Art 17 (Chapter 8, Section 3, Sub-section 5) Investment Chapter of the EU–Vietnam Free Trade Agreement.

[161] On this problem see Chapter 7, at 7.3.2.2.

Morris v Australia) that an abuse of rights finding remains case-specific, the clause in its current version seems to considerably raise the bar to finding a strategic, possibly 'last-minute' restructuring as invalid, in particular as future claimants might quickly adapt to the heightened requirements of proving alternative reasons in light of the arbitral tribunal's holding in *Philip Morris v Australia*.[162]

Yet, despite the discussed problems, the inclusion of clauses in new IIAs that 'codify' the 'pre-existing/foreseeable dispute' jurisprudence is in principle a good way to ensure an arbitral tribunal will remain 'on the right track' in interpreting restructuring claims. However, to be effective and avoid any (bad) 'interpretative surprises', the reference to the 'main purpose' of the restructuring should in any case be eliminated.

8.3 Preliminary Conclusions

It has been seen that many States have indeed started to include, though to differing extent, more treaty shopping-restrictive language in newly negotiated investment treaties. In view of the currently limited chances of success of 'political' solutions to restrict the practice of treaty shopping, the treaty-based approaches seem for now to constitute the most appropriate way to rein in treaty shopping provided a corresponding policy decision has been taken by the State(s) in question.

Based on the different clauses examined in this chapter, a State wishing to make future investment treaties (or existing ones, in the case of subsequent agreements) as 'treaty shopping-proof' as possible could be advised to include or modify the following clauses:

- For the preamble, include an explicit expectation of reciprocity of protection;
- For the notion of natural person as investor, include an effective and dominant nationality requirement in the case of dual nationality and/or explicitly exclude claims by host State nationals;
- For the notion of legal person as investor, include the requirement of substantive business activities for the investor to qualify as covered investor, and clarify the indicators for finding substantial business activities;
- If substantive business activities are not required to qualify as protected investor under the IIA, alternatively include a denial of benefits clause giving the right to deny benefits to mailbox companies owned or controlled by either third or host State nationals and explicitly specifying that the clause may be exercised at any time, even after the beginning of an arbitral proceeding;
- For the notion of control, clarify that control means effective control and that in case of doubt, the burden of proof is reversed, requiring the investor to show that his control is effective;

[162] *Philip Morris Asia v Australia* (n 92) para 582.

- For the notion of 'foreign control' within the meaning of Article 25(2)(b), specify that foreign control must exist before the dispute arises and clarify that foreign control also means effective control; potentially clarify whether any first-found qualifying nationality will suffice the criteria of foreign control or rather whether ultimate control must be found out;
- For the notion of investment, include a formulation that can be interpreted as imposing an active relationship between the investor and its investment;
- For the notion of investment, provided a corresponding infrastructure and/or implementation capacity by the host State exists, include the obligation of the investor to disclose ownership and control structures, possibly as a pre-condition for being entitled to bring an investment claim, and/or clarify under which circumstances a corporate restructuring is permitted;
- For the question of the temporal scope of the treaty and the dispute settlement clause, explicitly exclude disputes that have arisen before the entry into force of the IIA or explicitly exclude the acts or facts giving rise to a later dispute that have occurred before the entry into force of the IIA.

On the other hand, clauses that incorporate (more or less literally) the 'pre-existing/foreseeable dispute' line of jurisprudence are an innovative approach to address the issue of time-sensitive restructuring, but should be handled with caution given the high fact-sensitivity of this jurisprudence, and they should in any cause do away with the 'sole' or 'main purpose' doctrine. A general clarification that a claim based on an abuse of process is excluded may be another appropriate way of addressing time-sensitive restructuring and has the advantage of covering other possible procedural 'misbehaviour', but this also presupposes that the arbitral tribunal will refer to the 'pre-existing/foreseeable dispute' jurisprudence out of its own initiative.

9

The Role of the Principle of Good Faith in Treaty Shopping

9.1 Introduction

As could be seen throughout the various chapters, disputing parties and arbitral tribunals have attached a possible lack of good faith in bringing an investment dispute based on treaty shopping to a variety of legal principles, institutions, or interpretative methods.[1] Thus, respondents have often tried to persuade the arbitral tribunals to ask for a 'genuine link' of the putative investor-claimant or to 'pierce its veil' in order to find the 'real' beneficiary of the investment claim. Arbitral tribunals have interpreted the notion of investment to require the investor to have made a contribution (so as to test whether the economic transaction was a real or only a sham transaction) or to have acquired the investment in good faith. Many of them have assumed the exclusion of disputes existing at the time of the strategic change of nationality even in the absence of a treaty-based exclusion clause to this effect, and they have applied the abuse of rights doctrine to determine whether the strategic change of nationality was done at a moment when a future dispute was foreseeable. It is no exaggeration to state that the potential for variable application of the principle of good faith is wide, with some cases being open to alternative applications or approaches, as has also been seen for example in the *Vannessa Ventures* or the *Alapli Elektrik* cases.[2]

The principle of good faith is thus pervasive and undoubtedly key to understanding the distinction between a 'legitimate nationality planning' and 'abusive treaty shopping'. However, as seen above, good faith may come in many different expressions and manifestations. The question therefore arises whether all of these applications and/or interpretations are equally correct or appropriate for judging the lawfulness of a claim based on a strategic change of nationality. This question seems particularly important for older international investment agreements (IIAs) that do not contain 'tailor-made' clauses to counter the potential for treaty shopping in a treaty-based manner as seen in Chapter 8.

[1] In this sense also *KT Asia Investment Group BV v Republic of Kazakhstan* ICSID Case No ARB/09/8, Award (17 October 2013) para 126.

[2] See *Vannessa Ventures Ltd v Bolivarian Republic of Venezuela*, ICSID Case No ARB(AF)/04/6, Award (16 January 2013) para 113; *Alapli Elektrik BV v Republic of Turkey*, ICSID Case No ARB/08/13, Decision on Annulment (10 July 2014).

This chapter will propose a systematization of arbitral tribunals' uses and applications of the principle of good faith and its manifestations or concretizations in drawing the distinction between a 'legitimate nationality planning' and 'abusive treaty shopping'. What will be seen is that arbitral tribunals have, broadly speaking, recurred to two methodological approaches when trying to make the distinction subject of this research: the 'interpretative' approach on the one hand and the 'application of the principle of good faith and its concretizations' approach on the other. Indeed, depending on the wording of the clauses under interpretation and personal 'legal preferences', arbitral tribunals have used both approaches to try and balance the countervailing interests inherent in an investment claim based on treaty shopping, even if the existence of a good faith examination in the interpretative approach is much less readily apparent than in the 'application' approach. The decision in *Phoenix Action v Czech Republic* has arguably played a particular role in the development of tribunals' approaches, thus warranting a separate analysis, constituting the point of transition from the 'interpretative approach' to the autonomous application of the abuse of rights doctrine and setting a de facto precedent for more recent arbitral decisions dealing with the question.

Given its nature for variable manifestations and concretization, but also its potential for controversy, it seems necessary to first examine the normative status of the principle of good faith, its functions and its concretizations before discussing the correctness or appropriateness of the different good faith emanations relevant to the question of treaty shopping found in arbitral jurisprudence and scholarship. Based on these findings, the chapter will close by proposing a more coherent conceptual approach towards the use of the principle of good faith and its emanations in drawing the line between a 'legitimate nationality planning' and 'abusive treaty shopping'.

9.2 The Normative Status of the Principle of Good Faith and its Functions

There are few principles in international law that are as widely and historically recognized in their importance and pervasiveness as the principle of good faith. Since the ages of time, good faith has been a major factor of social cohesion, instrumental to a peaceful coexistence of individuals and nations. Good faith not only governs contractual relations between private parties, but also treaty relations between States from the time of 'formation [of the treaties] to their extinction'.[3] It even reaches beyond treaty relations, being capable of creating certain obligations from unilateral declarations, as the International Court of Justice (ICJ) held in the *Nuclear Tests* case.[4] Good faith also plays an important role in international dispute

[3] Bin Cheng, *General Principles of Law as Applied by International Courts and Tribunals* (Stevens and Sons 1953) 106.

[4] *Nuclear Tests (Australia v France) (Merits)* [1974] ICJ Rep 253, 268–69.

settlement, infusing predictability and reasonableness into state behaviour, serving as an interpretative tool for courts and tribunals and restraining legal formalism and arbitrariness.[5]

The principle of good faith can thus be found in variegated codifications, such as the duty to fulfil one's obligations in good faith as in Article 2(2) of the Charter of the United Nations, the duty to settle disputes in good faith as in Article 33 of the Charter of the United Nations, paragraph 5 of the 1982 Manila Declaration on the Peaceful Settlement of International Disputes,[6] or Article 3.10 of the Dispute Settlement Understanding,[7] the duty to cooperate in good faith as in Article 86 of the Rome Statute of the International Criminal Court,[8] the duty to perform and interpret a treaty in good faith and not to defeat its object and purpose before its entry into force, as seen in Articles 18, 26, and 31 Vienna Convention on the Law of Treaties (VCLT), etc. Moreover, it has developed over time into related principles or concepts such as legitimate expectations, *pacta sunt servanda*, estoppel, acquiescence, equity, *abus de droit*, and others.

Given its prominence and universal recognition, there is no doubt that the principle of good faith qualifies as either general principle of law within the meaning of Article 38(1)(c) of the Statute of the ICJ, as general principle of international law and/or as rule of customary international law.[9] This has also been confirmed by international courts and tribunals.[10] There can also be hardly any doubt that the principle of good faith is applicable in investor–State arbitration and thus applies to foreign investors.[11]

[5] Andreas Ziegler and Jorun Baumgartner, 'Good Faith as a General Principle of (International) Law' in Andrew Mitchell, M Sornarajah, and Tania Voon, *Good Faith and International Economic Law* (Oxford University Press 2015) 9.

[6] Peaceful Settlement of Disputes between States, GA Res 37/10, UN GAOR, 37th sess, 68th plen mtg, Agenda Item 122, Annex, UN Doc A/RES/37/10 (15 November 1982).

[7] Marrakesh Agreement Establishing the World Trade Organization, opened for signature 15 April 1994, 1867 UNTS 3 (entered into force 1 January 1995) Annex 2 (Understanding on Rules and Procedures Governing the Settlement of Disputes) 1869 UNTS 401.

[8] Opened for signature 17 July 1998, 2187 UNTS 90 (entered into force 7 January 2002).

[9] See, eg, Marion Panizzon, *Good Faith in the Jurisprudence of the WTO* (Hart Publishing 2006) 11; Ian Brownlie, *Principles of Public International Law* (Oxford University Press, 5th edn 2008) 19; Andrew Mitchell, 'Good Faith in the WTO Dispute Settlement' (2006) 7 Melb J Intl L 339, 345.

[10] See, eg, Appellate Body Report, *United States—Import Prohibition of Certain Shrimp and Shrimp Products*, WTO Doc WT/DS58/AB/R (adopted 6 November 1998) para 158; *Phoenix Action Ltd v Czech Republic*, ICSID Case No ARB/06/5, Award (15 April 2009) para 77; *Mobil Corporation, Venezuela Holdings BV, Mobil Cerro Negro Holding, Ltd, Mobil Venezolana de Petróleos Holdings, Inc, Mobil Cerro Negro, Ltd, and Mobil Venezolana de Petróleos, Inc v Bolivarian Republic of Venezuela*, ICSID Case No ARB/07/27, Decision on Jurisdiction (10 June 2010) para 175.

[11] See, eg, *Inceysa Vallisoletana SL v Republic of El Salvador*, ICSID Case No ARB/03/26, Award (2 August 2006) para 234–39; *Phoenix Action v Czech Republic* (n 10) para 107; *ConocoPhillips Petrozuata BV, ConocoPhillips Hamaca BV and ConocoPhillips Gulf of Paria BV v Bolivarian Republic of Venezuela*, ICSID Case No ARB/07/30, Decision on Jurisdiction (3 September 2013) para 274; *Abaclat and Others v Argentine Republic*, ICSID Case No ARB/07/5, Decision on Jurisdiction and Admissibility (4 August 2011) para 646 (formerly known as Giovanna a Beccara and Others); Eric De Brabandere, '"Good Faith", "Abuse of Process" and the Initiation of Investment Treaty Claims' (2012) 3 JIDS 609, 619; Hervé Ascencio, 'Abuse of Process in International Investment Arbitration' (2014) 13 Chin J Intl L 763, 779.

The role of the principle of good faith in investor–State arbitration can thus not be overrated. As a general principle of law, it reunites (quasi-) constitutional qualities that make it an invaluable companion in the fragmented body of law that is international investment law. For one, general principles of law have the capacity to unify the legal system, and thus to contribute to legal security, by transporting some basic legal ideas both from one branch of international law to another and within specific branches of international law.[12] The quest to overcome fragmentation is not only relevant for the broader area of international law, but also for international investment law.

General principles of law also contribute to a flexibilization of the legal system. As Kolb noted:

> A system containing only precise and fixed legal rules does not exist, because it would not be viable. Social life is at once too multifaceted and too evolutionary to be able to be caught in some strict normative categories.[13]

This tends to be true for domestic law, yet international law is even less susceptible to quick changes because its formation and development depend to a large extent on the consent and consensus of States, found in treaties or custom. This applies even more to international investment law. Though based on thousands of IIAs, thus showing extraordinary treaty-making dynamics, these IIAs remain valid and thus (in principle) immutable for periods of ten to twenty years at a time. Good faith then allows to weigh circumstantial grounds into formal rules of consent or to soften the formal correctness of acts, thus avoiding harsh results and bringing flexibility into the legal relationship.[14]

The above-mentioned virtues would seem to make the principle of good faith and its emanations the perfect candidate for a more coherent approach towards judging the validity of a claim based on a strategic change of nationality under international investment law.

However, this eulogy on the qualities of the principle of good faith as a general principle of law should not mask the fact that good faith is an inherently abstract and value-oriented notion that without further concretization remains vague. It is in particular the related risk of being accused of 'judicial activism' that causes most adjudicators to treat the principle with awe, if not apprehension.[15] In this sense, the

[12] Markus Kotzur, 'Good faith', *Max Planck Encyclopedia of Public International Law* (Oxford Public International Law) para 14, available at <http://opil.ouplaw.com>; Robert Kolb, 'Principles as Sources of International Law (With Special Reference to Good Faith)' (2006) 53 NILR 1, 27. Similar Ole Fauchald, 'The Legal Reasoning of ICSID Tribunals—An Empirical Analysis' (2008) 19 EJIL 301, 312: '[General principles of law] could be expected to play a significant role in international investment law. One reason is that there is a close substantive relationship between public international law, private international law, and domestic law in relation to international investments ... General principles of law can thus be a 'common denominator' for and function as a bridge between these three sources of law.'

[13] Kolb, 'Principles as Sources' (n 12) 28.

[14] Ibid.

[15] Kotzur (n 12) para 26; Bernardo Cremades, 'Reflections on Good Faith in Investor-State Arbitration' in Peter Gauch, Franz Werro, and Pascal Pichonnaz (eds), *Mélanges en l'honneur de Pierre Tercier* (Schulthess 2008) 779, 785.

controversial question for many international tribunals has been whether to apply the principle of good faith as an autonomous source of obligation, in other words whether States (or investors) could violate an obligation of good faith independently of any more concretized duties. Both the ICJ and the Appellate Body of the World Trade Organization (WTO) have rejected this.[16]

Even though they have to this authors knowledge never explicitly discussed this question, investment arbitral tribunals have shown themselves somewhat less reluctant in assuming the applicability of an independent good faith obligation, in particular in connection with the acquisition of an investment contrary to domestic laws or international public policy (such as the case of bribery or corruption).[17] Indeed, one might wonder whether there isn't potentially more space for investment arbitral tribunals to explore the boundaries of an independent good faith obligation, given the normally relatively broad applicable law clauses, lesser adjudicatory limitations than those applying for example for the WTO Dispute Settlement Body, and limited annulment grounds. In a similar vein, one could argue that accusing a foreign investor of bad faith is possibly politically less sensitive than accusing a State of bad faith.[18]

And yet, fact is that in cases of claims based on strategic changes of nationality, arbitral tribunals have remained very careful with bad faith verdicts, trying to attach their disapproval of the circumstances surrounding the strategic change of nationality, wherever possible, to treaty-based interpretations or the abuse of rights/abuse of process doctrine, using the 'bad faith hammer' only very rarely, usually in cases of outright fraud.[19]

The following two sections will examine and systematize the two different approaches arbitral tribunals have used in order to make the distinction between 'legitimate nationality planning' and 'abusive treaty shopping': on the one hand the interpretation of treaty-based notions that are relevant for jurisdictional purposes (section 9.3), and on the other hand the application of manifestations and concretizations of the principle of good faith (section 9.4).

[16] See, eg, *Nuclear Tests (Australia v France) (Merits)* [1974] ICJ Rep 253, 268–69; *Border and Transborder Armed Activities (Nicaragua v Honduras) (Jurisdiction and Admissibility)* [1988] ICJ Rep 69, 105; confirmed in *Land and Maritime Borders (Cameroon v Nigeria) (Preliminary Objections)* [1998] ICJ Rep 275, 297; Appellate Body Report, *United States—Continued Dumping and Subsidy Offset Act of 2000*, WTO Doc WT/DS217/AB/R, WT/DS234/AB/R (adopted 27 January 2003). But see Robert Kolb, *La Bonne Foi en Droit International Publique* (Presses Universitaires de France 2000) 157–58.

[17] Stephan Schill and Heather Bray, 'Good Faith Limitations on Protected Investments and Corporate Structuring' in Andrew Mitchell, M Sornarajah, and Tania Voon (eds), *Good Faith and International Economic Law* (Oxford University Press 2015) 88ff.

[18] See in this sense International Law Commission, 'First Report on Diplomatic Protection' Report of the fifty-second session (2000) UN Doc A/CN.4/506, para 108: 'Faced with the choice between finding that Liechtenstein had acted in bad faith in conferring nationality on Nottebohm and finding that he lacked a "genuine link" of attachment with Liechtenstein, the Court preferred the latter course as it did not involve condemnation of the conduct of a sovereign State.'

[19] See at 9.4.3.

9.3 The Interpretative Approach Towards Treaty Shopping

Treaty interpretation has a key importance in deciding whether a strategic change of nationality should be considered 'legitimate nationality planning' or 'treaty abuse'. Indeed, many of the arbitral tribunals have had recourse to the interpretative methods or rules codified in Articles 31 and 32 VCLT in order to interpret specific notions contained in the International Centre for Settlement of Investment Disputes (ICSID) Convention and the IIAs under interpretation, such as the notions of investor, investment, and dispute. However, as seen, the resulting arbitral approaches have sometimes been rather heterogenic, often raising more questions than answering them.

The principle of good faith finds differing expression in treaty interpretation. As pointed out by De Brabandere and Van Damme, one may distinguish between the 'objective' and the 'subjective' function of the principle of good faith.[20] As for the former, '[i]n forming the basis for treaty interpretation under international law, good faith serves an objective function, that is, a function relating to the process of interpretation'.[21] The latter, on the other hand, concerns 'good faith's establishment of a general standard of behaviour for treaty interpreters by requiring that they act reasonably, fairly. In that sense, the principle of good faith has a subjective function, that is, one relating to the interpreter'.[22] It is mainly its objective function that will interest us in this section.

Article 31(1) VCLT provides that '[a] treaty shall be interpreted in good faith in accordance with the ordinary meaning to be given to the terms of the treaty in their context and in the light of its object and purpose'. Different elements must thus be taken into account in the interpretation of a treaty term, namely the ordinary meaning of the term under interpretation, the context of the term, the object and purpose of the treaty, and the obligation to interpret in good faith.

However, the Convention does not say anything about how these different elements interact in practice nor does it establish a hierarchical order in this respect.

It seems generally accepted that even though the 'ordinary meaning' of a term can normally be considered the 'starting point of any interpretation',[23] the interpretative process would be incomplete if it did not take into account all the elements mentioned in Article 31(1).[24] Indeed, as remarked by the tribunal in *Aguas del Tunarí*, the interpretative process is one of:

> progressive encirclement where the interpreter starts with (1) the ordinary meaning of terms of the treaty, (2) in their context and (3) in light of the treaty's object and purpose,

[20] Eric De Brabandere and Isabelle Van Damme, 'Good Faith in Treaty Interpretation' in Andrew Mitchell, M Sornarajah, and Tania Voon, *Good Faith and International Economic Law* (Oxford University Press 2015) 38.

[21] Ibid. [22] Ibid.

[23] Romesh Weeramantry, *Treaty Interpretation in Investment Arbitration* (Oxford University Press 2012) para 3.32. Similar Anthony Aust, *Modern Treaty Law and Practice* (Cambridge University Press 2000) 188.

[24] Andrés Rigo Sureda, *Investment Treaty Arbitration, Judging Under Uncertainty* (Cambridge University Press 2012) 22–23.

and by cycling through this three step inquiry iteratively closes in upon the proper interpretation.[25]

Good faith informs this whole interpretative process and in this sense at all times 'hovers' over the aforementioned interpretative methods, helping 'to justify choices in applying Articles 31 to 33 of the VCLT' and to identify 'other tools, principles or even values that can be taken into account in interpreting treaties, despite the absence of any express reference to them in the VCLT'.[26]

9.3.1 Ordinary meaning

Arbitral tribunals have often based their reasoning on the 'ordinary meaning' approach in order to distinguish an acceptable from an unacceptable claim based on treaty shopping. The 'ordinary meaning' approach has also been termed by the International Law Commission (ILC) as 'the very essence of the textual approach'.[27]

As seen in Chapter 4, the 'ordinary meaning' or 'textual' approach has prevailed in virtually all cases of strategic changes of nationality brought under Article 25(2)(a) and 25(2)(b) first clause ICSID Convention.[28] In the case of natural persons claiming as investor, tribunals have so far always refused to 'supplement' the notion of investor with unwritten additional 'genuine link' requirements, both in the case of single and dual nationalities. In the case of foreign-incorporated legal persons as investor–claimants, arbitral tribunals have, absent any additional treaty-based requirement in the notion of investor, equally let the 'textual' approach prevail, rejecting attempts to interpret the notion of investor in the light of the 'piercing the corporate veil' doctrine.[29] However, in conformity with what was said earlier, tribunals have in these cases usually confirmed the ordinary meaning of the term 'investor' by recourse to its context and the object and purpose of the treaty.[30]

As for the contribution requirement found to be relevant in a number of cases,[31] some arbitral tribunals have also relied on an interpretation of the 'ordinary

[25] *Aguas del Tunarí SA v Plurinational State of Bolivia*, ICSID Case No ARB/02/3, Decision on Respondent's Objections to Jurisdiction (21 October 2005) para 91.

[26] De Brabandere and Van Damme (n 20) 42–43. Similar Mark Villiger, *Commentary on the 1969 Vienna Convention on the Law of Treaties* (Martinus Nijhoff 2009) 'Article 31' N 8.

[27] International Law Commission, *Yearbook of the International Law Commission* (1966) Vol II, 221 (para 12).

[28] For the exception of *Venoklim Holding BV v Bolivarian Republic of Venezuela*, ICSID Case No ARB/12/22, Award (Spanish) (3 April 2015) see above in Chapter 4, at 4.3.1.1 and 4.3.1.3.

[29] On the 'piercing of the corporate veil' doctrine see below at 9.4.2.

[30] See, eg, *Tokios Tokelės v Ukraine*, ICSID Case No ARB/02/18, Decision on Jurisdiction (29 April 2004) para 31; *Rompetrol Group NV v Republic of Romania*, ICSID Case No ARB/06/3, Decision on Respondent's Preliminary Objections on Jurisdiction and Admissibility (18 April 2008) para 85; *ADC Affiliate Limited & ADMC Management Limited v Republic of Hungary*, ICSID Case No ARB/03/16, Award (2 October 2006) paras 357–59; *Saluka Investments BV v Czech Republic*, UNCITRAL, Partial Award (17 March 2006) para 241; *Yukos Universal Ltd (Isle of Man) v Russian Federation*, UNCITRAL, PCA Case No AA 227, Interim Award on Jurisdiction and Admissibility (30 November 2009) para 415. See also below at 9.3.3.

[31] See Chapter 5, at 5.4.1.

meaning' of the notion of investment under the ICSID Convention,[32] though others have favoured an object and purpose-based interpretation.[33]

9.3.2 Context

Arbitral tribunals also often recur to a context-based interpretation, though they do not always explicitly name it as such. Context can be provided for example by:

> (a) words or sentences found in close proximity to those terms; ... (c) other articles in the treaty; (d) the use of an identical or similar term in other articles of the treaty; ... (f) the definition of a term as providing the context for other terms in the same treaty ...[34]

One instance in which an arbitral tribunal arguably recurred to a context-based interpretation without explicitly saying so was in *Pac Rim Cayman v El Salvador*, when the tribunal interpreted the denial of benefits (DOB) clause in Article 10.12.2 Central American Free Trade Agreement (CAFTA) as having retrospective effect because the consent to arbitration in Article 10.16.2 CAFTA was 'necessarily qualified from the outset' by the DOB clause.[35]

Likewise, in the cases of *Burimi v Albania* and *National Gas v Egypt*, the tribunals used the 'host State bias' contained in Article 25(2)(a) ICSID Convention as interpretive context in order to interpret the notion of 'foreign control' in Article 25(2)(b) second clause, again without explicitly saying so.[36]

In a similar vein, even though tribunals tend not to identify it as such, clarifications for example in the IIA or in a Protocol forming integral part of the IIA, containing definitions or examples of what should be understood as 'control' for the purposes of the IIA (be it for the notion of investor, investment or DOB clause), can arguably be considered context within the meaning of Article 31(1) VCLT.[37]

9.3.3 Object and purpose

Other arbitral tribunals have placed the main emphasis on the object and purpose-based interpretative method in making the distinction between a 'legitimate nationality planning' and 'treaty abuse'. As already seen in Chapter 8, the object and purpose of a treaty is usually contained in the preamble.[38]

[32] *KT Asia v Kazakhstan* (n 1) para 165; *Quiborax SA, Non Metallic Minerals SA and Allan Fosk Kaplún v Plurinational State of Bolivia*, ICSID Case No ARB/06/2, Decision on Jurisdiction (27 September 2012) para 212.

[33] See, eg, *Phoenix Action v Czech Republic* (n 10) para 93; *Caratube International Oil Company LLP v Republic of Kazakhstan*, ICSID Case No ARB/08/12, Award (5 June 2012) para 350.

[34] Weeramantry (n 23) para 3.54.

[35] *Pac Rim Cayman LLC v Republic of El Salvador*, ICSID Case No ARB/09/12, Decision on the Respondent's Jurisdictional Objections (1 June 2012) para 4.90.

[36] See Chapter 4, at 4.2.2.

[37] Similar Florian Franke, *Der personelle Anwendungsbereich des internationalen Investitionsschutzrechts* (Nomos 2012) 158.

[38] But cautioning against the overreliance on the preamble see Richard Gardiner, *Treaty Interpretation* (Oxford University Press 2008) 186.

For IIAs, arbitral tribunals have sometimes greatly relied on the purpose of an IIA to protect foreign investors and stimulate the flow of capital and technology through the reciprocal encouragement and protection of foreign investment.[39] This has led these tribunals to adopt interpretations that have sometimes been termed as (too) 'investor-friendly' and have been evoked in connection with legitimacy concerns.[40] For the purposes of this research, relying on the object and purpose of protecting foreign investments and stimulating the flow of capital and technology has for example led to interpreting the notion of control as meaning 'legal control'[41] or denying retroactive effect to the exercise of the DOB clause.[42]

However, not all object and purpose-based interpretations are necessarily 'investor-friendly'. Thus, the stated objective of promoting the economic relations between the parties of the bilateral investment treaty (BIT) prompted the tribunal in the *Lao Holdings v Laos* decision to second-guess the nature of the claimants' investment:

> In the present case, as in Phoenix, it is difficult to discern any fresh economic investment arising out of the restructuring that would advance the purposes of the Treaty which, according to its preamble, exists 'to extend and intensify the economic relations between [the Parties], particularly with respect to investments by the nationals of one Contracting Party in the territory of the other Contracting Party'.[43]

In a similar vein, the objective of *reciprocal* protection of investments found in the UK–Tanzania BIT was one of the reasons for the tribunal to dismiss the claim for lack of 'active contribution' in *Standard Chartered Bank v Tanzania*.[44]

The purpose of the ICSID Convention to further *international* investment respectively to constitute a forum for *international* investment disputes has also been an important objective taken into account by arbitral tribunals in a number of cases. Thus, in the *Phoenix Action* case, the tribunal held that:

> The purpose of the ICSID system is not to protect nationals of a Contracting State against their own State: the system was clearly 'designed to facilitate the settlement of disputes

[39] See, eg, *Aguas del Tunarí v Bolivia* (n 25) paras 153 and 241; *Tokios Tokelės v Ukraine* (n 30) para 31; *Franz Sedelmayer v Russian Federation*, SCC, Award (7 July 1998) paras 58–59.

[40] On the issue of 'pro-investor bias' see, eg, Weeramantry (n 23) paras 6.98-6.106; Susan Franck, 'The Legitimacy Crisis in Investment Treaty Arbitration: Privatizing Public International Law Through Inconsistent Decisions' (2004–2005) 73 Fordham L Rev 1521, 1578. Similar Trinh Hai Yen, *The Interpretation of Investment Treaties* (Martinus Nijhoff 2014) 97–98.

[41] *Aguas del Tunarí v Bolivia* (n 25) paras 246, 264.

[42] *Plama Consortium Limited v Republic of Bulgaria*, ICSID Case No ARB/03/24, Decision on Jurisdiction (8 February 2005) paras 161–62, 165; *Liman Caspian Oil BV and NCL Dutch Investment BV v Republic of Kazakhstan*, ICSID Case No ARB/07/14, Award (22 June 2010) para 225; *Yukos v Russia* (n 30) paras 456–59; *Ascom and Stati v Republic of Kazakhstan*, SCC, Award (19 December 2013) para 745; *Pan American Energy LLP and BP Argentina Exploration Company v Argentine Republic*, ICSID Case No ARB/03/13, Decision on Preliminary Objections (27 July 2006) para 204.

[43] *Lao Holdings NV v The Lao People's Democratic Republic*, ICSID Case No ARB(AF)12/6, Decision on Jurisdiction (21 February 2014) para 79.

[44] *Standard Chartered Bank v United Republic of Tanzania*, ICSID Case No ARB/10/12, Award (2 November 2012) para 270.

between States and foreign investors' with a view to 'stimulating a larger flow of private international capital into those countries which wish to attract it'.[45]

In a similar vein, the tribunal in *National Gas v Egypt* based the dismissal of the case on the object and purpose of the ICSID Convention being a forum for *international* investment disputes.[46]

9.3.4 Special case: *Phoenix Action v Czech Republic*

The already variously mentioned *Phoenix Action* decision is of special interest, not only because it can be considered one of the precursor decisions for the more recent line of jurisprudence that applies the abuse of rights/abuse of process doctrine, but also because of its dual consideration of the principle of good faith as an element in the notion of investment under the ICSID Convention and in the (implicit) application of the abuse of rights doctrine. The special treatment of the principle of good faith thus warrants a more in-depth discussion.

The tribunal held in relevant parts that 'the purpose of the international protection through ICSID arbitration cannot be granted to investments that are made contrary to law'.[47] Though it later confirmed that in this case, there was no issue with the legality of the investment,[48] it seemed to extrapolate from this finding that the purpose of ICSID arbitration was to deny access to international investment arbitration 'if such protection would run contrary to the general principles of international law, among which the principle of good faith is of utmost importance'.[49] It then discussed various manifestations of the principle of good faith, such as the requirement to 'deal honestly and fairly with each other, to represent their motives and purposes truthfully, and to refrain from taking unfair advantage', the prohibition of abuse of rights, the requirement that 'the international conventions granting protection to foreign investors through arbitration … be applied in good faith', and the requirement that an investment must be performed in good faith.[50]

From these examples, the tribunal concluded that it 'is concerned here with *the international principle of good faith as applied to the international arbitration mechanism of ICSID*'.[51] Though this sounds as if the tribunal was applying an independent good faith obligation, unattached to any particularization of either national or international good faith principle, this is in reality not what the tribunal meant, as became at once apparent when it continued to conclude that it had:

> to prevent an abuse of the system of international investment protection under the ICSID Convention, in ensuring that only investments that are made in compliance with the international principle of good faith and do not attempt to misuse the system are protected.[52]

[45] *Phoenix Action v Czech Republic* (n 10) para 88.

[46] *National Gas SAE v Arab Republic of Egypt*, ICSID Case No ARB/11/7, Award (3 April 2014) para 136.

[47] *Phoenix Action v Czech Republic* (n 10) para 102.

[48] Ibid, para 113.

[49] Ibid, para 106.

[50] Ibid, paras 107–11.

[51] Ibid, para 113 (emphasis in original).

[52] Ibid.

The tribunal thus inferred its authority to prevent an abuse of the ICSID system from the purpose of the ICSID Convention and the BIT, which it found to lie in the protection of lawful and bona fide investments. This is how it inferred the necessity of the two additional '*Salini*-esque' criteria for the notion of investment under the Convention.

The question obviously arises why the tribunal had to go to such doctrinal lengths to arrive at this conclusion. Why did it not simply enquire, after finding early on that it did not have jurisdiction *ratione temporis* over 'claims arising prior to … the date of Phoenix's alleged investment',[53] at which time the claims (respectively the dispute) subject of the ICSID proceedings arose? As we have already seen in Chapters 6 and 7, the tribunal could have disposed of the case merely by finding a lack of jurisdiction *ratione temporis* and would not even have needed to venture into the discussion of a possible abuse of rights/abuse of process, due to its subsidiary nature and the fact that its discussion should be reserved for the question of whether a future dispute was sufficiently foreseeable.[54] What does then distinguish this case in its facts from other cases such as *Mobil v Venezuela, Pac Rim v El Salvador, Tidewater v Venezuela*, etc.? Certainly not the fact that the ultimate owner of the Israel-incorporated claimant, Mr Beno, was a fugitive from Czech fiscal authorities, since the tribunal confirmed that this fact did not make the investment unlawful.[55] In a similar vein, there was no deceitful or fraudulent conduct in the sense of the facts in *Cementownia v Turkey* and *Europe Cement v Turkey*, where in both cases the transfer of shares was evidently faked.[56] It is clear that the conduct of the owner of the Claimant was brazen by any means, so the tribunal was clearly correct in dismissing the case and imposing the totality of the costs of the proceedings and defence on the Claimant. However, in this author's opinion, the tribunal did not have to go through a purpose-oriented interpretation of the notion of investment under the ICSID Convention in order to sanction the abusive initiation of the ICSID proceedings for the pre-existing dispute.

Of course, this is easy to say in hindsight. The dual approach of the *Phoenix Action* decision undoubtedly has the merit of laying the conceptual basis for the transition from an interpretative approach to the application of the abuse of rights/abuse of process doctrine as an autonomous standard, which took place in the decisions succeeding *Phoenix*, such as *Mobil, Pac Rim, Tidewater*, etc. and where the same circumstantial elements as in *Phoenix* were examined as part of the abuse of rights/abuse of process objection.[57] However, the use of the finality of the abuse of rights/abuse of process objection within the notion of investment is redundant and should be avoided. Indeed, as seen further above, the tribunal developed the additional good faith criterion within the notion of investment based on an extrapolation of the jurisprudence that dealt with the problem of the legality of the investment in cases of corruption, bribery or cases of fraud and deceit. This jurisprudence

[53] Ibid, para 67. [54] See Chapter 7, at 7.3.2.1.
[55] *Phoenix Action v Czech Republic* (n 10) para 113. [56] See below at 9.4.3.
[57] Similar Ascencio (n 11) 778–79.

has often supplemented the notion of investment—sometimes based on an explicit 'in accordance with host State laws' clause in the BIT, sometimes not—with the (international law) principle of good faith.[58]

However, the crucial difference between these cases and a claim brought on the basis of a corporate restructuring is that while an investment acquired by recourse to bribery, corruption, etc. is, due to the widely acknowledged prescription of such acts, in itself tainted, a corporate restructuring, or more fundamentally the use or interposition of mailbox companies, is not in itself unlawful and thus does not as such incriminate the investment. Rather, it is the circumstances surrounding the corporate restructuring, and in particular the objective pursued with it, that may make the finality of the claim—but not the investment itself—objectionable.

It is true that in this particular arbitral case, 'the dividing line between using good faith for the purposes of interpretation or application is difficult to draw'.[59] Indeed, the tribunal seems to have placed its interpretative reasoning (also) within the frame of the principle of systemic integration, codified in Article 31(3)(c) VCLT.[60] This provision makes it possible to take into account, together with the context, 'any relevant rules of international law applicable in the relations between the parties'. Customary international law and general principles of law may thus be used as 'interpretive arguments in relation to treaty provisions'.[61]

Importantly, however, this is not the same as applying customary international law or general principles of law directly as independent sources of law. Whether tribunals may directly apply customary international law or general principles of law arguably depends on the applicable law clause. Virtually all IIAs foresee the applicability of international law, sometimes in conjunction with the domestic law of the host State.[62] For ICSID proceedings, Article 42(1) of the Convention also provides that in the absence of an agreement by the parties on the applicable law, 'the Tribunal shall apply the law of the Contracting State party to the dispute (including its rules on the conflict of laws) and such rules of international law as may be applicable'. Yet, the problem with integrating the abuse of rights doctrine as part of the interpretative process through Article 31(3)(c) VCLT lies in its methodological imprecision. Indeed, the application of the abuse of rights doctrine presupposes the existence of a right, which first has to be confirmed by recourse to treaty interpretation.[63] By integrating the analysis of the abusive circumstances into this first interpretive step, the tribunal therefore omits the second step, directly concluding at the absence of a right.

[58] See, eg, *Yaung Chi Oo Trading Pte Ltd v Government of the Union of Myanmar*, ASEAN ID Case No ARB/01/1, Award (31 March 2003) para 58; *Gustav FW Hamester GmbH & Co KG v Ghana*, ICSID Case No ARB/07/24, Award (18 June 2010) paras 123–24; *Plama Consortium Ltd v Bulgaria*, ICSID Case No ARB/03/24, Award (27 August 2008) paras 138–41.

[59] De Brabandere and Van Damme (n 20) 80.

[60] *Phoenix Action v Czech Republic* (n 10) paras 77–78.

[61] Fauchald (n 12) 309.

[62] See, eg, Art 13(6) of the 1995 Australia–Argentina BIT; Art X(4) of the 1991 Canada–Argentina BIT.

[63] Similar Franke (n 37) 166–67.

To be clear, this is not to say that this is necessarily and under all circumstances wrong as concerns the result. In the case of the WTO Agreements, which leave the WTO Dispute Settlement Body with a (at least in explicit terms) narrow applicable law clause,[64] this may be a way to avoid that the WTO Agreements are 'read in clinical isolation from public international law'.[65] This has for example been the approach of the Appellate Body in *US–Shrimp* in interpreting the Chapeau of Article XX General Agreement on Tariffs and Trade (GATT), taking account of the abuse of rights doctrine.[66] However, this would normally not seem necessary in the case of IIAs and/or the ICSID Convention, given the relatively broad applicable law clauses as mentioned further above. In this case, the main concern would appear to lie in the potential blurring of the distinction interpretation versus application of the law[67] and the attendant consequences in terms of qualifying the objections as being directed at the jurisdiction of the tribunal or at the admissibility of the claim, a distinction that, as will be seen further below, does matter.[68]

9.3.5 Discussion

As can be seen, the 'objective' function of the principle of good faith plays a more important role than its 'subjective' function in making the distinction between 'legitimate nationality planning' and 'abusive treaty shopping' by recourse to interpretative methods. Though there has been a tendency in former years to emphasize the object and purpose of protection of foreign investors, in more recent decisions arbitral tribunals seem to have been intent on trying to balance potentially contradictory purposes contained in IIAs or the ICSID Convention in their interpretative approaches.

Yet, given the inherent subjectivity in treaty interpretation,[69] even an arbitral tribunal focusing exclusively or mainly on the object and purpose of protection of foreign investment may surely hardly be said to have interpreted the IIA or ICSID

[64] See Article 3.2 of the Understanding on Rules and Procedures Governing the Settlement of Disputes (DSU): 'The Members recognize that it serves to preserve the rights and obligations of Members under the covered agreements, and to clarify the existing provisions of those agreements in accordance with customary rules of interpretation of public international law. Recommendations and rulings of the DSB cannot add to or diminish the rights and obligations provided in the covered agreements.' See also Article 19.2 DSU. But see Joost Pauwelyn, *Conflict of Norms in Public International Law: How WTO Law Relates to Other Rules of International Law* (Cambridge University Press 2003) 460ff for the proposition that 'the fact that the substantive jurisdiction of WTO panels is limited to claims under WTO covered agreements does not mean that the applicable law available to a WTO panel is necessarily limited to WTO covered agreements.'

[65] Appellate Body Report, *United States—Standards for Reformulated and Conventional Gasoline*, WTO Doc WT/DS2/AB/R (adopted 29 April 1996) 18.

[66] Appellate Body Report, *United States—Shrimp* (n 10) paras 158–59.

[67] On this problem see also Duncan French, 'Treaty Interpretation and the Incorporation of Extraneous Legal Rules' (2006) 55 ICLQ 281, 287–91.

[68] See below at 9.4.4.

[69] See in this sense also *Certain Expenses of the United Nations (Advisory Opinion)* [1962] ICJ Reports 151, 184 (Judge Spender): 'the ordinary and natural sense of words may at times be a matter of considerable difficulty to determine. What is their ordinary and natural sense to one may not be so to another. The interpreter not uncommonly has, what has been described as, a personal feeling towards certain words and phrases. What makes sense to one may not make sense to another. Ambiguity may lie hidden in the plainest and most simple of words even in their natural and ordinary meaning.'

Convention in bad faith. Even the 'alternative good faith' approaches as seen in *Alapli Elektrik v Turkey* (dismissal of the case on grounds of lack of 'active contribution' vs dismissal on grounds of abuse of process)[70] would seem to attest more to personal 'legal preferences' or 'legal convictions' without for that matter necessarily being incorrect or even less so done in bad faith.[71]

The same applies in this author's opinion to tribunals' textual approaches towards upholding jurisdiction *ratione personae* in cases of claims by mailbox companies.[72] It may be unwelcome for States from a policy perspective, yet in the absence of a wide-ranging prescription of mailbox companies,[73] it seems difficult to argue that '[t]he arbitrator who finds jurisdiction may not be acting in good faith in permitting a possibly fraudulent scheme to found jurisdiction', [74] the mailbox company as such not being a fraudulent scheme.

9.4 Application of the Principle of Good Faith or One of its Concretizations

Arbitral tribunals have also discussed the principle of good faith or some of its concretizations in order to draw the line between a 'legitimate nationality planning' and 'treaty abuse'. Indeed, as seen in Chapter 4, Respondents have regularly invoked the 'genuine link' and the 'piercing of the veil' theory. In other cases, arbitral tribunals have examined the existence of fraud or an abuse of rights/abuse of process.

As will be explained over the following pages, it is submitted that the distinction between a 'legitimate nationality planning' and 'treaty abuse' is most adequately captured by the application of the abuse of rights/abuse of process doctrine or the case of fraud. The 'genuine link' and 'piercing of the veil' theory, on the other hand, do in this author's opinion not constitute adequate tools to identify treaty abuse.

9.4.1 'Genuine link' theory

As has already been seen, the 'genuine link' doctrine does not have a place in international investment arbitration. Not only is it a theory that in customary international law only applies in the case of dual nationalities, thus not being applicable in the case of a single nationality. But even so, international investment law establishes a clear *lex specialis* framework that—in the absence of explicit, treaty-based 'genuine link' requirements—does not permit recourse to the *lex generalis* that is the

[70] See in Chapter 5, at 5.4.3 and 5.4.4.

[71] Even though if anywhere at all, it is in this author's opinion with respect to the development of the 'active contribution' requirement where the risk of 'judicial activism' becomes most apparent.

[72] See the discussion in Chapter 4, at 4.3.1.3.

[73] See the proposal in Chapter 8, at 8.1.2.

[74] M Sornarajah, 'Good Faith, Corporate Nationality, and Denial of Benefits' in Andrew Mitchell, M Sornarajah, and Tania Voon, *Good Faith and International Economic Law* (Oxford University Press 2015) 117, 125.

(customary) international law of diplomatic protection, thus attesting to a formal and consent-based approach towards the notion of natural person as investor.[75]

This is not to say that strategic changes of nationality by natural persons (other than the invocation of dual nationalities) could not occur, even though they are more seldom than strategic changes of nationality by legal persons. Rather, the argument is that to judge the validity of such a potential strategic change of nationality, the 'genuine link' doctrine cannot be considered the answer.

Indeed, it is submitted that a potential strategic change of nationality by a natural person is more adequately captured by recourse to the abuse of rights doctrine than the 'genuine link' theory. There is no reason why the approach developed by arbitral tribunals in more recent jurisprudence, which distinguishes as to whether the change of nationality occurred at a time when a dispute was pre-existing or whether a future dispute was foreseeable,[76] should not be equally adequate and applicable to the question of the validity of a strategic change of nationality by a natural person. Possibly different functions of nationality in diplomatic protection and in international investment law[77] in any case do not seem to justify such differentiation, as in both cases, the question is really the same: how should international (investment) law deal with potential manipulations of nationality? Framing the corresponding legal arguments by recourse to the abuse of rights doctrine would have the advantage of providing for a more coherent approach towards the question of the validity of strategic changes of nationality, as it would unify the legal discourse and legal reasoning.

9.4.2 'Piercing of the corporate veil' doctrine

As also seen in Chapter 4, Respondents in investment arbitration have often invoked the so-called 'piercing of the veil' doctrine with the aim of asking the arbitral tribunal to disregard the formal claimant and search for, or consider, another (natural or legal) person as the 'true' claimant.

In the context of investment arbitration, this doctrine is commonly based on the ICJ's holding in the *Barcelona Traction* case, where, as already examined in Chapter 3, the tribunal found that the firm distinction between the company and its shareholders could under exceptional circumstances be disregarded.[78] It has thus far exclusively been invoked in connection with jurisdiction *ratione personae*. However, in the case of foreign-incorporated investor–claimants, arbitral tribunals have always rejected the application of the 'piercing of the veil' doctrine on the facts of the case.

Thus, in *Tokios Tokelés*, the tribunal reviewed the relevant holding of the ICJ in *Barcelona Traction* and found that:

> The Respondent has not shown or even suggested that the Claimant has used its status as a juridical entity of Lithuania to perpetrate fraud or engage in malfeasance. The Respondent

[75] See Chapters 3 and 4. [76] See Chapters 6 and 7.

[77] Robert Sloane, 'Breaking the Genuine Link: The Contemporary International Legal Regulation of Nationality' (2009) 50 Harv Intl L J 1, 52.

[78] *Barcelona Traction, Light and Power Co (Belgium v Spain) (Judgment)* [1970] ICJ Rep 3, 39 (para 56).

has made no claim that the Claimant's veil must be pierced and jurisdiction denied in order to protect third persons, nor has the Respondent shown that the Claimant used its corporate nationality to evade applicable legal requirements or obligations … The Claimant made no attempt whatever to conceal its national identity from the Respondent … The Claimant manifestly did not create Tokios Tokelés for the purpose of gaining access to ICSID arbitration under the BIT against Ukraine, as the enterprise was founded six years before the BIT between Ukraine and Lithuania entered into force.[79]

Similarly, the tribunal in *ADC Affiliate v Hungary* acknowledged that:

> Although that principle [ie piercing of the corporate veil] does exist in domestic legal practice in some jurisdictions, it is rarely and always cautiously applied. Further, it would be inapplicable in this case. The reason is that this principle only applies to situations where the real beneficiary of the business misused corporate formalities in order to disguise its true entity and therefore to avoid liability.[80]

The tribunals in *Rumeli Telekom v Kazakhstan* and *KT Asia v Kazakhstan* decided in a similar manner.[81]

Interestingly, these arbitral tribunals seemingly took the international law status of the doctrine for granted. Some commentators appear to share this opinion.

Sange Addison-Agyei, for example, endorses the 'piercing of the veil' doctrine such as expressed by the ICJ in *Barcelona Traction* and proposes to apply it, in the context of the ICSID Convention, in those cases where the investor uses treaty shopping in order 'to prevent the evasion of legal requirements or of obligations'.[82] In her opinion, the investor who, as a third or host State national, sets up a mailbox company with the sole aim of benefitting from the advantages of ICSID arbitration, tries to evade the legal requirements under Article 25 ICSID Convention, thus fulfilling the third category proposed by the ICJ.[83] This should, in her view, apply irrespectively of whether the mailbox company was set up prior to or after the making of the investment and even irrespectively of whether damages have already happened.[84] However, in case the aim of benefitting from the advantages of ICSID arbitration was not the sole aim of the corporate structuring, she proposes the application of the 'piercing of the veil' doctrine in case the investor was trying to evade the nationality requirements in a 'conscious and purposeful way'.[85]

Addison-Agyei's proposal to apply the 'piercing of the veil' doctrine irrespectively of whether the mailbox company was set up prior to or after the making of the investment and even irrespectively of whether damages have already happened is clearly contradicted by arbitral jurisprudence and thus difficult to maintain. Indeed, as has already been seen in detail, arbitral jurisprudence nowadays makes a marked difference as to whether damages (or more correctly a dispute) have

[79] *Tokios Tokelés v Ukraine* (n 30) paras 55–56.
[80] *ADC Affiliate v Hungary* (n 30) para 358.
[81] *Rumeli Telekom AS and Telsim Mobil Telekomunikasyon Hizmetleri AS v Republic of Kazakhstan*, ICSID Case No ARB/05/16, Award (29 July 2008) para 328; *KT Asia v Kazakhstan* (n 1) paras 126–39.
[82] Sange Addison-Agyei, *Nationality Planning und Treaty Shopping im Internationalen Investitionsrecht* (Frankfurt aM, Peter Lang 2012) 132, 136.
[83] Ibid, 136. [84] Ibid, 137. [85] Ibid, 137–38.

already occurred at the time of the restructuring or not.[86] The multi-tiered, multi-jurisdictional corporate structuring, in particular through the strategic interposition of mailbox companies, may be undesirable for States for policy reasons, but it is not unlawful *in abstracto* as can be seen from the wide-ranging State practice in this regard. This is why circumstances of the corporate restructuring matter and short of situations of 'fraud or malfeasance', arbitral tribunals have to look into the motives for the restructuring. However, motives pertaining to the subjective sphere and thus being inherently difficult to prove, arbitral tribunals have started to infer the motives from more verifiable, objective facts, such as the timing of the restructuring and the pre-existence of a dispute. The proposal to enquire into whether the 'conscious purpose' of the restructuring was to gain access to protection where otherwise none would exist is therefore as impracticable as the 'sole purpose' doctrine examined further above.[87]

Another commentator, Albert Badia, extensively examines the 'piercing of the veil' doctrine in the context of his claim that this doctrine should be used to attribute wrongdoings by State-owned enterprises to host States in investment arbitration.[88]As methodological underpinning, Badia contends that the 'piercing of the veil' doctrine falls 'into the third and fourth sources of international law, as set out by Article 38(1) of the Statute of ICJ'.[89] To substantiate his claim, he affirms that 'the veil-piercing doctrine emanates from a broader principle of equity' and contends that '[i]nternational Courts do not hesitate to resort to remedies based on equity where there are no specific rules to apply', which leads him to conclude that 'veil-piercing is an equitable principle of law recognized in all legal systems'.[90]

To corroborate this claim, Badia then analyses in the next chapter veil-piercing scenarios under municipal law. Having elaborated on the conditions required for finding the existence of a general principle of law,[91] he finds that 'the corporation, as a legal genus, is present in all legal systems and traditions of law. So it is indeed a "general principle of law recognized by civilized nations"'.[92] In a next step, he questions whether 'the attributes of independence, legal personality and limited personality, which are inextricably linked to corporations, can be considered "general principles of law recognized by civilized nations"', not without conceding that '[b]y default, legal principles are very difficult to classify … [and] come in a bewildering number and forms, and intertwine forming clusters and families'.[93] From this, he again concludes that 'veil-piercing is a general principle of 'law', or more concretely 'a composite of, at least, three primary principles: the principle of good faith, the theory of the abuse of rights and the rule of equity',[94] which he further nuances into the conclusion that 'it is an equitable remedy aimed to address the abuse of rights and to ensure the exercise of good faith in relation to a body corporate'.[95] He then goes on to examine manifestations of a 'veil-piercing doctrine' under English, US,

[86] See Chapters 6 and 7. [87] See Chapter 7, at 7.3.2.3.

[88] Albert Badia, *Piercing the Veil of State Enterprises in International Arbitration* (Kluwer Law International 2014).

[89] Ibid, 40. [90] Ibid, 40–41. [91] Ibid, 45–47. [92] Ibid, 47.

[93] Ibid. [94] Ibid, 48. [95] Ibid, 49.

German, and French law, including corresponding jurisprudence,[96] not without conceding here and there that '[t]here is a great range of tests to apply, and many inconsistencies arise between one case and another'[97] and that 'far from being flat and uniform, veil-piercing is an ever-evolving and bewildering area of the law'.[98] He also reviews 'corporate law doctrines' such as the 'enterprise entity liability theory', the 'alter ego doctrine' and the 'groups of companies doctrine', admitting that courts in England, the United States, and France have shown differing receptiveness towards these doctrines.[99]

Badia's analysis is highly instructive in its effort to identify and describe different corporate and non-corporate law doctrines and theories with a 'piercing of the veil' effect. However, despite the wealth of examples given, the present author remains sceptical with respect to the existence of a veritable international law doctrine called 'piercing of the veil'. This is not to deny the existence of variegated municipal law doctrines, applicable in differing fields of law, that may have a 'veil-piercing' *effect*. However, this does not necessarily translate into a uniform international law doctrine, be it in the form of customary international law or as a general principle of law.

Indeed, it is submitted that the 'piercing of the veil' doctrine is no more than a figurative description of an intended effect (that is the disregarding of the separation between corporate entities and their shareholders). To attain this effect, approaches and conditions vary widely according to whether domestic or international law is concerned, and even within the realm of international law, it is arguably difficult to attach one single and precise meaning to it. Other scholars have made the same point.[100]

The method employed by the ICJ in *Barcelona Traction*, the mechanical transposition of municipal law into international law, has already been criticized in Chapter 3.[101] The lack of exact contours either in domestic or in international law of this supposed doctrine has equally been pointed out further above. In particular the use of the relativizing 'the veil is lifted, *for instance*'[102] raises the question how an international law-based doctrine or principle could be established if the conditions for its applicability are only approximate.[103] Indeed, as already mentioned in Chapter 3 above, the ICJ visibly understood its holding only as a *general* holding, followed by two more concrete situations justifying in its opinion the 'piercing of the veil' (now also found in Article 11 of the Draft Articles on Diplomatic Protection).

The lack of contours of a so-called 'piercing of the veil' international law doctrine can also be seen in its haphazard use, ascribing differing meanings to it, in other ICJ

96 Ibid, 54–74. 97 Ibid, 56. 98 Ibid, 62. 99 Ibid, 63–74.

100 See, eg, Yaraslau Kryvoi, 'Piercing the Corporate Veil in International Arbitration' (2011) Global Business Law Review 169–70. Similar Markus Perkams, 'Piercing the Corporate Veil in International Investment Agreements' in August Reinisch and Christina Knahr (eds), *International Investment Law in Context* (Eleven International Publishing 2008) 93, 100.

101 See Chapter 3, at 3.2.2.2.2.

102 *Barcelona Traction* (n 78) 38–39 (para 56).

103 Tellingly, the Court does not elaborate further on its normative status.

decisions. Thus, in the Advisory Opinion on the *Legality of the Threat or Use of the Nuclear Weapon*, Judge Guillaume wondered in his Separate Opinion whether, given the political pressure:

> the requests for opinions could still be regarded as coming from the Assemblies which had adopted them or whether, *piercing the veil*, the Court should not have dismissed them as inadmissible [emphasis added].[104]

In *Oil Platforms*, Judge Ranjeva declared that in view of diversionary tactics employed by the Parties, 'the Court has "pierced the veil" of the dispute, relying directly on acts, conduct and statements contemporaneous with the events having given rise thereto'.[105]

As can be seen from the aforementioned examples, the use of the term 'piercing the veil' has no more than figurative character. Crucially, however, a reference to a 'piercing the veil' doctrine or principle is blatantly absent in the *Diallo* case, which is where one would expect to find a discussion relating to it, were one to assume as correct its international law status. Rather, the Court in this decision discusses (but in the end rejects) the possibility of protection 'by substitution' as a corrective to the continued upholding, under customary international law, of the restrictive shareholder standing.[106]

So how can what is commonly referred to as 'veil-piercing' be classified in normative terms? Badia qualifies the 'piercing of the veil' doctrine as an 'equitable remedy aimed to address the abuse of rights and to ensure the exercise of good faith in relation to a body corporate'.[107]

That equity has a role to play has also been confirmed by other tribunals.[108] Equity being an emanation of the principle of good faith and as such also being recognized as general principle of law,[109] one could stop the analysis at this point. However, equity is a difficult concept straddling notions of law, fairness, reasonableness and justice. The use of equity is further complicated by the fact that one must distinguish between various forms of equity—equity *infra legem*, equity *praeter legem*, and equity *contra legem*—and in particular the latter two invite dissent and uncertainty.[110]

[104] *Legality of the Threat or Use of Nuclear Weapons (Advisory Opinion)* [1996] ICJ Rep 226 (para 2) (Separate Opinion Judge Guillaume).

[105] *Oil Platforms (Iran v United States) (Judgment)* [2003] ICJ Rep 161 (para 3) (Vice-President Ranjeva).

[106] *Ahmadou Sadio Diallo (Guinea v Democratic Republic of Congo) (Preliminary Objections)* [2007] ICJ Rep 582, 614–16 (paras 87–95).

[107] Badia (n 88) 49.

[108] See *Barcelona Traction* (n 78) 48–50 (paras 92–101); ibid, 85 (para 35) (Separate Opinion Judge Fitzmaurice); *Harza v Iran*, Case No 232-97-2 (2 May 1986) 2 Iran–US CTR 76, 110; *Foremost Tehran Inc v Iran*, Case No 220-37/231-1 (11 April 1986) 10 Iran–US CTR 228, 240; *Nasser Esphahanian v Bank Tehran*, Case No 31-157-2 (29 March 1983) 2 Iran–US CTR 157, 166. See also the Respondent's submission in *Phoenix Action v Czech Republic* (n 10) para 34.

[109] See Ziegler and Baumgartner (n 5) 35–36.

[110] See, eg, Vaughan Lowe, 'The Role of Equity' (1988–1989) 12 Austr Year Book of Int L 54, 61; Prosper Weil, 'L'Équité dans la jurisprudence de la Cour Internationale de Justice' in Vaughan Lowe and Malgosia Fitzgerald (eds), *Fifty Years of the International Court of Justice: Essays in Honour of Sir Robert Jennings* (Cambridge University Press 1996) 121, 131; Francesco Francioni, 'Equity' in Rüdiger

The question is of course whether recourse to equity is necessary at all. As becomes apparent from various international decisions, it seems to this author that the situations found as warranting the 'piercing of the veil' in case of a strategic change of nationality should better be captured by recourse to the principle of good faith and its concretizations, most importantly fraud and the abuse of rights doctrine.

Indeed, the Iran–United States Claims Tribunal found in *Esphahanian v Bank Tehran*, referring to the *Flegenheimer* case,[111] that:

> There is precedent for denying jurisdiction on equitable grounds in cases of fraudulent use of nationality. Such a case might occur where an individual disguises his dominant or effective nationality in order to obtain benefits with his secondary nationality not otherwise available to him.[112]

The arbitral tribunal in *KT Asia v Kazakhstan* also zeroed in on possible fraud or the abuse of a legal personality:

> Relying primarily on Barcelona Traction, certain cases, including ADC, Rumeli and Tokios Tokelés, have indeed acknowledged the possibility of piercing the corporate veil to 'prevent the misuse of the privileges of legal personality' or where the 'real beneficiary of the business misused corporate formalities in order to disguise its true identity and to avoid liability'. Assuming for the sake of argument that one were to follow that line, it would require a showing of abuse of the corporate form, which is not present here.[113]

The tribunal's holding in *Tokios Tokelés* also raises doubts as to whether there really is a difference between the cases of 'abuse of corporate form or legal personality in order to disguise its true identity and to avoid liability' and the abuse of rights/abuse of process doctrine. Indeed, as already seen further above, the tribunal found that:

> None of the Claimant's conduct with respect to its status as an entity of Lithuania constitutes an abuse of legal personality … The Claimant manifestly did not create Tokios Tokelés for the purpose of gaining access to ICSID arbitration under the BIT against Ukraine, as the enterprise was founded six years before the BIT … entered into force. Indeed, there was no evidence in the record that the Claimant used its formal legal nationality for any improper purpose.[114]

This reasoning sounds conspicuously akin to the reasoning employed by various tribunals in more recent decisions applying the abuse of rights/abuse of process doctrine, focusing on the timing element as objective element for the purpose pursued with the restructuring.[115] Moreover, as already seen in Chapter 7, the 'abuse

Wolfrum (ed), *Max Planck Encyclopedia of Public International Law* (Oxford University Press) para 17, available at <http://opil.ouplaw.com>.

[111] *Flegenheimer (Italy-United States)* (1958) 14 RIAA 327, 378.

[112] *Esphahanian v Bank Tehran* (n 108) 166.

[113] *KT Asia v Kazakhstan* (n 1) para 134.

[114] *Tokios Tokelés v Ukraine* (n 30) para 55–56.

[115] See, eg, *Phoenix Action v Czech Republic* (n 10) para 92; *Aguas del Tunarí v Bolivia* (n 25) para 330; *Millicom International Operations BV and Sentel GSM SA v Senegal*, ICSID Case No ARB/08/20, Decision on Jurisdiction of the Arbitral Tribunal (16 July 2010) para 84.

of corporate form or of legal personality in order to disguise its true identity and/or to avoid liability' is arguably nothing else but the exercise of an existing right for a purpose not sanctioned by the law, in other words, an abuse of rights.

It is therefore submitted that the situations commonly referred to as warranting the 'piercing of the veil' in the case of treaty shopping are better captured by recourse to the principle of good faith and its concretizations, most importantly fraud and the abuse of rights/abuse of process doctrine. This would also respond to the call for a more principled approach towards the principle of good faith respectively the abuse of rights/abuse of process doctrine (advocated for with good reason by other scholars)[116] and lay to rest a doctrine that only adds to an incoherent approach towards the question of the validity of a claim based on treaty shopping.

9.4.3 Fraud

Though constituting rare instances, investment arbitral tribunals have indeed been willing to make a bad faith finding in cases of (attempted) fraud with respect to strategic changes of nationality, thus rejecting the claims.

Three of the most egregious cases of fraud in this aspect can be found in the cases *Cementownia v Turkey*,[117] *Europe Cement v Turkey*,[118] and *Libananco v Turkey*.[119] All cases were part of wider litigation efforts by the Turkish entrepreneurial Uzan family and companies controlled by them who tried to contest a new Electricity Market Law introduced by Turkey in 2003 allegedly expropriating their investments.[120] In these three cases, the putative investor–claimants fraudulently asserted the transfer of shares allegedly transferring the ownership of the investment in question. In other words, the claimants fraudulently asserted ownership of an investment that in fact did not exist. However, even though the facts were comparable, the treatment of these cases by the arbitral tribunals in terms of the bad faith findings differed.

After reviewing the facts of the case, the arbitral tribunal in *Cementownia* found that:

> Here the Claimant's conduct is not even close to proper conduct. Had Cementownia actually proven that on May 30, 2003, it legally acquired the shares of CEAS and Kepez, there would still be the question of whether this was treaty shopping of the wrong kind, in the words of Phoenix Action, 'a transfer of the national economic interests to a foreign company in an attempt to seek protections under a BIT.' The problem for the Claimant is that the evidence shows that it did not even interpose itself between Mr. Kemal Uzan and the

[116] Tania Voon, Andrew Mitchell, and James Munro, 'Legal Responses to Corporate Manoeuvering in International Investment Arbitration' (2014) 5 JIDS 41, 65; similar Ascencio (n 11) 785.

[117] *Cementownia "Nowa Huta" SA v Republic of Turkey*, ICSID Case No ARB(AF)/06/2, Award (17 September 2009).

[118] *Europe Cement Trade & Investment v Republic of Turkey*, ICSID Case No ARB(AF)/07/2, Decision on Jurisdiction (13 August 2009).

[119] *Libananco Holdings Co Limited v Republic of Turkey*, ICSID Case No ARB(AF)/06/8, Award (2 September 2011).

[120] See Chapter 1, at 1.1.3.

Republic of Turkey. The transaction that would pose the issue of whether the corporate veil should be pierced was fabricated. The Claimant's conduct in bringing the instant claim fails to meet the requisite standard of good faith conduct. The claim is manifestly ill-founded.[121]

The tribunal expressed its disapproval of the attempted fraud in exceptionally clear terms:

The Arbitral Tribunal is of the opinion that the Claimant has intentionally and in bad faith abused the arbitration; it purported to be an investor when it knew that this was not the case. This constitutes indeed an abuse of process. In addition, the Claimant is guilty of procedural misconduct: once the arbitration proceeding was commenced, it has caused excessive delays and thereby increased the costs of the arbitration. As can be seen by the ICSID case-law … the misconduct of an arbitration proceeding leads generally to the allocation of all costs on the party in bad faith. As the present case concerns an accumulation of liabilities—abuse of process and procedural misconduct—there is good cause for the Arbitral Tribunal to go beyond the general sanction and to declare that the Claimant has brought a *fraudulent* claim against the Republic of Turkey.[122]

It thus allocated the full costs onto the claimant.[123]

The tribunal in *Europe Cement* similarly found that:

The circumstantial evidence points strongly to the conclusion that Europe Cement did not own shares in CEAS and Kepez at the relevant time … Indeed, the evidence points to the conclusion that the claim to ownership of the shares at a time that would establish jurisdiction was made fraudulently.[124]

Referring to the decisions in *Inceysa v El Salvador* and *Phoenix Action*, it added that:

In the above cases, the lack of good faith was present in the acquisition of the investment. In the present case, there was in fact no investment at all, at least at the relevant time, and the lack of good faith is in the assertion of an investment on the basis of documents that according to the evidence presented were not authentic … Such a claim cannot be said to have been made in good faith. If, as in Phoenix, a claim that is based on the purchase of an investment solely for the purpose of commencing litigation is an abuse of process, then surely a claim based on the false assertion of ownership of an investment is equally an abuse of process.[125]

However, the tribunal in *Europe Cement* refrained from making a finding that the claim was 'manifestly ill-founded',[126] yet allocated the full costs onto the claimant.[127]

As in the other cases, the tribunal in *Libananco* found that there were 'many evidential gaps … as well as serious discrepancies for which no satisfactory explanation has been given',[128] so that it considered that the Claimant had not proved that it owned the shares in CEAS and Kepez at the critical date.[129] However, it

[121] *Cementownia v Turkey* (n 117) paras 156–57.
[122] Ibid, para 159 (emphasis in original).
[123] Ibid, para 178.
[124] *Europe Cement v Turkey* (n 118) para 167.
[125] Ibid, para 175.
[126] Ibid, para 176.
[127] Ibid, para 185.
[128] *Libananco Holding v Turkey* (n 119) para 533.
[129] Ibid, para 536.

made no finding as to whether the claim was to be considered an abuse of process or manifestly ill-founded. Yet, it also ordered the claimant to pay to Respondent a substantial part of its incurred legal fees and expenses.[130]

In particular the cases of *Cementownia* and *Europe Cement* show that these arbitral tribunals equated the lack of good faith found in the fraud attempts with the abuse of rights/abuse of process doctrine.[131]

However, the question is whether fraud *should* be equated with an abuse of rights/ abuse of process. As Bin Cheng held in his seminal work on general principles of law, *fraus omnia corrumpit*, in other words, fraud vitiates everything and is thus 'the antithesis of good faith'.[132] The ILC, in the Draft Articles on the Law of Treaties, also found that '[f]raud, when it occurs, strikes at the root of an agreement in a somewhat different way from innocent misrepresentation and error … it destroys the whole basis of mutual confidence between the parties'.[133] The legal maxims *ex dolo malo non oritur action* (an action does not arise from fraud) and *nemini dolos suus prodesse debet* (nobody must profit from his own fraud) should clearly be understood in the same way.[134]

Indeed, in the quoted cases above, and unlike in the other corporate restructuring cases such as *Phoenix, Mobil, Pac Rim*, etc., there effectively was no (qualifying) investment at all that could have given a right to commence investment arbitration.[135] Hence, properly speaking, there was no right that could be abused. Fraud thus arguably comes as close as it can get to (a violation of) an independent obligation to act in good faith.[136]

Arguably, the purposeful attempt to deceive the host State over the true ownership or conceal the national identity of the investment could be likened to a case of fraud and treated in a similar way as the cases above, even though such cases of deceit could possibly also be dismissed by recourse to an 'in accordance with host State law' clause if contained in the IIA, as the motive to use 'straw men' or

[130] Ibid, para 569.

[131] The procedural misconduct during the arbitral proceedings by the claimants, as found for example by the tribunal in *Cementownia* in the causing of additional delays, can also be considered an abuse of process, see, eg, Ascencio (n 11) 767. But being not directly relevant for the purposes of this research, it will not further be analysed here.

[132] Cheng (n 3) 158.

[133] ILC Commentary on Art 46 [now Art 49], in International Law Commission, *Yearbook of the International Law Commission* (1966) Vol II 244 (para 1).

[134] See *Inceysa v El Salvador* (n 11) 240.

[135] Similar De Brabandere (n 11) 620, 628–29.

[136] Similar De Brabandere (n 11) 620: 'in case there is no "original" right to file a claim, for example, because the court or tribunal has no jurisdiction, one cannot theoretically consider such an action an "abuse of process" or "abuse of right" since there is no (procedural) right that can be abused. The abusive submission of a claim by a foreign investor, while knowing that there is no legal basis to found the claim, should thus be categorized as a breach of the principle of "good faith", rather than an "abuse of process" or "abuse of rights".' See also ILC, 'First Report on Diplomatic Protection' (n 18) para 118: 'Customary international law recognizes that a nationality acquired by fraud, negligence or serious error may not be recognized … This principle may be consolidated in a requirement of good faith. A conferment of nationality will be recognized for the purpose of diplomatic protection if it is not made in bad faith (footnotes omitted)'. See also *Cementownia v Turkey* (n 117) para 157: 'The Claimant's conduct in bringing the instant claim fails to meet the requisite standard of good faith conduct.'

'dummies' will often be triggered precisely by corresponding restrictions in domestic law.[137] However, arbitral tribunals have so far always rejected arguments by Respondents that the use of mailbox companies constituted such deceitful conduct on the facts of the case.[138] This shows that the simple fact of host State or third State nationals controlling the foreign-incorporated claimant/mailbox company is not enough, absent further fraudulent circumstances, to find 'deceit'.

9.4.4 The abuse of rights/abuse of process doctrine

From the above follows that the abuse of rights/abuse of process doctrine is the 'natural candidate' for judging the validity of a claim based on a strategic change of nationality in a more 'principled' manner, provided the arbitral tribunal has not dismissed its jurisdiction on interpretative grounds or has not found any fraud (though the latter case will arguably remain rather exceptional).

As a general principle of law, the abuse of rights/abuse of process doctrine reunites all the (quasi-)constitutional qualities needed to build a bridge between international investment law and public international law and instil a more 'principled' approach into arbitral decision-making.[139]

However, an important question that remains as of yet inconsistently answered is whether the abuse of rights/abuse of process doctrine should be treated as a jurisdictional or an admissibility objection.[140]

Indeed, this question is not merely one of academic importance. If the arbitral tribunal dismisses jurisdiction, 'there is no possibility for the parties to re-submit the claim to the tribunal', while if the tribunal declares the claim to be inadmissible, 'there is no legal obstacle in a resubmission of the claim once the admissibility requirements are met'.[141] On the other hand, if the claim is dismissed on grounds

[137] As was the case for example in *Fraport AG Frankfurt Airport Services Worldwide v Republic of the Philippines*, ICSID Case No ARB/03/25, Award (16 August 2007).

[138] *Niko Resources (Bangladesh) Ltd v People's Republic of Bangladesh, Bangladesh Petroleum Exploration & Production Company Limited ("Bapex") and Bangladesh Oil Gas and Mineral Corporation ("Petrobangla")* ICSID Case No ARB/10/11 and 10/18, Decision on Jurisdiction (19 August 2013) para 197; *Autopista Concesionada de Venezuela CA (Aucoven) v Bolivarian Republic of Venezuela*, ICSID Case No ARB/00/5, Decision on Jurisdiction (27 September 2001) paras 127–32; *ADC Affiliate v Hungary* (n 30) para 358; *Tokios Tokelés v Ukraine* (n 30) paras 55–56.

[139] See Kolb, 'Principles as Sources' (n 12) 27–36.

[140] See, eg, *Société Générale in Respect of DR Energy Holdings Limited and Empresa Distribuidora de Electricidad del Este, SA ('EDE Este') v Dominican Republic*, LCIA Case No UN 7927, Award on Preliminary Objections to Jurisdiction (19 September 2008) paras 110, 121; *Mobil v Venezuela* (n 10) para 206; *Pac Rim v El Salvador* (n 35) para 2.110; *Tidewater Inc, Tidewater Investment SRL, Tidewater Caribe, CA, Twenty Grand Offshore, LLC, Point Marine, LLC, Twenty Grand Marine Service, LLC, Jackson Marine, LLC and Zapata Gulf Marine Operators, LLC v Bolivarian Republic of Venezuela*, ICSID Case No ARB/10/5, Decision on Jurisdiction (8 February 2013) para 198. This question was seemingly left open by the tribunal in *Renée Rose Levy and Gremcitel SA v Republic of Peru*, ICSID Case No ARB/11/17, Award (9 January 2015) para 181, however, in the end, the tribunal used language clearly pointing at an admissibility question, ibid, para 195 ('Therefore, the tribunal is precluded from exercising jurisdiction over the dispute.')

[141] De Brabandere (n 11) 617. Of course, how a time-sensitive restructuring, found to constitute an abuse of rights/abuse of process, could be cured is another question.

of lack of jurisdiction, there is usually the possibility for annulment of the decision (Article 52 of the ICSID Convention), while if it is dismissed on grounds of inadmissibility of the claim, no such possibility exists.[142]

The uncertainty reigning in this respect can also be seen in the inconsistent terminology used by different arbitral tribunals who have tried to systematize their approaches towards the principle of good faith respectively the abuse of rights/abuse of process doctrine.[143]

Thus, for example, the arbitral tribunal in *Abaclat* distinguished between 'material good faith' on the one hand, which it understood as referring to the 'context and the way in which the investment was made, and for which the investor seeks protection', and 'procedural good faith' on the other hand, which it defined as referring to the 'context and the way in which a party, usually the investor, initiates its treaty claim seeking protection for its investment'.[144] 'Material good faith' may, according to the *Abaclat* tribunal, be examined within the frame of the tribunal's jurisdiction or as relating to the legality of the investment, and can thus be considered either a question of consent (and thus jurisdiction) or a question of the merits.[145] By contrast, 'procedural good faith' may be addressed 'within the context of jurisdiction or within the context of admissibility', that is, as an 'issue of consent and thus of jurisdiction where one party considers procedural aspects to be key components of the consent of the host State' or as an 'issue of admissibility, where the key question is whether the way in which the investor initiated the proceedings, although in accordance with the applicable provisions, aim to obtain a protection, which he is—under the principle of good faith—not entitled to claim'.[146]

The tribunal in *ST-AD GmbH v Bulgaria* distinguished between two categories of abuse of process: 'systemic abuse' as understood as 'manipulation of the international system of investment arbitration' or 'bad faith in the initiation of the arbitration' on the one hand, and 'procedural abuse', as understood as 'bad faith in the conduct of the arbitration' on the other.[147] However, it did not draw any conclusions as to whether either one should be treated as a question relating to jurisdiction, admissibility or the merits.

[142] Ibid.

[143] This uncertainty is also reflected in the alternative framing of the objections by Australia against the claim by Philip Morris Asia, see *Philip Morris Asia Limited v Commonwealth of Australia*, UNCITRAL, PCA Case No 2012-12, Australia's Response to the Notice of Arbitration (21 December 2011) para 31: 'In such circumstances, there could be no "investment" for the purposes of Article 10 of the BIT and any reliance on Article 10 of the BIT would constitute an abuse of rights. It follows that the arbitral tribunal lacks jurisdiction or that the claims that PM Asia now seeks to bring under the BIT are inadmissible.' But see in the award the tribunal's characterization of the abuse of rights objection as admissibility question, *Philip Morris Asia Limited v Commonwealth of Australia*, UNCITRAL, PCA Case No 2012-12, Award on Jurisdiction and Admissibility (17 December 2015) (redacted version) para 588.

[144] *Abaclat and Others v Argentina* (n 11) para 647.

[145] Ibid, para 648.

[146] Ibid, para 649.

[147] *ST-AD GmbH v Republic of Bulgaria*, UNCITRAL, PCA Case No 2011-06, Award on Jurisdiction (18 July 2013) paras 404–06.

The tribunal in *Vannessa Ventures* refrained from trying to clad the principle of good faith in specific terminology and rather pointed out the case-specific (but also controversial) nature of its application:

One of us considers that, on the facts of this case, there was no good-faith investment and that the BIT does not cover investments not made in good faith, and accordingly the tribunal lacks jurisdiction. The majority accepts that good faith has an important role in the analysis but considers that, in the absence of a treaty provision ascribing some different effect to the principle of good faith, it is only in circumstances where the application of good faith as a principle of national law invalidates the acquisition of the investment that a lack of good faith means that there is no "investment" for jurisdictional purposes. In other circumstances, the question of good faith does not go to jurisdiction but is a matter to be considered by the Tribunal when exercising its jurisdiction and to be applied in the context of admissibility and/or application of the substantive protections of the Treaty at the merits phase.[148]

It is certainly true, and it has been recalled throughout this book, that conceptual approaches towards the application of the principle of good faith may vary depending on the circumstances of the case so that no single and uniform solution will likely be found. In this respect, this author also shares De Brabandere's criticism of the terminology used by the *Abaclat* tribunal as being confusing and potentially overlapping,[149] and fully endorses his proposal to rather 'categorize "good faith" claims as either being directed at the jurisdiction of the tribunal, even when dealt with at the stage of the merits, or at the admissibility of the claim' as being much clearer.[150] The problem with the terminology used by the *ST-AD* tribunal, on the other hand, is that although on its face more straightforward, the notion of 'systemic abuse' may again be understood as either going at the jurisdiction, the admissibility of the claim or the merits. This terminology does therefore not appear to have much added value either.

9.5 A (More) Systematic Approach Towards the Use of the Principle of Good Faith and its Emanations in Cases of Treaty Shopping

With the above in mind, a (more) systematic approach towards the use of the principle of good faith and its emanations and concretizations—in particular the abuse of rights/abuse of process doctrine—in cases of strategic changes of nationality will now be proposed. Far from pretending that there is a single, 'catch-all' answer to the treatment of treaty shopping in investment arbitral jurisprudence, systematization of the approach will arguably help to 'streamline' the legal questions at issue and therefore contribute to more homogeneity in arbitral reasoning, thereby reducing blurry lines and enhancing legal predictability.

148 *Vannessa Ventures v Venezuela* (n 2) para 113.
149 De Brabandere (n 11) 615. But see Ascencio (n 11) 779.
150 De Brabandere (n 11) 616.

The starting point of the analysis is the rather straightforward observation (already mentioned several times further above) that a potential abuse of rights presupposes the existence of a right. Indeed, as already Hersch Lauterpacht has held, '[t]here is no right however well established, which could not, in some circumstances, be refused recognition on the ground that it has been abused'.[151]

The right potentially being abused in the case of strategic changes of nationality is the right to bring investment arbitration proceedings against the host State under certain circumstances. Investment arbitration being dependent on the existence of consent by the host State, the question of when such a right arises is determined by the terms of the instrument containing this consent. In the case of investment treaties, these terms are normally contained in the dispute settlement clause and may vary depending on the specificities contained in the investment treaty under interpretation. Thus, an investor obtains a direct right to sue the host State for alleged breaches of the investment treaty only if he fulfils all the requirements stipulated in the dispute settlement clause, that is, if he qualifies as 'investor' and has made an 'investment' as defined by the relevant clauses in the treaty; if a 'dispute' exists;[152] depending on whether the treaty contains the principle of non-retroactivity (and on which approach the arbitral tribunal takes in this respect)[153] or a (single or double) exclusion clause, if the dispute has already arisen before the change of nationality or not, etc.[154] Whether these (jurisdictional) requirements are fulfilled, the arbitral tribunal will have to determine through interpretation of the relevant terms and application to the facts.[155] *Thus, whether a right to commence arbitral proceedings exists is in the first place a question directed at the jurisdiction of the tribunal, which has to be determined by recourse to treaty interpretation. By contrast, once this right has been established, the question, as part of the admissibility of the claim, is whether it has been abused under the specific circumstances of the case.*[156]

The above leads to another observation. As we have seen in Chapters 4 to 7 and above in this chapter, tribunals have shown a clear tendency for attaching a possible lack of good faith in the bringing of the investment claim based on a strategic change of nationality to treaty-based notions and only in a subsidiary manner to the abuse of rights/abuse of process doctrine. Two closely linked factors would seem to explain this almost natural preference for an interpretative approach. For one, though no official hierarchy exists as between the sources of international law,

[151] Hersch Lauterpacht, *The Development of International Law by the International Court* (Stevens and Sons 1958) 164.

[152] See in this sense Franke (n 37) 168–69.

[153] See Chapter 6, at 6.4.1.2 above.

[154] This is without prejudice to admissibility requirements that also may be contained in the dispute settlement clause, such as cooling-off periods, exhaustion of local remedies, the requirement that no more than three years have elapsed since the investor knew (or should have known) of the existence of the alleged breach, see, eg, Art 1116(2) NAFTA. See also Andrea Steingruber, *Consent in International Arbitration* (Oxford University Press 2011) paras 11.08–11.27.

[155] Similar Franke (n 37) 166–67.

[156] Similar De Brabandere (n 11) 620; John Gaffney, 'Abuse of process in Investment Treaty Arbitration (2010) 11 JWIT 515, 533. This would also seem to suggest that for the reasons explained at 9.3.4, the abuse of rights doctrine does not work in the context of the principle of systemic integration.

general principles of law are considered subsidiary in character as opposed to treaty or customary international law. Indeed, when the Statute of the Permanent Court of International Justice was drafted, general principles of law were conceived of to fill potential gaps left by treaty and customary law.[157] More importantly, though, the threat of being accused of 'judicial activism' often enough seems to temper any adjudicator's willingness to venture too far into 'unchartered good faith territory', as also remarked by Cremades:

> When an arbitrator decides on specific claims based on a legislative text he enjoys an interpretative precision that he lacks when basing his decisions on the general principles of law, specifically on the principle of good faith. Therefore, the logical hesitation that exists in practice and in doctrine makes recurring to good faith replete with legal insecurity or, in a worst case scenario, leads to a risk of arbitrariness ... Nevertheless, any judicial or arbitral decision, as a human activity, has a strong discretionary content subject to personal valuation. Therefore, arbitrators are extraordinarily cautious in their decisions when they must apply the principle of good faith.[158]

Though it may sound like a truism, it follows from the above that a more systematic approach towards the principle of good faith respectively the abuse of rights/abuse of process doctrine would warrant that when judging the validity of a claim based on a strategic change of nationality, interpretative approaches (should) come before the application of the abuse of rights/abuse of process doctrine. In other words, it seems correct and a sound decision for tribunals to try and attach a possible objection to a corporate structuring or restructuring primarily to treaty-based notions open to interpretative methods before applying the abuse of rights/abuse of process doctrine.

It may not always be obvious, but even when interpreting key jurisdictional notions, tribunals do incorporate a good faith judgment on the change of nationality, though in an implicit, or 'coded', way. Indeed, qualifying a claim for example as 'using the ICSID Convention for purposes for which it was clearly not intended'[159] or expressing 'serious concerns about the nature and extent of Claimant's interest in Venezuela, and about the distinction between the making of an investment and the buying of a legal claim against the host State'[160] is arguably another way for passing judgment on the propriety of the claim, even though not in a similarly explicit way as saying that the claim was abusive (or even that the claimant acted in bad faith, in particular since an abuse of rights arguably does not require a bad faith finding).[161] Though seemingly treaty-based, the finding of necessity for an 'active contribution'

[157] Alain Pellet, 'Article 38' in Andreas Zimmermann, Christian Tomuschat, and Karin Oellers-Frahm (eds), *The Statute of the International Court of Justice: A Commentary* (Oxford University Press, 2nd edn 2012) para 278.

[158] Bernardo Cremades, 'Good Faith in International Arbitration' (2011–2012) 27 Am U Intl L Rev 761, 785.

[159] See, eg, *Vacuum Salt Production Limited v Government of the Republic of Ghana*, ICSID Case No ARB/92/1, Award (16 Feb 1994) para 54; *National Gas v Egypt* (n 46) para 146.

[160] *Vannessa Ventures v Venezuela* (n 2) para 121.

[161] In this sense also *Philip Morris Asia v Australia* (n 143) para 539.

requirement as seen in *Standard Chartered Bank* and *Alapli Elektrik* also seems to attest to this implicit good faith examination.

This being said, arbitral tribunals do appear to make a distinction between a dismissal on jurisdictional grounds and one on grounds of abuse of rights/abuse of process, and this seemingly for reasons of cost allocation.[162] For example, though dismissing the claim for lack of 'foreign control', the arbitral tribunal in *National Gas* thought that the 'choice of corporate structure was made in good faith for legitimate fiscal reasons'[163] and ordered each party to bear its own costs. The tribunal in *Caratube v Kazakhstan* also rejected the Respondent's contention that Claimant's investment was not *bona fides*, finding no 'sufficient proof in the present case that the nationality shelter was the exclusive motivation for the transaction' and allocated only a portion of the Respondents costs on the Claimant.[164] By contrast, the tribunal in *Renée Rose Levy and Gremcitel v Peru* opined that:

> A finding of abuse of process justifies an award of costs against the unsuccessful party. Thus, the Claimant shall pay for the entirety of the costs of the proceedings, i.e. for the costs of the Arbitral Tribunal and for the costs of the proceedings.[165]

The proposed differentiation also implies that for the questions of jurisdictional relevance that remain inconsistently decided by arbitral tribunals (such as whether the notion of control means legal or effective control, whether for the notion of foreign control the nationality of the ultimate controller is decisive or whether the exercise of the DOB clause has retrospective or prospective effect), the main remedy, in view of the subjectivity inherent in treaty interpretation, is more rigorous treaty drafting as seen in the preceding chapter. By contrast, the inconsistencies observed in the application of the abuse of rights/abuse of process doctrine are more difficult to remedy through more rigorous treaty drafting due to its highly fact-intensive nature. Indeed, as seen in Chapter 8, the attempt undertaken in the investment chapter of the EU–Singapore FTA to incorporate the pre-existing dispute/foreseeable future dispute jurisprudence (and thus constrain a tribunal's discretion in this respect) has shown the difficulty, if not to say the limits, of trying to 'codify' doctrines as fact-intensive as the abuse of rights/abuse of process doctrine. Here, then, arbitral tribunals will be called upon to lay particular emphasis on applying the jurisprudence on the notion of dispute and its foreseeability in a differentiated manner to the facts of the case.

Remains the question whether the risk of subjective bias outweighs the benefits of the principle of good faith and its emanations or whether there is even hardly any place for them in judging the validity of a claim based on treaty shopping. [166] This research has argued that the dividing line between a 'legitimate nationality planning' and 'abusive treaty shopping' would be impossible to draw without the

[162] Similar De Brabandere (n 11) 629.
[163] *National Gas v Egypt* (n 46) para 146, 156–57. Similar in *KT Asia v Kazakhstan* (n 1) para 205.
[164] *Caratube v Kazakhstan* (n 33) paras 465, 494–95.
[165] *Renée Rose Levy and Gremcitel v Peru* (n 140) para 201.
[166] In this sense seemingly Schill and Bray (n 17) 116.

principle of good faith and its manifestations, among which the abuse of rights/abuse of process doctrine. This being said, some safeguards do need to be taken.

For one, a clear separation of the methodological steps, and thus the priority of the interpretative approach as seen above, would seem to lower the risk of subjective bias commonly associated with the principle of good faith. On the other hand, and as already mentioned above, a cautious approach is warranted with respect to the judicial development of new doctrines or additional, unwritten requirements, even if on its face treaty-based such as the 'active contribution' requirement. In a similar vein, a more consistent application of the abuse of rights/abuse of process doctrine would seem to require a more careful application of the jurisprudence on the notion of dispute or its foreseeability to the facts of the case. This is so because even though the question of whether a dispute existed at the time of the restructuring is not part of the abuse of rights/abuse of process doctrine properly speaking (but overlaps with jurisdiction *ratione temporis*),[167] the question of whether a dispute existed or was foreseeable at the time of the restructuring arguably captures the value judgment inherent in making the distinction between a 'legitimate nationality planning' and 'abusive treaty shopping'. At either leg of the jurisprudential test, this value judgment should be exercised, whether in a differentiated analysis of the notion of dispute that does not automatically equate the starting point of the dispute with the occurrence of the alleged breach, or otherwise in the analysis of its foreseeability, having due regard to an 'objectivized' investor horizon.

Thus checked, there is in this author's opinion no reason why the principle of good faith and its manifestations, in particular the abuse of rights/abuse of process doctrine, should not be an adequate tool for increasing coherence of investment arbitral decision-making with public international law, thereby enhancing predictability of the jurisprudence and furthering legal security.[168]

9.6 Preliminary Conclusions

This chapter has shown that the principle of good faith and its emanations play a key role in drawing the distinction between a 'legitimate nationality planning' and 'abusive treaty shopping'. In this sense, it has been argued that arbitral tribunals recur to two methodological approaches when seeking to make this distinction, the 'interpretative' approach on the one hand side and the 'application of the principle of good faith and its emanations' approach on the other hand. Indeed, in both approaches, arbitral tribunals attempt to balance the countervailing interests inherent in an investment claim based on treaty shopping and infuse a value judgment on the purpose of the strategic change of nationality, though in the case of the interpretative approach in more implicit terms.

[167] See Chapter 7, at 7.3.2.1.

[168] In this sense also Voon, Mitchell, and Munro, 'Legal Responses' (n 116) 65; similar Ascencio (n 11) 785.

As for the application of the principle of good faith and its concretizations, it has been seen that both the 'genuine link' and the 'piercing of the corporate veil' theories should, in the absence of corresponding treaty-based requirements, be laid to rest in the discussions subject of this research. By contrast, the abuse of rights/abuse of process doctrine and, in exceptional cases, fraud as the 'antithesis of good faith' offer all the legal tools needed to deal appropriately with the question of validity, under international investment law, of a claim based on treaty shopping.

Conclusions

What is treaty shopping and how may a 'legitimate nationality planning' be distinguished from 'treaty abuse'? This is the question this book has set out to explore, analysing systematically and comprehensively both customary international law as well as investment law and arbitral jurisprudence relevant to this question.

As has been seen, no single, 'catch-all' answer may be expected to this question. This is per se not particularly surprising. First of all, there is no common understanding of the term 'treaty shopping', and once this definitional obstacle has been overcome, one notes that there is no universal prohibition of either this practice or the vehicle primarily associated with it, the so-called mailbox or shell company. Yet, treaty shopping is beset with a negative connotation. And sure enough, treaty shopping does raise some important policy issues,[1] making this practice (understandably) undesirable for States. *How* undesirable is only gradually transpiring to States party to IIAs. Second, no uniform answer should also be expected because of the fragmented nature of international investment law, mandating arbitral tribunals to interpret each IIA with often distinct treaty language in its concrete (mostly bilateral) relationship, yet functioning in a de facto multilateralized governance system.[2] In this peculiar ordering system, then, nationality still holds the 'key to the club', yet at the same time is increasingly easily acquired through corporate structuring or restructuring, in particular through the use of mailbox companies.

This paradox has put arbitral tribunals before the value judgment at issue: is it 'nationality planning' or 'treaty abuse', what is the role of nationality, and why should corporate structuring be allowed while corporate restructuring prohibited? Arbitral tribunals have shunned to answer these (almost philosophical) questions, engaging instead in punctual analyses of the legal questions at issue. This, of course, should not be read as a complaint as this is what they are entrusted with, but it has contributed to a piecemeal approach towards this value judgment that has only more recently started to be couched in more systematic terms.

With the afore-said in mind, the following conclusions may be drawn.

[1] See Chapter 2.

[2] See Stephan Schill, 'Ordering Paradigms in International Investment Law: Bilateralism—Multilateralism—Multilateralization' in Zachary Douglas, Joost Pauwelyn, and Jorge Viñuales (eds), *The Foundations of International Investment Law* (Oxford University Press 2014) 109ff.

The Customary International Law Position on Treaty Shopping

The analysis of the customary international law on the question of changes of nationality in Chapter 3 has shown that customary international law is traditionally wary of possible nationality-related abuses and has, as a consequence, taken a restrictive stance towards the question of shareholder standing. By contrast, international investment law has developed markedly different rules and approaches towards the question of a (strategic) change of nationality. Indeed, the role of customary international law for the purposes of this research is limited. Beyond the possible invocation of customary international law through the principle of systemic integration and the reference to customary international law in prior decisions by the Permanent Court of International Justice (PCIJ) and International Court of Justice (ICJ), investment arbitral tribunals have established a clear *lex specialis* approach with respect to the investment law system so that the approaches taken by the ICJ in *Barcelona Traction* and in *Diallo* have been uniformly rejected by arbitral tribunals.[3]

Treaty Shopping by Natural Persons

For the case of strategic uses/changes of nationality by natural persons, we have seen in Chapter 4 that this kind of treaty shopping usually functions through the invocation of a dual nationality. Arbitral tribunals have in this respect uniformly rejected to import the customary international law-based 'genuine link' requirement in the absence of a corresponding treaty-based requirement in the IIA, attesting to the *lex specialis* character of the international investment law system.[4] The only bar to the invocation of a dual nationality may be found in the 'host State bias' contained in Article 25(2)(a) International Centre for Settlement of Investment Disputes (ICSID) Convention.[5] This means that claims under other arbitral rules (such as United Nations Commission on International Trade Law (UNCITRAL) rules) by a dual national holding host State nationality remain possible unless the invoked international investment agreement (IIA) contains an explicit exclusion to this effect. Arbitral tribunals have also started to recognize the potential for 'circumventions' of the 'host State bias' in Article 25(2)(a) ICSID Convention by the use of interposed corporate entities controlled by (host State) dual nationals, interpreting the notion of 'foreign control' in Article 25(2)(b) second clause in the light of Article 25(2)(a) ICSID Convention.[6]

Whether the abuse of rights/abuse of process doctrine (in particular in the jurisprudence distinguishing between a pre-existing and foreseeable future dispute) could be applied to a change of nationality properly speaking by a natural person

[3] See Chapter 3, at 3.4.
[4] See Chapter 4, at 4.2.1.
[5] See Chapter 4, at 4.2.2.
[6] See Chapter 4, at 4.2.2 and 4.2.3.

has so far (at least as far as publicly known) not been decided by arbitral tribunals. However, in this author's opinion, there is no reason why this line of jurisprudence should not apply to the same extent as in the case of changes of nationality by legal persons.

Treaty Shopping by Legal Persons

For the case of strategic changes of nationality by legal persons (in other words corporate structuring and restructuring), we have also seen in Chapter 4 that most cases, and indeed most legal problems and inconsistencies, arise in this scenario, potentially touching objections to jurisdiction *ratione personae, ratione materiae*, and/or *ratione temporis*, as well as objections on grounds of abuse of rights/abuse of process.

With respect to objections to jurisdiction *ratione personae*, we have seen that it is in cases of claims brought under Article 25(2)(b) first clause ICSID Convention where the legal problems are nowadays most settled. Indeed, arbitral tribunals have developed and maintained a very clear formal and consent-oriented approach towards the use of mailbox companies in the absence of additional treaty-based requirements, virtually uniformly rejecting arguments aimed at 'piercing the corporate veil'.[7] States wishing to exclude the use of mailbox companies as potential investor-claimants are therefore well advised to prescribe additional substantive requirements for the investor to benefit from IIA protection, such as the requirement of 'substantive business activities'.[8] Alternatively, States may also include a denial of benefits (DOB) clause in the IIA. However, inconsistent jurisprudence as to whether the exercise of the DOB clause has retrospective or prospective effect only may relativize the usefulness of this provision.[9]

More arbitral inconsistency exists in cases of claims brought under Article 25(2)(b) second clause ICSID Convention. This concerns in particular the question of whether the notion of 'foreign control' should be understood as requiring purely legal/formal control or rather effective/de facto control, being understood that a formal approach towards the notion of 'foreign control' condones the use of corporate structures set up and interposed by host or third State nationals with the aim of bringing the investment under the protection of the intended treaty, while requiring de facto control considerably raises the bar to this effect. Though some arbitral tribunals have established the presumption that majority shareholding (that is, the formal control position) implied effective control, others have shown themselves prudent enough to look for actual control (even in the case of majority shareholding) when they had doubts about the true nature of the investor (respectively its investment). Indeed, as seen, given the specific objectives of the ICSID Convention to provide a forum and framework for *international* investment disputes, there are

[7] See Chapter 4, at 4.3.1. [8] See Chapter 4, at 4.3.2. [9] See Chapter 4, at 4.3.3.

good reasons to argue that the notion of 'foreign control' should be understood as meaning effective or actual control as opposed to merely formal control.[10]

A similar uncertainty exists with respect to the question of how far up the corporate tier an arbitral tribunal should look in order to validate or invalidate the finding of 'foreign control'.[11] Should it stop once it has found the requisite nationality, or should it continue its enquiries until the ultimate level of control, even if this leads to the invalidation of foreign control, for example because the ultimate controller of the investment is a host State national? While some arbitral tribunals have stopped in their enquiries once they have found a qualifying nationality, others have looked into ultimate control, dismissing the cases where the ultimate controller was found to be a host State national. This seems correct, also in view of the submission that 'foreign control' should be understood as effective control. Yet, any such finding will greatly depend on the availability of information on ownership/control structures and the burden of proof in this respect.

In Chapter 5, we have seen that arbitral attention has been increasingly centering on questions relating to jurisdiction *ratione materiae*, raising questions with respect to the notion of investment both under IIAs and the ICSID Convention. In order to counter the restrictive effects of the *Barcelona Traction* jurisprudence, modern investment treaties nowadays virtually uniformly protect shareholding as an investment. Moreover, arbitral tribunals have rather consistently found that IIAs protect not only direct but also indirect investments, and this is even in cases where the IIA is silent on whether indirect investments should be covered.[12] This leads to a very broad potential standing of shareholders and raises questions that, as it would seem, have not yet been conclusively answered by arbitral jurisprudence. Thus, for example, is it enough for an investor, originally without a qualifying nationality, to acquire assets qualifying under the targeted investment treaty for nominal value? Is it enough for a parent company to reshuffle (qualifying) corporate assets in favour of an entity holding the requisite nationality? And finally, is it enough for any entity along the chain of a corporate group to claim ownership or control of (qualifying) assets that any of its subsidiaries might hold, or does the investor-claimant actually have to make an 'active' contribution?

Arbitral tribunals (including non-ICSID tribunals) have by now found a fairly coherent line as to the fact that the payment of a nominal price for the investment alone—in the absence of further elements indicating a 'bad faith' or 'sham transaction'—does in principle not disqualify the investment.[13] In a similar vein, questions of jurisdiction *ratione temporis* (did the reshuffling, i.e. the acquisition of the qualifying investment, take place at a moment when a dispute already existed?) would also seem to be relevant in order to provide answers. Yet, what remains to date rather unclear is what qualifies as an 'active' as opposed to a 'passive' contribution and how the latter relates to a (in principle protected) indirect investment.[14]

[10] See Chapter 4, at 4.3.4.1.
[11] See Chapter 4, at 4.3.4.2.
[12] See Chapter 5, at 5.2.2.
[13] See Chapter 5, at 5.4.1.2.
[14] See Chapter 5, at 5.4.3.

Indeed, the judicial development of an 'active contribution' requirement as an element to pass (implicitly) judgment on the 'propriety' of the claim raises the question how far an arbitral tribunal may go in reading additional (unwritten) requirements into a treaty text. The same question arguably arises with respect to an unwritten 'good faith' requirement as additional element inherent in the notion of investment under the ICSID Convention. Most arbitral tribunals have clearly rejected such additional 'good faith' requirement.[15]

As for objections to jurisdiction *ratione temporis*, Chapter 6 has arguably shown the overriding importance of the notion of dispute for judging the propriety of a claim based on a strategic change of nationality. Indeed, arbitral tribunals have established an increasingly consolidated line of jurisprudence that dismisses jurisdiction *ratione temporis* if the strategic change of nationality has occurred at a time when the dispute already existed. Yet, many questions and inconsistencies remain in this respect.

First, arbitral tribunals have not been unanimous in finding that jurisdiction *ratione temporis* should be rejected if a dispute existed at the time of the change of nationality. While many tribunals have based their reasoning on the (customary) principle of non-retroactivity, some have objected that the exclusion of pre-existing disputes is not necessarily the same as the exclusion of pre-existing acts or facts leading to the (alleged) breach of the obligation.[16]

Second, arbitral tribunals have been rather incoherent in determining the point in time when a dispute has started to exist.[17] Even though a well-established and nuanced jurisprudence by the PCIJ and ICJ exists on the notion of dispute,[18] arbitral tribunals often tend to equate the (alleged) breach of the obligation with the occurrence of a dispute, and this even in cases where the business relationship has over time become increasingly conflictive. This *may* be correct, but need not in *all* cases, in particular in cases of continuous or composite acts, making a nuanced treatment of the notion of dispute necessary.[19] The same risk of arbitral subjectivity exists for the question whether in a series of host State acts and measures affecting the investor, the tribunal is faced with a single (broadly framed) or two or more separate (narrowly framed) disputes.[20] As has been shown, the determination of when a dispute has come into being has crucial importance for dismissing (or not) a claim based on a strategic change of nationality.

As for continuous nationality potentially at stake in a change of nationality, it has been seen that the (controversial) customary international law-based continuous nationality requirement has no place in the *lex specialis* investment law system.[21] Investment treaties, including the ICSID Convention, implicitly or explicitly mandate that the claimed nationality must exist only at the moment of the (alleged) breach (so-called *dies a quo*) and the moment of the bringing of the claim (so-called *dies ad quem*). A change of nationality beyond that moment therefore has

[15] See Chapter 5, at 5.4.4.
[16] See Chapter 6, at 6.4.1.2.
[17] See Chapter 6, at 6.4.2.
[18] See Chapter 6, at 6.4.2.2.
[19] See Chapter 6, at 6.4.2.3.
[20] See Chapter 6, at 6.4.2.3.3.
[21] See Chapter 6, at 6.3.

no incidence on the competence of the tribunal, even though it might be taken into account within the merits phase. Furthermore, the transfer of an investment between persons of the same nationality (thus not leading to a change of nationality) remains possible even after the occurrence of the (alleged) breach.

Chapter 7 has finally shown the relevance of the abuse of rights/abuse of process doctrine in distinguishing a 'legitimate nationality planning' from 'treaty abuse'. Indeed, arbitral tribunals have in recent years increasingly recurred to this manifestation of the principle of good faith and thereby developed a line of jurisprudence that is more or less consolidated by now and distinguishes as to whether at the time of the change of nationality, there was a pre-existing dispute (in which case the tribunal would lack jurisdiction *ratione temporis*) or, in its absence, whether a future dispute was (sufficiently) foreseeable (in which case the claim would be inadmissible on grounds of an abuse of rights/abuse of process).[22] As has been seen, the focus on the timing element is a consequence of the need to 'objectify' the motives for the change of nationality and thus to eschew the potential for manipulation inherent in asking for the 'sole purpose' of the transaction.

The increasing consolidation of this line of jurisprudence is a welcome development that is in principle suitable to further predictability in arbitral decision-making. Yet, inconsistent application of the 'foreseeability' test somewhat relativizes this conclusion,[23] and in general, arbitral tribunals have arrived at abuse of process judgments only very rarely, thus putting up a high barrier for considering a claim based on a strategic change of nationality abusive. In this respect, it could also be observed that arbitral tribunals have been more willing to dismiss possibly 'invalid' claims based on the interpretation of treaty-based notions, thus avoiding the explicit 'abuse', respectively 'bad faith', verdict.[24]

Indeed, the important role of the principle of good faith in drawing the line between a 'legitimate nationality planning' and 'treaty abuse', and arbitral tribunals' use and application of it, has warranted in this author's opinion a separate chapter. It has been submitted that the principle of good faith, in particular in the manifestations it finds in treaty interpretation as well as in the concretizations of fraud and abuse of rights/abuse of process, holds the key for purposes of this research.[25] By contrast, neither the 'genuine link' nor the 'piercing of the corporate veil' theories are in this author's opinion appropriate legal tools to approach the question of treaty shopping.[26] The same applies to the 'sole purpose doctrine' and the maxim *nemo dat quod non habet*, both figures being more adequately captured by the abuse of rights/abuse of process doctrine and its concretization in the 'pre-existing/foreseeable dispute' jurisprudence.[27]

Responding to fears about the risk for arbitral subjectivism inherent in the use of the principle of good faith, this research concedes that this risk does exist. However, it may be kept at bay if arbitral tribunals place the relevant legal questions in the

[22] See Chapter 7, at 7.3.2.1. [23] See Chapter 7, at 7.3.2.2.
[24] See Chapter 9, at 9.5. [25] See Chapter 9, at 9.4.3 and 9.4.4.
[26] See Chapter 9, at 9.4.1 and 9.4.2. [27] See Chapter 7, at 7.3.2.3 and 7.4.

proposed methodological order and take a principled approach towards certain key questions (in particular the notion of dispute and its foreseeability).

Transfer of Claims

Finally, as could be seen, arbitral decisions have only very rarely treated the question of transfers of claims. This may be due to the fact that when they do happen, they would usually seem to raise sensitive questions of jurisdiction *ratione temporis*. If a claim has already arisen at the time of the transfer, this means that a dispute is very likely to have already come into existence or to have been foreseeable for the investor. The line of jurisprudence that, as seen above, distinguishes between the existence of a pre-existing and the foreseeability of a future dispute would therefore also be applicable to the case of a transfer of claim, rendering the investment claim either moot for lack of temporal jurisdiction or inadmissible on grounds of an abuse of rights/abuse of process.

States' Possible Approaches Towards Treaty Shopping

In view of the above analysis, what can States do if they want to guard themselves against the uncertainties arising from the observed inconsistencies in the treatment of treaty shopping by arbitral jurisprudence? It has been argued that political approaches aimed at solving the problems arising from treaty shopping at their root, such as the negotiation of a uniform multilateral investment framework, the prescription of mailbox companies or the negotiation of new treaties without investor–State dispute settlement clauses, are possible, yet under current political circumstances for the time being not very realistic options (at least for the former two).[28] Particular emphasis must in this author's opinion therefore be placed on more careful treaty drafting in newly negotiated IIAs and other tools enhancing States' 'interpretative control' if these wish to restrict treaty shopping.

In this respect, the analysis of a wide sample of IIAs with the aim of taking stock of current treaty practice and identifying possible policy approaches and/or treaty wording has shown that States are becoming increasingly attentive to the practice of treaty shopping. Yet, while some have started to explore innovative ways in newer IIAs to restrict it, many others still leave the door wide open to treaty shopping.[29]

In conclusion, treaty shopping will remain possible in the absence of a profound overhaul, that is, multilateralization of the international investment law system, but in the absence of such multilateralization, States and arbitral tribunals both have their roles in curbing the phenomenon.

[28] See Chapter 8, at 8.1. [29] See Chapter 8, at 8.2.

Annex

The following table lists in a non-exhaustive and cursory way the most important arbitral decisions analysed in Chapters 4 to 7 categorized according to the key legal question(s) at stake.

Abbreviations:
AT: Arbitral tribunal
bc: because
btw: between
JD: Jurisdiction

Case name	Arbitral forum/ rules	Case No	Type of decision	Date of decision	Key legal finding	Where
Natural person: 'Genuine link' requirement (single nationality)						
Feldman v Mexico	ICSID	ARB(AF)/ 99/1	Interim Decision on Preliminary JDal Issues	6 Dec 2000	No 'genuine link' requirement in IIL	4.2.1.1
Siag and Vecchi v Egypt	ICSID	ARB/05/15	Decision on JD	11 April 2007	No 'genuine link' requirement in IIL	4.2.1.1
Micula et al v Romania	ICSID	ARB/05/20	Decision on JD and Admissibility	24 Sept 2008	No 'genuine link' requirement in IIL	4.2.1.1
Oostergetel et al v Slovak Republic	UNCITRAL	—	Decision on JD	30 April 2010	No 'genuine link' requirement in IIL	4.2.1.1
Natural person: 'Genuine link' requirement (dual nationality)						
Olguín v Paraguay	ICSID	ARB/98/5	Award	26 July 2001	No 'genuine link' requirement in IIL	4.2.1.2
Champion Trading Company et al v Egypt	ICSID	ARB/02/9	Decision on JD	21 Oct 2003	Idem	4.2.1.2
Pey Casado et al v Chile	ICSID	ARB/98/2	Sentence Arbitrale	8 May 2008	Idem	4.2.1.2

Case name	Arbitral forum/ rules	Case No	Type of decision	Date of decision	Key legal finding	Where
Serafín García Armas y Karina García Gruber	PCA (UNCITRAL)	2013-3	Decision on JD	15 Dec 2014	No 'genuine link' requirement in IIL; but claim by (host State) dual national possible under UNCITRAL rules	4.2.1.2
Natural person: 'foreign control' through dual (host State) national						
Burimi SRL and Eagle Games v Albania	ICSID	ARB/11/13	Award	29 May 2013	AT dismissed JD because of ultimate (dual) host State national control	4.2.2
National Gas v Egypt	ICSID	ARB/11/7	Award	3 April 2014	Idem	4.2.2
Legal person: Mailbox company, third State national-controlled						
Saluka Investments v Czech Republic	PCA (UNCITRAL)	--	Partial Award	17 March 2006	AT accepted third State national-controlled mailbox company in the absence of additional treaty-based requirements	4.3.1.2
ADC Affiliate v Hungary	ICSID	ARB/03/16	Award	2 Oct 2006	Idem	4.3.1.2
Niko Resources v Bangladesh et al	ICSID	ARB/10/11	Decision on JD	19 Aug 2013	Idem	4.3.1.2
Gold Reserve Inc v Venezuela	ICSID	ARB(AF)/09/1	Award	22 Sept 2014	Idem	4.3.1.2
Legal person: Mailbox company, host State national-controlled ('round-tripping')						
Wena Hotels v Egypt	ICSID	ARB/98/4	Proceeding on the JD	25 May 1999	AT accepted claim by foreign-incorporated claimant ultimately controlled by dual (host State) national	4.3.1.1

Case name	Arbitral forum/ rules	Case No	Type of decision	Date of decision	Key legal finding	Where
Tokios Tokelés v Ukraine	ICSID	ARB/02/18	Decision on JD	29 April 2004	AT accepted JD *ratione personae* for host State-controlled foreign-incorporated mailbox company in the absence of additional treaty-based requirements	4.3.1.1
Rompetrol v Romania	ICSID	ARB/06/3	Decision on Respondent's Preliminary Objections on JD and Admissibility	18 April 2008	Idem	4.3.1.1
Yukos Universal Ltd v Russia	PCA (UNCITRAL)	AA 227	Interim Award on JD and Admissibility	30 Nov 2009	Idem	4.3.1.1
Alpha Projektholding v Ukraine	ICSID	ARB/07/16	Award	8 Nov 2010	Idem	4.3.1.1
KT Asia Investment Group v Kazakhstan	ICSID	ARB/09/8	Award	17 Oct 2013	Idem	4.3.1.1
Venoklim Holding BV v Venezuela	ICSID	ARB/12/22	Award	3 April 2015	AT dismissed claim by Netherlands-incorporated claimant because of ultimate effective control by Venezuelan companies and nationals (claim based on Venezuelan Investment Law)	4.3.1.1

Case name	Arbitral forum/ rules	Case No	Type of decision	Date of decision	Key legal finding	Where
Legal person: Notion of 'foreign control': legal or de facto control						
Vacuum Salt v Ghana	ICSID	ARB/92/1	Award	16 Feb 1994	AT required effective control in case of minority shareholding	4.3.4.1.2
Autopista Concesionada de Venezuela (Aucoven) v Venezuela	ICSID	ARB/00/5	Decision on JD	27 Sept 2001	AT found legal control sufficient for majority shareholding	4.3.4.1.2
Compagnie d'Exploration du Chemin de Fer Transgabonais v Gabon	ICSID	ARB/04/5	Decision on JD	19 Dec 2005	AT required effective control for combined minority shareholding	4.3.4.1.2
Caratube International Oil Co v Kazakhstan	ICSID	ARB/08/12	Award	5 June 2012	AT required effective control despite majority shareholding	4.3.4.1.2
Legal person: Notion of 'foreign control': first qualifying nationality or ultimate control						
Amco Asia Corporation et al v Indonesia	ICSID	ARB/81/1	Award on JD	25 Sept 1983	AT stopped at first tier for finding 'foreign control'	4.3.4.2.1
SOABI v Sénégal	ICSID	ARB/82/1	Decision on JD	19 July 1984	AT accepted qualifying nationality at second-tier level	4.3.4.2.1
Compagnie d'Exploration du Chemin de Fer Transgabonais v Gabon	ICSID	ARB/04/5	Decision on JD	19 Dec 2005	AT accepted first qualifying nationality, (but left open possible exception where host State control could be proven)	4.3.4.2.1

Case name	Arbitral forum/ rules	Case No	Type of decision	Date of decision	Key legal finding	Where
TSA Spectrum v Argentina	ICSID	ARB/05/5	Award	19 Dec 2008	AT enquired into ultimate control which turned out to be host State control, dismissing JD *ratione personae*	4.3.4.2.1
National Gas Company v Egypt	ICSID	ARB/11/07	Award	3 April 2014	Idem	4.3.4.2.1
Denial of benefits clause: Retrospective or prospective effect						
Plama v Bulgaria	ICSID	ARB/03/24	Decision on JD	8 Feb 2005	Prospective effect	4.3.3
Pan American Energy et al v Argentina	ICSID	ARB/03/13	Decision on Preliminary Objections	27 July 2006	Idem	4.3.3
Empresa Eléctrica del Ecuador v Ecuador	ICSID	ARB/05/9	Award	2 June 2009	Retrospective effect	4.3.3
Liman Caspian Oil et al v Kazakhstan	ICSID	ARB/07/14	Award	22 June 2010	Prospective effect	4.3.3
Ulysseas Inc v Ecuador	PCA (UNCITRAL)	--	Interim Award	28 Sept 2010	Retrospective effect	4.3.3
Pac Rim Cayman v El Salvador	ICSID	ARB/09/12	Decision on the Respondent's JD and Objections	1 June 2012	Idem	4.3.3
Khan Resources et al v Kazakhstan	PCA (UNCITRAL)	2011-09	Decision on JD	25 July 2012	Prospective effect	4.3.3
Ascom Stati v Kazakhstan	SCC	V (116/2010)	Award	19 Dec 2013	Idem	4.3.3
Guaracachi America Inc et al v Bolivia	PCA (UNCITRAL)	2011–17	Award	31 Jan 2014	Retrospective effect	4.3.3

Case name	Arbitral forum/ rules	Case No	Type of decision	Date of decision	Key legal finding	Where
Notion of 'control' in IIAs						
Aguas del Tunarí v Bolivia	ICSID	ARB/02/3	Decision on JD	21 Oct 2005	AT accepted legal control for case of majority shareholding	4.3.4.3.1
International Thunderbird Gaming Corporation v Mexico	UNCITRAL	--	Award	26 Jan 2006	AT required effective control for case of minority shareholding	4.3.4.3.1
Yukos v Russia	PCA (UNCITRAL)	AA 227	Interim Award on JD and Admissibility	30 Nov 2009	AT accepted legal control for purposes of the DOB clause under the ECT	4.3.4.3.1
Mobil v Venezuela	ICSID	ARB/07/27	Decision on JD	10 June 2010	AT accepted legal control for case of majority shareholding	4.3.4.3.1
Guardian Fiduciary Trust v Macedonia	ICSID	ARB/12/31	Award	22 Sept 2015	AT required effective control despite majority shareholding	4.3.4.3.1
Notion of investment: 'contribution' requirement						
Société Générale et al v Dominican Republic	LCIA (UNCITRAL)	UN 7927	Award on Preliminary Objections to JD	19 Sept 2008	AT accepted acquisition of shares at nominal value	5.4.1.2
Caratube International Oil Co v Kazakhstan	ICSID	ARB/08/12	Award	5 June 2012	AT accepted acquisition of shares at nominal value if plausible economic motivation	5.4.1.2

Case name	Arbitral forum/ rules	Case No	Type of decision	Date of decision	Key legal finding	Where
Quiborax SA, Non Metallic Minerals SA and Allan Fosk Kaplún v Bolivia	ICSID	ARB/06/2	Decision on JD	27 Sept 2012	Donation of shares not sufficient for contribution requirement in the absence of post-investment contributions	5.4.1.2
Vannessa Ventures Ltd v Venezuela	ICSID	ARB(AF)/04/6	Award	16 Jan 2013	AT accepted acquisition of shares at nominal price	5.4.2.1
KT Asia Investment Group v Kazakhstan	ICSID	ARB/09/8	Award	17 Oct 2013	AT found no contribution in case of reshuffling of assets in the absence of post-investment contributions	5.4.2.1
Renée Rose Levy de Levi v Peru	ICSID	ARB/10/17	Award	26 Feb 2014	AT accepted donation of shares despite lack of contribution bc no change of nationality was involved	5.4.2.1
Gold Reserve Inc v Venezuela	ICSID	ARB(AF)/09/1	Award	22 Sept 2014	AT accepted intra-group share swap bc investor made post-investment contributions	5.4.2.1
OI European Group BV v Venezuela	ICSID	ARB/11/25	Award	10 March 2015	AT accepted transfer of shares without payment bc of post-investment contributions	5.4.2.1

Case name	Arbitral forum/ rules	Case No	Type of decision	Date of decision	Key legal finding	Where
Notion of investment: 'active contribution' requirement						
Alapli Elektrik v Turkey	ICSID	ARB/08/13	Award Decision on Annulment	16 July 2012 10 July 2014	Dismissal of case, but split approach by AT: 'Active contribution' requirement by one arbitrator, additional 'good faith' requirement by another	5.4.3
Standard Chartered Bank v Tanzania	ICSID	ARB/10/12	Award	2 Nov 2012	AT dismissed the case for lack of 'active contribution' by the investor	5.4.3
Notion of investment: 'good faith' requirement						
Phoenix Action Ltd v Czech Republic	ICSID	ARB/06/5	Award	15 April 2009	AT read additional good faith requirement into notion of investment, dismissing JD	5.4.4.
Saba Fakes v Turkey	ICSID	ARB/07/20	Award	14 July 2010	AT rejected 'good faith' requirement in the absence of treaty-based requirement	5.4.4
Alapli Elektrik v Turkey	ICSID	ARB/08/13	Award Decision on Annulment	16 July 2012 10 July 2014	Dismissal of case, but split approach by AT: 'Active contribution' requirement by one arbitrator, additional 'good faith' requirement by another	5.4.4

Case name	Arbitral forum/ rules	Case No	Type of decision	Date of decision	Key legal finding	Where
Quiborax SA, Non Metallic Minerals SA and Allan Fosk Kaplún v Bolivia	ICSID	ARB/06/2	Decision on JD	27 Sept 2012	Additional 'good faith' requirement rejected	5.4.4
Vannessa Ventures Ltd v Venezuela	ICSID	ARB(AF)/ 04/6	Award	16 Jan 2013	Additional 'good faith' requirement rejected	5.4.4
Continuous nationality requirement						
Loewen v United States	ICSID	ARB(AF)/ 98/3	Award	26 June 2003	AT required continuous nationality until the time of the award	6.3.1
Yukos v Russia	PCA	AA 227	Interim Award on JD and Admissibility	30 Nov 2009	AT rejected continuous nationality requirement as found in *Loewen*	6.3.2
Teinver v Argentina	ICSID	ARB/09/1	Decision on JD	21 Dec 2012	AT rejected continuous nationality requirement as found in *Loewen*	6.3.2
Temporal jurisdiction: notion and timing of dispute (pre-existing dispute)						
Pac Rim Cayman v El Salvador	ICSID	ARB/09/12	Decision on the Respondent's JD and Objections	1 June 2012	AT equated (alleged) breach of obligation with dispute and found no pre-existing dispute	6.4.2.3.2
ST-AD GmbH v Bulgaria	PCA (UNCITRAL)	2011-06	Award on JD	18 July 2013	AT equated (alleged) breach of obligation with dispute, but found pre-existing dispute	6.4.1.2

Case name	Arbitral forum/ rules	Case No	Type of decision	Date of decision	Key legal finding	Where
ConocoPhilipps et al v Venezuela	ICSID	ARB/07/30	Decision on JD and Merits	3 Sept 2013	AT found no pre-existing dispute bc Claimant withdrew early protest against the announced measure	6.4.2.3.1
Lao Holdings NV v Laos	ICSID	ARB(AF)/ 12/6	Decision on JD	21 Feb 2014	AT equated (alleged) breach of obligation with dispute and found no pre-existing dispute	6.4.2.3.2
Cervin Investissements & Rhone Investissements v Costa Rica	ICSID	ARB/13/2	Decision on JD	15 Dec 2014	AT equated (alleged) breach of obligation with dispute and found no pre-existing dispute	6.4.2.3.2
Renée Rose Levy and Gremcitel SA v Peru	ICSID	ARB/11/17	Award	9 Jan 2015	AT equated (alleged) breach of obligation with dispute and found no pre-existing dispute	6.4.2.3.2
Philip Morris Asia Ltd v Commonwealth of Australia	PCA (UNCITRAL)	2012-12	Award	17 Dec 2015	AT equated (alleged) breach of obligation with dispute and found no pre-existing dispute	6.4.2.3.3

Case name	Arbitral forum/ rules	Case No	Type of decision	Date of decision	Key legal finding	Where
Abuse of rights/abuse of process: pre-existing/foreseeable dispute						
Mobil Corporation et al v Venezuela	ICSID	ARB/07/27	Decision on JD	10 June 2010	AT distinguished between pre-existing and future disputes and found abuse of rights only for restructuring in view of pre-existing disputes	7.3.1
Pac Rim Cayman v El Salvador	ICSID	ARB/09/12	Decision on the Respondent's JD and Objections	1 June 2012	AT found the dispute not to be foreseeable and rejected abuse of process (but JD dismissed for treaty claims because AT accepted retrospective effect of DOB clause)	7.3.1
Tidewater et al v Venezuela	ICSID	ARB/10/5	Decision on JD	8 Feb 2013	AT found that future dispute was not 'reasonably' foreseeable	7.3.1
ConocoPhilipps et al v Venezuela	ICSID	ARB/07/30	Decision on JD and Merits	3 Sept 2013	AT did not enquire into foreseeability of a future dispute	7.3.1

Case name	Arbitral forum/ rules	Case No	Type of decision	Date of decision	Key legal finding	Where
Lao Holdings NV v Laos	ICSID	ARB(AF)/ 12/6	Decision on JD	21 Feb 2014	AT did not examine foreseeability of dispute bc Claimant had not raised abuse of process objection with respect to the entire arbitration	7.3.1
Cervin Investissements & Rhone Investissements v Costa Rica	ICSID	ARB/13/2	Decision on JD	15 Dec 2014	AT rejected abuse of process objection bc Respondent could not prove abusive purpose of the restructuring	7.3.1
Renée Rose Levy and Gremcitel SA v Peru	ICSID	ARB/11/17	Award	9 Jan 2015	AT found abuse of process bc the dispute was foreseeable with a 'very high probability'	7.3.1
Philip Morris Asia Ltd v Commonwealth of Australia	PCA (UNCITRAL)	2012-12	Award	17 Dec 2015	AT found the dispute to be 'reasonably foreseeable' for the investor and dismissed the claim on grounds of abuse of rights	7.3.1

Case name	Arbitral forum/ rules	Case No	Type of decision	Date of decision	Key legal finding	Where
'Nemo dat quod non habet'						
Banro American Resources Inc and SAKIMA v DRC	ICSID	ARB/98/7	Award	1 Sept 2000	AT did not accept the claim based on a transfer of shares from a non-qualifying to a qualifying nationality	7.4
Mihaly International Corporation v Sri Lanka	ICSID	ARB/00/2	Award	15 March 2002	AT did not accept claim based on an assignment of claims	7.4
ST-AD GmbH v Bulgaria	PCA (UNCITRAL)	2011-06	Award on JD	18 July 2013	AT found pre-existing dispute, thus lack of JD ratione temporis, but also found abuse of process (on grounds of '*nemo dat quod non habet*')	6.4.2.3.4 and 7.4
Fraud						
Europe Cement v Turkey	ICSID	ARB(AF)/07/2	Decision on JD	13 Aug 2009	AT dismissed case bc of faked investment	9.4.3
Cementownia "Nowa Huta" v Turkey	ICSID	ARB(AF)/06/2	Award	17 Sept 2009	Idem	7.3.1 and 9.4.3
Libananco Holdings v Turkey	ICSID	ARB(AF)/06/8	Award	2 Sept 2011	Idem	9.4.3

Bibliography

Abi-Saab Georges, 'The International Law of Multinational Corporations: A Critique of American Legal Doctrines' (1971) Annales d´études internationales-Genève 97

Acconci Pia, 'Determining the Internationally Relevant Link between a State and a Corporate Investor' (2004) 5 JWIT 139

Addison-Agyei Sange, *Nationality Planning und Treaty Shopping im Internationalen Investitionsrecht* (Frankfurt aM, Peter Lang 2012)

Aguirre Luzi Roberto and Love Ben, 'Individual Nationality in Investment Treaty Arbitration: The Tension Between Customary International Law and Lex Specialis' in Bjorklund Andrea, Laird Ian, and Ripinsky Sergey (eds), *Investment Treaty Law: Current Issues III* (British Institute of International and Comparative Law 2008) 183

Aldrich George, *The Jurisprudence of the Iran-United States Claims Tribunal* (Oxford, Clarendon Press 1996)

Alexandrov Stanimir, *Reservations in Unilateral Declarations Accepting the Compulsory Jurisdiction of the International Court of Justice* (Martinus Nijhoff 1995)

Alexandrov Stanimir, 'The Baby Boom of Treaty-based Arbitrations and the Jurisdiction of ICSID Tribunals: Shareholders as "Investors" and Jurisdiction Ratione Temporis' (2005) 19 LPICT 19

Alschner Wolfgang, 'Regionalism and Overlap in Investment Treaty Law—Towards Consolidation or Contradiction?' (2014) 17 JIEL 271

Alvarez José, *The Public International Law Regime Governing International Investment* (Martinus Nijhoff 2011)

Alvik Ivar, *Contracting with Sovereignty, State Contracts and International Arbitration* (Oxford, Hart Publishing 2011)

Amerasinghe Chittharanjan, 'Jurisdiction Ratione Personae Under the Convention on the Settlement of Investment Disputes Between States and Nationals of Other States' (1974–1975) 47 BYIL 227

Amerasinghe Chittharanjan, 'The International Centre for Settlement of Investment Disputes and Development Through the Multinational Corporations' (1976) 9 Vand J Transnatl L 793

Amerasinghe Chittharanjan, *Local Remedies in International Law* (Cambridge University Press 1990)

Amerasinghe Chittharanjan, 'Interpretation of Article 25(2)(b) of the ICSID Convention' in Lillich Robert and Brower Charles N (eds), *International Arbitration towards "Judicialization" and Uniformity?* (New York, Transnational Publishers 1994) 223

Amerasinghe Chittharanjan, *Diplomatic Protection* (Oxford University Press 2008)

Arnold Brian, *International Tax Primer* (Kluwer Law International, 3rd edn 2016)

Ascencio Hervé, 'Abuse of Process in International Investment Arbitration' (2014) 13 Chin J Intl L 763

Badia Albert, *Piercing the Veil of State Enterprises* (Kluwer Law International 2014)

BBC, 'TTIP trade deal: Germans rally in Hanover against EU-US trade deal' (23 April 2016), available at <http://www.bbc.com/news/world-europe-36120560> (last accessed on 15 September 2016)

Baelz Kilian and Baldwin Teresa, 'The End of the Real Seat Theory (Sitztheorie): The European Court of Justice Decision in Überseering of 5 November 2002 and its Impact on German and European Company Law' (2002) 3 Germ L J 1

Beauvais Joel, 'Regulatory Expropriations under NAFTA: Emerging Principles and Lingering Doubts' (2002) 10 NYU Environmental L J 245

Bekker Pieter, 'Is Arbitration Based on "Treaty Shopping" in Jeopardy' *Kluwer Abitration Blog* (17 June 2009) available at <http://kluwerarbitrationblog.com/2009/06/17/is-arbitration-based-on-treaty-shopping-in-jeopardy> (last accessed on 15 September 2016)

Bell Andrew, *Forum Shopping and Venue in Transnational Litigation* (Oxford University Press 2003)

Ben Hamida Walid, 'The Notion of Investor: Comment on Sedelmayer v Russia, Generation Ukraine, Inc. v Ukraine, Tokios Tokelés v Ukraine, Plama Consortium Ltd. v Bulgaria, and Petrobart Ltd. v Kirghizstan' (2006) 4 OGEL 33

Bentolila Dolores, 'Shareholders' Action to Claim for Indirect Damages in ICSID Arbitration' (2010) 2 Trade, Law and Development 87

Besson Samantha, 'The Sovereign, the Investor and the Arbitrator' in Peter Gauch, Franz Werro, and Pascal Pichonnaz (eds), *Mélanges en l'honneur de Pierre Tercier* (Schulthess 2008) 745

Berman Franklin, 'Evolution or Revolution?' in Brown Chester and Miles Kate (eds), *Evolution in Investment Treaty Law and Arbitration* (Cambridge University Press 2011) 658

Bischoff Jan Asmus and Happ Richard, 'Ratione Materiae' in Marc Bungenberg, Jörn Griebel, Stephan Hobe, and August Reinisch (eds), *International Investment Law, A Handbook* (CH Beck, Hart Publishing and Nomos 2015) 495

Bjorklund Andrea, 'The Emerging Civilization of Investment Arbitration' (2008–2009) 113 Penn St L Rev 1269

Blyschak Paul M, 'Yukos Universal v Russia: Shell Companies and Treaty Shopping in International Energy Disputes' (2010–2011) 10 Rich J Global L & Bus 179

Borchard Edwin, *The Diplomatic Protection of Citizens Abroad or The Law of International Claims* (New York, The Banks Law Publishing 1927)

Borg-Barthet Justin, 'Free at last? Choice of Corporate Law in the EU Following the Judgment in VALE' (2013) 62 ICLQ 503

Braun Tillmann Rudolf, *Ausprägungen der Globalisierung: Der Investor als partielles Subjekt im Internationalen Investitionsrecht, Qualität und Grenzen dieser Wirkungseinheit* (Nomos 2011)

Briggs Herbert, 'Barcelona Traction: The Jus Standi of Belgium' (1971) 65 AJIL 327

Broches Aron, 'The Convention on the Settlement of Investment Disputes Between States and Nationals of other States', Académie de droit international (1972) 136 Recueil des Cours 330

Brower Charles and Sharpe Jeremy, 'Multiple and Conflicting International Arbitral Awards' (2003) 4 JWI 211

Brower Charles, Brower II Charles and Sharpe Jeremy, 'The Coming Crisis in the Global Adjudication System' (2003) 19 Arb Intl 415

Brower Charles and Schill Stephan, 'Is Arbitration a Threat or a Boon to the Legitimacy of International Investment Law' (2009) 9 Chi J Intl L 471

Brower Charles and Schill Stephan, 'Regulating Counsel Conduct before International Arbitral Tribunals' in Bekker Pieter, Dolzer Rudolf, and Waibel Michael (eds), *Making Transnational Law Work in a Global Economy*, Essays in Honour of Detlev Vagts (Cambridge University Press 2010) 488

Brower II Charles, 'Structure, Legitimacy and NAFTA's Investment Chapter' (2003) 36 Vand J Transnatl L 37
Brower II Charles, 'Reflections on the Road Ahead: Living with Decentralization in Investment Treaty Arbitration' in Rogers Catherine and Alford Roger (eds), *The Future of Investment Arbitration* (Oxford University Press 2009) 339
Brownlie Ian, *Principles of Public International Law* (Oxford University Press, 5th edn 2008)
Brundtland Gro, *Our Common Future: The Report of the World Commission on Environment and Development* (Oxford University Press 1987)
Buchanan Allan, 'The Legitimacy of International Law' in Besson Samantha and Tasioulas John (eds), *The Philosophy of International Law* (Oxford University Press 2010) 79
Buchanan Allan and Keohane Robert, 'The Legitimacy of Global Governance Institutions' in Lukas Meyer (ed), *Legitimacy, Justice and Public International Law* (Cambridge University Press 2009) 29
Buergenthal Thomas, 'The Proliferation of Disputes, Dispute Settlement Procedures and Respect for the Rule of Law' (2006) 22 Arb Intl 495
Bungenberg Marc, 'The Division of Competences Between the EU and its Member States in the Area of Investment Policies' in Marc Bungenberg, Jörn Griebel, and Steffen Hindelang (eds), *International Investment Law and EU Law, European Yearbook of International Economic Law*, Special Issue (Berlin, Springer 2011) 29
Bungenberg Marc, 'The Scope of Application of EU (Model) Investment Agreements' (2014) 15 JWIT 402
Burgstaller Markus, 'Investor-State Arbitration in EU International Investment Agreements with Third States' (2012) 39 LIEI 207
Burgstaller Markus, 'Nationality of Corporate Investors and International Claims against the Investor's Own State' (2006) 7 JWIT 857
Burriez Délphine, 'Le treaty shopping procedural d´incorporation dans le contentieux arbitral transnational' (2010) 25 ICSID Review-FILJ 394
Byers Michael, 'Abuse of rights: An Old Principle, A New Age' (2002) 47 McGill L J 391
Caflisch Luzius, 'The Protection of Corporate Investments Abroad in the Light of the Barcelona Traction Case' (1971) 31 ZaöRV 162
Cassese Antonio, *International Law* (Oxford University Press 2005)
Cassese Antonio, Gaeta Paola, Baig Laurel, Fan Mary, Gosnell Christopher, and Whiting Alex, *Cassese's International Criminal Law* (Oxford University Press, 3rd edn 2013)
Chaisse Julien, 'Promises and Pitfalls of the European Union Policy on Foreign Investment—How will the New EU Competence on FDI affect the Emerging Global Regime?' (2012) 15 JIEL 51
Cheng Bin, *General Principles of Law as Applied by International Courts and Tribunals* (Stevens and Sons 1953)
Cheng Tai-Heng, 'Precedent and Control in Investment Treaty Arbitration' in Bjorklund Andrea, Laird Ian, and Ripinsky Sergey (eds), *Investment Treaty Law: Current Issues III* (British Institute of International and Comparative Law 2008) 149
Choudhury Barnali, 'Recapturing Public Power: Is Investment Arbtration's Engagement of the public Interest Contributing to the Democratic Deficit?' (2008) 41 Vand J Transnatl L 775
Chung Olivia, 'The Lopsided International Investment Law Regime and its Effect on the Future of Investor-State Arbitration' (2006–2007) 47 Va J Intl L 953
Commission Jeffery P, 'Precedent in Investment Treaty Arbitration: A Citation Analysis of a Developing Jurisprudence' (2007) 24 J Intl Arb 129

Convention on the Settlement of Investment Disputes between States and Nationals of Other States, Documents Concerning the Origin and the Formation of the Convention, Vol II (Washington DC 1968)

Côté Christine, *A Chilling Effect? The impact of international investment agreements on national regulatory autonomy in the areas of health, safety and the environment*, Doctoral thesis, London School of Economics (February 2014) available at <http://etheses.lse.ac.uk/897/8/Cote_A_Chilling_%20Effect.pdf> (last accessed on 15 September 2016)

Cottier Thomas, 'The Legitimacy of WTO Law', NCCR Trade Regulation Working Paper No 2008/19 (November 2008), available at <http://phase1.nccr-trade.org/images/stories/publications/IP2/The_Legitimacy_of_WTO_Law_cottier_final%200808.pdf> (last accessed on 15 September 2016)

Crawford James, *The International Law Commission's Articles on State Responsibility, Introduction, Text and Commentaries* (Oxford University Press 2005)

Crawford James, 'Investment Arbitration and the ILC Articles on State Responsibility' (2010) 25 ICSID Review-FILJ 127

Cremades Bernardo, 'Resurgence of the Calvo Doctrine in Latin America' (2006) 7 Bus L Intl 53

Cremades Bernardo, 'Reflections on Good Faith in Investor-State Arbitration' in Gauch Peter, Werro Franz, and Pichonnaz Pascal (eds), *Mélanges en l'honneur de Pierre Tercier* (Zürich, Schulthess 2008) 779

Cremades Bernardo, 'Good Faith in International Arbitration' (2011–2012) 27 Am U Intl L Rev 761

Cuniberti Gilles, 'Parallel Litigation and Foreign Investment Dispute Settlement' (2006) 21 ICSID Review-FILJ 381

Dahlquist Joel and Peterson Luke Eric, 'Analysis: $12 billion arbitration vs. Russia by exiled oligarch may be next test case by arbitrators' willingness to let dual-nationals sue their own State' *IA Reporter* (23 September 2015) available at <www.iareporter.com>

D'Amato Anthony, 'Good Faith' in Rudolf Bernhardt (ed), *Encyclopedia of Public International Law* (Amsterdam, North Holland Publishing Company 1992) Vol 2, 600

De Andrade Levy Daniel, *L'abus de l'ordre juridique arbitral: Contributions de la doctrine de l'abus de droit à l'arbitrage international*, Thèse de doctorat, Université Panthéon Assas (Paris II) (2013)

De Broe Luc, *International Tax Planning and Prevention of Abuse*, Volume 14 of Doctoral Series (Amsterdam IBFD 2008)

De Búrca Gráinne, 'The Quest for Legitimacy in the European Union' (1996) 59 Modern Law Review 349

Delaume George, 'ICSID Arbitration and the Courts' (1983) 77 ASIL 784

Delaume George, 'Le Centre International pour le Règlement des Différends relatifs aux Investissements (CIRDI)' (1982) 109 JDI 797

Delbrück Jost, 'Exercising Public Authority Beyond the State: Transnational Democracy and/or Alternative Legitimation Strategies?' (2003) 10 Ind J Global Legal Stud 29

De Brabandere Eric, '"Good faith", "Abuse of Process" and the Initiation of Investment Treaty Claims' (2012) 3 JIDS 609

De Brabandere Eric and Van Damme Isabelle, 'Good Faith in Treaty Interpretation' in Mitchell Andrew, Sornarajah M, and Voon Tania (eds), *Good Faith and International Economic Law* (Oxford University Press 2015) 37

DiMascio Nicholas and Pauwelyn Joost, 'Nondiscrimination in Trade and Investment Treaties: Worlds Apart or Two Sides of the Same Coin' (2008) 102 AJIL 48

Dimopoulos Angelos, *EU Foreign Investment Law* (Oxford University Press 2011)

Dimopoulos Angelos, 'The Compatibility of Future EU Investment Agreements with EU Law' (2012) 39 LIEI 447
Dimpsey Mariel, *The resolution of international investment disputes* (Utrecht, Eleven International Publishing 2008)
Dodge William, 'Investor-State Dispute Settlement Between Developed Countries: Reflections on the Australian-United States Free Trade Agreement' (2006) 39 Vand J Transnatl L 1
Dolzer Rudolf and Schreuer Christoph, *Principles of International Investment Law* (Oxford University Press, 2nd edn 2012)
Douglas Zachary, 'The Hybrid Foundations of Investment Treaty Arbitration' (2003) 74 BYIL 151
Douglas Zachary, *The International Law of Investment Claims* (Cambridge University Press 2009)
Duchesne Matthew, 'The Continuous-Nationality-of Claims Principle, Its historical development and current relevance to investor-State investment disputes' (2004) 36 Geo Wash Intl L Rev 783
Dupont Pierre-Emmanuel, 'The Notion of ICSID Investment: Ongoing "Confusion" or "Emerging Synthesis"?' (2011) 12 JWIT 245
Endicott Timothy, 'Law and Language' in Jules Coleman and Scott Shapiro (eds), *The Oxford Handbook of Jurisprudence and Philosophy of Law* (Oxford University Press 2004) 935
European Commission, 'Communication, Towards a comprehensive European international investment policy' COM(2010)343 final (07.07.2010) 3, available at <http://trade.ec.europa.eu/doclib/docs/2010/july/tradoc_146307.pdf> (last accessed on 15 September 2016)
European Commission, 'Fact Sheet, Investment Protection and Investor-to-State Dispute Settlement in EU Agreements' (November 2013) available at <http://trade.ec.europa.eu/doclib/docs/2013/november/tradoc_151916.pdf> (last accessed on 15 September 2016)
EU Commission, 'Commission proposes new Investment Court System for TTIP and other EU trade and investment negotiations' Press Release (16 September 2015) available at <http://europa.eu/rapid/press-release_IP-15-5651_en.htm> (last accessed on 15 September 2016)
European Parliament, 'Resolution of 6 April 2011 on the future European international investment policy' (2010/2203(INI)) available at <www.europarl.europa.eu/sides/getDoc.do?pubRef=-//EP//TEXT+TA+P7-TA-2011-0141+0+DOC+XML+V0//EN> (last accessed on 15 September 2016)
Fauchald Ole, 'The Legal Reasoning of ICSID Tribunals—An Empirical Analysis' (2008) 19 EJIL 301
Faya Rodriguez Alejandro, 'The Most-Favored-Nation Clause in International Investment Agreements- A Tool for Treaty Shopping?' (2008) 25 J Intl Arb 89
Feldman Mark, 'Setting Limits on Corporate Nationality Planning in Investment Treaty Arbitration' (2012) 27 ICSID Review-FILJ 281
Fiedler Patrick, Hunter Robert and Klemm Ulrich, 'Chapter H. Policy Issues: Is the Current Status of Law and Treaty Practice Satisfactory?' in ILA German Branch/Working Group, *The Determination of the Nationality of Investors under Investment Protection Treaties*, Heft 106 (2011) 79, available at <http://telc.jura.uni-halle.de/sites/default/files/BeitraegeTWR/Heft%20106.pdf> (last accessed on 15 September 2016)
Fitzmaurice Gerald, 'The Law and Procedure of the International Court of Justice 1951–54: Treaty Interpretation and Other Treaty Points' (1957) 33 BYIL 203

Fortese Fabricio, 'In new Costa Rica ruling, arbitrators weigh allegations of abusive restructuring and whether all BIT claims meet prima facie test' *IA Reporter* (24 December 2014) available at <http://www.iareporter.com>

Francioni Francesco, 'Equity' in Rüdiger Wolfrum (ed), *Max Planck Encyclopedia of Public International Law* (Oxford University Press) available at <http://opil.ouplaw.com>

Franck Susan, 'The Legitimacy Crisis in Investment Treaty Arbitration: Privatizing Public International Law Through Inconsistent Decisions' (2004–2005) 73 Fordham L Rev 1521 (quoted: Susan Franck, 'Legitimacy Crisis')

Franck Susan, 'Development and Outcomes of Investment Treaty Arbitration' (2009) 50 Harv Intl L J 435

Franck Susan, 'The ICSID Effect? Considering Potential Variations in Arbitration Awards' (2010–2011) 51 Va J Intl L 825

Franck Susan, 'Rationalizing Costs in Investment Treaty Arbitration' (2010–2011) 88 Wash U L Rev 769

Franck Thomas, *The Power of Legitimacy Among Nations* (Oxford University Press 1990)

Franke Florian, *Der personelle Anwendungsbereich des internationalen Investitionsschutzrechts* (Nomos 2013)

French Duncan, 'Treaty Interpretation and the Incorporation of Extraneous Legal Rules' (2006) 55 ICLQ 281

Friedman Howard, *Publicly Held Corporations, A Lawyer's Guide* (Oxford University Press 2011)

Gaffney John, 'Abuse of process in Investment Treaty Arbitration' (2010) 11 JWIT 515

Gaffney John, 'Jurisdiction ratione temporis of ICSID Tribunals: Lucchetti and Jan de Nul considered' (2006) 3 TDM, available at <http://www.transnational-dispute-management.com>

Gaillard Emmanuel, 'Chronique des Sentences Arbitrales' (2009) JDI (Clunet) No 1 355

Gallus Nick, *The Temporal Scope of Investment Protection Treaties* (British Institute of International and Comparative Law 2008)

Gantz David, 'An Appellate Mechanism for Review of Arbitral Decisions in Investor-State Disputes: Prospects and Challenges' (2006) 39 Vand J Transnatl L 39

García Bolívar Omar, 'Sovereignty v Investment Protection: Back to Calvo' (2009) 24 ICSID Review-FILJ 464

García Bolívar Omar, 'Economic Development at the Core of the International Investment Regime' in Brown Chester and Miles Kate (eds), *Evolution in Investment Treaty Law and Arbitration* (Cambridge University Press 2011) 586

García Bolívar Omar, 'The Issue of a Foreign Company Wholly Owned by National Shareholders in the Context of ICSID Arbitration' (2005) 2 TDM, available at <http://www.transnational-dispute-management.com>

Gardiner Richard, *Treaty Interpretation* (Oxford University Press 2008)

Gastrell Lindsay and Le Cannu Paul-Jean, 'Procedural Requirements of "Denial-of-Benefits" Clauses in Investment Treaties: A Review of Arbitral Decisions' (2015) 30 ICSID Review-FILJ 78

Gaukrodger David, 'The Legal Framework Applicable to Joint Interpretive Agreements of Investment Treaties' OECD Working Papers on International Investment 2016/1 (OECD 2016) available at <http://www.oecd-ilibrary.org/docserver/download/5jm3xgt6f29w.pdf?expires=1462177183&id=id&accname=guest&checksum=A771D43EF45E3E523C7FAB28E46E7C17> (last accessed on 15 September 2016)

Gaukrodger David and Gordon Kathryn, 'Investor-State Dispute Settlement: A Scoping Paper for the Investment Policy Community' OECD Working Papers on International Investment No 2012/3 (OECD 2012) available at <http://www.oecd.org/daf/inv/investment-policy/WP-2012_3.pdf> (last accessed on 15 September 2016)

Gazzini Tarcisio, 'The Role of Customary International Law in the Field of Foreign Investment' (2007) 8 JWIT 691

Gehring Markus and Newcombe Andrew, 'An Introduction to Sustainable Development in World Investment Law' in Cordonier Segger Marie-Claire, Gehring Markus and Newcombe Andrew, *Sustainable Development in World Investment Law* (Kluwer Law International 2011) 3

Geiger Rainer, 'The Multifaceted Nature of International Investment Law' in Sauvant Karl (ed), *Appeals Mechanism in International Investment Disputes* (Oxford University Press 2008) 17

Geiger Rainer, 'Regulatory Expropriations in International Law: Lessons from the Multilateral Agreement on Investment' (2002) 11 NYU Environmental L J 94

Gill Judith, 'Is There a Special Role for Precedent in Investment Arbitration?' (2010) 25 ICSID Review-FILJ 87

Guillaume Gilbert, 'The Use of Precedent by International Judges and Arbitrators' (2011) 2 JIDS 5

Guillaume Gilbert, 'Advantages and Risks of Proliferation: A Blueprint for Action' (2004) 2 JICJ 300

Guillaume Gilbert, 'The proliferation of international judicial bodies: The outlook for the international legal order', Speech by His Excellency Judge Gilbert Guillaume, President of the International Court of Justice, to the Sixth Committee of the General Assembly of the United Nations (27 October 2000) available at <http://www.icj-cij.org/court/index.php?pr=85&pt=3&p1=1&p2=3&p3=1> (last accessed on 15 September 2016)

Gurudevan Naveen, 'An Evaluation of Current Legitimacy-based Objections to NAFTA's Chapter 11 Investment Dispute Resolution Process' (2004–2005) 6 San Diego Intl L J 399

Hallward-Driemeier Mary, 'Do Bilateral Investment Treaties Attract Foreign Investment? Only a Bit … And They Could Bite' in Sauvant Karl and Sachs Lisa (eds), *The Effect of Treaties on Foreign Direct Investment: Bilateral Investment Treaties, Double Taxation Treaties, and Investment Flows* (Oxford University Press 2009) 349

Harlow Carol, 'The Concepts and Methods of Reasoning of the New Public Law: Legitimacy' LSE Law, Society and Economy Working Paper 19/2010, available at <http://papers.ssrn.com/sol3/papers.cfm?abstract_id=1713633> (last accessed on 15 September 2016)

Harlow Carol, 'Global Administrative Law: The Quest for Principles and Values' (2006) 17 EJIL 187

Hébert Jean-François, 'Abuse of Corporate Nationality and the Jurisdiction of International Investment Tribunals' (2010) 1 J Arb & Med 119

Heiskanen Veijo, 'Of Capital Import: The Definition of "Investment" in International Investment Law' in Hoffmann Anne (ed), *Protection of Foreign Investments through Modern Treaty Arbitration,* ASA Special Series No 34 (May 2010) 51, available at <http://www.lalive.ch/data/publications/vhe_Of_capital_import;_The_definition_of_'investment'_in_international_investment_law.pdf> (last accessed on 15 September 2016)

Helfer Laurence R, 'Forum Shopping For Human Rights' (1999–2000) 148 U Pa L Rev 285

Hepburn Jarrod, 'Mauritius to face first known BIT claim over revoked banking licence' *IA Reporter* (9 November 2015) available at <http://www.iareporter.com>

Higgins Rosalyn, 'Aspects of the Case Concerning the Barcelona Traction, Light and Power Company, Ltd.' (1971) 11 Va J Intl L 327

Higgins Rosalyn, *Problems and Process: International Law and How We Use it* (Oxford, Clarendon Press 1994)

Higgins Rosalyn, 'Time and the Law: International Perspectives on an Old Problem' (1997) 46 ICLQ 501

Higgins Rosalyn, 'A Babel of Judicial Voices' (2006) 55 ICLQ 791

Hirsch Moshe, *The Arbitration Mechanism of the International Centre for the Settlement of Investment Disputes* (Martinus Nijhoff 1993)

Human Rights Council, 'Protect Respect and Remedy: a Framework for Business and Human Rights: Report of Special Representative of the Secretary-General on the issue of human rights and transnational corporations and other business enterprises, John Ruggie' (2011) UN Doc A/HRC/8/5

Hunter Robert, 'Is a Corporation's Entitlement to the Protection of an Investment Treaty a Question Solely of Form or is it also a Question of Substance?' in ILA German Branch, Working Group, *The Determination of the Nationality of Investors under Investment Protection Treaties*, Heft 106 (2011) 37, available at <http://telc.jura.uni-halle.de/sites/default/files/BeitraegeTWR/Heft%20106.pdf> (last accessed on 15 September 2016)

ICSID Secretariat, 'Possible Improvements of the Framework for ICSID Arbitration' Discussion Paper (22 October 2004) available at <https://icsid.worldbank.org/apps/ICSIDWEB/resources/Documents/Possible%20Improvements%20of%20the%20Framework%20of%20ICSID%20Arbitration.pdf> (last accessed on 15 September 2016)

ICSID, 'Report of the Executive Directors on the Convention on the Settlement of Investment Disputes between States and Nationals of Other States', ICSID Doc 2 (18 March 1965)

ICSID, 'Suggested Changes to the ICSID Rules and Regulations' Working Paper of the ICSID Secretariat (12 May 2005) available at <https://icsid.worldbank.org/apps/ICSIDWEB/resources/Documents/Suggested%20Changes%20to%20the%20ICSID%20Rules%20and%20Regulations.pdf> (last accessed on 15 September 2016)

International Law Association, Committee on Formation of Customary (General) International Law, 'Final Report, Statement of Principles Applicable to the Formation of General Customary International Law' (ILA 2000)

International Law Association, 'New Delhi Declaration on the Principles of International Law Related to Sustainable Development' (London, ILA 2002)

International Law Commission, 'First Report on Diplomatic Protection' Report of the Fifty-second Session (2000) UN Doc A/CN.4/506

International Law Commission, *Yearbook of the International Law Commission* (1966) Vol II, UN Doc A/CN.4/SER.A/1966/Add.1

International Law Commission, 'Fourth Report on Diplomatic Protection' Report of the Fifty-fifth Session (2003) UN Doc A/CN.4/530

International Law Commission, 'Seventh Report on Diplomatic Protection' Report of the Fifty-eighth Session (2006) UN Doc A/CN.4/567

International Law Commission, 'Draft Articles on Diplomatic Protection with commentaries' Report of the Fifty-eighth Session (2006) UN Doc A/CN 4/L 684

International Law Commission, 'Conclusions of the work of the Study Group on the Fragmentation of International Law: Difficulties arising from the Diversification and

Expansion of International Law' Report of the Study Group of the International Law Commission, Fifty-eighth Session (2006), A/CN/L.702

International Law Commission, 'First Report on subsequent agreements and subsequent practice in relation to Treaty Interpretation' Report of the Sixty-fifth Session (2013) UN Doc A/CN.4/660

Jagusch Stephan and Sinclair Anthony, 'Part II, Denial of Advantages under Article 17(1)' in Coop Graham and Ribeiro Clarisse (eds), *Investment Protection and the Energy Charter Treaty* (Juris Publishing 2008) 17

Jennings Robert and Watts Arthur (eds), *Oppenheim's International Law*, Vol I, Peace, Introduction and Part I (London and New York, Longman, 9th edn 1996)

Jennings Robert and Watts Arthur (eds), *Oppenheim's International Law*, Vol I Peace, Parts 2 to 4 (London and New York, Longman, 9th edn 1996)

Joubin-Bret Anna, Rey Marie-Estelle, and Weber Jörg, 'International Investment Law and Development' in Cordonier Segger Marie-Claire, Gehring Markus, and Newcombe Andrew (eds), *Sustainable Development in World Investment Law* (Kluwer Law International 2011) 15

Jones David Lloyd, 'The Iran-United States Claims Tribunal: Private Rights and State Responsibility' (1984) 24 Va J Intl L 259

Jones Mervyn, 'The Nottebohm Case' (1956) 5 ICLQ 230

JT/GSW, 'Thousands protest in Berlin against industralized farming' *Deutsche Welle* (17 January 2015) available at <http://www.dw.de/thousands-protest-in-berlin-against-industrialized-farming/a-18198089> (last accessed on 15 September 2016)

Kahale III George, 'The new Dutch sandwich: The issue of treaty abuse' *Columbia FDI Perspectives*, No 48 (October 10, 2011) available at <http://ccsi.columbia.edu/files/2014/01/FDI_48.pdf> (last accessed on 15 September 2016)

Kalotay Kalman, 'Does it matter who invests in your country' Columbia FDI Perspectives, No 66, (April 30, 2012) available at <http://ccsi.columbia.edu/files/2014/01/FDI_66.pdf> (last accessed on 15 September 2016)

Kapeliuk Daphna, 'The Repeat Appointment Factor: Exploring Decision Patterns of Elite Investment Arbitrators' (2010) 96 Cornell L Rev 49

Keohane Robert, 'Reciprocity in International Relations' (1986) 40 Intl Org 1

K.G., 'Protesting about power prices' *The Economist* (15 February 2013) available at <http://www.economist.com/blogs/easternapproaches/2013/02/bulgarias-electricity-prices> (last accessed on 15 September 2016)

Kingsbury Benedict, 'Foreword: Is the Proliferation of International Courts and Tribunals a Systemic Problem?' (1998–1999) 31 NYU J Intl L & Pol 679

Kingsbury Benedict and Schill Stephan, 'Investor-State Arbitration as Governance: Fair and Equitable Treatment, Proportionality and the Emerging Global Administrative Law' IILJ Working Paper 2009/6, available at <http://www.iilj.org/publications/documents/2009-6.KingsburySchill.pdf> (last accessed on 15 September 2016)

Kinnear Meg, Bjorklund Andrea, and Hannaford John, *Investment Disputes Under NAFTA: An Annotated Guide to NAFTA Chapter 11* (Kluwer Law International, 2006) last updated: March 2008, available at <http://www.kluwerarbitration.com>

Kirtley William Lawton, 'The Transfer of Treaty Claims and Treaty-Shopping in Investor-State Disputes' (2009) 10 JWIT 427

Kiss Alexandre, 'Abuse of Rights' *Max Planck Encyclopedia of Public International Law* (Oxford Public International Law) available at <http://opil.ouplaw.com>

Kleinheisterkamp Jan, 'Investment Protection and EU Law: The Intra- and Extra-EU Dimension of the Energy Charter Treaty' (2012) 15 JIEL 85

Kleinheisterkamp Jan, 'Is there a need for Investor-State Arbitration in the Transatlantic Trade and Investment Partnership?' (14 February 2014) available at <http://papers.ssrn.com/sol3/papers.cfm?abstract_id=2410188> (last accessed on 15 September 2016)

Kokott Juliane, Interim Report on 'The Role of Diplomatic Protection in the Field of the Protection of Foreign Investment' in International Law Association, Report of the Seventieth Conference, New Delhi (2002)

Kolb Robert, *La Bonne Foi en Droit International Publique* (Presses Universitaires de France 2000)

Kolb Robert, 'Principles as Sources of International Law (With Special Reference to Good Faith)' (2006) 53 NILR 1

Kolb Robert, 'General Principles of Procedural Law' in Andreas Zimmermann, Christian Tomuschat, and Karin Oellers-Frahm (eds), *The Statute of the International Court of Justice: A Commentary* (Oxford University Press, 2nd edn 2012) 871

Kotzur Markus, 'Good faith' *Max Planck Encyclopedia of Public International Law* (Oxford Public International Law) available at <http://opil.ouplaw.com>

Kreindler Richard, 'Are Tribunals Setting New Limits on Access to International Arbitration?' (2010) 25 ICSID Review-FILJ 37

Krisch Nico and Kingsbury Benedict, 'Global Governance and Global Administrative Law in the International Legal Order' (2006) 17 EJIL 1

Krishan Devashish, 'Thinking about BITs and BIT Arbitration: The Legitimacy Crisis that never was' in Weiler Todd and Baetens Freya (eds), *New Directions in International Economic Law, In Memoriam Thomas Wälde* (Martinus Nijhoff, 2011) 107

Kryvoi Yaraslau, 'Counterclaims in Investor-State Arbitration' LSE Legal Studies Working Paper (5 August 2011) No 08/2011, available at <http://papers.ssrn.com/sol3/papers.cfm?abstract_id=1891935> (last accessed on 15 September 2016)

Kulovesi Kati, *The WTO Dispute Settlement System, Challenges of the Environment, Legitimacy and Fragmentation* (Kluwer Law International 2011)

Kurtz Jürgen, 'The Australian Trade Statement on Investor-State Dispute Settlement', ASIL Insights Vol 15, Issue 22 (2 August 2011) available at <http://www.asil.org/insights/volume/15/issue/22/australian-trade-policy-statement-investor-state-dispute-settlement> (last accessed on 15 September 2016)

Kurtz Jürgen, 'The Paradoxical Treatment of the ILC Articles on State Responsibility in Investor-State Arbitration' (2010) 25 ICSID Review-FILJ 200

Kussmaul Heinz, Richter Lutz, and Ruiner Christoph, 'Corporations on the Move, the ECJ off Track: Relocation of a Corporation's Effective Place of Management in the EU' (2009) 6 Europ Company L 246

Kwasniewski Nicolai, 'Anger in Cyprus: They Can't Just Penalize Us Because of the Banks' *Spiegel Online* (19 March 2013) available at <http://www.spiegel.de/international/europe/anger-in-cyprus-over-euro-crisis-bank-levy-plan-a-889724.html> (last accessed on 15 September 2016)

Lamm Carolyn, Greenwald Brody and Young Kristen, 'From World Duty Free to Metal-Tech: A Review of International Investment Treaty Arbitration Cases Involving Allegations of Corruption' (2014) 29 ICSID Review-FILJ 328

Lauterpacht Hersch, *The Function of Law in the International Community* (Clarendon Press 1933)

Lauterpacht Hersch, 'Survey of International Law in Relation to the Work of Codification of the International Law Commission' (1949) UN Doc A/CN.4/1/Rev.1

Lauterpacht Hersch, *The Development of International Law by the International Court* (Stevens and Sons 1958)

Lavranos Nikos, 'Protecting its Exclusive Jurisdiction: The MOX Plant-Judgment of the ECJ' (2006) 5 LPICT 479
Leal-Arcas Rafael, 'Towards the Multilateralization of International Investment Law' (2009) 10 JWIT 865
Lee Eunjung, 'Treaty Shopping in International Investment Arbitration: How often has it occurred and how has it been perceived by tribunals?' LSE Working Paper Series 2015, No 15–167, available at <http://www.lse.ac.uk/internationalDevelopment/pdf/Dissertations/WP167.pdf> (last accessed on 15 September 2016)
Lee John, 'Resolving Concerns of Treaty Shopping' (2015) 6 JIDS 1
Legum Barton, 'Defining Investment and Investor: Who is Entitled to Claim?' (2006) 22 Arb Intl 521
Lillich Richard, 'The Rigidity of Barcelona' (1971) 65 AJIL 522
Lowe Vaughan, 'The Role of Equity' (1988–1989) 12 Austr Year Book of Intl L 54
Lowe Vaughan, 'Shareholders' Rights to Control and Manage from Barcelona Traction to ELSI' in Nisuke Ando and others (eds), *Liber Amicorum Judge Shigeru Oda* (Kluwer Law International 2002) 269
Lowenfeld Andreas, *International Economic Law* (Oxford University Press, 2nd edn 2008)
Luttrell Sam and Weeramantry Romesh, *Submission in respect of the Trade and Foreign Investment (Protecting the Public Interest) Bill 2014*, available at <http://globalarbitrationreview.com/cdn/files/gar/articles/Submission_in_respect_of_the_Trade_and_Foreign_Investment_Protecting_the_Public.pdf> (last accessed on 15 September 2016)
Mann FA, 'The Protection of Shareholders' Interests in the Light of the Barcelona Traction Case' (1973) 67 AJIL 259
Mann FA, 'Notes: British Treaties for the Promotion and Protection of Investment' (1981) 52 BYIL 241
Marian Cornel, 'Who is Afraid of Nottebohm? Reconciling the ICSID Nationality Requirement for Natural Persons with Nottebohm's "Effective Nationality" Test' (2011) 28 J Int Arb 313
Markert Lars, 'International Investment Law and Treaty Interpretation—Problems, Particularities and Possible Trends' in Hofmann Rainer and Tams Christian (eds), *International Investment Law and General International Law, From Clinical Isolation to Systemic Integration* (Nomos 2011) 53
Mbengue Makane Moise, 'Preamble' *Max Planck Encyclopedia of Public International Law* (Oxford Public International Law) available at <http://opil.ouplaw.com>
McLachlan Campbell, 'Investment Treaties and General International Law' in Bjorklund Andrea, Laird Ian, and Ripinsky Sergey, *Investment Treaty Law: Current Issues III* (British Institute of International and Comparative Law 2008) 105
McLachlan Campbell, *Lis Pendens in International Litigation* (Martinus Nijhoff 2009)
McLachlan Campbell, Shore Laurence, and Weiniger Matthew, *International Investment Arbitration—Substantive Principles* (Oxford University Press 2007)
McRae Donald, 'The WTO Appellate Body: A Model for an ICSID Appeals Facility?' (2010) 1 JIDS 371
Mendelson Maurice, 'Runaway Train: Continuous Nationality Rule from the *Panevezys-Saldutiskis Railway Case* to *Lowen*' in Todd Weiler (ed), *International Investment Law and Arbitration: Leading Cases* (Cameron May 2005) 97 (quoted: Mendelson, 'Runaway Train')
Mendelson Maurice, 'Issues Relating to the Identity of the Investor' in Rovine Arthur W (ed), *Fordham Papers 2010, Contemporary Issues in International Arbitration and Mediation* (Brill/Martinus Nijhoff 2011) 22

Metzger Stanley, 'Nationality of Corporate Investment under Investment Guaranty Schemes: The Relevance of Barcelona Traction' (1971) 65 AJIL 532

Miles Kate, 'Reconceptualising International Investment Law' in Kolsky Lewis Meredith and Frankel Susy (eds), *International Economic Law and National Autonomy* (Cambridge University Press 2010) 295

Mistelis Loukas and Baltag Crina, 'Denial of Benefits and Article 17 of the Energy Charter Treaty' (2008–2009) 113 Penn St L Rev 1301

Mitchell Andrew, 'Good Faith in WTO Dispute Settlement' (2006) 7 Melb J Intl L 339

Mitchell Andrew, Munro James, and Whittle Devon, 'Vannessa Ventures Ltd v The Bolivarian Republic of Venezuela' (2014) 15 JWIT 305

Montt Santiago, *State Liability in Investment Treaty Arbitration* (Hart Publishing 2009)

Muchlinski Peter, *Multinational Enterprises and the Law* (Oxford University Press 2007)

Muchlinski Peter, 'The Diplomatic Protection of Foreign Investors: A Tale of Judicial Caution' in Binder Christina, Kriebaum Ursula, Reinisch August, and Wittich Stephan (eds), *International Investment Law for the 21th Century: Essays in Honour of Christoph Schreuer* (Oxford University Press 2009) 341

Muchlinski Peter, 'Corporations and the Uses of Law: International Investment Arbitration as a "Multilateral Legal Order"', Oñati Socio-Legal Series, Vol 1, No 4 (2011)—Socio-Legal Aspects of Adjudication of International Economic Disputes, available at <http://papers.ssrn.com/sol3/papers.cfm?abstract_id=1832562> (last accessed on 15 September 2016)

Murphy Sean, 'The ELSI Case: An Investment Dispute at the International Court of Justice' (1991) 16 Yale J Intl L 391

NAFTA Free Trade Commission, 'Recommendation on Non-disputing Party Participation' (7 October 2004) available at <http://www.sice.oas.org/tpd/nafta/Commission/Nondispute_e.pdf> (last accessed on 15 September 2016)

Neumayer Eric and Spess Laura, 'Do Bilateral Investment Treaties increase Foreign Direct Investment to Developing Countries?' (2005) 33 World Dev 1567

Newcombe Andrew and Paradell Lluís, *Law and Practice of Investment Treaties, Standards of Treatment* (Kluwer Law International 2009)

O'Connor John, *Good Faith in International Law* (Dartsmouth Publishing Company 1991)

OECD, 'Transparency and Third Party Participation in Investor-State Dispute Settlement Procedures, OECD Working Papers on International Investment (OECD 2005) available at <http://www.oecd.org/daf/inv/investment-policy/WP-2005_1.pdf> (last accessed on 15 September 2016)

OECD, 'Guidelines for Multinational Enterprises' (2011 Edition) available at <http://www.oecd.org/daf/inv/mne/48004323.pdf> (last accessed on 15 September 2016)

OECD, 'Roundtable on Freedom of Investment 18' Summary of Roundtable discussions by the OECD Secretariat (20 March 2013) available at <http://www.oecd.org/investment/investment-policy/18thFOIRoundtableSummary.pdf> (last accessed on 15 September 2016)

OECD, 'Action Plan on Base Erosion and Profit Shifting' (OECD 2013) available at <http://www.oecd.org/ctp/BEPSActionPlan.pdf> (last accessed on 15 September 2016)

OECD, 'Preventing the Granting of Treaty Benefits in Inappropriate Circumstances', Action 6—2015 Final Report (OECD 2015) available at <http://www.oecd-ilibrary.org/docserver/download/2315331e.pdf?expires=1461341716&id=id&accname=guest&checksum=3206A82136A7D3BE726F36C4B64C47CF> (last accessed on 15 September 2016)

Ortino Federico, 'Legal Reasoning of International Investment Tribunals: A Typology of Egregious Failures' 3 (2012) JIDS 31

Panayi Christiana, *Advanced Issues in International and European Tax Law* (Hart Publishing 2015)

Panizzon Marion, *Good Faith in the Jurisprudence of the WTO* (Hart Publishing 2006)

Paparinskis Martins, 'Barcelona Traction: A Friend of Investment Protection Law' (2008) 8 Baltic YIL 105

Parisi Francesco and Ghei Nita, 'The Role of Reciprocity in International Law' (2003) 36 Cornell Int'l L J 93

Paulsson Jan, 'Continuous Nationality in Loewen' (2004) 20 Arb Intl 213

Paulsson Jan, 'Jurisdiction and Admissibility' in *Global Reflections on International Law, Commerce and Dispute Resolution*, Liber Amicorum in honour of Robert Briner, ICC Publication 693 (November 2005) 601

Paulus Andreas, 'Reciprocity Revisited' in Fastenrath Ulrich and others (eds), *From Bilateralism to Community Interest—Essays in Honour of Judge Bruno Simma* (Oxford University Press 2011) 113

Pauwelyn Joost, *Conflict of Norms in Public International Law: How WTO Law Relates to Other Rules of International Law* (Cambridge University Press 2003)

Pellet Alain, 'Article 38' in Andreas Zimmermann, Christian Tomuschat, and Karin Oellers-Frahm (eds), *The Statute of the International Court of Justice: A Commentary* (Oxford University Press, 2nd edn 2012)

Perkams Markus, 'Piercing the Corporate Veil in International Investment Agreements' in Reinisch August and Knahr Christina (eds), *International Investment Law in Context* (Eleven International Publishing 2008) 93

Perkams Markus, 'The Determination of Nationality of Investors in International Investment Agreements (IIAs)—Taking Stock of the Criteria Used in Modern Investment Law' in ILA German Branch, *The Determination of the Nationality of Investors under Investment Protection Treaties* (March 2011) 13, available at <http://telc.jura.uni-halle.de/sites/default/files/BeitraegeTWR/Heft%20106.pdf> (last accessed on 15 September 2016)

Peters Anne, 'Unequal Treaties' *Max Planck Encyclopedia of Public International Law* (Oxford Public International Law) available at <http://opil.ouplaw.com>

Peterson Luke Eric, 'Argentina by the numbers: where things stand with investment treaty claims arising out of the Argentine financial crisis' *IA Reporter* (1 February 2011) available at <http://www.iareporter.com>

Peterson Luke Eric, 'Poland wins investment treaty arbitration with EU; Government sits on growing cache of unpublished rulings' *IA Reporter* (7 February 2012) available at <www.iareporter.com>

Peterson Luke Eric, 'South Africa pushes phase-out of early bilateral investment treaties after at least two separate brushes with Investor-State Arbitration' *IA Reporter* (24 September 2012) available at <http://www.iareporter.com>

Peterson Luke Eric, 'Brussels' thinking on future of extra-EU Investor-State Dispute Settlement comes into focus after much give and take with Member-States' *IA Reporter* (22 October 2012) available at <http://www.iareporter.com>

Peterson Luke Eric, 'In two recent arbitrations, Prof. William W. Park holds that wholly passive ownership is not enough for claimants to enjoy investment treaty protection' *IA Reporter* (18 January 2013) available at <http://www.iareporter.com>

Peterson Luke Eric, 'Analysis: India invites comments on Draft Model Investment Treaty; Text offers radical departure, and calls to mind Norway's past efforts at revision' *IA Reporter* (24 March 2015) available at <http://www.iareporter.com>

Peterson Luke Eric, 'Infringement proceedings initiated by European Commission against five States over intra-EU BITs' *IA Reporter* (18 June 2015) available at <http://www.iareporter.com>

Peterson Luke Eric, 'Analysis: European Commission's newly released investment treaty model departs in significant ways from recently concluded Canada Pact' *IA Reporter* (17 September 2015) available at <http://www.iareporter.com>

Potestà Michele, 'Bilateral Investment Treaties and the European Union. Recent Developments in Arbitration and Before the ECJ' (2009) 8 LPICT 225

Protopsaltis Panayotis, 'The Challenge of the Barcelona Traction Hypothesis: Barcelona Traction Clauses and Denial of Benefits Clauses in BITs and IIAs' 11 (2010) JWIT 561

Qureshi Asif, 'An Appellate System in International Investment Arbitration?' in Muchlinski Peter, Ortino Federico, and Schreuer Christoph (eds), *Oxford Handbook of International Investment Law* (Oxford University Press 2008) 1154

Radi Yannick, 'The Application of the Most-Favoured-Nation Clause to the Dispute Settlement Provisions of Bilateral Investment Treaties: Domesticating the "Trojan Horse"' (2007) 18(4) EJIL 757–774

Redfern Alan and Hunter Martin, *Law and Practice of International Commercial Arbitration* (Sweet and Maxwell 2004)

Reed Lucy, 'The De Facto Precedent Regime in Investment Arbitration: A Case for Proactive Case Management' (2010) 25 ICSID Review-FILJ 95

Reed Lucy and Davis Jonathan, 'Ratione Personae' in Bungenberg Marc, Griebel Jörn, Hobe Stephan and Reinisch August (eds), *International Investment Law, A Handbook* (CH Beck, Hart Publishing and Nomos 2015) 614

Reinhold Steven, 'Good Faith in International Law' (2013) 2 UCL Journal of Law and Jurisprudence 40

Reinisch August, 'The Use and Limits of Res Judicata and Lis Pendens as Procedural Tools to Avoid Conflicting Dispute Settlement Outcomes' (2004) 3 LPICT 37

Reinisch August, 'Expropriation' in Peter Muchlinski, Federico Ortino, and Christoph Schreuer (eds), *Oxford Handbook on International Investment Law* (Oxford University Press 2008) 407

Reinisch August, 'The Issues Raised by Parallel Proceedings and Possible Solutions' in Waibel Michael, Kaushal Asha, Chung Kyo-Hwa, and Balchin Claire (eds), *The Backlash against Investment Arbitration* (Kluwer Law International 2010) 113

Reinisch August, 'Articles 30 and 59 of the Vienna Convention on the Law of Treaties in Action: The Decisions on Jurisdiction in the Eastern Sugar and Eureko Investment Arbitrations' (2012) 39 LIEI 157

Reisman W. Michael and Sloane Robert, 'Indirect Expropriation and its Valuation in the BIT Generation' (2003) 74 BYIL 115

Reisman W. Michael and Vinnik Anna, 'What Constitutes an Investment and Who Decides?' in Rovine Arthur (ed), *Fordham Papers 2010, Contemporary Issues in International Arbitration and Mediation* (Martinus Nijhoff 2011) 50

Rigo Sureda Andrés, *Investment Treaty Arbitation, Judging under Uncertainty* (Cambridge University Press 2012)

Ripinsky Sergey and Rosert Diana, 'European Investment Treaty Making: Status Quo and The Way Forward (A Development Perspective)' (2013) 10 TDM, available at <http://www.transnational-dispute-management.com>

Roberts Anthea, 'Power and Persuasion in Investment Treaty Arbitration: The Dual Role of States' (2010) 104 AJIL 179

Romano Cesare, 'The Proliferation of International Judicial Bodies: The Pieces of the Puzzle' (1998–1999) 31 NYU J Intl L & Pol 709

Rosenne Shabtai, *The Law and Practice of the International Court 1920–2005*, Vol II, Jurisdiction (Martinus Nijhoff 2006)

Roulet Jean-David, *Le Caractère Artificiel de la Théorie de l'Abus de droit en Droit International Public* (Neuchâtel, Éditions de la Baconnière 1958)

Rubins Noah and Love Ben, 'Ratione Temporis' in Bungenberg Marc, Griebel Jörn, Hobe Stephan, and Reinisch August (eds), *International Investment Law: A Handbook* (CH Beck, Hart Publishing and Nomos 2015) 481

Salacuse Jeswald, 'The Emerging Global Regime for Investment' (2010) 51 Harv Intl L J 427

Salacuse Jeswald and Sullivan Nicholas, 'Do BITs Really Work? An Evaluation of Bilateral Investment Treaties and Their Grand Bargain' (2005) 46 Harv Intl L J 67

Sauvant Karl, 'The times they are a-changin'—again—in the relationship between governments and multinational enterprises: From control, to liberalization to rebalancing', *Columba FDI Perspectives*, No 69 (May 21, 2012) available at <http://ccsi.columbia.edu/files/2014/01/FDI_69.pdf> (last accessed on 15 September 2016)

Schill Stephan, 'Do investment treaties chill unilateral State regulation to mitigate climate change?' (2007) 24 J Intl Arb 469

Schill Stephan, *The Multilateralization of International Investment Law* (Cambridge University Press 2009)

Schill Stephan, 'Enhancing International Investment Law's Legitimacy: Conceptual and Methodological Foundations of a New Public Law Approach' (2011–2012) 52 Va J Intl L 57

Schill Stephan, 'Luxembourg Limits: Conditions for Investor-State Dispute Settlement under Future EU Investment Agreements' (2013) 10 TDM, available at <http://www.transnational-dispute-management.com>

Schill Stephan, 'Ordering Paragidms in International Investment Law: Bilateralism—Multilateralism—Multilateralization' in Zachary Douglas, Joost Pauwelyn, and Jorge Viñuales (eds), *The Foundations of International Investment Law* (Oxford University Press 2014) 109

Schill Stephan, 'Editorial: The German Debate on International Investment Law' (2015) 16 JWIT 1

Schill Stephan and Bray Heather, 'Good Faith Limitations on Protected Investments and Corporate Structuring' in Mitchell Andrew, Sornarajah M, and Voon Tania (eds), *Good Faith and International Economic Law* (Oxford University Press 2015) 88

Schlemmer Engela, 'Investment, Investor, Nationality and Shareholders' in Peter Muchlinski, Federico Ortino, and Christoph Schreuer (eds), *The Oxford Handbook of International Investment Law* (Oxford University Press 2008) 51

Schreuer Christoph, 'Calvo's Grandchildren: The Return of Local Remedies in Investment Arbitration' (2005) 4 LPICT 1

Schreuer Christoph, 'Consent to Arbitation' (2005) 2 TDM, available at <http://www.transnational-dispute-management.com>

Schreuer Christoph, 'Shareholder Protection in International Investment Law' (2005) 2 TDM, available at <http://www.transnational-dispute-management.com>

Schreuer Christoph, 'What is a Legal Dispute?' in Isabelle Buffard, James Crawford, Alain Pellet, and Stephan Wittich (eds), *International Law between Universalism and Fragmentation: Festschrift in Honour of Gerhard Hafner* (Martinus Nijhoff 2008) 959

Schreuer Christoph, 'Nationality Planning' in Rovine Arthur W (ed), *Contemporary Issues in International Arbitration and Mediation: The Fordham Papers 2012* (Martinus Nijhoff 2013) 17

Schreuer Christoph, Malintoppi Loretta, Reinisch August, and Sinclair Anthony (eds), *The ICSID Convention: A Commentary* (Cambridge University Press 2009)

Schreuer Christoph and Weiniger Matthew, 'A Doctrine of Precedent?' in Muchlinski Peter, Ortino Federico, and Schreuer Christoph, *Oxford Handbook of International Investment Law* (Oxford University Press 2008) 1189

Schwarzenberger Georg, *International Law as Applied by International Courts and Tribunals*, Vol I (Stevens and Sons, 3rd edn 1957)

Schwarzenberger Georg and Brown Edward D, *A Manual of International Law* (Milton, Professional Books, 6th edn 1976)

Schwebel Stephen, 'In defense of bilateral investment treaties' *Columbia FDI Perspectives*, No 135 (2014), available at <http://ccsi.columbia.edu/files/2013/10/No-135-Schwebel-FINAL.pdf> (last accessed on 15 September 2016)

Shan Wenhua, 'From "North-South Divide" to "Private-Public Debate": Revival of the Calvo Doctrine and the Changing Landscape of International Investment Law' (2006–2007) 27 Nw J Intl L & Bus 631

Shan Wenhua, 'Towards a Balanced Liberal Investment Regime: General Report on the Protection of Foreign Investment' (2010) 25 ICSID Review-FILJ 421

Shany Yuval, *The Competing Jurisdictions of International Courts and Tribunals* (Oxford University Press 2003)

Shaw Malcolm, *International Law* (Cambridge University Press, 6th edn 2008)

Simma Bruno, *Das Reziprozitätselement in der Entstehung des Völkergewohnheitsrechts: Alfred Verdross zum 80. Geburtstag gewidmet* (München, Fink 1970)

Simma Bruno, *Das Reziprozitätselement im Zustandekommen völkerrechtlicher Verträge* (Berlin, Duncker und Humblot 1972)

Simma Bruno, 'Reciprocity' in Wolfrum Rüdiger (ed), *Max Planck Encyclopedia of Public International Law* (Oxford Public International Law 2012) 651

Sinclair Anthony, 'Investment Protection for "Mailbox Companies" under the 1994 Energy Charter Treaty, A note on one aspect of the Decision on Jurisdiction in *Plama Consortium Ltd. v. Republic of Bulgaria*' (2005) 2 TDM, available on <http://www.transnational-dispute-management.com>

Sinclair Ian, *The Vienna Convention on the Law of Treaties* (Manchester University Press 1984)

Skinner Matthew, Miles Cameron, and Luttrell Sam, 'Access and advantage in investor-state arbitration: The law and practice of treaty shopping' (2010) 3 JWELB 260

Sloane Robert, 'Breaking the Genuine Link: The Contemporary International Legal Regulation of Nationality' (2009) 50 Harv Intl L J 1

Smeureanu Ileana, *Confidentiality in International Commercial Arbitration* (Kluwer Law International 2011)

Smith David, 'Shifting Sands: Cost-and-Fee Allocation in International Investment Arbitration' (2010–2011) 51 Va J Intl L 749

Soloway Julie and Tollefson Chris, 'NAFTA's Chapter 11: Investment Protection, Integration and the Public Interest' (2003) 9 Choices 1, available at <http://irpp.org/wp-content/uploads/assets/research/new-research-program/new-research-article-6/vol9no2.pdf> (last accessed on 15 September 2016)

Sornarajah Muthucumuraswamy, 'A Coming Crisis: Expansionary Trends in Investment Treaty Arbitration' in Sauvant Karl (ed), *Appeals Mechanism in International Investment Disputes* (Oxford University Press 2008) 39

Sornarajah Muthucumuraswamy, 'Portfolio Investments and the Definition of Investment' (2009) 24 ICSID Review-FILJ 516

Sornarajah Muthucumuraswamy, 'Towards Normlessness, The Ravage and Retreat of Neo-Liberalism in International Investment Law' in Sauvant Karl (ed), *Yearbook on International Investment Law and Policy 2009–2010* (Oxford University Press 2010) 595

Sornarajah Muthucumuraswamy, *The International Law on Foreign Investment* (Cambridge University Press, 3rd edn 2010)

Sornarajah Muthucumuraswamy, 'Evolution or revolution in international investment arbitration? The descent into normlessness' in Brown Chester and Miles Kate (eds), *Evolution in Investment Treaty Law and Arbitration* (Cambridge University Press 2011) 631

Sornarajah Muthucumuraswamy, 'Good Faith, Corporate Nationality, and Denial of Benefits' in Mitchell Andrew, Sornarajah M, and Voon Tania (eds), *Good Faith and International Economic Law* (Oxford University Press 2015) 117

Spears Suzanne, 'The question of more policy space in a new generation of international investment agreements' (2010) 13 JIEL 1037

Steingruber Andrea Marco, *Consent in International Arbitration* (Oxford University Press 2011)

Stern Brigitte, 'In Search of the Frontiers of Indirect Expropriation' in Rovine Arthur W. (ed), *Contemporary Issues in International Arbitration and Mediation, The Fordham Papers 2007* (Martinus Nijhoff 2008) 29

Stern Brigitte, 'Are There New Limits on Access to International Arbitration?' (2010) 25 ICSID Review 26

Stoll Peter-Tobias, 'The World Trade Organization as a Club: Rethinking Reciprocity and Common Interest' in Ulrich Fastenrath and others (eds), *From Bilateralism to Community Interest—Essays in Honour of Judge Bruno Simma* (Oxford University Press 2011) 172

Susman AM, 'Notes, The Barcelona Traction Case' (1971) 12 Harv Intl L J 91

Teichmann Christoph, 'The Downside of being a Letterbox Company' (2012) 9 Europ Company L 180

Teichmann Christoph, 'Report from Germany' (2008) 5 Europ Company L 189

Thorn Rachel and Doucleff Jennifer, 'Disregarding the Corporate Veil and Denial of Benefits Clauses: Testing Treaty Language and the Concept of "Investor"' in Waibel Michael, Kaushal Asha, Chung Kyo-Hwa, and Balchin Claire (eds), *The Backlash against Investment Arbitration* (Kluwer Law International 2010) 3

Tienhaara Kyla, 'Regulatory Chill and the Threat of Arbitration' in Brown Chester and Miles Kate (eds), *Evolution in Investment Treaty Law and Arbitration* (Cambridge University Press 2011) 606

Titi Aikaterini, *The Right to Regulate in International Investment Law* (Nomos 2014)

Topcan Utku, 'Abuse of the Right to Access ICSID Arbitration' (2014) 29 ICSID Review-FILJ 1

Trevino Clovis, 'Arbitrators toss out ICSID claim against Peru due to abusive restructuring of investment' *IA Reporter* (18 January 2015) available at <http://www.iareporter.com>

Trinh Hai Yen, *The Interpretation of Investment Treaties* (Brill Martinus Nijhoff 2014)

Uchkunova Inna, 'Drawing a Line: Corporate Restructuring and Treaty Shopping in ICSID Arbitration' *Kluwer Arbitration Blog* (6 March 2013) available at <http://kluwerarbitrationblog.com/blog/2013/03/06/drawing-a-line-corporate-restructuring-and-treaty-shopping-in-icsid-arbitration> (last accessed on 15 September 2016)

UNCITRAL, 'Settlement of Commercial Disputes: Preparation of a Legal Standard on Transparency in Treaty-based Investor-State Arbitration' Note by the Secretariat, (New

York, 4–8 February 2013) A/CN.9/WG.II/WP.176, available at <http://daccess-dds-ny.un.org>/doc/UNDOC/LTD/V12/577/83/PDF/V1257783.pdf?OpenElement> (last accessed on 15 September 2016)

UNCTAD, 'Lessons from the MAI' UNCTAD Series on issues in international investment agreements (United Nations 1999) available at <http://unctad.org/en/docs/psiteiitm22.en.pdf> (last accessed on 15 September 2016)

UNCTAD, 'International Investment Arrangements: Trends and Emerging Issues' UNCTAD Series on International Investment Policies for Development (United Nations 2006) available at <http://unctad.org/en/docs/iteiit200511_en.pdf> (last accessed on 15 September 2016)

UNCTAD, 'Investor-State Disputes: Prevention and Alternatives to Arbitration' UNCTAD Series on International Investment Policies for Development (United Nations 2010) available at <http://unctad.org/en/Docs/diaeia200911_en.pdf> (last accessed on 15 September 2016)

UNCTAD, 'Scope and Definition, A Sequel' UNCTAD Series on Issues in International Investment Agreements II (United Nations 2011) available at <http://unctad.org/en/docs/diaeia20102_en.pdf> (last accessed on 15 September 2016)

UNCTAD, 'World Investment Report 2012—Towards a New Generation of Investment Policies' (United Nations 2012) available at <http://unctad.org/en/PublicationsLibrary/wir2012_embargoed_en.pdf> (last accessed on 15 September 2016)

UNCTAD, 'Transparency, A Sequel' UNCTAD Series on Issues in International Investment Agreements II (United Nations 2012) available at <http://unctad.org/en/PublicationsLibrary/unctaddiaeia2011d6_en.pdf> (last accessed on 15 September 2016)

UNCTAD, 'IIA Issues Note, Latest Developments in Investor-State Dispute Settlement' Issues Note No 1 (April 2012) available at <http://unctad.org/en/PublicationsLibrary/webdiaeia2012d10_en.pdf> (last accessed on 15 September 2016)

UNCTAD, 'IIA Issues Note, The Rise of Regionalism in International Investment Policymaking: Consolidation or Complexity?' Issues Note No 3 (June 2013) available at <http://unctad.org/en/PublicationsLibrary/webdiaepcb2013d8_en.pdf> (last accessed on 15 September 2016)

UNCTAD, 'Investor-State Dispute Settlement, A Sequel' UNCTAD Series on Issues in International Investment Agreements II (United Nations 2014) available at <http://unctad.org/en/PublicationsLibrary/diaeia2013d2_en.pdf> (last accessed on 15 September 2016)

UNCTAD, 'World Investment Report 2014, Investing in the SDGs: An Action Plan' (United Nations 2014) available at <http://unctad.org/en/publicationslibrary/wir2014_en.pdf> (last accessed on 15 September 2016)

UNCTAD, 'IIA Issues Note, Recent Trends in IIAs and ISDS' Issues No 1 (February 2015) available at <http://unctad.org/en/PublicationsLibrary/webdiaepcb2015d1_en.pdf> (last accessed on 15 September 2016)

UNCTAD, 'World Investment Report 2015—Reforming International Investment Governance' (United Nations 2015) 115, available at <http://unctad.org/en/PublicationsLibrary/wir2015_en.pdf> (last accessed on 15 September 2016)

UNCTAD, 'Taking stock of IIA Reform' IIA Issues Note No 1 (March 2016) available at <http://unctad.org/en/PublicationsLibrary/webdiaepcb2016d1_en.pdf> (last accessed on 15 September 2016)

Vandevelde Kenneth, 'A Brief History of International Investment Agreements' (2005–2006) 12 UC Davis J Intl L & Pol 157

Van Harten Gus, *Investment Treaty Arbitration and Public Law* (Oxford University Press 2007)

Van Harten Gus, 'Pro-Investor or Pro-State Bias in Investment-Treaty Arbitration? Forthcoming Study Gives Cause for Concern' Investment Treaty News (13 April 2012) available at <http://www.iisd.org/itn/2012/04/13/pro-investor-or-pro-state-bias-in-investment-treaty-arbitration-forthcoming-study-gives-cause-for-concern/> (last accessed on 15 September 2016)

Van Harten Gus, *Arbitral Behaviors in Asymmetrical Adjudication: An Empirical Study of Investment Treaty Arbitration*, Osgoode Hall Law School, Research Paper No 41/2012, available at <http://ssrn.com/abstract=2149207> (last accessed on 15 September 2016)

Van Harten Gus and Loughlin Martin, 'Investment Treaty Arbitration as a Species of Global Administrative Law' (2006) 17 EJIL 121

Van Harten Gus and others, Public Statement on the International Investment Regime (31 August 2010) available at <http://www.osgoode.yorku.ca/public-statement-international-investment-regime-31-august-2010/> (last accessed on 15 September 2016)

Van Os Roos and Knottnerus Roeline, *Dutch Bilateral Investment Treaties, A Gateway to 'Treaty Shopping' for Investment Protection by Multinational Companies* (SOMO 2011) available at <http://papers.ssrn.com/sol3/papers.cfm?abstract_id=1974431> (last accessed on 15 September 2016)

Van Weeghel Stef, *Improper Use of Tax Treaties* (Kluwer Law International 1998)

Villiger Mark, *Commentary on the 1969 Vienna Convention on the Law of Treaties* (Martinus Nijhoff 2009)

Von Bogdandy Armin and Venzke Ingo, 'Beyond Dispute: International Judicial Institutions as Lawmakers' (2011) 12 Germ L J 979

Voon Tania, Mitchell Andrew, and Munro James, 'Legal Responses to Corporate Manoeuvering in International Investment Arbitration' (2014) 5 JIDS 41

Voon Tania, Mitchell Andrew, and Munro James, 'Good Faith in Parallel Trade and Investment Disputes' in Mitchell Andrew, Sornarajah M, and Voon Tania, *Good Faith and International Economic Law* (Oxford University Press 2015) 60

Watts Arthur, 'Nationality of claims: some relevant concepts' in Lowe Vaughan and Fitzmaurice Malgosia (eds), *Fifty Years of the International Court of Justice: Essays in Honour of Sir Robert Jennings* (Cambridge University Press 1996) 424

Weeramantry J Romesh, *Treaty Interpretation in Investment Arbitration* (Oxford University Press 2012)

Weil Prosper, 'L'Équité dans la jurisprudence de la Cour Internationale de Justice' in Vaughan Lowe and Malgosia Fitzgerald (eds), *Fifty Years of the International Court of Justice: Essays in Honour of Sir Robert Jennings* (Cambridge University Press 1996) 121

Weiler Joseph HH, *The Constitution of Europe. Do the New Clothes Have an Emperor? And Other Essays on European Integration* (Cambridge University Press 1999)

Weiniger Matthew and Ormsby Harry, 'Treaty Column: Contrasting approaches to "contribution"' *Global Arbitration Review*, Vol 9 Issue 2, available at <http://www.globalarbitrationreview.com>

Werlauff Eric, 'Pro Form a Registration of Companies: Why a Brass Plate in the Host Country Is Enough in Some Respects, but Not in Others' (2010) 7 Europ Company L 25

Werlauff Erik, 'A "Copenhagen Effect"? Denmark's Answer to Centros: A Far-Reaching Company Law Reform Aimed at Strengthening the "Free Movement of Companies"' (2009) 6 Europ Company L 160

Whytock Christopher, 'The Evolving Forum Shopping System' (2010–2011) 96 Cornell L Rev 481

Wisner Robert and Gallus Nick, 'Nationality Requirements in Investor-State Arbitration' (2004) 5 JWIT 927

Williams David and Foote Simon, 'Recent developments in the approach to identifying an "investment" pursuant to Article 25(1) of the ICSID Convention' in Brown Chester and Miles Kate (eds), *Evolution in Investment Treaty Law and Arbitration* (Cambridge University Press 2011) 42

Wouters Jan and Hachez Nicolas, 'The Institutionalization of Investment Arbitration and Sustainable Development' in Cordonier Segger Marie-Claire, Gehring Markus, and Newcombe Andrew (eds), *Sustainable Development in World Investment Law* (Kluwer Law International 2011) 615

Wyler Eric, *La règle dite de la continuité de la nationalité dans le contentieux international* (Presses universitaires de France 1990)

Yackee Jason Webb, 'Do Bilateral Investment Treaties Promote Foreign Direct Investment? Some Hints Form Alternative Evidence' (2010–2011) 51 Va J Intl L 397

Yannaca-Small Katia, 'Improving the System of Investor-State Dispute Settlement: An Overview' OECD Working Papers on International Investment, Number 2006/1, available at <http://www.oecd.org/china/WP-2006_1.pdf> (last accessed on 15 September 2016)

Yannaca-Small Katia, 'Definition of "Investment": An Open-ended Search for a Balanced Approach' in Yannaca-Small Katia (ed), *Arbitration under International Investment Agreements* (Oxford University Press 2010) 243

Ziegler Andreas and Baumgartner Jorun, 'Good Faith as a General Principle of (International) Law' in Mitchell Andrew, Sornarajah M, and Voon Tania, *Good Faith and International Economic Law* (Oxford University Press 2015) 9

Zuleta Eduardo, Saldarriaga Andrea and Vohryzek-Griest Ana, 'Treaty Planning: Current Trends in International Investment Disputes that Impact Foreign Investment Decisions and Treaty Drafting' in Fernández-Ballesteros Miguel Angel and Arias David (eds), *Liber Amicorum Bernardo Cremades* (Madrid La Ley 2010) 1207

Index

abus de droit, *see* abuse of rights
abuse of process, *see* abuse of rights
abuse of rights 2–3, 19, 48–49, 67–68, 73, 99, 146–66, 176, 194–95, 201–33, 235–36, 246, 269, 274, 276, 278–79, 282, 287–92, 294, 296–98, 300–08, 310–11, 314–15
  abuse of discretion 204
  admissibility 163, 165, 216, 220–21, 275, 290, 301–04
  'main purpose' 228, 274–77
  nemo dat quod non habet 155, 205, 229–32, 233, 314
  'sole purpose' 7, 95, 110, 154, 161, 203–05, 207, 209, 216, 221–22, 231, 233, 250, 253, 275, 277, 294, 314
  timing of dispute 181, 194
  see also dispute
access to justice 37–39, 64
  see also denial of justice
acquiescence 280
African Court of Human Rights 15
annulment 60, 182, 282, 302
appellate tribunal 55
arbitrariness 56, 280, 305
arbitration
  ad hoc 38, 55, 106, 115, 146
  applicable law 274, 282, 289, 290
  costs 56, 58, 60–61, 64–65, 115, 198, 215, 221, 231, 288, 299, 306
  institutional 45, 106
  see also investor–State dispute settlement
arbitrator
  bias 54, 58–59
  repeat appointment 55
Articles on Responsibility of States for Internationally Wrongful Acts, *see* Draft Articles on State Responsibility

bad faith, *see* good faith
Barcelona Traction, *see* diplomatic protection
Base erosion and profit shifting 241
BEPS, *see* Base erosion and profit shifting
bilateral investment agreements, *see* international investment agreements
bribery 265, 282, 288–89
  see also corruption
BRICS 22

Calvo doctrine 64
CETA, *see* Comprehensive Economic and Trade Agreement
civil law 38, 80
common law 32, 80
Comprehensive Economic and Trade Agreement, *see* Table of Treaties
control
  effective 107, 113, 122–23, 126, 132, 134–39, 256–61, 266, 276–77, 306
  'foreign control' 2, 21, 27, 92, 97–100, 103, 120–34, 137–38, 168, 174, 182, 234, 260–61, 277, 285, 306, 310–12
  legal 121, 123, 125–27, 134–38, 234, 256–58, 286, 306
  level of 121, 127–33, 312
  notion of 92, 120–23, 125, 134–38, 256–59, 276, 286, 306
  ownership, *see* ownership
control theory, *see* nationality
corporate restructuring 9, 116, 118, 152, 165–66, 176, 181–83, 190, 192, 194, 199, 201–05, 208–10, 212, 214, 216–18, 220, 224–28, 233, 261, 272–74, 277, 289, 294, 300, 309
corporation
  corporate structuring 8, 10–11, 13–14, 19, 39, 48, 64, 77, 102, 121, 140, 147–48, 160, 163–64, 166–69, 202, 204–07, 215, 219, 246, 264, 272–73, 282, 292–94, 305, 309, 311
  see also corporate restructuring
  diplomatic protection, *see* diplomatic protection
  mailbox company, *see* mailbox company
  nationality of, *see* nationality, legal person
  'piercing of the veil', *see* 'piercing of the veil'
  'round-tripping', *see* 'round-tripping'
  see also multinational enterprise
corruption 265, 274, 282, 288–89
cost allocation 60, 306
  see also arbitration
customary international law 3, 9, 27–29, 31, 38, 41, 45, 53, 68–70, 73–75, 77–78, 80–81, 83–91, 96, 101, 113, 169–72, 175, 178, 202, 210, 234–35, 246–47, 261, 269, 280, 289, 291–92, 295–96, 300, 305, 309–10, 313
  see also diplomatic protection

damages 18, 71, 84, 89, 146, 159, 170, 184, 192, 206
debt restructuring 24, 60–61
denial of benefits 2, 36, 47–48, 92, 104, 108, 112, 114, 116, 118–19, 121, 137, 235, 249–51, 254–55, 276, 285, 311
  retrospective effect 100, 117–20, 138, 235, 250, 254–56, 285, 306, 311
denial of justice 38

diplomatic protection 1–2, 9, 20, 27–31, 33, 39, 42, 44, 53, 68, 70, 73, 75, 77–79, 81, 84–86, 88–89, 91, 93, 95, 171–72, 206, 241, 292
Barcelona Traction, *see* Table of Cases
Diallo, *see* Table of Cases
continuous nationality requirement 86–91, 234–35, 313
Draft Articles on Diplomatic Protection 29, 31, 72–74, 77, 85–86, 88–89, 98, 171, 295
exhaustion of local remedies 29, 64, 170, 304
Nottebohm, *see* Table of Cases
shareholder 18, 29–31, 53, 75, 77–80, 82–85, 88–89, 91, 101, 103, 105, 115, 122, 124–27, 136, 145–46, 153, 170, 199, 234, 261, 273, 292, 295–96, 310, 312
dispute
double exclusion clause 177–78, 192, 224, 270–71, 304
foreseeability of 176, 181–82, 194–96, 201, 205, 208, 211–12, 215–22, 224–28, 232–33, 236, 246, 261, 274–78, 288, 292, 306–07, 310, 314–15
identity of 196–200
notion of 166, 176, 181–85, 188–90, 193, 195–96, 199–201, 220, 226–27, 233, 236, 270, 272, 306–07, 313, 315
parallel, *see* multiples proceedings
pre-existence of.... 161, 175–233, 270–71, 273–77, 288, 292, 294, 306, 310, 313–15
single exclusion clause 177, 190, 214, 270
dispute settlement clause 27, 112, 159, 168, 175–77, 180–81, 188, 195, 200, 241, 265, 267, 270, 272, 277, 304, 315
see also investor–State dispute settlement
Doha Round 23
domestic law 70, 74, 83, 98, 106, 249, 273, 281–82, 289, 301
Draft Articles on State Responsibility 28, 159, 179, 183–84
Draft Articles on Diplomatic Protection, *see* diplomatic protection
due process 54

economic development 59, 148, 264
effet utile, *see* treaty interpretation
equity 280, 294, 296–97
see also shareholding
estoppel 280
European Union 17, 24–26, 76, 240, 243, 249
Common Commercial Policy 24
extra-EU BITs 24–27
intra-EU BITs 24–26
expectations 41, 43, 117–20, 193, 216, 280
expropriation 18, 107, 168, 170, 173, 183, 194, 199, 206, 212, 223–24, 272

fair and equitable treatment 193
forum shopping 1, 8–9, 15–17, 19, 33, 38, 64, 110, 131, 248

general principle of law 80, 83, 202, 274, 280–81, 294–96, 301
'genuine link' doctrine, *see* nationality
good faith 4, 19, 35, 48, 68, 73, 75, 110, 112–13, 131, 149, 160–65, 202–04, 207, 209, 220, 226, 228, 232, 237, 244, 255, 264–65, 273, 278–84, 286–308, 313–14
abuse of process, *see* abuse of process
abuse of rights, *see* abuse of rights
bad faith 133, 160, 162, 164, 204–05, 211, 214, 217, 227, 231, 235, 282, 291, 298–300, 302, 305, 312, 314
fraud 35, 61, 79, 112, 138, 204, 208, 228, 274, 282, 288, 291–92, 294, 297–301, 308, 314
'genuine link', *see* nationality
interpretation, *see* treaty interpretation
nemo dat quod non habet, *see* abuse of rights
'piercing of the veil', *see* 'piercing of the veil'
'sole purpose', *see* abuse of rights

host State laws 161, 289

ICSID
Convention, *see* Table of Treaties
disputes, *see* Table of Cases
incorporation theory, *see* nationality
Inter-American Court for Human Rights 15
International Chamber of Commerce 17, 45
International Court of Justice 3, 9, 44, 71, 94, 176, 178, 185, 262, 279, 310
disputes, *see* Table of Cases
Statute, *see* Table of Treaties
International Criminal Court 15, 280
International Criminal Tribunal for Rwanda 15
International Criminal Tribunal for the former Yugoslavia 15
international economic law 15, 46
international investment agreements
agreements, *see* Table of Treaties
bilateral, *see* Table of Treaties
disputes, *see* Table of Cases
see also dispute settlement
International Law Commission 26, 28, 72, 89, 108, 159, 210, 284
International Monetary Fund 22
international tax law 7–8
International Tribunal for the Law of Sea 15
interpretation, *see* treaty interpretation
investment
'active' contribution 48, 140, 150, 153, 155, 158–60, 264–65, 267, 286, 291, 305, 307, 312–13
agreements, *see* international investment agreements

contribution 144, 148–55, 157, 159, 164–65, 235, 264, 278, 284
notion of 48, 140–50, 154–55, 158–64, 163–65, 256, 261–62, 264–65, 267, 277–78, 285, 287–89, 312–13
economic motivation 150, 264
good faith, *see* good faith
indirect 2, 48, 134, 140, 142–43, 145–47, 156, 158–60, 164–65, 206, 235, 262–63, 265, 312
nominal payment 150–53, 155, 162, 235, 264, 312
origin of capital 104, 106, 109, 268–69
risk 155
Salini criteria 148–49, 155, 264
shareholding, *see* shareholding
Investment Court System 55, 240
investor
nationality, *see* nationality
mailbox company, *see* mailbox company
investor–State contract 232, 273
investor–State dispute settlement 7, 10–11, 15, 23, 27–28, 36, 60–63, 64, 142, 179, 213, 239, 241–43, 272–73, 315
ISDS, *see* investor-State dispute settlement
ius cogens 35
ius standi, *see* standing

jurisdiction
ratione personae 2–3, 48, 67–68, 92–138, 140, 250, 291–92, 311
ratione materiae 2–3, 48, 67–68, 134, 140–64, 229, 235, 311–12
ratione temporis 2–3, 48, 67–68, 133, 154, 164–200, 205, 211, 214–17, 219–21, 230–32, 235, 246, 269, 288, 307, 311–15

law of aliens 27, 82, 85
legitimacy
accountability 37, 51–52
crisis or concerns 23, 37, 43, 49
democratic legitimation 52, 56
meaning of 49–52
'public–private divide' 52, 58, 61, 65
rule of law, *see* rule of law
transparency, *see* transparency
legitimate expectations, *see* expectations
level-playing field 63–65
lex generalis 90, 247, 291
lex specialis 31, 89–90, 93, 95–96, 98, 171–72, 234, 247, 291, 310, 313
lis pendens, *see* multiple proceedings
London Chamber of International Arbitration 45

MAI, *see* Multilateral Agreement on Investment
mailbox company 1, 92, 108–10, 113, 115, 121, 131–32, 137, 253, 255, 291, 293, 301, 309
Manila Declaration on the Peaceful Settlement of Disputes between States, *see* United Nations General Assembly
MFN, *see* most-favoured nation
minimum standard of treatment 85, 170
MNE, *see* multinational enterprise
most-favoured nation 11, 36, 46, 57
Multilateral Agreement on Investment 20, 22, 240
multilateralization 45–46, 240, 309, 315
multinational enterprise 2
multiple proceedings 15–17, 19, 53, 60, 164, 248, 263
identity test 18
lis pendens 18
res judicata 18

nationality
change of 10, 12, 34, 48, 67–69, 73, 88, 92, 150, 154, 158, 166–67, 169–70, 172, 174–76, 182–83, 192–93, 196, 201, 210–11, 215, 219–22, 224–29, 232–37, 240, 246, 265, 269, 271, 275, 278, 281–83, 292, 297, 301, 304–05, 307, 310, 313–14
continuity of 86, 154, 166, 169–175, 235, 313
control theory 77, 79, 85, 101–02, 144–45
customary international law, *see* diplomatic protection
dual 1, 11, 33, 72, 92, 94–95, 97, 99, 138, 246–47, 276, 310
effective 72, 94, 96, 246–48, 297
'genuine link' theory 2, 72–73, 80–81, 92–95, 97–99, 109, 136, 138, 234, 246, 278, 282, 284, 291–92, 308, 310, 314
host State 96–99, 103, 108, 121, 126, 128,130–33, 138–39, 174, 234, 246–48, 252–53, 260–61, 276, 293, 310, 312
incorporation theory 32, 74–75, 79–81, 85, 88, 101–02, 108, 241, 249
legal person 74–85, 99–138
natural person 71–74, 92–98
permanent resident 94–95, 144, 246, 248–49
planning 1, 4, 8, 10, 33, 64, 68, 160, 182, 196, 202, 226, 237, 278–79, 282–83, 285, 290–91, 293, 306–07, 309, 314
seat theory 75–76, 101–02
single 72–73, 93–95, 98, 246, 291

OECD 7, 10, 15–16, 19, 22, 60, 240–41
origin of capital, *see* investment

pacta sunt servanda 35, 37, 41, 280
Permanent Court of International Justice 28, 35, 70, 176, 185, 187, 272, 305, 310
disputes, *see* Table of Cases

Philip Morris Asia v Australia, *see* Table of Cases
'piercing of the veil' 2, 80, 83–84, 91–92, 101, 104, 113, 129, 145, 234, 294, 291–98, 308, 314
precedent 2, 20, 32–33, 42, 53, 72–73, 81, 97, 120, 132, 279, 297
principle of non-retroactivity 166, 177, 179–81, 183, 195, 200–01, 215, 235, 269–70, 304, 313
public policy 24, 163, 194, 265, 282

ratione personae, *see* jurisdiction
ratione materiae, *see* jurisdiction
ratione temporis, *see* jurisdiction
real economic activities 14, 47, 77, 114–16, 250–51, 253
  see also substantive business activities
reciprocity 36, 39–49, 65, 154, 245–46, 256, 269, 276
regionalism 23, 240
regulatory chill 62–63, 65
'round-tripping' 13, 26, 102–03, 105–06, 108, 111, 242
rule of law 50, 52, 59, 203

Salini criteria, *see* investment
seat theory, *see* nationality
shareholder, *see* diplomatic protection
shareholding
  equity 106, 156, 257, 268, 280
  majority 78, 97, 103, 107, 113, 123, 125–26, 128, 132, 134–36, 139, 156–57, 258–60, 311
  minority 2, 18, 121, 123–26, 132, 134–36, 139, 141, 156, 259
  voting rights 122–25, 134, 136, 259–60
shell company, *see* mailbox company
small and medium-sized enterprise 64
sovereignty 21, 35–37, 58
  sovereign consent 34, 37, 39, 65, 112, 129
standing 1–2, 12, 15, 18–20, 26–28, 33, 44–45, 48, 53, 84–85, 100, 116, 122, 131, 140, 142, 146, 152, 173, 197, 234, 261, 268, 296, 310, 312
state responsibility 27–28, 191
Stockholm Chamber of Commerce 17, 45
substantive business activities 48, 114–15, 235, 241, 276, 311
sustainable development 24, 59–61, 65
  Sustainable Development Goals 59
  public–private partnerships 59

tobacco plain packaging 194–95, 218
  see also Philip Morris Asia v Australia
TPP, *see* Trans-Pacific Partnership
Trans-Pacific Partnership, *see* Table of Treaties
Transatlantic Trade and Investment Partnership, *see* Table of Treaties
transfer of claims 11, 14, 39, 315
transparency 52, 55–56, 58, 61
  amicus curiae 56
treaty interpretation
  context 112, 156, 161, 180, 207, 244–45, 283–85, 289
  effet utile 255, 258
  good faith, *see* good faith
  'host State bias' 99, 138, 247, 285, 310
  joint interpretation 243–44
  object and purpose 58, 104, 107, 112–14, 117, 130, 132, 134, 156, 174, 207, 224–45, 280, 283–87, 290
  preamble 24, 35, 39–40, 42, 103, 148, 157, 215, 244–46, 276, 285–86
  systemic integration 90, 289, 304, 310
  see also Table of Treaties, Vienna Convention on the Law of Treaties
treaty negotiation 36
TTIP, *see* Transatlantic Trade and Investment Partnership

umbrella clause..... 11
UNCITRAL, *see* United Nations Commission on International Trade Law
United Nations Commission on International Trade Law 17, 45, 96, 247, 310
  Arbitration Rules 17, 55–56, 96–97, 99, 106, 118, 138, 247
  disputes, *see* Table of cases
United Nations General Assembly 21
  Manila Declaration on the Peaceful Settlement of Disputes Between States 280

venire contra factum proprium 48

Washington Consensus 22
World Trade Organization 11, 209, 240, 280, 282
  Dispute Settlement Body 15, 55, 282, 290
  Disputes, *see* Table of Cases
  Treaties, *see* Table of Treaties